Vængesø and Holmegaard

Vængesø and Holmegaard

Ertebølle Fishers and Hunters on Djursland

Søren H. Andersen

East Jutland Museum

Moesgaard Museum

Aarhus University Press

Vængesø and Holmegaard
Ertebølle Fishers and Hunters on Djursland

By Søren H. Andersen
East Jutland Museum Publications vol. 4
© Museum Østjylland and Aarhus University Press 2018

Translation from Danish: Anne Bloch and David Earle Robinson | HSLS
Graphic design: Jørgen Sparre
Typesetting: Ea Rasmussen
Cover illustration: Flemming Bau
Printed by Narayana Press, Denmark

ISBN 978 87 7124 886 9

AARHUS UNIVERSITY PRESS
Finlandsgade 29
8200 Aarhus N, Denmark
www.unipress.dk

Oxbow Books Ltd
The Old Music Hall, 106–108 Cowley Road
Oxford, OX4 1JE
United Kingdom
www.oxbowbooks.com

ISD
70 Enterprise Drive
Bristol, CT 06010
USA
www.isdistribution.com

Published with the financial support from

Dronning Margrethe II's Arkæologiske Fond
Farumgaard-Fonden
The Danish Agency for Culture and Palaces
KrogagerFonden
Den Hielmstierne-Rosencroneske Stiftelse
Lillian og Dan Finks Fond

Contents

Preface

· ·

This book presents the collated results of a number of archaeological investigations undertaken on Djursland over a period of almost 40 years. It begins with the findings of the excavations carried out around the former marine lagoon of Vængesø in the northeastern part of the Helgenæs peninsula. Then follows an overview of an excavation undertaken at the site of Holmegaard, located on the former Stubbe Fjord complex. One of the sites (Vængesø I) has been published previously (in 1975), but the interpretation of this locality has been revised in the light of research and the results of other investigations undertaken over the intervening four decades.

A crucial precondition for the excavations carried out by the Vængesø lagoon was the extensive, long-standing survey work and collecting undertaken by former market gardener and enthusiastic amateur archaeologist Poul Poulsen (1927-2016) over the course of a lifetime on northern Helgenæs. His work resulted in professional archaeological attention being focussed on this part of Denmark for almost 40 years. Further to this was a professional desire to employ this delineated marine area in an attempt to obtain a more cohesive impression of whether several archaeologically coeval coastal settlements could possibly have functioned together and, if so, in what way.

A number of friends and colleagues have provided assistance and support during this work – both in excavations in the field and in the subsequent post-excavation analysis. Ole Poulsen (East Jutland Museum) deserves many thanks for his ever-reliable assistance throughout. T.D. Price, (University of Wisconsin) has helped with suggestions and advice and is also warmly thanked. Particularly warm thanks go to Tina, who has been a great help with the layout of the tables. Flemming Bau is thanked for permission to use one of his drawings as the motif for the front cover of this book. And thanks to good friends and colleagues G.N. Bailey, N. Milner and Harry Robson (all University of York); also to East Jutland Museum for help and economic support for the production of this book: Jørgen Smith-Jensen, Lutz Klassen, Ernst Stidsing, Lisbeth Wincentz, Jakob Vedsted and Esben Kannegaard. Esben Kannegaard has been both a good friend and colleague with whom I have discussed and debated many archaeological questions over the years. Gitte Gebauer, National Museum of Denmark, and Niels H. Andersen, Moesgaard Museum, are thanked for help with the pottery from Vængesø II; Helle Juel-Jensen (Aarhus University) for her work in writing the report on the excavation of this settlement and for useful professional comments and suggestions. Also Jette Sunesen, Aarhus, and a group of energetic amateur archaeologists from the Aarhus area deserves thanks for their help in processing the large finds assemblage and their efforts in the field during the excavation of Vængesø III.

The faunal material was analysed in exemplary fashion by Inge B. Enghoff, Natural History Museum of Denmark, Copenhagen, who both participated in the excavation of Vængesø III and also provided much constructive input during the extended process of post-excavation analysis. The faunal assemblage was subsequently published in her doctoral thesis of 2014: *Regionality and biotope exploitation in Danish Ertebølle and adjoining periods.*

Jesper Olsen and Marie Kanstrup, Aarhus AMS Centre, Aarhus University, are thanked for assistance with the radiocarbon dates.

The Danish Agency for Culture, Moesgaard Museum and the University of Aarhus have granted funding for the investigations. Finally, I would also like to extend thanks to my colleague and friend Benny Staal for permission to mention his excavation at Statoil, Kalundborg, and to my colleague Peter Vang Petersen of the National Museum of Denmark.

Last, but definitely not least, special thanks go to Lone R. Andersen and Nina H. Nielsen, both for the exemplary way in which they undertook the excavation of Vængesø III and for their assistance with cleaning and sorting of finds, redrawing of plans etc.

The book was translated into English by David Earle Robinson and Anne Bloch, HSLS, Ebeltoft, and the layout work by Ea Rasmussen, warm thanks to all three for their excellent cooperation during this work.

The artefact drawings were produced by Pia Brejnholt (PB), Søren Timm Christensen (STC) and Orla Svendsen (OS), who are all also warmly thanked.

Søren H. Andersen

1 Vængesø: Geology, topography and research history

1.1 Geology and topography

Vængesø is located on the northeast coast of the Helgenæs peninsula, which extends south of Mols on the southern coast of Djursland. Djursland is itself a peninsula, projecting east from the central eastern coast of Jutland (Fig. 1a). Vængesø today is a wetland area, situated between the marine bays of Begtrup Vig and Ebeltoft Vig (Fig. 2). About 10 km to the south lies the northern tip of the island of Samsø and about 14 km to the west is the city of Aarhus.

The Helgenæs peninsula is triangular in outline and measures c. 7 km (N-S) by 4-5 km (E-W – broadest to the north). Its landscape is sharply undulating, reaching heights of c. 50-60 m a.m.s.l. and, in one instance (Ellemandsbjerg), as much as 81 m a.m.s.l.

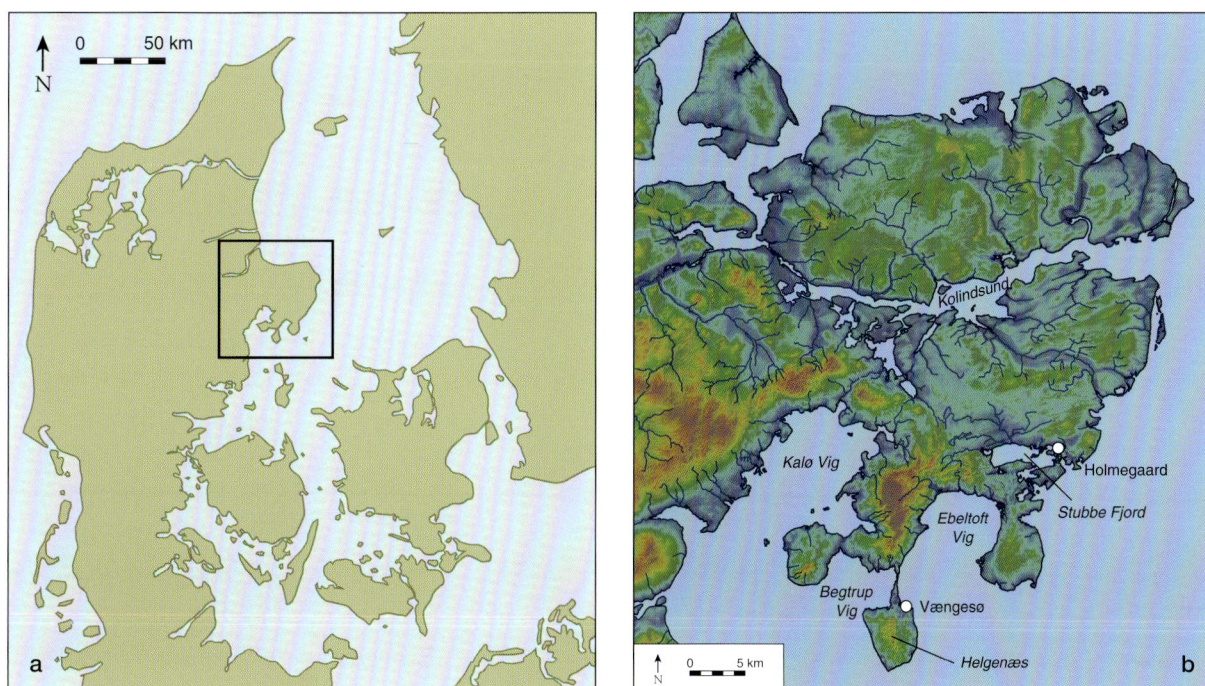

Fig. 1. a) The location of the Djursland peninsula in Denmark. b) The approximate relationship between land and sea on Djursland in Ertebølle (Late Atlantic) times, with the localities of the Vængesø lagoon and Holmegaard marked. Modified after Klassen (2014).

Topographically and environmentally the peninsula is characterised by extreme variation, with the landscape continually alternating between steep-sided hills and small peat- or water-filled hollows. The subsoil consists of fluvioglacial deposits of sand, gravel and sandy clay. The most common soil type is coarse sand (Fig. 2). Importantly, there are no rivers or large freshwater watercourses on the peninsula.

The waters around Helgenæs are deep by Danish standards – especially to the south and southwest, where they reach a maximum of 56 m. To the east are depths of 12-16 m and a shallower area, Skadegrund, lies to the southeast (Fig. 2). The coast almost everywhere takes the form of steep erosion slopes, which must have developed during the period of highest sea level in prehistoric times.

The area has risen c. 4-4.3 m since the Stone Age and almost all coasts show clear evidence of heavy marine erosion in the form of high fossil cliffs and broad beach-ridge systems. These are especially evident to the northeast and to the southwest, towards Sletterhage (Jessen 1920, 93; Mertz 1924, 23), and there are areas of raised seabed both to the northwest, southwest and northeast (Fig. 2).

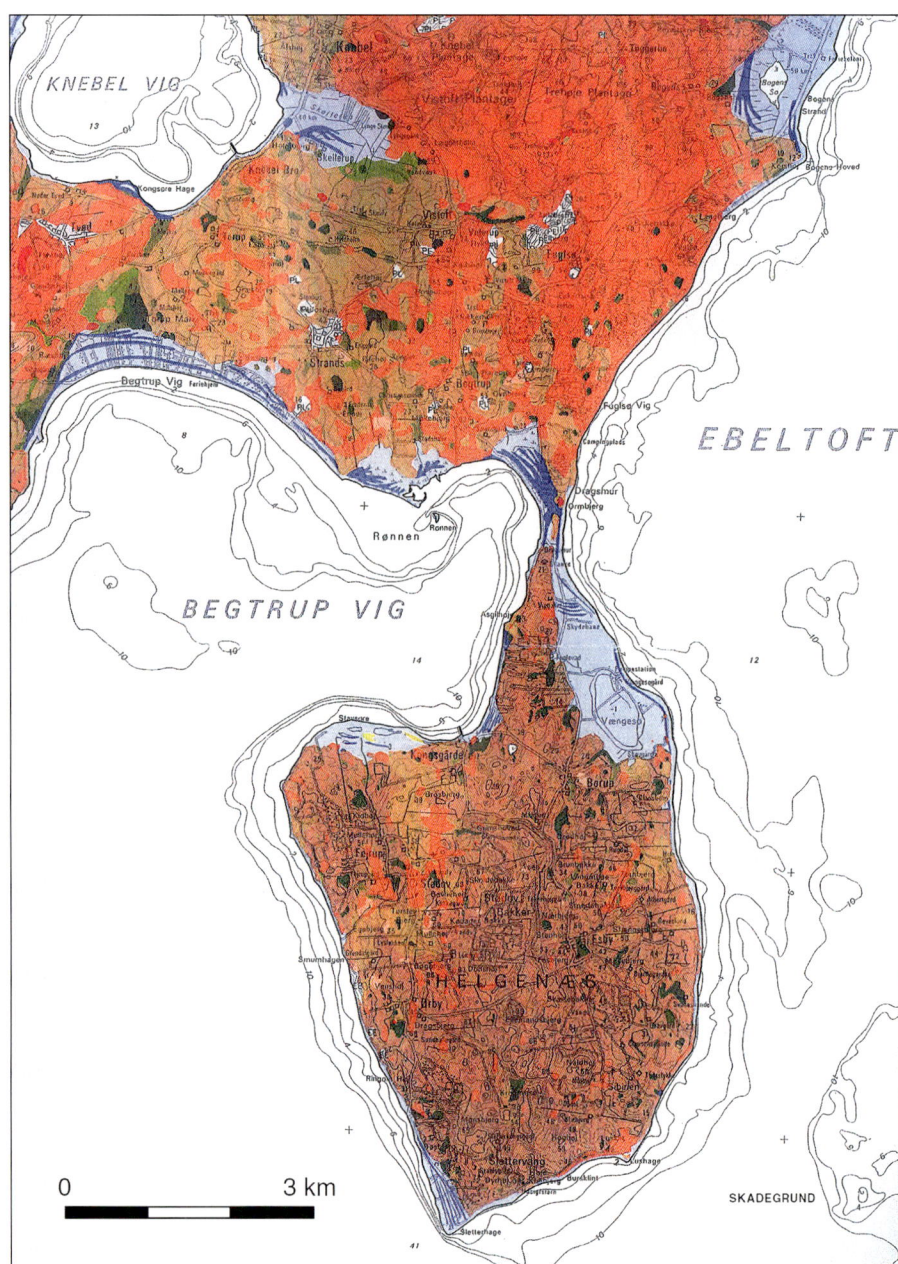

Fig. 2. Soils map for Helgenæs and the southern part of Mols. Marine deposits, raised seabed and beach ridges are shown in blue. Fluvioglacial sand and gravel are shown in dark brown and red, till is shown in light brown. Freshwater deposits are shown in green. Reproduced with permission from GEUS, Copenhagen.

In prehistory, Helgenæs was at various times (depending on the sea level) separated from, or joined on to, the southern part of Mols by a narrow strip of land running north-south called "Draget", which consists of several small islands and a system of beach ridges. The islands have steep erosion slopes to the west and, especially, to the east, towards Ebeltoft Vig.

Vængesø must originally have been an open lagoon facing out towards Ebeltoft Vig, but during the course of the Atlantic period, a system of beach ridges developed from north and south, gradually transforming it into a lagoon or sack-shaped inlet. Archaeological investigations at the Vængesø settlements show that the highest sea level must have been c. 3.9-4 m a.m.s.l., which is consistent with the geological estimate mentioned above. For the history of Vængesø over the last 300-400 years, reference is made to a recent account by Vedsted (2014, 38-51). Central to this story is the draining of the area for agriculture in the 19th and 20th centuries. Water recently returned to Vængesø when the area was converted into a freshwater lake – a nature reserve for birdlife.

The Vængesø basin (Fig. 3) is oval in outline with its greatest length (1-1.5 km) in a north-south direction, while its width (to the south) is c. 0.8 km. In the Stone Age it held a small bay or lagoon, the southernmost part of which was cut off and closed towards Ebeltoft Vig by a c. 1 km long barrier. This was formed of two small islands linked by an extended beach ridge connected to Helgenæs to the south. The archaeological evidence shows that this beach ridge must have been formed in Early Atlantic times. To the northeast, there was a c. 1 km wide opening out towards Ebeltoft Vig. This explains the presence opposite this opening, on the ENE coast of Helgenæs, of a high, steep fossil erosion slope, while further to the south, where the coast was more protected by the aforementioned small islands and the beach ridge, the coastal slope quickly reduces in height and becomes less steep. The Core Archive at GEUS (Geological Survey of Denmark and Greenland) contains geological descriptions of a number of cores taken in and around Vængesø, which reveal series of marine deposits of as much as 7-10 m in thickness. The inlet must therefore have been of considerable depth in the Stone Age, and even though Vængesø was partially closed towards Ebeltoft Vig at this time, it must nevertheless have contained seawater that was sufficiently fresh and nutrient-rich for oyster banks to be formed within it. The presence of kitchen middens has been established in at least five or six locations, with oysters constituting the dominant species. There must therefore have been at least one or more shell banks in Vængesø where Stone Age people could gather these marine invertebrates.

In the Stone Age, the area must have resembled present-day Stavns Fjord and Besser Rev on Samsø. Along the shores of the Vængesø bay/lagoon are between eight and ten coastal settlements from the Mesolithic and Neolithic. These relate in particular to the final part of the Ertebølle culture, but in a few places there are also finds from the slightly earlier Middle Ertebølle period. Further to these are several localities with evidence of Neolithic settlement – especially from the Early Neolithic Funnel Beaker culture. These sites have the character of either kitchen middens (eight examples) or coastal settlements with no shell deposits (the remainder; Fig. 3). Common to all of them is that they are (with the exception of Vængesø III) small in area relative to Ertebølle sites seen elsewhere in Jutland (see Tab. 8). In addition, a large number of axes (core, flake and greenstone axes) have been collected over the years from littoral areas bordering Vængesø and the nearby coast (Fig. 167). Archaeological excavations were carried out at four localities (all kitchen middens) between 1973 and 2005 (Fig. 3). The other localities have not been archaeologically investigated but their existence has been demonstrated by surface collection of artefacts or by test pitting. From a rather wider perspective, it should be pointed out that a number of further Ertebølle settlements have been localised within a short distance of Vængesø, several of which are (archaeologically) contemporaneous with the localities associated with the Vængesø lagoon (see Fig. 3).

Within a 5 km radius of Vængesø today, the proportions of land and sea are c. 37% and 63%, respectively. If this radius is increased to 10 km,

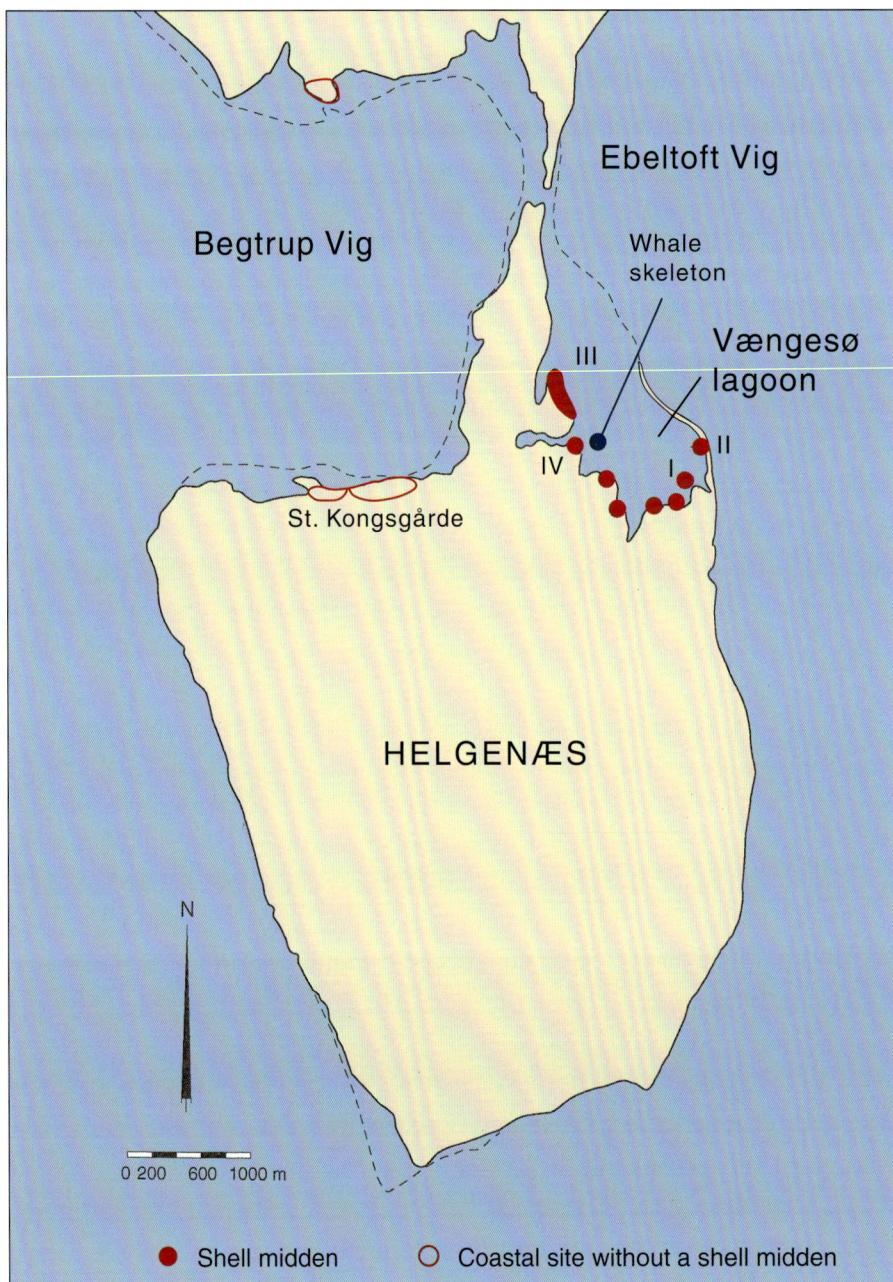

Fig. 3. Map of Vængesø and Helgenæs, showing known Stone Age settlements (predominantly from the Late Ertebølle culture) and the find spot for a whale skeleton dating from the Early Bronze Age.

these proportions change to c. 31% land and c. 69% sea. The situation was probably roughly the same in the Stone Age, as no great changes in land and sea area have occurred since prehistory. This means that two thirds of the local area comprised marine biotopes. The 5 km zone is dominated by shallow coastal marine waters, but the resource area within the 10 km zone also includes open sea, represented by all of Begtrup Vig and Ebeltoft Vig, with water depths of 12-16 m, as well as a large part of southern Mols (Fig. 2). From this, it is clear that marine biotopes must have played an important role relative to the subsistence economies of these settlements. In topographic and environmental terms, they therefore differ from contemporaneous Ertebølle coastal sites where marine biotopes generally only constituted around 30-50% of the local area. As a consequence, the Vængesø sites do not match any of the recognised criteria relating to the topographic location of coastal settlements of the Ertebølle culture on mainland and must therefore be more closely associated with the group of localities found on "outer islands" (Andersen, S.H. 1998, 24).

1.2 Research history

A.P. Madsen of the National Museum of Denmark visited Helgenæs in 1897 and undertook a minor excavation in a small kitchen midden on a little holm (former islet) at the southern end of Vængesø (subsequently referred to here as Vængesø I; Fig. 4). This investigation revealed that the kitchen midden consisted of a shell layer with a maximum thickness (at the foot of the holm) of c. 40-50 cm and almost exclusively comprised of oyster shells (*Ostrea edulis*), with a few shells of cockle (*Cerastoderma edule*) and, sporadically, periwinkle (*Littorina littorea*). There was also a good quantity of flint debitage and a number of blades and cores, as well as borers and 17 flake axes, plus a few marrow-split bones. In 1920, the skull of a fin whale (*Balaenoptera* sp.; identified by H. Winge) was found during ploughing about 100 m out in the marine sand and shingle layers off the southwestern shore of Vængesø. The rest of the whale skeleton was not located and excavation conditions did not permit a clear investigation of the finds circumstances. The discovery attracted a good deal of attention because, during excavation of the cranium, some Stone Age tools were found "in the vicinity" (eight flakes and two greenstone axes of Ertebølle type as well as three flakes). It was then (see Ch. 5.5) interpreted as remains associated with the butchering of a stranded whale in Ertebølle times (Nordmann 1936, 127-128). In 1991, the whale skull was radiocarbon dated to 1205-945 BC cal (1 σ; K-5661: 2890 ± 80 bp), i.e. the transition between the Early and Late Bronze Age. This showed that there was no chronological association between the whale skull and the Ertebølle tools found nearby (information on the date kindly provided by P.V. Petersen, National Museum of Denmark).

The numerous settlements that now lie beneath the arable fields of the Vængesø area have attracted the attention of many amateur archaeologists, and market gardener Poul Poulsen, of Borup on Helgenæs, has been particularly active in this respect. Poul Poulsen has carried out extensive field-walking and surface collection of artefacts over the last 20-30 years – predominantly on the

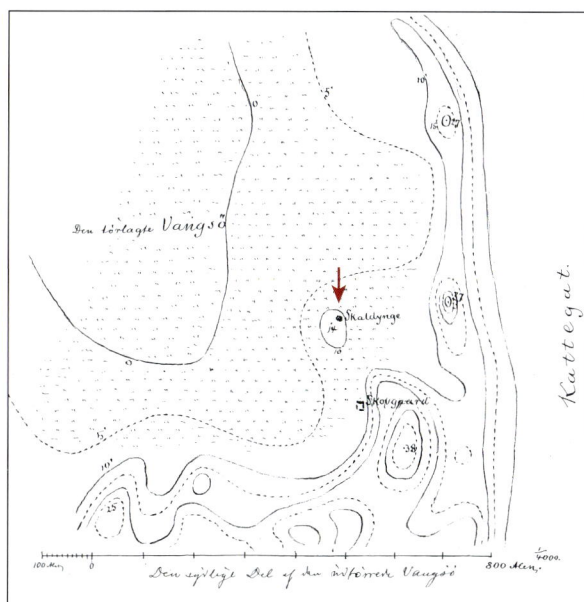

Fig. 4. The southeastern part of Vængesø, showing the Vængesø I settlement (arrowed). After an original from 1897 by A.P. Madsen (in the archives of the National Museum of Denmark).

sites around Vængesø, but also over a large part of northern Helgenæs. These activities resulted in a large collection of archaeological artefacts which is now held by East Jutland Museum. Without fear of exaggeration, it can be said that this area is probably one of the most intensively surveyed areas in Denmark and, in addition to the settlements, a significant number of single finds have been recorded around Vængesø (see Fig. 167).

As the individual Stone Age settlements did not function in isolation, but formed part of social and economic complexes with other settlements, I have found it both relevant and interesting to carry out regional projects aimed at illuminating some of these links, where possible. This work has taken place at Norsminde Fjord (Andersen 1976) and later around the former Bjørnsholm Fjord in northwest Himmerland (Andersen in prep.). Similar investigations have also been undertaken in smaller areas, where the limited size of the localities makes it easier to obtain a sharper picture of settlement function and subsistence economy. This was one of the reasons that Vængesø was selected as a suitable area for an investigation of the aforementioned type.

In addition to the investigation of the whale skull outlined above, archaeological excavations have been undertaken on numerous occasions at several Stone Age settlements: Vængesø I: total excavation of a settlement surface with kitchen midden (excavation in plan by the National Museum of Denmark and Moesgaard Museum in 1974); Vængesø II: excavation of a section trench and settlement surface with kitchen midden (excavation in plan and in section by Moesgaard Museum 1975 and 1979); Vængesø III: excavation of a settlement surface with kitchen midden (excavation in plan by Moesgaard Museum and East Jutland Museum in 1998-2004); Vængesø IV: excavation of three minor sections through kitchen midden (excavation in section by Moesgaard Museum in 1976).

2 Vængesø I "Svendhøj"

This locality lies in the southern part of Vængesø and appears today as a small, well-defined moraine hummock (sandy clay) that in the Stone Age was surrounded on all sides by earlier marine deposits of sand, gravel and peat (parish record no. 19, Helgenæs parish, Mols Søndre district, Randers county, Moesgaard Museum archive no. 4466). Today the area is occupied by meadows and cultivated or fallow land. In the Stone Age, the hummock must have appeared as a very small islet which, depending on the sea level, measured c. 20-40 × 20-40 m. Only to the south was a shoal with shallow water, and it was also here that there was the shortest distance to dry land (Figs. 4 and 5). The hummock's highest point is now located around 4 m a.m.s.l. As the highest level of the Stone Age sea is said to have been c. 3.9-4.3 m a.m.s.l. (Jessen 1920, 93; Mertz 1924, 23), this means that the islet must, at least occasionally (and certainly during the Stone Age sea-level maximum), either have been completely inundated by the sea or extremely inaccessible. This concurs with the fact that the worked flint shows evidence of the alkaline effect of the sea-water (bleaching) and is also slightly water-worn. Due to its modest size, the islet had neither freshwater nor other forms of raw materials such as bone, antler and so on. These had to be transported to the site. Across the entire islet, but especially on its eastern side, are the ploughed-up shells and shell fragments of marine invertebrates. In addi-tion to large quantities of worked flint, oyster shells dominate the picture, in particular within a c. 10 × 10 m (100 m²) area near the top of the islet and on its northeastern slope. This was presumably the location of the small kitchen midden partially investigated by the National Museum in 1897 (see above). Over the course of the subsequent century, this has been completely removed by ploughing. Worked flint has also been found at the foot of the islet, but this is considerably more water-worn than that found higher up. The artefacts collected here indicate a presence during a slightly earlier phase (early/middle part) of the Ertebølle culture than the finds found at a higher level on the slope and during the excavation. The latter was carried out on the ESE side of the islet in 1974 and covered an area of 35 m². The findings have been published previously (Andersen, S.H. 1975b, 9-48) and have subsequently been referred to in the international archaeological literature (Newell 1981, 249-250, Fig. 10.2; Rowley-Conwy 2013, 141-142). The excavation revealed this to be a very small, well-defined settle-ment. Beneath the plough soil was an undisturbed (*in situ*), charcoal-rich culture layer – representing a settlement area – dating from the Late Ertebølle period, while there were no traces of a refuse layer running down the slope of the islet. No stratifica-tion of the culture layer was observed during the investigation and this is consistent with the entire finds assemblage dating exclusively to the Late

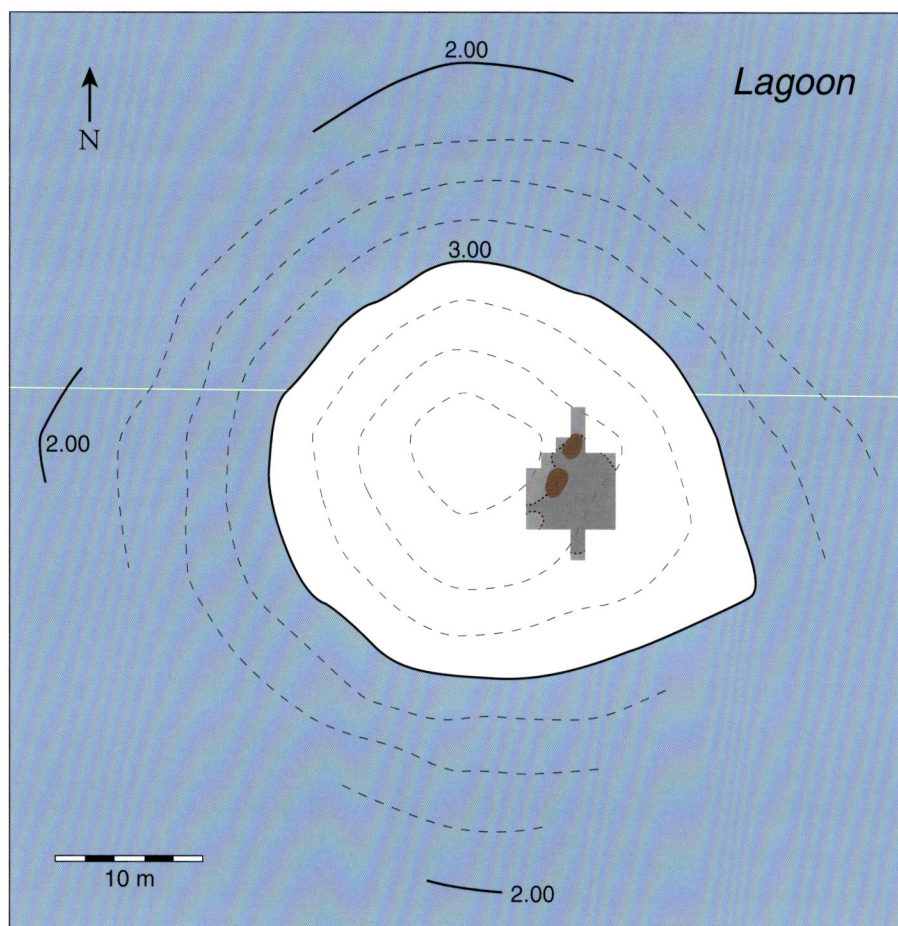

Fig. 5. Contour map of the islet with the Vængesø I settlement, showing the location and size of the excavated area. Also evident are the terrace and the stone-set hearths. A thick contour line marks 2 and 3 m a.m.s.l., equidistance between broken contour lines is 20 cm.

Ertebølle culture. Finds earlier or later than this were not demonstrated. The distribution plans, shown below, should be evaluated in the light of the fact that the finds from the 1974 excavation were only recorded with reference to a grid of 1 m² squares – in contrast to the situation at all the other Vængesø settlement excavations, where cultural remains were recorded according to a system of 3D coordinates.

2.1 Stratigraphy

The subsoil consisted of fluvioglacial sand, over which was a sandy, exceptionally charcoal-rich culture layer containing worked flint (+O and ±R; see explanation below), numerous cooking stones and scattered bones and pottery, in addition to scattered shell fragments of oysters, cockles, mussels (*Mytilus edulis*) and periwinkles. Above the culture layer was a layer of sandy soil (the plough soil).

2.2 Settlement structures

2.2.1 Terrace

During excavation of the culture layer, the existence was demonstrated of a small level terrace measuring 5-6 × 3-4 m (15-24 m²) and extending from the edge of the slope into the side of the islet, where it formed a c. 5-30 cm high step. The latter must originally have been somewhat higher but had been reduced due to later erosion and ploughing. How much has been removed over the years is, however, not known. The terrace lay at c. 3.60 m a.m.s.l. Its very limited extent, and the fact that it was located on the side of the islet opposite the mouth of Vængesø, facing out towards Ebeltoft Vig, shows that it was not formed by marine erosion but must have been the result of digging out and levelling of the slope in order to make it more suitable for occupation. On the terrace was an up to c. 30 cm thick, well-protected, *in situ* culture layer consisting of black, extremely charcoal-rich fill containing flint. The state of this flint can be described using the formulae +O and –R. O is an expression of the degree of surface transformation of the flint such that +O is a white, totally transformed surface, ±O is flint with partial surface transformation and –O is a primary, non-transformed, black-grey surface. In the same way, R is an expression of the degree of water-wearing of the flint, where –R is non-water-worn flint, ±R is slightly water-worn and +R is heavily water-worn (Troels-Smith 1939, 491-492; Andersen, K. 1985, 45). In addition to flint, the culture layer also contained numerous cooking stones, scattered animal bones and a little pottery, as well as small patches of marine invertebrate shells. On the terrace lay scattered (field-) stones, but these were most numerous towards the outer edge and on the slope running down to the prehistoric shore. This obviously means that the actual terrace surface, i.e. the central settlement area, was cleared of stones in order to make it more suitable for occupation. Similar phenomena have been observed at Late glacial settlements, for example Stoksbjerg Bro (Pedersen 2009, 79).

2.2.2 Hearths

On the terrace was a rounded-oval concentration of heat-affected stones forming a single layer with a diameter of c. 1 m (Fig. 6). This feature was originally perceived as a somewhat larger hearth of c. 2.5 m in length and rather more oval in form. However, re-analysis of the original excavation data shows that the feature comprised two smaller and rounder hearths, with a diffuse extension reaching further to the northeast than originally described (Andersen 1975a, 15-16, Fig. 6). The hearths lay up against the "rear edge" of the terrace (Fig. 6). Both their form and their content of the heat-brittled stones show that these are two stone-built hearths of the type well-known from many Ertebølle settlements in Jutland, for example Ertebølle itself (Madsen et al. 1900, 25-27), and also seen at Vængesø III (Ch. 4.2.2.1). Furthermore, the feature's interpretation as two hearths is supported by the considerable quantities of charcoal in this area and the fact that the greatest amount of pottery was found directly around it.

Cooking stones were also found in the culture layer. These are common finds on many Ertebølle settlements and in several cases they form layers of considerable extent, for example at Bloksbjerg (Westerby 1927, 23-24, Figs. 8-9 and references), Sønderholm (Jønsson/Pedersen 1983, 174-176, Figs. 4-5), Flynderhage (Gabrielsen 1953, 5-16), Norslund (Andersen/Malmros 1966, 37) and Ringkloster (Andersen, S.H. 1998, 26). Ash hearths (Ch. 4.2.2.2) were not found on the terrace or in the culture layer.

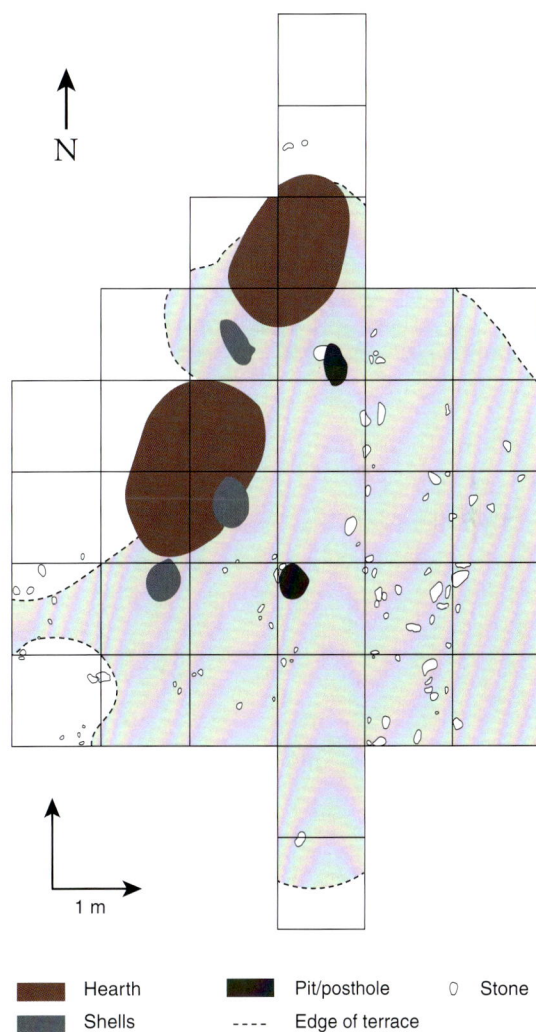

Fig. 6. Excavation trench showing the terrace (grey shade), hearths, postholes, large stones and three small shell concentrations. Note that the area in front of the hearths has been cleared of larger stones.

2.2.3 Shell concentrations

On the terrace were three small heaps of marine invertebrate shells, primarily composed of oysters but also containing cockles, mussels and periwinkles. These were located close to the hearths and presumably represent the remains of meals following the collection and consumption of these marine invertebrates. The heaps measured 40-50 cm in diameter and 5-10 cm in thickness (Fig. 6). A similar situation, with a small patch of shells found close to a hearth, was encountered at the Ertebølle settlement of Sindholt Nord near Hadsund (Andersen, S.H. 2004, 33, Fig. 12) and in association with a similar feature at Vegger (Simonsen 1952, 203-206, Fig. 4). Finally, it should be remembered that there was still a kitchen midden on this islet in the 19th century, as this was investigated by A.P. Madsen in 1897 (see Chapter 1.2).

2.2.4 Pits/postholes

On the terrace were also two pot-shaped pits which contained no finds. These had a diameter of c. 35 × 45 cm and a uniform depth of c. 13-18 cm. They were aligned along, and approximately in the middle of, the terrace, at a distance of c. 1-1.5 m from its "rear edge". The two pits were c. 2 m apart (Fig. 6). They could be either postholes associated with a "building" that stood on the terrace, or other features associated with the occupations.

2.2.5 Summary

Even though this locality has been a cultivated field since the 19th century, when A.P. Madsen made his visit, the distribution of worked flint and shells on the surface of the field, together with the size of the islet, shows that this was a very small settlement with an associated kitchen midden and an (occupation) platform (cut into the slope). It was here that people lived and from where they threw food waste and other rubbish down on to the shore, although no actual refuse layer has been found at the site. An analysis of the settlement surface (the terrace) shows that this was functionally differentiated (hearths, pits, postholes etc.). From the description given in the excavation report of the investigation in 1897, it appears that the kitchen midden ran down the slope immediately below the terrace.

2.3 The finds

2.3.1 Flint

A total of 8291 pieces of worked flint were recovered. Of these, 371 are tools and 7920 represent flint debitage. The complete tool inventory includes all the Ertebølle culture's groups of flint tools; in addition there is (thick- and thin-walled) pottery and a little worked red deer antler. The finds were clearly restricted to the terrace. Down the slope, however, a few squares were found to contain large quantities of waste from flint-working. These presumably represent debitage thrown down the slope in connection with 'tidying up operations' during occupation of the terrace (Fig. 7). The concentration of finds was particularly dense around the hearths, but there were also many tools on the southern part of the terrace: scrapers, borers, burins, transverse arrowheads and truncated flakes.

2.3.1.1 Debitage, technique and primary flint-working

The culture layer contained c. 240 pieces of white-burnt flint, constituting c. 3% of the total flint assemblage from the settlement. The amount of burnt flint present at Vængesø I appears to be greater than at other coeval Ertebølle settlements. This is true both in absolute terms and also, in particular, in relation to the (small) size of the locality. On this point there is, however, some similarity with the coeval settlement of Vængesø III (Ch. 4.3.1.1; Fig. 112). The distribution of the burnt (fire-crazed) flint shows a tendency towards two separate concentrations, located respectively to the north and to the south of the terrace. This supports the conclusion that there were two hearths (Fig. 7).

The assemblage includes all the stages of tool production and use: flint debitage, flint cores, blades, tools and worn-out discards. The blades were struck using indirect, soft technique. The percussion bulb is weakly developed and in almost all

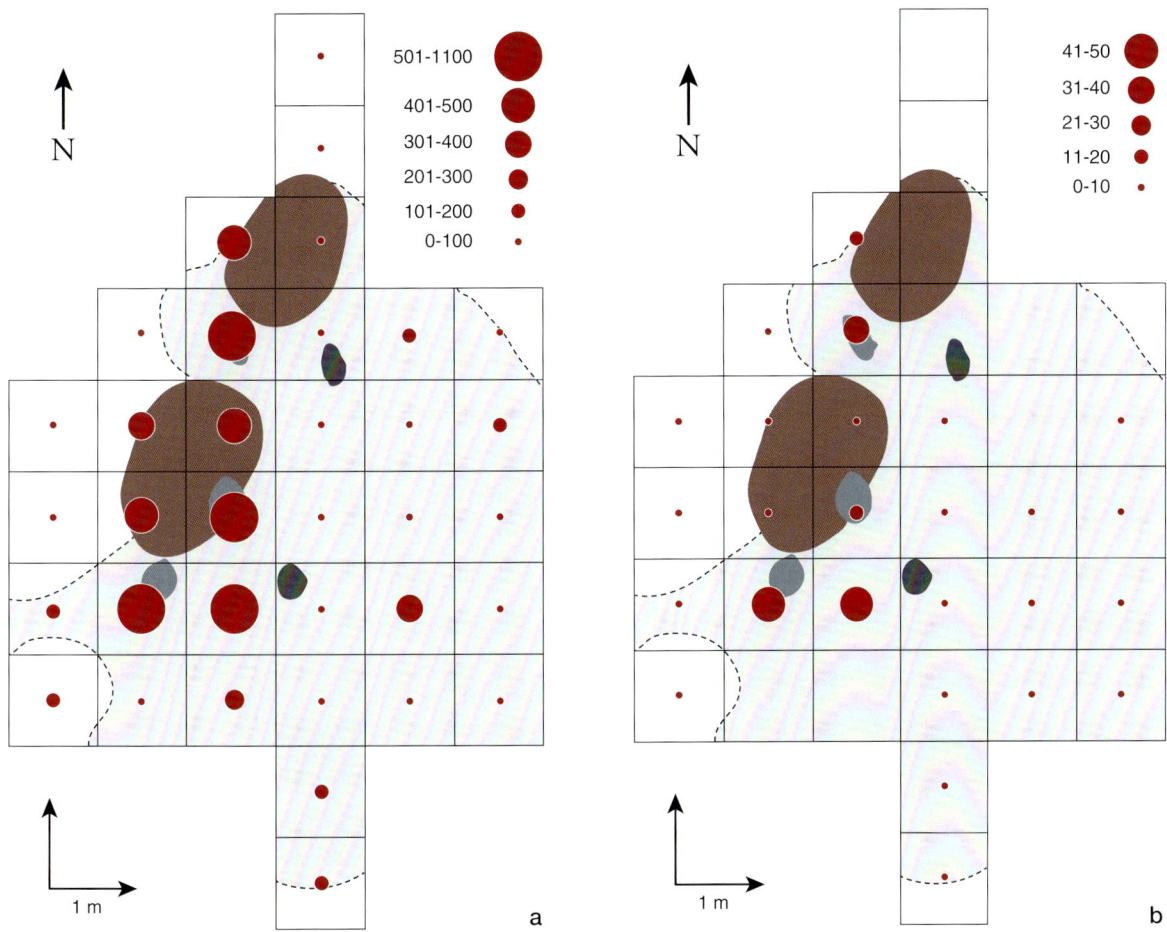

Fig. 7. a) Distribution of flint debitage and b) fire-brittled flint across the excavation trench.

cases a "lip" is evident at the platform remnant. Percussion bulbs are only exceptionally found. The platform remnants are narrow and oval and measure c. 0.2 × 0.8 cm. The percussion point is in many cases not identifiable. No traces were observed of preparation on the blade platform remnants, which are smooth. The "front" of the flakes, i.e. the dorsal side, shows retouch at the percussion bulb end and there are almost always traces of preparatory trimming (Madsen 1992, 93-131).

The flint technique evident at Vængesø I is characteristic of blade production. Out of a total of 960 blades, 312 are A-blades (32.5%), 624 are B-blades (65%) and 24 are microblades (2.5%). The ratio of A- to B-blades is higher at this settlement than at the other coeval settlements at Vængesø, and on Djursland in general.

Blade cores are represented by 80 examples, of which 45 are conical with one platform (56.3%), 31 have two platforms arranged at an angle (38.7%), three are cylindrical with two parallel platforms, three have several platforms (nodules) and there is one discoid core. The blade cores have a circular distribution with the centre of gravity close to the hearth area at the centre of the excavation. From here, their frequency decreases in all directions. In contrast to what one might expect, there was only a slight coincidence between the centres of gravity for the flint debitage and the blade cores (Figs. 7 and 8). Tool working and blade production apparently did not take place within the same area of the settlement.

Core flakes are represented by 207 examples, of which core-side flakes comprise c. 46% and core-edge flakes c. 27%.

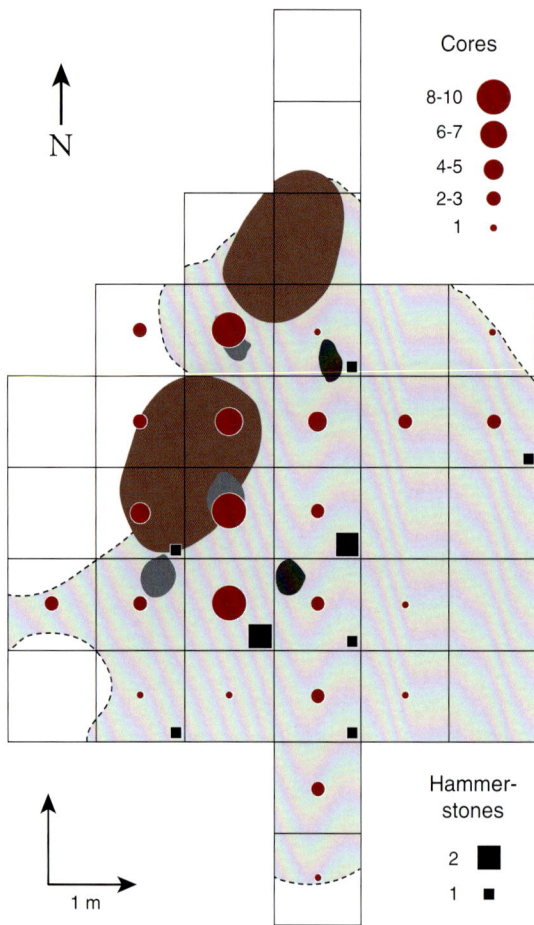

Fig. 8. Distribution of blade cores and hammerstones across the excavation trench. The cores lie close to the hearths, while the hammerstones lie in front of the hearths.

2.3.1.2 Artefacts from secondary working

Scrapers constitute 10% of the tools made on blades and flakes (Fig. 9). *Blade scrapers* are only represented by two examples (1%; Fig. 9a), whereas there are numerous *simple* (seven examples; Fig. 9b-c) and *denticulate flake scrapers* (eight examples). The latter type was very common at the Vængesø I and III settlements, but is otherwise rare at the coeval settlements in eastern Jutland, where blade scrapers are either universal or dominant, for example at Dyrholmen II (Mathiassen et al. 1942, 20) and Norslund layers 0+1 (Andersen/Malmros 1966, 76-77). Denticulate flake scrapers are also known from other settlements around the Vængesø lagoon (Vængesø II and III), from

the Ertebølle settlement of Ølby Lyng near Køge (Petersen, E.B. 1971, 8-9, Figs. 2-3) and Dyngby I at Saxild (unpublished; Moesgaard Museum archive no. 3954). The frequent occurrence of this scraper type at the Vængesø sites must reflect a special function at the Ertebølle settlements in this area. Two scrapers were made on symmetrical flat-flaked flake axes, while the other flake scrapers were made on irregular, elongate or circular flakes which in eight cases had a more or less cortex-covered dorsal side. The length of the denticulate flake scrapers is 3.1-8.6 cm, their width 2.7-8.2 cm and their thickness 0.7-2.8 cm. The blade scrapers were both made on irregular B-blades and their length is 7.2-9 cm, their width 2.8-2.9 cm and their thickness 0.8-1.2 cm.

Borers are similarly few in number (11 examples). This group is dominated by *flake borers* (seven examples), but there are also four *blade borers* (Fig. 10a). One flake borer was made on a flat-flaked, symmetrical flake axe. All the flake borers have a clearly defined tip relative to the grip. The length of the flake borers is 5.5-11.2 cm, their width 2.9-5.4 cm and their thickness 0.6-2.6 cm. The blade borers were made on short, irregular B-blades, where the tip is at the distal end and on the longitudinal axis of the original (raw) blade. None of these borers has a clearly defined tip. Their length is 4.9-6.4 cm, their width 2-2.6 cm and their thickness 0.2-0.6 cm.

Burins are represented by 18 examples. *Angle burins on a break* dominate this group with ten examples (Fig. 11).The raw material used comprised both coarse flakes and regular A-blades. In two cases, the burins were made on axes, respectively an asymmetrical flake axe and an axe unidentifiable to type. Five angle burins were made on regular blades, while the remainder were all flakes. The assemblage only includes a single angle burin on concave transverse retouch, which is a little unusual as this is a type that is otherwise common at other coeval eastern Jutish Ertebølle settlements. The burins were found in particular in the grid squares to the south of the hearth area. Their length is 6.2-9.9 cm, their width is 2.4-2.8 cm and their thickness is 0.4-1 cm.

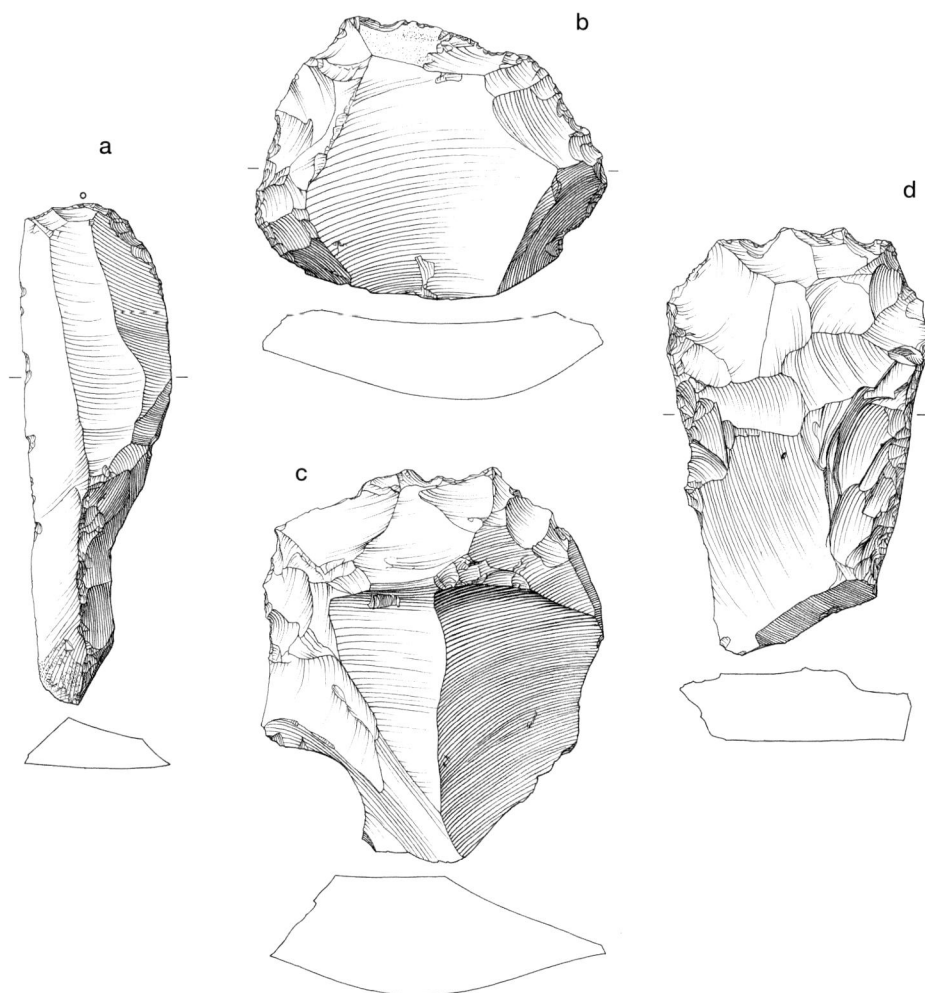

Fig. 9. a) Blade scraper. b-c) Denticulate flake scrapers. d) Denticulate flake scraper on a flake axe. Scale 3:4. Drawing: Orla Svendsen.

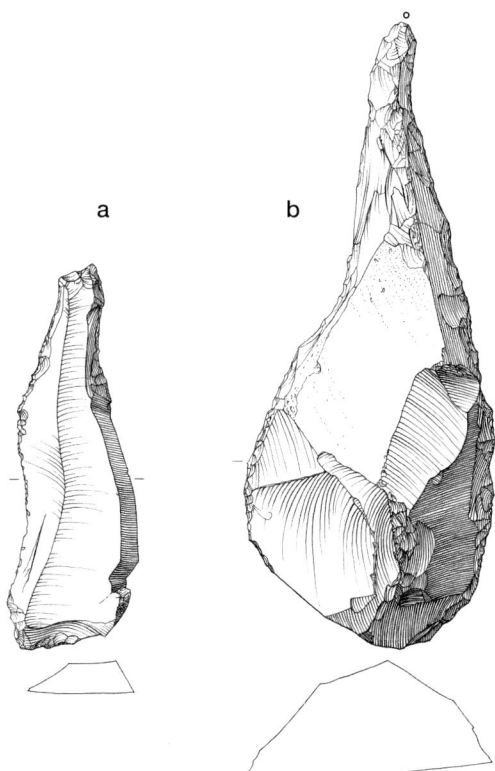

Blades with concave truncation constitute the absolute dominant tool type, with 20 examples (10.5% of all the blade tools; Fig. 13). The raw material used comprised blades in 18 cases and discoid flakes in two others. Seventeen examples have distal truncation and three have truncation at their proximal end. The truncated examples were found in the SSE part of the excavation (Fig. 12). Their length is 5.4-9.6 cm, their width 1.3-3.3 cm and their thickness 0.3-1.8 cm. In addition, there are three examples with straight truncation, three with straight and oblique truncation and six with slightly convex truncation – all made on blades. In this group, there are grounds to note the examples where the raw material comprised coarse, short,

◄ *Fig. 10. a) Blade borer. b) Flake borer. Scale 3:4. Drawing: Orla Svendsen.*

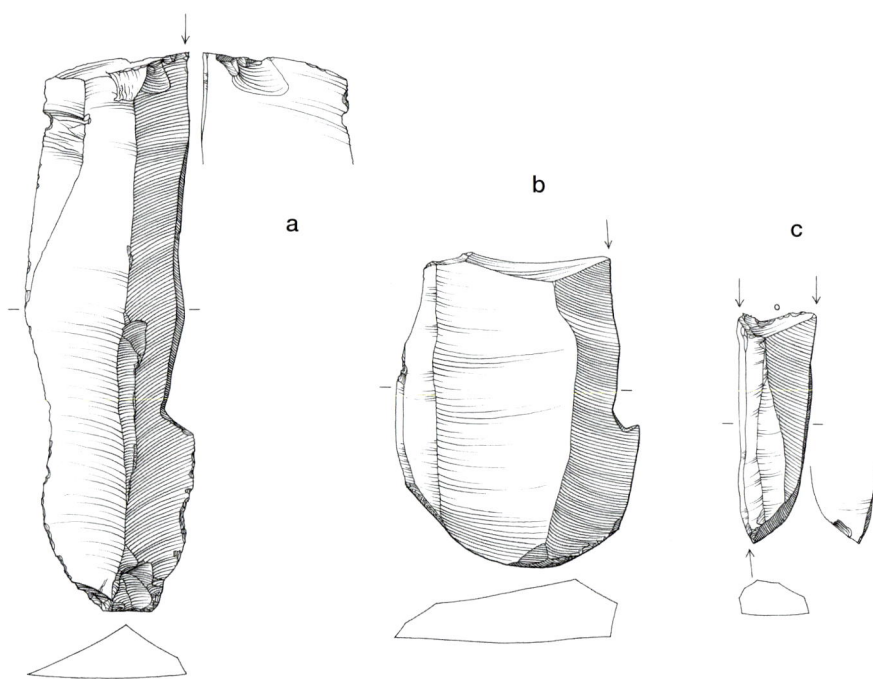

Fig. 11. a-b) Angle burins on a break. c) Mixed multi-burin on concave truncation. Scale 3:4. Drawing: Orla Svendsen.

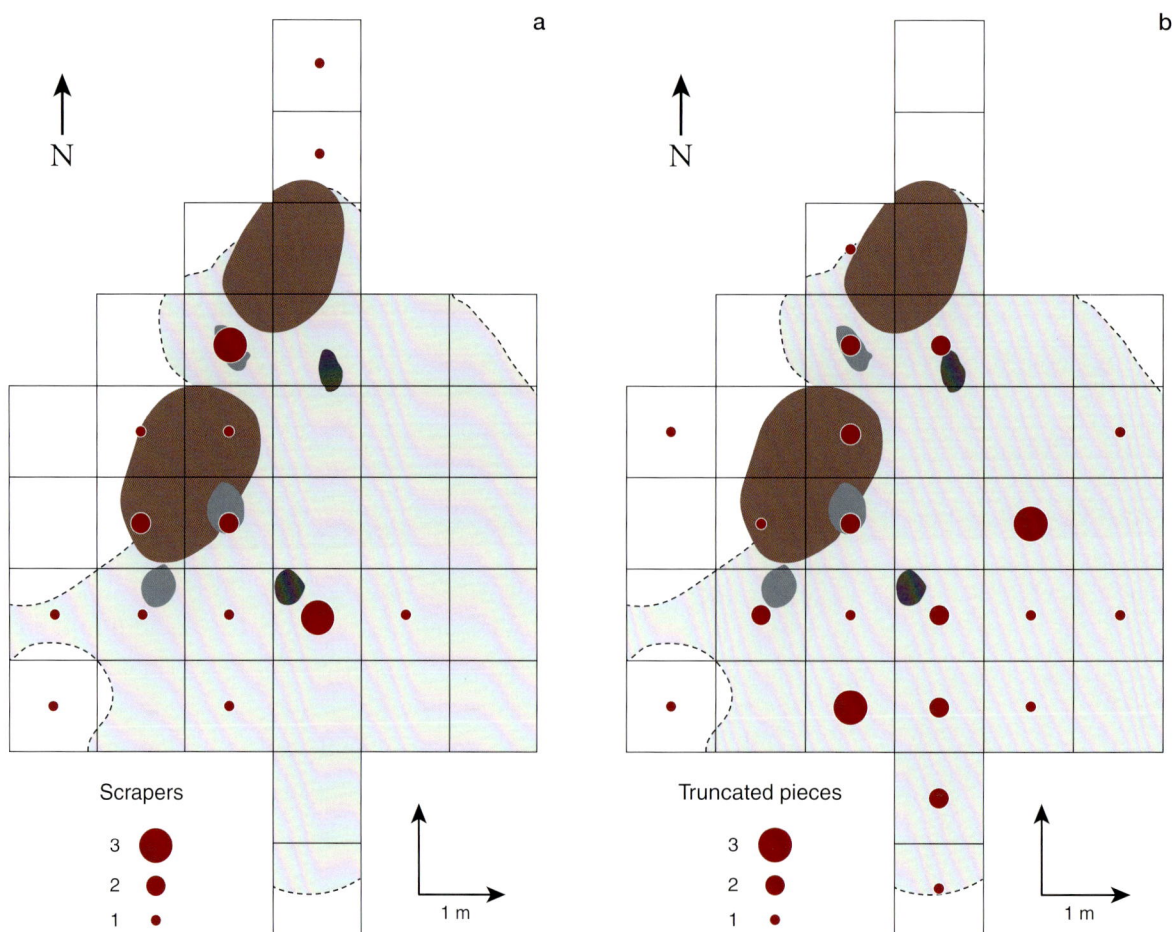

Fig. 12. a) Distribution of scrapers and b) truncated pieces across the excavation trench.

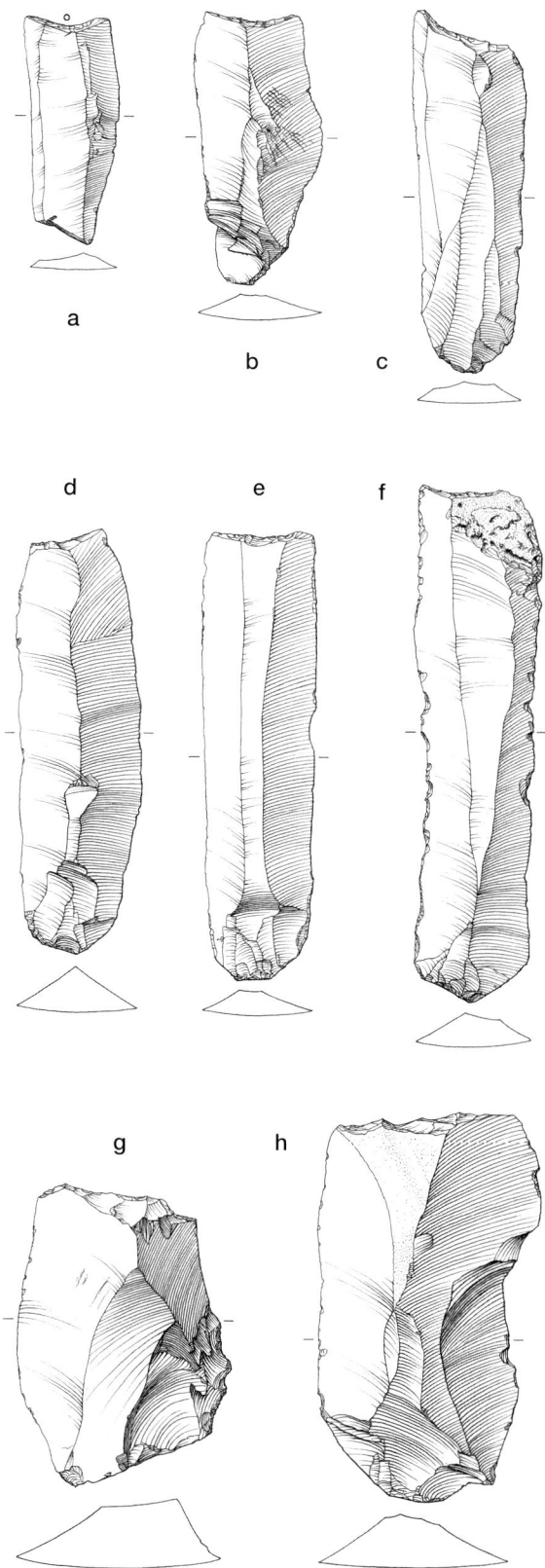

Fig. 13. a-d) Blades with concave and e-f) with straight truncation. g-h) Truncated pieces on short, wide flakes, cf. also Fig. 50d. Scale 3:4. Drawing: Orla Svendsen.

thick flakes. The length of these pieces is 4.5-9.4 cm, their width 1.7-3.4 cm and their thickness 0.3-0.9 cm. A single blade has a retouched "grip" or "handle" at the percussion bulb end, where the grip section is only slightly demarcated relative to the edges ("western Danish variant"; Fig. 16a; Andersen, S.H. 2009, 68).

Blades with a finely denticulate edge are represented by four examples (2%), of which one is denticulate on both edges (Fig. 14a). The raw material was in three cases a very regular blade, while the fourth was made on a rather more irregular flake. Their length is 6.4-12.4 cm, their width 1.4-3.2 cm and their thickness 0.3-1.4 cm.

Pieces with coarse denticulation are represented by 14 examples (5.5% of all the flake tools). The group is dominated by denticulate flakes (nine examples), while the rest were made on irregular blades. The raw material comprised irregular flakes, all with a

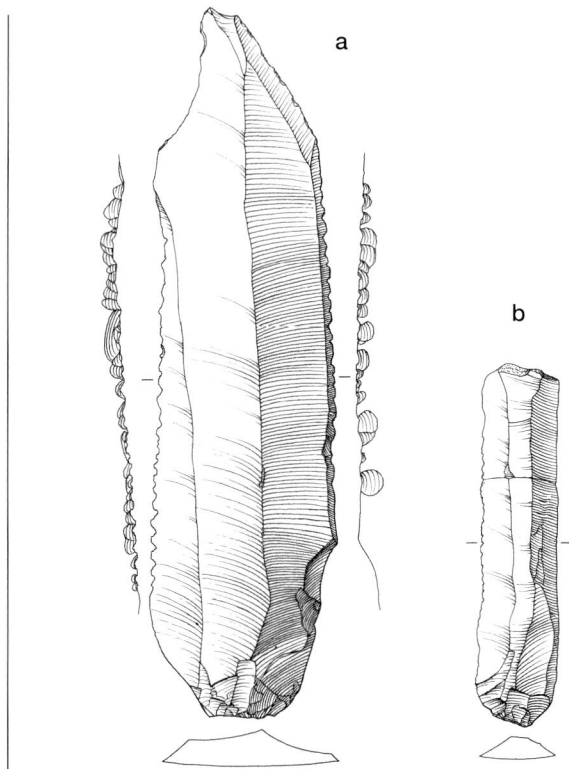

Fig. 14. Blades with finely denticulate edge (saws). a) Denticulation along both sides. b) Denticulation along one side. Scale 3:4. Drawing: Orla Svendsen.

dorsal cortex covering. Five flakes only have denticulation on one edge, while one has this on both longitudinal edges. Their length is 5.1-8.5 cm, their width 3.4-7.6 cm and their thickness 1.2-3.4 cm.

Notched pieces are common and are represented by 25 examples, of which 12 were made on blades and 13 on flakes (Fig. 15a-c). Of the former group, seven were made on regular blades and five on irregular blades. On seven examples, the notch was produced by normal retouch, while the remainder have reverse retouch. Ten examples have only one notch, while two have two notches in the same edge. Their length is 4.4-12.3 cm, their width 1.4-4.2 cm and their thickness 0.4-2.5 cm.

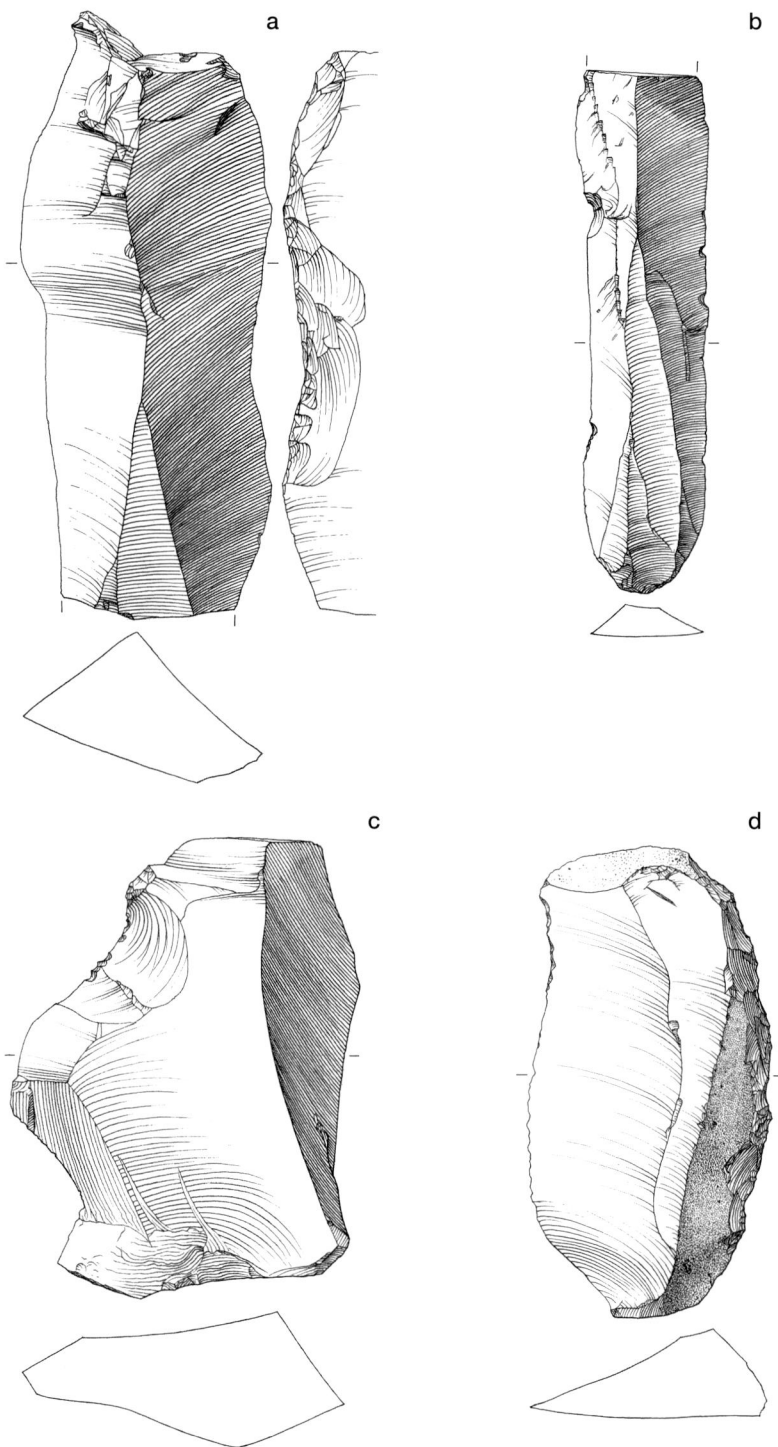

Fig. 15. a-c) Notched flakes and blades. d) Flake with curved dorsal trimming. Scale 3:4. Drawing: Orla Svendsen.

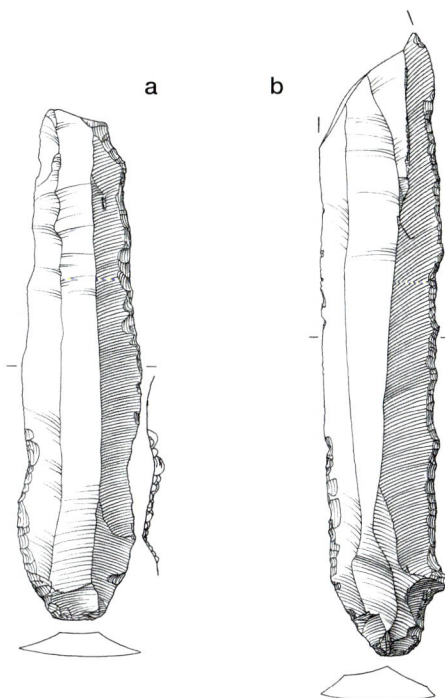

Fig. 16. Blades with contiguous edge retouch. Blade a has handle retouch. Scale 3:4. Drawing: Orla Svendsen.

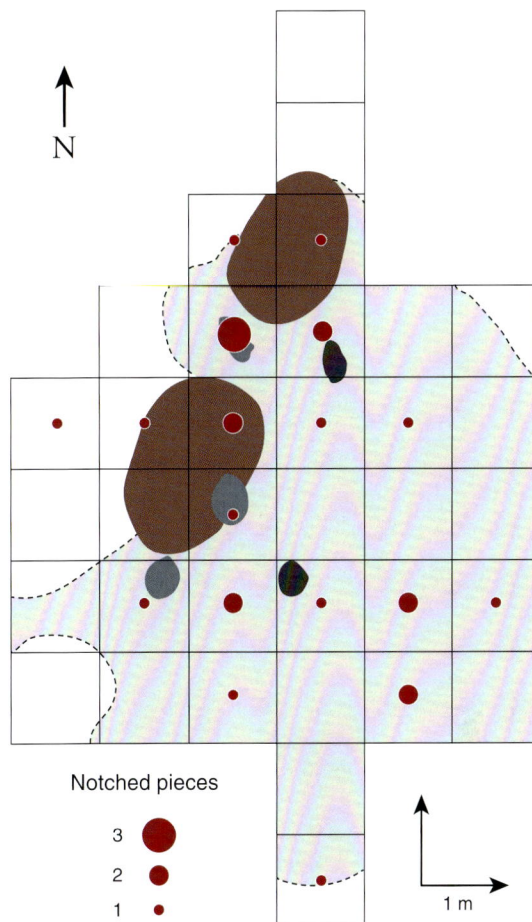

Notched pieces

3

2

1

Fig. 17. Distribution of notched pieces.

Notched flakes constitute an irregular group and six of them have a dorsal cortex covering. In ten cases the notch was made by normal retouch, while in three cases it was made by removing (striking off) part of the edge of the blank (preform). Eight examples have one notch, one example has two notches and a further example has three notches. Their length is 2.4-10.4 cm, their width 2.1-8 cm and their width 0.7-2.8 cm.

Blades and flakes with continual edge retouch are represented by 16 examples (Fig. 16a-b). Of these, 12 were made on regular blades and four on irregular blades. Seven blades have retouch along one edge, while nine have retouch on both edges. Their length is 6.1-11.2 cm, their width 1.6-3.4 cm and their thickness 0.4-0.9 cm. Fig. 17 shows the distribution of the notched tools and tools with continual edge retouch.

Two blades have a coarse, *curved back* (Fig. 15d).

The group of *transverse arrowheads* (48 examples; 25.2% of the blade tools) is characterised by symmetrical points with a straight edge and very strongly flared edge corners (39 examples; 81.2% of all arrowheads; Fig. 18b-h). One example was made on a biconvex flake (Fig. 18j) and could therefore possibly be earlier (and thereby a trace of earlier visits to the islet). The type with parallel edges and a slightly or markedly oblique edge is very poorly represented. Two transverse arrowheads must be classified as "large transverse arrowheads" (Fig. 18k). If these arrowheads are compared with corresponding examples from for example Norslund layer 2, the examples from Vængesø have more strongly concave sides (Andersen/Malmros 1966, 5-54). The distribution of the transverse arrowheads across the excavated area is shown in Fig. 19.

The *axe group* is extensive and dominated by flake axes, which constitute 85.3% of the total. On the other hand, the 25 *core axes* constitute 14.6% of the total; symmetrical axes dominate this latter

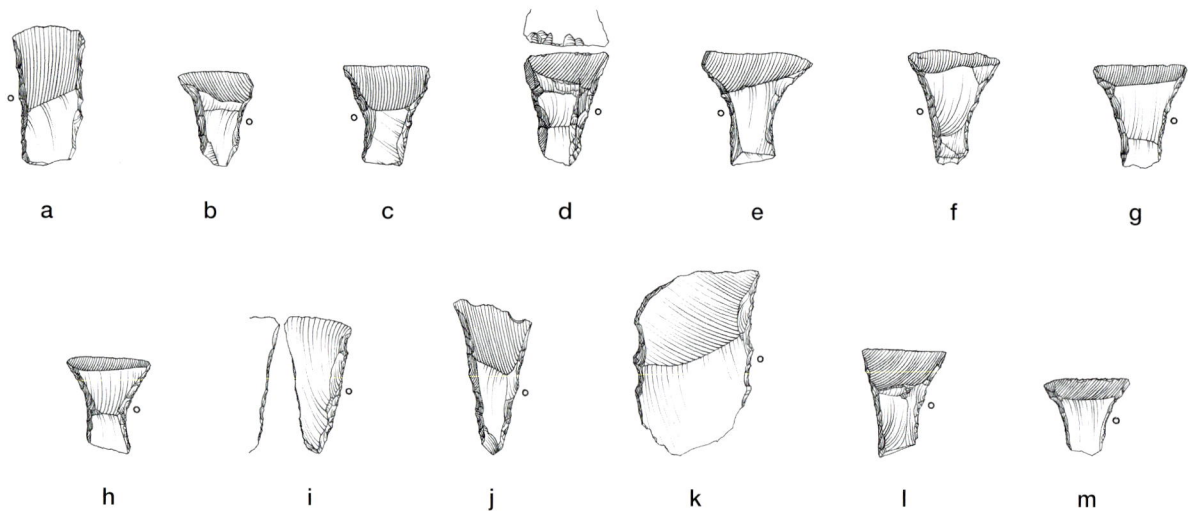

Fig. 18. Selection of transverse arrowheads; i) is on a biconvex flake. The dominant type at Vængesø I is symmetrical with strongly concave sides. Scale 3:4. Drawing: Orla Svendsen.

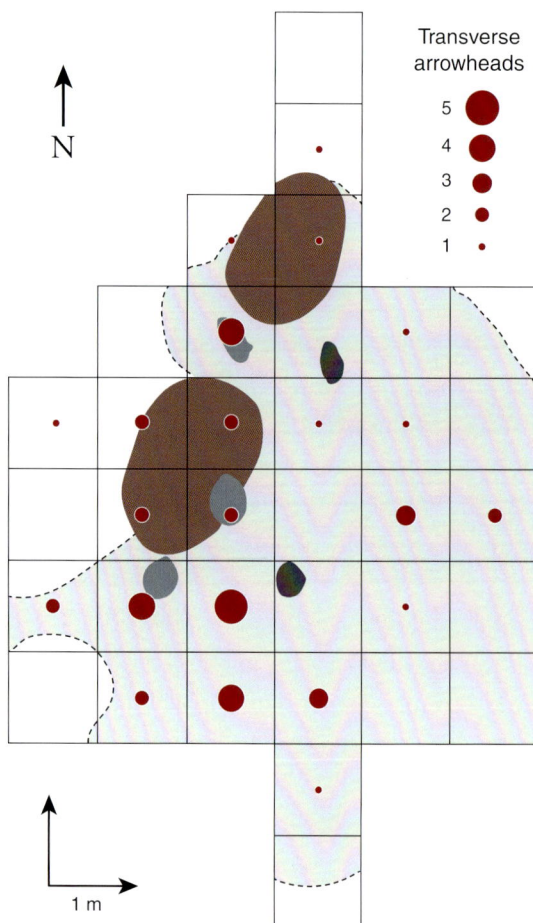

Fig. 19. Distribution of transverse arrowheads across the excavation trench.

group. There are four symmetrical axes, of which one has double-sided specialised edge trimming (Fig. 20), and four symmetrical adzes, of which one has specialised edge trimming. The assemblage also includes four asymmetrical axes as well as a number of butt sections from broken axes. The symmetrical axes are all regular with a median length of c. 10 cm, a median width of c. 3.2 cm and a median thickness of c. 3.1 cm. Their edge is 1.9-2.4 cm. The symmetrical adzes measure 6.7-9.2 cm in length, 3.8-4.6 cm in width and 2.4-3.6 cm in thickness: The edge width of these examples is 1.7-2.4 cm. One symmetrical adze has unilateral, specialised edge trimming. The asymmetrical core axes form a uniform group, but are smaller and less regularly worked than the symmetrical forms. Their median length is c. 7.4 cm, median width c. 3.5 cm and median thickness c. 2.2 cm. As for broken butt sections, two can cautiously be said to come from adzes and one is presumably from an axe. The others are completely unidentifiable with respect to their original type/edge orientation.

Flake axes, with 135 examples, constitute the commonest tool form in the assemblage (Fig. 21). Rejuvenation is a commonly occurring feature and is evident on 34.6% of the axes. This frequency corresponds to the situation encountered at the

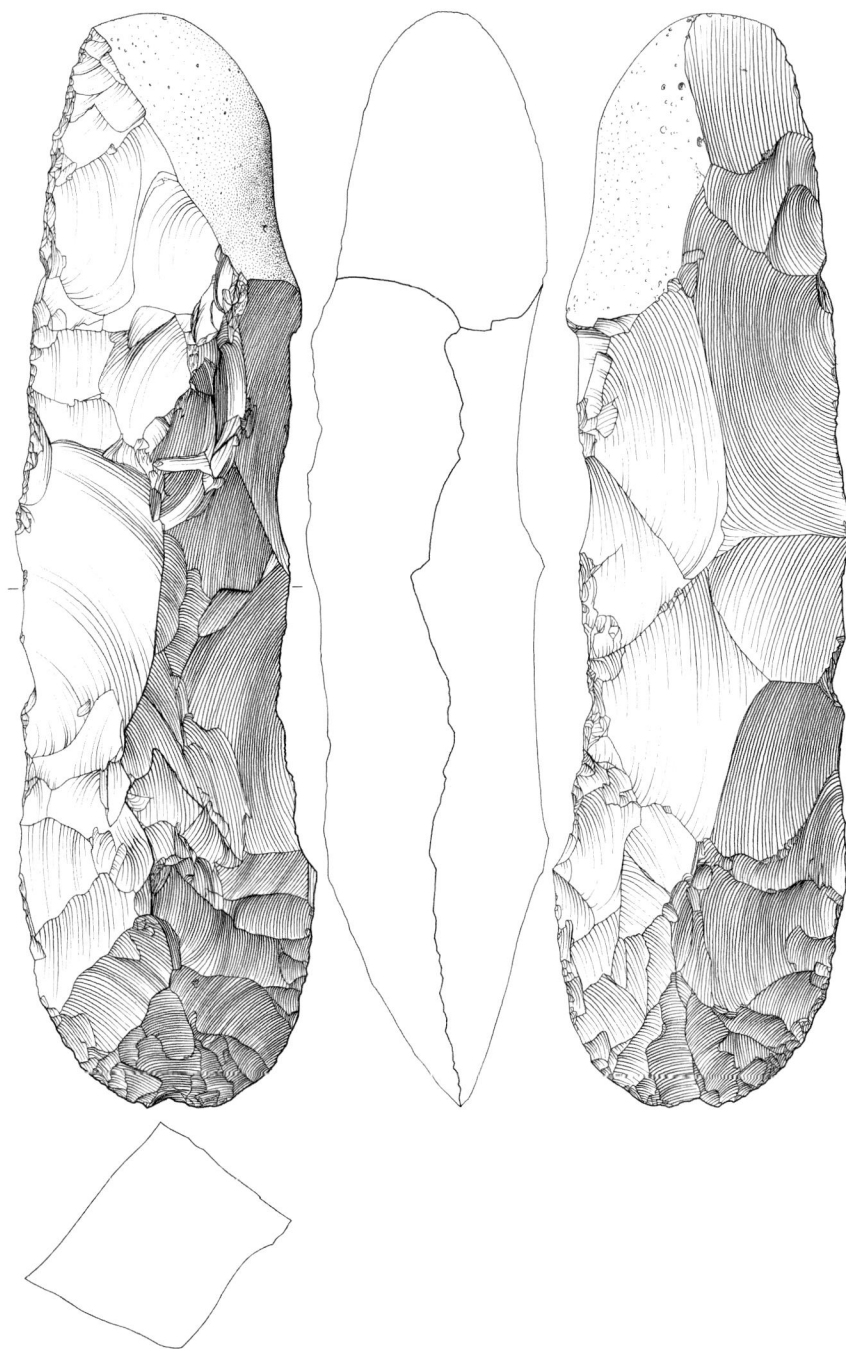

Fig. 20. Symmetrical core axe with double-sided, specialised edge working. Scale 3:4. Drawing: Orla Svendsen.

coeval settlement of Ronæs Skov on the west Funen coast of the Little Belt, where 33.6% of the flake axes show traces of edge rejuvenation (Andersen, S.H. 2009, 76-77). For all the flake axes, their median length is 7.8 cm, their greatest width 4.8 cm, width 3 cm from the butt 3.5 cm and their greatest thickness 2 cm. The flake axes were found across the entire occupation surface but especially close to, and to the south of, the hearths (Fig. 22). The type can be divided up into edge-trimmed flake axes

(four examples), asymmetrical flat-flaked flake axes (13 examples), symmetrical flat-flaked flake axes (105 examples) and atypical flake axes (nine examples). The symmetrical flat-flaked variant is prominent and represents 78% of the total. Among the latter, examples with very concave sides are dominant (Fig. 21a-c), but examples with either parallel or weakly concave sides are also represented (Fig. 21d-e). Two flat-flaked flake axes had been further worked into coarse scrapers (Fig. 9d), and

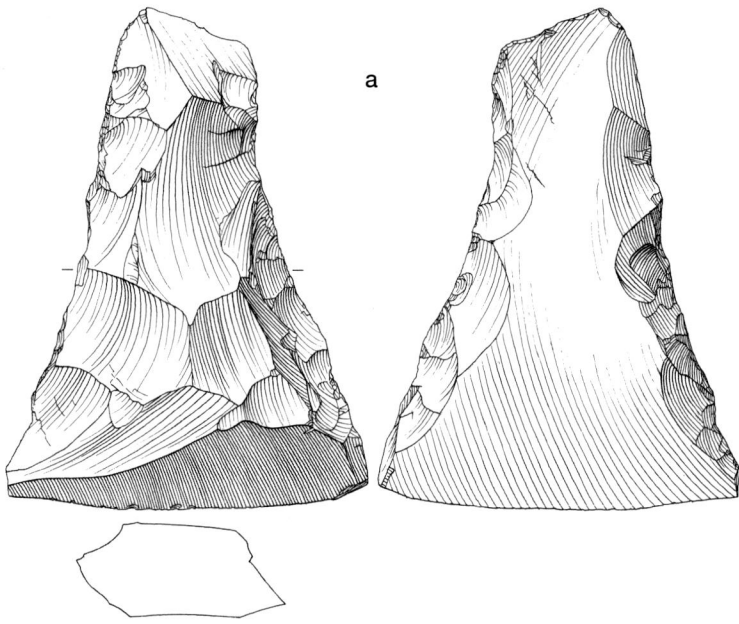

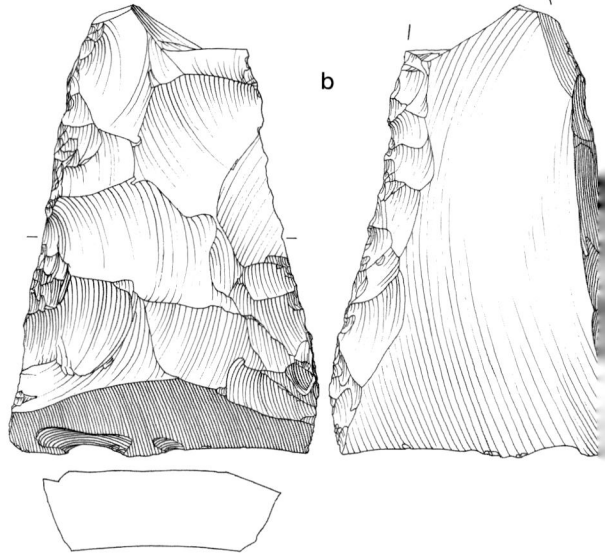

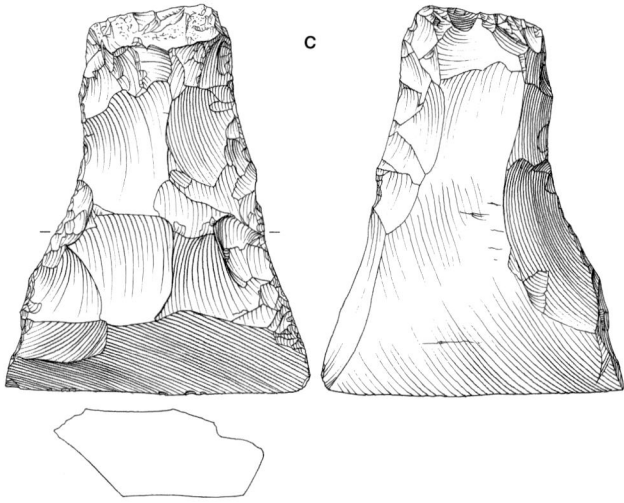

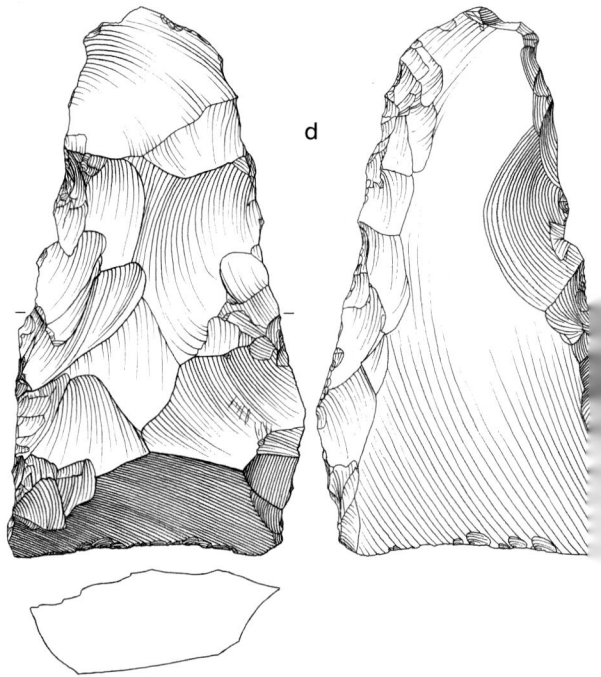

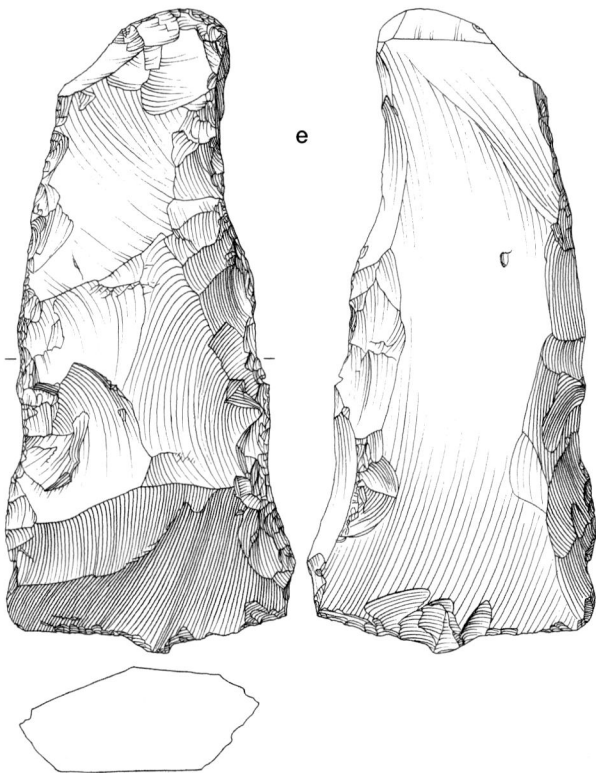

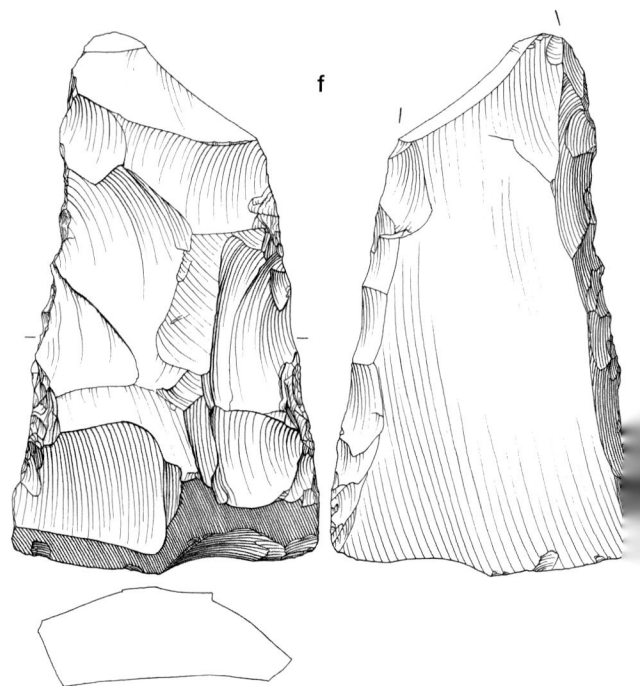

one had been reused/reworked as a symmetrical borer. Finally, an asymmetrical, flat-flaked flake axe has been (re-)used as an angle burin on a break. The reuse of flake axes is a well-known feature of settlements from the Late Ertebølle culture and is seen for example at Ordrup Næs (Becker 1939, 244, Figs. 11-12) and Ronæs Skov (Andersen, S.H. 2009, 74, 76, Fig. 47c-e) and also at the other settlements around Vængesø (Fig. 131b). The median value for the length of the flat-flaked flake axes is 8.6 cm, greatest width 4.9 cm, width 3 cm from the butt 3.5 cm and greatest thickness 2 cm. If these dimensions are compared with corresponding measurements from Norslund layer 0, it becomes apparent that the axes from Vængesø I are both longer and wider than those from Norslund. The butt width and thickness are, on the other hand, exactly the same (Andersen/Malmros 1966, 45-47). The assemblage also includes a single edge flake from a symmetrical, flat-flaked flake axe (Fig. 23).

The assemblage also includes 11 *flake chisels*, of which seven are symmetrically flat-flaked (6.4% of the axe group; Fig. 24). The latter type is a very characteristic artefact of the latest Ertebølle culture in eastern Jutland. One of the symmetrical chisels shows evidence of edge rejuvenation. Two chisels are made on recycled, symmetrical flat-flaked flake axes, where a narrow edge has been created on the central axis and clearly "demarcated" from the rest

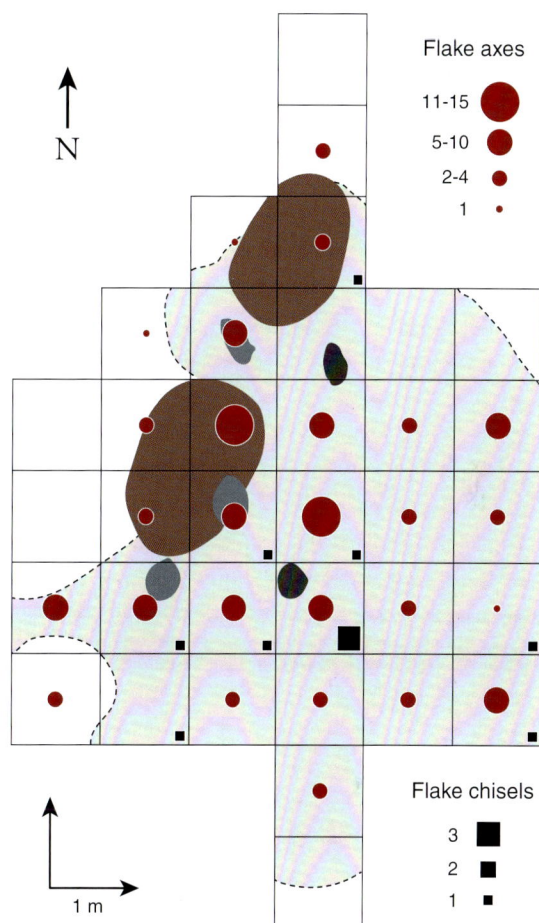

Fig. 22. Distribution of flake axes and flake chisels across the excavation trench. The two types are found in different squares on the terrace.

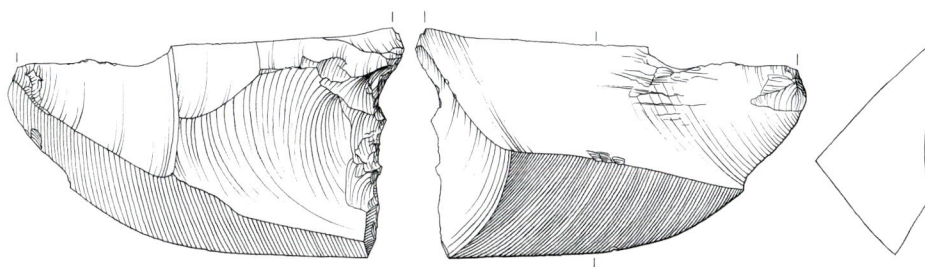

Fig. 23. Struck-off edge section from a symmetrical, flat-flaked flake axe. Unsuccessful attempt at rejuvenation. Scale 3:4. Drawing: Orla Svendsen.

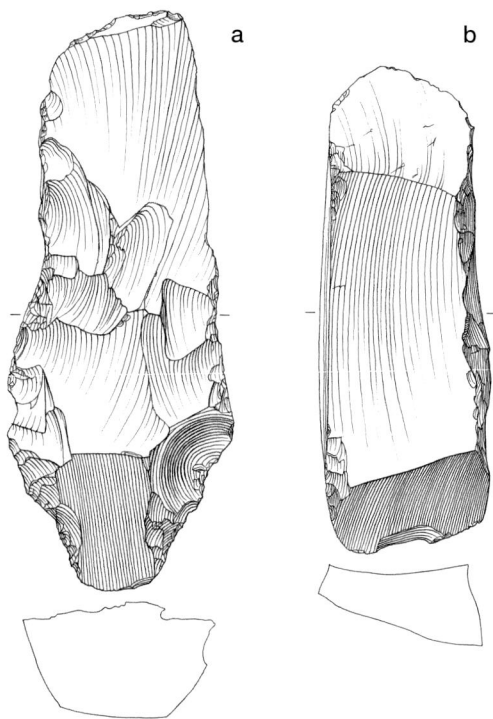

Fig. 24. Symmetrical flake chisels. One side of example b) is formed by a hinge fracture, a typical feature of Late Ertebølle chisels in eastern Jutland. Scale 3:4. Drawing: Orla Svendsen.

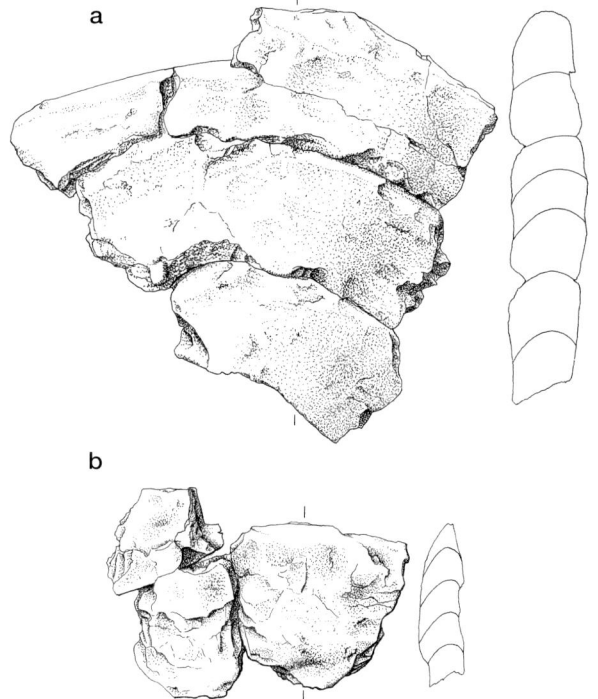

Fig. 25. Examples of coil-constructed Ertebølle pottery. a) Thick-walled ware constructed in reverse U-technique. The sherd comes from the lower part of a pointed-based vessel. b) Thin-walled ware constructed in the same technique. Scale 3:4. Drawing: Orla Svendsen.

of the piece by two carefully worked "shoulders" (Fig. 24a). The length of the symmetrical flat-flaked chisels is 6.4-10.3 cm, the width 2.6-3 cm and their thickness fluctuates between 1.1 and 1.8 cm. Two flake chisels stand out from the rest because they were made on flakes with "hinge fractures" such that this fracture constitutes one of the long sides (Fig. 24b). This slightly unusual form is regularly seen at settlements from the Late Ertebølle culture. The length of these two examples is 8.1-12.2 cm, their width 2.8-3 cm and their thickness 1.5-1.7 cm. The distribution of flake chisels on the settlement is shown in Fig. 22.

The flint inventory also contains four *spherical hammerstones*, each with a diameter of c. 6 cm. The use/function of these hammerstones is unknown, but the convincing theory has been proposed that they could have been used in the production of greenstone axes (Nicolaisen 2009, 855). There appears to be a tendency for hammerstones to occur on the periphery of the finds distribution, i.e. outside the terrace and towards the ESE (Fig. 8).

2.3.2 Greenstone

No *greenstone axes* were found in the excavation, but P. Poulsen had previously, during surface collection on this settlement, found three examples with a blunt and rounded butt, as well as an edge fragment.

2.3.3 Pottery

In addition to flint artefacts, *potsherds* were also present in the culture layer (a total of 62 examples), of which 56 are of a thick ware with a wall thickness of more than 1 cm, and five are of thinner ware with a wall thickness of less than 1 cm. One could not be measured. Unfortunately, none of the sherds are from rim sections or are ornamented and none have any other special characteristics. The sherds show that the pottery was made using so-called U-techniques; they represent at least eight pottery vessels. The form (curvature) of one of the sherds shows that it comes from close to the base of a pointed-based vessel of Ertebølle type (Fig. 25). The thick-walled sherds could, on the basis of their structure, tempering and thickness, all be assigned to the Ertebølle culture. The age of the thin-walled sherds is slightly less certain. These could theoretically be from the Neolithic, but their tempering, firing and structure tend to indicate an origin in a late phase of the Ertebølle culture. Thin-walled sherds from pointed-based vessels have been found at other sites, especially from the culture's final phase in western Denmark (Mathiassen et al. 1942, 62; Troels-Smith 1967, 516). A good example of this is seen at Vængesø II, where it was extremely difficult to distinguish between thin-walled Ertebølle pottery and Early Neolithic Funnel Beaker pottery. Consequently, a significant proportion of the thin-walled side sherds could only be assigned with great difficulty to one or other of these two periods. The potsherds formed a concentration in the middle of the hearth area, which is consistent with the fact that it was here cooking etc. took place (Fig. 26).

2.3.4 Antler

The finds include the c. 7.2 cm long tip of a *fabricator* (Fig. 27a) and a piece (c. 3 × 2.5 cm) from the edge of an *antler axe* (Fig. 27b). There is also a fragment from the base of an antler tine with a distinct transverse saw mark at its broad end. The latter may be the missing base from the aforementioned fabricator. Based on the character and date of the finds assemblage as a whole, the edge fragment must be from an axe of T-form. The small num-

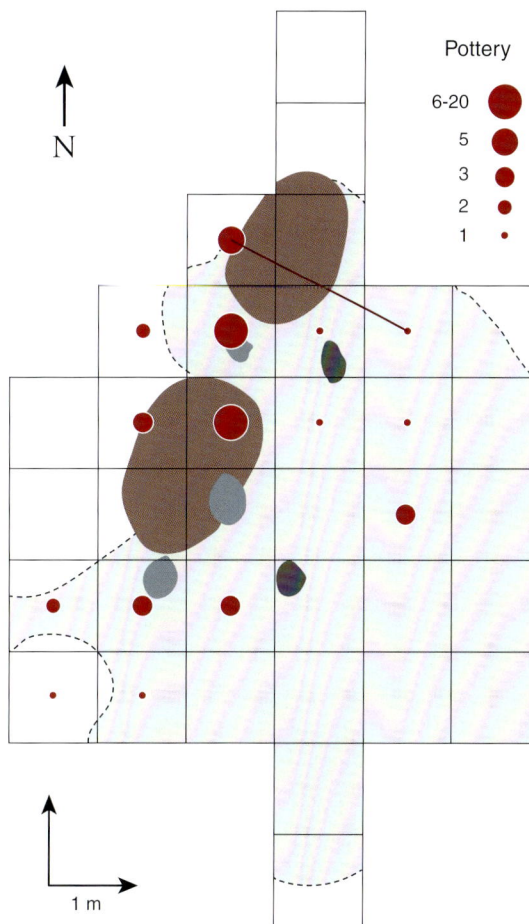

Fig. 26. Distribution of Ertebølle pottery across the excavation trench. Ertebølle sherds are generally found close to the hearths. Sherds that belong together are joined with a thin line.

ber of antler and bone tools is remarkable, given that there was originally a small kitchen midden at the site. Similarly, the complete absence of bone points and waste from bone- and antler-working should be noted. This can hardly be due to the preservation conditions at the site, but must mean that these bone points did not form part of the Ertebølle population's equipment here. The probable correctness of the latter view is underlined by the absence, or virtual absence, of such tools from the two other contemporaneous and closely adjacent Ertebølle settlements of Vængesø II and III and is apparently a regional characteristic of this settlement group.

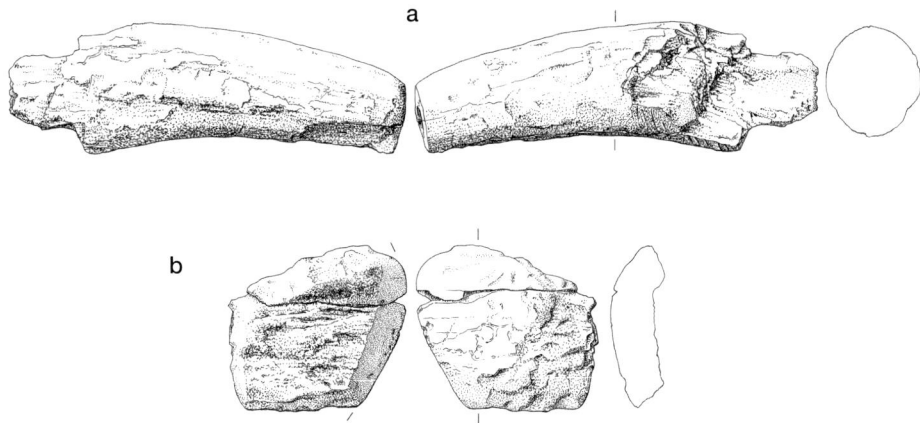

Fig. 27. Tools of red deer antler. a) Point of a fabricator. b) Fragment from the edge of an antler axe. Scale 3:4. Drawing: Orla Svendsen.

2.4 Dating

A typological assessment of the total finds assemblage clearly indicates a date for this settlement in the Late Ertebølle culture. The criteria on which this conclusion is based comprise the relationship between the various types of transverse arrowheads, with domination of the type with a strongly flared edge, the relationship between core axes and flake axes, with the latter type with a strongly flared edge being clearly dominant and the presence of core axes with bifacial edge trimming. The flat-flaked flake chisels are also a characteristic component of the tool inventory. Further to this is the dominance of thick-walled, coil-constructed pottery.

There is also chronological evidence from the radiocarbon dating of a whale bone (identified to the order Cetacea; AAR-8298: 5479 ± 45 bp) which gave an age of 4362-4263 BC cal (1 σ); the $\delta^{13}C$ value of this sample is -14.11‰. This date corresponds to the Late Ertebølle culture and there is therefore accordance between the archaeological-typological and the scientific dates for this locality. It should, however, be noted that artefact collection on the "islet" has yielded types (including dihedral burins etc.) that must originate from use of the site during Early/Earliest Ertebølle culture (cf. the previously mentioned transverse arrowhead made on a biconvex flake).

This and all subsequently-cited radiocarbon dates have been calibrated using the most recent calibration curve, as of autumn 2016.

2.5 Faunal remains and seasonality

Scattered through the culture layer were eight pieces of splintered bone from a large whale (infraorder Cetacea). There were also bones of aurochs (*Bos primigenius*), ox (*Bos* sp.), red deer (*Cervus elaphus*), roe deer (*Capreolus caprelous*), wild boar (*Sus scrofa*), dog (*Canis familiaris*), grey seal (*Halichoerus grypus*), seal (*Phoca* sp.), porpoise (*Phocaena phocaena*) and various birds (class Aves), which unfortunately could not be identified to species (Andersen S.H. 1975b, 42; identifications by U. Møhl, Zoological Museum, Copenhagen). Conversely, no fishbones were found – a consequence first and foremost of the prevailing preservation conditions and the excavation methods employed. Judging from the occurrence of bone fragments in the excavated grid squares, wild boar was the commonest species followed by whale and red deer.

Collecting is documented by the marine molluscs. The bone splinters of large whale (Fig. 28) were of particular interest because, in relation to the limited extent of the settlement, they occurred in remarkably large numbers. At least two were fragments of vertebral epiphyses, derived from the bone's solid, dense bone mass (outer layer). These bones do not show definite signs of working, but all have cloven and fractured surfaces, which suggest that they were hammered and chopped into pieces while fresh. The length of the bone fragments is c. 7.5-13.5 cm, their width 1.5-4 cm and their thickness c. 1.5-2 cm. They were found scattered across the settlement surface but without any obvious concentrations (Fig. 29). Considering the size of the bones associated with large species of whale, one can only wonder about what happened to the remainder of the animals. One possibility is that, in Atlantic times, Vængesø was a lagoon in which, due to the topography, large whales regularly became stranded, and this knowledge was systematically exploited by the Ertebølle fishers and hunters. Targeted exploitation of a particular area's "stranded" whales has

been described from New Zealand, where the indigenous population have, up to the present day, exploited whales that regularly strand in bays with particularly shallow water (Dudok van Heel 1962, 473). Pieces of crushed whalebone are not unusual finds at Ertebølle settlements in eastern Jutland. For example, similar bone splinters from a large whale were found in layer 3 at the Norslund settlement (see U. Møhl in Andersen/Malmros 1966, 108-109) and these showed traces of fire/burning.

Despite the limited size of the faunal assemblage recovered from Vængesø I, the remains of marine mammals are common and must, at least to some degree, reflect economic activities. Given the small size of the islet, it is difficult to imagine that it sustained an independent population of forest animals. All the bones recovered therefore probably represent provisions brought along

Fig. 28. Example of a bone splinter from a large whale. The piece shows clear evidence of axe cuts (arrowed). Photo: Photo/Media Department, Moesgaard Museum.

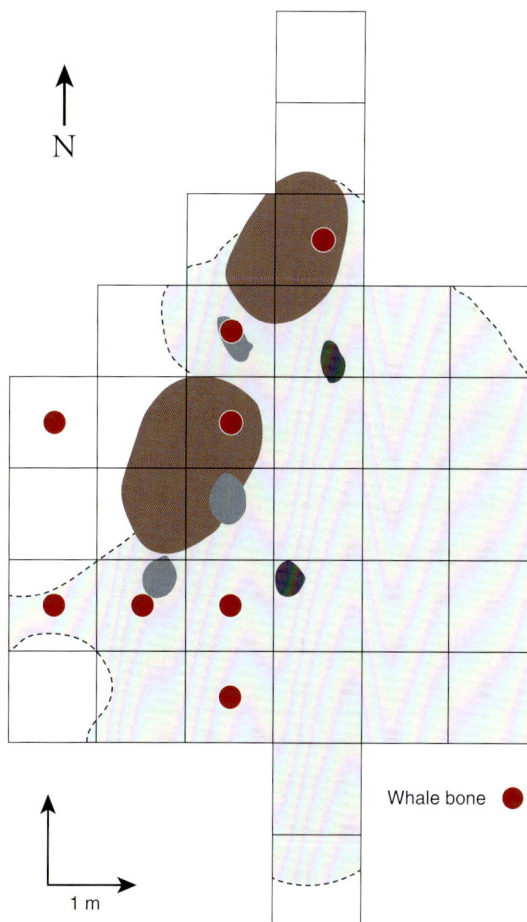

Fig. 29. Excavation plan showing the distribution of bone splinters from large whales.

during visits to the site. As for the season during which the Ertebølle hunters and fishers occupied the islet, a non-shed roe deer antler shows that they spent time there during the period from spring to early winter, i.e. the summer half of the year (Enghoff 2011, 193). But the faunal remains do not reveal anything about visits at other times of the year.

2.6 Settlement type

A small islet with a domed surface such as this could not have been occupied by very many people. Then there was the lack of drinking water (though this could have been obtained by sailing to one of the springs in the surrounding area). These factors harmonise well with a settlement and culture layer/kitchen midden of very limited extent and thickness and the modest nature of the finds assemblage that was recovered. Seen as a whole, the tool inventory suggests that the site should be interpreted as a small (hunting) camp that was occupied occasionally/seasonally for one or more periods of short duration by a small group of hunters for the purposes of fishing, hunting marine animals and so on.

The site must be seen in conjunction with one or more of the other contemporaneous Ertebølle localities associated with the lagoon, for example in relation to a larger settlement such as Vængesø III (Fig. 3). The finds assemblage shows that transverse arrowheads were produced on the islet. Similarly, the splintered whale bones could be remains arising from the production of harpoons, as these have in several instances been found to be made of whalebone, including an example from the nearby site of Vængesø II (Andersen, S.H. 1977, 49-50, Fig. 5). The numerous cooking stones at Vængesø I must reflect settlement activities that required considerable amounts of hot or boiling water. The group of denticulate flake scrapers is also interesting, and it is difficult to know how the occurrence and function/use of these scrapers should be explained. The contemporaneous settlement of Ølby Lyng, close to Køge Bay, also yielded tools of this kind, which were interpreted as being in-

volved in the processing of animals bagged during the passing seasonal migration of smaller marine mammals, for example seals, porpoises and so on (Petersen, E.B. 1971, 17). A similar explanation is conceivable for the denticulate flake scrapers found at Vængesø I. Seen from an overall perspective, and compared with the finds assemblages from the other excavated localities, the core axes at this site were more numerous and more regular in form than those from the other Vængesø sites (Vængesø II and III).

The terrace is indicative of a settlement surface, or at least part of one, containing several different structures. An analysis of the distribution of the various finds categories on this surface reveals no clear patterns, but in several cases it does provide some suggestions as to original activity areas that have been more or less erased by later occupations (Asher 1968). The terrace at Vængesø I is very reminiscent of a similar structure at the small locality of Vegger in Halkær Bredning (Simonsen 1952, 199-226). Here was a terrace with a pointed-oval outline that had been cut into the side of a steep coastal slope in the same way as at Vængesø I. The feature, which was irregular in outline, measured c. 5.5 in length and had a maximum width of c. 2.5 m; consequently it covered an area of about 13.7-15 m². Its surface sloped downwards towards the prehistoric shore (Simonsen 1952, 204, Figs. 5-6). The Vegger site also had heaps of cooking stones/stone-set hearths and small concentrations of shells on the surface. Even though there is a considerable degree of uncertainty associated with this latter site with regard to the excavation method employed and, in particular, the subsequent recording and interpretation (Sørensen 1993, 28; Rowley-Conwy 2013, 141), and even though the observational conditions at Vegger were difficult, the structure found does show great similarity to the terrace encountered at Vængesø I: i.e. the "cutting" of a terrace into the slope, the form and size of this structure and the features present on the actual (floor) surface.

The conclusion is that this type of terrace is a characteristic feature of small, restricted settlements at sites with a sloping occupation surface.

3 Vængesø II "Egehøj"

This locality (parish record no. 39, Helgenæs parish, Mols Søndre district, Randers county; Moesgaard Museum archive no. 1850) is situated in the southeastern part of Vængesø, c. 250 m northeast of Vængesø I (Fig. 3). The settlement is located within a c. 10 m wide hollow in a steep-sided, saddle-shaped hill, which to the east borders the present-day coast (Ebeltoft Vig), while the other sides are bounded by raised and reclaimed areas of sea-floor sediments. This hill, which was an elongated island in the Stone Age Vængesø lagoon, measures c. 70 × 80 m (N-S/E-W) and has two peaks; the easternmost is the highest (c. 5.3 m a.m.s.l.), while the westernmost is somewhat lower and only reaches c. 4 m a.m.s.l. The hill is part of a north-south orientated beach-ridge system that in the Stone Age sheltered Vængesø from the more open water of Ebeltoft Vig. Its eastern side was steep due to (marine) erosion, while the other sides had a more even fall down towards the contemporaneous shore. The location of the settlement, and the height of the beach-ridge system (at c. 2.5-3 m a.m.s.l.), makes it difficult to assess when and to what extent the beach ridge was dry enough to permit settlement and when it possibly constituted a partly submerged reef. The size of the island therefore varied, depending on the sea level at different times. At the Stone Age maximum (when the sea level was c. 4-4.3 m above present), the size of the island was c. 40 × 50 m. As the lower part between the two hilltops lies at c. 3-3.85 m a.m.s.l., it must have been inundated at this time and during periodic high water/storm surges. At this sea level there would only have been a c. 10 m wide dry area, or "saddle", between the two hilltops – and probably even less (Fig. 30).

The location of the settlement in the "saddle" was ideal, because this is the only approximately flat place on the relatively steep-sided island. At the same time, it provided a good view out across Ebeltoft Vig and was also sheltered from the wind coming from the open sea to the east. With the sea level at c. 3 m above present, the dry area would have been significantly larger, c. 56 × 63 m (3528 m²), encompassing both the eastern and western hilltops and the area between them (Fig. 30). The cultural deposits are concentrated in particular within a c. 16 × 6 m area (c. 96 m²) between the two hilltops and by the foot of the highest hill, where they have been well protected from erosion. But worked flint is also found on the western and southern sides of the island, facing in towards the Vængesø lagoon.

Numerous flint tools, representing Ertebølle types (many finds), can be collected everywhere across the field surface, but there are also some examples from various phases of the Neolithic (few finds). It is important to emphasise that the topography narrowly restricted occupation of this island to the area between the two hilltops. In 1975, amateur archaeologist Poul Poulsen excavated a test pit in this saddle, which led to the discovery of an undisturbed kitchen midden containing

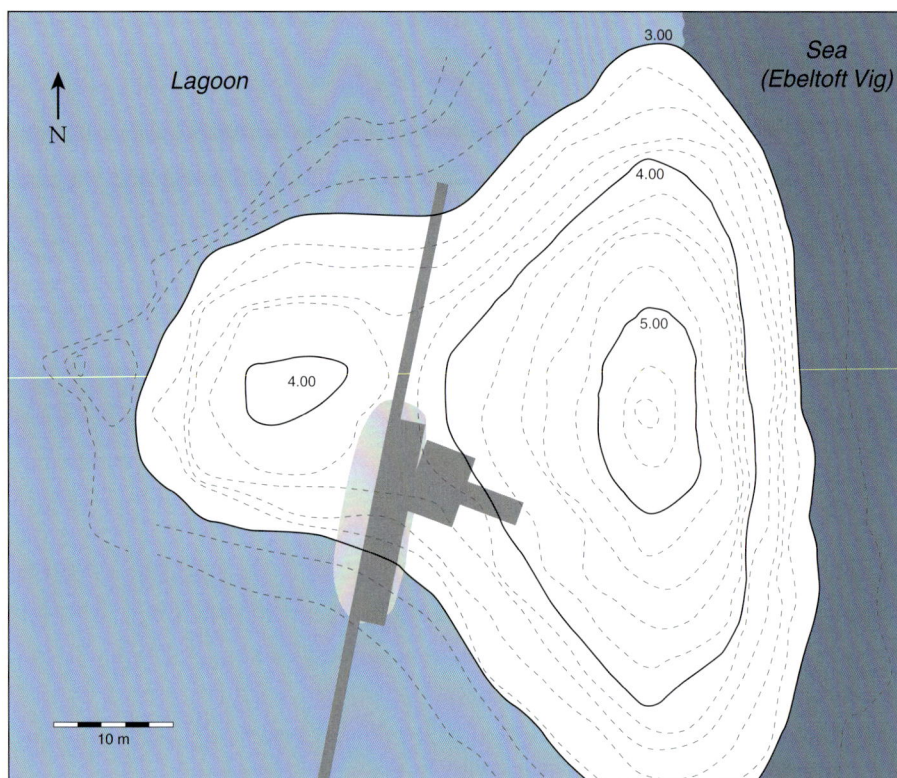

Fig. 30. Contour map of the island with Vængesø II. To the east, the former island borders the present-day shore facing Ebeltoft Vig. On the plan, the excavation trench is shown in the saddle between the two hilltops. A thick contour line marks 3, 4 and 5 m a.m.s.l., equidistance between broken contour lines is 20 cm. The light grey area indicates the distribution of the Ertebølle shell midden.

Ertebølle artefacts (lowermost), overlain by a layer containing Neolithic pottery. This gave rise to further excavations in subsequent years, resulting in the investigation of a total area of 130 m². The latter included a 1 m wide and 57 m long north-south-oriented trial trench, and a rectangular 73 m² trench, which was excavated in 1975 and 1979 (Fig. 31). In conjunction, these trenches resulted in the investigation of more or less the entire area in the saddle. It is therefore estimated that almost all the settlement surface has been examined. The area containing worked flint covers c. 1200 m². The extent of the cultural deposits and the distribution of the artefacts, compared with the topography, shows that a small settlement is represented at this locality.

The area investigated in 1975 was excavated in 10 cm thick layers, with the finds kept separate according to metre square and layer, while the trench investigated in 1979 was excavated such that all tools, potsherds and faunal remains were recorded in a system of 3D coordinates, and flint debitage was collected in 10 cm layers from individual squares. As the cultural deposits were shallow,

most squares on the saddle had, in practice, just one or two excavation layers, whereas there could be three to five excavation layers in the adjacent areas (Fig. 32).

In spite of the sandy/gravelly subsoil, the preservation conditions for organic remains (bone and antler) were good in the kitchen midden and in the underlying pre-midden layer. As a consequence, a large faunal assemblage was recovered, as well as some tools of bone and antler.

3.1 Stratigraphy

The following stratigraphy was recorded in the long trial trench (Fig. 33):

1) The subsoil consisted of brownish-yellow sandy clay, encapsulating a number of larger stones (moraine deposits). During the excavation, the surface of the subsoil formed an even curve from north to south, rising from c. 2.7 -3.5 m a.m.s.l. Midway between the two hilltops was a c. 10 m long stretch where the surface of the moraine was relatively even and horizontal (Fig. 30).

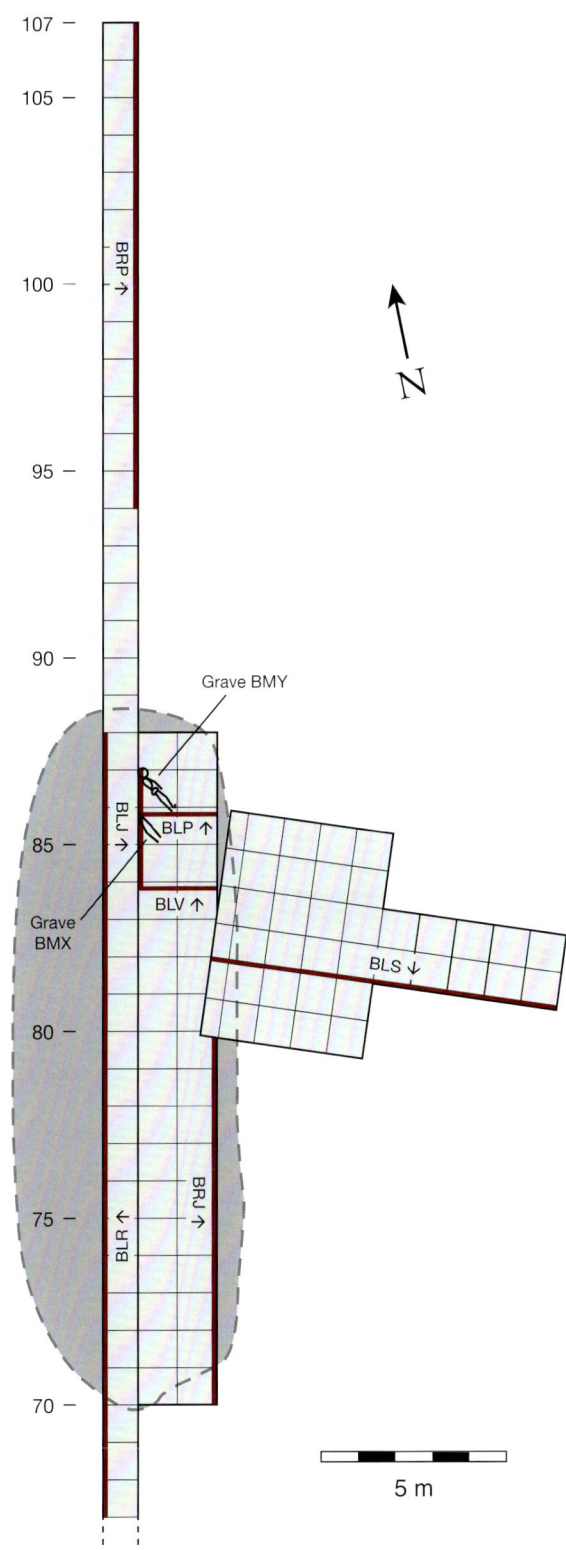

107 –	
105 –	
	BRP →
100 –	
95 –	
90 –	Grave BMY
85 –	BLJ → , BLP ↑
	BLV ↑
Grave BMX	BLS ↓
80 –	
75 –	BLR ← , BRJ →
70 –	

N

5 m

Fig. 31. Plan of the excavated area, showing the sections (red lines) and the horizontal extent of the kitchen midden in the excavation trenches (broken line). The viewing directions for the sections are shown with arrows. The two graves (BMX and BMY) are also marked.

2) Above this was an up to 20 cm thick black, sandy culture layer containing scattered shells of oysters, cockles, mussels and periwinkles. There was also a significant content of artefacts of flint, diabase, bone and antler, as well as pottery, charcoal and numerous cooking stones. Faunal remains were similarly abundant. This layer was a so-called "pre-midden layer" (Andersen S.H. 2000, 368), which lay at a level of 2.8-3.6 m a.m.s.l.

3) It was overlain by a c. 15-25 cm thick kitchen midden layer, which consisted of horizontally-oriented oyster shells (dominant species) and shells of cockles, mussels and periwinkles, together with artefacts of flint, diabase, bone and antler, as well as pottery, charcoal and scattered cooking stones. In the highest parts of the excavation, the kitchen midden lay partly over the pre-midden layer and partly directly over the subsoil. It could be followed up to a level of c. 3-3.5 m a.m.s.l. (midway in the saddle).

4) Towards the north, the shell midden overlay a c. 50 cm thick layer of yellowish-brown (marine) sand (at c. 2.6 m a.m.s.l.), containing local 2-5 cm thick sloping stripes of charcoal and scattered flint artefacts representing Ertebølle types that were heavily water-worn and had a completely leached, white surface.

5) Above the kitchen midden in the saddle was a c. 5-10 cm thick, charcoal-rich, sandy culture layer containing numerous fist-sized stones which, in the majority of cases, were heat-shattered (cooking stones), together with pottery dating from the earliest part of the Early Neolithic Funnel Beaker culture.

6) There then followed a c. 10-15 cm thick layer of black, charcoal-rich sand containing abundant cooking stones, pebbles and shingle, which could be followed up to a level of c. 3.6 m a.m.s.l. Higher up the hillside this had been ploughed away. The layer contained potsherds

Fig. 32. The excavation in progress in 1979, with skeleton BMY exposed (in the foreground). The picture shows (from the left) market gardener P. Poulsen, Helgenæs, who discovered the settlement, Keeper of National Antiquities P.V. Glob and the author. Photo: Rita Geertz.

▶ *Fig. 33. North-south section (eastern face of squares 107-94/50 and the western face of squares 67-87/50) through the settlement area in the middle of the depression and the adjacent raised marine deposits. 1 Brownish-grey sandy soil (plough soil) containing flint artefacts (+O and +R). 2 Black, sandy layer with shingle, containing flint (±O and -R), pottery and numerous (Neolithic) cooking stones. 3 Greyish-brown sandy soil containing comminuted shell (marine). 4 Kitchen midden with horizontal shells of marine invertebrates – predominantly oysters, but also of cockles, mussels and periwinkles, flint (-O and -R), animal bones and cooking stones. 5 Black, sandy culture layer (pre-midden layer) with scattered shells of marine invertebrates: oysters, cockles, mussels and periwinkles, flint (-O and -R), animal bones and cooking stones. 6 Secondary pit (black, sandy fill with numerous cooking stones and a little comminuted shell) (Neolithic). 7 Yellowish-brown sandy moraine clay. The position of radiocarbon-dating sample (OxA-117) is indicated.*

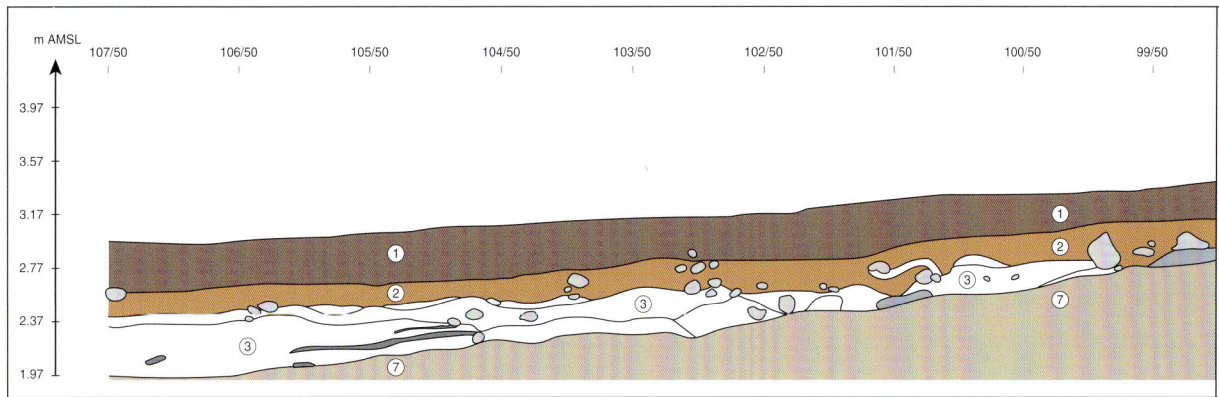

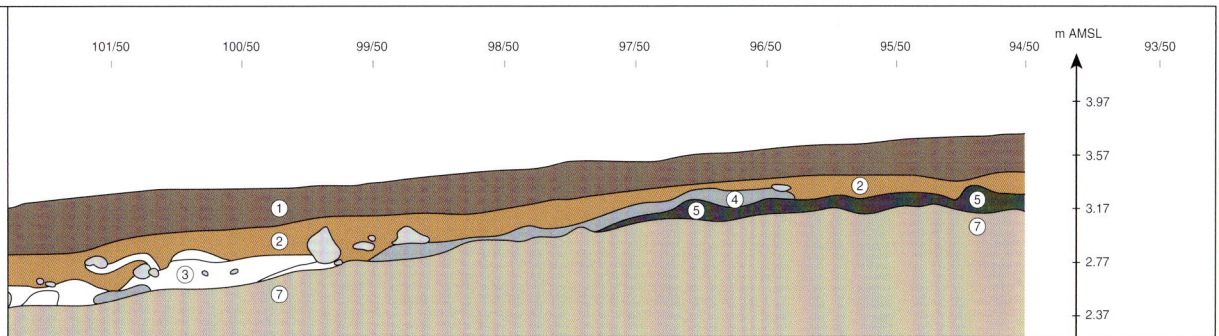

BRP East section

BLR West section

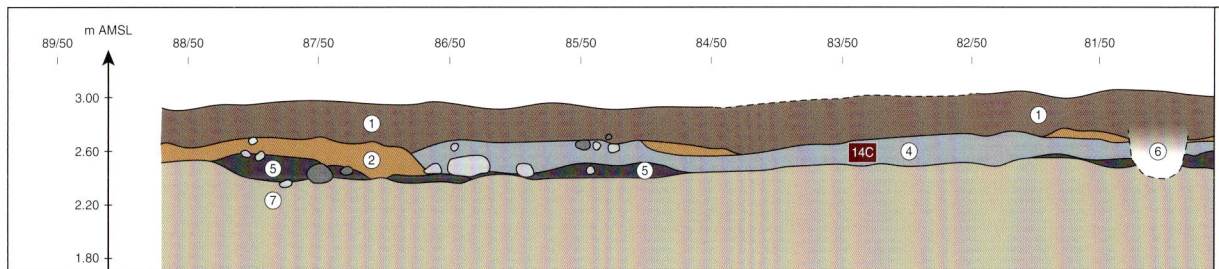

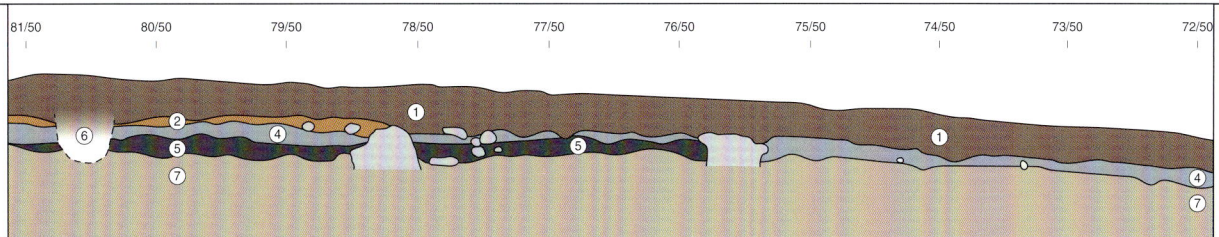

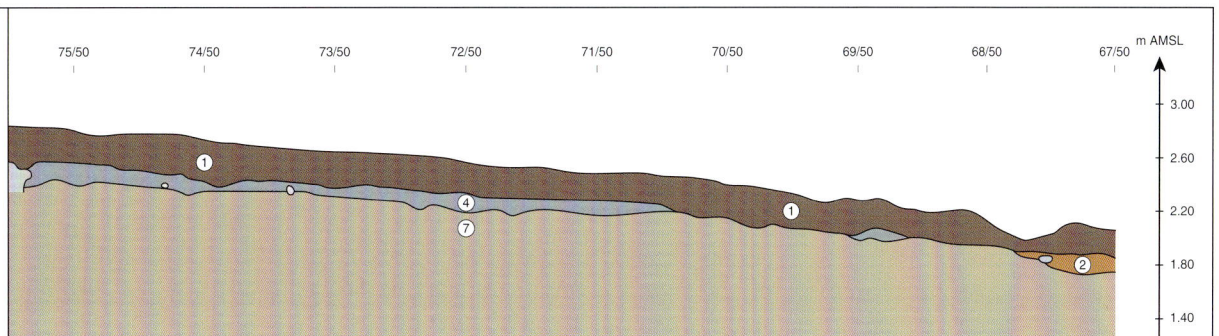

from vessels with a vertically striped belly (Middle Neolithic Funnel Beaker culture (MN A I), Single Grave culture and Late Neolithic/ Bronze Age.

7) The stratigraphy terminated uppermost in a 25-40 cm thick, brown sandy soil layer (plough soil) containing flint artefacts dating from the Late Neolithic/Early Bronze Age (up to a level of c. 3.7 m a.m.s.l.).

The the plough soil and cultural deposits contained worked flint, and this displayed an increasing degree of surface transformation and water-wear from the base of the stratigraphy upwards. Both to the north and south of the central settlement area, the trial trench was continued out into the adjacent marine layers of sand and shingle, but without *in situ* refuse layers being encountered in these deposits. In this respect, the situation at the settlement corresponds to that observed at Vængesø I, where there was a similar absence of the refuse layers containing organic remains that are known from numerous other coastal settlements of the Ertebølle culture in Jutland and on Funen; for example Dyrholmen (Mathiassen et al. 1942), Brabrand (Thomsen/Jessen 1906) and Tybrind Vig (Andersen, S.H. 2013). Apart from a few stripes of charcoal in the neighbouring marine sand layers, the culture layers appear to have been deposited on stable dry land. It is important to emphasise that the entire stratigraphy rarely had a total thickness of more than 20-30 cm and was irregular everywhere, displaying several disturbances resulting from the various visits to, and occupations of, the locality. Because the sequence of culture layers is so relatively shallow and it can be assumed that artefacts etc. could have slipped or rolled down into the saddle from the adjacent hillsides, artefacts from different periods frequently lay mixed together within the same layer. The disturbances have particularly impacted on the uppermost Neolithic culture layer, while the deeper Ertebølle layers were not affected to any significant degree. The analysis of the finds has, however, shown that the great majority of the artefacts and the faunal remains can securely be assigned to the Ertebølle culture. Definite types from the Neolithic are few in number and comprise primarily pottery, axe blanks and a few flat-flaked flint tools dating from the Late Neolithic/ Early Bronze Age.

On the basis of the stratigraphy and the character of the artefacts recovered, the following geological sequence can be cautiously outlined:

At some time in the Middle/Late Ertebølle culture there was a settlement on the island. This became inundated due to a rise in sea level (transgression), during which the culture layer was eroded and a thick sand layer was deposited on the SSW part of the island, which contained heavily water-worn flint artefacts (mostly flake axes). Subsequently, the sea level fell (regression) and a new settlement was established in the island's saddle (the pre-midden layer). The settlement continued and the kitchen midden then accumulated. Later, there was yet another rise in sea level and the kitchen midden became inundated, leading to the deposition of a charcoal-rich sand layer with substantial shingle content. This layer was found to contain pottery from the earliest phase of the Middle Neolithic Funnel Beaker culture (MN A I), revealing it to be coeval with or later than this phase, c. 3300-3200 BC. There then followed yet another fall in the sea level (regression), after which the exposed surface lay open for repeated brief visits during the rest of the Neolithic/Earliest Bronze Age.

The horizontal distribution of the artefacts and the culture layers shows that these are located primarily in the central flat area of the saddle between the two hilltops. The spatial distribution of the tools reveals no clear activity areas, which is probably due to all functions having been undertaken within a very restricted area. At the same time, it must be assumed that there was a certain mixing of the finds that had slipped or rolled down from the neighbouring hillsides. Consequently, various distribution analyses of flint artefacts did not reveal any clear concentrations. In the trial trench to the south and north, the finds concentration was found to be low.

3.2 The kitchen midden

The kitchen midden covered a contiguous area of c. 18 × 7 m, but was also evident as small patches of shells that measured c. 0.5 × 3 m and were c. 15-25 cm in thickness. The material therefore covered an area of c. 126 m² and must be seen as representing a small kitchen midden with a thin shell layer (Fig. 31). Apart from small areas showing secondary disturbance, the shell layer was an *in situ* accumulation. It was dominated by oyster shells, which constituted c. 50% of the shell mass, but carpet mussels, blue mussels and periwinkles were also common. On the other hand, there were only a few shells of cockles (Tab. 2). Within the deposit were several small, well-defined heaps of shells of a single species of marine mollusc, so-called "meal heaps". The shell midden contained numerous artefacts, especially of flint with a light-blue/whitish surface and no trace of water-wear. Further to these, the contents included charcoal, cooking stones, pottery and faunal remains. The great majority of these cultural traces could be assigned to the Late Ertebølle culture. However, there was also a little pottery of Early Neolithic Funnel Beaker type in the upper part of the shell layer, a dating which is supported by a radiocarbon date of 3629-3135 BC (K-2444).

3.3 Settlement features and structures

Considering the size of the excavation trench, and its location in the place that was best suited to occupation on the island, i.e. the saddle, there were on the whole few settlement features and structures at the site. Immediately beneath the plough soil was a layer of stones, varying in size from that of a fist to a child's head, which were particularly abundant within a c. 6-8 m broad band running north-south on the highest part of "the saddle". Below this followed yet another horizon containing stones, but in significantly fewer numbers and in several cases either grouped in more discrete heaps or in such a way that they constituted structures in the form of rows or curves. These structures could be dated to the Ertebølle culture. Culture layers

everywhere at the locality contained numerous fist-sized cooking stones, but a c. 32 m long stretch in the highest parts of the saddle was almost free of stones. To the north, there were stones over a c. 5-6 m long stretch, after which the stone scatter ceased. To the south, there was a stone layer along a c. 8-9 m strip. The stoneless part therefore presumably constitutes the actual settlement area, from where cooking stones and other settlement refuse were thrown out or slipped/rolled down the hillside. This interpretation is supported by the fact that it was also here, in this stone-less area, that the inhumation graves were discovered (see later). To the north, the stone carpet was not as well-delimited and dense as to the south. In the virtually stone-less area on the highest part of the saddle were three circular concentrations of stones measuring 0.75-1 m in diameter. In two cases, these lay on top of the kitchen midden and must therefore be Neolithic in date (Fig. 37).

3.3.1 Stone layers

Directly east of the north-south-oriented trial trench, a pavement containing a mixture of cooking stones and stones not obviously heat-affected covered an area of c. 6 × 10 m on one of the hillsides running down towards the saddle (Fig. 34). The stones were particularly large to the west and became smaller up the hillside to the east. To the west, this stone carpet terminated in an elongated (north-south) area measuring c. 2 × 2 m and delimited by a single row of stones. The stratigraphy and the artefacts recovered here suggest that this feature dates from the Neolithic. It was not clearly delimited to the south and east, but declined in intensity towards the north. Similar features have been described from the settlements of Ørnekul on Nekselø (Becker 1952a, 64, 68-69, 71-72, Figs. 3, 5, 6-8), Bloksbjerg (Westerby 1927, 23-24, Figs. 8-9), Sønderholm (Jønsson/Pedersen 1983, 175-176, Figs. 4-5), Dybdal in northern Djursland (Boas 2001, 148, Fig. 6) and Smakkerup Huse (Price/Gebauer 2005, 54, Fig. 2.16). Common to all of these is that they are evident as relatively irregular layers containing stones of various sizes, which, in the majority of cases, are heat/fire-affected. The location of these various stone layers is most indicative of them being discarded, worn-out cooking stones – an explanation that can similarly be applied to Vængesø II.

Fig. 34. a) Excavation photo of the stone setting from the Neolithic (seen from the west). Photo: Søren H. Andersen. b) Excavation plan of the stone setting. It measures c. 8 x 10 m and extends from the saddle a little way up the hillside to the east, cf. Figs. 30 and 31.

The stone covering and the stratigraphy at the site both correspond closely to the situation described at the coastal settlement of Selbjerg on the Limfjord (Marseen 1953, 103-104).

Stone features were encountered over the kitchen midden in a further two places: A small circular stone setting (c. 20 × 20 cm), probably a small hearth, and an oval stone setting (c. 60 × 50 cm), presumably also a (slightly larger) hearth. The two latter features also date from the Neolithic.

To the west, the main stone layer covered a feature consisting of a single row of stones of the size of a child's head, which formed a horseshoe-shaped curve. The artefacts recovered, together with the stratigraphy, indicate that this structure must belong to the Ertebølle culture. In squares 101-102/50 was a circle with a diameter of c. 80 cm made up of a single row of fist- to head-sized stones (Fig. 35). It lay on the surface of the marine sand and must therefore be dated to the Late Ertebølle culture. No clear parallels are evident in the literature, so its interpretation remains open. There were generally few stones to the south, but in three places those present formed small, discrete concentrations (c. 40-50 cm in diameter), consisting of a dense layer of stones: These features can also be dated to the Late Ertebølle culture. In addition to the aforementioned stone layers, a semicircular feature was encountered that was formed of a single row of smaller, fist-sized stones (c. 2 m long north-south and c. 1-2 m wide). Further to this was a subrectangular, slightly diffuse stone layer, which continued up the hillside to the southeast, but was clearly delimited to the north and west by a single row of stones. Apart from this, the area was completely free of stones.

3.3.2 Terrace

The subsoil on the highest part of the saddle was level (in contrast to an expected, more domed appearance, based on the topography) over a c. 10-15 m long stretch (north-south; Fig. 36) at c. 3.6-3.8 m a.m.s.l.. At the same time, section BLP, which ran across the saddle at its highest point, showed that the hill's eastern (steep) side had been cut into by c. 25-30 cm (Fig. 36). As a consequence of the excavation and recovery of the two skeleton graves in the neighbouring squares, it was not possible to obtain more precise dimensions for this levelling of the hillside. However, it must have extended at least c. 2 m east-west and c. 7-8 m north-south, and this terrace was therefore oriented roughly north-south, i.e. along the saddle, and had an area of at least 14-16 m². The earthworks and consequent levelling of the surface must have been an attempt to make the sloping (and steep) terrain more even and thereby better suited to occupation. This is an important observation, because all indications are that a terrace was also cut into the hillside at this site and that it was of the same size and shape as those described from the Vængesø I and III settlements (Ch. 2.2.1 and 4.2.1). The terrace at Vængesø II was covered by the kitchen midden and must accordingly be of the same age or older than the latter, which dates from the Late Ertebølle culture.

3.3.3 Pit

In square 80/51, a pot-shaped pit was found with a diameter of c. 40-45 cm and a depth of c. 30 cm. Its fill comprised charcoal-rich sand mixed with shells. The stratigraphy showed that it had definitely been cut down through both the kitchen midden and the pre-midden layer. Unfortunately, it contained no date-conferring artefacts, but based on the stratigraphic observations it must be post-Ertebølle culture. It presumably dates from the Middle or Late Neolithic.

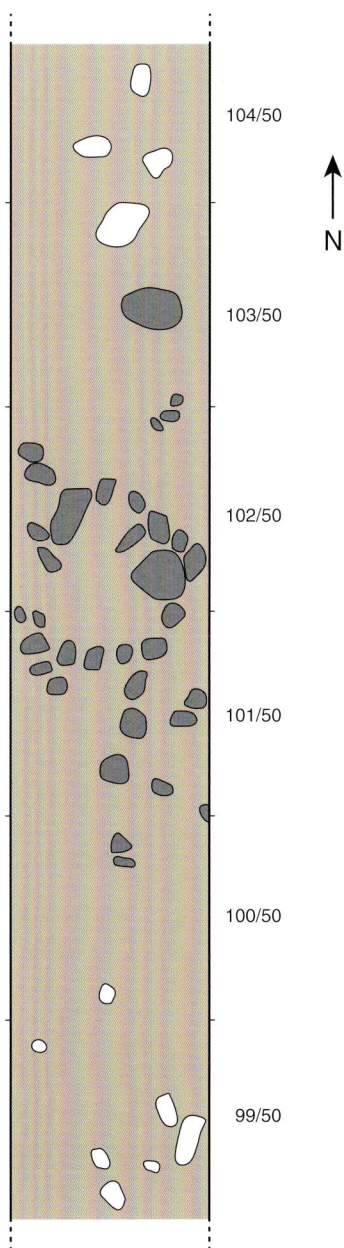

Fig. 35. Circle of stones dating from the Ertebølle culture.

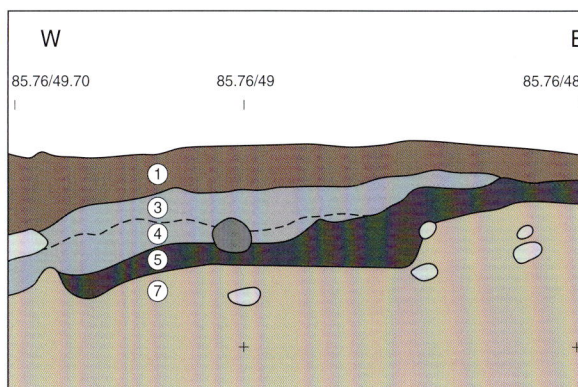

Fig. 36. Transverse section BLP (east-west) through the culture layer. Clearly evident in the stratigraphy is the marked step in the surface of the subsoil towards the hillside. This presumably relates to the cutting of a terrace of the same kind as those seen on the other settlements around the Vængesø lagoon. 1 Brownish-grey sandy soil (plough soil). 3 Layer of comminuted shell. 4 Kitchen midden with horizontal oyster shells. 5 Black, sandy culture layer (pre-midden layer). 7 Yellow-brown sandy till.

3.3.4 Hearths?

Vængesø II apparently had no stone-set hearths of the kind evident at both Vængesø I and III – and at many other Ertebølle settlements in Jutland, for example Ertebølle *locus classicus* (Madsen et al. 1900, 25-27). Conversely, discrete concentrations of fist-sized stones, forming a single layer, were found in three places directly over the kitchen midden (Fig. 37); these measured 50 × 35, 50 × 50 and 40 × 50

cm in diameter, respectively. They were therefore clearly smaller than the stone-built hearths seen in kitchen middens at other sites. Moreover, the stones showed signs of the effects of heat and fire. No concentrations of charcoal and/or fire-brittled flint were observed in association with these stone concentrations. Their stratigraphic position indicates that they are later than the Ertebølle kitchen midden and must therefore be presumed to be Neolithic in date, cf. Holmegaard (Figs. 179-180).

Neither were there any examples of the grey, ash hearths that were so common at Vængesø III (and in other Danish kitchen middens). The absence of ash hearths is also underlined by the similar absence of the reddened patches of subsoil sand that were observed in many places at Vængesø III (Fig. 111; Canti/Linford 2000, 385ff). All in all, it can be concluded that no definite hearths were found associated with the Ertebølle horizon at Vængesø II.

3.4 Inhumation graves

During the excavation, two inhumation graves were discovered positioned immediately side-by-side (Figs. 38-40). They were both oriented NNW-SSE, with the head in a northerly direction. The graves lay on the highest part of the saddle, i.e. they were located on the terrace, which further underlines that this was the central habitation area on the island. Both graves were cut down through the kitchen midden and were therefore later than this. The southwestern skeleton (BMX) lay in the pre-midden layer and had been disturbed in the Stone Age. The skull was missing, and the ribs and part of the vertebral column lay in a secondary position. Given the close vicinity of the neighbouring grave and the nature of the stratigraphy, it seems likely that this grave was disturbed when the pit was dug for the northeastern grave (BMY), which must therefore be the later of the two. Skeleton BMX was that of an adult, the age and gender of whom could not be securely determined, but probably female (Andersen, S.H. et al. 1986, 41). The individual was c. 1.6 m in height. Slight changes are evident due to arthritis in the right elbow, and two vertebrae in the vertebral column have collapsed and are par-

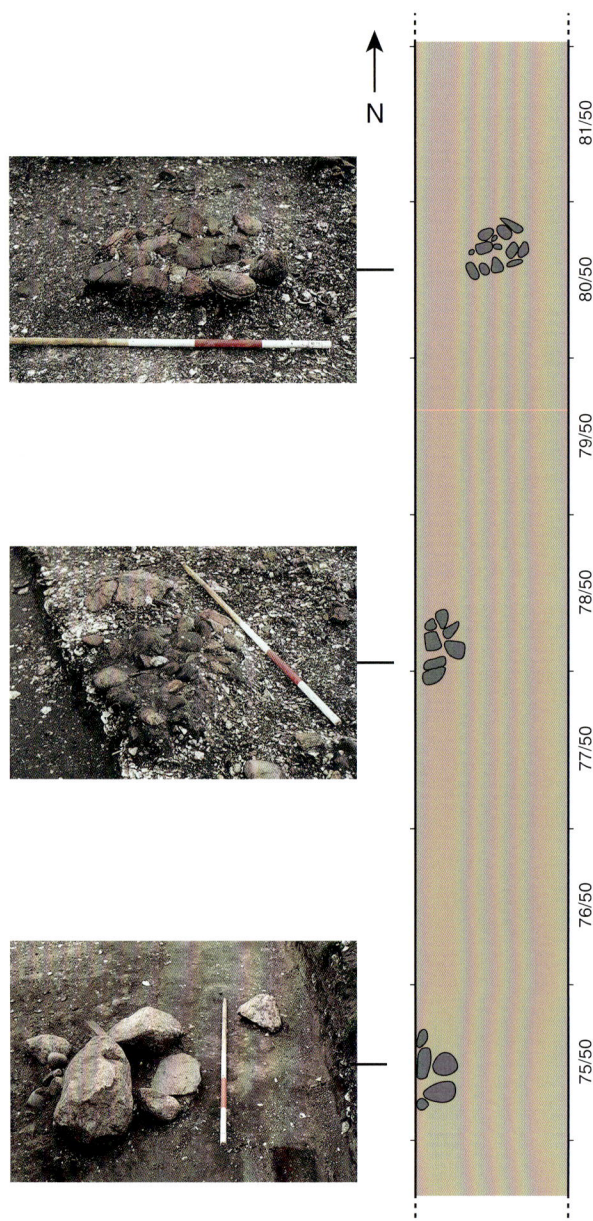

Fig. 37. Well-defined small stone concentrations of Neolithic age on top of the Ertebølle shell midden. Similar features were observed at the Holmegaard site, cf. Figs. 179-180. Photo: Søren H. Andersen.

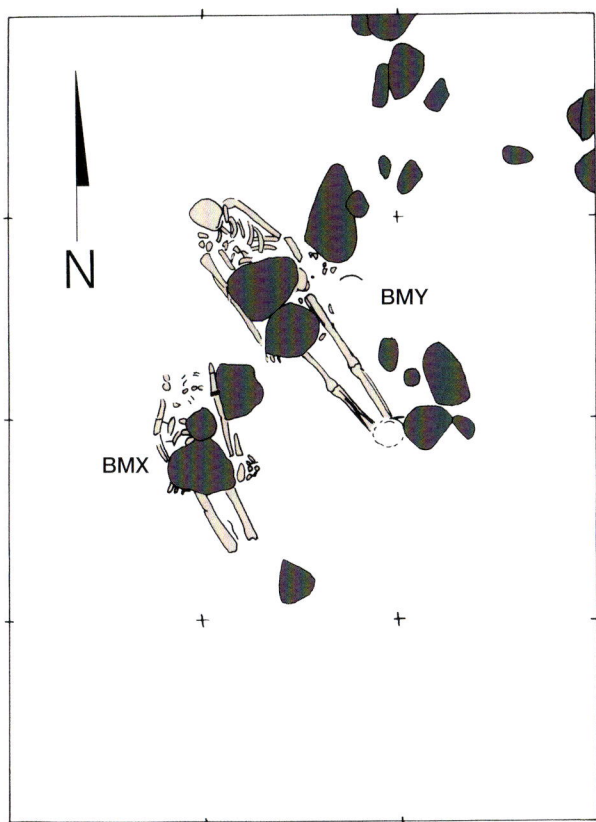

Fig. 38. Plan of the two graves (BMX and BMY). Both skeletons are covered by large stones, which lie over the lower abdomen and hips, cf. the Holmegaard grave, Figs. 185-186. Drawing: Helle Juel Jensen.

tially fused. The northeastern skeleton (BMY) lay on the surface of the subsoil, and digging by the right shoulder has left a clear feature in the subsoil. This skeleton therefore lay slightly deeper than the first. The grave was completely undisturbed and was later taken up intact in a block and exhibited at Moesgaard Museum. The individual lay outstretched in a supine position with arms and hands placed alongside their body. The feet were close together, with all the bones together, suggesting that they had been bound. The person interred in grave BMY was a man of 20-35 years of age; he was dolichocephalic and had a moderately broad face. He shows no traces of caries or other dental illnesses, but has, on the other hand, heavy tooth wear. He was c. 1.65 m tall. On his skull, on the left side of the frontal bone, is a c. 2-3 cm long, c. 1 cm wide and c. 0.5 cm deep healed lesion (Fig. 41). On the "front" of the eleventh thoracic vertebra (chest region) is a round lesion measuring c. 1 × 0.5 cm, which could very well have been caused by an arrow, a spear or similar and was probably the cause of death. This injury shows that the grave can be assigned to the group of Stone Age graves in which lesions are evident on the skeleton, for example those found at Korsør Nor, Tybrind Vig, Bøgebakken etc.

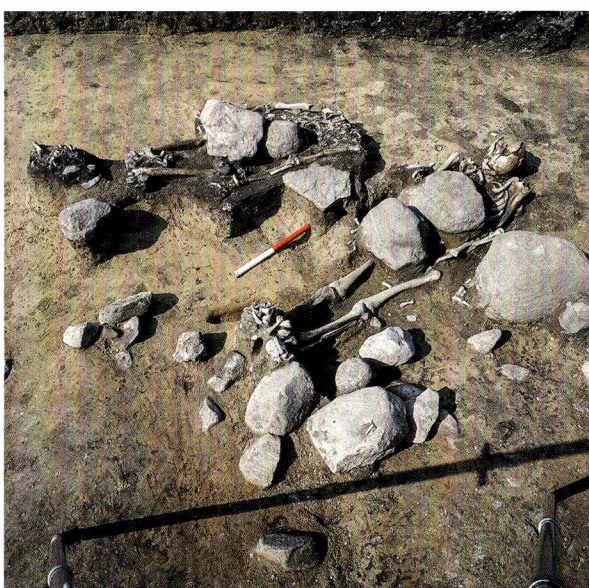

Fig. 39. Graves BMX and BMY, seen looking northwest. The two graves lie in situ. Photo: Søren H. Andersen.

Fig. 40. Grave BMY seen looking northeast. The lower abdomen and hip region is partly covered by a large stone. Photo: Søren H. Andersen.

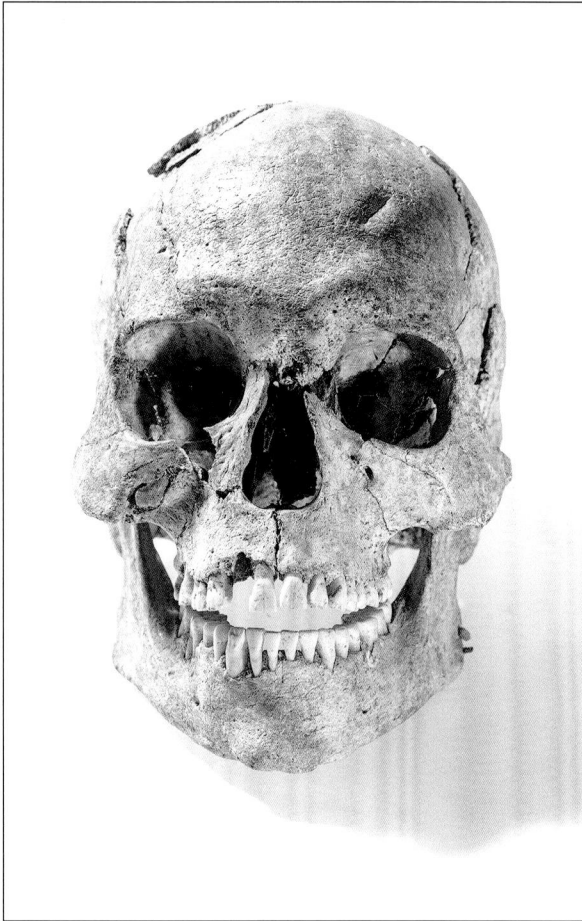

Fig. 41. The skull from grave BMY, showing a furrow in the left frontal bone. The injury must have been caused by a blow with a sharp weapon (axe?). Photo: Photo/Media Department, Moesgaard Museum.

No grave goods were found associated with these graves, but large stones had been placed around and over them. In the southwestern grave there was a large and a medium-sized stone over the skeleton's hip region and its left side. The northeastern skeleton had had two large stones placed over the abdominal and hip regions, and there was a further large stone partially underneath the left foot. Because of the pressure exerted by the weight of these stones, the skeleton had been pressed downwards such that it appeared slightly curved in longitudinal section. The presence of large stones over the abdominal and pelvic regions of the skeletons corresponds to the situation observed in the Ertebølle grave at Holmegaard (Ch. 7.3; Fig. 185-

186), where there were also two large stones over the corpse's shinbones and feet (Figs. 185-187). This use of (large) stones in Mesolithic graves was also observed in grave 10 at Bøgebakken, in eastern Zealand, where four large and two smaller stones had been placed around the lower legs and feet of the interred corpse (Albrethsen/Petersen 1977, 9, 12, 13, Figs. 11-12).

The two graves were initially radiocarbon dated to, respectively, 4041-3809 BC cal (1 σ; K-3920, 5156 ± 70 bp; BMX) and 4142-3815 BC cal (1 σ; K-3921, 5181 ± 65 bp; BMY)(Andersen, S.H. et al. 1986, 40-41). Both skeletons proved to have high $\delta^{13}C$ values (respectively -11.2‰ and -11.1‰), which shows that a significant proportion of the individuals' food was of marine origin (Andersen, S.H. et al. 1986, 40-42; Meiklejohn et al. 1998, 204-205; Fischer/Kristiansen 2002, 348-349, 360; Fischer et al. 2007, 2132-2133, 2137). Subsequently, corrective dating analyses were undertaken on the skeletons, resulting in revised ages of, respectively, 5156 ± 70 bp (4040-3810 BC cal) and 5181 ± 65 bp (4140-3820 BC cal), and the respective $\delta^{13}C$ values were -12.7‰ and -12.6‰ (Fischer et al. 2007, 2132-2133, 2136-2137). The bones were also analysed for their content of the nitrogen isotope ^{15}N, giving values of 15.7‰ and 16.1‰ (Fischer et al. 2007, 2132-2133). These analyses indicate that these two individuals existed almost completely, but not quite exclusively, on food from the marine environment (Fischer et al. 2007, 2144, Fig. 4). The dates show that the two people interred here are from the time around the transition between the Mesolithic and the Neolithic, i.e. Ertebølle culture/Funnel Beaker culture (c. 3950 BC). Depending on the correction factor employed, the dates fall either at the end of the Ertebølle culture or in the earliest part of the Funnel Beaker culture (Fischer 2002, 360: "probably Neolithic").

The scientific dates for the two graves can be supplemented by the stratigraphic observations, which show that the southwestern skeleton must be the earliest and the northeastern skeleton the latest. The time difference between the two burials cannot, however, have been particularly great, as the scientific dates indicate. The stratigraphy also shows that the two graves are later than the Ertebølle kitchen midden, which is dated to c. 4459-4075 BC (OxA-117). The two graves are of exceptional importance in scientific terms, because they belong to a period from which there are virtually no other well-preserved skeletons (Fischer 2002, 348-349, Fig. 22.4).

In addition to the two graves, a number of scattered human bones were encountered during the excavation. Some could come from the disturbed grave BMX, but this cannot be true of all of them as the disarticulated bones represent at least one further individual. This suggests that there could have been further, now completely disrupted, graves at the site.

Inhumation graves from the Ertebølle culture/earliest Funnel Beaker culture remain a rarity – especially in Jutland. In this respect, however, Djursland constitutes an interesting exception. Apart from the two graves at Vængesø II, an Ertebølle grave was also found on the southernmost part of Vængesø III, (Figs. 160-161; Asingh 2000, 32-33).

Moreover, there was an Ertebølle grave at the Holmegaard kitchen midden (Ch. 7.3) and six graves at the kitchen midden at Nederst in Kolindsund (Nielsen/Petersen 1993, 76-81; Kannegaard 2016). From the Fannerup area (also in Kolindsund), there are traces of at least one definite Ertebølle grave (Rasmussen 1990, 31-41). Finally, there is a report of at least five graves being found at Koed (a little further west in Kolindsund). Some "pits" were discovered here, cut into the subsoil beneath a kitchen midden, which contained skeletal remains stained with red ochre (Rasmussen 1990, 39). A radiocarbon analysis of one of them gave a date of c. 4250 BC (K-3750; Danish National Museum archive no. 826/44, A 40529-32).

3.5 Finds from the Ertebølle culture

3.5.1 Flint

3.5.1.1 Debitage, technique and primary working

The flint assemblage is characterised by a quantity of debitage and tools that are all of a grey, calcareous flint type. The cores are on fist-sized, elongate or round flint nodules with "old" cortex on the surface. These clearly represent local flint nodules that were gathered from the beach ridge by the settlement.

The flint nodules on this settlement are slightly larger, i.e. longer and thicker, than those from Vængesø III (Ch. 4.3.1.1). The flint from the plough soil and excavation layer 1 has a white, transformed surface and is water-worn to varying degrees, while the flint from layer 2 (and possibly deeper layers – the kitchen midden and pre-midden layer) either has a primary, untransformed surface or is whitish blue; it is never water-worn. There are two splintered flint nodules, both large examples, weighing 2 and 0.39 kg, respectively. Due to surface transformation of the flint, its varying degree of water-wear and the calcareous precipitations present, it was not possible to carry out wear analysis or refitting.

The form of the percussion bulb on the flint artefacts is either strongly or only slightly protruding. The percussion bulb is generally well-defined and often shows a clear "lip"; percussion bulb scars are only rarely seen. The platform remnants are narrow and oval, measuring c. $0.8 \times 0.2 \times 0.3$ cm. The percussion (impact) point is in most cases not discernible due to surface transformation. The platform face is in almost all cases smooth and without preparation, but in two cases the platform is cortex-covered. The dorsal side of most flakes has retouch at the percussion bulb (proximal) end. Between 10 and 20% of the flakes are, however, without retouch and the dorsal side is consequently irregular with a triangular cross-section – often with a projection ("horn") on this side. The flint technique must be characterised as "soft".

The amount of flint debitage is greatest in layer 1, with 10-158 pieces/m^2. In layer 2 there are between 2-90 pieces/m^2, and in layer 3, 34-100 pieces/m^2. A total of 3943 large and 243 small flakes were recorded, as well as 11 large outer flakes. Flakes from the working of flake axes (primarily edge flakes) were observed on 12 occasions. The flint debitage weighs a total of 55.323 kg. Its distribution across the settlement shows no clear, well-defined concentrations like those encountered at many coeval Ertebølle settlements (e.g. Vængesø III and

Holmegaard; Ch. 4.2.2.2, Fig. 108). There is, however, a tendency for the flint debitage and tools to be associated with clusters of stones. This is true in squares 101-103/50, where a concentration of stones is surrounded by flint tools – especially flake axes and transverse arrowheads. A higher concentration of flint tools is evident in squares 58a-62, 76a-79 and 80a-62 (at the edge of the saddle).

A total of 239 pieces of *fire-brittled flint* were recorded, of which 185 are white-burnt and 54 have a grey/greyish-black crazed surface. On average, there are three to four pieces of greyish-black heat-affected flint per square metre and excavation layer. Burnt flint constitutes c. 5.7% of the entire flint assemblage, which could indicate very intensive occupation (Pedersen 2009, 122).

The percentage values are clearly higher than at the two neighbouring sites of Vængesø I and III, where burnt flint comprises 3% and 3.3-3.5%, respectively (Ch. 2.3.1.1 and 4.2.2.3). This difference is difficult to explain. It could be due either to the settlement at Vængesø II having been more intensively occupied than the two other localities, or the combined effects of the thin culture layer and repeated visits to the site. In the latter case, the use of fire could have affected flint in the older, slightly deeper and not particularly well-protected layers.

With very few exceptions, the *cores* from this settlement are short, very irregular and have large cortex-covered areas, and only two show regular, parallel flake scars. They measure between 3.5 and 10.5 cm in length and are derived from local fist- to child's-head-sized round/oviform flint nodules with cortex. The dominant core type has one platform and is represented by 41 examples, while 34 cores are elongate-oviform and seven are flat. There are ten cores with two platforms (four with platforms at an angle and six with parallel platforms), and a further 15 cores with several irregular platforms ("nodules/cores with several platforms"). Most of the cores with one platform are on elongate, rounded flint cobbles, on which a simple platform has been created with a single transverse blow (Fig. 42a-c). These cores have therefore a cortex-covered surface and terminate distally (at the end opposite to the platform) in the natural rounding of the cobble. On the whole, this core type is characterised by irregularity and only two examples have a short, worked dorsal surface. None of the cores shows clear signs of special platform preparation, and in two cases the platform is cortex covered. If the lengths of the blocks from Vængesø II and Vængesø III are compared, it is evident that those from Vængesø II are slightly larger/longer. This difference is probably because the beach ridges at Vængesø II provided the opportunity to select slightly longer flint nodules than those available in the fluvioglacial deposits around Vængesø III. Compared with those from other Ertebølle settlements in eastern Jutland, the blade cores from Vængesø II (and Vængesø III) should definitely be categorised as "short" and irregular, reflecting limited access to good flint. A variant of this core group consists of seven cores, of which six are cortex-covered outer flakes with a denticulate edge. These cores are of the same type as seen at both Vængesø I and III (Fig. 42d). The type displays an even transition to denticulate flake scrapers. Their dimensions range from $5 \times 4 \times 3$ cm to $11 \times 6 \times 3$ cm. *Cores with two platforms* are few in number and are, like the previous group, characterised by great irregularity. Only two examples display regular blade scars (Fig. 43). These cores are between 6 and 9.5 cm in length. *Cores with several platforms* are irregular, spherical and have cortex-covered surfaces. Their dimensions range from $5 \times 4 \times 3$ cm to $8 \times 7 \times 6$ cm. *Core flakes* are few in number, showing that adjustment of the platform and edges of the cores only rarely took place. Core side flakes are represented by a sin-

▶ *Fig. 42. a-c) Cores with one platform. The raw material comprised short, elongate or round flint nodules with cortex-covered surface on which, with a single blow, a platform was produced at one end. One of these cores shows further dorsal trimming (c). d) Flat core with one platform. This form displays a gradual morphological transition to denticulate flake scrapers. Scale 3:4. Drawing: Søren Timm Christensen.*

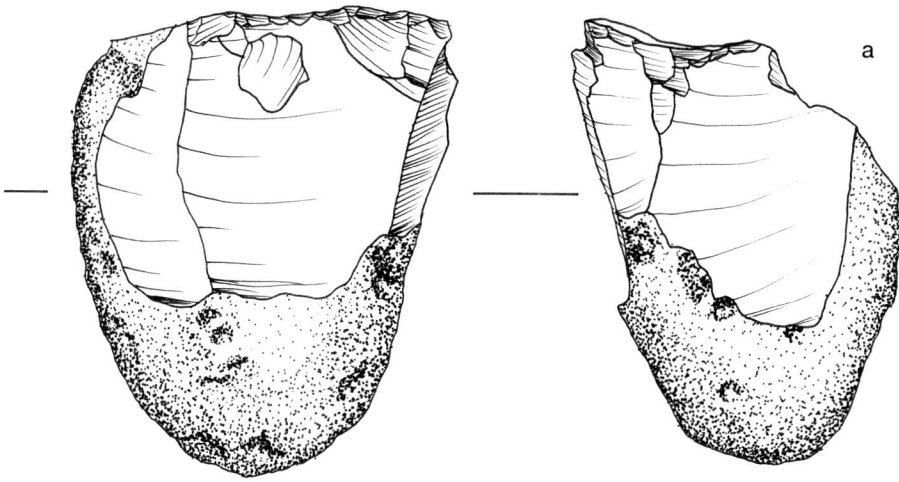

a

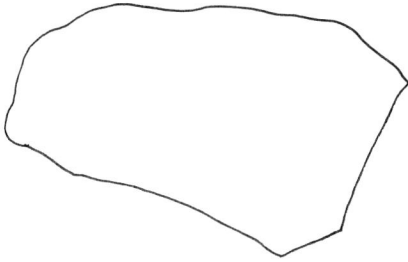

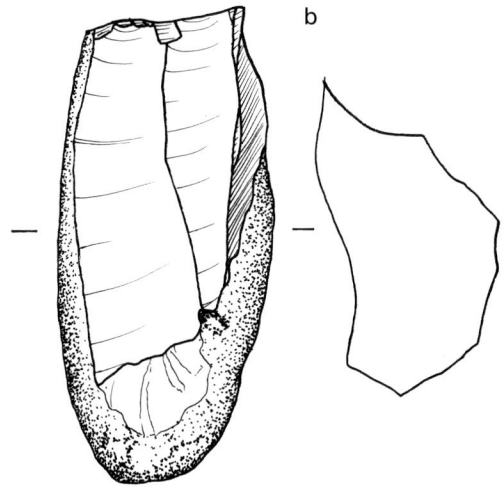

b

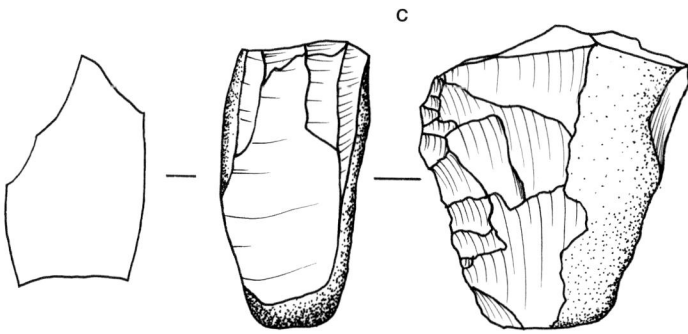

c

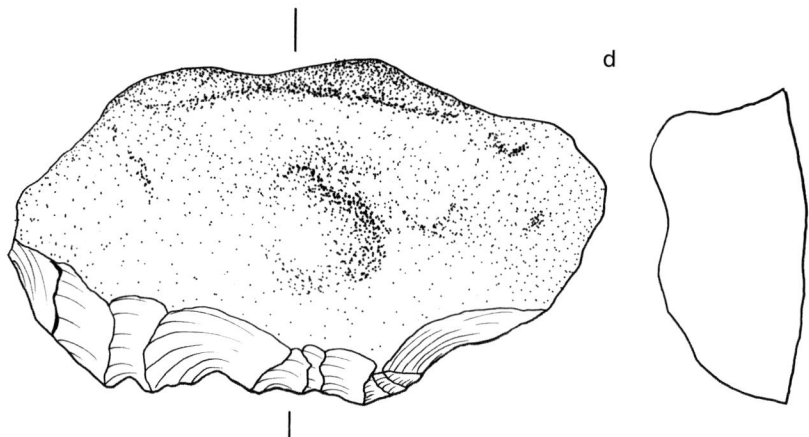

d

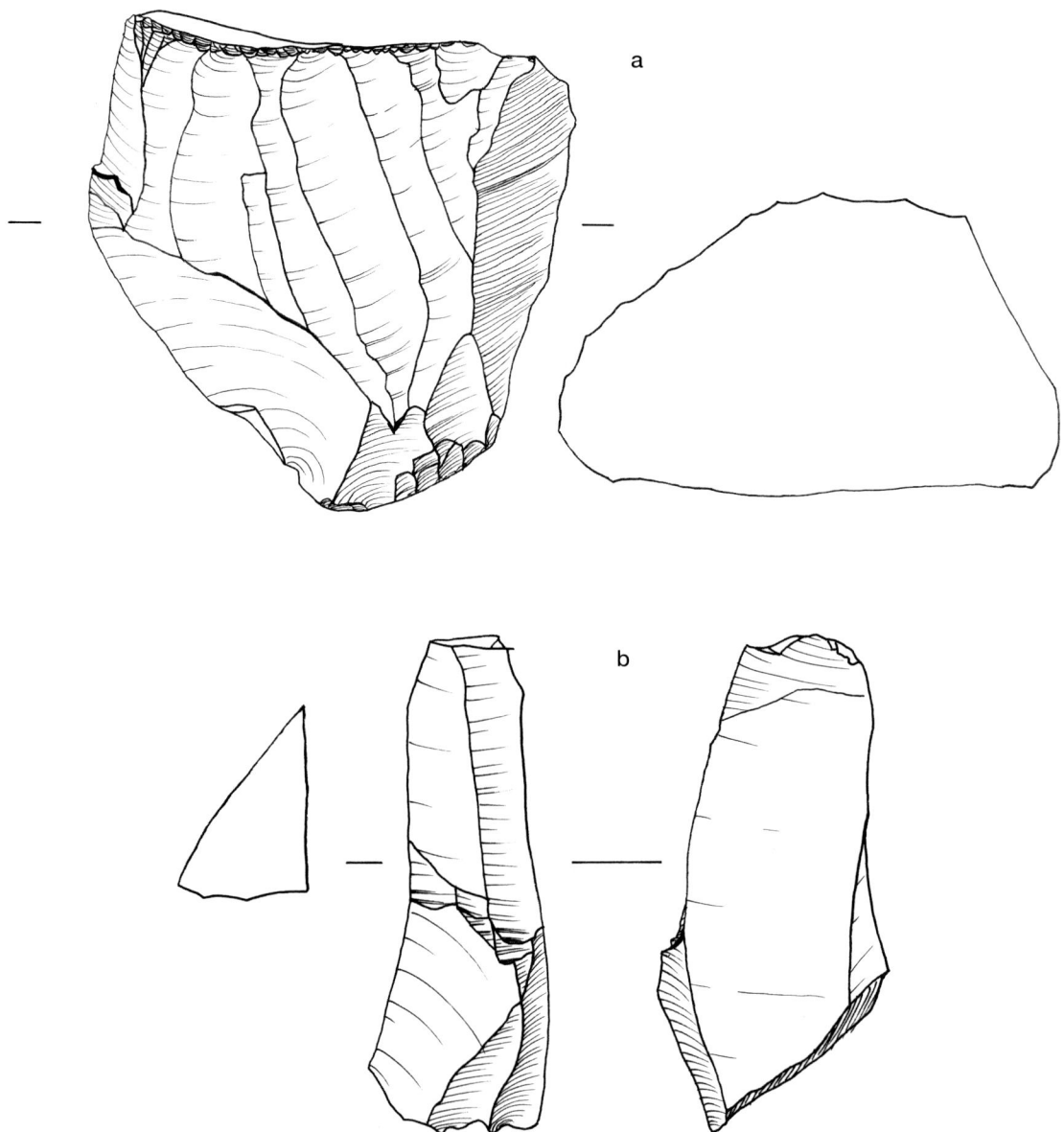

Fig. 43. Cores with two platforms that are either parallel (a) or form an angle (b). This group contains the most regular examples. Scale 3:4. Drawing: Søren Timm Christensen.

gle irregular example of triangular cross-section. Slight retouch along the sides shows that this piece was used secondarily for cutting, sawing work. Its length is 7.5 cm and its width 5 cm. There are eight examples of *core edges*. These are very irregular pieces, all struck along a platform edge. They are triangular in cross-section and semicircular or straight-sided in outline. They are 2.8-7 cm long. There is one example of a *core base* (fragment). This is a crescent-shaped, irregular piece of a platform that had been used secondarily as a knife. The edge

has large chips resulting from use. Its length is 8.9 cm and its width 4.7 cm. The distribution of the cores in the excavated area is shown in Fig. 44.

The blade assemblage is characterised by a major dominance of short, irregular B-blades. A significant proportion of the blades have dorsal cortex at their distal end – a feature that results from the use of short cores with cortex-covered surfaces (Fig. 45b). The dominant blade type has a single longitudinal dorsal rib, while examples with two or more parallel dorsal ribs are exception-

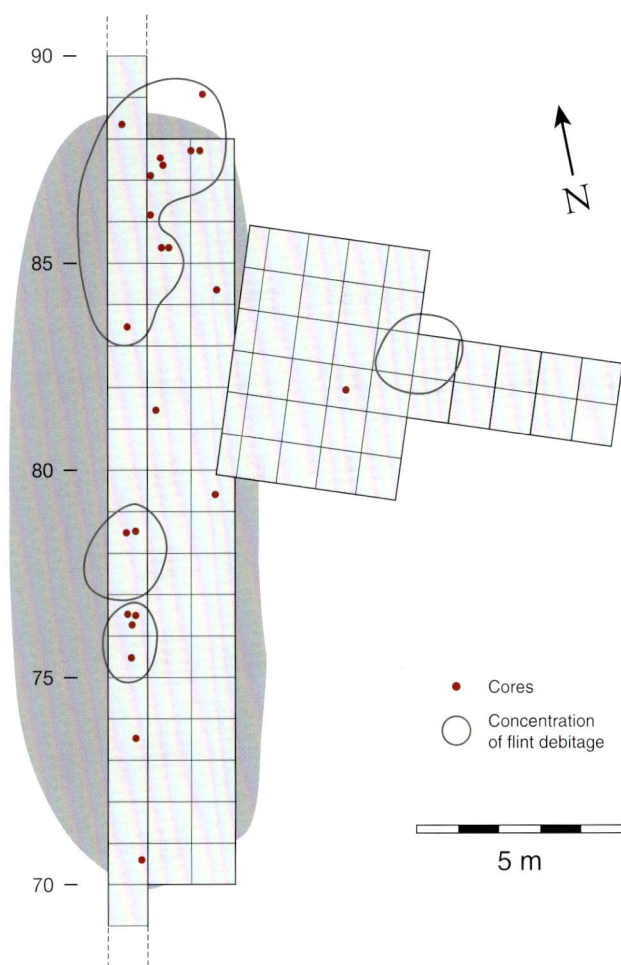

Fig. 44. The distribution of cores and flint debitage across the excavation trench.

Cores

Concentration of flint debitage

5 m

ally few in number (Fig. 45b). Regular A-blades are rare, being only represented by four examples (Fig. 46a-b). Conversely, 62 B-blades were recorded (Fig. 46c-j). These are generally irregular and short and characterised by a clear percussion bulb, but with no percussion bulb scar. The platform remnant is either small and relatively narrow or oval and narrow. In many cases the proximal end of the blades shows trimming, but there are also blades with no dorsal trimming here. Thirteen *preparation flakes* were recorded (Fig. 46k). *Micro blades* are rare and only six pieces have been assigned to this category.

Crested blades are very rare and only represented by three examples, of which two are primary and one is secondary. The small number of backed

blades from this locality is due to a combination of the knapping technique employed and the available raw material, the small size of which did not permit the trimming of the blocks prior to actual blade production. One of the backed blades is a coarse, thick primary blade with a central ridge. Its thickness is 1.7 cm and it was struck using hard, direct technique. The other is a secondary backed blade, which is only backed at its distal end. Its length is 9.7 cm and its width 3.1 cm. A total of 60 proximal ends, 11 middle pieces and 38 distal ends of blades were recorded (Fig. 45b).

All in all, the flint-knapping technique was influenced by the poor locally-available raw material. The cores are short and irregular and adjustment of the cores during blade production occurred only rarely. Crested blades are very few in number and the blades are totally dominated by short, irregular examples.

3.5.1.2 Artefacts from secondary working

The *scraper* group is very small and comprises only c. 2.9% of the tool inventory of flakes and blades (see Tab. 9).

Blade scrapers are rare and only represented by three examples, of which one has a pointed snout and a notch in one edge (Fig. 47a). The raw material for this was a regular A-blade measuring 6-7 cm in length and 2.6 cm in width. Pointed blade scrapers occur regularly in Jutland's Ertebølle culture, for example at Aggersund (Andersen, S.H. 1979a, 25, Fig. 13a). The two other pieces are, respectively, the broken end of a (fire-brittled) scraper made on an A-blade, and a more irregular scraper made on a B-blade (Fig. 47b). The latter is 6.1 cm long, 3.4 cm wide and has fine reverse edge retouch on one side of the percussion bulb. The assemblage also includes two atypical scrapers made on irregular flakes, where the distal end forms a narrow, pointed/snout-shaped scraper edge. A small "horn" has been produced on the edge of one of these scrapers. The two scrapers are, respectively, 4.6 and 7.3 cm long and 4.2 and 3.6 cm wide.

Borers constitute 15.4% of all the artefacts arising from secondary working; the largest proportion seen at any of the lagoon's settlements (see Tab. 9).

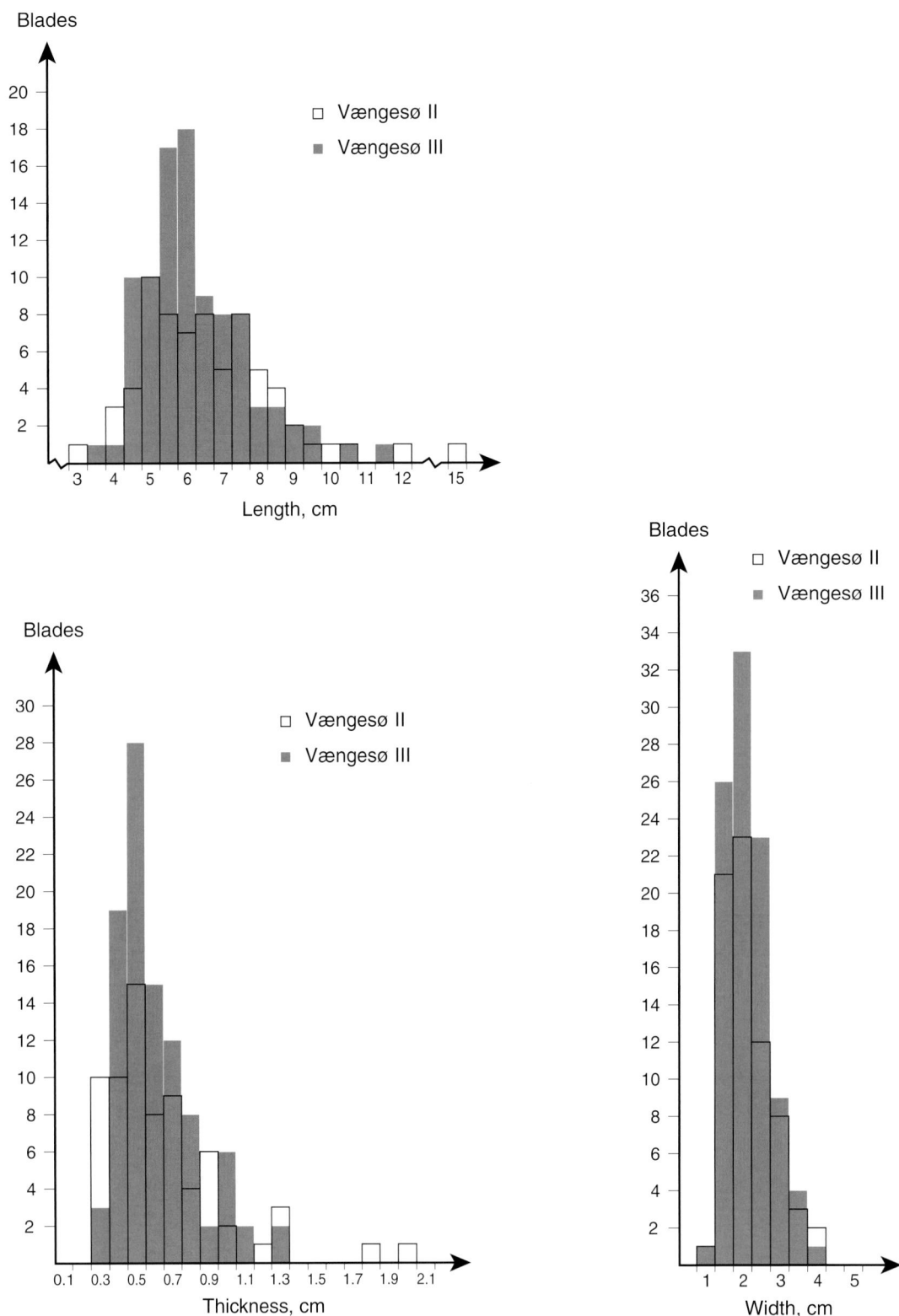

a

▲▶ *Fig. 45. a) Comparative diagrams showing the length, width and thickness of the blades from Vængesø II and Vængesø III. The Vængesø II blades are shorter and thicker than those from Vængesø III, cf. Fig. 128. b) Abundance of the various blade types and fragments of blades. Compare with Fig. 127, where corresponding totals are given for Vængesø III. From this it is obvious that the blade-production techniques at Vængesø II and II are identical.*

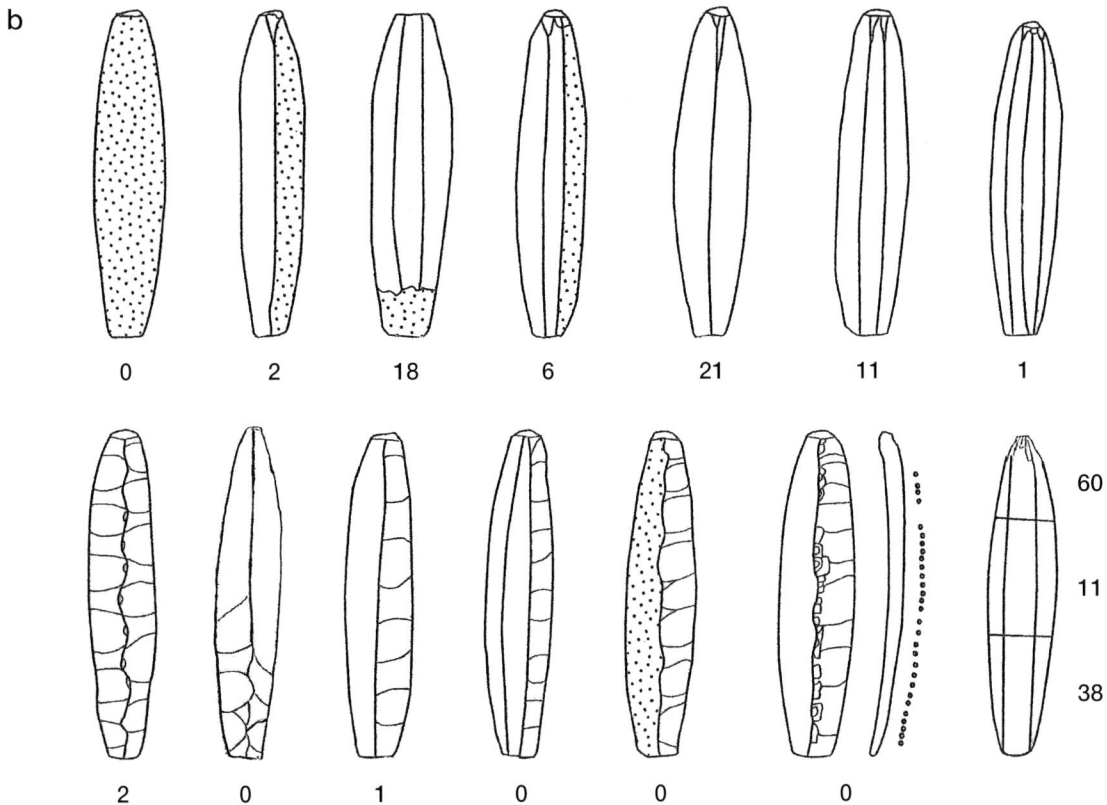

b

0	2	18	6	21	11	1

						60
2	0	1	0	0	0	11
						38

Flake borers are represented by eight examples, of which six have a "shouldered" point (Fig. 48c). The raw material for these was elongate flakes. The group is of uniform size, with the exception of one piece, which is somewhat larger. Their length ranges from 4.4-10 cm, but most have a length of 4-6 cm.

Blade borers are also few in number and the type without shoulders is represented by two examples on B-blades (Fig. 48a-b). One measures 9.1 cm in length and 2.3 cm in width, the other 11.7 cm in length and 2.6 cm in width. *Borer tips* are represented by three examples, of which two are on A-blades, while the third is the tip of a borer that broke with a diagonal fracture. These pieces are triangular in cross-section. The first two are 4.5 and 8 cm in length, respectively, while the third is 2.5 cm. Seven *core borers/thick borers* were also recovered. Of these, five have a worked, shaped tip, forming shoulders with the handle, while the tip and handle on the two others show an even, straight, uninterrupted transition. The latter two are very closely related in form to "picks". Two pieces are made from

calcareous (Danien) flint. Their tips are short, c. 4 cm long, and have a triangular or rhombic cross-section. The length of the core borers is 8.1-10.7 cm. There is a single *needle-shaped drill*. This is a narrow piece with heavily and steeply retouched edges such that its cross-section is trapezoid. Its length is 6.1 cm and its width 1.2 cm. The category *irregular borers* includes four examples, of which three are on elongate, irregular flakes with a short tip at the distal end. The fourth piece is on a short flake. Their length is 4.7-6.7 cm. Finally, there is an *atypical borer*. This piece is irregular and heavily water-worn with a partially dissolved surface. It has a thick tip, which forms clear shoulders with the handle section, and the tip is broken off. The length of this borer is 6.3 cm and its width at the handle is 7.5 cm.

Burins are extremely few in number and constitute only c. 2.4% of the secondarily-worked artefacts, which is the lowest proportion encountered at any of the Vængesø settlements (see Tab. 9). Only one example was found of each of the following variants: *Symmetrical dihedral burin* on a thick,

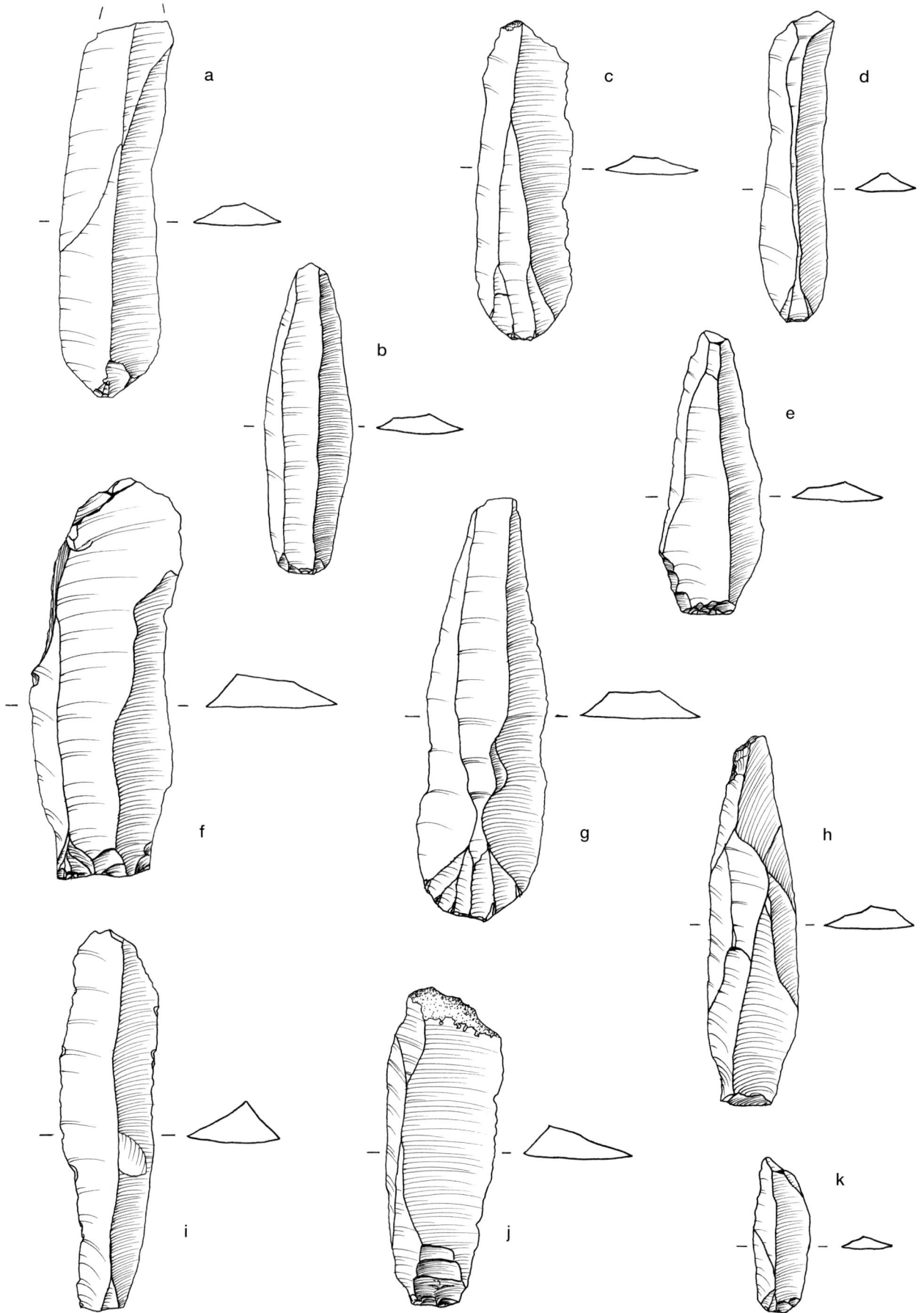

Fig. 46. a-j) Blades. k) Preparatory flake. The blades from this settlement are generally short and irregular due to the nature of the local raw material. Scale 3:4. Drawing: Søren Timm Christensen.

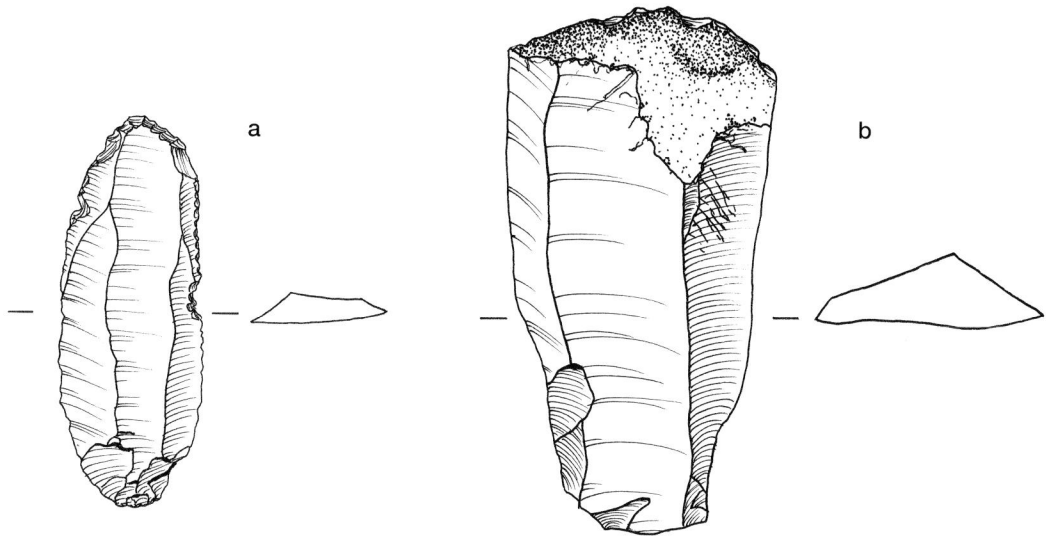

Fig. 47. a) Pointed blade scraper. b) Atypical scraper on a coarse flake. Scale 3:4. Drawing: Søren Timm Christensen.

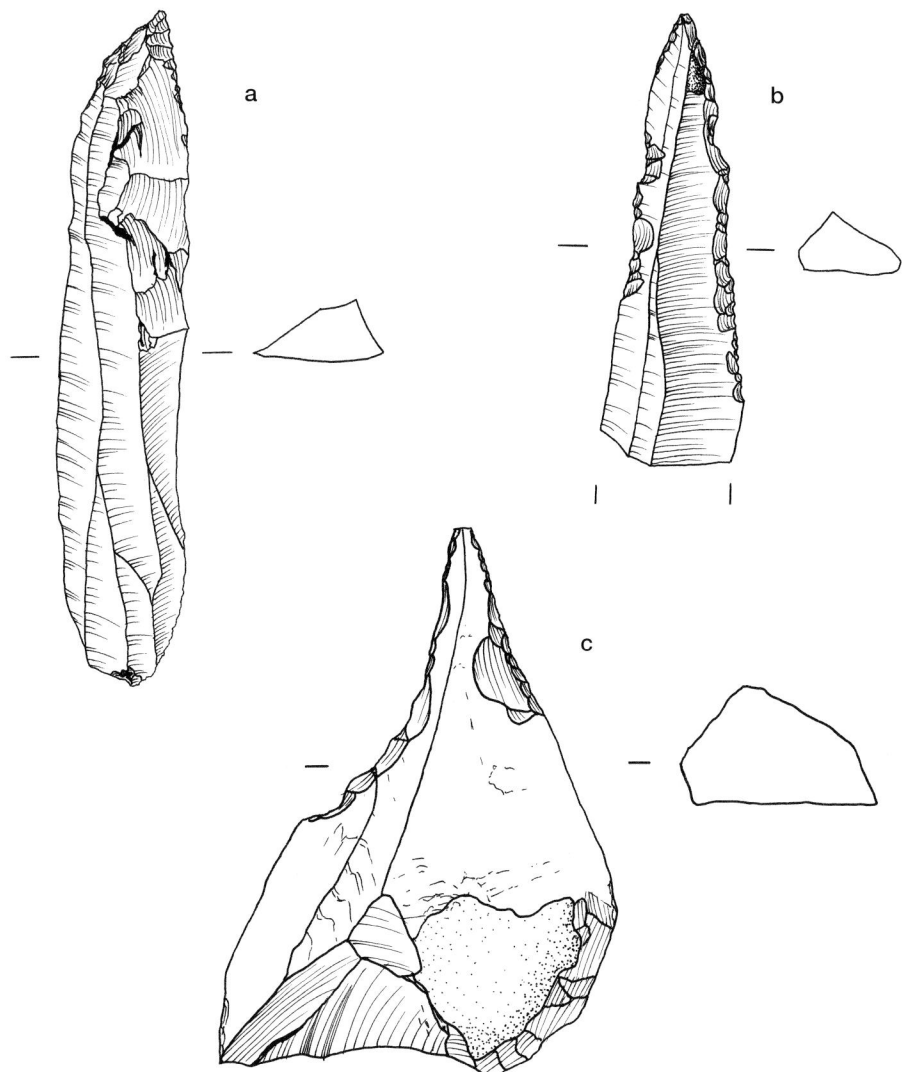

Fig. 48. Borers. a) Blade borer with an oblique point. b) Point of a symmetrical blade borer. c) Flake borer. Scale 3:4. Drawing: Søren Timm Christensen.

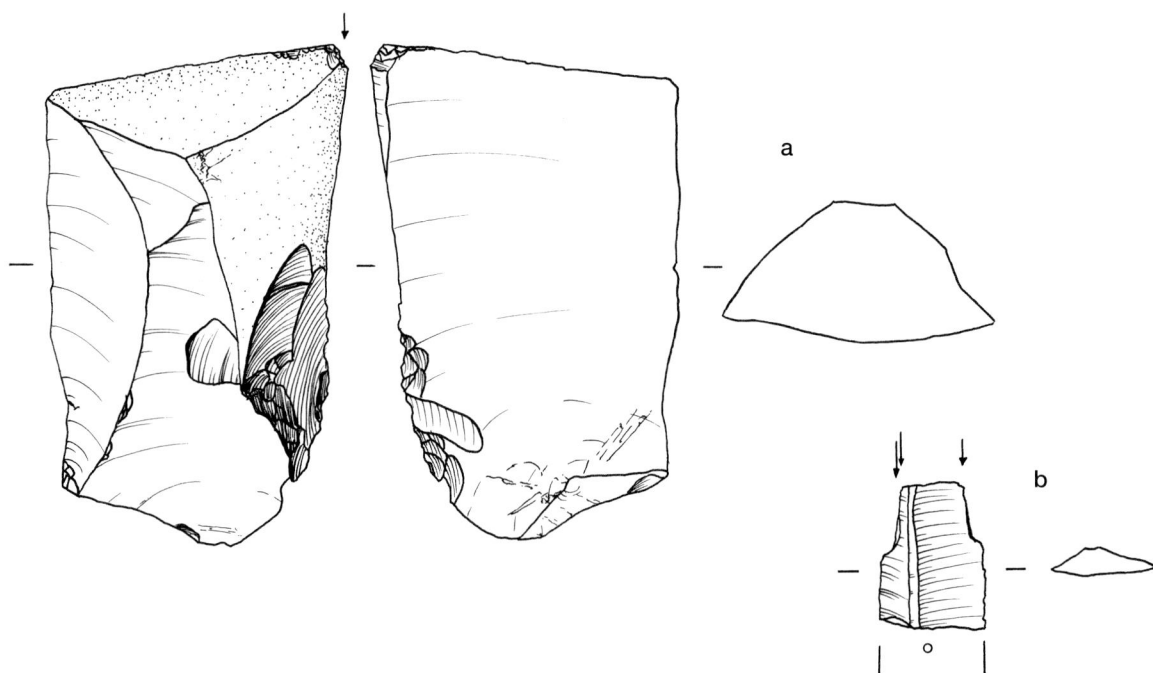

Fig. 49. a) Angle burin on a cortex-covered flake. b) Multi-burin on a blade. Scale 3:4. Drawing: Søren Timm Christensen.

regular blade. At the proximal end of the piece is a burin edge, while the distal end originally had a tang that was severed with a transverse blow and subsequently used as the basis for an (angle) burin blow. Typologically, this piece falls completely outside the rest of the tool inventory (which can be dated to the Late Ertebølle culture) and must belong to an earlier settlement. Similar burin types are characteristic of the Early Ertebølle culture and are known for example from Norslund layers 3-4 (Andersen/Malmros 1966, 73-74, Figs. 23-24). The length of the example from Vængesø II is 7.9 cm, its width 3.7 cm and its thickness 1.6 cm. An *angle burin on a break* (on a thin A-blade) measures 4.8 cm in length and 2.5 cm in width. There is a single *angle burin on a natural surface* (Fig. 49a). An *angle burin on a transverse blow* (proximal) and with edge retouch is on a thick flake, which measures 6.4 cm in length, 4.8 cm in width and 1.9 cm in thickness. Finally, there is a *multi-burin on a break* in the form of the broken end of a regular A-blade (Fig. 49b).

Truncated pieces constitute 26.2% of all the blade tools and are thereby clearly the most dominant tool type at this settlement (see Tab. 9). To a very

great degree, the 63 examples characterise the tool inventory at this site. The raw material for them was generally regular A-blades, but in a number of cases very broad blades were selected. These are often triangular in outline, with the truncation always being found at the broad distal end (Fig. 50d). A similar shaping of the truncated blades is also seen in the assemblage from Vængesø III. This type is otherwise rare at coeval Ertebølle settlements in eastern Jutland, where the preferred raw material for these tools was regular, narrow blades/flakes with parallel edges (e.g. Norsminde: Andersen, S.H. 1991, 27, Fig. 13,10). They presumably represent a local variant of this tool type. The often very broad, long and regular blades that constituted the majority of the raw material for these truncated pieces differ from all the other flake artefacts and blade cores, which are all short and irregular. Moreover, none of the core flakes recovered appears to originate from core forms other than those described above. Finally, an examination of the blade pieces reveals that there are no fragments of broad blanks in this group. The impression gained is therefore that the blades, which in the majority of cases were the raw material for a number of the truncated pieces, were not manufactured on this "island" but must have originated at another locality.

Concave truncation is the most common variant, represented by 51 examples (Fig. 50). In 11 cases, the raw material comprised large, broad blades, 11 were made on narrow regular blades and 18 on short, broad flakes. In four cases, raw materials were selected with a triangular or trapezoid outline, and with the greatest width at their distal end, i.e. at the truncated edge (Fig. 50d). This group contains the largest and most regular blade tools in the Vængesø II assemblage, and both size and the regularity of these pieces clearly differ from the other blade artefacts. Similarly, large blades/flakes with concave truncation are also represented at Vængesø III, but in considerably smaller number (three examples). This group includes a piece with slight edge truncation at the percussion bulb end, where the other edge has a c. 3 cm long, coarsely denticulate section. Another piece has a short point at one corner of the concave truncation. All the pieces are truncated distally, but one also has proximal, reverse and irregular truncation. Furthermore, two pieces are fire-brittled and four are water-worn. All the pieces have chips in one or both edges as a result of being used as knives. One truncated piece stands out from the rest of the group by being unusually small. It is 2.3 cm long and 1.3 cm wide, but wear traces on one (the longest) edge show that, despite its small dimensions, this was nevertheless also used as a knife. The length of the large pieces is 6.3-11.2 cm, their width 3.4-4.9 cm and their thickness 0.6-1.4 cm. The length of the regular blades with concave truncation is 4.5-10.4 cm, their width 1.5-2.9 cm and their thickness 0.2-0.5 cm. The dimensions of the short, broad truncated flakes are 2.4-5.6 cm (length), 4.2-5 cm (width) and 1-1.3 cm (thickness).

Blades with concave distal truncation and handle section are common and are represented by 11 examples, of which two are broken across diagonally (Fig. 51b-d). This variant clearly differs from the other truncated pieces because narrow, regular A-blades were chosen with a length of 5.8-8.4 cm and a width of 1.7-3.2 cm. In all cases, these are tools on which the truncated sections are short (c.

2-2.5 cm) and continue evenly into the side edges ("the Jutland form"). They never have a sharply demarcated handle section like that seen on this type at the Ertebølle settlements on northern and eastern Funen and on Zealand (Andersen, S.H. 2013, 308-310, Fig. 7.6b). Two of the pieces have propeller retouch and four examples only have retouch on one side of the percussion bulb (proximal) end (Fig. 51b).

Seven pieces have concave retouch, one has irregular retouch and two are broken across. This type occurs on many Ertebølle settlements in western Denmark, but is not common and the Vængesø II assemblage is the largest from Jutland. One piece, on an A-blade, has a *double, slightly convex truncation* (Fig. 50h). Its length is 8 cm and its width 3.3 cm. Similarly, there is only a single example of a piece with *concave truncation and dorsal working/trimming* (Fig. 50i). Three blades have *diagonal, straight truncation*. Both were made on regular blades. The truncation is at the distal end (Fig. 51f). Their length is, respectively, 4.2 and 8.9 cm and their width 1.8 and 2.8 cm. Three short blades have *diagonal concave truncation* (Fig. 52b-c). In all cases, the retouch is at the distal end. Their length is 5.7-6.9 cm and their width 2.3-3.8 cm. There were 11 finds of *broken-off end pieces of truncated blades*. Of these, one has straight, three have straight-diagonal and seven have concave truncation. One piece has proximal truncation, while the others have distal truncation. Two pieces are made from very broad blades of the kind described under pieces with concave retouch. Two examples have a triangular outline with truncation at the broad end, as also described above. Their length is 0.5-6.3 cm and their width 1.8-3.3 cm.

The distribution of the truncated pieces across the excavation area is shown in Fig. 53a. Thick, evenly tapering *B-blades with heavily trimmed edges*, but without a point, occur in two cases, of which one shows dorsal cortex. One measures 8.6 cm in length and 2.7 cm in width, while the other is 7.4 cm long and 2.7 cm wide.

"Knives" are represented by two examples. One is very regular and has an evenly curved, worked edge. Its length is 6.7 cm and its width 1.8 cm (Fig.

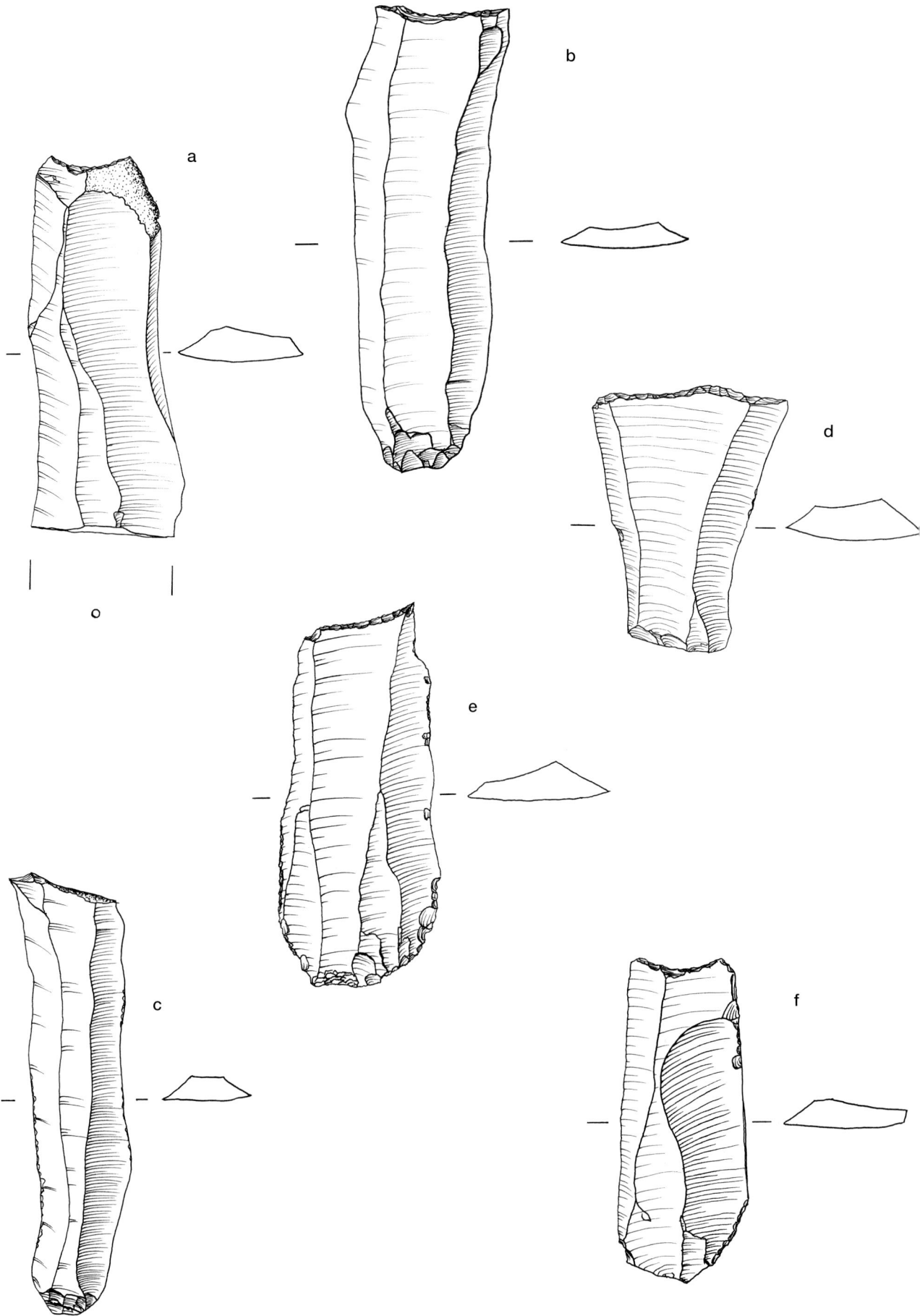

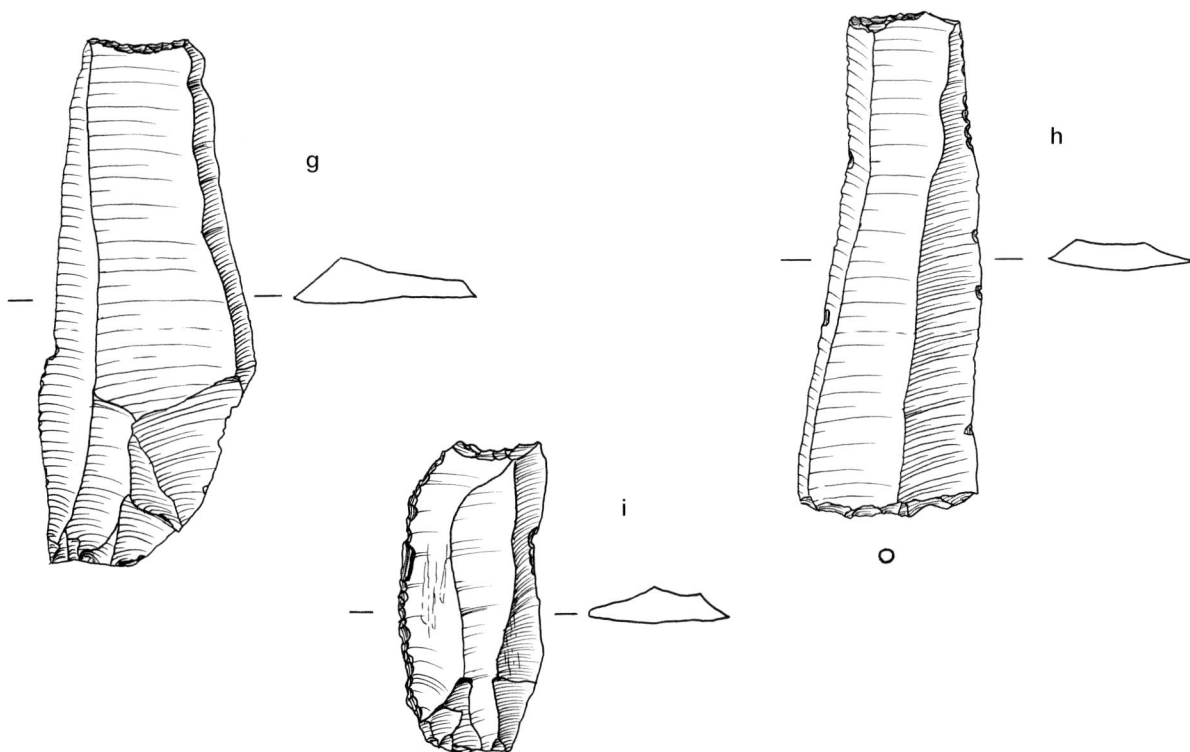

Fig. 50. a-b) Large blades with concave, distal truncation. c) Blade with oblique, distal trunc-
ation. d) Short, wide flake of triangular form with distal truncation. e) Blade with oblique, concave
and distal truncation. f-g) Smaller blades with straight, concave distal truncation. h) Blade with
double truncation. i) Blade with concave truncation and arched dorsal trimming. Scale 3:4.
Drawing: Søren Timm Christensen.

52a). The other is an irregular, partially cortex-covered flake, on which a natural cortex-covered and diagonal edge has formed a finger support, while the opposite edge is concave and denticulate (heavy wear). Its length is 9.4 cm and its width 3.9 cm.

Flakes and blades with a finely denticulate edge are few in number (c. 4.2%) and were only found in two cases. These comprise a regular blade, on which both edges are denticulate, and a curved flake on which the concave edge is denticulate (Fig. 52d-e). The blade measures 10.7 cm in length and 2.5 cm in width, while the curved piece is 5 cm in length and 2.5 cm in width. The few examples of this type contrast with the situation at Vængesø III, where the finely denticulate pieces are more prominent. There are also a few pieces with coarse denticulation of one edge (Fig. 54a-b). Fig. 54c shows a *piece with a deep notch.* This latter form was only found in one case.

Transverse arrowheads (Fig. 55) are represented by 95 examples (Tab. 1). If the latter table is compared with similar summaries from other Ertebølle sites in eastern Jutland, it is apparent that the Vængesø II site's Ertebølle layer should be dated to the Late Ertebølle culture. This relative date is completely consistent with the rest of the Ertebølle tool inventory and the available radiocarbon dates. The first group of transverse arrowheads with parallel sides includes an example on a biconvex flake and this also has reverse retouch. The raw material, form and working suggest that this piece is probably Neolithic. One transverse arrowhead is fire-brittled and two arrowheads have double-sided reverse edge retouch. One arrowhead has a pointed base (Fig. 55a). If attention is turned to the length-width ratio of these arrowheads, it can be seen that, for the type with strongly concave sides, their dimensions lie within very narrow limits. Their

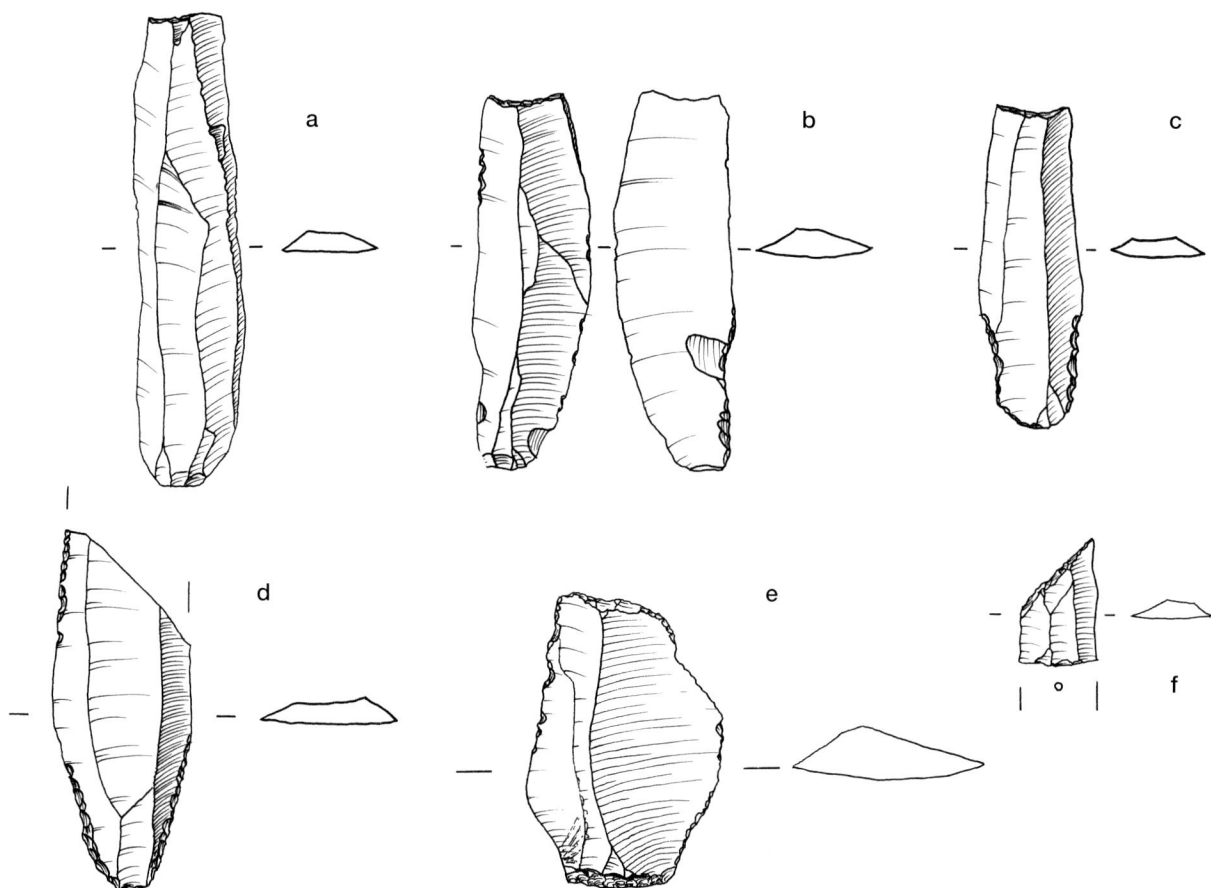

Fig. 51. a-c) Slender blades with concave, distal truncation, of which b) has one-sided (and reverse) edge retouch (handle retouch) at its proximal end; c) has double-sided retouch (handle retouch) at its proximal end. d) Broken blade with worked handle. e) Short flake with irregular, distal truncation. f) Point of a blade with oblique, straight and distal truncation. Scale 3:4. Drawing: Søren Timm Christensen.

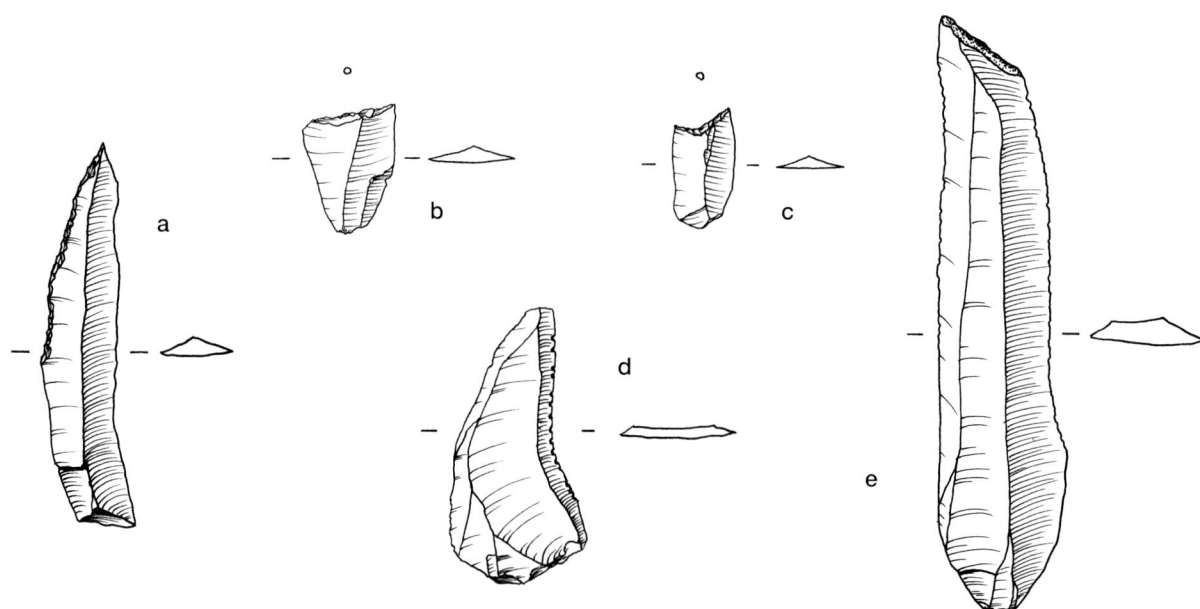

Fig. 52. a) Blade with arched dorsal trimming. b-c) small flakes with concave, oblique proximal truncation (preforms for transverse arrowheads). d) Flake and e blade with a finely denticulate edge. Scale 3:4. Drawing: Søren Timm Christensen.

length is between 1.6 and 2.2 cm and their width between 1.2 and 2 cm. As for the type with slightly concave sides, these pieces are generally slightly longer (1.8-2.4 cm) and with a narrower edge (1-1.6 cm) than the first type (Fig. 56).

A summary of all the use damage (i.e. from being fired) evident on the arrowheads reveals that 49 examples (61.2%) have chips in the edge, ten (12.5%) lack a base and 21 (26.2%) have a broken-off edge corner. If these percentages are compared with the corresponding data from Vængesø III, the two sites differ in that there are more arrowheads with chips in the edge at Vængesø II than at Vængesø III, while the other types of edge damage are similar between the two sites. If the use damage is examined relative to arrowhead type, the type with parallel or slightly concave sides shows the following picture: Nine have a broken base, six have a broken-off edge corner and 19 have chips in the edge. An arrowhead of this type has such heavy use damage that one of the edge corners has a "burin blow" (Fig. 55c). Of the type with heavily concave sides, seven have a broken base, six have a broken-off edge corner (in two cases a "burin blow" has been formed by the arrowhead striking

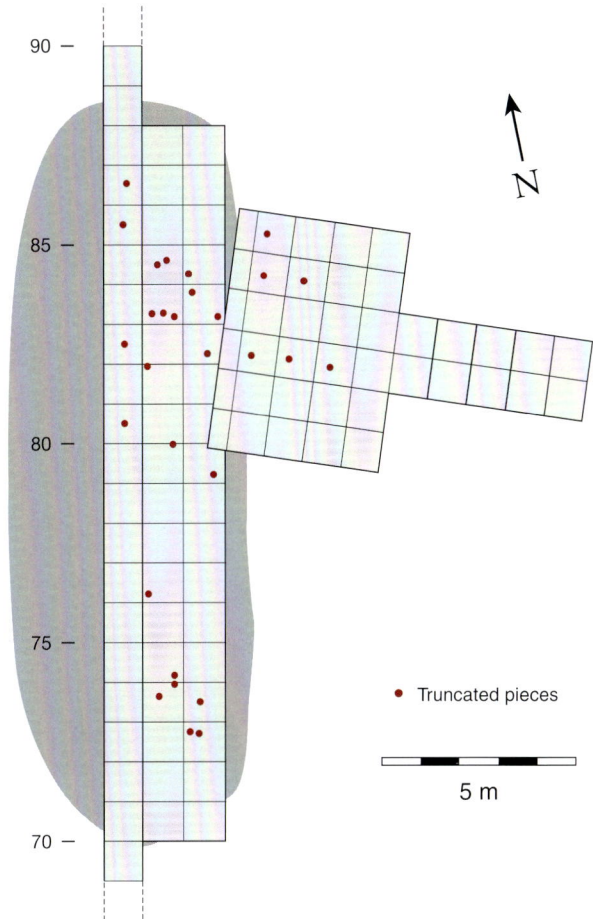

a

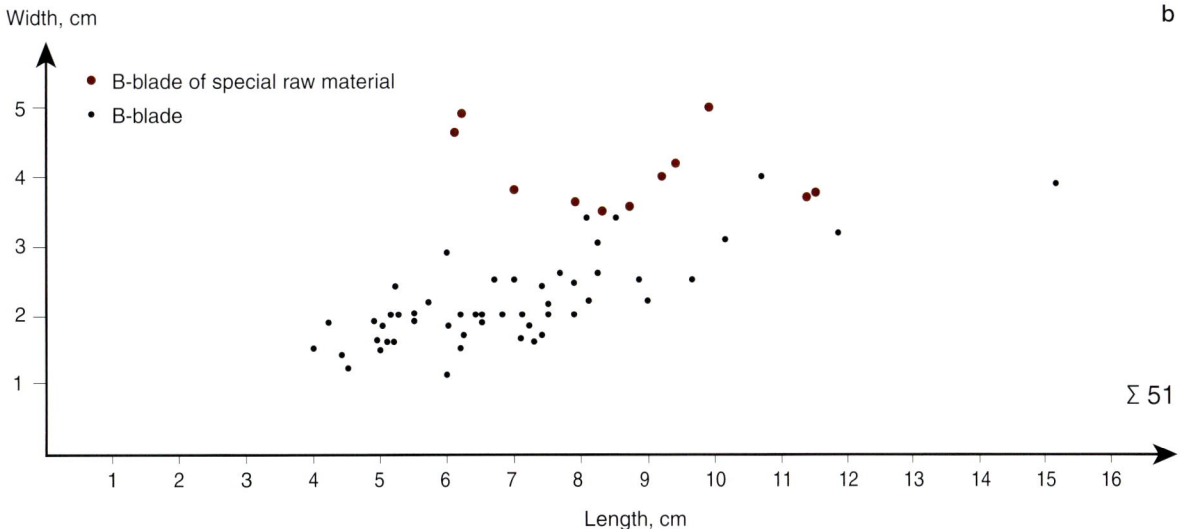

b

Fig. 53. a) Distribution of truncated pieces across the excavation trench. b) Diagram showing corresponding length-width measurements for the large blades with concave truncation and a selection of 51 B-blades from Vængesø II. It is clearly evident from the measurements that special raw materials (blanks) were chosen for the truncated pieces as these generally are both longer and (in particular) wider than the blades.

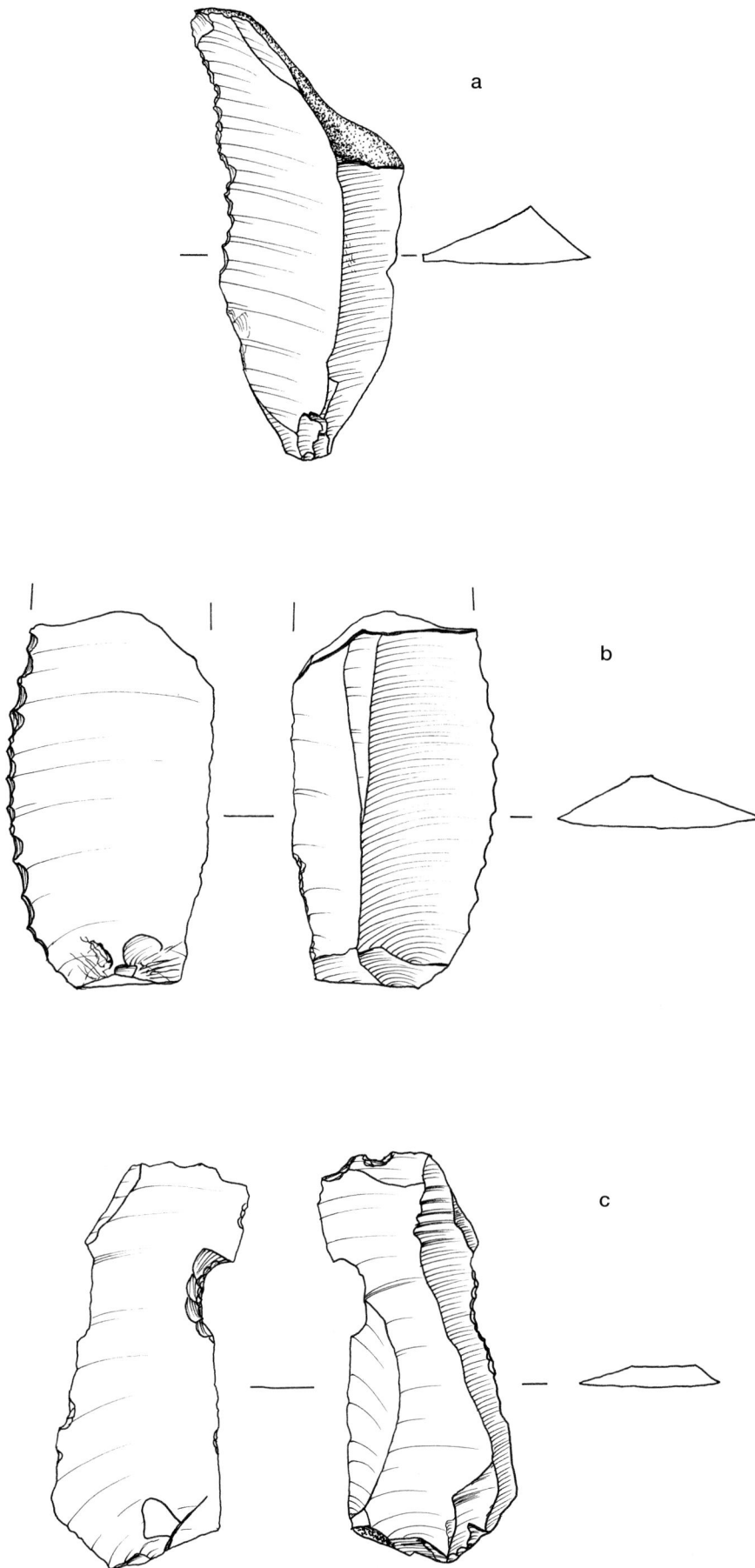

Fig. 54. a-b) Flake with coarse denticulation. c) Piece with a deep notch. Scale 3:4. Drawing: Søren Timm Christensen.

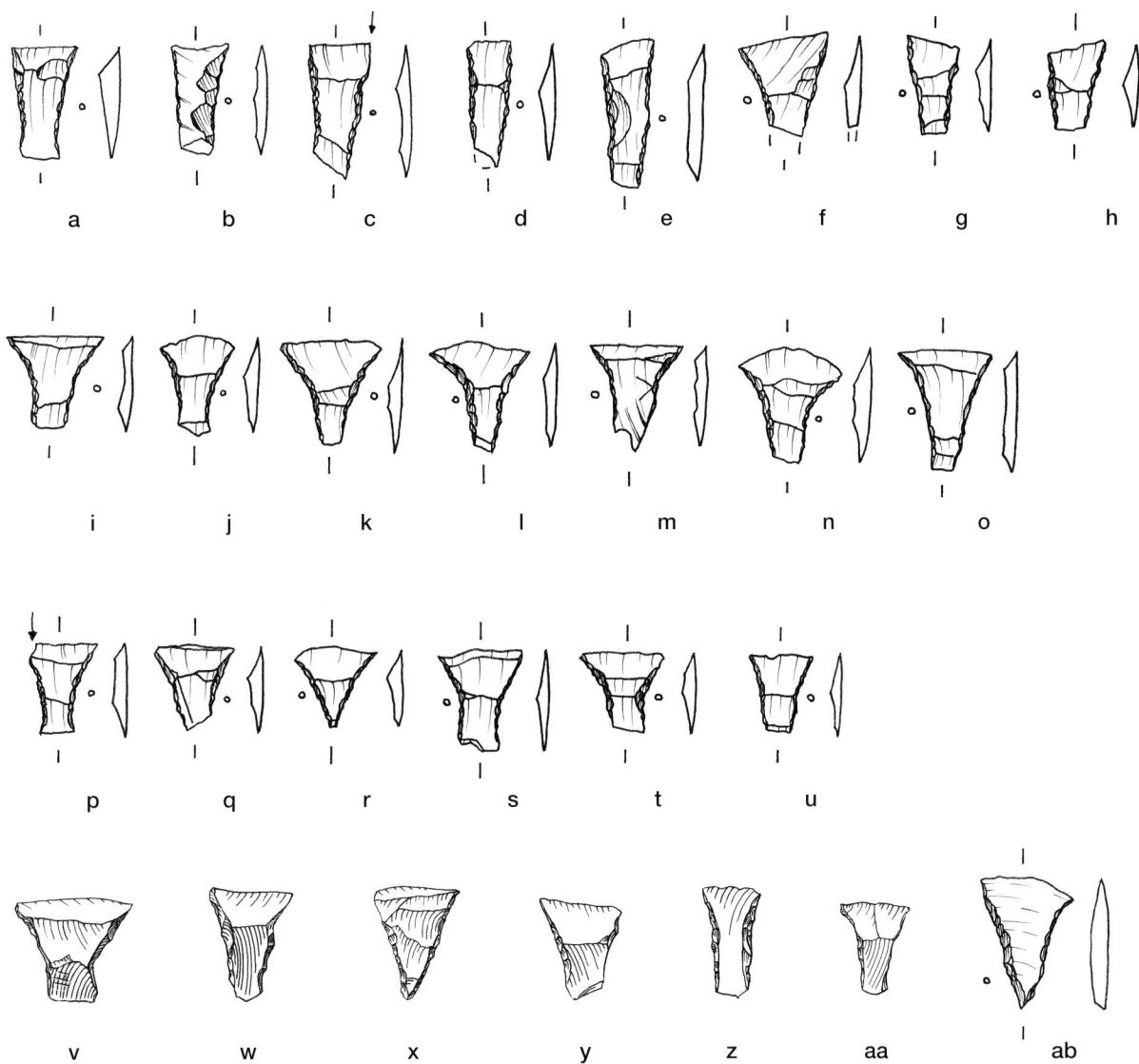

Fig. 55. Selection of transverse arrowheads. The dominant type is symmetrical with strongly concave sides. Some have an oblique edge (e-h) and a few others have a pointed base (x and ab). The preferred raw material was thin flakes. Two arrowheads (z and ab lowermost) were made on biconvex flakes. Arrows indicate heavy impact fractures. Scale 3:4. Drawing: Søren Timm Christensen.

a hard material, possibly bone (Fig. 55p)), and 31 clearly show chips in their edge. Of the type with a slightly oblique edge, four have a broken-off base, two have a broken-off edge corner and 12 have chips in their edge. Finally, arrowheads with a very oblique edge have in one case a broken base, one has a broken edge corner and five show chips in their edge. One of the latter type is on a biconvex flake and three have a pointed base. If this

summary is compared with that from a similar investigation at the contemporaneous settlement of Ronæs Skov (on the Little Belt coast in western Funen), a difference is seen in the distribution of the use damage among the arrowheads. At Ronæs Skov, arrowheads with a broken-off edge corner dominate, followed by examples with chips in the edge. Conversely, transverse arrowheads with a broken base are more frequent at Vængesø II and

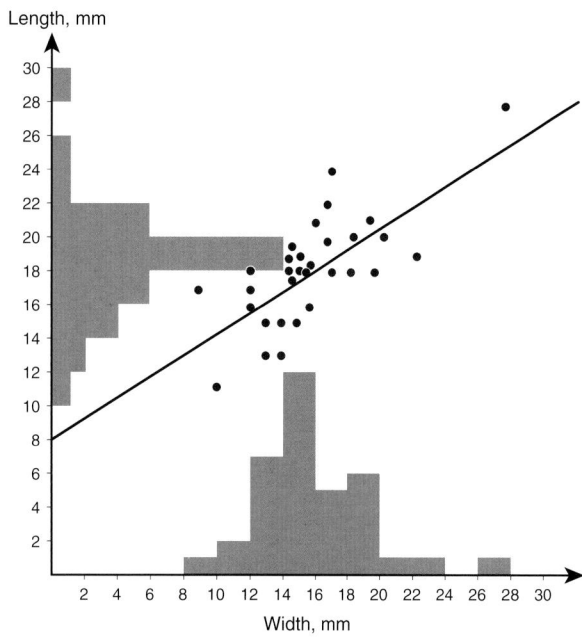

a

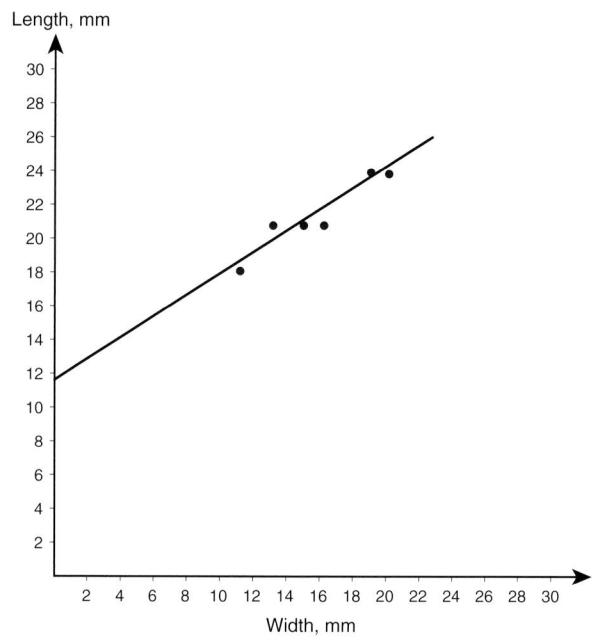

b

c

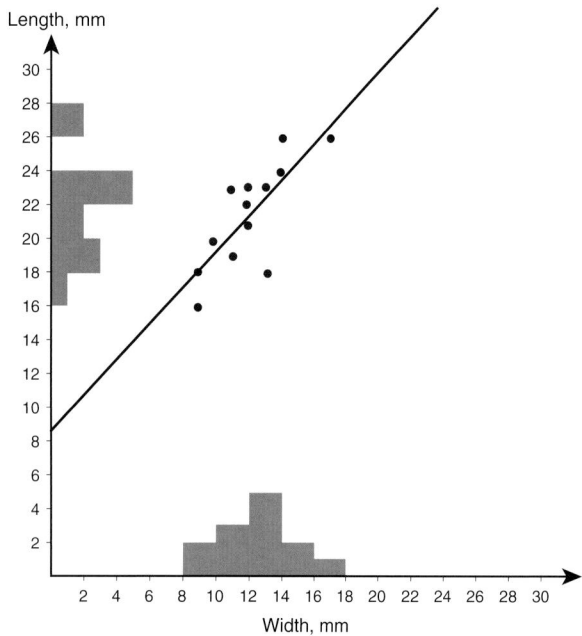

d

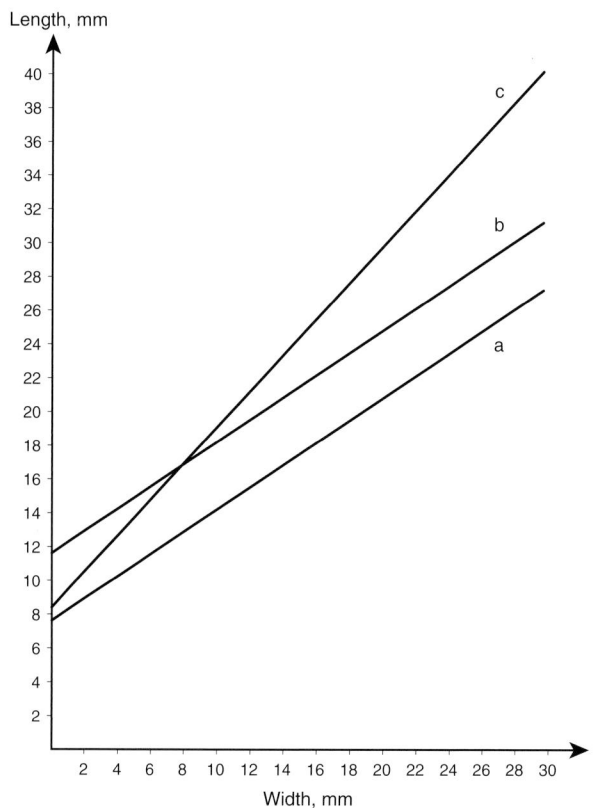

Fig. 56. a) Length and width of the transverse arrowheads with strongly concave sides and a straight edge, b) with a pointed butt, straight edge and weakly concave sides, c) is arrowheads with a straight edge and weakly concave sides. d) Cumulative diagram of trend lines.

III than at Ronæs Skov. As the total number of arrowheads is significantly less at Ronæs Skov than at the Vængesø settlements, these relative differences should be taken with some reservation (Andersen, S.H. 2009, 71, Fig. 43).

Pointed, trimmed core tools ("*picks*"), elongate, oval in outline and with a tri- or quadrangular cross-section are represented by two examples, of which one has a broken-off tip. These are core tools, the edges of which run together to form a point, while the opposing end is blunt or unworked. Their length ranges from 8.5 to 10 cm and their width is c. 3.5 cm. Also included in this group is a large pick, which is elongate-oval in outline and has an equilateral, triangular cross-section. The trimming is coarse, but all the sides are carefully worked. The piece was apparently originally pointed at both ends, though these were later broken off. The coarse shaping could suggest that this is a preform for a (large) core axe (adze) with a specialised edge. Its length is 20 cm and its width/thickness is 5.3-5.8 cm.

A projection of the assemblage's axes onto the surveyed sections shows that the majority lay in the deepest part of the kitchen midden and in the pre-midden layer, while the middle and upper parts of the kitchen midden layer only contained few axes and chisels. It is also evident that there is a tendency for the core axes to lie deeper than the flat-flaked flake axes and flake chisels. As the core axes are, however, few in number, no clear trends can be deduced from their distribution. The axe group comprises c. 5.8% core axes, 85.4% flake axes and 8.7% flake chisels.

In the *core axes*, fragments dominate with 12 examples, while *symmetrical adzes with specialised edge treatment* and *asymmetrical core axes* (oblique axes) are only represented by one example each. The asymmetrical core axe is a small, regular example with a length of 8.5 cm and a width of 3.7 cm. The *symmetrical core axe has double-sided edge treatment* (Fig. 57a) and judging from the edge flakes, there were originally further examples of this type on the settlement. Its length is 14.5 cm, its width 5.9 cm and its thickness 4.2 cm. Among the core axes fragments, *butt fragments* dominate with nine examples. Two examples are made from a grey, calcareous type of flint. Eight examples are broken transversely and

display a flat, fractured surface, while one example has been broken longitudinally and terminates in a "fishhook fracture". All the fragments have a trapezoid or semicircular cross-section. Apart from two examples (from a large symmetrical axe and from a symmetrical adze of triangular cross-section), the other fragments cannot be identified to axe type. Two fragments have been secondarily employed as flake cores, where the fracture has served as a platform. Their length is 6-10 cm, their width 2.6-4 cm and their thickness 2.3-3.5 cm. One fragment comes from the *middle of a symmetrical axe*. It is 5.5 cm in length, 4.7 cm in width and 2.5 cm in thickness. A fragment of an *edge section* is from a symmetrical axe with a double-sided trimmed edge (Fig. 57b). The width of the edge is 4.8 cm, which shows that this was a relatively large core axe. Another edge flake comes from a *narrow-edged symmetrical core chisel* with double-sided, specialised edge trimming (fire-brittled). It is 4.9 cm in length and 2.7 cm in width (Fig. 57c). Both the latter pieces, which can be assigned to the Ertebølle occupation of the site, have double-sided specialised edge trimming.

The commonest axe form at this settlement is the *flake axe*, which is represented by 205 examples (Fig. 58). The most dominant of these is the symmetrical, flat-flaked variant with c. 83%. The raw material was bryozoan flint. In one case, use was though made of a whitish-yellow, very calcareous type of flint. Characteristic edge and surface flakes from the manufacture of flat-flaked flake axes were also recorded from this locality, but in much fewer numbers than would be expected, given the number of flake axes and in comparison with for example Vængesø III. The number of production flakes from the manufacture of flake axes does not match the large number of flake axes that have been excavated. With considerable caution, this discrepancy could perhaps be explained by a number of the flake axes not having been manufactured at this settlement. Instead, they were perhaps brought along on various visits to the site and therefore originated from one or more other settlements in the area.

There are also two pieces of butts of *edge-trimmed flake axes*. The few examples present show that this type is rare and probably originates from visits to the

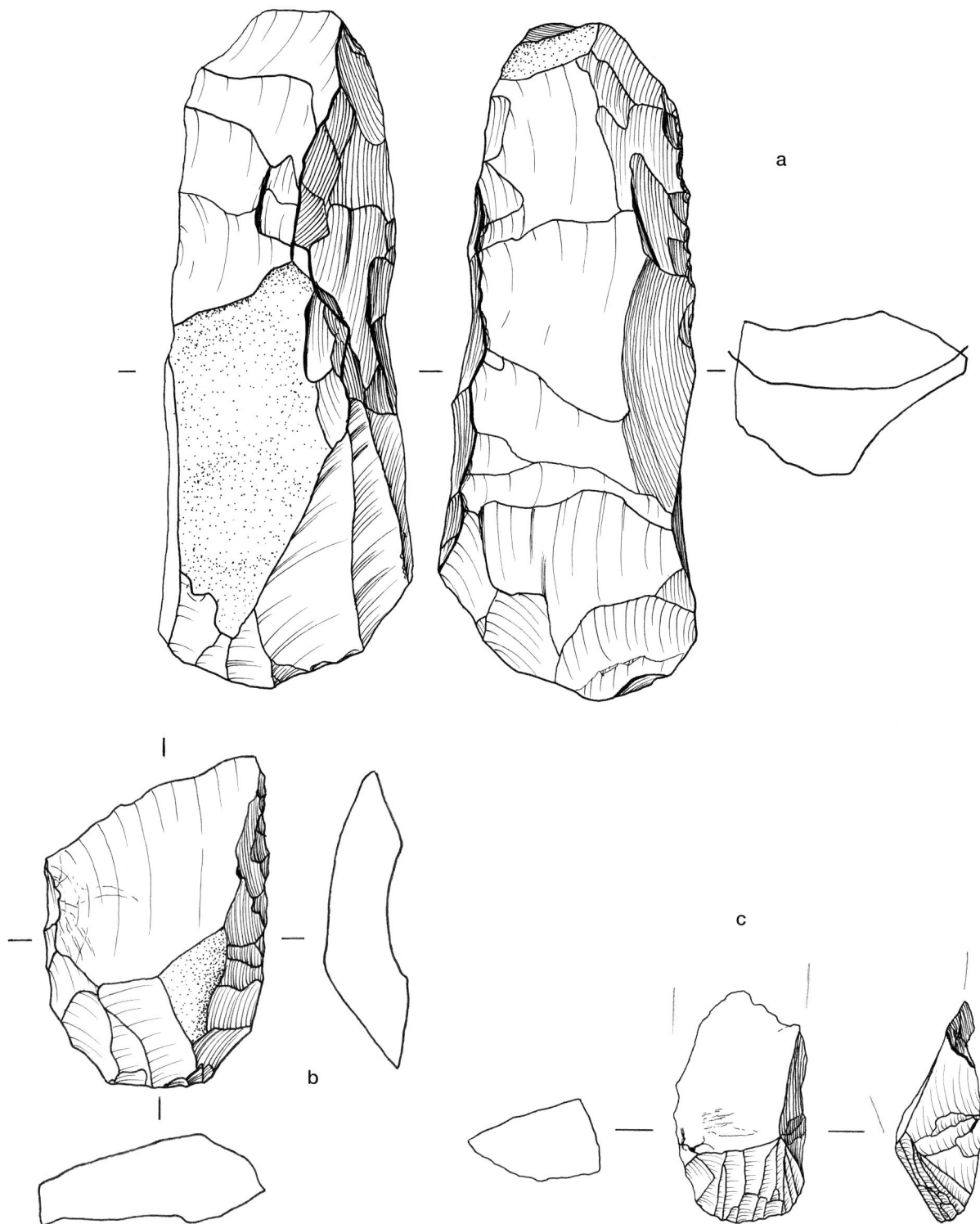

Fig. 57. a) Symmetrical core axe. b) Edge flake from a symmetrical core axe with bifacial, specialised edge working. c) Edge flake from a symmetrical core chisel, also with a bifacial, specialised edge. Scale 3:4. Drawing: Søren Timm Christensen.

▶ *Fig. 58. Flake axes. a-b) Flat-flaked symmetrical flake axes with parallel sides. c-d) Flat-flaked symmetrical flake axes with strongly concave sides and a broader edge (the dominant type at Vængesø II). e) Flat-flaked flake axe with irregular sides. f) Flat-flaked flake axe with convex sides. The dominant type at this site is a flat-flaked and symmetrical axe with strongly concave sides and broad edge. Scale 3:4. Drawing: Søren Timm Christensen.*

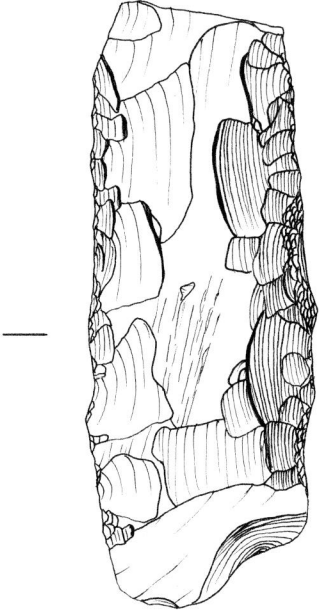

a

b

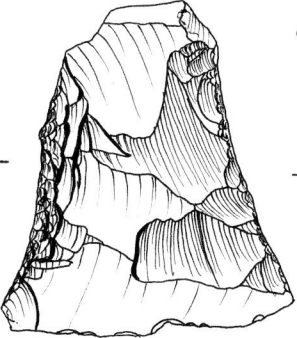

c

d

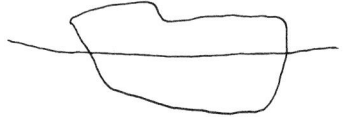

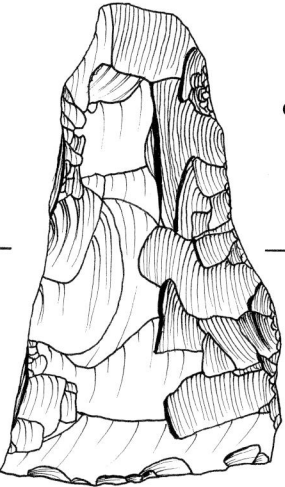

e

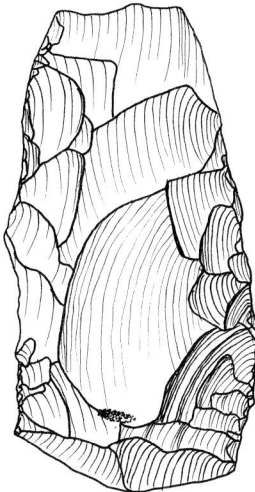

f

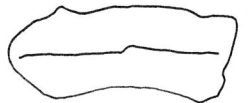

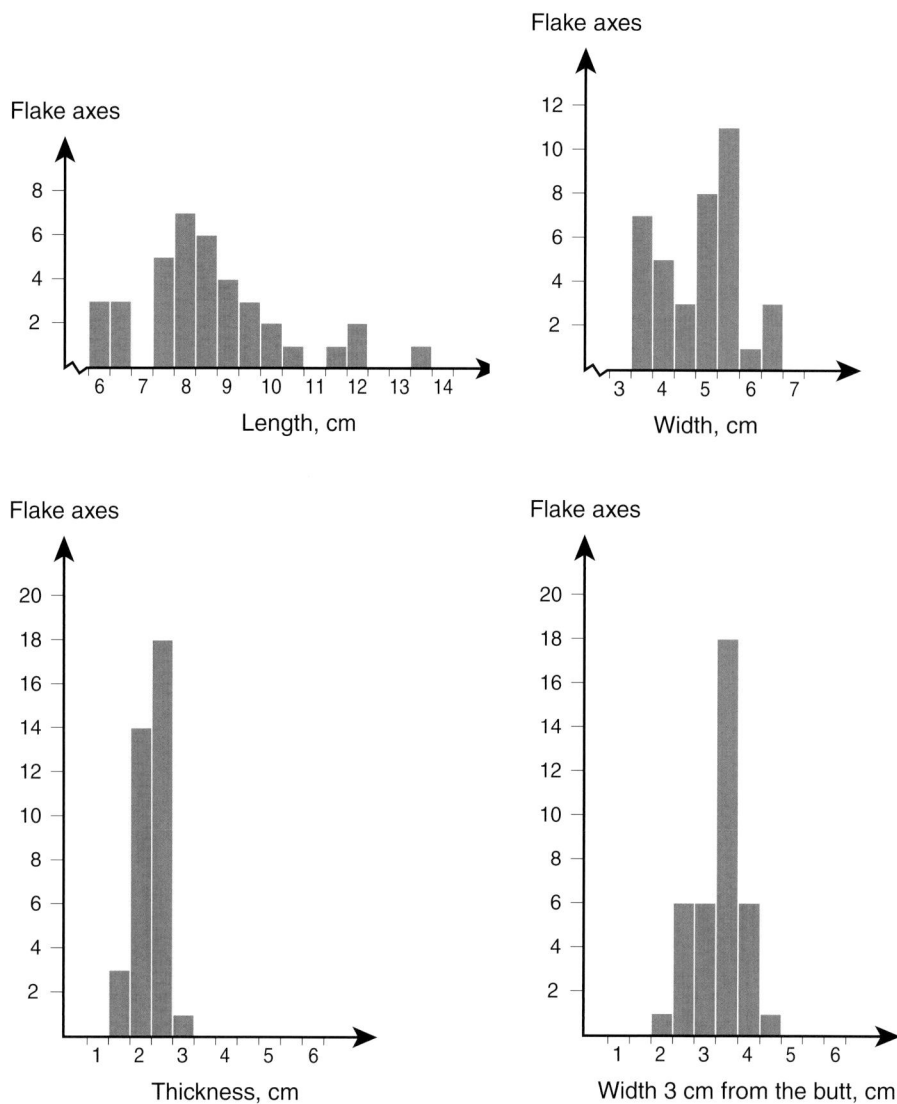

Fig. 59. Diagrams showing the maximum length, maximum width (at the edge), greatest thickness and width 3 cm from the butt of the flat-flaked flake axes.

	Total	Flake axe type, outline				Average edge width, cm	Average length, cm
Vængesø III	102	0	17 (16.6%)	57 (55.8%)	28 (27.4%)	4.94	7.51
Vængesø II	47	3 (6.3%)	6 (12.7%)	17 (36.1%)	21 (44.6%)	4.86	8.56

Fig. 60. Diagram showing the side morphology and edge of the flat-flaked flake axes from Vængesø II and III. The dominant type is clearly that with strongly concave sides, which is a late feature in the Ertebølle culture of eastern Jutland, cf. Fig. 145. The diagram shows that the flake axes become shorter and develop broader edges over time.

site during the Early Ertebølle culture. This conclusion is supported by the fact that these pieces are slightly water-worn. There are 152 *symmetrical flat-flaked flake axes* and 18 *asymmetrical flat-flaked flake axes*. One flat-flaked flake axe has *specialised edge trimming* on both edge faces – a very rare form that is only known from the settlements of the very latest Ertebølle culture, for example Norslund layers 0+1 (Andersen/Malmros 1966, 47, Fig. 6), Rønæs Skov (Andersen, S.H. 2009, 73) and the latest Ertebølle settlements on Zealand (Johansson 1999, 23). A random sample of 47 flat-flaked flake axes revealed that 21 have strongly concave sides, 17 have slightly concave sides, six have parallel sides, three have convex sides and three have irregular sides. If attention is turned to the contour of the edge (seen looking towards the broad side of the axe), an examination of a random sample of 59 axes shows that 26 (44%) have a convex edge and 14 (23.7%) have a straight

edge, while 19 (32.2%) have an oblique or concave edge. If the edge is viewed from in front, there are 35 examples (59.3%) with an oblique-convex edge, followed by 12 examples (20.3%) with a straight edge and nine (15.2%) with a convex edge, while three are completely irregular. The mean for the edge width is 4.9 cm and 8.6 cm for the length (Fig. 60). As for the form of the sides of the flat-flaked flake axes, reference is made to Fig. 60.

The flint assemblage from Vængesø II also includes 33 *atypical flake axes*. This group is characterised by very irregular pieces that vary in form, size and working. Finally, there are eight fragments of flake axes. Of these, two are side flakes, three are parts of an edge, one is a regular edge rejuvenation piece and two are struck-off edge corners.

The flake axes from Vængesø II almost all show *wear traces* on their edge or face, but these are of very variable extent and intensity (Fig. 61). *Edge re-*

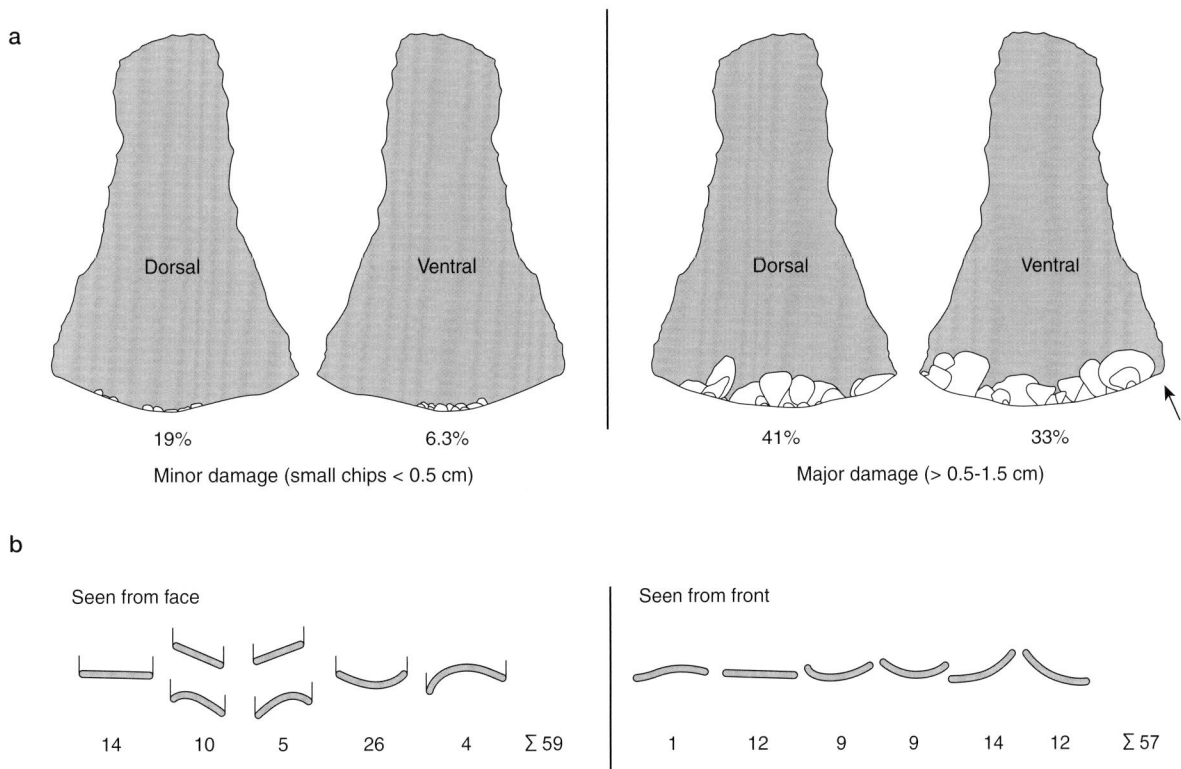

Fig. 61. a) Diagram showing wear traces at the edge, b, the line of the edge, seen from the face and in front, of the flake axes. b) The wear to the edge is classified as small chips (less than 0.5 cm) and major damage (0.5-1.5 cm). In addition to wear damage to the edge, many of the flake axes show major damage to the corners of the edge (arrowed), cf. Fig. 145 a. Most of the axes have a convex edge seen from the face, which is straight or slightly oblique seen from the front.

juvenation can be demonstrated in 13 cases (8.6%), with one axe showing edge rejuvenation attempts from both edge corners. This is a considerably lower frequency than for example at Vængesø I (34,6%) but similar to Vængesø III (6%), Ronæs Skov (33.6%; Andersen, S.H. 2009, 76) and at Norslund layers 0, 1 and 2, where rejuvenation was identified on 49% of the axes (Andersen/Malmros 1966, 47). *Edge flakes* from flake axes were found in 11 instances, of which three were recovered from the same excavation layer and square. There are also two fragments of flake axe edges. The most common form of *use damage* is that one, or possibly both, edge corners have been broken or struck off (possibly also worn down) as a consequence of numerous small chips (spall removal; 26 examples). Other use damage is evident in three axes that are broken in the middle, one has a broken

edge and five lack part of the butt, which has been broken off. This type of damage indicates tension in the shaft and has previously been described in connection with the contemporaneous Ertebølle assemblage from Ronæs Skov on the Little Belt coast in western Funen (Andersen, S.H. 2009, 73, Fig. 46b and e). Fifty-nine flake axes have *scale-like spalls on their edge faces* (33 examples on the dorsal side and 26 examples on the ventral side), 20 axes have fine, small spalls on the sides of the edge (15 on the dorsal side and five on the ventral side; Fig. 61). Five axes have a completely worn-down (blunt) edge, which suggests working in a hard material (antler and/or bone). *Four flat-flaked flake axes have been reused* – one as a coarse scraper, two were converted into chisels and two have an (angle) burin in an (edge) corner. Modification and reuse of flake axes as other forms of tools is a charac-

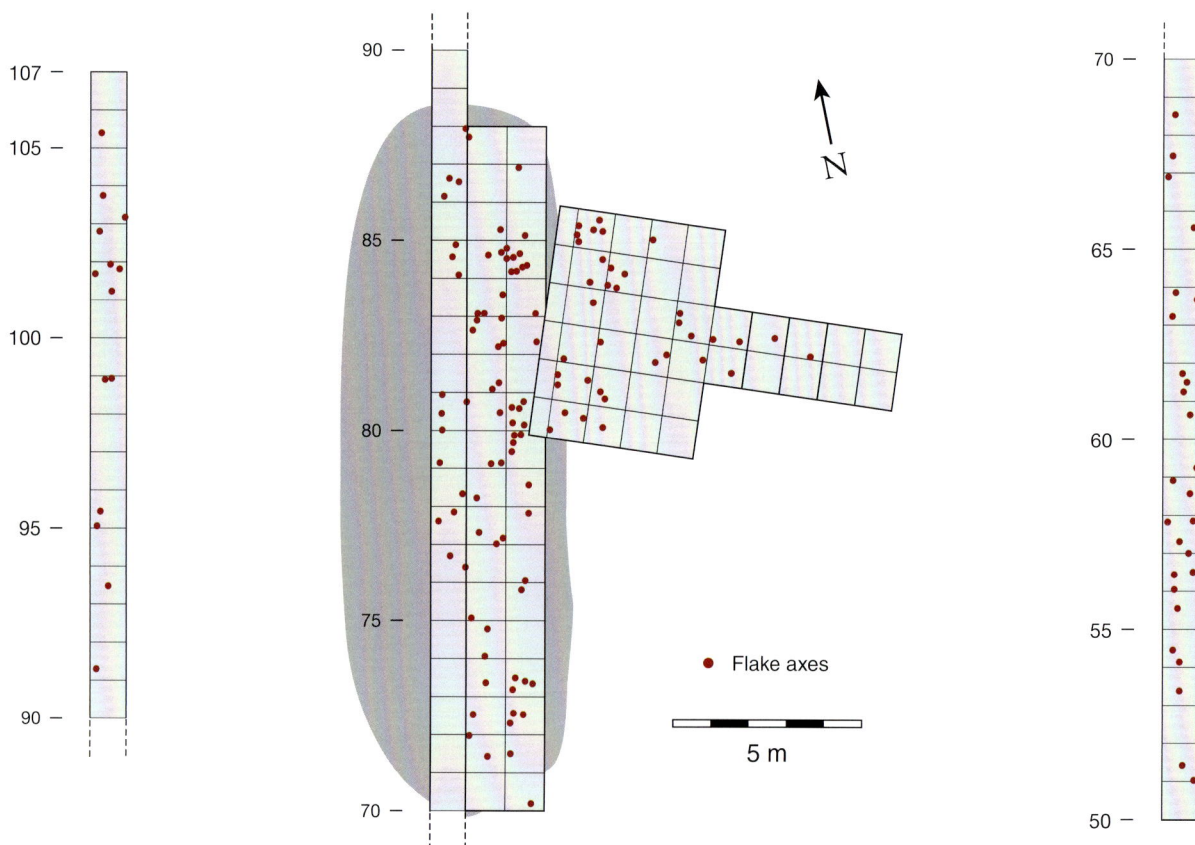

Fig. 62. *The distribution of flake axes across the excavation trench. They were found all over the settlement surface, though with a tendency towards a concentration in the saddle and to the south towards the lagoon.*

teristic feature of the flat-flaked flake axes of the Late/Latest Ertebølle culture. It is seen at Vængesø I and III and at other contemporaneous Ertebølle settlements, for example Rønæs Skov (Andersen, S.H. 2009, 73-74, Fig. 47d-e).

The flake axes occur across the entire excavated area, but with a centre of gravity in the saddle (Fig. 62). Even though the assemblage gives the impression of a large number of flake axes at Vængesø II, the total is not so great relative to the excavated area and in comparison to other coeval coastal settlements, for example Norslund (layers 0+1), where 108 flake axes were recovered from a smaller excavated area (Andersen/Malmros 1966, 76). The axes were measured and their dimensions are shown in Fig. 59. If they are compared with corresponding examples from Vængesø III, it becomes apparent that the Vængesø II flake axes are longer and have a broader edge and a slightly narrower butt (Fig. 145). They are also longer than the flake axes from both Rønæs Skov and Norslund (Andersen, S.H. 2009, 75, Fig. 48).

Flake chisels are common and are represented by 21 examples, in addition to two fragments, corresponding to 8.7% of the axe group. Chisels are defined as having an edge width of less than 3 cm (Andersen, S.H. 2009, 80). The numerous chisels arc a characteristic element of this settlement, which is consistent with a date in the Late/Latest Ertebølle culture, when this tool type was common on the settlements of eastern Jutland. *Symmetrical flat-flaked flake chisels* constitute the most prominent form, with 15 examples, and appear to be a very homogeneous group (Fig. 63). One chisel has a completely dissolved surface and is also heavily water-worn; another is fire-brittled. On two examples (and a fragment) the edge is very narrow and clearly forms shoulders relative to the rest of the piece; these tools were made on reworked flake axes. *Edge-trimmed flake chisels* are only represented by a single example. This is a regularly worked, narrow and parallel-sided piece, on which both sides have been trimmed along their entire length; it is semicircular in cross-section. Its length is 8 cm and its width 3.3 cm. Three chisels are classified as asymmetrical flat-flaked and one as atypical, while

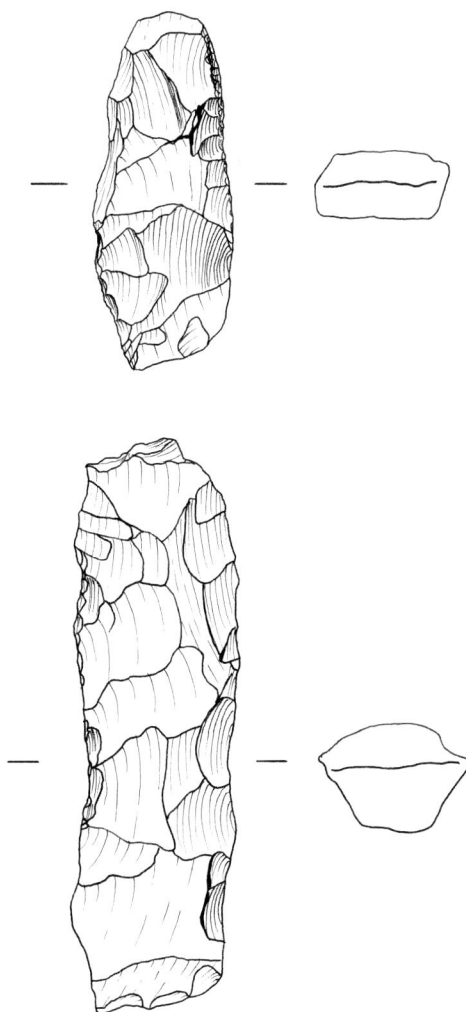

Fig. 63. Flat-flaked symmetrical flake chisels. Scale 3:4. Drawing: Søren Timm Christensen.

the two recorded fragments include a broken-off edge section of a symmetrical flat-flaked chisel. The length of the chisels is 5.1-11.1 cm and their width 2.7-3.7 cm (measured in the middle). Their thickness is 1.2-2.2 cm. The course of their sides differs markedly from that of the flake axes. On five examples the sides follow a convex course, whereas they are parallel on nine examples and on one piece they are slightly concave (on one atypical chisel the sides are completely irregular).

Eight *burin spalls* also feature in the assemblage. Of these, six are straight-sided with a triangular cross-section (primary flakes) and two have a quadrangular cross-section (secondary flakes). Their length is 2.4-4.4 cm.

A *tanged arrowhead* is made from a short, slender blade which is almost straight in profile. At the distal end, a point has been shaped with oblique truncation. At the percussion bulb end, a tang has been created which forms a clear shoulder relative to one side, while the retouch on the other side shows a more even transition from tang to side edge. Midway between the tip and the tang is a short section with retouch on one side. The percussion bulb is broken off. The form and working of the arrowhead provides only a hint of a date. There is greatest similarity with a slender tanged point of Lateglacial age (Ahrensburg culture; Petersen/Johansen 1993, 23, Figs. 4,31, 11), but it is also just possible that it represents an irregular A-arrowhead of the Pitted Ware culture (Becker 1951, 175, 189, Figs. 6,1-4, 8). As the arrowhead was found deep in the stratigraphy, it seems most likely that it dates from the Lateglacial and thereby demonstrates activity at the site in the final part of the Upper Palaeolithic. Its length is 4.3 cm, its width 1.7 cm and its thickness 0.3 cm.

Five crushing stones were found in the form of *flint spheres* that had become rounded by intensive use, which caused their surface to become covered with closely-spaced crushing marks. One of these spheres is of a calcareous type of flint. These spheres are c. 5-11.5 cm in diameter; three have a diameter of c. 5-6.2 cm, while two are somewhat larger (c. 8.5 and 10-11.5 cm). Similar spherical crushing stones are characteristic of the Late Ertebølle settlements in eastern Jutland and on Funen and are also known from both Vængesø I and III (Ch. 2.3.1.2), Ringkloster (Andersen, S.H. 1975a, 53-54, Fig. 43) and Tybrind Vig (Andersen, S.H. 2013, 107-108, Fig. 2.22). The dating of the above finds corresponds to the situation at Vængesø III, where the spherical crushing stones were also associated with deposits from the Late Ertebølle culture.

Flint nodules with crushing marks are represented by three examples. These are irregular, elongate pieces of flint. In one case, a "nodule" was used, and in another a flake core with a platform. This third piece is on an irregular, elongate flint nodule. Crushing is evident on the sides and ends of the pieces. The largest piece measures 7 cm in length.

Flakes with a chipped edge and crushing marks are represented by two examples. The largest of these measures 11.5 × 8.3 × 3.7 cm.

Three pieces can be classified as worked flint. One of these is oval and the working had the aim of forming a point.

3.5.2 Stone

Greenstone axes are represented by four examples (Fig. 64), all made of a fine-grained, pale grey-green to dark-green diabase. Two pieces are almost intact and only have damage to the edge, while the others are in the form of fragments, respectively a middle piece and a piece of the edge. The fractured surface on one of the axes runs at right angles to the longitudinal axis of the axe, while the other is a so-called bending fracture. The surface is finely polished and all the axes have a round cross-section. One has a blunt butt, while the other is more pointed. The latter shows clear wear polish extending c. 5-6 cm forwards from the butt across the surface of the axe. The length of the intact greenstone axes is 11.7-12.4 cm and their diameter is c. 4.2-4.4 cm across the edge, which in one case is tongue-shaped. These axes were all located deep in the stratigraphy and belong to the Ertebølle occupation of the site.

In addition to the artefacts that could be securely identified, a piece of stone (diabase) was found with a very degraded surface, though with a smooth part. This artefact is elongate/pointed-oval and has an irregular, round cross-section. Due to the erosion, it is not possible to determine whether the smooth section represents a piece of the original surface of a glacial erratic or a remnant from polishing. If the latter is the case, it could represent a broken greenstone axe or a preform for one. Its length is 11.5 cm, its width 4.3 cm and its thickness 3.8 cm.

A single *Limhamn axe* of greenstone was recovered (Fig. 65). This is a resharpened axe with a triangular outline, a pointed butt and an oval cross-section. The surface is polished, but the sides of the butt still show clear traces of the working. On one of the longitudinal sides the polishing forms narrow facets. The length of the axe is 10.3 cm, its edge

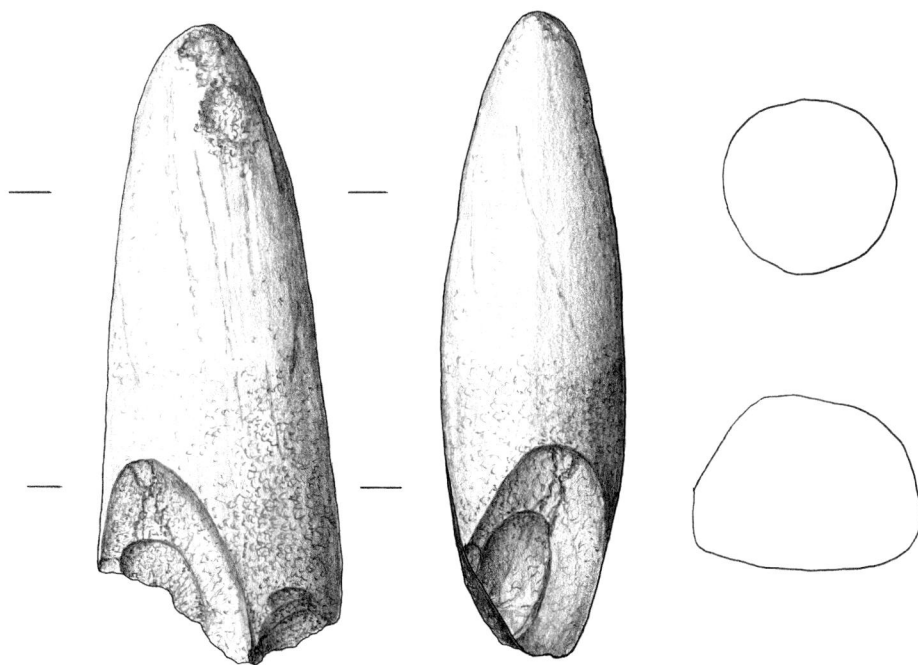

Fig. 64. Diabase axe with a pointed butt. Scale 3:4. Drawing: Søren Timm Christensen.

Fig. 65. Limhamn axe of diabase. Photo: Photo/Media Department, Moesgaard Museum.

width 5 cm and its thickness 3.5 cm. The Limhamn axe is a characteristic type for the Ertebølle culture east of the Great Belt and in Scania (Petersen, P.V. 1984, 14, Fig. 11; Sørensen 2007, 184-187, Fig. 2), but so far it has not been found in its classic form at Ertebølle settlements in Jutland. A small stone axe was found at Dybdal, northeast Djursland (Boas 2001, 152, Fig. 12), which, in principle, must be classified as a Limhamn axe. However, both in its size and its working it differs from the Zealandic-Scanian axes and the axe from Vængesø II. The Limhamn axe from Vængesø is therefore a new and unusual find in Jutland. As Helgenæs belongs to the part of Jutland located closest to northwest Zealand (c. 50 km away as the crow flies), the axe is probably an indication of contact(s) across the Kattegat in the Late Ertebølle culture. This idea is given further support by a rim sherd found at Vængesø III (Ch. 4.3.3; Fig. 152b), which is very similar to a rim sherd found on the coeval Ertebølle settlement of Ordrup Næs (Becker 1939, 263, Fig. 21c). In eastern Jutland, dotted Ertebølle potsherds have been found at Brabrand, Ringkloster and settlements on Norsminde Fjord (Andersen, S.H. 1998, 42-43, 51, Fig. 39).

From Vængesø II there are 22 *diabase flakes* with clearly evident percussion bulbs, which show that greenstone was worked on the site (Fig. 66a-c). All size categories are represented, from small splinters measuring c. $3 \times 0.9 \times 0.3$ cm to large flakes measuring c. $9.2 \times 7.3 \times 2.3$ cm. There is also a large three- to four-sided *greenstone boulder* with worked sides, on which only a small part of the original surface is still preserved (Fig. 66d). The raw material was presumably washed-out basalt boulders from the beach ridges and their slightly different mineralogical composition (phenocrysts etc.) shows that several different diabase boulders were worked at the settlement.

These very characteristic flakes were found almost exclusively within a c. 2-3 m wide and almost 1.5 m long area in the middle part of the saddle. Outside this area, one flake was found in a square to the north and four were recorded from a square to the south. This collection of flakes situated close together suggests either that this square metre was one of the places where working of greenstone took place or that they represent a heap of waste flakes thrown out into the lagoon by the settlement (Fig. 67). The majority of the flakes come from the kitchen midden and therefore belong to the Late Ertebølle culture. Their presence shows that greenstone axes were produced at the site. As a few pieces come from the Neolithic layers, it is possible that axe production also took place during this period, even though it is more likely that these had become secondarily mixed up in the later deposits. Corresponding diabase flakes are actually very rare on Mesolithic settlements, but a single example was recorded during a trial excavation of a small kitchen midden "Anemoneskoven" near the Meilgaard midden in northern Djursland (unpublished, Djurslands Museum (now East Jutland Museum) archive no. 2401). Two flakes were also found on a Late Mesolithic inland settlement at Ravning in Vejle Ådal. These measure, respectively, 9.4×5.7 cm and 9.2×5.5 cm (Moesgaard Museum archive no. 1743). New excavations at the Havnø kitchen midden have yielded a single, similar diabase flake (Andersen, S.H. 2008). On the coast, erosion gave easier access to a larger range of washed-out greenstone boulders than was the case inland, where it must have been considerably more difficult to find sufficient suitable raw material. The observations at Vængesø II show that, at least occasionally, collection and subsequent rough shaping of the diabase axe blanks took place on coastal sites. This conclusion fits with the observations from Holmegaard, where there were traces of local manufacture of greenstone axes (Ch. 7.4.2). The fact that greenstone axes (and Limhamn axes on Zealand) were produced locally is consistent with the results of an investigation on Zealand, which concluded that these axe types were produced locally from diabase boulders collected on the shore (Nicolaisen 2009, 855). As in Jutland, diabase flakes are very rare on Zealand's Ertebølle settlements and have only been recorded at Gøngehusvej 7 (from the production of a single greenstone axe) and Lollikhuse (Nicolaisen 2009, 856).

Thin slabs of fine-grained stone – presumably sandstone or slate – were recorded in three instances. All of them have one or two broken edges, while the other edges are rounded, showing that these are natural, split slabs. They are completely flat and their surfaces show no clear evidence of grinding or polishing marks. One slab does, however, have a broad concavity on one side, but this is probably due to wear. The largest slab measures c. 10 × 11 cm and is 0.6-0.8 cm thick. Two pieces were found close to each other and are of the same colour and type of stone, so it seems likely that they come from the same (large) slab. Unfortunately, they could not be fitted together. If they actually are from the same slab, it must have measured at least c. 20-25 × 20-25 cm. Even though these stone slabs do not show clear traces of grinding or polishing, their presence in the culture layer, and the fact that they are broken, demonstrate that they must have been systematically gathered and subsequently used at the settlement. They belong to the Ertebølle occupation of the site.

Quartzite hammerstones are represented by three examples. These are selected, oval, unworked cobbles with crushing marks at one or both pointed ends. One is a regular flat, oviform stone with crushing marks and chipping at its pointed end, as well as slight crushing marks at its broad end. Its length is 6 cm, its width 4.7 cm and its thickness 2.5 cm. There is also a flat, circular quartzite stone with scattered crushing marks along its edge. Its length is 7.1 cm, its width 6.3 cm and its thickness 2.4 cm. The third example is a flat, rounded-oval stone with an oval cross-section and with crushing marks in two places along the edge (mostly at the pointed end). The length of this latter hammerstone is 6.7 cm, its width 6 cm and its thickness 3 cm.

An *oviform stone of fine-grained granite* has slight crushing marks on both points and has been used as a hammerstone. It is 6.4 cm long, 5.2 cm wide and 3.6 cm thick.

An *oval net sinker of limestone* can be highlighted as a stone artefact associated with the marine environment (Fig. 68; Andersen, S.H. 1981b, 133, 1995, 57, Fig. 18). The stone is pointed-oval, gutti-form (drop-shaped) in outline and with a sub-rectangular cross-section and rounded edges. At its pointed end is a biconical hole, formed by

pecking from both sides. The broad end is damaged in that the original edge has been struck off. Its length is 10.4 cm, its greatest width c. 6 cm and its thickness c. 2 cm. It was found in the kitchen midden and can therefore be dated to the Late Ertebølle culture. This type is exceptionally rare, but three similar pieces are known from the Ertebølle kitchen midden at Kolind (Mathiassen et al. 1942, 37-46; Mathiassen 1948, no. 116). The example from Vængesø is important as it shows that net-fishing was practised from this settlement.

The *butt of a shoe-last axe*, broken in the shaft hole, constitutes an exotic element at the settlement (Fig. 69). Its broad faces are flat, while one of the narrow sides is rounded and the other is flat. The fragment is rectangular in outline. The raw material was a greenish-black stratified stone. The shaft hole is cylindrical, with a diameter of 2.2 × 2.3 cm. It forms a slightly oblique angle with the broad faces. The length of the fragment is 6.6 cm, its width 5.9 cm and its thickness 2.7 cm. This is a rare, foreign type, the occurrence of which is unusual at this kind of settlement. The fragment can, with some reservation, be referred to the "Böken" type which, on the basis of its European contexts, can be seen to be coeval with the Late Ertebølle culture (Klassen 2004, 28-29, Abb. 9-10). The fragment from Vængesø was unfortunately found in a disturbed layer in the kitchen midden, but is said to have been located "deep" in the shell midden. Comparison with other dates for this horizon at the settlement gives a rough date of c. 4400-4000 BC, thereby providing an indirect date for this type in eastern Jutland. In the rest of Jutland, shoe-last axes of the same form are only known from Brabrand and from Åle in northwest Himmerland (Andersen, S.H. 1995, 62, Fig. 25; Klassen 2004, 409-410).

3.5.3 Antler and bone

Tools of antler and bone are few in number but they do include several of the Ertebølle culture's characteristic types. With a few exceptions, pre-forms and waste from the production of antler and bone weapons and tools are absent.

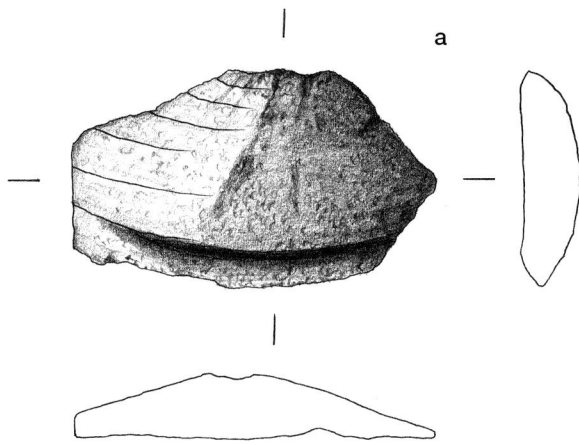

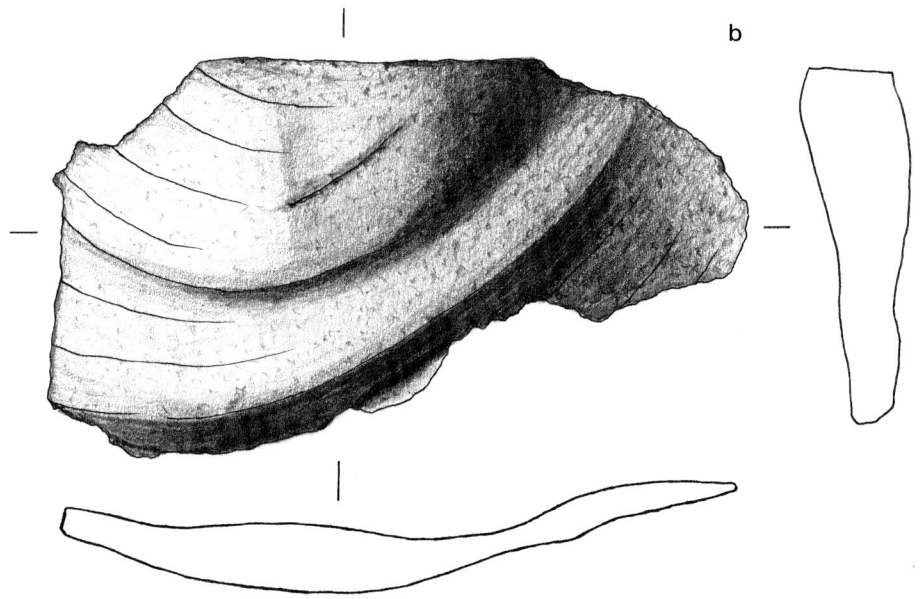

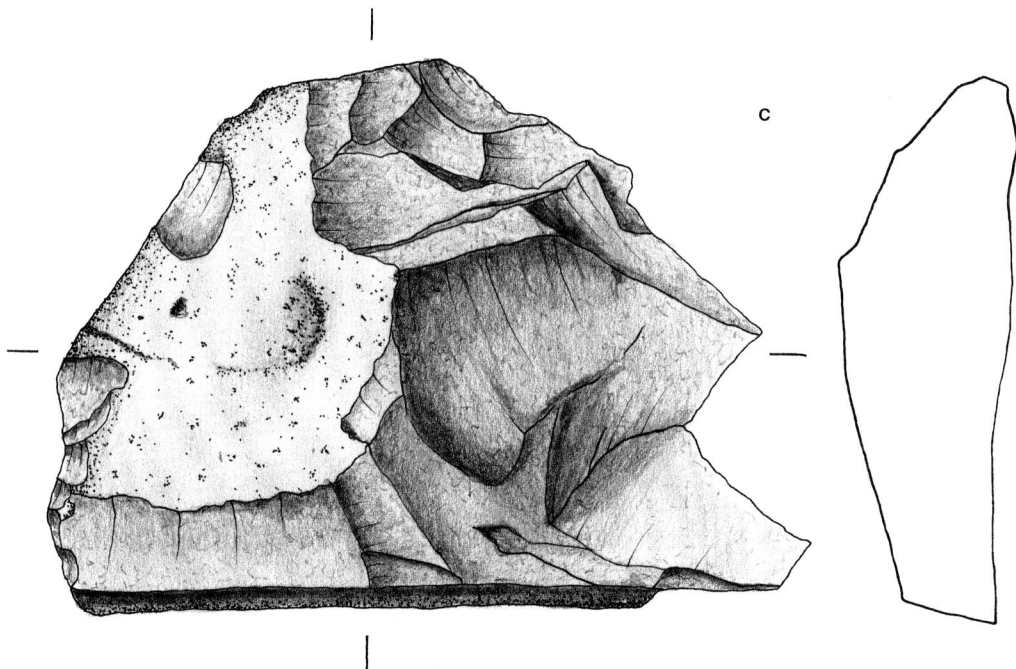

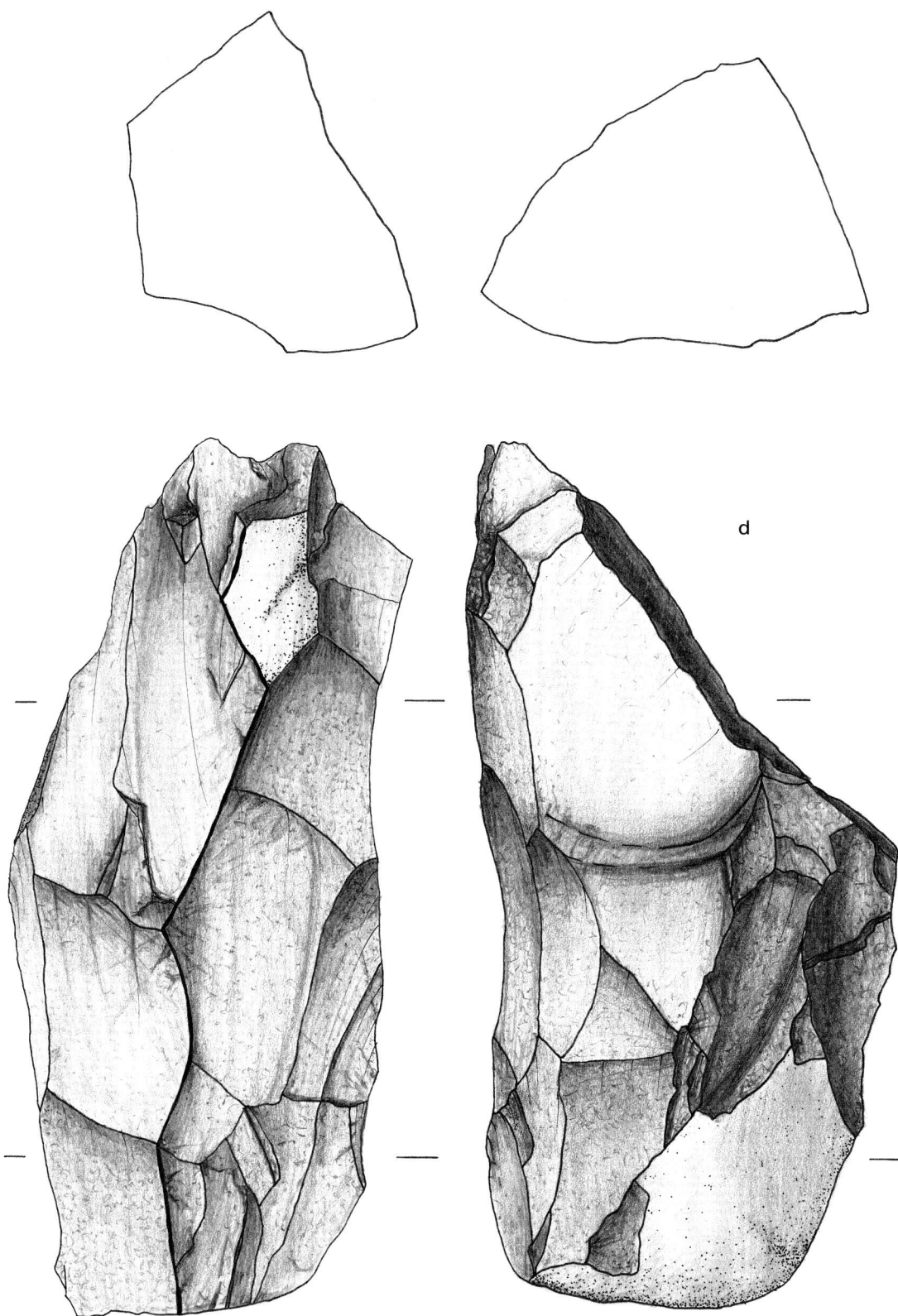

▲▲ *Fig. 66. a-c) Diabase fragments; waste from the production of diabase axes. d) Pointed piece of diabase with tri-/quadrangular cross-section. Scale 3:4. Drawing: Søren Timm Christensen.*

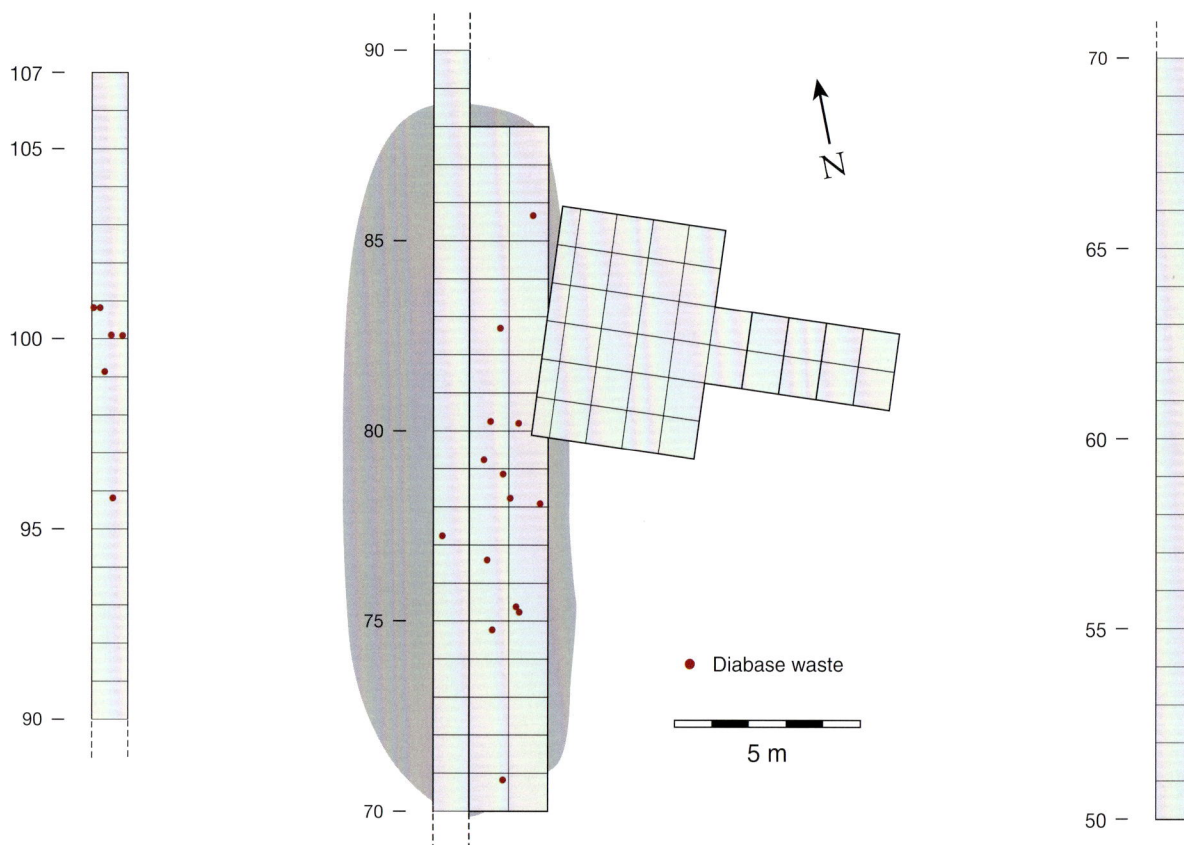

Fig. 67. Distribution of diabase waste fragments across the excavation trench. These were mostly concentrated within a limited area (c. 7 x 3 m) in the saddle. Two squares to the north contained five fragments located close together (and a further fragment lying 3.2 m away). This concentration reflects either that working of diabase axes took place here (presumably on the prehistoric shore) or that a heap of waste fragments was thrown out into the sea from the settlement.

The assemblage includes an *atypical antler axe* with a shaft hole at the burr (Fig. 70). The raw material was a non-shed, slender red deer antler from a young animal. The piece of antler between the burr and the skull has been retained, but it terminates in a carefully worked, spherical rounding from which the frontal bone has been completely removed. Most of the burr has similarly been cut away, but a c. 3 cm long piece, extending obliquely out from the shaft hole, has been retained. This is an axe (rather than an adze) with a slightly oblique edge that is damaged due to a piece having been chipped off. The surface has been scraped smooth but is without ornamentation. The shaft hole is oval and runs obliquely through the antler. At one side, the hole measures 2.8 × 1.7 cm and, at the other, 3 × 1.8 cm. The form, the raw material, the

smooth-scraped surface, the oblique shaft hole and the short, blunt burr show that this was originally an antler shaft that was subsequently reused as an antler axe. It is therefore an example of "recycling", as also underlined by the fact that had this been a "proper" antler axe, then (according to the dating of the settlement layer to the Late Ertebølle culture) it should have been a T-shaped axe. This piece helps to highlight the local shortage of raw materials on this small island – in this case antler. Smooth-scraped unornamented shafts are a characteristic type at settlements in Jutland from the Late/Latest Ertebølle culture (e.g. Flynderhage: Andersen, S.H. 1981b, 36). This is consistent with the date from Vængesø, where the piece was found in the kitchen midden and therefore belongs to the Late Ertebølle culture. The length of the axe is 22.3 cm, its width at the shaft hole 3 cm and its thickness opposite the shaft hole 3.3 cm.

A *fabricator* made from an antler tine. This is a 4.4 cm long, broken-off tine from the edge of which four chips had been struck off during use (Fig. 71).

Ulnar daggers are represented by four examples, of which two are made from ulnar bones (*Ulna dextra*) of red deer (*Cervus elaphus*) and two from the ulnar bones (*Ulna dextra* and *Ulna sinistra*) of dog (*Canis familiaris*; Fig. 72). The two pieces of red deer bone are well preserved, but the outermost tip on one of them is broken off, and this piece also has tooth marks (presumably made by a dog). Compared with the other ulnar daggers of this type, these are relatively short, which suggests they have been resharpened. They are 10.7 and 11.7 cm in length, respectively. The two other daggers are more slender and lack their outer tip. Their length is 9 and 9.3 cm, respectively. Ulnar daggers, with their characteristic tongue-shaped, blunt-edged tip, could have been used as bodkins/skinning knives when working with hides. In his presentation of the Brabrand assemblage, T. Thomsen mentions just such a function for similar tools used by the Inuit of the Bering Strait

Fig. 68. Flat, guttiform piece of limestone with a hole, perhaps a net sinker. Photo: Photo/Media Department, Moesgaard Museum.

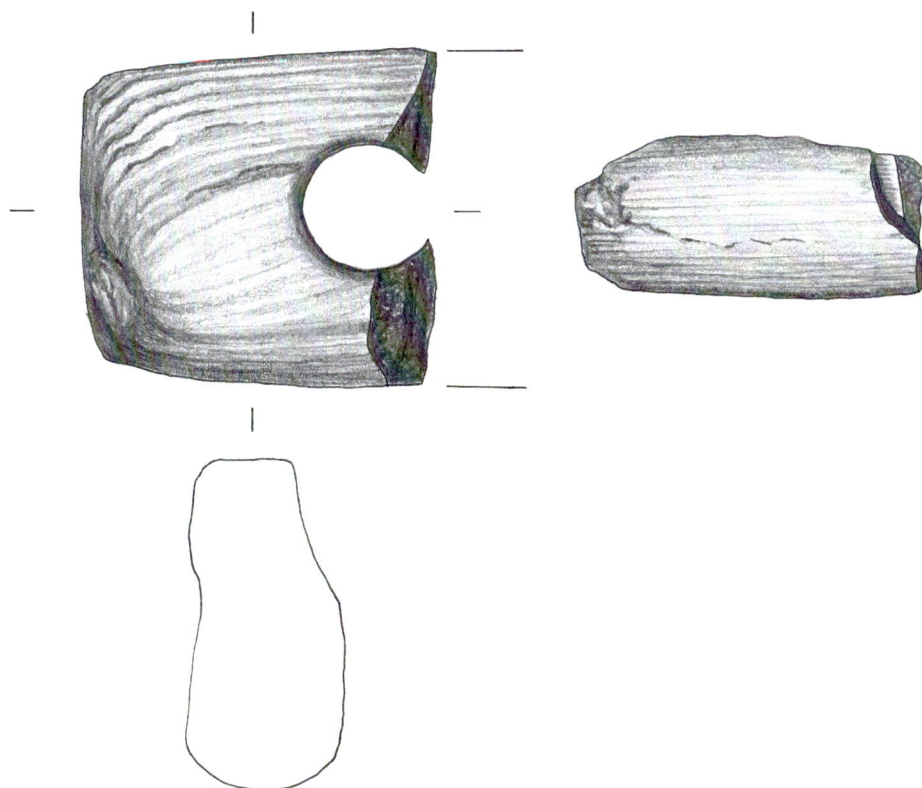

Fig. 69. Butt section of a shoe-last axe, broken at the shaft hole. It is made of a central European kind of stone and is "an exotic element" at the Vængesø lagoon – and on the Djursland peninsula. Scale 3:4. Drawing: Søren Timm Christensen.

(Thomsen/Jessen 1906, 33 lower). Ulnar daggers, which have only been found at this one settlement in the Vængesø area, suggest that prey were skinned and hides processed on the site.

Points of mammal bone are represented by nine examples, of which the longest is 20 cm (Fig. 73a-d). These are pencil-shaped with a round or oval cross-section and show no trace of the original surface of the raw material. Three points are intact, five are represented by bases, one of which has a flat, tongue-shaped curvature, and the final example is a broken-off tip. Excavations of Ertebølle settlements in Jutland have shown that bone points with a round or quadrangular cross-section are the most recent variant of this artefact type, and this is completely consistent with the situation at Vængesø, which dates from the Late Ertebølle culture.

Points made of bird bone are represented by two examples (Fig. 73e-f). One of these is a narrow, split bone splinter, which is 6.6 cm long and 0.5 cm wide and has had its tip broken off. The other is the broken-off tip of a piece with a "syringe tip", which is 4.6 cm long and 0.9 cm in diameter. It is the only example of this type from the Vængesø localities.

The finds from this settlement also include the front part of a single-rowed *harpoon* with three barbs (Fig. 74). The base has been broken off and the outer tip of two of the barbs is also missing. The raw material is whalebone, and the harpoon has been so heavily worked that the original surface of the bone has been completely removed. The harpoon is straight in profile and oval in cross-section. Its length is 12.3 cm, its width at the break 2 cm and its thickness 1.3 cm. It is therefore sturdier than the harpoons made of red deer antler (Andersen, S.H. 1997, 50, Fig. 5). Unfortunately, the harpoon is a stray find so it cannot be dated with certainty. It could therefore be from either the Ertebølle culture

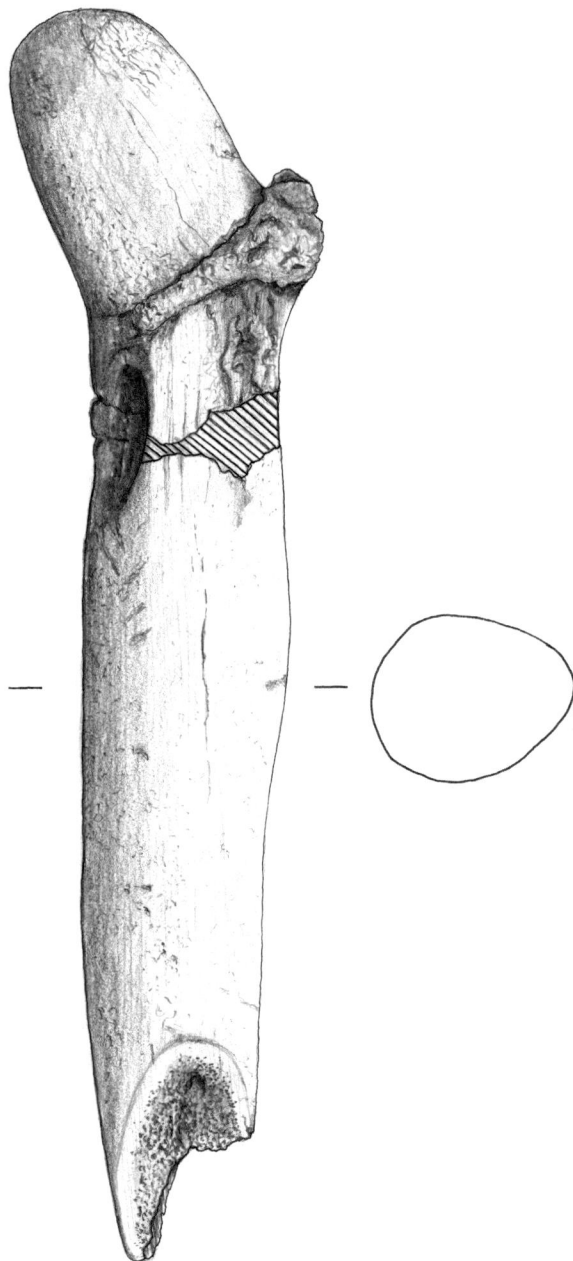

Fig. 70. Atypical antler axe made from a piece of antler shaft (an example of "re-use"). Scale 3:4. Drawing: Søren Timm Christensen.

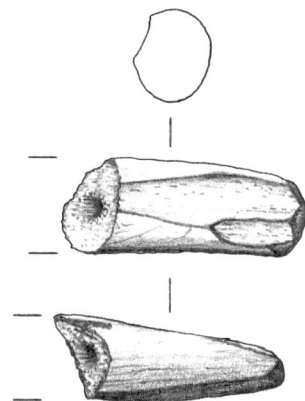

Fig. 71. Broken-off point of a fabricator made from a red deer antler tine. Scale 3:4. Drawing: Søren Timm Christensen.

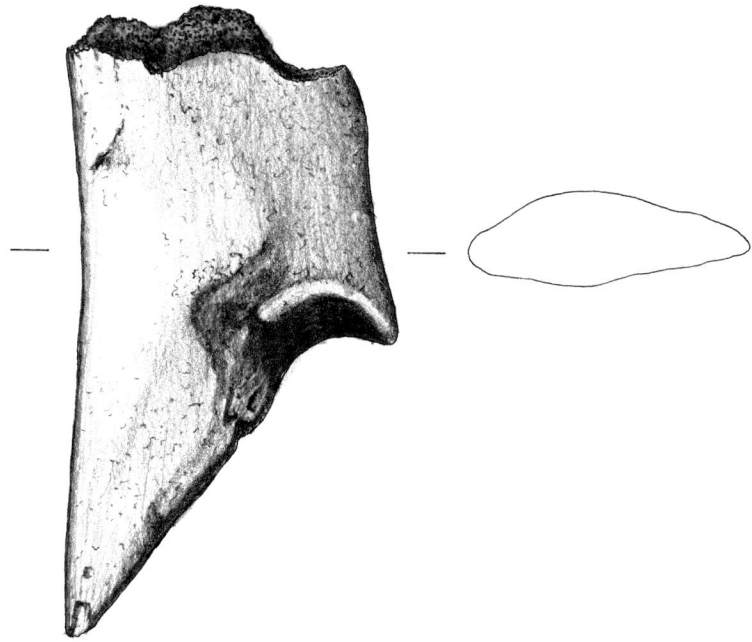

Fig. 72. Dagger of red deer ulna. The dagger has been heavily resharpened. Scale 3:4. Drawing: Søren Timm Christensen.

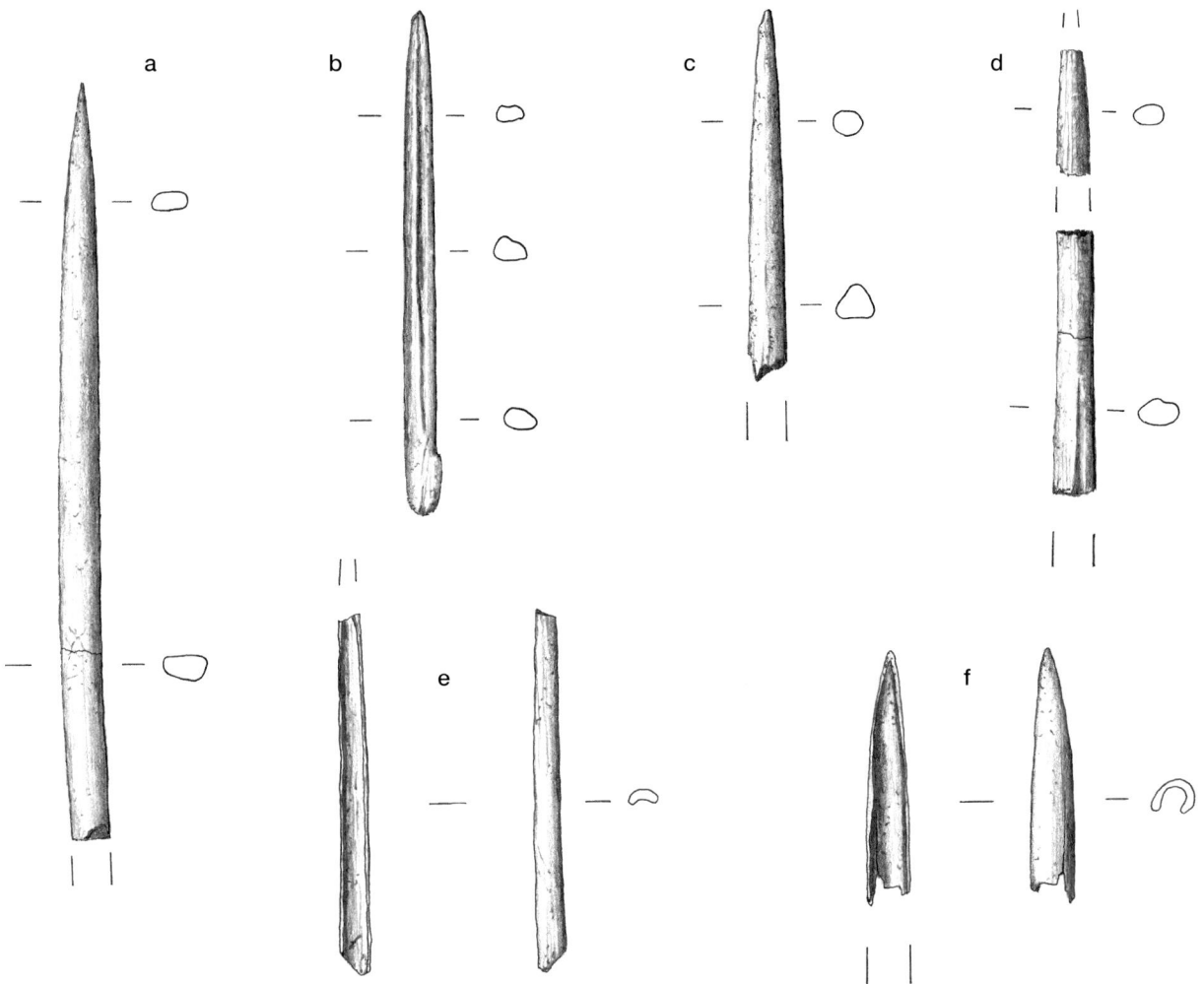

Fig. 73. a-d) Bone points of mammal bone with a round or oval cross-section. e-f) Bone points made from splinters of bird bone. Scale 3:4. Drawing: Søren Timm Christensen.

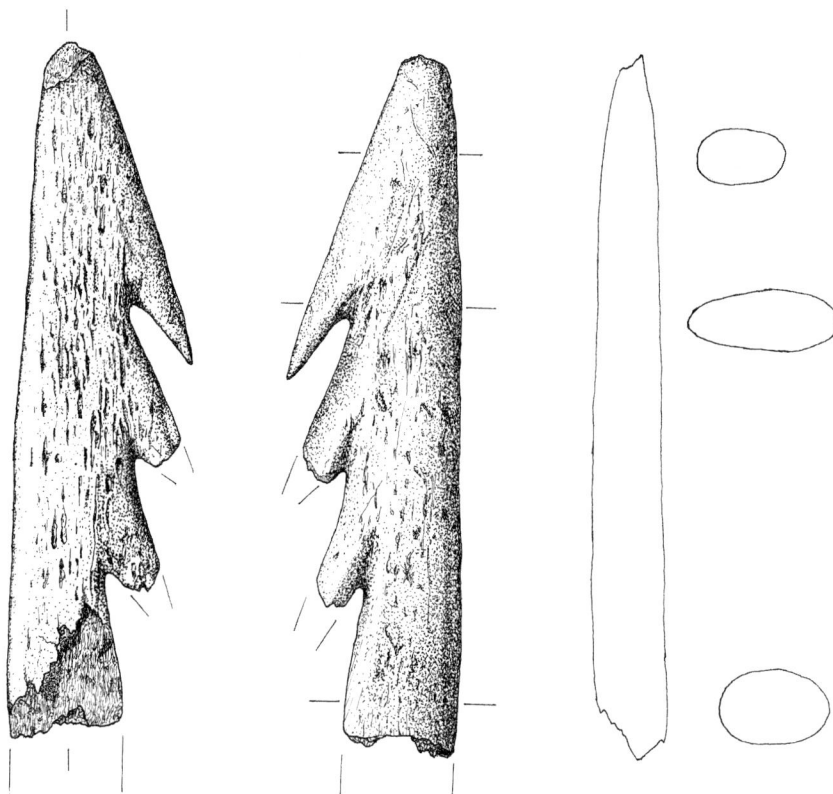

Fig. 74. Single-row harpoon made of whalebone. The harpoon is broken in the middle of the shaft so the base is missing. Drawing: Søren Timm Christensen.

or the Neolithic. However, based on its similarity with other well-dated pieces, it can cautiously be assigned to the Ertebølle culture. In terms of its form, it is a variant of Ertebølle harpoons of type A (Andersen, S.H. 1972, 73-125).

Other pieces of worked bone and antler that should be mentioned comprise an irregular bone splinter with a smooth-scraped edge and a piece of bone showing traces of encircling sawing marks. These could be waste from the production of either bone points or fishhooks, as seen at Bjørnsholm (Andersen, S.H. 1993, 23, Fig. 22) and Tybrind Vig (Andersen, S.H. 2013, 270-272, Fig. 4.51). The two pieces measure c. 2.2 × 1.2 cm and 5 × 1.3 cm, respectively.

The assemblage also includes two unshed roe deer *antlers*. One is broken in the middle of the main beam, which is still attached to a piece of the frontal bone. And a complete antler displays many transverse cut marks between the burr and the frontal bone. At the tip are longitudinal scratches, suggesting that the otherwise unworked antler was used for work that involved stabbing and pressing movements. The two pieces are 11.2 and 17.2 cm long, respectively.

A 5 cm long *piece of red deer antler tine* has been cut through obliquely at one end and at right angles to the longitudinal axis at the other. This type has been described previously (Andersen, S.H. 2013, 248-249, Fig. 4.34) and is interpreted as waste from the production of fabricators. There is also the outer tip of an unworked red deer antler tine which is broken off at the opposite end. It was found in the kitchen midden. Its length is 9 cm.

In two cases, split-off *strips of red deer antler cortex* were encountered. Both of these have been illustrated previously (Andersen, S.H. 1997, 84, Fig. 29 left). One is the curved part of the tip of a tine where, at the base, traces can be seen of where it had been cut off, while the remainder of the surface is unworked. Working traces along the edges show that it was split off from the tine using "groove-and-splinter technique", and the antler's porous (inner) side has been scraped away. It is rectangular in cross-section. The other piece is a flat, slightly bent strip of antler with clear traces of groove-and-splinter technique on both edges. It tapers evenly towards one end, the outer part of which is broken off. The surface of this piece is also unworked, but at its base are traces from where it was cut through. The length of the pieces is, respectively, 13.5 and 16.4 cm, their width at the base c. 2.3 cm and their thickness c. 2.3 cm. They can be dated to the Ertebølle culture (Fig. 75a).

The finds assemblage also includes two flat, straight pieces of *split whalebone*, which have also been illustrated previously (Andersen, S.H. 1997, 84, Fig. 27 centre and right). These have parallel sides with clear traces of groove-and-splinter technique, and their broad faces have been scraped smooth. The strips are worked such that the outer side of the bone forms one of the side surfaces. They are subrectangular in cross-section. One piece is broken at both ends; it measures 6.6 cm in length, 2.8 cm in width and 0.6 cm in thickness. The pieces are so similar to each other that they probably represent parts of the same object (but they cannot be fitted together). They come from the Ertebølle horizon at the settlement (Fig. 75b-c).

These four strips could represent preforms for harpoons – presumably of the Ertebølle culture's A-type (Andersen, S.H. 1997, 80-86, Figs. 5-11), but they could just as well (or perhaps more so) represent material that was brought along (and discarded) as raw material for the production of harpoons at the settlement. An argument in favour of the latter interpretation is the assemblage's total lack of waste from the production of tools and weapons of antler. Whether one or other of these explanations is true, the finds confirm that the use of harpoons was one of the activities undertaken at the site and that both red deer antler and whalebone were employed as raw materials for these. Judging from the overall finds picture from the Ertebølle culture, harpoons were commonly manufactured from whalebone. This choice could have been based on the raw material's toughness and resistance to breakage, and also on hunting-ritual circumstances (Andersen, S.H. 1997, 84).

Splinters of bones of large whales are represented by ten examples (Fig. 76), one of which shows clear chop marks, which were presumably made with an axe (Andersen, S.H. 1997, 86, Fig. 31). These pieces are all elongate, quadrangular in cross-section and

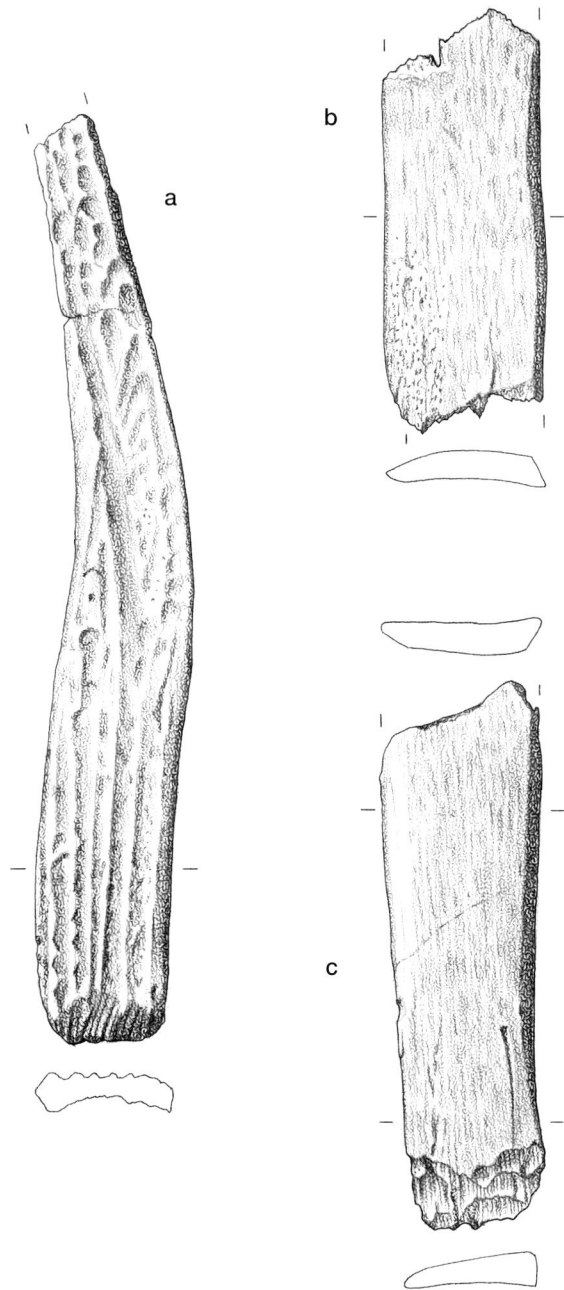

Fig. 75. Split-off strips of red deer antler (a) and whalebone (b-c). As no antlers or antler waste were found at the site – the antler strip (a) must have been brought to the island from another location. Scale 3:4. Drawing: Louise Hilmar.

measure 4.5-35 cm in length, 1.5-16 cm in width and 1-2 cm in thickness. In all cases, they consist of pieces of the bone's hard, dense outer wall. One piece shows a clear axe mark made with a chipped convex edge that was 3.5-4 cm wide (core axe or greenstone axe). The surface of this piece also shows longitudinal traces from scraping. One piece has a 0.75 × 0.5 cm subrectangular aperture – possibly a trace left by an attempt to divide the bone up into smaller pieces. The finds context shows that the whale bones come from the pre-midden layer and the kitchen midden, i.e. they can be dated to the Late Ertebølle culture. The situation is similar to that at Vængesø I, where there were also numerous pieces of bones of large whales (Ch. 2.5; Andersen, S.H. 1975b, 42-45). It cannot be determined from the remains whether these pieces of bone represent remains of prey taken to the site or material that was brought along for local production of harpoons.

3.5.4 Ertebølle pottery

During the excavation, 119 pieces of pottery were recorded, most of which lay singly in the culture layer, but in eight cases there were small clusters of potsherds. Pottery was encountered throughout the entire stratigraphy. As a rule, the thick-walled pottery and the definite Ertebølle types were found in the deepest part and at the base, while all the ornamented rim and side sherds of definite Neolithic types are from the upper and uppermost layers. In spite of the large number of finds, this element of the artefact assemblage is generally poorly preserved. The sherds are frequently less than 2 cm in length and width; very few measure

Fig. 76. Selection of splintered bones of large whale, cf. Fig. 83. Photo: Photo/Media Department, Moesgaard Museum.

more than c. 3-5 cm. The great majority of the pottery comprises completely uncharacteristic thin-walled side sherds, probably due in the first instance to the assemblage being exclusively comprised of coarse settlement/household vessels. As only very few sherds have characteristic profiles or ornamentation, it is difficult to arrive at a more precise date for the majority of the assemblage. In particular, it is very difficult to distinguish securely between the thin-walled Ertebølle pottery and the Early Neolithic Funnel Beaker pottery, when not dealing with rim sherds, ornamented sherds or possibly bases.

Most of the side sherds are brownish-black/brownish-red in colour. They are constructed in oblique lamella N-technique or oblique U-technique, and their thickness lies between 0.7 and 1 cm. Sherds of definite Ertebølle vessels are few in number and only six to eight pointed-based vessels can be securely identified, even though the actual number was probably slightly greater. No sherds were found of the characteristic Ertebølle boat-shaped "lamps". There are three pointed bases, which come from the pre-midden layer and the kitchen midden (Fig. 77). Further to these is a thin-walled sherd with a curvature that shows it comes from the lower part, close to the base, of a pointed-based vessel. A thin-walled rim sherd has fingernail imprints along the upper edge, and as this feature is characteristic of Ertebølle pottery, it can be dated accordingly (this is also consistent with its position in the stratigraphy). Further to these are ten uncharacteristic side sherds with a thickness greater than 1 cm. Finally, there are two collections of uncharacteristic thick-walled side sherds which, given their wall thickness (1-1.2 cm) and their deep stratigraphical position, can be assigned to the Ertebølle culture. Based on their wall thickness, tempering form and construction, 17 uncharacteristic side sherds are cautiously identified as thin-walled Ertebølle ware.

3.5.5 Conclusion: Finds from the Ertebølle culture

The flint tool assemblage recovered from the Ertebølle layers at Vængesø II is not large, but it contains all this culture's characteristic types. In particular, the large number of blades with concave truncation characterises this site – both in relation to other settlements around the lagoon and especially relative to other contemporaneous Ertebølle settlements in Jutland. The raw material for these artefacts differs markedly from those used for the cores and other blades and flakes found at the site and it was presumably brought to the site from somewhere with access to better flint. Further to these are a large number of transverse arrowheads, in which the completely dominant type comprises short, broad examples with markedly concave sides. Flat-flaked flake axes and flake chisels are also very prominent. Flake axes with concave side edges are the most common type. Finally, spherical flint crushing stones are a further characteristic type encountered at this site. Diabase flakes, from the local production of greenstone axes, constitute a new feature. Bone tools are dominated by bone points with a round or quadrangular cross-section, representing a late type within this tool category (Andersen, S.H. 2013, 267), while artefacts of antler are very few in number. A completely new type in the tool inventory of the Ertebølle culture comprises preforms/raw material for harpoons of antler and whalebone. Pottery is represented by pointed-based vessels, but these only occur as single sherds. The presence of "lamps" has not been securely demonstrated. Overall, this artefact assemblage shows that the Ertebølle deposits should be dated to the Late Ertebølle culture.

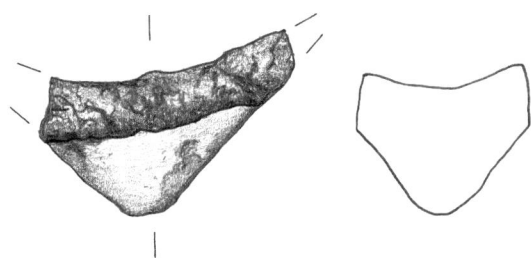

Fig. 77. Pointed base from an Ertebølle vessel. Scale 3:4. Drawing: Søren Timm Christensen.

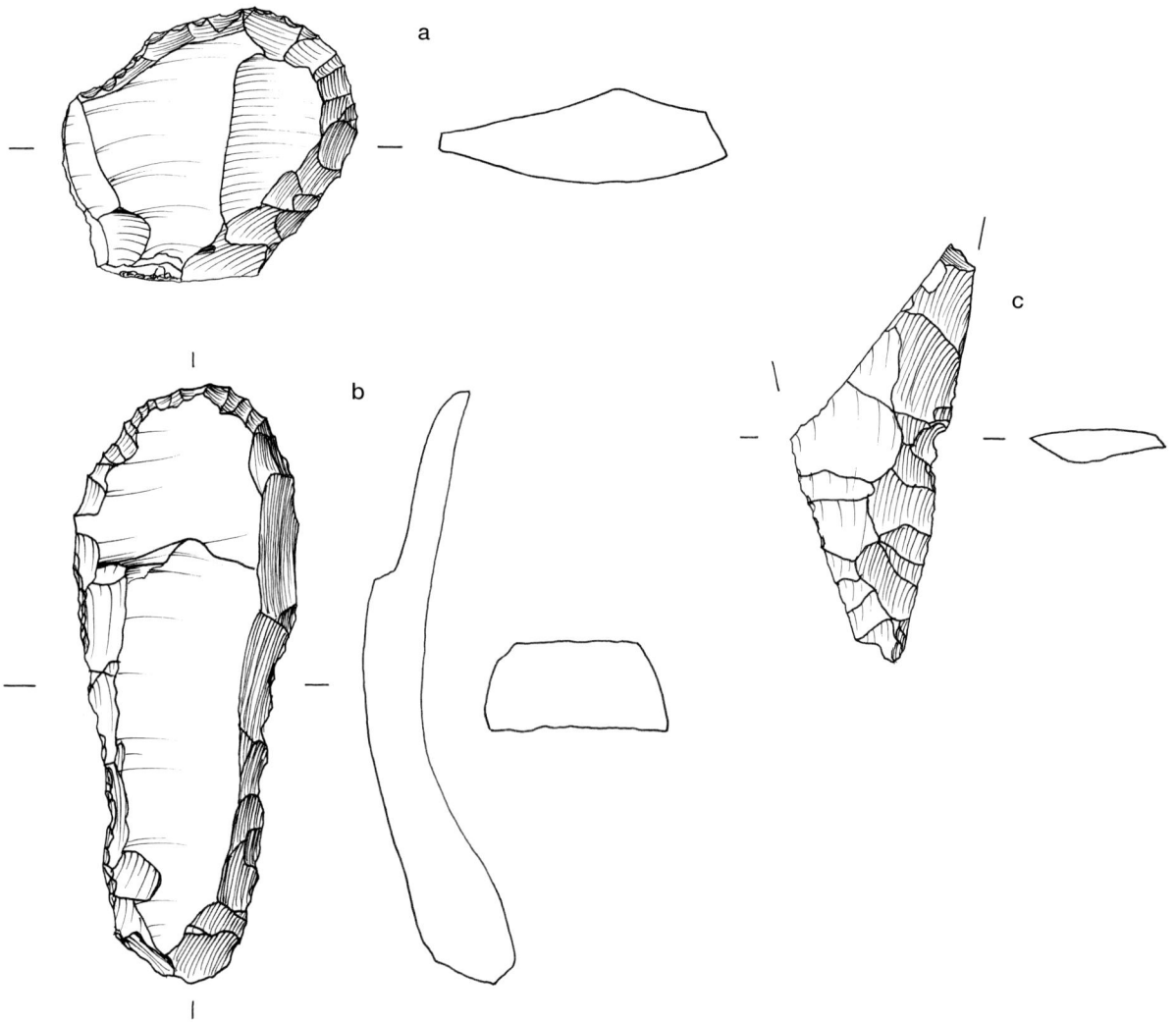

Fig. 78. a) Regular, circular flake scraper from the Neolithic. b) Spoon-shaped scraper from the Late Neolithic / Early Bronze Age. c) Tip of a flat-flaked dagger from the Late Neolithic/Early Bronze Age. Scale 3:4. Drawing: Søren Timm Christensen.

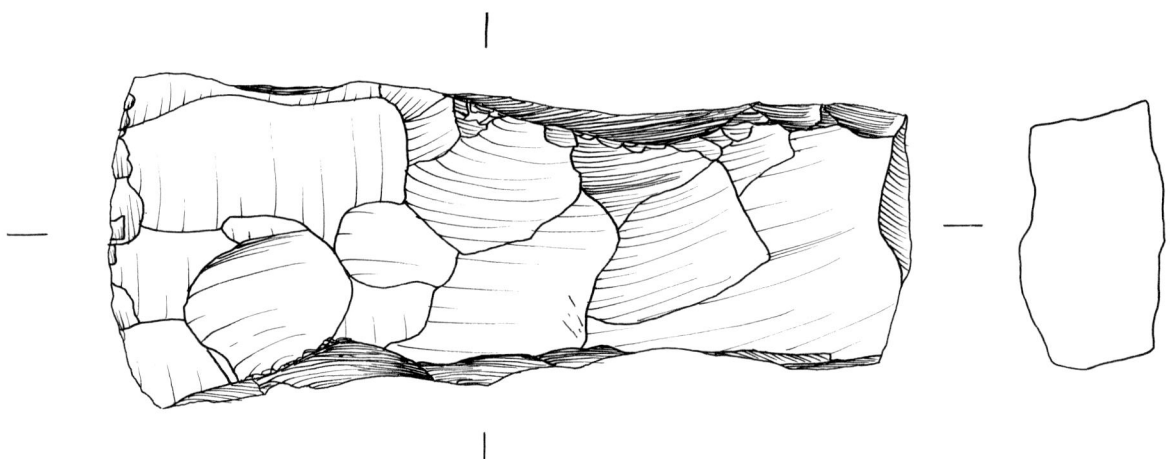

Fig. 79. Neolithic axe blank, presumably from the Late Neolithic / Early Bronze Age. Scale 3:4. Drawing: Søren Timm Christensen.

3.6 Finds from the Neolithic and Early Bronze Age

3.6.1 Flint

There are five *flake scrapers*, of which one is a regular scraper (Fig. 78a), while the four others are more irregular. Two pieces are on cortex-covered flakes. One scraper is more oval/guttiform in outline. As this is on a completely primary piece of flint, it differs from the other flint artefacts in the assemblage (which are almost all on surface transformed and slightly water-worn flint). The scrapers measure between 4.5 × 3.4 cm and 5.5 × 6.7 cm; one is larger (more elongate) and measures 6.6 × 8.3 cm. The flake scrapers are Neolithic, but a closer dating within this period is not possible.

Spoon-shaped scrapers are represented by five examples (Fig. 78b). The raw material was thick flakes which, through knapping, have acquired an elongate, guttiform outline with a regularly-formed handle at the distal end. One of the scrapers differs slightly from the others in that it is shorter and has a completely primary surface. On the ventral surface of this scraper are three small chips running from the edge and across the surface. Four scrapers have a transformed surface and the fifth has both a transformed surface and is water-worn. Their length is 5.1 11 cm and their width 2.7-4.2 cm. The spoon-shaped scrapers correspond to previously published examples (Boas 1983, 94, Fig. 4,1-8) and can be dated to the early part of the Early Bronze Age. At Vængesø II, all these scrapers were found in the plough soil and the upper part of the culture layer.

There are seven Neolithic *axe blanks* (i.e. roughouts), which represent various phases in the working of raw material to finished axe (Fig. 79). Three of these blanks are only coarsely worked and their surface still has large cortex-covered areas. Four display a later stage in the working, when a quadrangular cross-section has been created and a slightly flared edge. Finally, one roughout also has working showing that the aim was to produce a hollow edge. Despite their differences, it is clear that the intention in all cases was the production of short, thin-butted axes. One example has a triangular cross-section and possibly represents a

failed preform for a core axe. These artefacts are difficult to date typologically, but their form, size and tendency towards a flared and hollow edge indicate a date in the Late Single Grave culture or early part of the Late Neolithic. This is also consistent with their stratigraphic positions, which showed that these flint roughouts were all associated with the Neolithic visits represented in the stratigraphy. Moreover, the axes are of Danien flint, which is a characteristic of the majority of the axes from the Single Grave and Late Neolithic sites Bejsebakken, Fornæs and Myrhøj (Jensen, J.A. 1973, 86). The roughouts are 12.4-25.8 cm in length, 5.7-11 cm in width and 3-9 cm in thickness.

Three fist-sized, rounded-oval *flints with a (natural) hole* in the middle were recorded at Vængesø II, and in all cases flint of a calcareous type had been selected. Two have crushing marks at their ends and the third has retouched edges. As these flints are worked and represented by several examples, it is unlikely that they represent chance occurrences, but are systematically gathered stones (presumably from a nearby beach ridge). These stones with holes could have been used as sinkers for fishing nets. They measure 9.5-12 cm in length, 8-9 cm in width and 3-8 cm in thickness. Their finds circumstances indicate a date in the Neolithic. There are also two stones with holes from the Ertebølle horizon at Vængesø III.

The finds assemblage also includes an oval, guttiform piece of limestone, which has been split longitudinally and in its flat cleavage plane has a 1.5 cm wide and 0.3-0.4 cm deep longitudinal furrow. This furrow roughly follows the central axis of the stone, tapers evenly towards its ends and has a semicircular cross-section. Both its size and its form indicate a function as an *arrow-shaft smoother* (Glob 1952, no. 539). A similar artefact was found in an Early Neolithic shell layer in the kitchen midden of Krabbesholm I (Andersen, S.H. 2005), at the Mesolithic and Neolithic settlement of Store Nor I in Norsminde Fjord (unpublished, Moesgaard Museum archive nos. 2320 and 2890) and at Bjørnsholm (Andersen, S.H. 1993, 85, Fig. 28). As the piece was found in a disturbed layer (above the southwestern grave containing a skeleton), it is not possible to date it more closely at Vængesø II. Its length is 10.3 cm, its greatest width 5.8 cm and its thickness 2.6 cm.

The assemblage includes three blades of *flat-flaked daggers* of type I (Lomborg 1973, 35-44; Fig. 78). Two are broken at the transition between blade and hilt, while the third lacks its tip. There is also a flat-flaked arrowhead with a broken tip (use/shooting damage) and fragments of sickle blades. Further to these is the outer part of a fire-brittled, flat-flaked flint artefact – presumably the hilt of a dagger. These few artefacts all come from the latest cultural horizon and belong to the early part of the Late Neolithic.

The flat-flaked artefacts and the spoon-shaped scrapers show that the site was visited at the end of the Neolithic and/or in the Early Bronze Age for the purposes of fishing and marine hunting. A projection of these few types on to a section through the settlement layers shows that both the point of a flat-flaked dagger and a Late Neolithic arrowhead lie in the plough soil, i.e. at a clearly higher level than the other finds from this locality. This stratigraphic position is consistent with these artefacts being the latest traces of visits to the site.

3.6.2 Neolithic pottery

Early Neolithic pottery from the Funnel Beaker culture is present in the form of two thin rim sherds with, respectively, two and three horizontal cord motifs (probably from the same vessel; Fig. 80b). Further to these are six rim sherds bearing a clay moulding with finger impressions directly below the outer edge of the rim (Fig. 80a and c). These rim sherds come from a food storage jar of the Single Grave culture (Becker 1955, 66, Figs. 1-3, Plate III). The sherds are so uniform that they must come from the same vessel. This conclusion is supported by the fact that they were found within a limited area of c. 1 m² and in the same layer above the kitchen midden. Apart from the vessel from the Early Neolithic Funnel Beaker culture represented by the aforementioned ornamented rim sherds, there could have been further vessels from the same period, in which case these are represented by rim sherds with a thin smooth edge. A single side sherd comes from the neck/belly transition of a small, thin-walled funnel beaker, the upper part of the belly of which was ornamented with vertical cord impressions. This sherd can be dated to either a late part of the Early Neolithic Funnel Beaker culture or the first phase of the Middle Neolithic Funnel Beaker culture (MN A I). Eight coarse side sherds are ornamented with incised, vertical parallel stripes on their outer surface and are so uniform that they probably come from the same vessel, which must again be dated to the same phase (MN A I). Further to these are two thick rim sherds with an out-turned rim, which must come from the same vessel as they closely resemble each other with respect to form, firing and tempering and were both found in the uppermost excavation layer within the same square. These sherds also represent settlement/household pottery from the Single Grave culture (Fig. 80a and c). Around 50 uncharacteristic, thin-walled side sherds have generally been assigned to the Neolithic. If these sherds are compared with the well-defined rims etc., it seems likely that the great majority of them date from the Early or early Middle Neolithic Funnel Beaker culture.

There is pottery throughout the entire stratigraphic sequence of culture layers, but due to the often irregular course of the individual culture layers, and to secondary disturbances, the stratigraphic positions of the potsherds can only be employed with great caution and only as a rough indicative guide to their date. Finally, there are, as already mentioned, a considerable number of uncharacteristic, thin-walled sherds, which can only be rather insecurely dated to the end of the Mesolithic and the beginning of the Neolithic, respectively. It is evident that visits to the site in the Neolithic are characterised by pottery to a greater extent than those of the Ertebølle occupation. This picture corresponds to that evident at other coastal settlements on the "outer islands", for example Selbjerg in the Limfjord, where visits during the Neolithic were also characterised by potsherds from coarse household vessels – presumably because the activities during this period were concentrated around the storage, boiling and production of blubber and oil from hunted marine animals (Marseen 1953, 102-120 – especially 111-116).

Fig. 80. Neolithic pottery. a) Rim sherd with an ornamental moulding below the rim edge. b) Rim sherd from a vessel with decoration in the form of three rows of two-ply cord impressions. c) Rim sherd with a slightly out-turned rim. a) Single Grave culture, b) Early Neolithic Funnel Beaker culture, c) Single Grave culture or Late Neolithic. Photo: Photo/Media Department, Moesgaard Museum.

3.7 Dating

In addition to the dates for the two human skeletons, there are a further three radiocarbon dates from this site: An oyster shell from the top layers of the kitchen midden gave a date of 3629-3135 BC cal (K-2444), a whalebone (Cetacea sp.), also from the kitchen midden, gave a date of 5585 ± 35 bp, corresponding to 4450-4368 BC cal (1 σ; AAR-8299) and a bone of a wild boar (*Sus scrofa*), also from the kitchen midden, gave a date of 5475 ± 130 bp,

corresponding to 4459-4075 BC cal (1 σ; OxA-117; Andersen, S.H. et al. 1986, 41). The date (K-2444) for the oyster shell, which falls in the Neolithic, shows that marine molluscs were also gathered during this period, but to a lesser extent, such that coherent kitchen midden layers were not formed at this time. It is therefore likely that small parts of the kitchen midden could date from the Neolithic.

Both the radiocarbon dates and (particularly) the archaeological finds assemblage show that the settlement was occupied on numerous occasions during the course of the Stone Age. Apart from the Late Palaeolithic tanged arrowhead, the earliest datable finds from Vængesø II derive from one or more occupations during the Early/Middle Ertebølle culture. The traces from these occupations comprise the heavily water-worn flint artefacts (in particular flake axes) found in the marine sand layers extending out from the hillside and a few "scaled flakes". The few scattered finds from this phase are unfortunately not able to provide a basis for conclusions about the extent and possible duration of an occupation. There then follows a rich culture layer from the Late Ertebølle culture, which can be dated on the basis of its dominant and characteristic types. These comprise transverse arrowheads and flat-flaked symmetrical flake axes, as well as a few, but characteristic, symmetrical core axes with a double-sided specialised edge working, some flake chisels and several spherical flint crushing stones. Moreover, there are bone points with a round or quadrangular cross-section, which also constitute a late type within this culture. Finally, there are thin-walled potsherds from pointed-based vessels.

The shallow and, in places, disturbed stratigraphy makes it difficult to distinguish the individual layers and their content of cultural remains arising from the individual occupations. This is particularly significant with respect to all the non-period artefacts, first and foremost tools made on flakes and blades. The above-mentioned tool groups doubtless include simple flint artefact types from the Neolithic. Unfortunately, chronologically diagnostic artefacts are few in number, but they can, on the other hand, be securely assigned to the Early, Middle and Late Neolithic. They consist of a small group of flake scrapers and several ornamented potsherds from the Early and Middle Neolithic Funnel Beaker culture, which testify to occupations during these periods. This is also true of the later Single Grave and Pitted Ware cultures (pottery, axe blanks and a possible tanged arrowhead from the Pitted Ware culture), as well as characteristic flat-flaked flint tools/weapons (daggers, sickle blades, spoon-shaped scrapers) from the end of the Neolithic/

Earliest Bronze Age. The faunal remains include a few bones of sheep/goat which, on the basis of their stratigraphic position, must belong to the Neolithic, but unfortunately such that their date within this period cannot be determined more precisely.

3.8 Subsistence economy

Due to the kitchen midden's calcareous shell layers, the conditions for the preservation of organic remains (bone and antler) were particularly good in the Late Mesolithic deposits. During examination of the finds assemblage, it proved possible to reaticulate a small number of animal bones – wolf, whale, domestic pig or wild boar and cormorant – and in four cases also bones of humans. Mapping of

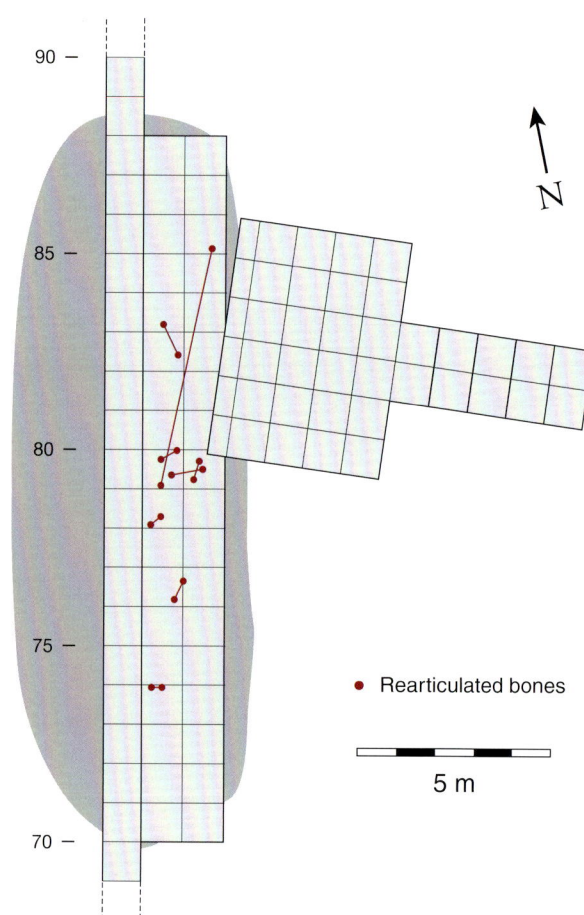

Fig. 81. Distribution of bones that could be rearticulated. In most cases, they lay close together in the saddle, but in one instance they were found c. 6 m apart.

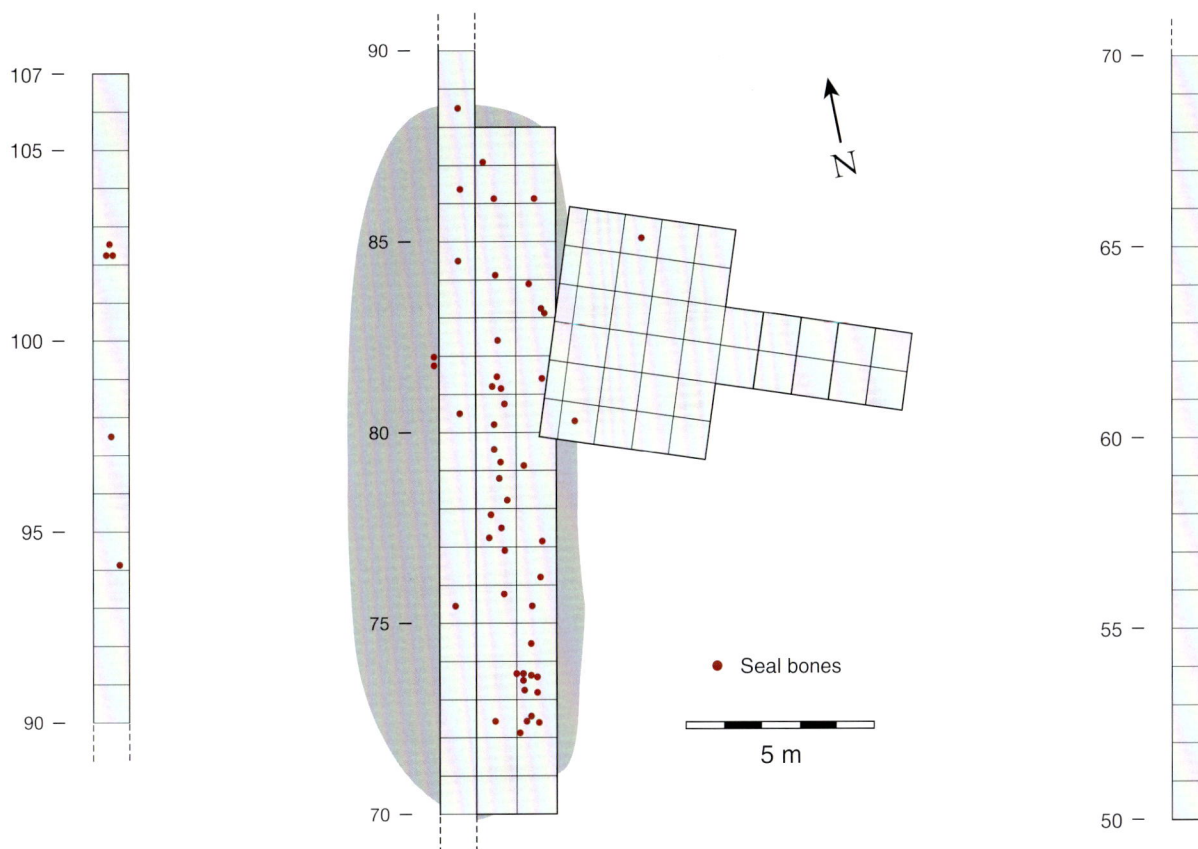

Fig. 82. Distribution of seal bones (all species). These bones were found in particular within a c. 16 x 3 m area in the saddle and in the ditch to the north.

these bones reveals that they were all found within an area of 12 × 2 m in the middle of the hollow (i.e. the saddle) between the two hilltops (Fig. 81). This bone assemblage was analysed and identified by P. Rowley-Conwy (mammals and birds) and I.B. Enghoff (mammals, birds and fish; Enghoff 2011, 193-194, Plates 33-35, 128-129. From an overall perspective, the faunal remains document a subsistence economy exhibiting greater marine influences than are usually evident at coastal settlements of the Ertebølle culture. An approximate examination of the relationship between terrestrial animals (meat animals), fur animals and marine mammals reveals relative proportions of 49.2%, 18.5% and 32.2%. This shows that marine mammals are very prominent and contribute to making this settlement distinctive in terms of its fauna and subsistence economy. In order to put the proportion of marine mammals at Vængesø II somewhat into perspective, the corresponding element of marine

mammals constitutes 26% (MN I) at the North German locality of Neustadt, which has deposits from the Ertebølle and Funnel Beaker cultures, and where seal hunting in particular is highlighted as being specially characteristic and important for the local subsistence economy (Glykou 2014). In general, investigations of faunal remains recovered from a number of North German Late Ertebølle and Early Neolithic coastal settlements reveal an increasing frequency of grey seal during this time (6300-4100 BC; Schmölcke et al. 2009, 209-211, Fig. 2, Tab. 3). Whether this was also the case in Denmark is uncertain, but it is something that should be checked (Tab. 10).

Terrestrial mammals are represented by wild boar (*Sus scrofa*), roe deer (*Capreolus capreolus*), red deer (*Cervus elaphus*), ox (both aurochs (*Bos primigenius*) and domesticated ox (*Bos taurus*)) and a couple of bones of sheep/goat (*Ovis aries/Capra capra*). The bones of definite domesticated animals derive from the Neolithic horizons. The Mesolithic deposits contain wild boar – the clearly most dominant species, followed by roe deer, whereas red deer, in contrast to the situation at many coeval Ertebølle settlements, is less prominent (Fig. 159). This could (as at Vængesø I and III) possibly be due to the small area of the locality, which means that it is unlikely to have supported a natural population of larger animals. Bones of dog (*Canis familiaris*) are also very prominent in the faunal remains, which is a further characteristic of this locality and corresponds to the situation at Vængesø III.

The category "fur animals" is, on the other hand, very poorly represented compared with Vængesø III and other contemporaneous Ertebølle settlements, comprising only single individuals of pine marten (*Martes martes*), otter (*Lutra lutra*),

polecat (*Mustela putoris*), beaver (*Castor fiber*) and badger (*Meles meles*), as well as possibly fox (*Vulpes vulpes*), wolf (*Canis lupus*) or dog. Again, this situation must be due to the locality's topography, which did not provide opportunities to hunt these animals.

The faunal remains show that the hunting of marine mammal species was very extensive and had an intriguing and prominent role in the subsistence economy (Enghoff 2011, 204). There are in particular numerous bones of seals (grey seal (*Halichoerus grypus*), ringed seal (*Phoca hispida*), harp seal (*Phoca groenlandica*) and common seal (*Phoca vitulina*)); these are otherwise rare in Danish assemblages from this time. Even though seal bones occur on most Ertebølle settlements on the coast, they are generally only represented by a few specimens. An example of this is seen at the con-

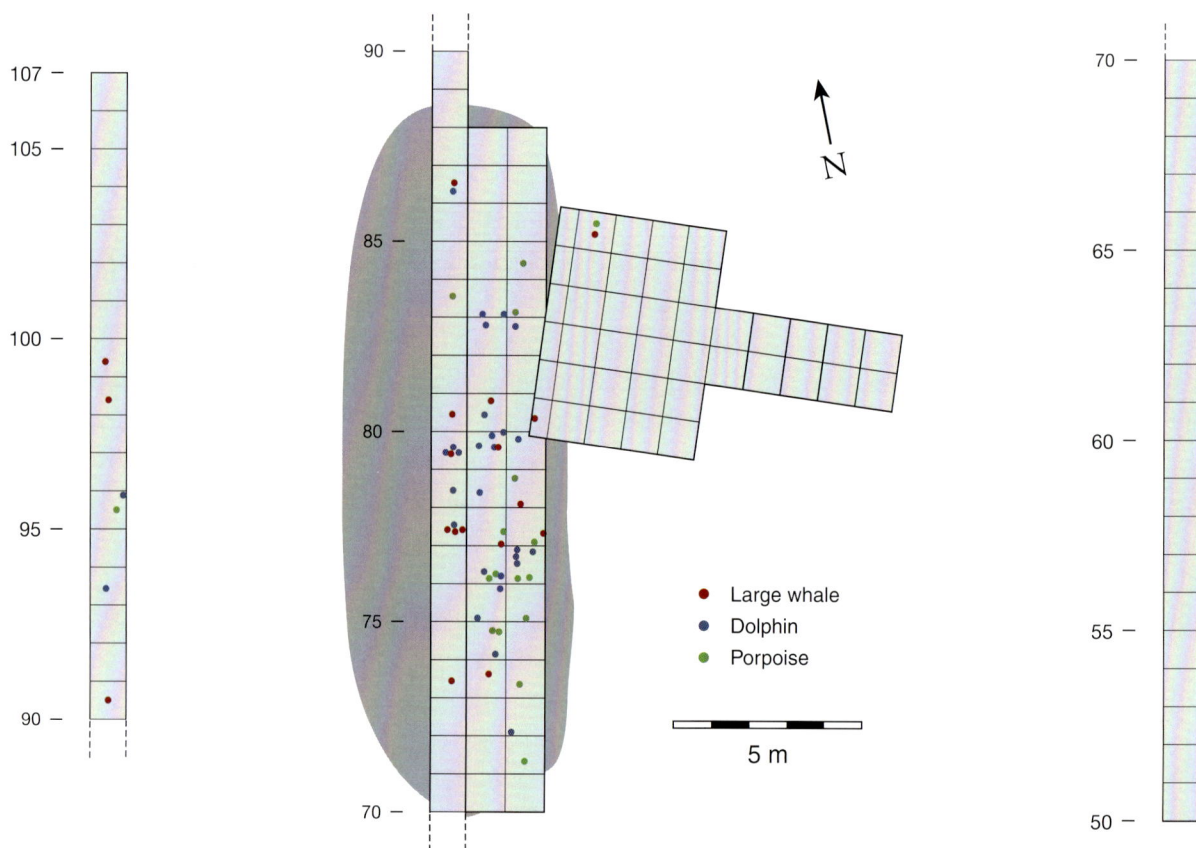

Fig. 83. *The distribution of bones of large whale, dolphin and porpoise. Most of the bones of these animals were found within the same restricted area in the middle of the settlement surface, corresponding to the distribution of the seal bones, but more concentrated, cf. Fig. 82.*

temporaneous settlement of Agernæs on northern Funen (Richter/Noe-Nygaard 2003, 27), which only yielded two seal bones, despite the fact that several harpoons were found at the site (Andersen, S.H. 1997, 53-56, Figs. 9-11).

Seal hunting presumably took place with clubs, but harpoons, bow and arrows and nets could also have been employed. The animals gave meat, blubber, oil, offal and blood as well as the raw materials of skin, bone and tooth/tusk (Figs. 82, 84). Vængesø II also yielded numerous remains of porpoise (*Phocoena phocoena*) and white-beaked dolphin (*Lagenorhynchus alberostris*), the vertebrae of which were mostly found in the pre-midden layer (Fig. 83). In addition to these are also a large number of bones of seal (unspecified) and remains of whales – both large and small species (unspecified). The whale bones were found concentrated (with a single exception) within an area of 10 × 3 m in the central part of the saddle (Fig. 83). A selection of splintered whale bones is shown in Fig. 76.

Birds are similarly very abundantly represented and this group is supremely dominated by a large number of remains of cormorant (*Phalacrocorax carbo*), giving Vængesø II a special faunal character, which it shares with Vængesø III, and which distinguishes these localities from almost all other coeval Ertebølle settlements. The cormorant is so prominent that the impression gained is of a colony being located in the immediate vicinity of the settlement. This view is reinforced by the presence of a femur of a very young bird, suggesting that the cormorants bred at the site or very close to it – see also the discussion associated with the description of the faunal remains from the settlement of Vængesø III (Ch. 4.5). Other bird species which help underline the settlement's links with the marine environment include numerous ducks, for example shelduck (*Tadorna tadorna*), northern pintail (*Anas acuta*), velvet scoter (*Melanitta fusca*) and goose (*Anser/Branta* sp.), as well as auks (*Alcidae*), for example razorbill (*Alca torda*), or guillemot (*Uria aalge*) and great auk (*Pinguinus impennis*). There is also the great crested grebe and little grebe (*Podiceps cristatus* and *Tachybabtus ruficollis*), red-throated loon (*Gavia stellata*), common loon (*Gavia immer*), swan (*Cygnus* sp.), common merganser (*Mergus merganser*) and gannet (*Morus bassanus*). Furthermore, remains of both white-tailed eagle (*Haliaeetus albicilla*) and osprey (*Pandion haliaetus*) have been identified.

Fishing activities undertaken from this settlement appear to have been extensive too, corresponding to those at Vængesø III. The range and relative proportions of fish species are the same at the two neighbouring settlements (Enghoff 2011, 200). Bones of flatfish, i.e. plaice/flounder/dab (*Pleuronectes platessa/Platichthys flesus/Limanda limanda*), cod (*Gadus morhua*) and unspecified members of the cod family (*Gadidae*) dominate. Further to these are the dorsal spines of spur dog (*Squalus acanthias*) and a few bones of eel (*Anguilla Anguilla*), herring (*Clupea harengus*), turbot or brill (*Psetta maxima/Scophthalmus rhombus*), weaver fish (*Trachinus draco*), haddock (*Melanogrammus aeglefinus*) and pollock (*Pollachius virens*).

Gathering activities are demonstrated by the kitchen midden's content of marine mollusc shells. An investigation of the species distribution was carried out on the remains from square 72/49. The sample was sieved through a mesh of 1-1.5 mm diameter (Tab. 2), and the analysis of the shells confirms the visual impression of the kitchen midden, i.e. that it is totally dominated by oysters. The length of the oyster shells in two different shell samples was measured. The smallest individuals fall in the range of 3-4.5 cm, and the largest are 8-8.5 cm in length. The average length for the two samples, each consisting of c. 60 shells, is, respectively, 5.24 and 6.25 cm, which corresponds to the size of the majority of the oysters on the Vængesø III settlement. The investigation also revealed that these are small individuals with thin shells, suggesting poor living conditions for this species. The size of the oysters from Vængesø II is markedly less than for the coeval kitchen midden at Ertebølle (*Locus classicus*), where the largest individuals have a length of 16 cm (Madsen et al. 1900, 80).

Overall, the faunal assemblage reveals a subsistence economy that to a very great degree was characterised by the surrounding marine environment. The fact that it was so reliant on the sea must be due to a combination of the settlement's location on a small island, which was surrounded by the sea and of a limited size such that virtually the only opportunity was to hunt animal groups from the marine environment. The subsistence economy was mixed, with the main emphasis on fishing, marine hunting and bird catching, supplemented by the gathering of marine invertebrates. This was combined with the hunting of terrestrial animals in the surrounding primeval forests. The dominant role of the marine biotope in the subsistence economy is further underlined by the ^{13}C and ^{15}N analyses of bones from the graves, which show that the two individuals buried here lived to a very great extent, but not exclusively, on the highest level of the marine food chain (Fischer et al. 2007, Fig. 4; Enghoff 2011, 194).

Fig. 84. Seal hunting in the Stone Age as depicted by Flemming Bau. After Nielsen (1981).

The faunal assemblage provides some indications of the period/periods during which the site was occupied. Razorbill and guillemot indicate winter visits and this is probably also true of the seal hunting, which presumably took place in late autumn and early winter (Glykou 2013, 104). Conversely, the roe deer antlers recovered with intact frontal bone suggest a visit in the summer half of the year. Analyses of the growth layers in the oyster shells reveal that these were gathered in late winter and/or early spring. The faunal remains from the Ertebølle culture therefore indicate activities at the site at several times of the year, but it is uncertain whether this means that it was visited during several short periods at different seasons for the purposes of exploiting specific seasonally available resources, or whether there was more long-term (permanent) year-round occupation. Furthermore, there is some uncertainty with respect to whether the site was visited at the same time of the year during the Ertebølle period as it was during the Neolithic, or whether there possibly were differences in seasonal use between the two periods. The few settlement features and structures (hearths etc.), the limited size of the locality and the shallowness of the kitchen midden deposits suggest, however, that it was repeatedly visited for short periods at different times of the year. The lack of "production flakes" from the manufacture of flake axes points in the same direction, as do the large, long, truncated blades, which were brought to the site from another locality. The numerous flake axes, which were probably used in particular to make the rods and poles for fish weirs, suggest that stationary fishing structures were constructed at the site. These structures do not, however, mean that there had to be permanent habitation here, as the Vængesø lagoon is of a size where it would have been possible to sail to the island from other nearby settlements in order to check/empty fish traps. Overall, these uncertainties mean that we cannot arrive at any definite conclusions with respect to the settlement's function in the subsistence economic pattern of the time and, perhaps most importantly, whether the site had the same function throughout the entire Stone Age, or whether this changed between the Mesolithic and the Neolithic. The most comprehensive use of the settlement was during the Late Ertebølle culture, but the site was also visited at the transition between the Ertebølle and earliest Funnel Beaker cultures, as documented by the two graves and the finds of Early Neolithic pottery. A few artefacts also reveal visits during several periods of the Neolithic and Early Bronze Age. The traces of occupation in the Neolithic are, however, restricted and are definitely only indicative of shorter stays.

Overall, this locality shows evidence of use from the end of the Mesolithic and through several periods of the Neolithic. It also documents the exploitation and significance of the marine biotope during a thousand-year period of the Stone Age.

3.9 Settlement type

Vængesø II belongs to the group of coastal stations located on "outer islands" and beach ridges, i.e. of the same type as the localities of Pandebjerg on Nekselø (unpublished, but mentioned in Brøndsted 1938, 334, 1957, 381), the small coastal localities on Sejrø (Liversage 1973, 86-96; Kempfner-Jørgensen/ Liversage 1985), Hjortholm on Samsø (Malmros 1995, 35-67), Selbjerg (Marseen 1953, 102-120), Vedbæk (Petersen et al. 1993, 61-69) and Rønbjerg Strandvolde by the Limfjord (Skousen 1998, 29-73). A common feature of these localities is that they are all small settlements (often kitchen middens) with shallow culture layers. Moreover, these sites show similarities in their subsistence economy, which was naturally heavily influenced by the surrounding marine environment, i.e. primarily fishing, marine hunting of seals and small whales and of seabirds. Located midway between the inlets of Begtrup Vig and Ebeltoft Vig, the Vængesø II site had an optimal situation with regard to exploitation of the marine resources of the area. It was also well positioned as an excellent lookout post across Ebeltoft Vig and the nearby beach ridges and small islands that were ideal resting places/ breeding grounds for seals and the like. This was a small settlement that had an unusual location on a small island surrounded by a lagoon and the open

sea. The topography determined that the relatively narrow saddle/hollow between the island's two hilltops could only have accommodated a single habitation unit.

The few settlement features and structures and the tool inventory, which is heavily dominated by truncated pieces, distinguish this locality from the larger, contemporaneous coastal settlements of the Ertebølle culture in eastern Jutland. Together with the marine-influenced subsistence economy, these observations suggest that Vængesø II functioned as a "specialised site", i.e. a hunting camp, the function of which was to exploit the surrounding marine biotope. This interpretation is supported by the presence at the site of large numbers of "knives" (blades with concave truncation), ulnar daggers and flake axes (used for making poles and rods for fish weirs). Consequently, this site is unlikely to have functioned in isolation, but must have formed part of a subsistence economic and social system that encompassed one or more (larger) contemporaneous localities. In this respect, it is obvious to highlight the nearby, and much larger, settlement of Vængesø III on the western coast of the lagoon (Fig. 169). As in the case of Vængesø I, the quickest and easiest access to the site must have been by watercraft, but periodically it was possible to reach the settlement from the south via the beach ridge. The archaeological-typological dating of the kitchen midden indicates the Late Ertebølle culture. The radiocarbon date for the whale bone shows that the Ertebølle settlement is coeval with the Ertebølle settlements of both Vængesø I and III. All three sites could therefore possibly have been in use at the same time.

Vængesø II is such a small locality that (like Vængesø I) it is unlikely to have had freshwater. Even though this could be compensated for by transporting water to the settlement by boat from nearby springs on Helgenæs or the southern part of Mols, this lack of water must nevertheless also have influenced the duration of the visits and probably also the number of people involved. At the same time, it would have been difficult to obtain some raw materials and food, which therefore had to be brought from the mainland (Helgenæs). The absence of waste from the production of tools of for example bone and antler emphasises the local lack of these materials. The reuse of the antler shaft, which had been converted into an antler axe, also points in this direction (Fig. 70). It is clear that the site's beach ridges were important as a source of raw materials for everyday tools. There was production of greenstone axes in the Mesolithic and thick-butted axes at the end of the Neolithic. Production of greenstone axes is an activity that has not previously been seen at Ertebølle settlements in Denmark, but has now also been demonstrated at Holmegaard (Ch. 7.4.2). The frequent occurrence of cooking/boiling stones, especially in the Neolithic deposits, testifies to extensive settlement activity involving the use of hot or boiling water. In addition to the excellent availability of the marine resources of fish, marine mammals and seabirds, the easy access to important raw materials, such as diabase/greenstone, in the beach ridges could perhaps also have provided a motive to visit this isolated spot. In the Neolithic, it appears that access to the fresh flint of the beach ridges could also have been significant.

3.10 Conclusion

Vængesø II is a small coastal locality that was occupied during several periods of the Stone Age and consequently demonstrates continuity of place in the period from c. 4500-1800 BC. The most comprehensive use took place during the Late Ertebølle culture, but more sporadic visits in the Early, Middle and Late Neolithic are also evident. The small size of the locality and its position on a narrow beach ridge between the Vængesø lagoon and Ebeltoft Vig meant that the subsistence economy was, to a very great extent, based on the surrounding sea, involving fishing, marine hunting of seals and whales and extensive hunting of seabirds. Fresh water, provisions and furs from the animals of the primeval forest, as well as raw materials (apart from flint and other stone) are unlikely to have been obtainable on the island and must, as was the case at Vængesø I, have been brought to the site from the nearby "mainland". The finds assemblage derives from a shallow kitchen midden deposit, and a terrace was apparently cut into the hillside in exactly the same way as was the case at the nearby and contemporaneous localities of Vængesø I and III. There are very few settlement features and structures associated with the occupations of the site during the Ertebølle culture. Conversely, there are several larger stone layers containing cooking/boiling stones that can be dated to the Neolithic. Two graves were also found at the settlement, dating from the transition between the Mesolithic and Neolithic – a period from which only very few burials have otherwise been recorded. The locality's situation, limited size and composition of its finds assemblage indicate a specialised function, which was directed towards exploiting the surrounding marine resources. The settlement was part of a system that encompassed other large localities (perhaps Vængesø III?). Vængesø II should be termed and interpreted as a hunting station or camp focussed on the exploitation of the marine biotope. Finally, mention should also be made of contacts across the sea with coeval Ertebølle settlements on northwestern Zealand, for example Ordrup Næs (Limhamn axe, pottery).

The locality is important and interesting in that it belongs to a group of coastal settlements with a marine-oriented subsistence economy which, at the same time, show continuity of marine hunting through a very long period of prehistory – in the case of Vængesø II from the Ertebølle culture to the Late Neolithic, i.e. almost 2000 years.

4 Vængesø III "Ishuset"

This is the largest settlement on the lagoon. It is evident today as a c. 150 × 45 m (N-S/E-W) kitchen midden, which overlies a culture layer rich in finds (the "pre-midden layer"). The parish records are no. 17 (northern part of the settlement) and no. 18 (southern part of the settlement), Helgenæs parish, Mols Søndre district, Randers county; Moesgaard Museum archive no. 4428; East Jutland Museum archive no. EBM 156 (grave). The kitchen midden extends NW-SE along a low, coastal erosion slope (c. 3.5-6.5 m a.m.s.l.; Fig. 85-86), and slopes evenly to the ENE, i.e. towards the now reclaimed lagoon area (Vængesø, see Ch. 1), the surface of which lies at a c. 2-3 m a.m.s.l. Above the slope, the landscape takes the form of an even plateau, at c. 6 m a.m.s.l., before continuing westwards into more undulating, evenly rising hilly terrain, which eventually reaches a level of c. 6-7 m a.m.s.l. As the plateau is the only piece of relatively level ground in this area, this is probably the reason why it was preferred for settlement in the Stone Age (see also below). Both to the north ("Fuglevad") and to the south, there were at the time small marine inlets, which extended inland from Vængesø a short way into the hilly landscape, such that the locality was bounded by salt water to the northwest, north, northeast, east and south. Only to the west was there a dry-land connection to the rest of Helgenæs (Fig. 3) and the opening of the Vængesø lagoon into the open sea of Ebeltoft Vig lay 600-700 m to the northeast. In a wider topographic context, this settlement lay very close to the northernmost, narrowest part of Helgenæs – very close to where it is joined on to Mols. To the west, there was only 800 m from the settlement, as the crow flies, to the inlet of Begtrup Vig (and further west to the Bay of Aarhus). In contrast to the settlements Vængesø I and II, which were located on small islands, and Vængesø IV on a peninsula, Vængesø III lay directly on the shore, close to the northern tip of Helgenæs itself, and therefore had a slightly different (and greater) topographic "depth" than these other sites. Compared with other Ertebølle settlements, Vængesø III's hinterland was of a completely different character and considerably smaller than for example those at Ertebølle (*locus classicus*), Norsminde etc. In the latter cases, their territory extended many kilometres inland (into the hinterland) and also encompassed a number of different biotopes. Vængesø III is located c. 1.2 km away from Vængesø I and II, which lay to the southeast, and c. 200 m from Vængesø IV (Fig. 3). In topographic terms, this settlement thereby occupied an intermediary position between island settlements and coastal settlements on a mainland (with an associated hinterland).

The locality has been known for many years and a considerable number of ploughed-up artefacts have been collected, especially of flint, but also a little pottery, as well as antler and scattered faunal remains. The finds date predominantly from the Late Ertebølle culture, but artefacts from the

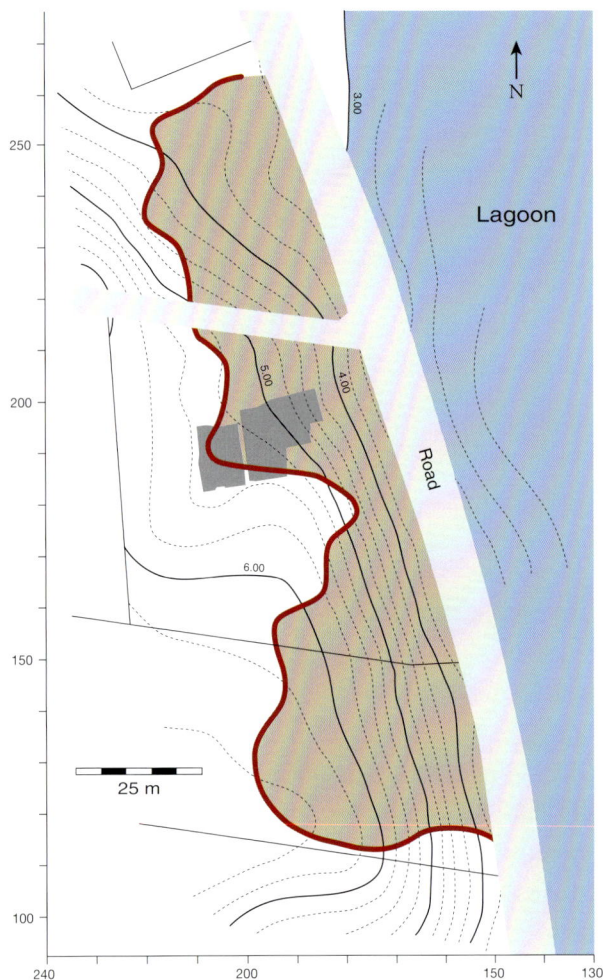

Fig. 85. Contour map of the settlement area at Vængesø III. A thick (red) line marks the outline and extent of the kitchen midden, based on the distribution of shells and flint debitage on the field surface. It is apparent that the kitchen midden has a natural division into a northern and a southern part. The location of the excavation trench is also shown (grey). Survey: Jan S. Carlsen.

Neolithic and pottery from the Bronze Age have also been picked up at the locality. These finds include a piece of a thin-butted polished stone axe, a hollow-ground thick-butted axe (Single Grave culture type) and a number of artefacts from the Late Neolithic, including pieces of flat-flaked daggers and several arrowheads. Finally, mention should be made of a coarse blade sickle of Late Bronze Age type.

The ploughed-up shells and artefacts on the surface of the field reveal that the kitchen midden was kidney-shaped in outline (Fig. 85). There is a narrower section in the middle which, in a simple way, divides the site into a southern (c. 65 × 45 m;

Fig. 86. The prehistoric coastal (erosion) slope and the level plateau behind it (to the right of the picture). The settlement was located at the foot of the slope and, in particular, up on the plateau. The Vængesø lagoon lay to the left and the modern road approximately follows the Stone Age coastline. Seen looking southwest. Photo: Søren H. Andersen.

Fig. 87. View of the northern part of Vængesø III following removal of the plough soil. The oval depression containing dark cultural deposits (pre-midden layer) and shells (kitchen midden) is seen clearly against the light-brown/yellowish-brown sand of the subsoil. Seen looking east. Photo: Søren H. Andersen.

c. 2900 m²) and a northern part (c. 85 × 25 m; c. 2100 m²), both of which lie at c. 3.5-5.5 m a.m.s.l. In total, the kitchen midden has therefore a length of c. 150 m and a width of between 10 and 45 m (Fig. 85). In Danish terms, this is therefore a substantial kitchen midden, covering at least 5000 m². In comparison, the Ertebølle kitchen midden measures c. 140 × 20 m (c. 2800 m²), Bjørnsholm c. 325 × 10-25 m (c. 8000 m²), Meilgaard c. 150 × 20 m (c. 3000 m²) and Nederst in Kolindsund c. 210 × 30 m (c. 6300 m²). The Vængesø III settlement is much larger than the other excavated localities in the Vængesø area, and this could be due to it having a particularly favourable position, where the lagoon opened out towards the sea (Ebeltoft Vig). The size of the kitchen midden, in conjunction with the findings from the other excavations, shows that it must consist of the remains from an (unknown) number of (habitation) units, the cultural deposits from which have become mixed together over time. A small section of the southern part and most of the northern part have been professionally investigated by archaeologists from, respectively, Syddjurs Museum/Ebeltoft Museum (now East Jutland Museum) in 1998 (P. Asingh and E. Kannegaard) and Moesgaard Museum (by the author, E. Kannegaard and archaeology students) in 2002-2005. Trial excavations and investigations

of the southern part of the settlement revealed that it had been greatly disturbed by secondary features, including several stone-filled cooking pits from the Bronze Age. The northern part of the locality was, on the other hand, virtually undisturbed. It was therefore decided to concentrate on the excavation of the northern *in situ* part. In the following, an account will only be given of the findings from the excavation of this part. However, finds from the other parts will be drawn into the analysis where relevant, including surface finds from the fields. All in all, the excavation therefore only covers a small portion of Vængesø III. It should be underlined that the southern and central parts of this kitchen midden have not been investigated and must definitely be scheduled and thereby secured against possible destruction in the future.

Below the plough soil was an oval feature (10-15 m) which marked a hollow in the surface of the subsoil and which was filled with kitchen midden deposits. It extended SW-NE across the plateau above the coastal slope and down the latter in a northeasterly direction (down towards the prehistoric shoreline; Fig. 87). This hollow was bounded on all sides by yellowish-brown subsoil sand. Elsewhere on the plateau were scattered minor features containing black, charcoal-rich fill. In the first phase of the excavation, the shell-filled hollow was

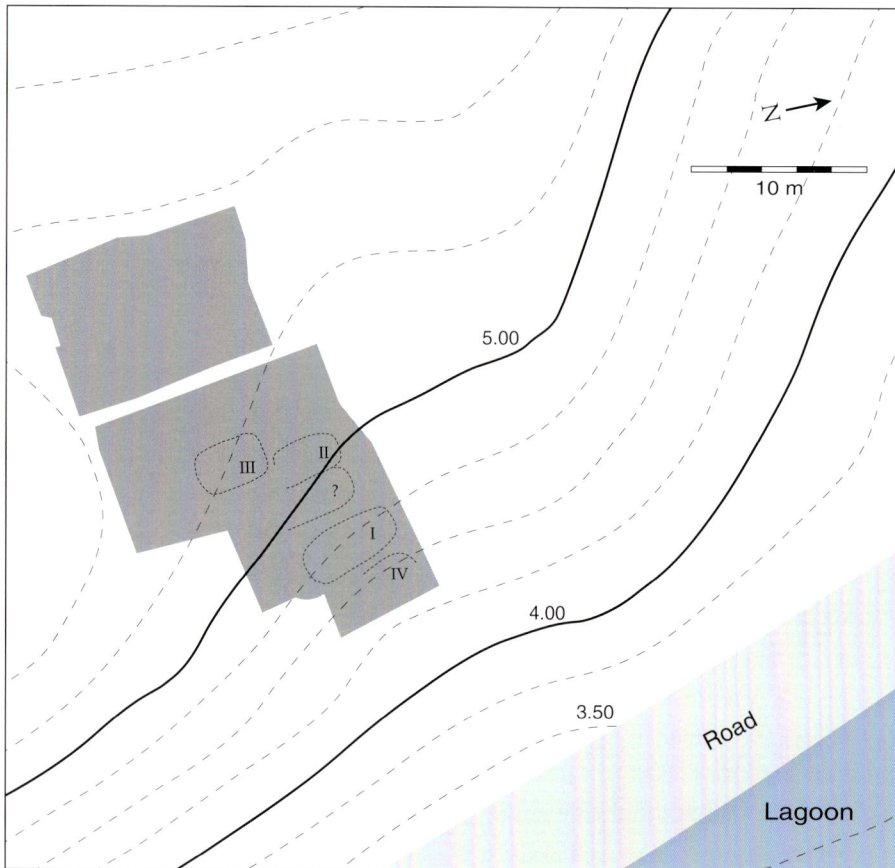

divided into four sections, referred to as the NW-, NE-, SW- and SE-areas. An area of c. 165 m² was subjected to systematic excavation, and in addition to this a further 34 m² was only partially investigated. In total, around 70-80% of the entire hollow was excavated. Consequently, this excavation was much more extensive, in terms of area, than those at the three other settlements at Vængesø and, in contrast to these, comprised one large continuous area. The excavation demonstrated that there were no refuse ("dump") deposits at the foot of the coastal slope. This could be due either to *post hoc* clearance of the surface (Binford 1982) or the fact that the dump now lies under the modern road (Olaf Ryesvej), which runs alongside, and very close to, the settlement area.

All tools/artefacts, bones, pottery and pieces of charcoal larger than 0.5 cm were recorded in a system of 3D coordinates, whereas flint debitage and uncharacteristic pieces of bone were collected in 0.25 m² squares and with respect to the local stratigraphy. The excavation layers were gener-

ally 2-3 cm thick and always respected any layer boundaries present. Both wet and dry sieving was undertaken, both in the field and subsequently at Moesgaard Museum, on a very large number of selected samples from the culture layers. At the same time, a considerable number of samples were taken for possible later scientific analysis. All the cultural deposits from a 0.5 m wide strip on either side of the east-west section, 478-485/500, were dry-sieved. A sample of c. 12 l from the pre-midden layer in square 482/501 was sent to the Zoological Museum, University of Copenhagen, for further analysis (Enghoff 2011, 154, 157, Tab. 41). In order to be able to keep a check on the stratigraphy, a number of sections were retained *in situ* in the excavation area until the final phase of the investigations, at which point they too were removed (Fig. 89a).

For the purposes of analysing the content of marine mollusc remains, material from an east-west baulk, which was 20 cm thick, 20 cm wide and 3.25 m long (volume 0.13 m³), was also taken as a sample.

a

b

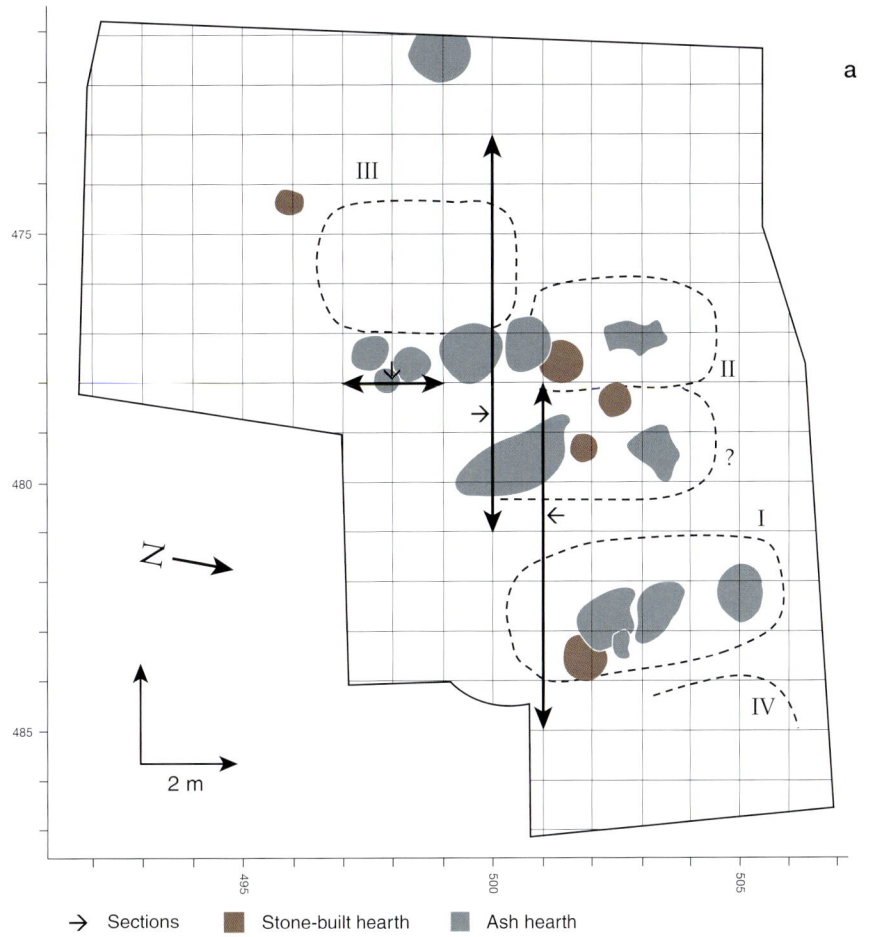

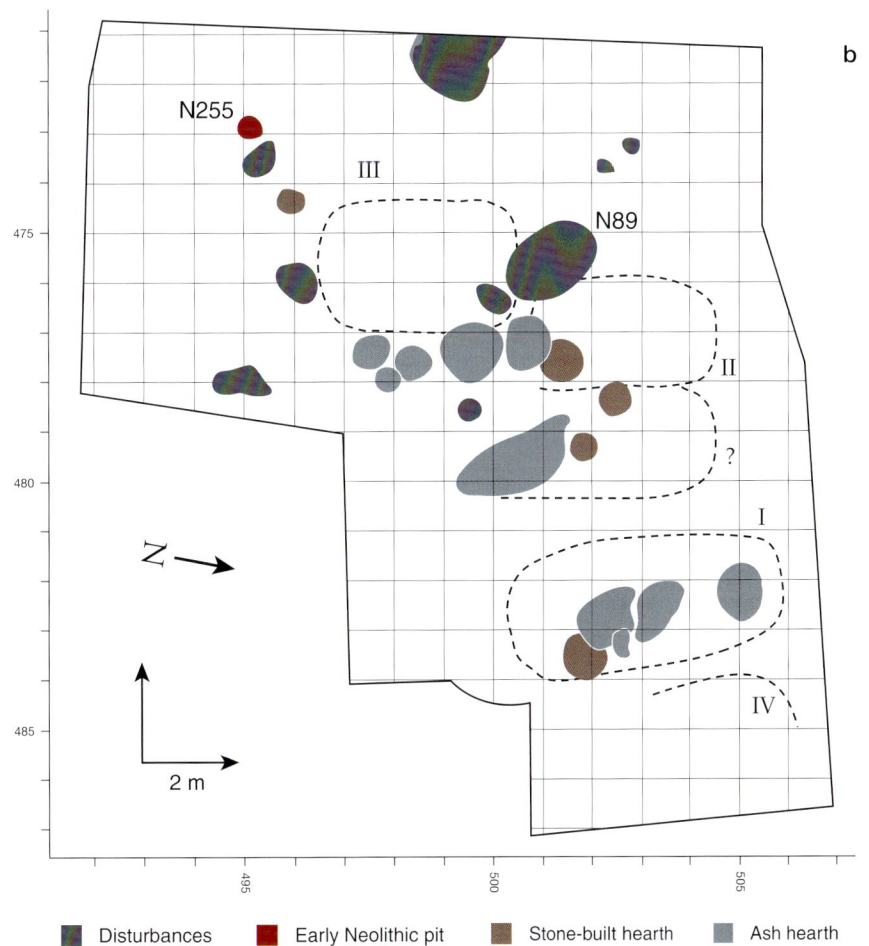

Fig. 89. a) Plan showing the surveyed and described sections with direction of view arrowed. Also shown are the hearths. b) Plan showing secondary pits, windthrows and other disturbances (animal burrows) (in black). N89 is a bathtub-shaped, stone-filled pit from the Bronze Age or Early Iron Age. N255 (red) is an Early Neolithic pit containing flint debris and an axe rough-out.

→ Sections | Stone-built hearth | Ash hearth

Disturbances | Early Neolithic pit | Stone-built hearth | Ash hearth

Disturbances were encountered in the form of secondary features, animal burrows and windthrows. It should be emphasised that the entire area had been under cultivation for many years, resulting in the upper (and latest) part of the original stratigraphy having been ploughed away. In several places there were secondary disturbances caused by minor windthrows, and in two cases there were larger examples. One of these measured c. 75 × 150 cm and the other c. 35 × 30 cm (Fig. 89b). In a few places, narrow, elongate disturbances resulting from animal burrows could be observed in the culture layer beneath the kitchen midden. In these cases, the overlying shell layer was, however, undisturbed. Further to these was a stone-filled cooking pit (N89), which was oviform in outline and measured c. 2 × 1.5 m (Fig. 89b). The pit cut down through the culture layers and into the upper part of the subsoil. On the basis of its content of head-sized cooking stones, charcoal-rich sandy soil and crushed mass of mussel shells, as well as 16 potsherds, this could be dated to the Bronze Age or Early Iron Age.

When it was initially thought that the 10 × 15 m shell-filled hollow in the surface of the subsoil could represent a partially sunken house foundation, two narrow intersecting trenches (N-S/E-W) were cut through the feature in order to gain an insight into its stratigraphy etc. From this, it was evident that the hollow had a more or less level, horizontal base and that the culture layer was a maximum of c. 30-40 cm thick (thickest approximately in the middle): From here it thinned out towards the edges. Beneath the kitchen midden was a c. 10-15 cm thick, charcoal-rich culture layer containing numerous cooking stones, the pre-midden layer (Andersen, S.H. 2000, 368), and below this was the subsoil (fine, yellowish-brown sand).

4.1 Stratigraphy

Uppermost was a c. 25 cm thick layer of greyish-brown, humus-rich, sandy plough soil which, within the limits of the hollow, had a sharply-defined lower boundary to an oyster-shell-dominated kitchen midden. Outside the hollow, the plough soil overlay fine,

yellowish-brown sand (the subsoil) and contained marine invertebrate shells and shell fragments, flint debitage and flint tools, cooking stones and a few pieces of bone and pottery. All these cultural remains show obvious traces of having been ploughed up from the underlying kitchen midden.

The kitchen midden, which lay at c. 4.5-5.5 m a.m.s.l., comprised shells of marine molluscs, mixed with other cultural remains, first and foremost animal bones (especially fishbones), charcoal, worked flint, cooking stones and pottery (Figs. 90-92, 99). On the basis of the deposit's composition and character (the degree of crushing/fragmentation of the shells), it was clear that the upper centimetres had more soil intermixed than the deeper deposits. The upper centimetres consisted of an up to c. 5 cm thick layer of much fragmented shells, primarily of cockles and mussels, with a few scattered potsherds and flint tools of Neolithic character. This layer overlay the kitchen midden and filled out irregularities in its upper surface. No date-conferring artefacts were found in this thin cockleshell horizon. However, as in the case of other kitchen middens, for example Norsminde, it is likely that this layer represents the last and deepest remains of a later, overlying horizon dating from the earliest part of the Neolithic, the Early Neolithic Funnel Beaker culture (Andersen, S.H. 1993, 38, Fig. 23). Associated with this layer was the base of a secondary pit (N255) which measured c. 40 × 50 cm. The pit contained a significant number of coarse flakes from the knapping of a flint roughout which also lay in it. The upper part of the pit had been removed by ploughing, while its base extended a few centimetres down into the surface of the kitchen midden. In addition to its stratigraphic position, a few potsherds date the pit to the Early Neolithic Funnel Beaker culture (see below).

Below this came a kitchen midden deposit of c. 25-40 cm in thickness. Its surface was uneven, with numerous small local pits and hollows. The deposit was dominated by shells of oysters, but also contained numerous cockles and carpet shells (*Venerupis corr.*), while shells of mussels (*Mytilus edulis*), periwinkles (*Littorina littorea*) and netted dog whelk (*Tritia reticulatae*) were less common. There were also shells of the small marine snail needle whelk (*Bittium reticulatum*) and scattered specimens of garden snail (*Cepaea hortensis*; Tab. 4). Further to these were many cooking stones, pieces of worked flint, bones, charcoal and a few potsherds. Several analyses of the layer revealed that shells of oysters dominated, constituting 55-72%, followed by cockles with 14-40% and periwinkles with 1-26%, while mussels and netted dog whelk were very few in number with only c. 1-2%. The shell layer also contained scattered occurrences of small oysters (less than 2-4 cm), while the largest individuals measured 11.3 cm in length. The presence of both carpet shells and small needle whelk, which are both salt-demanding species, shows that the sea was more saline at the time of the occupation than it is today, when these species are less common in inner Danish waters.

The kitchen midden contained many cultural remains – especially animal bones. It had a loose structure and the individual species often lay in delimited heaps and layers (Fig. 90c). In some places, in the deepest part, it did appear to consist of a more mixed shell mass than was the case higher up, where it comprised an almost pure oyster-shell layer. In one place was a c. 2 cm thick, black, horizontal stripe running through the kitchen midden, which contained numerous fishbones, a quantity of pottery, flint debitage and flint tools (Fig. 91). This horizon probably represents an old surface – a brief pause in the kitchen midden's depositional sequence – and it is possibly associated with the upper black ash layer of nearby hearth 131. If this is true, this finds-rich stripe shows that the kitchen midden must have accumulated over some time. In square 475-476/499, over a stretch of c. 1.5 m (east-west), a horizon was observed containing coarse flint flakes with a vertical distribution of c. 15 cm. This "flint layer" presumably also represents an old surface, on which flint debitage was deposited (see Fig. 91). Similar flint layers, marking pauses in the depositional rhythm (old surfaces), are also known from other kitchen middens, for example Ertebølle (Andersen/Johansen 1987, 46-47, Fig. 14). The flint from the kitchen midden had a pri-

mary surface and was not water-worn (-O, -R). In the southwestern part of the kitchen midden – in the deepest part of the shell layer at the transition to the underlying pre-midden layer – were two marked horizons that consisted of a c. 1-2 cm thick layer of fishbones. These covered a clearly delimited heap of periwinkle shells extending over an area of c. 2 × 2 m and c. 10 cm in thickness. Measurements of the oysters and cockles in a c. 25-30 cm thick series of layers through the shell deposit show that the average length of the oysters gradually decreases from the base upwards (from 6.75 to 6.23 cm), while the size of the cockle shells is more or less constantly around 2.4-2.6 cm (Fig. 93). As was the case at Vængesø II, where the oyster shells measured 6.25 cm in length, the shells were also small at Vængesø III. This leads to the conclusion that oysters did not have particularly good growing conditions in Vængesø at the time when the Ertebølle settlements were occupied.

Even though the culture layers' content of marine molluscs was everywhere dominated by oysters, and in most areas appeared as a homogeneous mass, the excavation also showed that in some places the layer contained discrete heaps of shells of a single mollusc species. For example, the layer was dominated by carpet shells over a 1 m² area in squares 477/496-497. Two discrete heaps of mussels, a heap of cockles, a local heap of oyster shells and four heaps of periwinkles were also demonstrated (Fig. 90c). Two of these small heaps were in the southern part of terrace I, while the others lay on the settlement surface, though concentrated in particular in and around the southern part of terrace II. The heaps often lay in close contact with a hearth, but in all cases only by an ash hearth. There were no examples where they lay by a stone-set hearth. The fact that all these heaps are located on the level settlement area shows that they were deposited where settlement activities, for example cooking, took place. These were the places where people were active – i.e. on the plateau where there was most activity (and of greatest duration). The heap of carpet shells measured c. 1 × 0.5 m, the cockle heap was c. 1 × 1 m, the two heaps of mussel shells were, respectively, 1 × 1 and 0.75 × 1

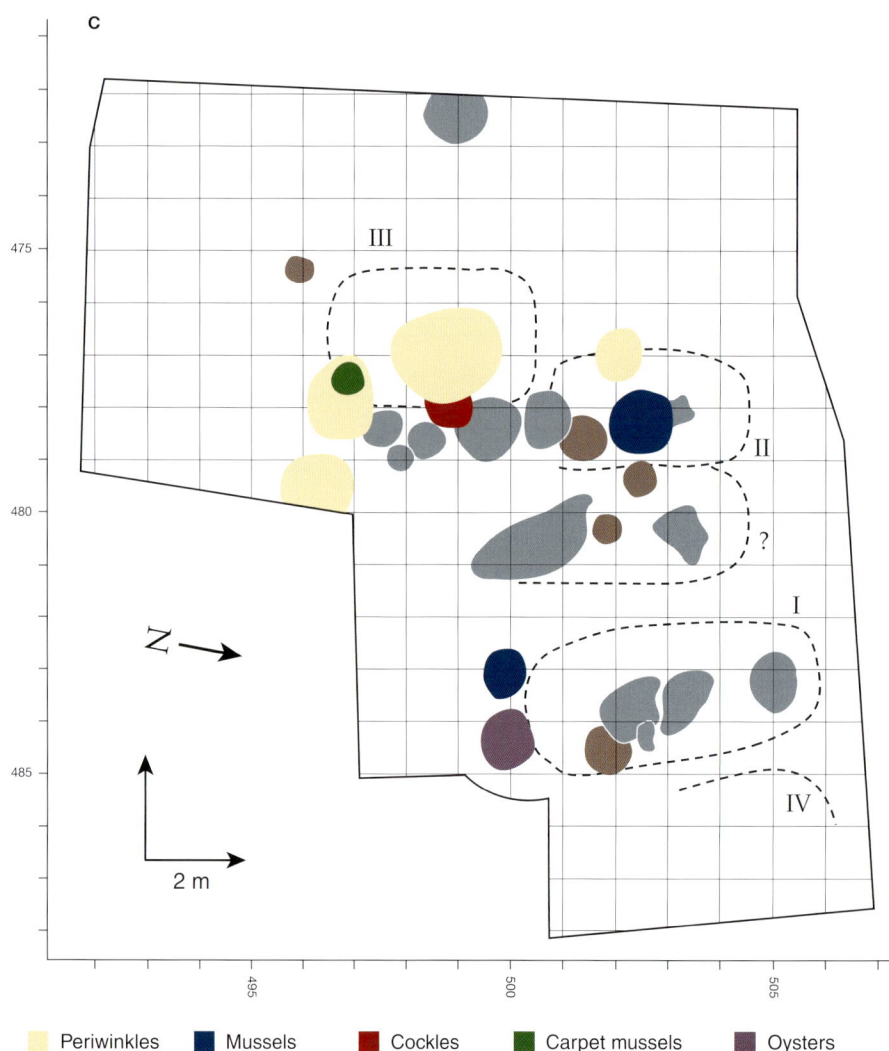

Fig. 90. a) Section
through the kitchen
midden. The layer
can be seen to contain
occasional cooking
stones and a minor
"meal heap" consisting
of periwinkle shells. b)
To the lower left, a thin
layer of oyster shells
can be seen wedged into
the base of the hearth
and continuing up into
its core, cf. Fig. 107.
c) Plan of the kitchen
midden showing small
local heaps of shells of
a single marine species.
These heaps are not
contemporaneous, but
must have been accu-
mulated over a period
of time.

| Periwinkles | Mussels | Cockles | Carpet mussels | Oysters |

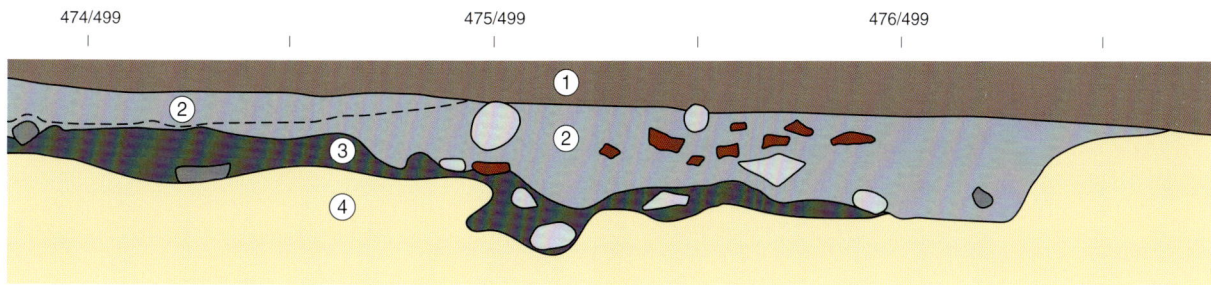

Fig. 91. The upper layer of the kitchen midden contained a local horizontal horizon of (coarse) flint flakes (red), showing that flint working had taken place on an earlier surface. 1 Ploughing horizon, 2 Kitchen midden, 3 Pre-midden layer, 4 Glacial sand.

m and, finally, the heap of oyster shells measured c. 1 × 1 m. One of the heaps of periwinkle shells was rather larger and measured c. 2 m in diameter and had a thickness of c. 10 cm in the middle. The second and third heaps both measured 1 × 1 m. The periwinkle shells formed a domed heap which was thickest towards the west. These heaps are interesting because they consisted almost exclusively of a single species and thereby differ markedly from the rest of the settlement's shell-rich layers. The size of the heaps and their uniform composition show that they represented the systematic and targeted gathering of an individual species within the settlement's resource area. The overall impression gained definitely suggests that these represent single refuse deposits – so-called "meal heaps". The volume of the aforementioned heap of periwinkle shells can be estimated to be c. 36 l and to contain 1116 gathered molluscs. If the meat from one periwinkle is estimated to weigh 1 g, this gives a total of c. 1.16 kg of mollusc meat. A similar, delimited heap of periwinkle shells lay in the eastern section of square 478-479/496-497, but this was slightly smaller, with a diameter of c. 1.6 m and a thickness at its centre of c. 10-15 cm. A third heap of periwinkle shells was recorded in square 479/495-496 (Fig. 90c). As the observations suggest that these shell heaps represent refuse/remains from meals relating to single episodes of short duration, the large numbers of snail shells must mean that there were several people involved in gathering them. Furthermore, their domed form and clear demarcation show that these heaps were swiftly covered

over and thereby avoided being levelled out and mixed with other settlement refuse.

Another interesting aspect of the kitchen midden deposits at this settlement is the high frequency of carpet shells, which otherwise only appear in very small numbers in Danish kitchen middens. Their presence in the latter case is interpreted as being the result of them being included by chance during the gathering of the other marine invertebrates (Madsen et al. 1900, 80-81). On the other hand, the many carpet shells at Vængesø III, all of uniform size, i.e. c. 4-5 cm, definitely shows that they were intentionally, systematically and selectively gathered, and on this point the locality differs from other Danish kitchen middens. Such intensive gathering of individual species from the adjacent marine environment must almost unavoidably have influenced the productivity of that environment. Perhaps the slight, but measurable, decrease in the size of oysters, which can be observed up through the kitchen midden, was a consequence of this (Fig. 93; Mannino/Thomas 2001, 1101-1114).

Given the ploughing-down of the site, which has been going on for a good number of years, the shell layer must originally have been both thicker and have extended even further out across the surrounding surface. A well-preserved and completely undisturbed sequence of deposits in a windthrow on the settlement surface gives an impression of the original stratigraphy and its depth. The sequence of deposits was as follows: Lowermost was light-brown/yellowish fine sand (subsoil), followed by 5-7 cm of greyish-black fine

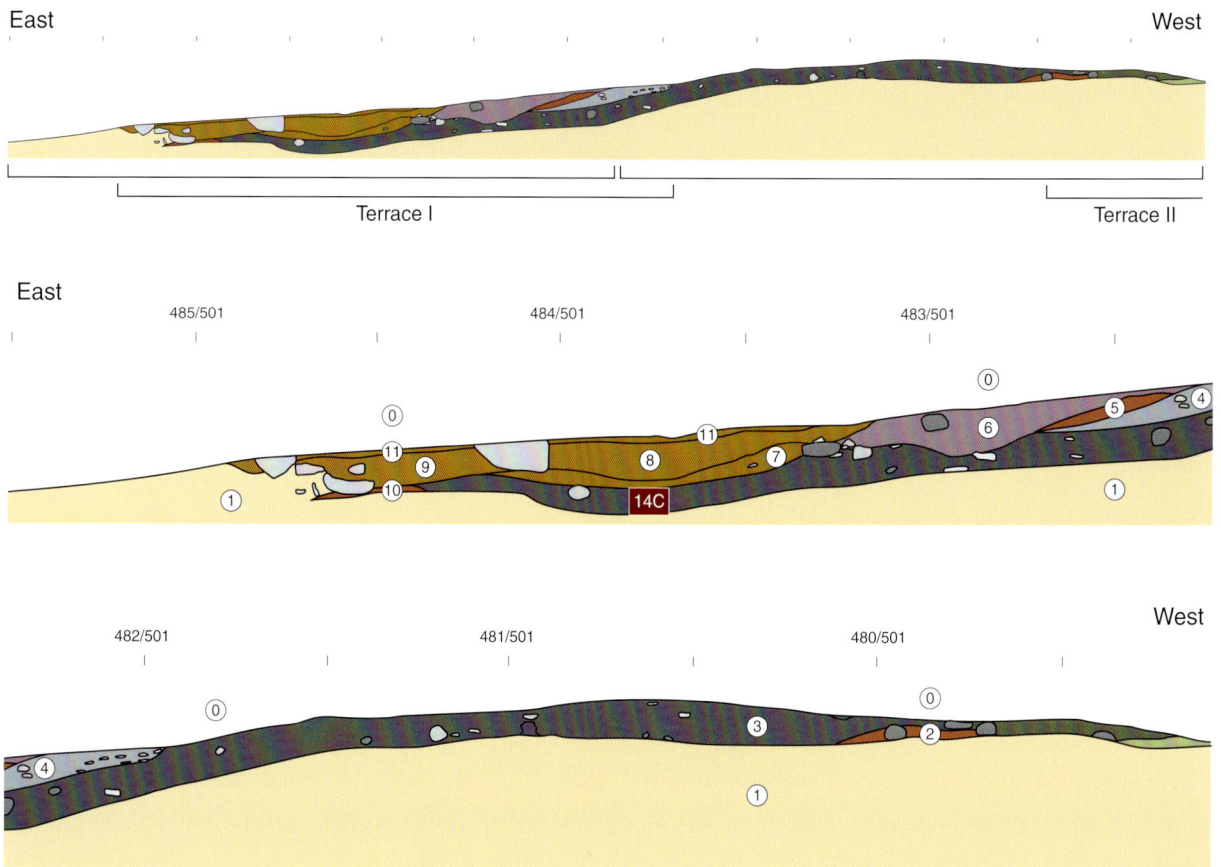

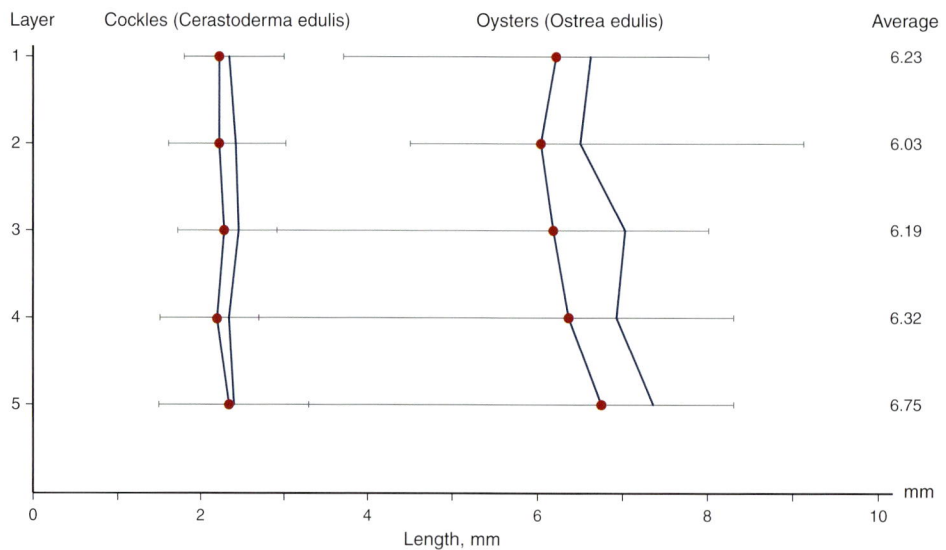

Fig. 93. Diagram showing the average size (length) of cockles and oysters through five layers in the kitchen midden. It is evident that, while the cockles are of more or less uniform size throughout the shell layer, the oysters become gradually smaller (shorter) from the base upwards. This phenomenon has been observed at numerous other Ertebølle kitchen middens in Jutland, for example Bjørnsholm, and could be either due to intensification of the collecting activities or environmental changes.

◄ *Fig. 92.* *Section evident in the south face of squares 479-485/501. The section cuts through terrace I (squares 480-485/501, to the left) and terrace II (squares 478-480/501, to the right). 0 Kitchen midden (removed before the drawing of the section). 1 Mottled subsoil – yellow-/olive-brown. 2 Fine clay-rich material. 3 Black culture layer – black-grey charcoal-stained sand with scattered shells, especially oysters, but also cockles and periwinkles, in addition to fishbones. Very rich in finds. At the transition between the shell layer and layer 3 there are more oyster shells, of which many are of large (old) individuals. 4 Very charcoal-rich layer with a major content of intact and crushed mussel shells, also occasional periwinkles, netted dog whelks and pullet carpet shells. Between layers 4 and 5, excavation of the section revealed a black-grey/brown sand-rich layer containing abundant fishbones and lowermost (i.e. directly over layer 4) a horizon of oyster shells which did not, however, form a continuous layer. 5 Yellowish-brown/reddish-brown sand-rich layer – possibly part of a hearth? 6 Mixed soil and shell layer (ratio of soil to shells 60-70:30-40%) containing intact and crushed shells, especially of oysters, but also cockles, mussels and periwinkles and a major content of fishbones. 7 Shell layer with a little soil (ratio between soil and shells 40-50:50-60%) containing mainly oyster shells, but also local concentrations of cockles and a few mussels. 8 Soil-rich shell layer containing, in particular, intact and crushed oyster shells. Appears a little compacted in the small hollow between the large stone and layer 6 (ratio of soil to shells 20-30:70-80%). Also containing a quantity of shells of mussels, cockles and periwinkles. 9 Soil and comminuted shell layer (ratio between soil and shells 50-60:40-50%); many intact oyster shells as well as periwinkles and crushed cockles (possibly a continuation of layer 7 or 8). 10 Soil and comminuted shell layer which predominantly consists of shells of oysters and periwinkles. 11 Soil and comminuted shell layer containing remains of mussels, cockles and oysters.*

The section was drawn and described after the kitchen midden had been removed. The uppermost layer in all squares had therefore originally been overlain by kitchen midden deposits (layer 0). The position of radiocarbon-dating sample LUS-7187 is indicated.

sand (pre-midden layer), then 20-25 cm of oyster shell deposit (kitchen midden). This corresponds to the stratigraphy encountered in the excavation. Over this was a 7-8 cm thick black layer of fine sand with shell fragments and fist-sized cooking stones, followed by a whitish-grey c. 10 cm thick layer of compacted oyster shells and comminuted mussel shells. Finally, there was a c. 25 cm thick black sand layer with a major content of crushed/fragmented cockle shells and scattered whole oyster shells, periwinkles and small stones (shingle). This entire depositional sequence was c. 70-75 cm in thickness. If this is compared with the deposits in the main hollow, it is apparent that the upper (and latest) part of the original sequence, i.e. c. 25-35 cm, has today been removed by ploughing. A general analysis of the total stratigraphy shows that it is the deposits which accumulated after the Mesolithic-Neolithic transition that have been removed by

ploughing. This conclusion is supported by the presence of the Neolithic pit (N255), which was cut down into the surface of the kitchen midden and where only the base remained *in situ*. Conversely, the stratigraphy also shows that the kitchen midden and the underlying pre-midden layer from the Ertebølle culture were still completely intact, which concurs with observations during the excavation. The overall conclusion drawn from the stratigraphy of the windthrow deposits is that this part of Vængesø III was originally a so-called "stratified kitchen midden", representing occupation from the Late Ertebølle to the Early Middle Neolithic Funnel Beaker culture (MN A I-II; Andersen, S.H. 2000, 375-376). The colour of the later layers, their content of charcoal, cooking stones and mollusc shells, and the degree of their fragmentation, give a clear indication that these post-date the Ertebølle culture and should probably be dated to the Neolithic.

Fig. 94. Two parts of the pre-midden layer, which consisted of a compact mass of fish waste (grey background matrix). Photo: Nina Helt Nielsen.

Fig. 95. Part of the pre-midden layer with animal bones in situ. a) Vertebra of a small whale, b) pelvic region of a cormorant, c) lower jaw (presumably of a seal) and quantities of fishbones (grey background matrix). Photos: Lone Ritchie Andersen.

The deepest part of the kitchen midden, i.e. at the transition from the underlying pre-midden layer, was diffuse and in many places characterised by several thin shell stripes (layers of shells c. 2-4 cm thick), which alternated with thin layers of black fill (cultural deposits). These shell layers consisted of relatively large oyster shells that commonly formed one or two horizontal courses and were frequently pressed down into the surface of the underlying pre-midden layer. They were very clear in the southwestern and northeastern parts of the excavated area. A large number of whale bones were also found towards the base of the midden. Down the hillside (towards the east), at least two to three distinct, 10-13 cm thick shell layers could be distinguished, separated by a c. 15 cm thick layer of shells mixed with soil, which must be interpreted as material that had slipped/eroded down from the occupation further up on the plateau. Collectively, these layers reveal the existence of several phases in the accumulation of the kitchen midden. As the stratigraphic transition between the underlying pre-midden layer and the kitchen midden is difficult to define – especially on the plateau and on the coastal slope – it was often necessary during the excavation to reach a qualified decision as to whether finds should be assigned to one or the other.

Below the kitchen midden (and especially north of the line 496.50) was a c. 5-15 cm thick, very charcoal-rich culture layer (the pre-midden layer), which lay at c. 4.50-5.25 m a.m.s.l. (Figs. 93-95). After the kitchen midden had been removed, the pre-midden layer was evident with an undulating surface, which occupied the entire large hollow that was observed at the beginning of the investigation. It had been well-protected at the base of the hollow by the overlying shell layer.

As is apparent from the above, the transition between the pre-midden layer and the kitchen midden was in many cases "fluid" and very difficult to delineate with certainty. This was especially true of the "plateau", where the pre-midden layer gradually disappeared towards the west.

Along the edge of the coastal slope was a c. 5 m long, c. 1-1.5 m wide and c. 10-15 cm thick "bank" of black cultural deposits, very rich in bones (especially fishbones) and settlement refuse (Fig. 114). This bank, which follows the eastern edge of terrace II, is perhaps a consequence of the clearing-out/digging away of fill layers on the terrace, but it could also be the result of the accumulation of refuse along the edge of the plateau. The bank lay between two clearly lower terraces, respectively to the east and west, later termed "terrace I" and "terrace II". These slightly sunken terraces were filled with kitchen midden material and were first identified when this had been removed during the excavation. From here, the pre-midden layer disappeared gradually, both towards the west and down the hillside to the east, where it came to an end at the foot of the slope. The layer was thickest in the middle (15 cm) and decreased from here in all directions. It lay obliquely down the slope and followed the hill's incline. Here, it consisted of at least 5-7 thin layers of black sandy material and several up to 10-12 cm thick sloping, local patches of shells, which measured c. 55-85 cm in diameter and were characteristic in that they only included a single mollusc species, either oysters or mussels.

The inclined deposition is further underlined by one or two stripes of large oyster shells, lying singly, which follow the downwards slope of the layers, and of the hill, to the east. This sequence of deposits on the hillside must have been formed by refuse arising from occupation higher up on the flat plateau and therefore represents at least a cor-

responding number of use visits/habitation episodes at this locality. The layer was rich in cultural remains such as worked flint (-O and -R), cooking stones, small potsherds and large fragments of pottery as well as substantial quantities of mammal and bird bones and, in particular, fishbones. There were many more bones at Vængesø III than is usual on the "dry" part of a settlement surface. There were abundant fishbones everywhere, but especially in the aforementioned north-south-oriented "bank", which had a dense concentration of fishbones, otoliths etc. The layer's appearance under excavation (Figs. 94-97) most resembled the culture layers encountered at the very finds-rich settlements of the Pitted Ware culture on Gotland. In relation to the overlying kitchen midden, there were also considerably more cooking stones in the pre-midden layer. Their concentration ranged from about 2-3 to 30-40 examples per m^2. The cooking stones did not, however, form a continuous layer, as seen at many other Ertebølle settlements of this date. As previously described, the culture layers at Vængesø III differ from those at other Danish Ertebølle settlements by virtue of the intensity of the cultural remains they contain – especially fishbones and bones of other animals. During the excavation of the southernmost part of Vængesø III, a similar thick culture layer was observed, which consisted primarily of concreted fishbones and seal and whale

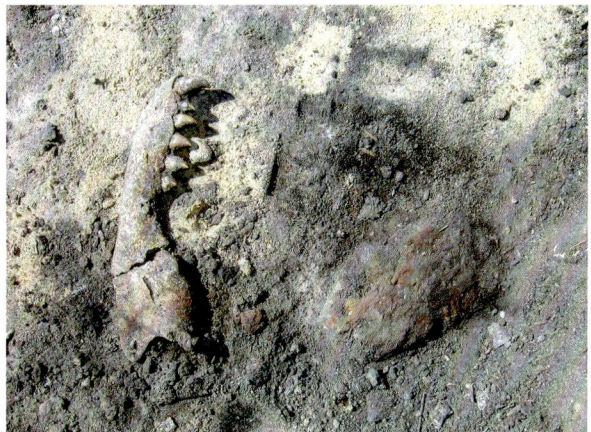

Fig. 96. Lower jaw of seal and degraded potsherd in situ *in the pre-midden layer. Photo: Lone Ritchie Andersen.*

Fig. 97. Lower jaw of a dog in situ *during excavation in the pre-midden layer. Photo: Lone Ritchie Andersen.*

Fig. 98. Terrace I after the pre-midden layer and the hearths had been removed. Seen looking north. Note the red colouration of the subsoil at the locations of the ash-rich hearths, cf. Fig. 111. Photo: Nina Helt Nielsen.

remains. The layer here was so thick and compacted that it still showed clear traces of the oil and had an unmistakable smell of train oil.

Beneath the pre-midden layer was the subsoil, which consists of fine, light-brown/yellowish-brown fluvioglacial sand, the upper 10-15 cm of which was characterised by small holes and burrows of small animals. The subsoil was observed between 4.25 and 5.5 m a.m.s.l. The upper c. 10 cm of the subsoil contained a small number of cultural remains, primarily flint artefacts, the presence of which must be due to them having been trodden down into the old ground surface during the earliest occupations of the site.

Prior to the first habitation, the sea had eroded a low coastal slope where the settlement came to be located. The sea level at this time, which, based on the archaeological and scientific dating evidence, would have been during the Atlantic period, corresponding to the Middle Ertebølle culture, i.e. c. 4600-4400 BC, must have been around 3.5-3.75 m a.m.s.l. The geological and archaeological studies show that the excavated area was never inundated by the sea, and this conclusion is consistent with the primary surface of the flint (-O and -R) artefacts.

The pre-midden layer was associated with habitation up on the plateau behind the slope, where the thin stripes of oyster shells show that marine invertebrates were occasionally, but infrequently, gathered and that this aspect of the subsistence economy was not of major consequence at this time. A kitchen midden was deposited on top of this layer during the Late Ertebølle culture, and its accumulation continued in the Early Neolithic. The depositional conditions show that the settlement (or part of it) gradually moved up the slope (presumably as a consequence of rising sea level), eventually ending up at the edge of the plateau, where the numbers of settlement features and finds were greatest. Finally, the relatively abundant areas with traces of flint-working and the slaughtering/butchering of prey, together with the discrete heaps of mollusc shells (consisting of a single species), show that parts of the depositional sequence was extremely "episodic". The occupation surface must have been covered immediately after it had been abandoned and without any extensive "clearing up" of any kind being undertaken. Otherwise, the shell heaps etc. would have become erased and mixed with other settlement waste. As a consequence of these depositional conditions, it was in many cases difficult or impossible during the excavation to determine whether finds should be assigned to the kitchen midden layer or the pre-midden layer. The finds assemblages from the two deposits are therefore examined together, and this decision is also justified by the archaeological and scientific dates, which indicate unanimously that the entire occupation sequence was of relatively short duration. Where possible, and in the case of finds of particular importance, their position relative to one or other of these culture layers will be given in the text. The scattered mollusc shells show that sporadic gathering of marine shellfish (especially oysters) took place during formation of the pre-midden layer. It was first later that gathering and consumption of these animals achieved such an extent that a kitchen midden accumulated.

4.2 Settlement features and structures

The Vængesø III settlement is characterised in particular by a large number of diverse structures and features, associated, first and foremost, with the pre-midden layer but also, to a lesser extent, with the kitchen midden. The existence has been demonstrated of elongate, rectangular, slightly sunken areas or working terraces, two to three different kinds of hearths, areas of reddened subsoil, pits, postholes, areas with traces of flint-working, concentrations of fishbones and patches/bodies of dug-up subsoil material.

4.2.1 Terraces

Terrace I was evident as a subrectangular, shallow depression, oriented north-south, i.e. parallel with the prehistoric shoreline (Figs. 88, 98). This was the easternmost of the three (possibly four) terraces and it lay between 4.5 and 4.75 m a.m.s.l. at the foot of the coastal slope. The terrace measured c. 6.5 × 2.75 m (N-S/E-W), i.e. it had an area of c.

17.9 m². Its edges were distinct – especially to the south and west, while to the east and especially to the northeast they were rather less clear. This was due to disturbance resulting from an animal burrow in this corner. The western and southern edges had a height of c. 15-30 cm relative to the surrounding terrain. The entire western edge was steep and along it ran a regular c. 10 cm wide band of mussel shells. The interpretation of the latter feature remains completely open: Does it represent the remains of some kind of wall fill? The distinct side edges, which stood sharp in the fine sand, showed that the feature must have become swiftly filled in after use. Otherwise, the edges would have collapsed and been trodden down (this was an actual problem encountered during the excavation!). The base was level – both longitudinally and transversely – and covered by a thin (c. 2-3 cm thick) layer of grey ash. On the base of the terrace were three to four ash hearths, running in a line down the central axis (hearth nos. 275, 7608 and 280 – from south to north), and with hearths 275 and 7608 slightly overlapping. Towards the southeast lay stone-set hearth 274 (Fig. 101). Beneath these hearths, the surface of the subsoil was clearly reddened along the central axis of the feature (Fig. 98). Terrace I was the best preserved of the terraces and almost completely undisturbed apart from the animal burrow in its northeastern corner. It lay directly on the surface of the subsoil and was covered by both the pre-midden layer and the kitchen midden. It is presumably the earliest feature of this type at the settlement.

The area between terraces I and II was characterised by many traces of activity – including two circular stone-set hearths (6318 and 6649) and two ash hearths (6911 and 6989). There was also a "bare" area with reddened subsoil sand, which must represent a trace of a hearth that had been removed. There could possibly also have been a terrace in this area (marked with ? on the plan Fig. 88).

Terrace II was evident as a subrectangular depression running north-south at a level of 5-5.25 m a.m.s.l. (Fig. 88). It was the middle terrace, which lay on the level terrain directly above and ran along the old (coastal) slope. Even though this feature lay higher than the other two terraces, it was parallel with terrace I and lay only c. 3 m away from it. Terrace II was rather more disturbed than terrace I – especially along its eastern side, as a result of intensive occupation during the Stone Age and the activities of burrowing animals. Despite this, the feature was relatively well-defined and could be seen to have dimensions of (at least) 5 × 2.5 m (corresponding to an area of c. 12.5 m²). The terrace had a flat base on which were three ash hearths (131, 6520 and 6524) arranged longitudinally (from south to north) along its middle. As in the case of terrace I, these hearths extended in a line.

Terrace III. During the excavation in 2004, a similar but rather smaller subrectangular sunken area was identified on the settlement surface: This was named terrace III. It was located c. 1-2 m southwest of terrace II, i.e. also on the plateau above the slope (Fig. 88) and was similarly oriented north-south. It measured c. 5 × 3 m, i.e. it had an area of c. 15 m². It was difficult to delimit to the south, but its boundary was evident as a curved area where the subsoil had a greater clay content and was therefore damper than the subsoil around it. The northern and northeastern parts of the feature were unfortunately disturbed by a secondary pit from the Bronze Age (Fig. 89b). The base was also flat in this case, but was more difficult to

identify than in the case of the two other terraces. This also differed on several further points from the other terraces. For example, it had no hearths and, consistent with this, no reddened areas of subsoil. Another difference was that the southern part contained a significantly greater quantity of cooking stones than was evident on the other terraces. Furthermore, there were discrete heaps of animal bones which must reflect that this was a slaughtering/butchering site (Fig. 115). These differences open up the possibility that this terrace was not of the same kind as terraces I and II, although of a related type.

Finally, there were possible traces of yet another feature, *terrace IV,* located at the lowest level at the foot of the excavation trench and with the same (north-south) orientation as the other three. Unfortunately, only the western edge could be identified as a shallow "step" in the hillside. This edge could be followed over a distance of c. 4 m and as it turned eastwards at each end, its width can be estimated as (at least) 2 m (Fig. 88).

The terraces described above represent features of a form and size that has not previously been demonstrated and described in association with the settlements of the Ertebølle culture. They were very uniform in size, form and orientation relative to the local terrain and had the same layout. They were subrectangular to oval in outline

Fig. 99. The southern end of terrace III seen looking north; east-west section in squares 476-477/499. At the base of the stratigraphy are one to two courses of large oyster shells and above these a solid layer of shells of cockles and periwinkles. Photo: Lone Ritchie Andersen.

and measured c. 5-7 m in length and c. 2.5-3 m in width: Their "floor" area was therefore c. 12.5-18 m². They all lay c. 15-30 cm deeper than the surrounding terrain. On their base, which was horizontal, there were, in the case of terraces I and II, a series of ash hearths running along their central axis. It could not be determined whether these represented successive use or one period of coeval activity. Furthermore, the terraces all lay close to and ran alongside the former shoreline. Stone-built hearths were, in two cases, encountered on the terraces and in one, possibly two, cases outside these (see section on the hearths). The numbers of finds from the terraces varied, but both terraces I and II were rich in finds. Moreover, they could be (archaeologically) coeval. Seen in relation to the local topography, the positioning of these features alongside the shoreline is the most logical choice, given that this provides level habitation surfaces that are well-suited to living/working on the sloping hillside. The same use of the topography is also evident in the terraces at Vængesø I, II and possibly also Vængesø IV. These similarities suggest that the terrace features represented the same kind of structure which, given their uniformity, differs from the previously presented Ertebølle dwelling sites. Lack of uniformity has so far been a problem with respect to the published Mesolithic dwellings, which have exhibited considerable variation in terms of form, size and contents (Simonsen 1952; Larsson, L. 1975; Sørensen 1993; Rowley-Conwy 2013, 137-154). On this point, the Vængesø terraces differ from the other possible Ertebølle dwellings by virtue of their great uniformity. So many points of similarity can be identified with respect to morphology and size between these three (possibly four) terraces in the hillside at Vængesø III and those found at Vængesø I and II that they must represent the same, or very similar, features. Do they represent the floors of partially sunken huts or activity platforms? No postholes were identified in association with them, or at least there were no traces of posts/poles greater than 2-5 cm in diameter, or which were systematically arranged. This could be because local biological activity has made it impossible to distinguish securely between possible rammed-in

posts and root channels or animal burrows. Traces of thin, rammed-in poles can therefore be considered to be inconsequential in the context of the excavation. The main argument for the existence of some form of construction (wall) along the edges of the terraces is the fact that the loose, dry sand of the subsoil would have collapsed and blurred the outlines of the features had there not been some form of support along the edges.

Terrace I is, as mentioned above, presumably the earliest of these features, as it lay on the surface of the subsoil and was overlain by both the pre-midden layer and the kitchen midden. The chronological relationship between the two other terraces (II and III) cannot be determined; they may be coeval. All terraces can, on the basis of the artefacts recovered, the stratigraphy and the radiocarbon dates for the pre-midden layer and the overlying kitchen midden, be dated to the Late Ertebølle culture, i.e. c. 4400-4200 BC. Terrace III has the same size and form as the two other terraces, but differs from these in its lack of hearths. It contains large quantities of fire-brittled stones (cooking stones), and the bones recovered indicate the existence of a slaughtering/butchering site for prey (Fig. 115). It should also be pointed out that, given the size of the excavated area and its location on the hillside, further similar terraces could well be situated both to the north and (perhaps especially) to the south (Figs. 85 and 88). The presence of hearths and settlement refuse on these terraces/depressions (at both Vængesø I and III) shows that people spent time here and carried out various activities (knapping flint, processing fish, butchering), which demanded both heat and light. A cautious interpretation is that these features could either represent some form of working platform or slightly sunken surface with an area of c. 12.5-18 m².

The terraces and their finds provide no immediate secure indication of the existence of a possible entrance, even though this must be considered likely. As this was a community that was strongly marine orientated, and which could have had stationary fishing structures located directly offshore from the settlement, it seems most likely that any opening or door to these terraces would have faced out towards the shore. In this way, visual contact could be maintained with the fishing structures, and navigation on the lagoon and the adjacent waters could also be monitored. Support for this conclusion is also provided by the fact that almost all the flint-working and fish-processing sites on the settlement surface are oriented such that the people undertaking these activities were facing out to sea.

The Vængesø terraces show similarities to the previously mentioned feature in the side of a coastal slope at Vegger (Halkær Enge) in Himmerland (Simonsen 1952, 199-299, Figs. 3-8). The Vegger feature is very similar to the Vængesø terraces, although the former is less regular. The archaeological finds date Vegger to the Middle/Late Ertebølle culture. A few years ago, part of an Ertebølle settlement was excavated on the outskirts of Kalundborg (at Statoil's oil refinery). This was a coastal settlement which lay on evenly sloping terrain running down towards a former Stone Age fjord. The excavation revealed several circular pits measuring 2-4 m in diameter, the significance of which was difficult to ascertain. In the same area were two elongate, subrectangular features which measured 6 × 3 m (18 m²) and 7 × 3 m (21 m²), respectively. These features lay parallel and followed the prehistoric shoreline, and one of them was cut 18 cm into the hillside in the same way as the features evident at Vængesø and Vegger (information kindly supplied by the excavator, B. Staal). The size, form and location relative to the sloping terrain of the two Kalundborg features were therefore very similar to the situations observed at Vængesø (Fig. 100).

A degree of similarity can also be identified between the Vængesø terraces and the rectangular, partially sunken feature beneath the kitchen midden at Lollikhuse (Roskilde Fjord). This has been interpreted as the outline/ground plan of a sunken hut (Sørensen 1993; 1995, 21, Fig. 2). The Lollikhuse feature, which was slightly diffuse in its delimitation, measured c. 6 × 4 m (i.e. an area of c. 24 m²) and was cut c. 10-20 cm into the subsoil. Along the edges of the sunken area were a few larger postholes and a greater number of smaller ones. It contained two hearths: a circular, stone-built example

and an ash hearth (Sørensen 1995, 21, Fig. 2). There was also a small pit in the subsoil containing a roe deer antler (Sørensen 1995, 23, Fig. 5). In terms of area, the floor at Lollikhuse was therefore slightly larger than the features encountered at Vængesø. This presumed dwelling at Lollikhuse was dated to the Early Ertebølle culture and was overlain by an oyster-dominated kitchen midden from the Late Ertebølle culture (Sørensen 1995, 20). As with the features at Vængesø and Halkær, the floor (i.e. dwelling) at Lollikhuse was also aligned with the coast (Sørensen 1995, 20, Fig. 1). It now appears that the same type of feature has been encountered in three to four cases (Vegger, Vængesø, Lollikhuse and possibly Kalundborg) at coastal settlements from the Ertebølle culture, and that common characteristics of these are their form, size and the fact that they were all cut slightly into the subsoil. Scanian Kongemose and Ertebølle settlements have also yielded several examples of hut/house floors that were sunken relative to the surrounding soil surface: i.e. the localities of Saxtorp, Hylligekroken, Ageröd I HC (Larsson, L. 1975), Hylteberga and, most recently, "Struktur 10 and 24" at Skateholm (Larsson, L. 1985, 197-209; 1988, 5-18). The Saxtorp feature measured c. 5.5 × 4.5 m (18 m²) and had a depth relative to the surrounding terrain of c. 50 cm. It was dated to the Early Ertebølle culture. At the inland settlement of Ageröd I HC there was an elongated surface (c. 8 × 3 m) covered with flat stones. This feature was dated to the Late Kongemose culture. Hylteberga is a further southern Swedish locality with a circular feature (3 m in diameter), cut c. 75 cm into the subsoil. This covered an area of c. 7 m² and is dated to the Kongemose/Early Ertebølle culture. A rectangular feature was observed at the southern Swedish settlement of Skateholm, "Struktur 24", which was also sunken c. 15 cm relative to the surroundings. This feature covered an area of c. 14.8 m² (Larsson, L. 1988, 5-18). Slightly sunken house foundations were demonstrated at the inland settlements of Bökeberg II and III (Karsten 1986, 65-89, 1991). In the recent investigations at Tågerup, four features (at least) were found that are interpreted as remains of houses. These include a round hut, which measured

Vængesø I

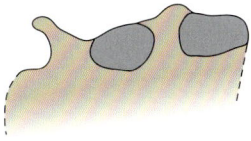

Vegger

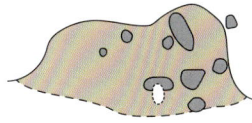

Lollikhuse

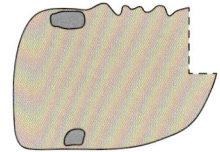

Vængesø III

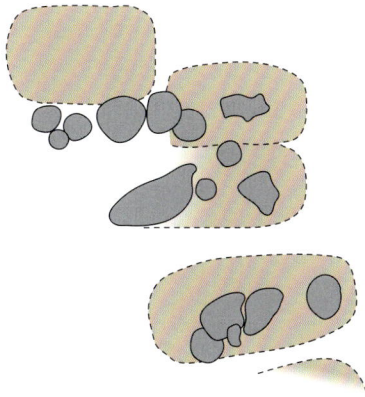

Egehøj

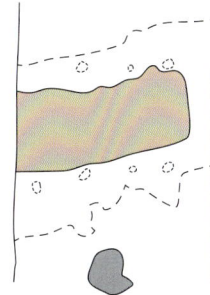

5 m

◼ Hearth

Kalundborg

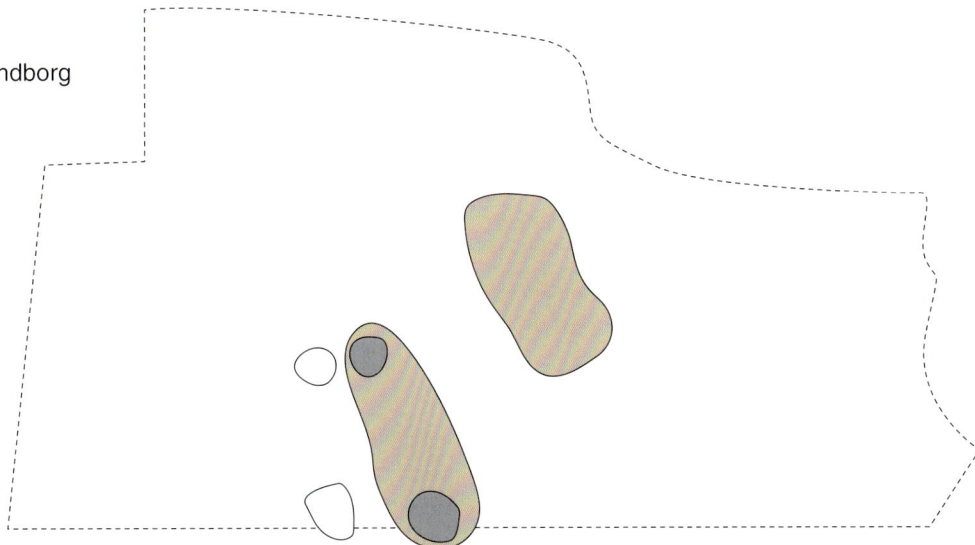

Fig. 100. Danish examples of terraces and hut outlines/floors from the Ertebølle culture. From top to bottom: Vængesø I, Vegger (Simonsen 1952), Lollikhuse (Sørensen 1995), Vængesø III, Egehøj (C.K. Jensen 2002) and Kalundborg (Staal 2009).

c. 7 × 8 m and had a depth of c. 17 cm relative to the surroundings. It is dated to the Early Ertebølle culture (Karsten/Knarrström 2003, 150-176). Further to this were three pits, which covered an area of c. 40-50 m², and an elongate feature, which measured c. 16 × 5 m and was c. 20 cm deep (Karsten/Knarrström 2003, 160). It was interpreted as the remains of a trapezoid longhouse (Karsten/Knarrström 2003, 150-151, Fig. 89).

In Denmark, possible house remains have also been recorded at the locality of Søholm 2 (Mahler 1993, 141-142) and at Kristrup/Egehøj, where there was a c. 3 × 5 m rectangular, sunken area, c. 20 cm in depth, with postholes at the edges and a few others in the middle (Fig. 100). On the floor were several layers of lime bark separated by layers of white sand, but no hearth. This feature is dated to the Late Ertebølle culture (Jensen, C.K. 2002, 40-46; Mandrup et al. 2003). Finally, there was also a round sunken feature at Nivå 10 (Late Kongemose/Early Ertebølle culture; Jensen, O.L. 2003; 2009). Traces of sunken dwellings (houses/huts) associated with Ertebølle settlements are therefore not unknown in Denmark, and related features have also been found at Ertebølle (*locus classicus*; Andersen/Johansen 1987, 37-40, Figs. 5-6), at the Åle kitchen midden in the former Bjørnsholm Fjord (unpublished) and at the inland settlement of Ringkloster (Andersen, S.H. 1998, 23, 27-29, Fig. 8). With regard to the elongate, rectangular house floors from the Ertebølle culture, reference can also be made to the possible bark floor found at the submerged settlement of Møllegabet II (Skaarup/Grøn 2004, 46-50, Fig. IVb, 11-15). In spite of the various differences, a common characteristic of all of these examples is that they are sunken, rectangular or round features with a (floor) area of c. 13-18 m².

Most recently, P. Rowley-Conwy has published a review of possible remains of Kongemose and Ertebølle dwellings (Rowley-Conwy 2013, 152). He argues that possible houses/huts associated with the kitchen middens stood on/in the shell heaps and that our difficulties in identifying them arise from the fact that the traces of these structures have been destroyed by later activities and occupations of the middens. In the light of the numerous excavations of kitchen middens in Jutland in recent years – both of the middens themselves and the areas around them, this view must be rejected. The observations, for example at Holmegaard (Ch. 7.2), indicate rather that possible houses/huts stood *behind* the shell middens, but that, at the same time, many everyday tasks took place *on top of* the shell heaps.

In an attempt to arrive at an interpretation of the features found on the settlement surface – especially the hearths – and their possible links with dwellings or working platforms, theoretical, standardised floor outlines were projected onto the plan of the settlement surface of Vængesø III in order to find out whether this produced any significant results. This was done such that the longitudinal rows of hearths and depressions were lined up with the central axis of the "theoretical floors", but also taking into account the local topography. In defining the size and form of these experimental floors, use was made of the smallest settlement units from Late Palaeolithic (Bro; Andersen, S.H. 1973) and Early Mesolithic times (Sværdborg II; Petersen, E.B. 1972), as well as the slightly larger and more rectangular unit from the Ertebølle period (Lollikhuse; Sørensen 1995, Fig. 2). The former all had a floor surface of c. 6 m in diameter, while the dimensions at Lollikhuse were c. 6 × 4 m. Well aware that possible dwellings at Vængesø III need *not necessarily* have been either of these dimensions or of these forms, this experiment shows that there was room on the settlement surface for at least three small "structures" or two larger ones. Consequently, it is interesting to see how a coincidence can be observed between the "theoretical floors" and terraces I and II. On grounds of size and topography, the three small structures could not have functioned at the same time, as there is an "overlap" between that in the middle and the two others. Conversely, the two other, slightly larger structures could well have stood on the plateau at the same time (without this necessarily having to be the case). Even though this is only an experiment, it does show that, in theory, there could have been several dwellings/floors of both sizes and forms on the settlement surface at the same time.

4.2.2 Hearths

Relative to other, contemporaneous Ertebølle settlements, Vængesø III is characterised by a large number of hearths within a limited area. In all, there were c. 15-20 features of this kind on the settlement surface. Two, perhaps three, types of feature have been demonstrated: Firstly, round, stone-built features made of fist-sized stones (five examples); secondly, round to elongate, domed heaps of reddish-brown/greyish-yellow ash with a little sand and clay and with small, grey, burnt shell fragments (13 examples) and a possible third type represented by a pit containing charcoal-rich sand and one or a few cooking stones. In order to distinguish clearly between stone-built hearths and possible heaps of discarded cooking stones (Fig. 116), it was decided to allow "regularity" and feature diameter to be the determinant criteria. In the following, stone-set hearths are defined as round, delimited concentrations of closely-spaced stones, with a diameter rarely exceeding 1 m. All other concentrations of cooking stones are classified as discarded hearth waste.

This is only the second time that an attempt has been made to classify the hearths of the Ertebølle culture (Sørensen 1993, 3-37, Fig. 4), possibly because attention has been focussed primarily on the artefacts and faunal remains from these settlements and only to a lesser degree on the feature types in themselves. Moreover, until a few years ago, occupation surfaces at Ertebølle settlements had neither been excavated nor published. Finally, hearths in particular were evaluated on the basis of their significance as *loci* for various settlement activities such as food preparation, flint-knapping etc. (Andersen/Johansen 1987, 46-47) and not as independent settlement features.

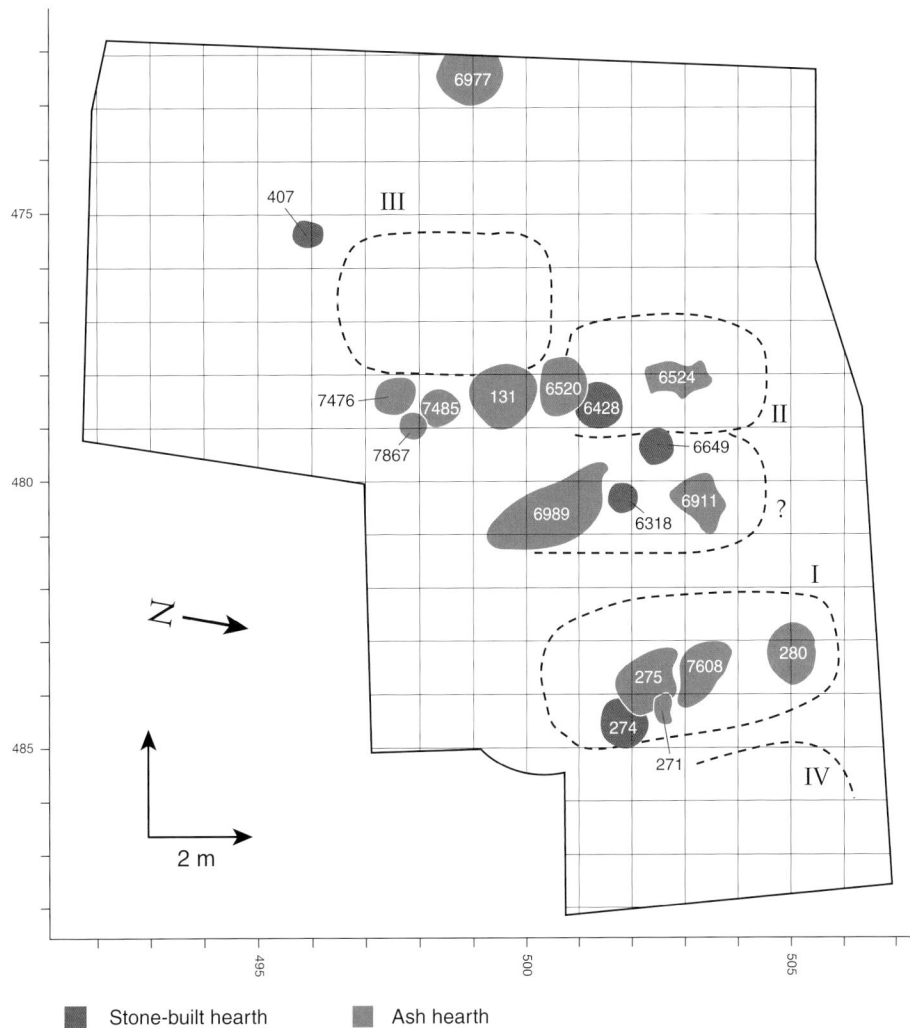

Fig. 101. Plan showing the location of the hearths on the settlement surface and in relation to the terraces. Grey: Ash hearths. Brown: Stone-set hearths. Pits containing charcoal and cooking stones, cf. Fig. 116.

The stone-built hearths at Vængesø correspond to Sørensen's type 1, the ash hearths to type 5 and the pit containing charcoal and cooking stones to type 4 (Sørensen 1993, 14, 16).

Within the excavated area, the grey-brown ash hearths lay in three north-south-oriented rows, roughly following the hillside in this direction, while the stone-built features were fewer in number and lay more dispersed across the plateau (Fig. 101). The ash hearths formed longitudinal rows along the central axes of terraces I and II, but not on terrace III. Both hearth types are well-known from other Ertebølle settlements, including the Ertebølle site itself (Madsen et al. 1900, 25-28; Andersen/Johansen 1987, 47-48), Norsminde (Andersen, S.H. 1991, 25), Bjørnsholm (Andersen, S.H. 1993, 73) and Lollikhuse (Sørensen 1995, 21, Fig. 2). From an overall perspective, the grey ash hearths are most common at settlements of the Ertebølle culture, and this was also the case at Vængesø III.

4.2.2.1 Stone-built hearths

Feature 274. Square 484/501-502. Round, stone-built, very regular hearth with a diameter of c. 70-80 cm. Unlike the other hearths of this type, this is the only example with both a level surface and consisting of one to two layers of stones. It lies on or within the top of the pre-midden layer and directly beneath a thin layer of oyster shells. This hearth appears to be stratigraphically earlier than (ash) hearth 275. The latter is wedged into hearth 274, such that it consists of two layers of stones at its western side, in contrast to only one layer at the eastern side.

Feature 6318. Square 480/501. Round, stone-built hearth with a diameter of c. 60 cm and consisting of 40 fist-sized stones, of which at least eight showed older cleavage surfaces (Fig. 102b). The feature lay at the bottom of the pre-midden layer in a small pit with a greasy, very charcoal-rich fill. The individual stones were up to 13 cm in diameter. The hearth was slightly pot-shaped and was c. 8 cm deeper in the middle than at the sides. The subsoil was slightly reddened in a c. 10 cm wide band around this feature. Of the 40 stones, 30 were of quartzite and ten of granite.

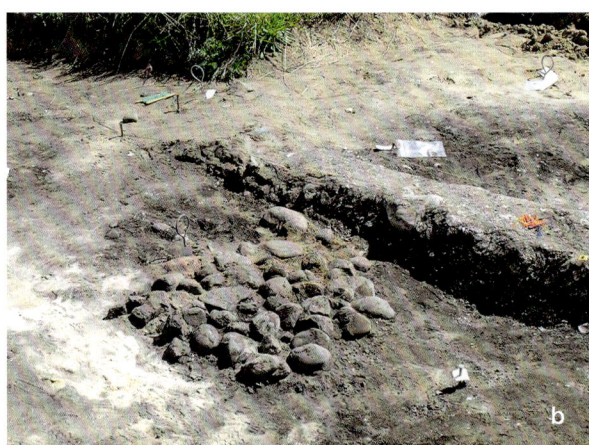

Fig. 102. a) Stone-set hearths 6649 and 6428. b) Stone-set hearth 6318. Photos: Nina Helt Nielsen.

Feature 6428. Square 478/501. Oval, stone-set hearth with a diameter of c. 70 × 85 cm. It was made up of 56 stones, in addition to which were c. 20 pieces of white-burnt flint of 8-13 cm in size, which lay in a single layer on top of the hearth stones (Fig. 103). Beneath the hearth there was reddened sand below a c. 5-7 cm thick layer of charcoal-rich sand. The hearth was stratigraphically older than ash hearth 7126, and it bordered ash hearth 7127. It lay on or in the top of the pre-midden layer and at a slightly higher level than stone-built hearth 6649.

Feature 6649. Square 479/502. Round, stone-set hearth in a pit which was covered by the pre-midden layer (Fig. 102a). Its diameter was c. 70-80 cm and it consisted of 31 stones of dimensions 8 × 8-13 × 13 cm. Of these, at least eight had older cleavage surfaces. In section, the feature was pot-shaped with a greatest depth in the middle of c. 5 cm. Beneath the stones was a c. 3-4 cm thick layer

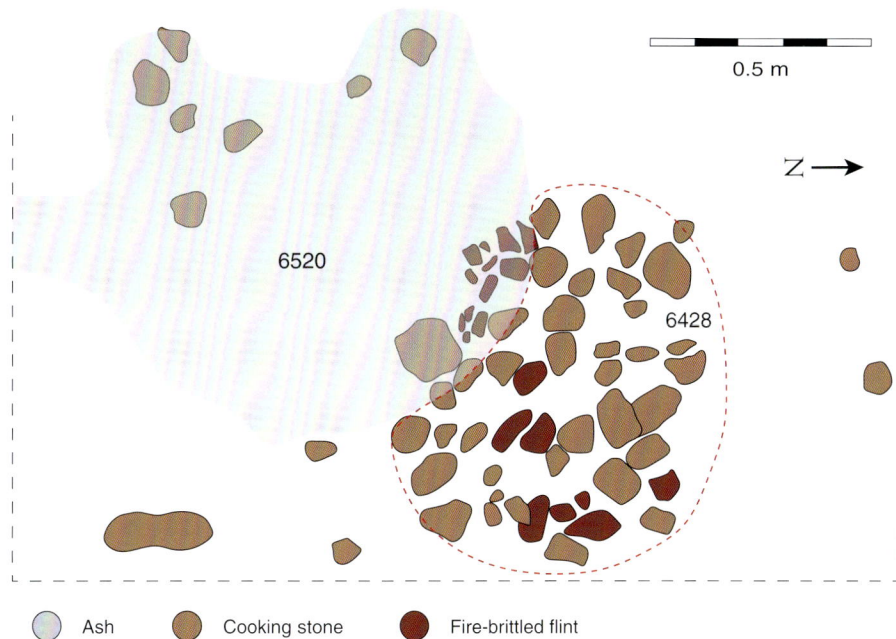

Fig. 103. Plan of stone-set hearth 6428 covered by ash hearth 6520. The white-burnt flint nodules uppermost in the hearth are marked in red. Drawing: Willy Hansen.

○ Ash   ● Cooking stone   ● Fire-brittled flint

6520

6428

0.5 m

z →

of sand containing scattered oyster shells, cockle shells and periwinkles. In the fill was a flint flake and a single fishbone. Of the 31 stones, 17 were of quartzite, nine of granite, four of gneiss and one of limestone.

Feature 407. Possibly the remains of a round, damaged hearth, marked by a semicircle of nine or ten heat-shattered stones and c. 50 cm in diameter. As this feature was disturbed and, moreover, lay in an area of the settlement characterised by particularly large numbers of cooking stones, it could represent a "chance" semicircular arrangement of stones at the base of the kitchen midden.

In addition to the well-defined hearths, it must also be assumed that many other features could have been reused, altered and partially robbed of stones that were subsequently used in other hearths.

All the stone-built hearths lay below the kitchen midden, i.e. either in the pre-midden layer or on the subsoil (Fig. 101). They were rounded or slightly oval, with a diameter of c. 60-80 cm and consisted of a single layer of closely-spaced, fist-sized and fire-affected stones. Two layers of stones were only evident at the sides of feature 274 in terrace I. Hearth 6428 also had an upper covering layer of white-burnt flint nodules (Fig. 103). This occurrence of flint in a hearth is very unusual and distinguishes this feature from all the others at Vængesø III.

Terrace I had a stone-set hearth at its eastern edge, a position which could perhaps suggest that the hearth post-dates the terrace. However, it could also be an indication that the two types of hearth were coeval, but had different functions. The three other stone-built hearths were either on terrace II or close by it (Fig. 101). As these three hearths lay very close together (less that 1 m apart), they can hardly have been in use at the same time. This conclusion is supported by a small difference in level between the features. With one exception, they have a slight but distinct depression in the middle, i.e. the surface appears a little pot-shaped (Fig. 104). Between the stones was black sand containing fine charcoal dust. On sectioning the features, it became evident that they all overlay pot-shaped pits containing a c. 3-4 cm thick layer of charcoal-rich sand, which were relatively clearly delimited downwards and peripherally. In two cases (6318 and 6428), there were reddened patches of subsoil beneath the features due to the effect of heat, but in both cases this effect was only weak.

Few cultural remains were found associated with the stone-built hearths. Large pieces of charcoal and accumulations of white-burnt flint were generally absent. Below stone-built hearth 274, at the edge of terrace I, there was however a small piece of calcined (white-burnt) human skull. In

Fig. 104. Section through a stone-set hearth. Below the stone layer is a shallow pit containing charcoal. Photo: Nina Helt Nielsen.

two cases, these features contained larger pieces of a pottery vessel, corresponding to observations at Ordrup Næs, where a pointed base was found jammed into a stone-set hearth (Becker 1939, 263). Similarly, two pointed bases were found standing in an ash hearth in the kitchen midden at Flynderhage in Norsminde Fjord, eastern Jutland (Andersen/Malmros 1985, 81-82, Fig. 4).

The types of stone used in one hearth comprised 17 pieces of quartzite, nine pieces of fine-grained granite, four pieces of gneiss and one piece of limestone. Another hearth contained 40 stones; 30 were of quartzite and ten of fine-grained granite. This small study shows that the types of stone chosen for these features were quite specific and that quartzite was the dominant type, followed by fine-grained granite.

On closer examination of the stones, it could be established in two cases (6318 and 6649) that there had been a degree of "recycling", i.e. that the stones had previously been heated (and thereby split). Recycling could be demonstrated because the stone fragments corresponding to the "old" cleavage surfaces were not present in the actual hearth, showing that they had been split while being used one or more times in another hearth. In some cases the stones had therefore a longer sequence of use at the settlement than would be otherwise assumed. The "recycling" of cooking stones in these hearths could be one of the explanations for the many scattered examples found in the culture layers.

The stone-built hearths at Vængesø III were slightly smaller than corresponding features in the Ertebølle shell midden and consequently contained fewer stones. In comparison, the two stone-set hearths found at Ertebølle measured 1.17 × 0.94 m (82 stones) and 1.6 × 1.15 m (126 stones; Madsen et al. 1900, 26). All the stone-built hearths at Vængesø III must, as already stated, have belonged to the earliest phase of the settlement. This conclusion is consistent with the observations at other Ertebølle kitchen middens, for example at Ertebølle (Madsen et al. 1900, 25-28, Fig. between pp. 26-27; Andersen/Johansen 1987, 47-48).

4.2.2.2 Ash hearths

Feature 131. Square 478/499. Round hearth with a clearly domed surface, the top of which was 15 cm above the surrounding surface, and its diameter was c. 1.2 m. It consisted of four layers (layers 3, 4a, 5 and 4b) – respectively two brown-grey ash layers (layers 4a and 4b), separated by a blackish-brown layer (layer 5), and terminating upwards in yet another thin, black ash layer (layer 3; Figs. 105, 109). The hearth lay on top of the pre-midden layer and was characterised by eight cooking stones located at its northern edge, where there were also several large solitary oyster shells.

Feature 271. Square 484/502. Elongated (east-west-oriented) hearth on terrace I, which measured 75 × 40 cm, and probably represented part of feature 275. The stratigraphic relationship between 271 and 275 is unclear and there was a similar uncertainty with respect to the relationship between feature 271 and stone-set hearth 274.

Feature 275. Square 483-484/501-502. Rounded-oval hearth, reddish-brown/yellowish-brown in colour, located on the central axis of terrace I. It measured 1.5 × 1.3 m. To the north, it bounded hearth 7608 and to the east, hearth 271 and stone-set hearth 274.

Feature 280. Square 483/504-505. Rounded-oval (east-west) hearth which measured 1.5 × 1.1 m and consisted of a c. 4 cm thick body of red-brown ash. It lay on the central axis of the northern end of terrace I and in extension of feature 7608, though with a gap of c. 50-60 cm.

Feature 6520. Square 478/500-501. Round hearth which measured 0.95 × 1.15 m and was irregular with numerous fist-sized stones along its southern edge. The ash contained numerous fishbones and at the southwestern edge of the hearth there was a c. 12 × 15 cm area with abundant flint splinters and flakes (flint-knapping site). It bounded stone-set hearth 6428.

Feature 6524. Square 478/502-503. Subrectangular, sandy hearth which measured 1.2 × 0.85 m and 14 cm in thickness. At its northern edge there was clear reddening of the subsoil sand, and five or six cooking stones lay close to or on its boundary. The ash contained numerous flint splinters and shell fragments.

Feature 6977. Square 472/498-499. Round hearth with a diameter of 1.2 m and a core with a diameter of c. 0.6 m. Uppermost was a 5 cm thick, light-brown, clay-rich layer containing a small amount of comminuted shell and occasional oyster shells. Below this was a c. 30 cm thick, black, charcoal-rich layer containing isolated oyster shells, followed by a 10 cm thick layer of light-brown ash. The overall thickness of the feature was 16 cm. The hearth rested directly on the subsoil, which was reddened.

Feature 6989. Square 480/500-501. Hearth consisting of a 2 cm thick, reddish-brown ash layer (Fig. 106).

Feature 6911. Square 480/503. Hearth consisting of a 2-4 cm thick, yellowish-brown ash layer with occasional flint splinters and fishbones.

Feature 7476. Square 478/497. Margin of an ash hearth which measured 50 × 15 cm (minimum dimensions). The hearth sloped, as it followed the northerly incline of the shell layer on the southern part of terrace II. Mass of fine, reddish-brown ash with shell fragments, some of which were burnt. Around the reddish-brown area was a 20 cm wide band of black-grey ash. Located in the kitchen midden layer.

Feature 7485. Square 478/498. Hearth, which measured 50 cm in diameter and consisted of fine, reddish-brown ash with burnt shell fragments. It lay at a slightly lower level than feature 7476.

Feature 7608. Square 483/503. Hearth on the central axis of terrace I. It was round, reddish-

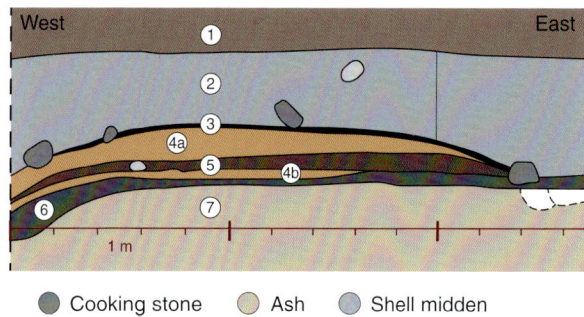

Fig. 105. Section drawing of the south face of squares 478-479/499, through ash-rich hearth 131, which was the settlement's largest and thickest. 1 Brown, sandy soil (plough soil). 2 Slightly sandy kitchen midden dominated by oyster shells and comminuted shell, worked flint (-O and -R), charcoal, animal bones (especially fishbones), a little pottery and scattered cooking stones, a few cockles, pullet carpet shells and periwinkles. Scattered small stones (less that 3-4 cm). 3 About 2 cm thick charcoal-rich ash layer. 4a-b Light-yellow/light-brown ash layer with scattered oyster shells and shell fragments that are heat/fire-affected. 5 Dark-brown/black sandy ash layer containing abundant flint debitage. 6 Black-grey sandy layer characterised by animal burrows, within which are shell fragments. 7 Light-yellow, fine sand (subsoil).

brown and measured 1.2 × 1.4 m; there was more sand towards the edges. To the south it bordered hearth 275. In the fill of this feature lay a fire-brittled core axe, some fire-brittled flint flakes and a small piece of burnt antler.

Feature 7867. Square 478/497-498. Area with yellowish-grey ash, which measured 50-75 cm in diameter and was 3 cm thick. It was located between 7476 and 7485. Interpreted as cleared-out hearth material.

There were in all about 13 features, but it is difficult to give a precise number as several lay so close together that it was difficult to delimit one from the other (Fig. 101). Sørensen uses the term "clay-rich" in reference to hearths of type 5 (ash hearths) and states that they could have been renewed several times and may contain scattered cooking stones (Sørensen 1993, 16). This corresponds fully to observations at

Vængesø III, where the features consisted of ash and had at their centre a grey/yellowish-brown core, surrounded by an up to 30 cm wide, blackish-brown periphery. In many cases, small pieces of grey-burnt shells could be observed – often of mussels and periwinkle. The composition of the hearths varied, with a lesser or greater sand content, but the main component was fine, pulverised grey ash, derived from burnt shells, together with a little sand and clay. The hearth ash readily took up moisture from the surroundings and thereby attained a greasy, clay-like consistency. In the first phase of the excavation, this was interpreted in terms of these hearths being comprised of clay. A sample from an ash hearth was treated with hydrochloric acid, which revealed that the ash consisted primarily of chalk/lime and a little sand. This test showed that the features result primarily from the gradual accumulation of ash derived from large quantities of burnt mollusc shells. Most of these hearths were round in outline, but could also be subrectangular or irregular. Their sizes ranged from 50 × 30 cm to 1.5 × 1.3 m and they were generally shallow features, with a thickness of only c. 1-3 cm. In two cases they were though considerably thicker, 15-16 cm (131 and 6977). The largest hearths of this type measured about 1-1.5 m in diameter and were domed in cross-section with the highest point at the centre. In two cases (the

Fig. 106. Section through ash-rich hearth 6989. Photo: Nina Helt Nielsen.

largest and thickest), stratification was evident in the form of differences in colour, density and charcoal content. Five layers could be identified in the largest hearth (Fig. 105); probably an indication that this was in use over a longer period. Beneath the hearths, the subsoil was almost always reddened in the same way as seen in some of the stone-set features (Fig. 111b). At Vængesø III, the ash hearths were often located close to the stone-set hearths, and the two types could possibly have had related but different functions. Almost all the ash hearths lay directly on the surface of the subsoil and as a consequence nothing can be said of their relative ages.

Fig. 107. The western edge of hearth 131, cf. layer 4b on Fig. 105. Photo: Nina Helt Nielsen.

In general, there were usually whole mollusc shells present in the ash hearths, as well as shell fragments, burnt shell mass and charcoal dust. There were also occasional bones – especially fishbones. Conversely, very few or no tools were found in the actual hearths. The scattered finds lay particularly at the base of the features, i.e. at the transition from the subsoil. In one instance, a small fire-brittled core axe lay at the base of one of these hearths. Most of the finds, and concentrations of finds – flint debitage from tool production, fishbones and a few burnt bird and mammal bones – were found at the edge of these hearths. The flint debitage shows that flint-knapping regularly took place in the vicinity (Fig. 108). Similarly, a charred hazelnut shell (*Corylus avellana*) was found in an

ash hearth, but as there was only a single nutshell, this is unlikely to represent evidence for the regular roasting of hazelnuts on the hearth. It more probably represents the remains from a meal which ended up there by chance. This corresponds to observations from other published Ertebølle settlements, where tools have only exceptionally been found in features of this type. Another characteristic was that a few scattered, fist-sized cooking stones were often found at their margin (Fig. 109). These finds circumstances give the impression that the cooking stones had a function associated with the hearth. They were heated with the intention of being used either on this hearth or somewhere else in the vicinity. The two largest hearths of this type (6977 and 131) had a similar stratigraphy, with

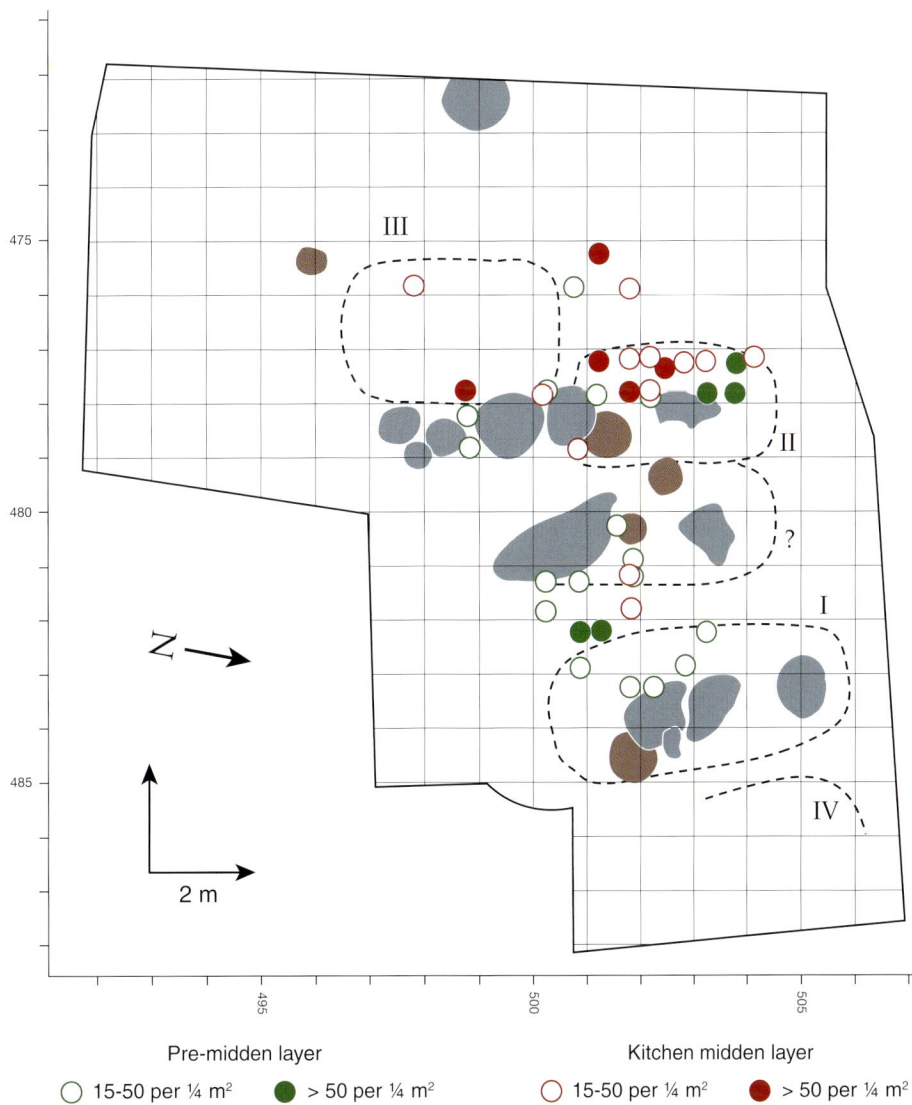

Fig. 108. Distribution of small well-defined flint-knapping areas with flint debitage in the kitchen midden and pre-midden layer. They lie, in particular, along the western edge of the hearths – especially in terrace II. These concentrations of debitage are a clear indication that flint-knapping took place close to the hearths – a feature also observed at Holme-gaard, cf. Fig. 181 AN.

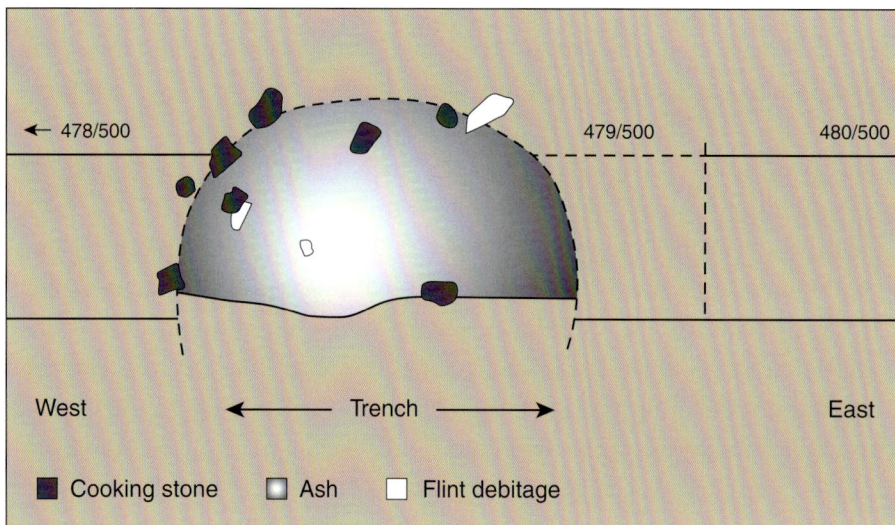

Fig. 109. Outline of ash hearth 131 with scattered cooking stones at its margin. cf. Fig. 105.

a black, charcoal-rich layer in the middle of the ash. In two cases, the ash hearths formed a stratigraphic sequence: No differences could be observed between the ash hearths in the kitchen midden and those in the pre-midden layer. In conclusion, it should be pointed out that there is a great similarity between these features and the hearths that, in several cases, have been found at the stern of the contemporaneous dug-out boats (Andersen, S.H. 2013, 189, Fig. 3.90).

Between hearths 131 and 7485 there was a 10-12 cm thick, black, sandy layer containing two larger stones, which measured 8 × 8 cm and 16 × 16 cm, respectively. In the same area was also a pit that measured c. 20 × 30 cm. The pit fill, which consisted of black, charcoal-rich sand, contained three cooking stones. This pit could represent a special type of hearth. Finally, on the western edge of ash hearth 280, there was a round pit with a black, charcoal-rich fill. This measured 30 cm in diameter and was 10 cm deep. It is possible that several of the larger pits could also belong to this type of hearth (Sørensen 1993, 16, Type 4; Figs. 116-117).

In several cases, smaller patches of the above-mentioned type of ash were encountered; these measured c. 10 × 10 cm and had a thickness of 1-1.5 cm. These areas could not be confidently interpreted as independent features – they were more probably the remains of either damaged or rebuilt hearths.

4.2.2.3 Discussion

The main differences between the stone-built and the ash hearths related to the occurrence of ash and cultural remains. The stone-built hearths contained much greater quantities of charcoal and charcoal dust than the grey ash hearths. Conversely, the grey ash was never found in the stone-built hearths. One explanation could be that the stone-built hearths had been used less intensely than the grey ash hearths, or perhaps that the ash had been removed from the stone-built hearths (in order to be able to use the heat from the stones again and again). Finally, the two hearth types could have had related, but different, functions. While all the observations indicate that the ash hearths actually were hearths, the situation is slightly less certain with respect to the stone-built features. Their construction and stratigraphy, which differ from those of the ash-hearth features, suggest they had another function. Another difference between the two feature types is that the subsoil was reddened below the stone-set hearths in only a few cases, while this was the norm in the case of the ash hearths. Moreover, there were no concentrations of fishbones and/or waste from flint-knapping at the edge of the stone-set features (as was the case with the other group of hearths). Neither was there any fire-brittled flint by or around the stone-built features. This situation appears to be much more general, because it has also been observed and mentioned previously in descriptions of hearths at the Ertebølle settlement of Lollikhuse by Roskilde Fjord (Sørensen 1993, 17). In two cases, an ash hearth (275) lay on top of a stone-built feature (274 and 6520 on 6428; Figs. 103, 110). This stratigraphic succession between the two types of hearth is quite common on Jutland's kitchen middens, for example Ertebølle (*locus classicus*; Madsen et al. 1900, 26), Norsminde (Andersen, S.H. 1991, 25) and Havnø (Andersen, S.H. 2008).

It is difficult to give an explanation for why the ash hearths at Vængesø III in several cases lie in rows and follow the central axis of the terraces. Do they represent one elongated and coeval hearth or do the observations reflect a successive series of hearths that have merely been displaced slightly relative to each other over a period of time? The observations during the excavation and the many, partially discrete features with traces of flint-knapping at the edge of the hearths suggest that there was not one, but rather several, successive features.

The location of the hearths on the settlement surface shows that the latter was divided up functionally. As the majority of these hearths lie so close together on the settlement surface, this has unfortunately resulted in the original activity traces present around and in the vicinity of these features becoming "blurred" or erased by later features and activities. There are several examples of how these two types of hearth lay very close to each other, for example on the best-preserved terrace I, where the stone-set hearth 274 lay below the ash hearth 275. The same applies to stone-built hearth 6428 and ash hearth 6520. Similar observations have not been published previously.

This situation could have arisen by chance, but the observed situation could perhaps also mean that they were in use at the same time, but for different activities. The fact that the two hearth types must have had a related function is also apparent from the fact that, in some cases, as described above, the ash hearths overlay the stone-built features. Where this was the case, it shows maintenance of hearth functions on the same spot on the settlement surface. From a wider perspective, there are two further differences it is important to

Fig. 110. Hearth 274 (stone-set) and ash hearth 275 at the southern end of terrace I. The ash hearth originally lay partially over the stone-set hearth. Photo: Nina Helt Nielsen.

be aware of: The number of stone-built features on the settlements is always significantly less than the number of ash hearths and, furthermore, the stone-built hearths are found almost exclusively at the base of, or deep in, the culture layers.

The conclusion reached here is that the ash and the stone-set features each represent hearths, but with different functions. Preparation of fish frequently took place by the ash hearths, as did knapping of flint. These kinds of activities were not demonstrated in association with the stone-built hearths, which more probably had a function (or functions) that required significantly greater and more long-lasting heat than the ash hearths; for example cooking, perhaps involving the processing of mollusc meat. Finally, it should be mentioned that several ethno-archaeological investigations show that indoor hearths are spatially restricted, while this is not often the case for corresponding outdoor features. At the same time, their area increases as a function of the duration of the occupation (Binford 1983, 138). If these circumstances are applied to the settlement surface at Vængesø III, they suggest that the ash hearths were located inside dwellings or perhaps under some form of cover. The fact that the hearths were used repeatedly and in approximately the same place can be explained by them being of a more permanent character on the settlement surface and by the work and effort that was

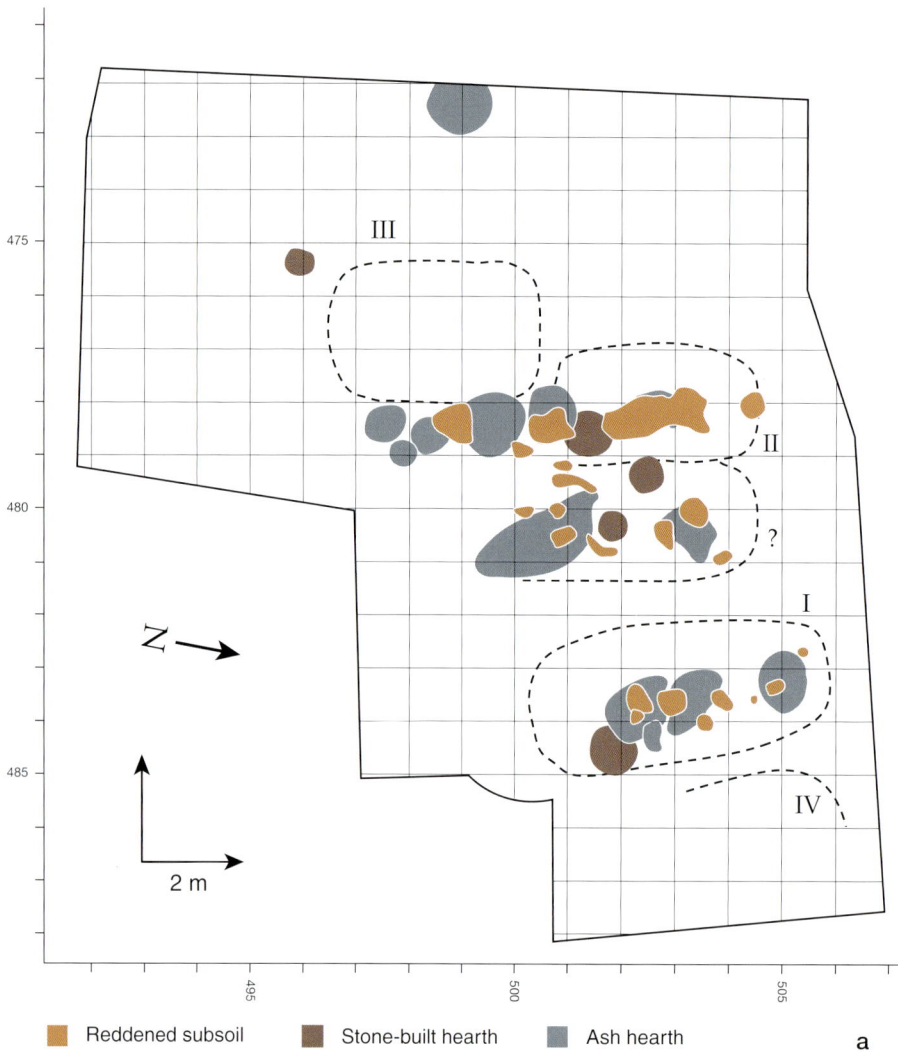

Fig. 111. a) Areas of reddened subsoil. Note how these form extended rows in terraces I and II. b) Section through an ash hearth and the reddened subsoil below. Photo: Søren H. Andersen.

Reddened subsoil ■ **Stone-built hearth** ■ **Ash hearth**

a

b

invested from the beginning in the construction of the terraces (digging and possibly building of a superstructure etc.). On subsequent visits, the terraces provided the most suitable working platforms on the sloping settlement surface.

As described above, the subsoil associated with the ash hearths was always reddened due to the effects of the heat (Fig. 111). In only one or two cases were the reddened areas not located directly beneath an ash hearth. The largest and most numerous reddened areas lay on or close to terrace II, while there were fewer examples and of smaller size on terrace I (and none at all on terrace III; Fig. 111). In contrast, there was only one instance of a small reddened border associated with a stone-set hearth (Fig. 104). This difference must mean that heat from the ash hearths could more easily effect the subsoil than was the case with the stone-set features. In turn, this suggests that the stone layer had, to some degree, a heat-insulating effect in these structures. In order to investigate this reddening of the surface of the subsoil, experiments were carried out which involved heating samples of sand from the settlement area. These showed that reddening occurs at temperatures above c. 600-700°C. It also became apparent that the stone-built hearths reached higher temperatures and – perhaps more importantly – retained these for a longer period than the ash hearths (Andersen/Kannegaard 2013, 3-7; Canti/ Linford 2000, 392f.). The places with reddened subsoil sand therefore most probably represent the effects of intense, local heating on the sand. In the few cases where the reddened areas were not in direct contact with or located beneath a hearth, these must be interpreted as traces of hearths which had subsequently been removed. One of these areas measured 48 × 50 cm and the other 40 × 60 cm. In the ash were numerous flint splinters, periwinkle shells and shell fragments, some of which were burnt. Uppermost in the ash layer there was a single cooking stone. Finally, there was an irregular clay-rich, reddened area which measured 1 × 1.2 m.

In general, heat-affected flint was common at Vængesø III and it occurred everywhere across the settlement surface in both the kitchen midden and the pre-midden layer. The greatest occurrence was seen particularly to the west and southwest of the ash hearths (Fig. 112). Concentrations of burnt flint have also been observed in association with kitchen middens on Zealand (Sørensen 1993, 17). On terrace I at Vængesø III, the burnt flint lay in particular in the southern parts of the feature, while on terrace II there was fire-brittled flint to the west and south of the hearths (Fig. 111). The fact that burnt flint was so widespread is unsurprising given the number of hearths present. Burnt flint was abundant on terrace III and along its eastern edge, alongside the row of ash hearths located here. In the kitchen midden, the burnt flint extended further to the south/southwest across the surface, as much as c. 2-3 m away from the terrace (Fig. 112). Burnt flint constitutes 3.3-3.5% of the entire finds assemblage, i.e. more or less the same proportion as at Vængesø I (Ch. 2.3.1.1). Even though no distinction was made in the analysis between the various degrees of fire-brittling (Fischer et al. 1979, 22; Sergent at al. 2006), it must be presumed that the great majority of the flint recorded as being burnt was of the white-burnt type. In general, the quantity of burnt flint appears to have been greater than at most other contemporaneous settlements. As a significant proportion of the fire-brittled flint is white-burnt, this can be taken as an indication of the high occupation intensity at Vængesø III, as flint must be exposed to heat for a longer time in order for it to acquire this white-burnt character (Pedersen, K.B. 2009, 122).

4.2.3 Large stones

This term was applied to unworked stones larger than c. 10 × 10 cm. In three cases, stones of this type lay in the pre-midden layer. They were oval in shape and in two cases measured c. 35 × 20 cm. The third stone was found at the edge of the pit in square 479/497 and measured c. 30 × 23 cm. None of these stones formed part of an identifiable feature or structure, as they lay without any apparent pattern. Neither were they surrounded by a characteristic concentration of finds which could suggest that they had been used in connection with particular settlement activities, for example

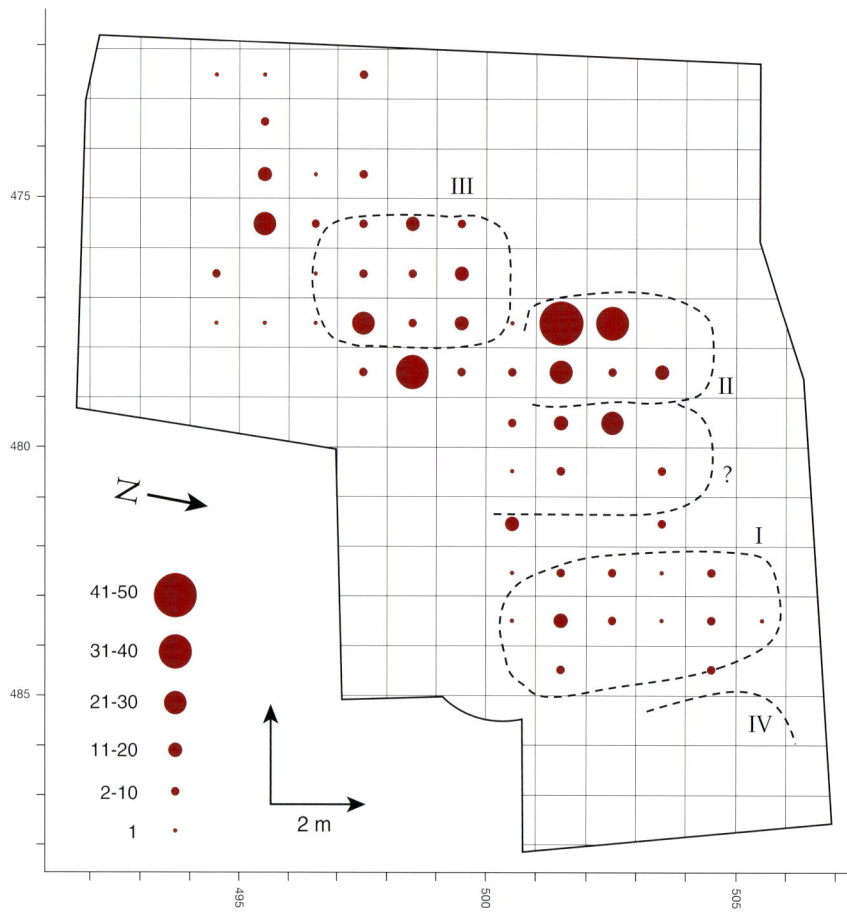

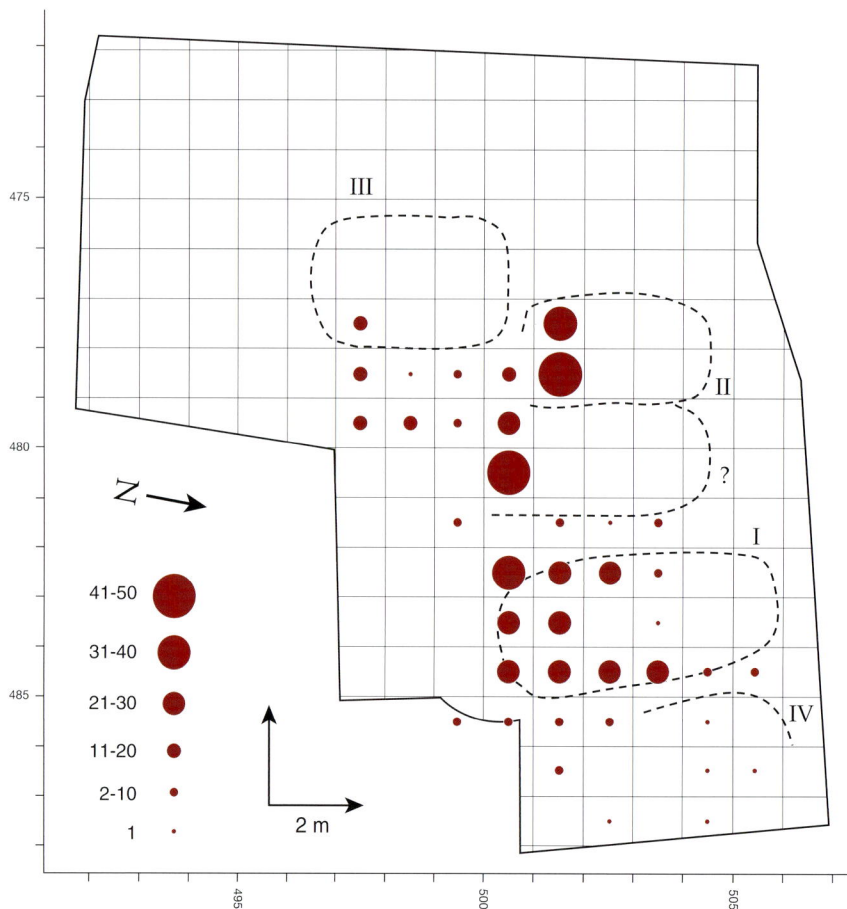

Fig. 112. a) Distribution of burnt flint in the kitchen midden and in the pre-midden layer. There is a concentration on terrace II. b) Distribution of burnt flint in the pre-midden layer with concentrations on terraces I and II.

flint-knapping, as was seen at Ertebølle (Andersen/Johansen 1987, 37-39, Figs. 5-6). It is possible, however, that these stones had a function in association with the occupation, for example as "furniture".

4.2.4 Postholes

Dark-coloured features interpreted as postholes were encountered in eight places on the excavation surface. These were all round-oval in outline and lay on the periphery of the large hollow, but unfortunately without forming any identifiable system or pattern (Fig. 89). It is not certain that they are coeval or that they were associated with one or more of the terraces. They measured 18-45 cm in diameter, were round-bottomed and had a depth of 7-26 cm. They contained a charcoal-rich, sandy fill, but unfortunately no date-conferring finds. They differed from the many other small features distrib-

uted across the excavated area, the size and form of which in the great majority of cases indicated that they were either traces of tree roots or animal burrows. Even though the postholes were smaller, more regularly rounded and round-bottomed, there was though a gradual transition to the "pits" evident on the settlement surface. The postholes could not be dated more closely than that they were contemporaneous with the Late Ertebølle culture.

4.2.5 Patches of subsoil

In four cases, small, clearly delimited areas ("patches") of yellowish-brown, sandy clay were encountered on top of the pre-midden layer and only found in association with this layer (Fig. 113). These were round or elongate in outline, measured c. 30 × 40 cm and were rarely more than 5 cm thick. Due to their different colour and consistency

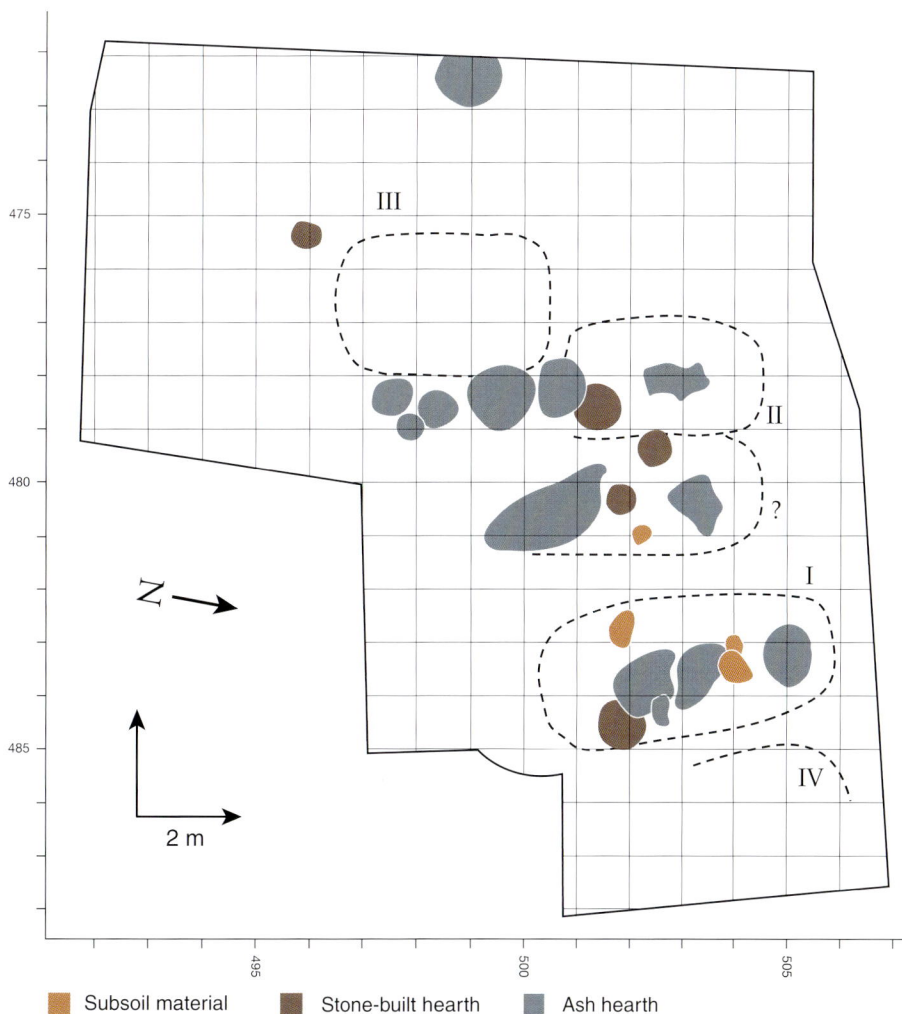

Fig. 113. The settlement surface showing the places where there are "patches" of subsoil material on top of the pre-midden layer – especially on terrace I. These small deposits most probably result from digging out small pits and/or postholes, which were not, however, observed or recorded during the excavation.

Subsoil material   Stone-built hearth   Ash hearth

relative to the black pre-midden layer, they were easy to identify and delimit. They were generally without finds, or almost so, but in one case did contain fish remains. This type of "feature" was identified in three cases on terrace I, and in one case directly to the west of this feature (Fig. 113). With the exception of terrace I, where there were two patches close to hearths, the other examples showed no clear associations with other forms of features across the settlement surface. The interpretation of these features is uncertain, but their occurrence by the hearths on terrace I and their content of fishbones could suggest that they were involved in some way in food production. In this respect, it should be pointed out that one square contained a body of yellowish-brown, clay-rich sand, measuring c. 45 × 20 cm and 10 cm in thickness, which was densely packed with fishbones.

4.2.6 Concentrations of fishbones

Large numbers of fishbones were evident everywhere in the cultural deposits, but at varying concentrations. In the kitchen midden, the fish remains were always found as small, discrete concentrations which measured c. 10-30 × 10-20 cm (Fig. 114). Conversely, the underlying pre-midden layer also contained actual "fish-bone layers", which could be up to 5 cm in thickness. The concentrations of fish remains were so great in the pre-midden layer that fishbones and scales were found stuck to a significant proportion of the worked flint. The greatest concentration of fish remains was found in the northeastern part of the excavation area, i.e. extending from the plateau down the slope towards the former shore (and terrace I). Here, it was possible to identify an actual layer of fishbones at the transition between the pre-midden layer and the

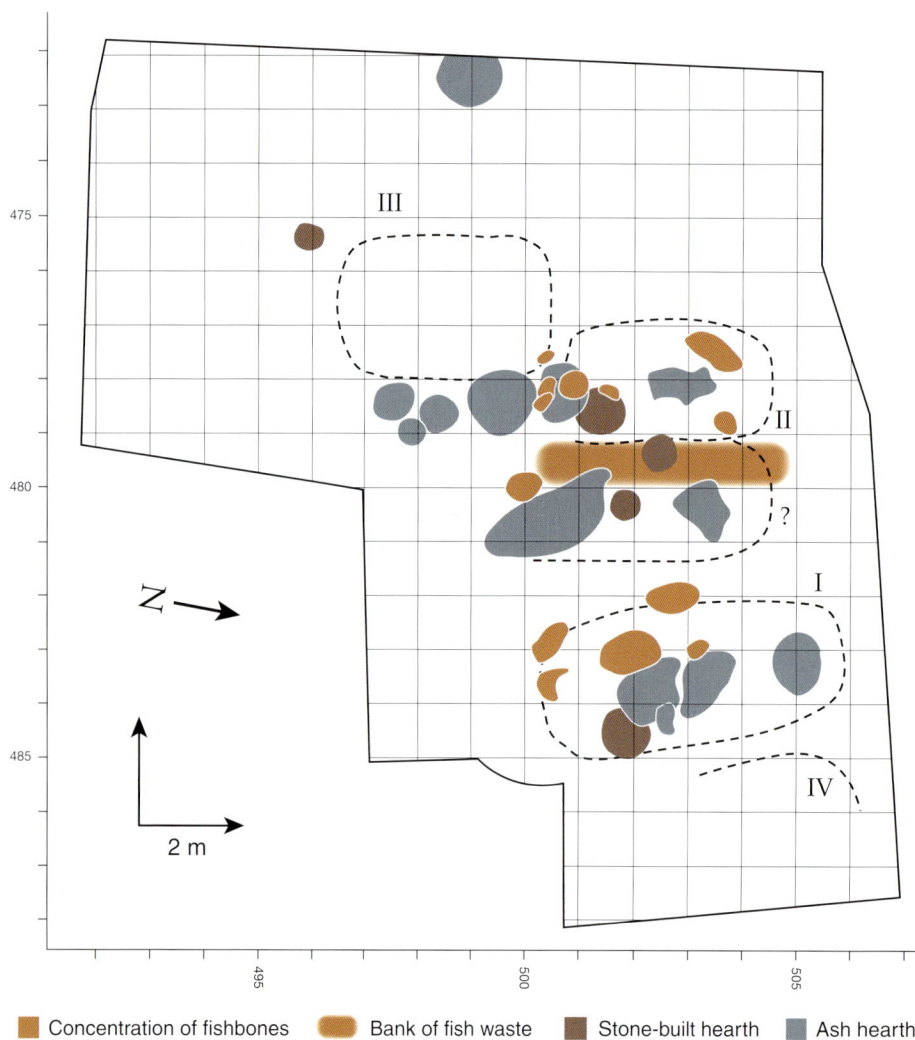

Fig. 114. Fishbones were found in all excavation units and layers. The illustration shows locations of particularly high concentrations of fishbones in the pre-midden layer. These lay especially along the western margin of the ash-rich hearths. The "bank" of fish waste running north-south between terraces I and II is also indicated. This bank could represent a "dump area" in front of terrace II.

Concentration of fishbones   Bank of fish waste   Stone-built hearth   Ash hearth overlying kitchen midden. This occurrence of fish waste on the settlement surface reflects perhaps that food waste etc. either slipped or was thrown down (perhaps both) the hillside from the settlement area up on the plateau. But it could also result from the cleaning of fish down on the shore. An uneven occurrence of fish waste across the settlement surface is a well-known phenomenon seen at many kitchen midden sites, as shown by observations at Norsminde (Andersen, S.H. 1991, 21, 26, Fig. 8b) and Ertebølle (Andersen/Johansen 1987, 46-47, Fig. 12).

In a few places, the amount of fish waste was particularly great. This was true of a semicircular area directly adjacent to and west of hearths 6524 and 6520 and hearths 7608 and 275 (Fig. 114). Further to this was a 1.2 m wide bank of fishbones and cultural remains in excavation strip 479. Then there was a thin but compact layer of fishbones above the heap of cockle shells found by hearth 131. Finally, it should be pointed out that similar discrete layers containing fishbones were observed in several places in sections in the southern part of the settlement during the initial trial excavations.

4.2.7 Slaughtering and butchering/skinning sites

During analysis of the faunal remains, it was discovered that the bones of a particular species often lay in discrete "heaps", both in the kitchen midden and in the pre-midden layer (Fig. 115). This was true of remains of pine marten (*Martes martes*), of which a heap was found containing parts of at least four animals (Enghoff 2011, 170-172), badger (*Meles meles*), juvenile dog (puppy; *Canis familiaris*) and seal (*Phoca* sp.). Cut marks on the bones show that these animals were slaughtered and skinned in particular areas of the settlement, for example directly east of and on terrace II, on the southern part of terrace III and directly to the east of this. Conversely, there was no clear evidence of this type of behaviour around terrace I. Traces of the slaughtering/skinning of particular prey animals, in the form of heaps of bones, have been found at numerous Ertebølle settlements in recent decades, for example Ring-

kloster (Andersen, S.H. 1975a, 84; Rowley-Conwy 1998, 95-96), Tybrind Vig (Trolle Lassen 1986, 123, Fig. 3; Andersen, S.H. 2013, 69-70, Fig. 1.35) and Agernæs (Richter/Noe-Nygaard 2003, 24, 40, Fig. 28). But while the finds at these various Ertebølle settlements were all located in the settlements' offshore refuse/dump areas, the slaughtering waste at Vængesø III derives from a dry surface – from the actual slaughtering site on the settlement area.

4.2.8 Cooking stones

Cooking stones were found in both the kitchen midden and the pre-midden layer, but in varying quantities and concentrations, from five to 15 examples per m². In the kitchen midden, they lay singly and scattered, while they were considerably more abundant in the pre-midden layer. Here, the concentration reached 10-15 examples per m², especially on terrace III to the south and southwest, but without any indication of the existence of a cohesive stone pavement. One explanation for the many cooking stones found in this particular feature could be that it functioned as a refuse area for worn-out cooking stones resulting from the activities that took place on terrace II and on the settlement surface. There was a row of fist-sized stones in squares 475-476/499, by hearth 131. The abundant cooking stones could either represent domestic refuse or the remains of demolished, stone-set hearths (possibly a mixture of the two). As mentioned previously in relation to the stone-set hearths, in at least two cases it could be established that a proportion of the stones found in the hearths represented "recycling". This shows that the cooking stones at the settlement had a dynamic "life cycle" with several periods of use.

4.2.9 Pits

Five pits were found during the excavation (Fig. 116). These were round or elongate in outline and had a pot-shaped base. Their length and width measurements varied between 35 and 140 cm and their depth was between 5 and 25 cm. The pits on terraces I and II were closely associated with a

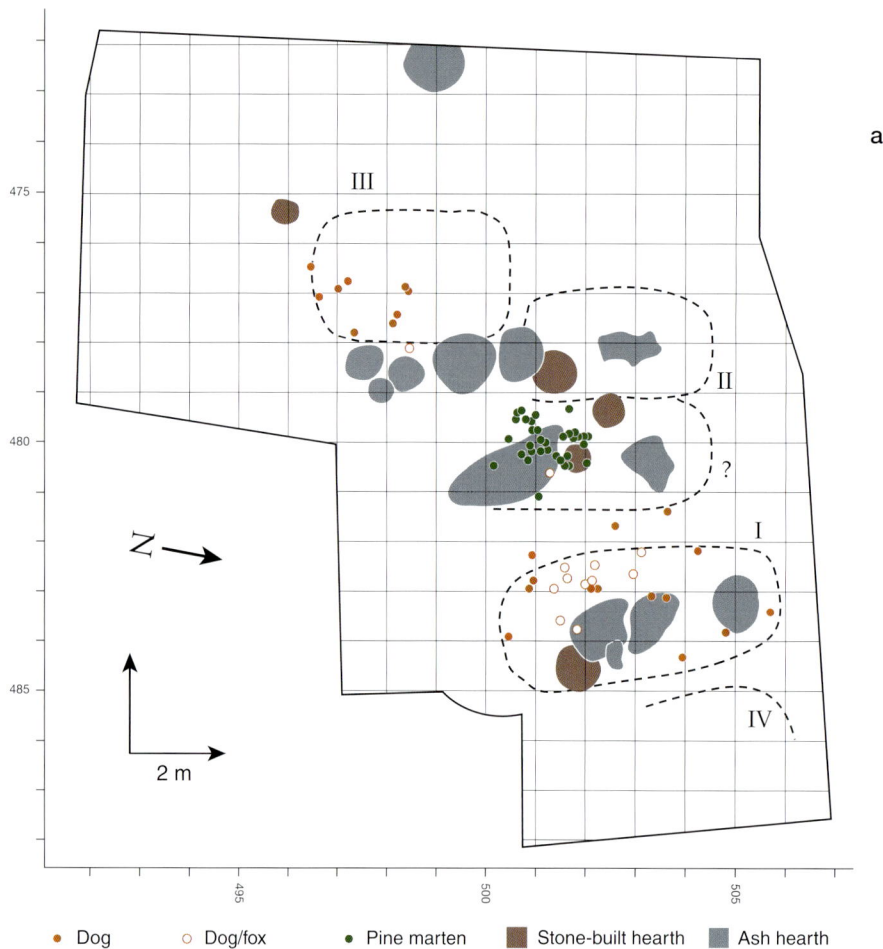

a

| ● Dog | ○ Dog/fox | ● Pine marten | ■ Stone-built hearth | ■ Ash hearth |

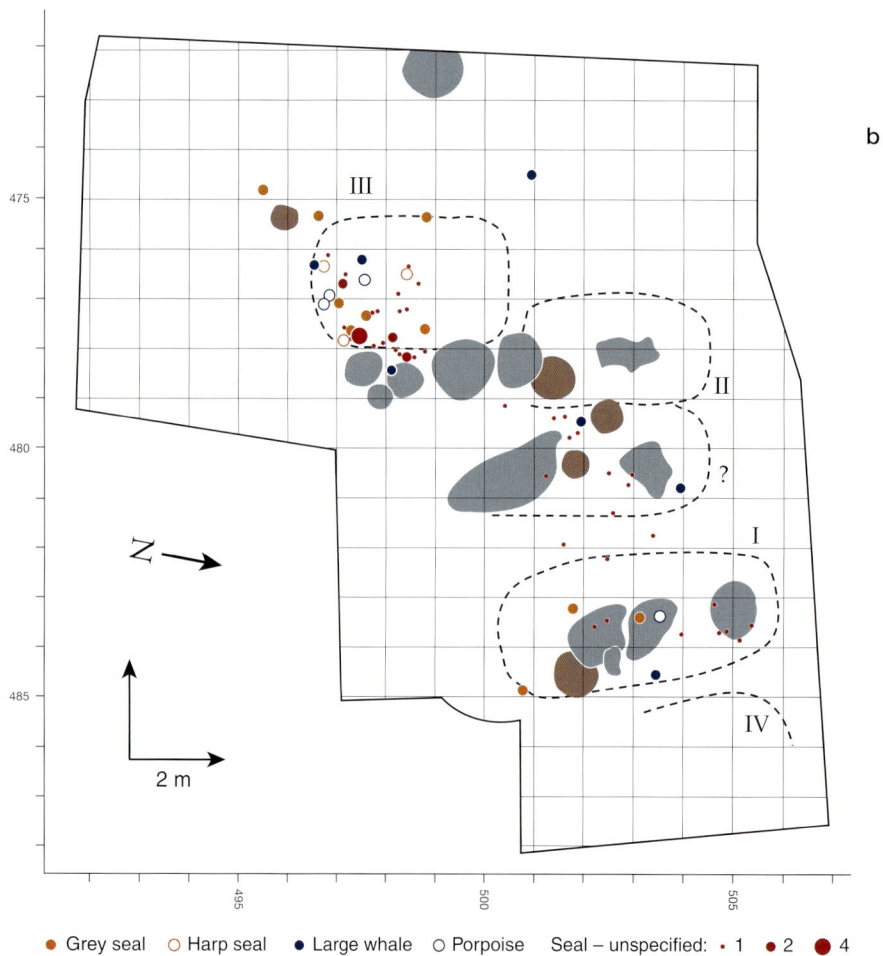

b

Fig. 115. a) Distribution of bones of dog, dog/fox and pine marten, which in several instances formed distinct concentrations (slaughtering sites). b) Seal (unspecified), grey seal, harp seal, large whale and porpoise. These bones were found, in particular, on the southern part of terrace III. Drawings: Nina Helt Nielsen.

| ● Grey seal | ○ Harp seal | ● Large whale | ○ Porpoise | Seal – unspecified: · 1 ● 2 ● 4 |

hearth (Fig. 116). In the other cases were no clear connections between the pit and other features. The pits had a charcoal-rich fill containing one to three scattered cooking stones. The largest pit measured 140 × 70 cm and had a black, charcoal-rich fill with abundant periwinkle shells. The fill also contained numerous flint flakes and splinters, of which some were fire-brittled. On the south-eastern edge of the pit there was a further round, c. 20 cm diameter and 5 cm deep, feature with a

brownish-black, humus-rich fill with no shells – possibly a posthole. Apart from its size, pit 6437 also clearly differed from the other pits due to its content of flint debitage. Flint-knapping apparently took place somewhere in the vicinity, after which the debitage etc. was put into the pit. In square 479/497 there was a c. 35 × 20 cm pot-shaped pit with a black, charcoal-rich sandy fill containing three fist-sized cooking stones. At the edge of the pit lay a large stone, which measured 30 × 23

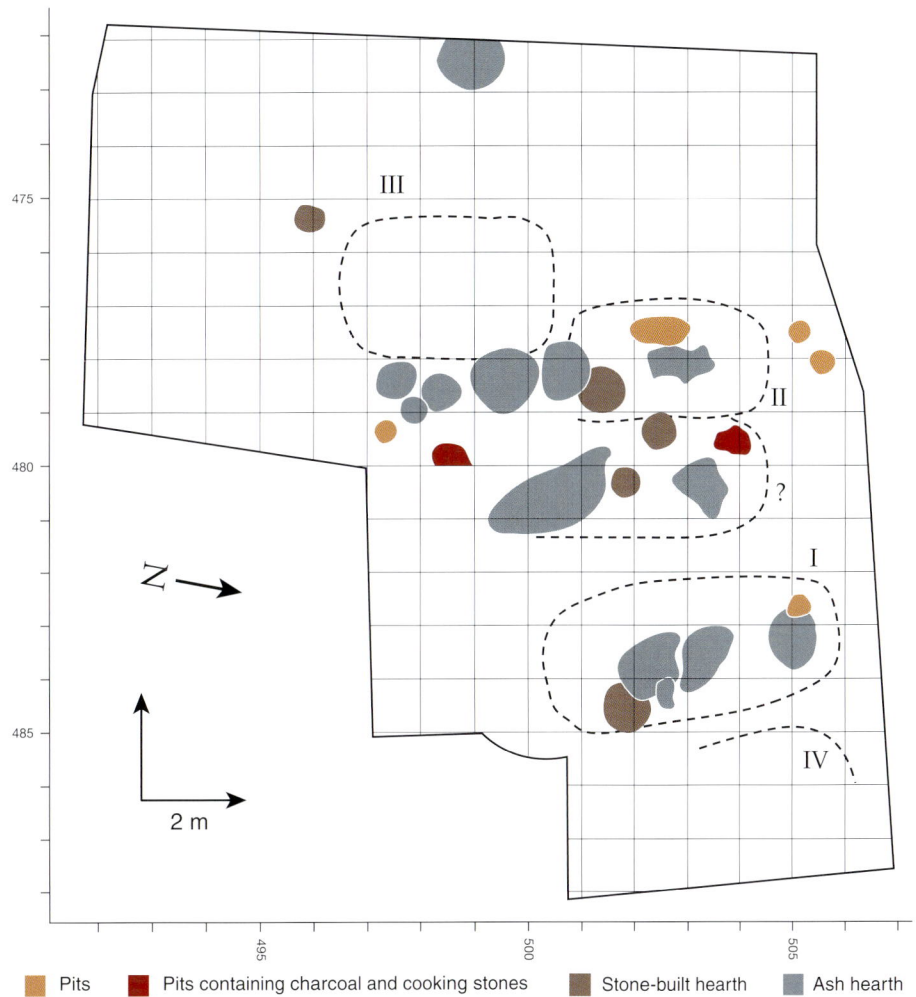

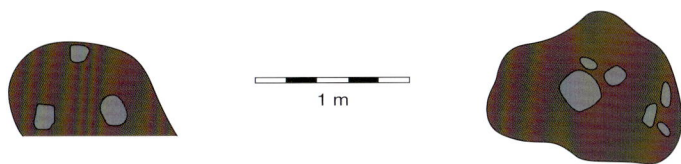

Fig. 116. a) Distribution of pits on the settlement surface. In two cases, the pits lay very close to the western side of a hearth. b) Two small pits were filled with charcoal and a few cooking stones, and perhaps represent a special type of hearth or cooking pit.

Pits
Pits containing charcoal and cooking stones
Stone-built hearth
Ash hearth

a

b

Fig. 117. Part of the settlement surface after the culture layers had been removed. Left behind are the stone-set hearths 6428 (far right), 6649 and 6318. There is also a small pit with a charcoal-rich fill and six stones in the foreground (arrowed), cf. Fig. 116. The western margin of terrace I can just be seen to the left of the picture. Seen looking south. Photo: Nina Helt Nielsen.

cm. There was also a pit in square 479/498 which measured 50 × 30 cm and had a fill of charcoal containing two cooking stones. This pit bordered an area of heat-affected sand that had an extent of c. 45 × 65 cm. These pits were very similar to the aforementioned hearth, which was situated in a pit, and in several cases it was a matter of judgement whether these features should be labelled as a pit or a pot-shaped hearth (Sørensen 1993, 15, Type 4). The presence of pits is important for the interpretation of this settlement's occupation type and function within the Ertebølle settlement complex around the Vængesø lagoon.

4.2.10 Flint-knapping sites

Discrete concentrations of small flint flakes (flakes less than 1 cm² in area) were encountered in 39 cases (Fig. 108). These "flint patches" are defined as areas on the settlement surface where there were more than 15 small flakes within an area of 0.25 m², and where the flakes formed a coherent and well-defined layer. The size of these patches varied between c. 20 × 20 and c. 50 × 50 cm and their thickness between 1 and 5 cm. They had a very diverse content of flakes, the total number of which could in some cases run into several hundreds.

There were 17 of these flint-knapping patches in the kitchen midden, of which five were particularly concentrated and contained more than 50 flint flakes. Nine of these patches lay along the western edge of terrace II and one lay on terrace III; there were none on terrace III. In almost all cases, the distribution of these flint-knapping patches followed the western edge of the ash hearths (Fig. 108). In addition were two flint concentrations that differed from the rest. One of these was the previously mentioned pit containing a Neolithic flint blank (N255; Fig. 89), and the other was a c. 1 m wide horizon uppermost in the kitchen midden, which contained isolated, scattered, large, coarse flakes. This "flint layer" had a maximum vertical extent of c. 15 cm and must mark an old surface on which flakes from nearby flint-knapping were scattered. This flint layer lay *in situ* and encapsulated within the oyster shells and must therefore be dated to the Late Ertebølle culture (Fig. 91).

On the settlement surface in the pre-midden layer there were 21 flint patches; of these, five had particularly high concentrations of flint flakes (Fig. 108). This distribution differs somewhat from that evident in the kitchen midden (Fig. 108). In the pre-midden layer there were flint-knapping sites on terrace I and in the area between terraces I and

II (and on II), where three patches were especially rich in finds. As mentioned previously, these flint-knapping sites also lay primarily along the western edge of the ash hearths in this layer, but there were also patches on the eastern side of some hearths. The overall picture from the pre-midden layer is of flint-knapping sites located to a very great extent at the edges of the hearths (Fig. 108). During the excavation of hearth 6524, large quantities of small-sized flint debitage (splinters) were found in the light-brown fill along its western edge, where the flint formed a well-defined, c. 1-3 cm thick horizon. The same was true for hearth 131 in the kitchen midden, where there was also abundant flint debitage along the western and northwestern edges of the feature. Two smaller patches with a similar concentration of flint debitage, both measuring c. 40 × 40 cm, were found in squares 478/498 and 475/501. There was also a small area (15 × 15 cm) containing abundant small pieces of flint debitage in square 477/501 (Fig. 108).

The flint concentration in square 483/501-502 contained a symmetrical, flat-flaked flake axe. Flake axes were also found at three other flint-knapping sites, and a patch in square 477/498 contained three flake axes. Finally, flakes from the working of a flake axe were found in square 482/501 (Fig. 118). One flint patch (square 483/501-502), which measured c. 70 × 55 cm, contained two flint nodules (raw material for further working).

Fig. 118. a) Flint concentration in the kitchen midden in square 482/501-502. A flake axe can be seen in the concentration (arrowed). Seen looking west. Photo: Nina Helt Nielsen. b) Flint concentration 255, which was c. 0.5 m in diameter and 3 cm thick. Photo: Lone Ritchie Andersen.

Common to all these flint concentrations was that they consisted of a very dense layer of quite small flint pieces, generally less than c. 1 cm across, and they all lay at the edge of the ash hearths – especially on their western and southwestern sides. Conversely, there were no knapping areas on the edges of the stone-built hearths. These observations show that the working/production of flake axes took place in the vicinity of the ash hearths, but not by those that were stone-built. It is not possible to determine whether the coincidence between the working of flint axes and the hearths is because flint-knapping generally took place by these hearths or because the production of these axes required the proximity of fire/heat. An identical observation was made during the excavation of the Ertebølle settlement at Holmegaard (Djursland), where flint debitage from the working of a flake axe was also found in the vicinity of an ash hearth (Fig. 181 AN; Ch. 7.2.5). These observations relating to the working of flake axes in the vicinity of hearths are new in the context of settlements of the Danish Ertebølle culture. In other instances, traces from the production of transverse arrowheads have been found by a hearth. In the Nederst kitchen midden in Kolindsund, abundant flint debitage from this process was found by one hearth in particular (Kannegaard 2013, 206). A similar "workplace" is mentioned in connection with the Ertebølle settlement at Ordrup Næs in northwestern Zealand. Here was an area of c. 1 m² (between two hearths), where four flake axes, 39 finished and 27 partly-made transverse arrowheads and 1330 pieces of flint debitage were found – "more than in any other square" (Becker 1939, 217). At Lollikhuse there was also a "workshop site" for the production of transverse arrowheads, but here it lay at some distance from the hearths (Sørensen 1995, 21, Fig. 2). Areas were also demonstrated at the Norsminde kitchen midden where flint-working had taken place close to the hearths (Andersen, S.H. 1991, 21, Fig. 8b, 26). Traces of flint-knapping in the vicinity of hearths is a general feature of Late Palaeolithic and Mesolithic settlements – not just in Denmark, but across all of northwestern Europe, for example in Belgium (Sergant et al. 2006, 1004).

The distribution of flint debitage on the plateau suggests that this constituted a "forward and backward toss zone" with large flakes and blades (Binford 1983, 149-156). I.e. the larger flakes and outer flakes were thrown backwards (to the southwest) on to the plateau, while the smaller flakes etc. lie where flint-knapping took place, close to the hearths (Figs. 108 and 119).

4.2.11 Analyses of charcoal and oyster shells

Random samples of 15 pieces of charcoal from the upper part of the kitchen midden were examined on two occasions. Two species were identified in one of the samples: oak (*Quercus* sp.) and elm (*Ulmus* sp.; P. Hambro Mikkelsen/C. Malmros, unpublished reports). The other sample showed a predominance of oak with three pieces, while ash (*Fraxinus* sp.) or elm (*Ulmus* sp.) was present in two cases; finally, there was a piece that could be lime (*Tilia* sp.). Flotation processing and analysis (P. Hambro Mikkelsen) revealed the presence in a sample taken from the pre-midden layer below the kitchen midden of seeds of fat hen (*Chenopodium* cf. *album* coll.) and vetch or vetchling (*Vicia/Lathyrus*). A sample from the kitchen midden contained seeds of fat hen, black bindweed (*Fallopia convolvulus*), persicaria (*Polygonum aviculare*), birch (*Betula* sp.), violet (*Viola* sp.) and longheaded poppy (*Papaver dubium*). As the majority of the seeds were uncharred, they could very well post-date the site or even be recent, but this question could be resolved by radiocarbon dating. Measurements of oyster and cockle shells from a c. 25-30 cm thick stratigraphic sequence through the kitchen midden directly east of hearth 131 revealed a decrease in both the maximum and the average length of the oyster shells from the bottom upwards (7.4-6.6 cm for the largest individuals and 6.75-6.23 cm for the average). Corresponding measurements of cockle shells did not display the same trend: the length of these shells remained constant around 2.2-2.3 cm (Fig. 93). If these measurements are compared with corresponding data from Vængesø II and other kitchen middens in Jutland, it is evident that the individuals at Vængesø III are of approximately the same size as those at Vængesø II (Tab. 8), but clearly smaller than those from for example Ertebølle and Havnø, where the largest shells had a length of 16 and 14-17 cm, respectively (Madsen et al. 1900, 80).

An analysis of the time of year at which the oysters were collected was performed on a random sample of 21 flat oyster shells. This revealed that 11 were gathered in the early spring, i.e. March/April and one during summer, June/July. The other shells could, for various reasons, not be determined in this respect (analyses kindly undertaken by N. Milner and H. Robson, University of York).

4.2.12 Conclusion

In spite of the fact that Ertebølle settlements have been excavated in Denmark for almost 150 years, almost all of these investigations have been undertaken in either finds-rich dump layers associated with kitchen middens or as minor sections and test pits. In only a few cases have larger settlement surfaces been investigated and published, for example at Ordrup Næs (Becker 1939, 205, Fig. 3), Vænget Nord (Jensen/Petersen 1985, 41-49, Fig. 1,10), Ertebølle (Andersen/Johansen 1987, 38-39, Figs. 5-6), Sønderholm (Jønsson/Pedersen 1983), Nivå 10 (Jensen, O.L. 2003, 2009; Jensen/Mørck in press) and Ringkloster (Andersen, S.H. 1998, 23, Fig. 8). The publication of Vængesø III is one of the first presentations of a large settlement surface from the Late Ertebølle culture in Denmark. Conversely, extensive settlement surfaces have been investigated at the two southern Swedish settlements of Tågerup (Karsten/Knarrström 2003) and Bökeberg III (Karsten 2001) and at the North German site of Rosenhof (Hartz 1999, 35-38, Abb. 9-11). The settlement surface at Vængesø III is characterised in particular by a large number of features of various kinds within a relatively small area. The numbers of artefacts, faunal remains and features bear witness to extensive activity at the site. However, in many cases this has also resulted in informative links and artefact distributions across the settlement surface, potentially being covered or blurred by later activities (Asher 1968, 50). The surface

of the pre-midden layer displayed an astonishing number of features and working/activity areas. First and foremost, there were (at least) three slightly sunken terraces, several types of hearth, pits, postholes and "drop-and-toss zones", as well as areas for the processing and preparation of fish. Further to these were concentrations of bones of specific prey animals etc., indicating the presence of slaughtering/skinning/butchering sites. A map of the finds intensity across the settlement shows that these were particularly abundant in two areas: Primarily along the edge of the plateau, i.e. at the eastern edge of terrace II, and also in and around terrace I. A large number of flake axes and transverse arrowheads were produced on the plateau, and the investigations reveal that it was divided up functionally. The many different types of finds, and especially the number of hearths and the amount of white-burnt flint, must be taken as an indication that the settlement was used over a considerable period. However, this was not so long that the traces left by earlier visits have been completely disturbed and erased by later occupations. The same indications are provided by the discrete heaps of bones of fur animals and seals and the shells of specific mollusc species. In most cases the hearths lie so close together that they can hardly have been in use at the same time, but must represent a number of different occupations/visits by small social units. If it is assumed that each hearth corresponds to one family group, the settlement must have been occupied or visited about 20 times. There may though have been fewer visits, as some hearths (some distance apart) could well have been used at the same time. Moreover, analyses of the settlement surface show that rebuilding and reuse of the hearths also took place, and that cooking stones were reused. It is difficult to ascertain whether the surface had been subject to clearance or tidying up as no areas were recorded within the excavated area that were characterised by special concentrations of particular kinds of refuse, for example on the edges of the settlement area. This applies not only to Vængesø III but to all the excavated settlements by the lagoon. This absence could be due to the fact that the individual occupations were of such short duration that "rubbish dumps" of this kind did not become established. However, it could also be that, for various reasons, these dumps were not observed during the excavations, i.e. they lay outside the excavated areas (Binford 1983, 190). Even though the traces of the various settlement activities have often been blurred or erased by later visits or occupations, it is nevertheless possible in many cases to identify activity areas etc. The delimited occurrence of traces of various working processes shows that there was functional organisation of the settlement surface with respect to both the coarse and fine working of flint, the location of the hearths, the slaughtering/butchering/skinning of animals, the deposition of individual heaps of marine mollusc shells and the processing/preparation of fish. If the traces of the various activities are compared between the pre-midden layer and the kitchen midden, it becomes evident that most activities and functions took place in the same locations. This is presumably also an indication that only a short time elapsed between the upper surface of the pre-midden layer and the active accumulation of the kitchen midden.

4.3 The finds

Both the kitchen midden and the pre-midden layer were very rich in finds. Their intensity was especially great on terrace II and the "plateau".

4.3.1 Flint

4.3.1.1 Raw material, debitage, technique and primary working

The flint from the pre-midden layer is completely fresh, whereas a slightly increasing bluish-white colouration of the flint can be observed in finds from higher up in the stratigraphy. Very few pieces of flint were found during the excavation that were water-worn and/or showed surface transformation. This is consistent with the local geology, which showed that the sea had not inundated all or part of the excavated area. The dominant flint was a blackish-grey, bryozoan-rich type, but in many

cases use had also been made of black, homogeneous flint of Senon type. A characteristic whitish-yellow, "milky-coloured" flint type also constituted a minor element of the flint debitage. The latter flint type was found in particular within a limited area in the central part of the excavated area. The flint nodules employed were generally small and irregular and had a cortex-covered surface ("old cortex"). No flint pieces were found with soft, fresh cortex as commonly seen for example on the coeval Ertebølle settlements on Mariager Fjord and the Limfjord, e.g. Ertebølle. Very few flint cores from Vængesø III exceed 12 cm in length – the great majority are smaller nodules that only measure c. 4-8 cm. One unworked flint nodule with old cortex over its entire surface was larger and measured c. 10.5 × 11 × 6 cm. Local flint had clearly been used, and this must come from fluvioglacial deposits in the area. In this respect, the findings from this settlement are completely consistent with the conclusions reached at Vængesø II, where use was made of local flint (but in this case from the beach ridges).

In two cases, flint nodules with a (natural) hole had been picked up and brought to the site. Even though they were both unworked, they could, on account of their form, have been used as weights for fishing nets or similar. Similar flint nodules with (natural) holes were encountered at Vængesø II, but there they are dated to the Neolithic. A slightly larger, cortex-covered flint nodule had, with three to four blows, been given a coarse dorsal ridge, but was then discarded. It measures c. 12 × 11.5 × 6 cm.

A map of the distribution of coarse (outer) flakes with a cortex-covered surface gives the impression that the initial working of the flint cores took place in particular in the southwestern part of the settlement (Fig. 120). It is evident that the first working took place especially within a c. 5 × 3-4 m area at terrace III and the southern part of terrace II. Conversely, no outer flakes were recorded on or around terrace I. Moreover, there was no evident general tendency for those flakes to be found near the hearths. Unlike the distribution of the "flint-knapping sites", which almost all lay in the vicinity

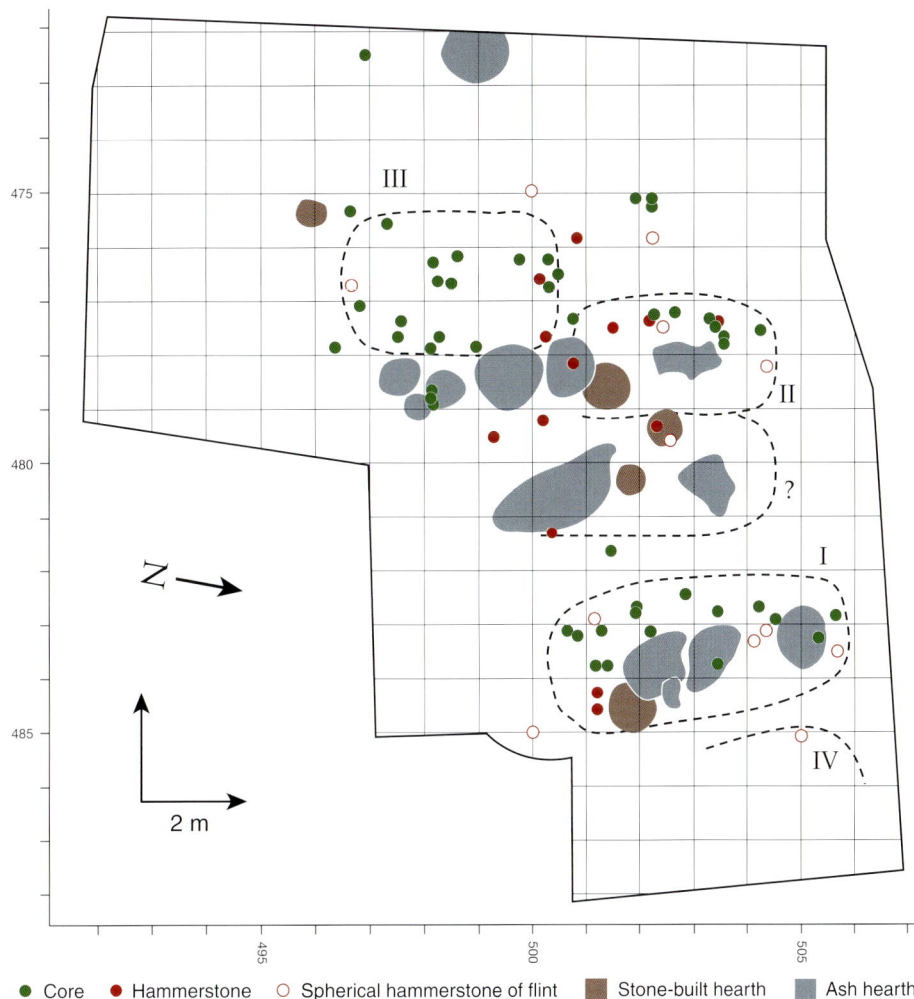

Fig. 119. Distribution of cores and hammerstones across the settlement surface; the cores are clearly restricted to the terraces.

● Core ● Hammerstone ○ Spherical hammerstone of flint ▪ Stone-built hearth ▪ Ash hearth

of (ash) hearths, this was not the case with the initial working of the blade cores, where only a minor proportion occurred in the vicinity of a hearth. The distribution of the flakes from the coarse working of the cores is of further interest in that these are in general particularly frequent in the areas that yielded numerous cores (Fig. 120). This part of the settlement surface was apparently preferred for coarser flint-knapping, while the finer working took place to a greater degree in the vicinity of the hearths. The distribution of quartzite hammerstones and spherical crushing stones of flint is shown in Fig. 119.

Due to the secondary calcareous precipitations and crusts of fishbones on the surface of the flint, it was not possible to carry out refitting or wear-trace analyses. Conversely, flint refitting was undertaken for the Neolithic flint blank mentioned above.

An examination of the assemblage revealed that only a third could definitely be assigned to either the kitchen midden or the pre-midden layer. Due to the complex and diffuse boundary between these two deposits, the remaining third could only arbitrarily be assigned to one or the other.

The excavation yielded a total 11,656 pieces of worked flint, weighing 131,804 kg. Of this total, 6176 pieces were from the kitchen midden and 5480 from the underlying pre-midden layer. The flint debitage from the kitchen midden has a frequency of between two and 478 pieces per m². A mapping of the flint debitage in this deposit reveals a much higher frequency along the western edge of terrace II and at the edge of the ash hearths that are located here. There is also abundant flint in the squares between terraces I and II – this area is in general the most flint-rich on the settlement

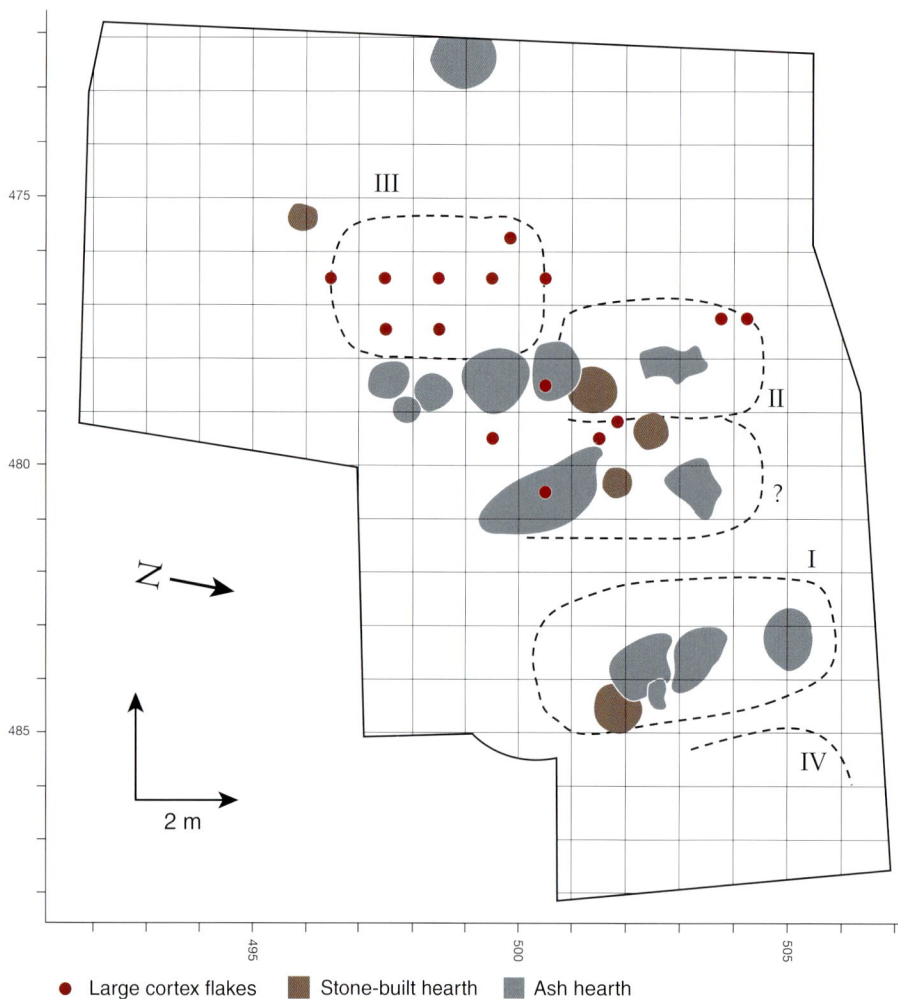

Fig. 120. Distribution of large cortex-covered outer flakes produced in the initial working of blade cores. These flakes only occurred around terraces II and III.

● Large cortex flakes   ■ Stone-built hearth   ■ Ash hearth

surface. There is also abundant flint debitage in terrace III (Fig. 120). Conversely, there is not much flint debitage on terrace I. With regard to the pre-midden layer, the flint concentration varies from one to 486 pieces per m². In this deposit, it is in particular the areas around the ash hearths on terrace I that are rich in flint. This is especially true on the western part of the terrace and in the squares further west from here (up the slope), towards terrace II.

There are 804 pieces of *fire-affected flint*, of which 395 came from the kitchen midden and 409 from the pre-midden layer. The burnt flint from the kitchen midden comprises 3.3% of the flint assemblage from that deposit, while that from the pre-midden layer constitutes 3.5%. It is found evenly distributed across the surface in both the kitchen midden and the pre-midden

layer (Fig. 112). If the ratio between burnt and unburnt flint is used as a measure of settlement intensity, as has been done for example in the case of the Lateglacial settlements in southern Zealand – with the occurrence of 2.5% burnt flint relative to the total debitage being used as the boundary between low and high settlement intensity – the value of 3.3% of burned flint at Vængesø III must be taken as an indication of high settlement intensity in both the pre-midden layer and the kitchen midden (Pedersen, K.B. 2009, 12).

Characteristic pieces of debitage from the working of flat-flaked flake axes (both edge/"wing" flakes and transverse flakes (Andersen, S.H. 2009, 78-79, Figs. 51-52)) were recorded in 372 cases, of which 14 are transverse flakes and 358 are edge flakes (further to these are 17 pieces of uncertain origin). Of these characteristic waste products, 205 are from the kitchen midden and 153 from the pre-midden layer. The fact that there are so few transverse flakes relative to wing-shaped edge flakes is presumably due to the former being more difficult to identify in the flint debitage than the latter. These flakes were found evenly distributed across the entire surface – both in the kitchen midden and in the pre-midden layer – showing that the working of the flat-flaked flake axes apparently took place everywhere on the settlement surfaces. However, it should be noted that, in several cases, working of flake axes can be demonstrated close to the hearths (Fig. 120).

Frost-cracked flint and unworked flint nodules were recorded in four cases.

The distribution of the flint debitage on the settlement surface (Fig. 120) shows that the flint in the kitchen midden lay in particular to the west of the hearths and also within a c. 5 × 5 m area to the south and southwest of terrace III (i.e. up on the "plateau"). In the pre-midden layer, particularly abundant flint was found by terrace I and within a c. 2 m wide band immediately outside (to the west of) this structure. On terrace II, the flint lay in a c. 1 m wide band to the west of the hearths and, finally, there was a rounded, delimited concentration (c. 3 × 3 m) in the middle of terrace III. (In evaluating Fig. 108, showing the distribution of flint debitage in the two cultural deposits, account must be taken of the fact that concentrations of flint debitage ("flint-knapping patches") heavily influence the totals in the various areas.)

The finds from Vængesø III show all stages of tool production at the site – from the primary working of blade cores and other cores to tool manufacture, resharpening/rejuvenation and finally actual discard. The blades were predominantly produced by "soft technique". The following account of the flint-working technique is based partially on B. Madsen's criteria (Madsen 1992, 105). The percussion bulb is weakly developed and often has a "lip" by the platform remnant. Percussion bulb scars are only exceptionally found. The platform remnants are narrow and oval and measure c. 0.2 × 0.8 cm. The point of percussion is, in

most cases, not visible. The platform remnant is smooth. The dorsal side of the flakes has, in almost all cases, retouch at the percussion bulb (proximal) end, i.e. the flakes show traces of preparation spalls and preparation flakes.

The blades from Vængesø III are characterised by 32 examples (c. 19%) without dorsal proximal retouch/preparation, otherwise the absolutely most dominant feature of the flint technology of the Ertebølle culture (Fig. 127). Instead, the Vængesø III blades have a projection (horn), such that the platform remnant is triangular in outline. This is also found on blades and flakes from the Vængesø II settlement (Ch. 3.5.1.1 and Fig. 45).

The *blade cores* from Vængesø III are dominated by small (short), cortex-covered and very irregular pieces, which distinguish the assemblage from those recovered from other coeval Ertebølle settlements, for example Tybrind Vig (Andersen, S.H. 2013, 80-84). The cores are so small that there are only a few on which the flake/blade scars are of a height, width and regularity that in any way fulfils the definition of a blade. This also means that, in many cases, it is difficult to distinguish the different core types and there is also a seamless transition between cores and "nodules". An explanation for the small cores must be sought in the fact that almost exclusive use had been made of local, spherical flint nodules which only exceptionally had dimensions greater than 5 cm. This kind of flint nodule is common in the local fluvioglacial deposits and it is clearly these that were collected and used for blade (flake) production. The small, short and irregular cores are also consistent with the small numbers of A-blades and backed blades. Viewed from a general perspective, the assemblage gives the impression of an "ad hoc production" based on local raw materials. One explanation for the small number of longer, more regular blades could perhaps be that these were not made at this settlement, but were brought from somewhere else. The great majority of the cores in the assemblage are from the pre-midden layer (61 examples as opposed to 14 from the kitchen midden), especially on terrace I and on and around terrace III, while there were no cores along the west side of terrace

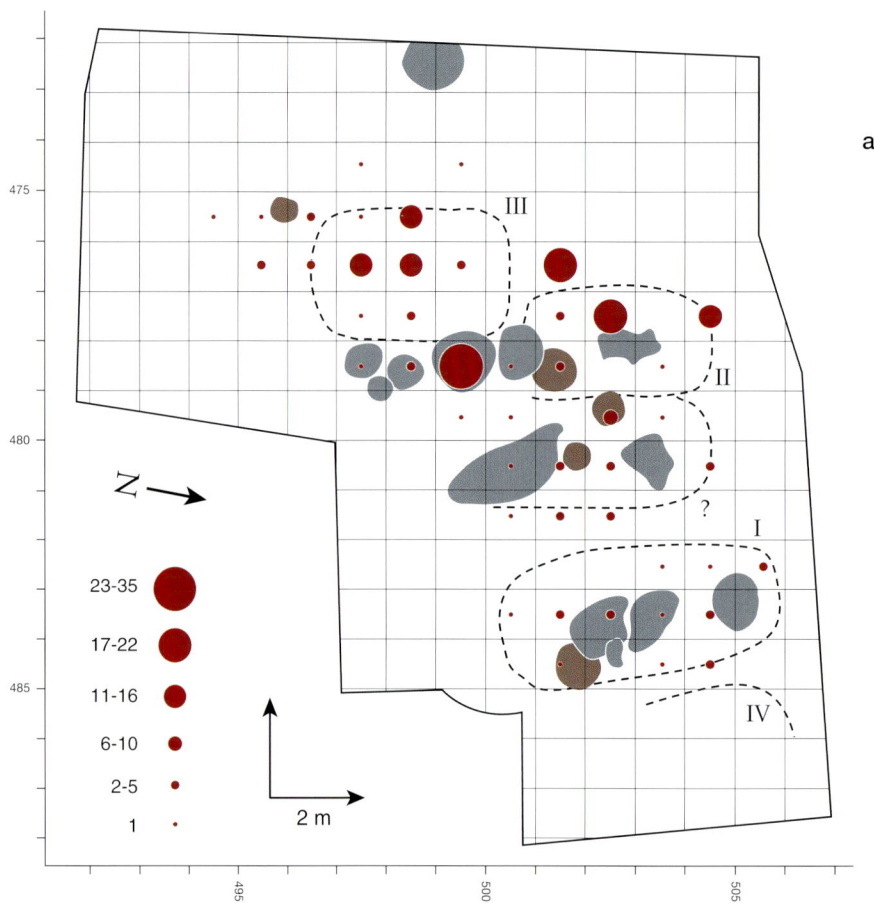

a

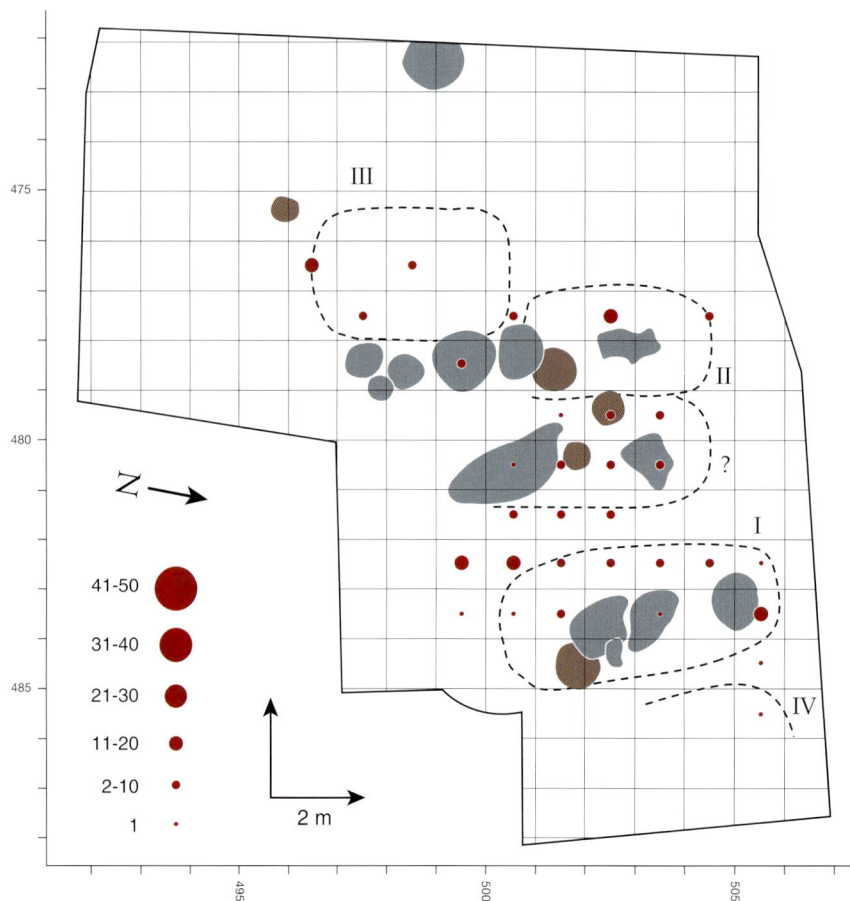

b

Fig. 121. The distribution of flakes resulting from the production of flake axes demonstrates that in the kitchen midden (a) this production was concentrated close to the hearths on terrace II, while in the pre-midden layer (b), production was on a smaller scale, but more evenly distributed, cf. Fig. 146.

II, where there were otherwise numerous occurrences of debitage from flint-working (Fig. 120). The fact that the cores from the pre-midden layer lay relatively delimited in association with terrace I can be taken as confirmation that these terraces were working platforms rather than house sites.

Cores with a single platform dominate the assemblage with 59 examples. They are characterised by great irregularity and variation in size. The raw material used was predominantly small, cuboid, locally gathered flint nodules with cortex, the greatest dimension of which rarely exceeds c. 5 cm. The largest/longest core of this type is a coarse, cortex-covered and very irregular flint nodule on which a platform has been created. Two blades were then struck off, after which the edge of the platform was destroyed (crushed) and any further work abandoned. This core measures 12 × 12 × 7 cm. Another discarded core is of a calcareous flint type. A single blow was used to create a rough back and a platform, from which two irregular flakes were struck. The core measures 11 cm in length and 5 cm in both width and thickness. The other cores of this type are all smaller (shorter) and measure c. 3.7-5 cm in length/height (Fig. 122). One example is fire-brittled. It is characteristic of this core type that the primary flint nodule was opened by the removal of a single, platform-creating flake, after which blades etc. were struck off. None of the cores shows traces of special platform preparation. Two cores of this type were formed from the butt of symmetrical core axes (their length is, respectively, 6.1 and 6.2 cm). Eight pieces represent a special form/variant as they have very short platform faces (2.2-4.5 cm) and, at the same time, are round or oval in outline with a serrated/denticulate edge (Fig. 122g-h). As a consequence of their size and form, it is difficult to distinguish these artefacts from denticulate flake scrapers. This variant of the core type has been described and illustrated previously (Andersen, S.H. 2009, 62-63, Fig. 33g). The cores measure 4.8-12 cm in length, 3.6-10.5 cm in width and 1.8-4 cm in thickness.

Cores with two platforms are represented by 20 examples, of which ten have parallel platforms and ten have platforms at an angle (Fig. 123). On the whole, these are irregular cores. Four of those with parallel platforms are cylindrical in form, and these are also the largest and most regular in the entire assemblage (Fig. 123a). Three examples were shorter and broader than the rest. The cores with two platforms are 3.8-9.7 cm in length.

The ten cores with two platforms *at an angle* are very irregular. All are cuboid in form and there is no distinct boundary to "nodules". One block of this type is, however, larger than the others and measures 6.3 cm in length, 9.4 cm in width and 4.5 cm in thickness.

Cores with numerous irregular platforms (nodules) and negative scars are represented by 89 examples, which are all small (short) and cuboid with cortex-covered sections on their surface. This type includes both completely exhausted flake cores and flint nodules showing sporadic dressing. The fact that this type was so prominent at this site is consistent with the small irregular cores and the raw material for blades and flakes being based on the local flint nodules. The largest measures c. 8 × 8 cm, but the majority are quite small, measuring only around 4-5 × 4-5 cm. One block has a single platform, from which short flakes were struck for the purpose of producing transverse arrowheads. Its length is 5.3 cm.

Discoid cores occur in four examples that, like the other cores, are very irregular. Their length is 7-11 cm, their width 8.5-10 cm and their thickness 2.5-6 cm.

Scaled flakes of Brovst type are only represented by one example. This is a flat, rectangular flake on which the short sides show retouch and from which a series of biconvex flakes have been struck across the ventral side of the piece. Continual edge retouch is visible along a 3.7 cm stretch of one longitudinal edge. It measures 7.9 × 5.5 cm.

Parts of platform sections are represented by 12 examples, which in four cases represent an entire (Fig. 124a), or most of, a core base, while the others constitute larger or smaller parts of core bases. The type is characterised by great irregularity and the pieces vary in size, with core base dimensions ranging from c. 2.9 × 3.6 cm to 8.7 × 8 cm and thickness from 0.8-2.9 cm.

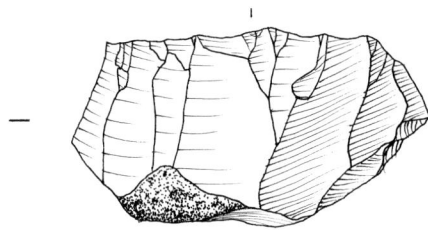
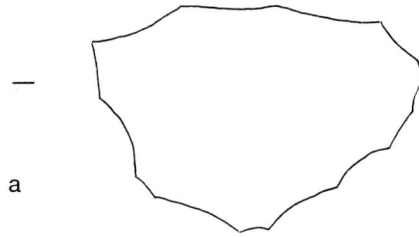

a

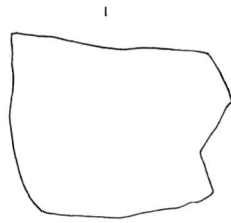

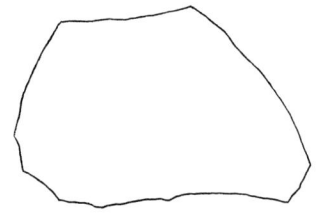

b

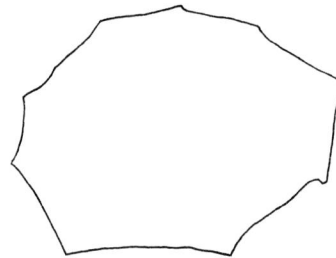

c

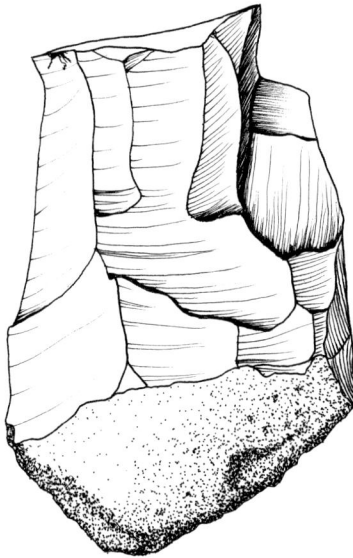

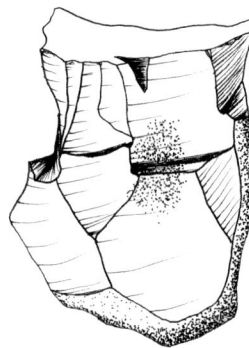
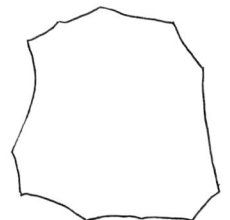

d

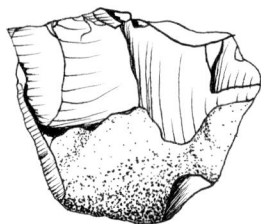

e

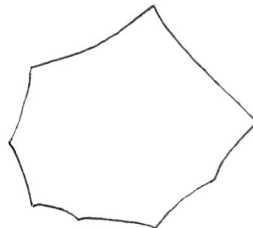

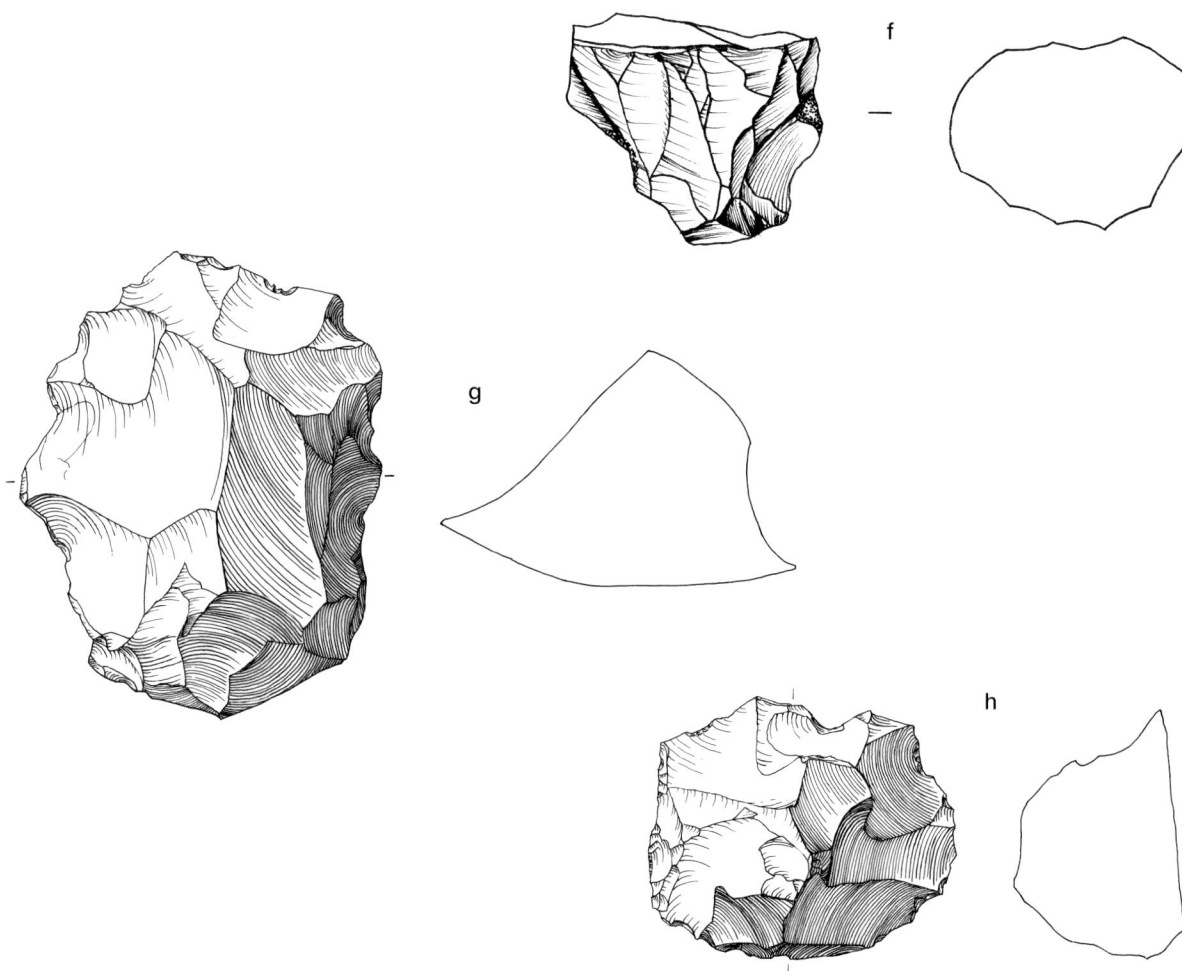

◄▲ *Fig. 122. a-e) Cores with a single platform. f) Core with two platforms. g-h) Denticulate cores/ scrapers. Scale 3:4. Drawing: Søren Timm Christensen.*

Flakes from *core faces* are the commonest type of core flake and are represented by 23 examples. This type is characterised by very irregular pieces, but it is nevertheless possible to distinguish between various variants of this kind of flake. Three pieces are from cylindrical cores with a length of 5.4-7.7 cm. Six pieces are from unipolar cores and consist of the core face, which extend from the platform to the core's opposing rounded or pointed end and thereby approach a "fishhook-shape". These are the longest, widest and thickest of this type and five of them terminate in a cortex-covered area (opposite the platform). Their length is 7.8-11.9 cm, their width 4-7.2 cm and their thickness 1-5 cm. One piece is fire-brittled. Five further pieces are similar to the aforementioned, but are shorter and tend towards being rectangular or rounded in shape and also end in a cortex-covered area. These flakes also come from unipolar cores, but are of considerably shorter form. Their length is 4.4-6.7 cm, their width 3.9-5.5 cm and their thickness 1.4-1.6 cm. The remaining examples comprise totally irregular pieces with part of a core face.

Block edges are represented by 25 examples and these are very variable with respect to both size and form. Five pieces include both an edge and enough of the flake side for it to be a matter of debate whether these should be termed core sides or core edges. Twelve pieces follow an edge and have a curved form, while the others are completely irregular. Two pieces take the form of small, slender flakes that have removed a narrow edge, and

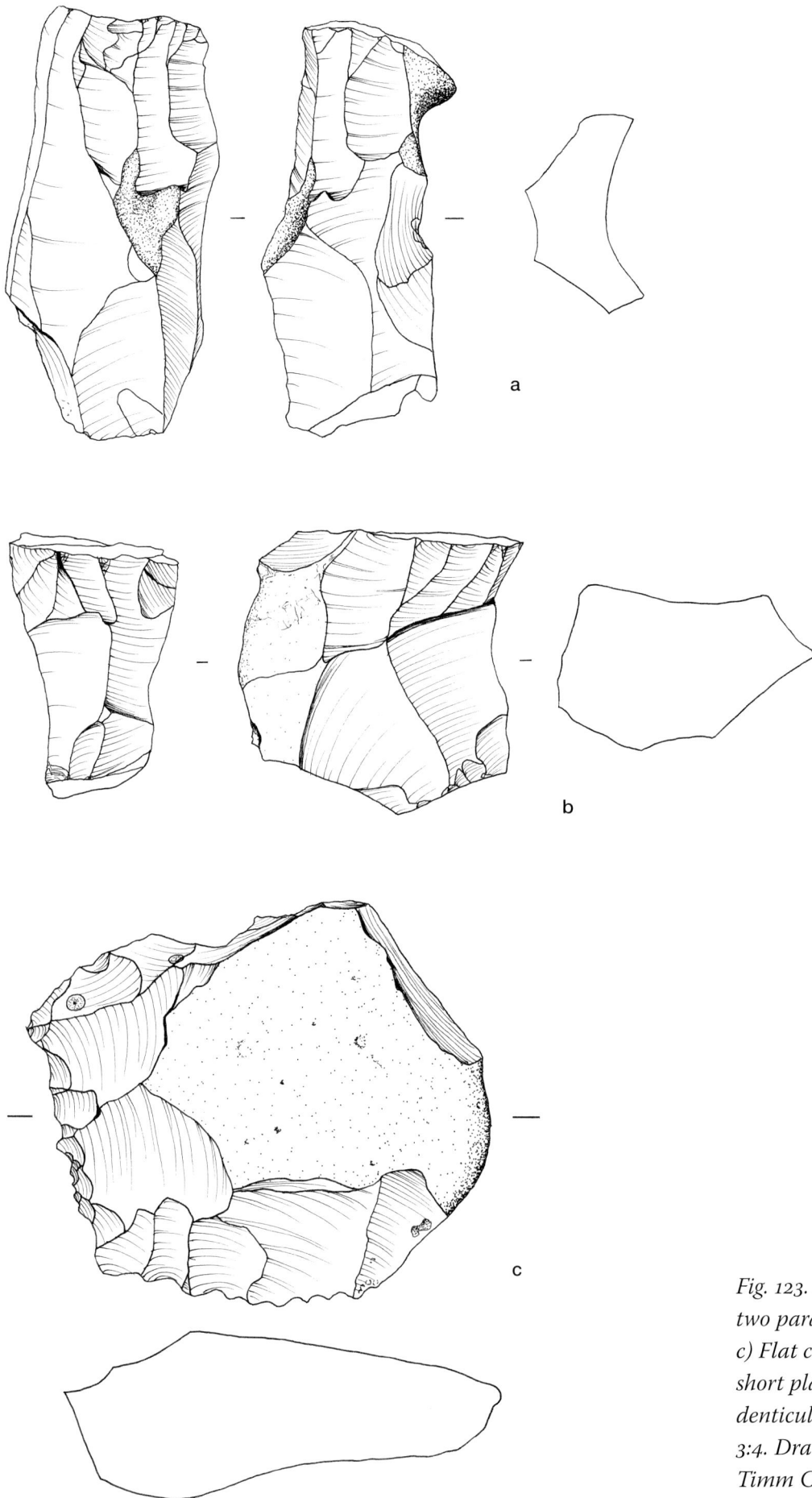

Fig. 123. a-b) Cores with two parallel platforms. c) Flat core with two short platforms and a denticulate edge. Scale 3:4. Drawing: Søren Timm Christensen.

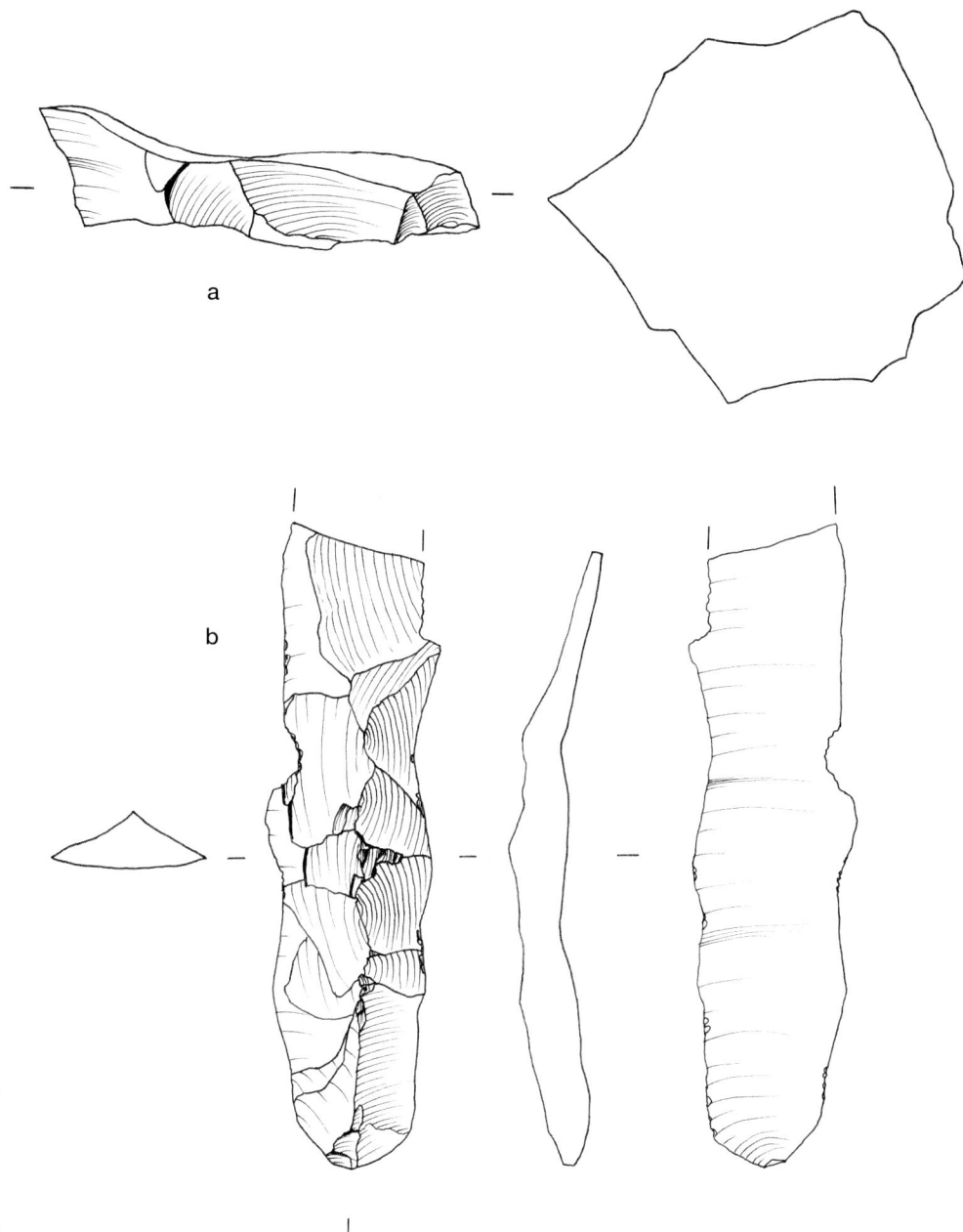

Fig. 124. a) Entire platform of core. b) Primary backed blade. Scale 3:4. Drawing: Søren Timm Christensen.

three other pieces have a coarse dorsal ridge, such that they may represent unsuccessful backed flakes. They vary in length from 2.7-11 cm.

The assemblage includes two large *flakes* which, apart from a few small chips here and there on the edges, are unworked. Given the extensive production of flake axes at this site, the small number of (unworked) flakes is surprising. The same applies to the absence of cores/remnants of cores that yielded the flakes for the axes. One of the flakes measures 11 × 11.5 × 2 cm and the other 13 × 13.5 × 3.5 cm.

A total of 54 *preparation flakes* have been identified: These are characterised by having an elongate, narrow, triangular outline with one or two longitudinal midribs on the dorsal side, giving them an equilateral, triangular cross-section (Fig. 125). They measure 2.9-5.2 cm in length and c. 0.8-2 cm in width.

The *blade* group comprises 171 pieces, which is a small total relative to the excavated area – and to other coeval Ertebølle settlements. Of these only 12 are regular A-blades, and 159 are B-blades (92.8%;

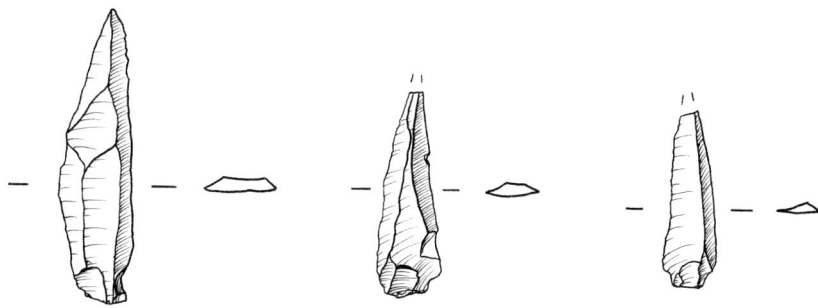

Fig. 125. Preparatory flakes. Scale 3:4. Drawing: Søren Timm Christensen.

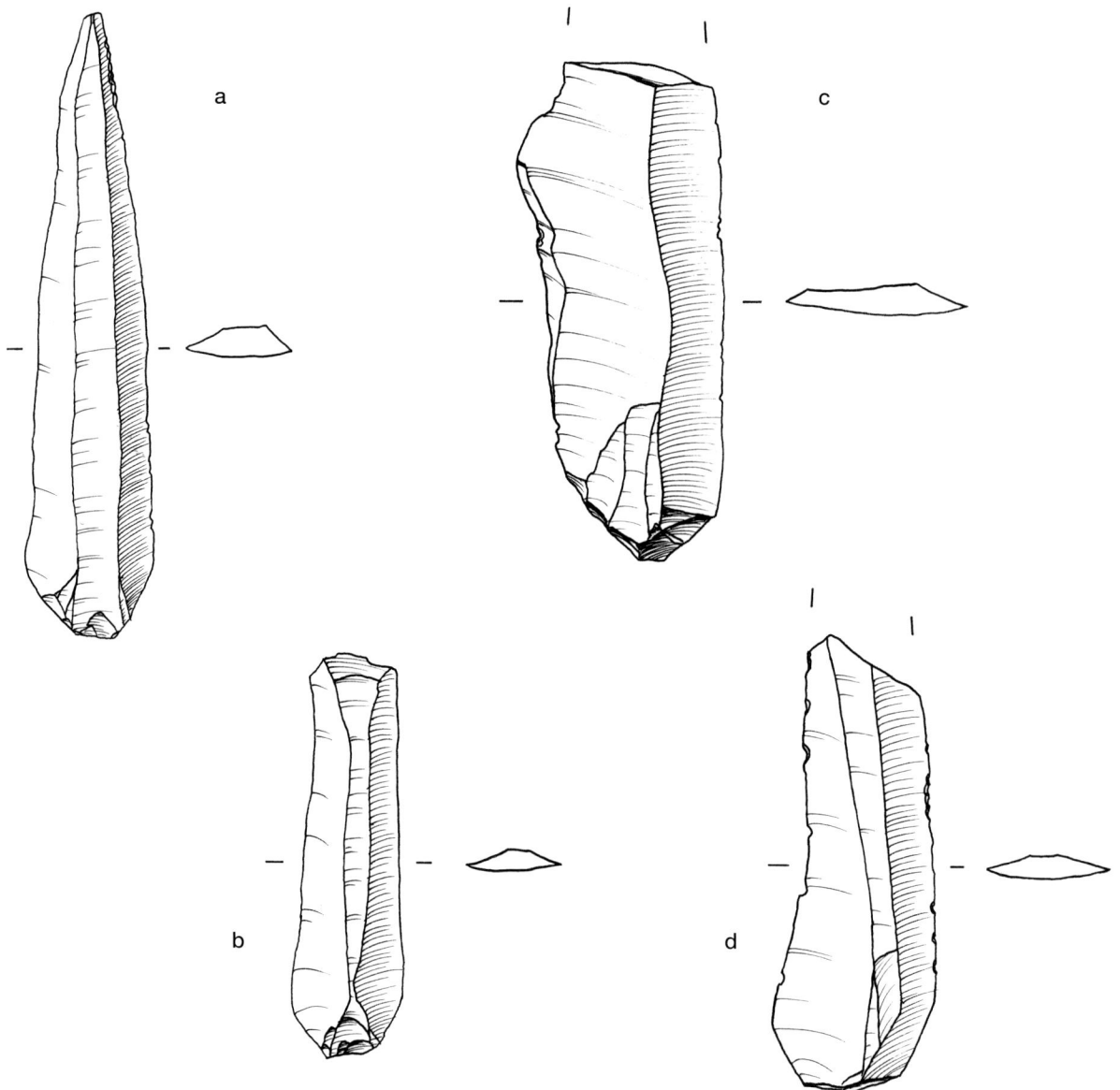

▲▶ *Fig. 126. a-b) A-blades. c-k) B-blades. The blades from Vængesø II and III are generally shorter and much more irregular than those from other coeval Ertebølle sites in eastern Jutland, e.g. Norsminde (cf. Stafford 1999). This is a function of the rather "poor" local raw material. Scale 3:4. Drawing: Søren Timm Christensen.*

Fig. 126). The small number of A-blades can probably be explained in part as being a consequence of the raw material almost only being able to yield short, irregular pieces. But it is also this group that has been predominantly used as raw material for tools – for the truncated pieces. If the blades that have been worked to produce tools are compared with the remainder of the group, there is an evident tendency for longer, more regular and (especially) broader blades to have been selected for tools. Around half of the blades have a dorsal ridge and about a quarter have a cortex-covered area dorsally at the distal end (Fig. 127). In four cases the A-blades are from the pre-midden layer and eight are from the kitchen midden. In the case of the B-blades, 96 are from the pre-midden layer and 53 from the kitchen midden. Two blades are fire-brittled and one has cortex on the platform

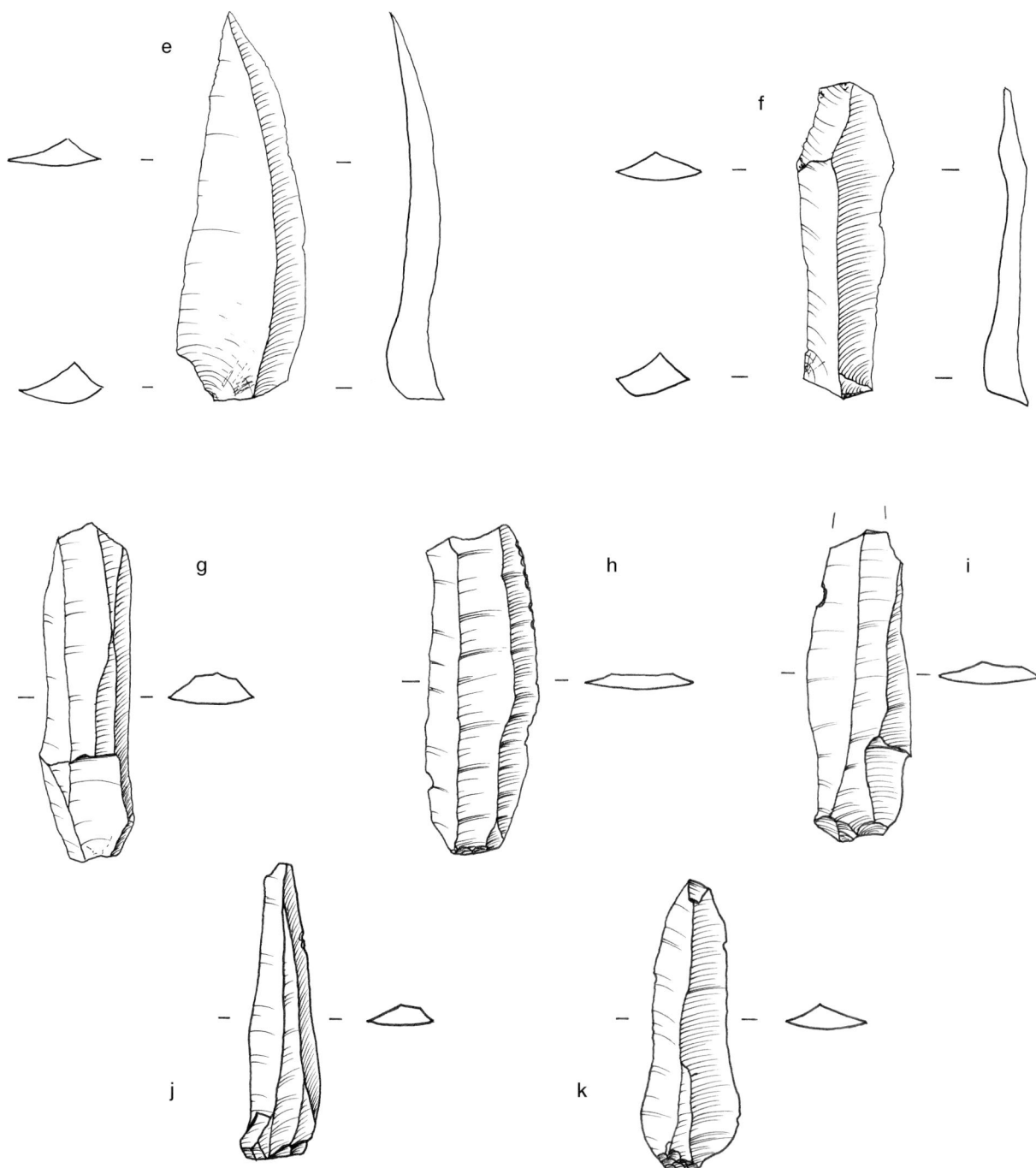

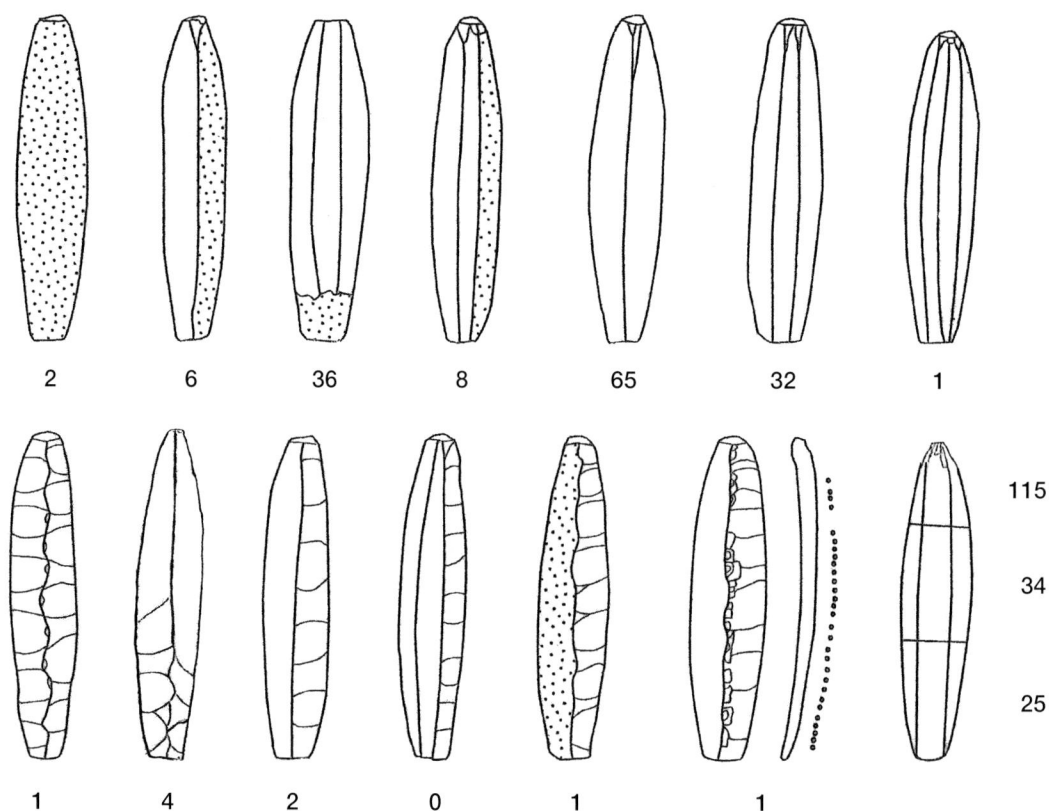

Fig. 127. The abundance of the various blade types and fragments at Vængesø III, cf. Figs 45b and 192c.

remnant. The length of the A-blades is 6.5-11.5 cm, with an average of 9.5 cm. The length of the B-blades is 3.5-11.5 cm, with an average of 6.1 cm. The width of the A-blades is 2-3 cm, with an average of 2.5 cm, while the B-blades have a width of 1-4 cm, with an average of 2.1 cm. For both groups, the average thickness is 0.6 cm (Fig. 128). The small number of wide, thin blades is characteristic of the assemblages from the Vængesø settlements and the form of the blade is, at the same time, a technological feature of the latest Ertebølle settlements in eastern Jutland. If the blade dimensions from the Vængesø settlements are compared with those from for example Holmegaard, it is evident that there is a tendency for the blades to become wider (and thinner) during the course of the Ertebølle culture. A parallel trend has previously been observed in the dimensions of blades from Åmosen in western Zealand (Andersen, K. 1981). The distribution of the blades across the settlement surface is shown in Fig. 129.

Backed blades are rare and are represented by only eight examples, and only one of these is a regular primary backed blade; this measures 10.8 cm in length and 2.5 cm in width (Fig. 124b). Two blades have a unilaterally worked back and one is a secondary backed blade. The pieces measure 7.3-9.8 cm in length, 1.8-2 cm in width and 0.8-1.3 cm in thickness. Finally, there is an irregular blade and a short fragment of a coarse backed flake as well as two distal pieces of blades, the backs of which bear a final remnant of previously struck backed blades. Compared with other coeval Ertebølle assemblages, the backed blades from Vængesø III are short; there is an identical situation at Vængesø II. The small number of short backed blades is completely consistent with the short and very irregular cores as well as the general impression gained of the flint technique at this locality. The flint cores were simply too small/short for them to be prepared adequately before blade production was commenced.

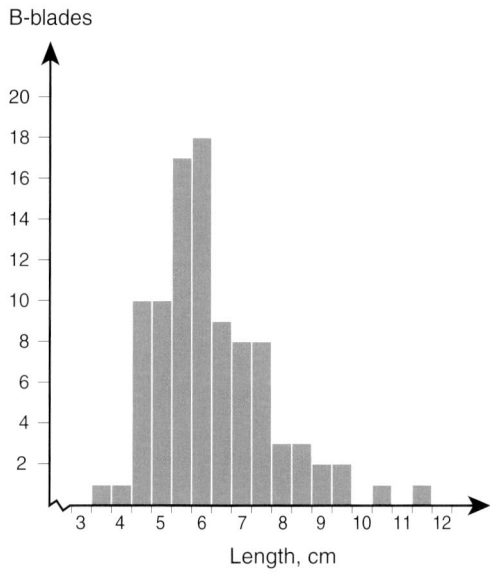

Fig. 128. B-blades from Vængesø III: length, width and thickness.

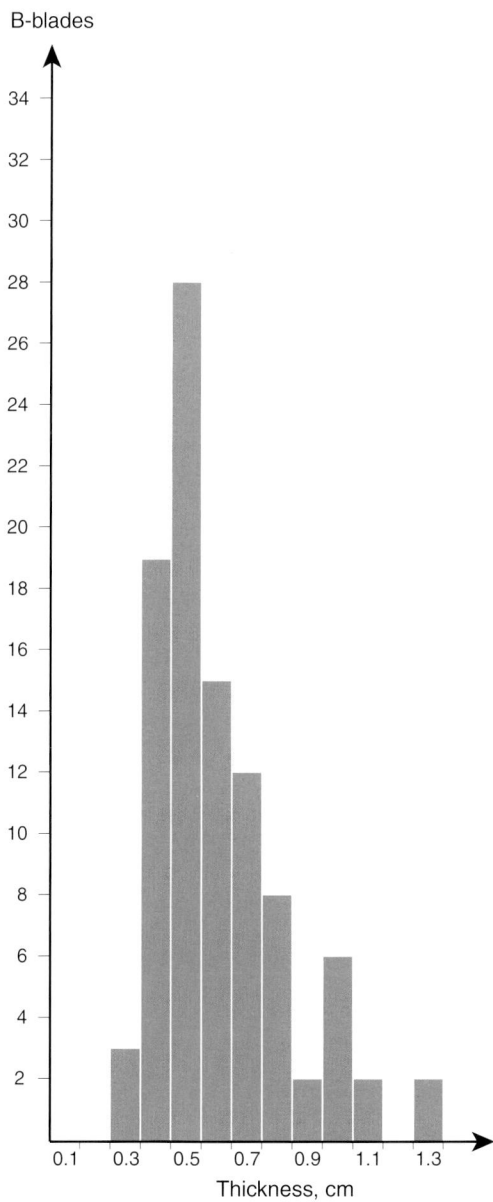

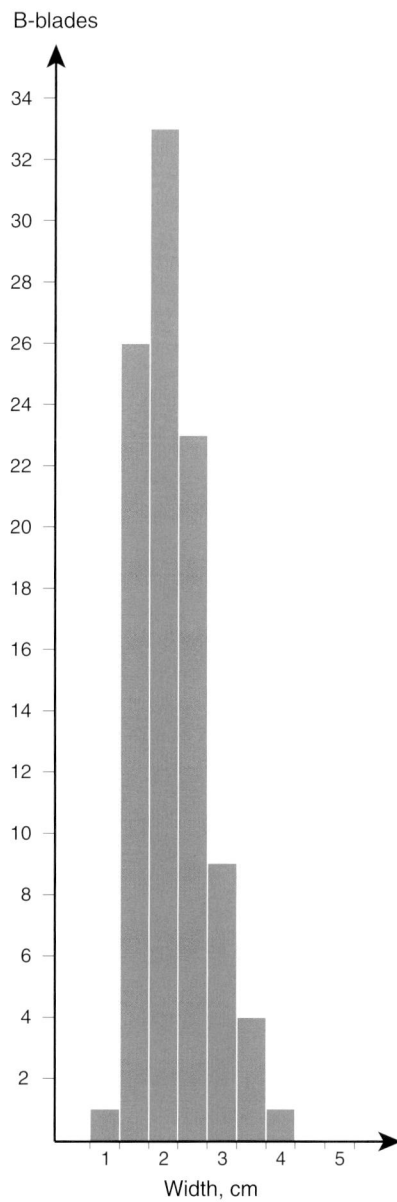

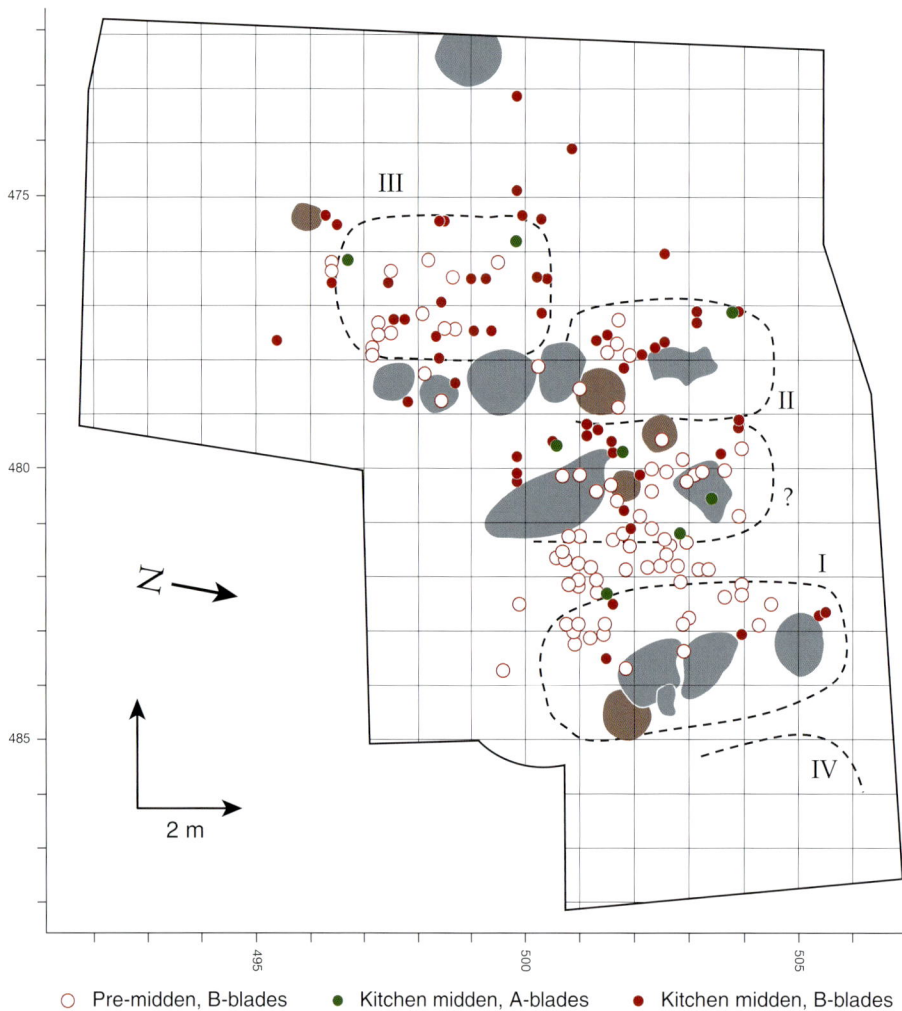

Fig. 129. Distribution of blades across the settlement surface.

○ Pre-midden, B-blades   ● Kitchen midden, A-blades   ● Kitchen midden, B-blades

Micro blades are very few in number – only nine examples were identified. These differ from the preparation flakes by having parallel edges and a trapezoid or rectangular cross-section. Their length is 3.6-4.3 cm and their width 0.7-1 cm.

Among the *blade fragments*, proximal ends are most frequent with 115 examples, followed by middle pieces with 34 examples and finally distal ends with 25 examples. The proximal ends include all the blade fragments with a well-preserved percussion bulb, which means that their length ranges from 2.5-10.3 cm. They are characterised by regularity and several appear to originate from A-blades. Seven pieces are fire-brittled, and wear and minor chips are evident on the edges. It has proved possible to refit a proximal part with a middle piece. The middle pieces have a fractured edge at each end and their length is 2.2-9.3 cm. Five examples

are fire-brittled, but most of these are short, being less than 3 cm in length. Many middle pieces show edge wear, which suggests they broke during use (sawing/cutting work). The distal pieces have a fractured edge and terminate either in a thin, sharp, tongue-shaped point or a hinge fracture. The 25 examples differ from the other blade fragments by not being fire-brittled and by only very rarely showing edge wear. Their length is 2.3-5.5 cm. A distal piece was refitted with a middle piece.

The overall impression gained from the cores, core flakes and blades is that these show great irregularity. The cores are small (short) and irregular and characterised by large cortex-covered areas. The flint assemblage shows that the raw material employed predominantly comprised small local flint nodules. Virtually none of the cores and core flakes provide evidence of the local production of regular blades, as also shown by the small number of A-blades found. The flint assemblage from Vængesø III gives the impression that the most regular blades and flint tools were perhaps brought along to the settlement from other places with easier access to large flint cores of high quality. The irregular flint technique is a distinctive feature of this settlement and it appears to be a general aspect throughout its period of use. On this point it resembles Vængesø II, where the flint-working was of a similar, irregular character.

4.3.1.2 Artefacts from secondary flint-working

Flake scrapers are represented by 12 examples (4.1% of the flake tools), of which one is a simple flake scraper, measuring 4.8 × 5.8 cm, and 11 are denticulate scrapers. The latter are on cortex-covered flakes with a distal, rounded denticulation. One is broken with an oblique diagonal fracture and another is fire-brittled. A small protruding "beak" has been worked in the edge of one of the scrapers. There is an even transition from denticulate flake scrapers to broad, flat cores, but the denticulate scrapers are, in this context, defined by a convex scraper edge, in contrast to the flat blocks, which do not have such a convex edge (Tixier 1963, 58, Fig. 13). Denticulate flake scrapers are also a characteristic element of Vængesø I (Ch. 2.3.1.2 and Fig. 9), but they are less prominent at Vængesø II. Similar scrapers are also mentioned and illustrated in connection with the submerged settlement of Rønæs Skov in the Little Belt (Andersen, S.H. 2009, 62-63, Fig. 33g). The scrapers measure from 3.3 × 4.7 cm to 6.4 × 6.1 cm.

Atypical scrapers are represented by two examples, of which one is on an elongate, irregular and cortex-covered flake with a narrow, tongue-shaped scraper edge. This piece measures 7.4 × 5.8 cm. The second example is on an elongate piece of flint (frost-cracked), on which a thin, irregular scraper edge has been worked and which continues into an edge with irregular chipping (wear traces).

There is only one *blade scraper* (plus a fragment). The raw material was a regular blade with irregular wear along the edges in the form of minor chipping. The scraper retouch follows an irregular, flared course with a notch. As the scraper – in contrast to the other flint tools in the assemblage – has a white, patinated surface, it is possible that it is older than the main settlement, perhaps a remnant from an earlier visit to the site. Its length is 7.5 cm and its width 2.3 cm. There is also a blade with a c. 1 cm wide section of (presumed) scraper retouch at its distal end. Most of the scraper edge has been broken off by an oblique fracture, which has split the distal end (presumably as a result of heavy wear). Its length is 6.7 cm and its width 2.5 cm.

There are two crescent-shaped pieces with a triangular cross-section and retouch along the edge. These are probably broken-off *edges from scrapers*. They measure 3.3 and 3.9 cm in length. Further to these is a piece of a broken-off scraper edge which follows a slightly irregular, flared course. This piece measures 2.3 cm. Similar scraper edges have previously been illustrated in connection with the publication of the Lateglacial settlement of Bro on northwestern Funen (Andersen, S.H. 1973a, 31, Figs. 39-40).

Borers are also few in number at this settlement and constitute only 6.5% of the blade tools. Blade borers are only represented by three examples (Fig. 130). Two have an offset tip (oblique borers) and the third is a blade borer with a symmetrical tip and shoulders. It is the most regular borer in the assemblage, for which the raw material was a broad, regular blade, the proximal end of which is broken off (Fig. 130a).

Only one *borer* was found, made on a short blade, the distal end of which has a short tip and a shoulder at one edge (Fig. 130c). Its length is 2.9 cm and its width 1.6 cm.

Flake borers are represented by six examples, of which five are on relatively short flakes and one is on an elongate, regular flake. Further to these is a borer that shows a transverse fracture. One piece has a broken-off tip. Their length is 6-8.8 cm and their width 3.5-7.5 cm.

Core borers are represented by seven examples, of which three are intact and four are broken-off tips. They are regular and have a clearly worked tip with a triangular-trapezoid cross-section. One piece has a fractured surface at both ends (Fig. 130d). Their length is 6.9-13.2 cm and their width and thickness 2.2-6.5 cm.

Finally, there are three *atypical borers*, two of which are elongate and have a triangular cross-section. In both cases, the tip has been broken off. The third borer in this group has a broad, tongue-shaped tip.

Burins are few in number at Vængesø III and are represented by only ten examples (3.2% of the flake tools). There are eight angle burins, a transverse burin and an atypical burin (Fig. 131). As the raw material in four cases comprised fragments of (flake) axes and for the remainder irregular flakes, this tool group is on the whole very heterogeneous with respect to form and size.

Fig. 130. Borers. a) Blade borer with shoulders. b) Flake borer. c) Drill. d) Core borer. e) Simple blade borer with symmetrical tip. Scale 3:4. Drawing: Søren Timm Christensen.

Four *angle burins* are on a surface created by a transverse blow. Of these, two are on the butt of a flake axe and two are on coarse flakes. Five burins are on a transverse break (one of which is on the butt of a flake axe), an angle burin is on a retouched notch and, finally, there is an atypical (possible) burin on a cortex-covered B-blade and an atypical burin on a fire-brittled edge.

If the distribution of the burins and burin spalls are mapped on the settlement surface, it becomes evident that these show great coincidence and in most cases were found in the same areas (Fig. 132). There are numerous burin spalls on terrace I and along the western edge of the hearths on terrace II, i.e. in the area where there are also numerous traces of flint-knapping. The

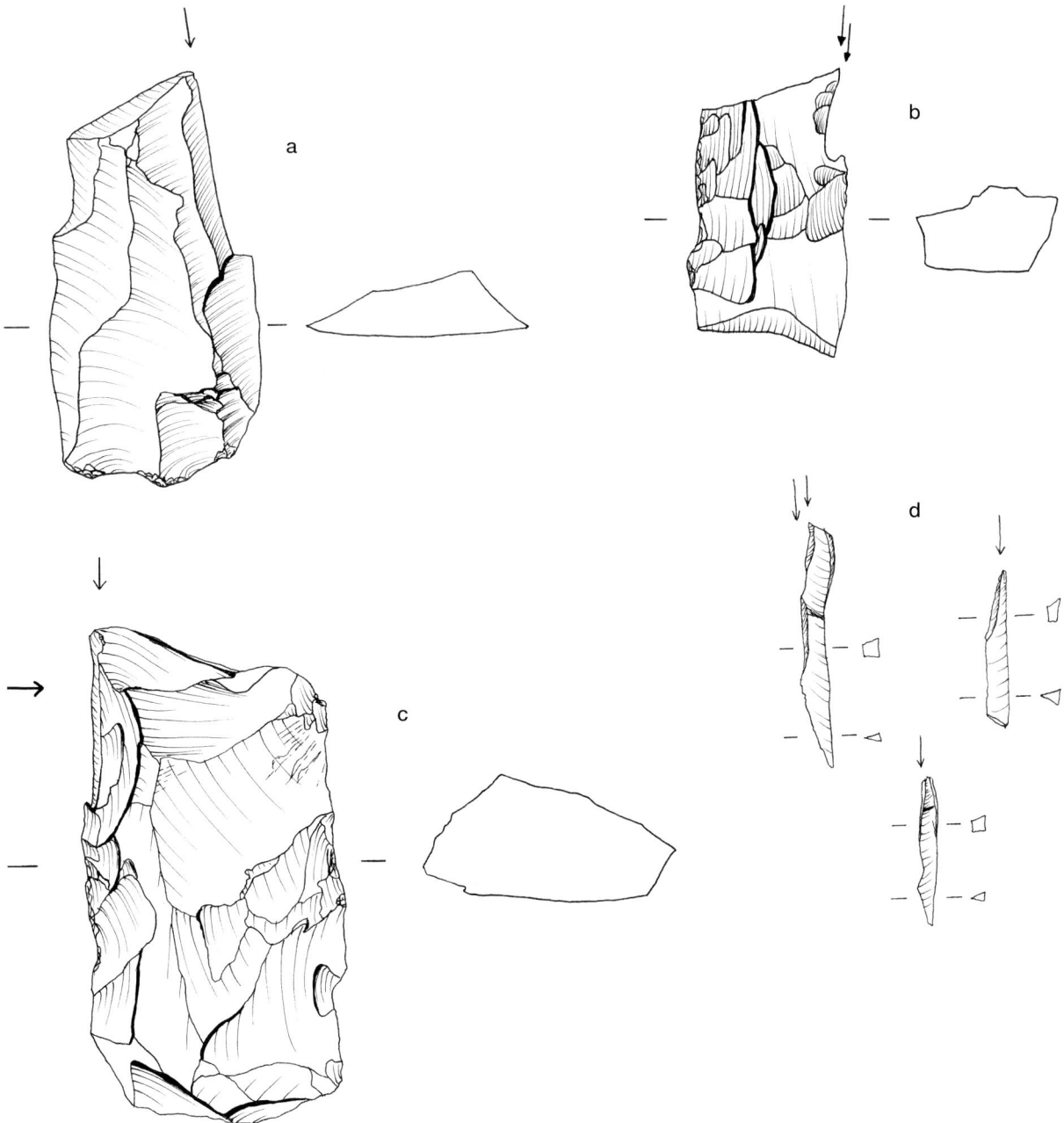

Fig. 131. Burins. a) Angle burin on a natural edge. b) Angle burin on flat-flaked flake axe. c) Angle burin on transverse blow (fragment of a core axe used as raw material). d) Burin spalls. Scale 3:4. Drawing: Søren Timm Christensen.

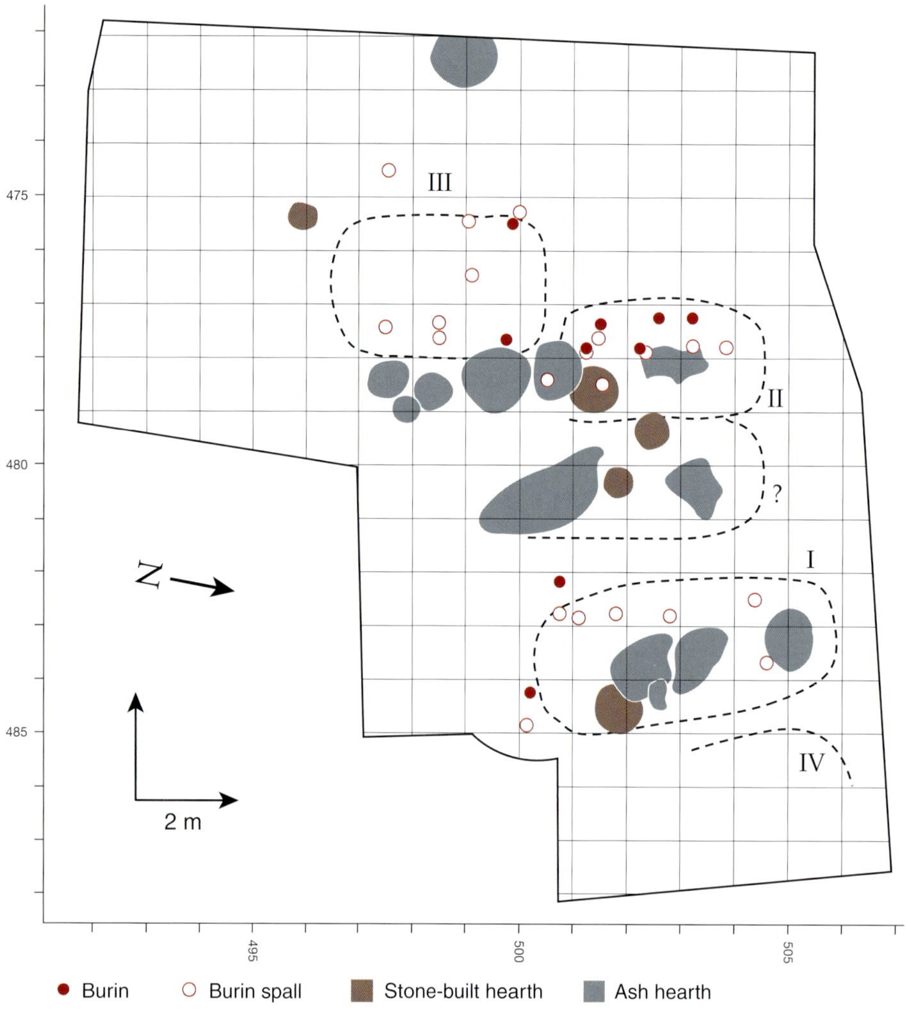

Fig. 132. The distribution of burins and burin spalls across the settlement surface. Most activities seem to be generally associated with the area to the west of the hearths.

length of the burin spalls is 6-10 cm and their width is 3-5.6 mm.

Truncated pieces are dominant among the flake tools with 37 examples, corresponding to 23.2% of the latter group. In most cases, raw material has been chosen that is triangular in outline and broadest at the distal end. Numerous pieces are on wide, thin A-blades. All show truncation at the distal end and the majority also have clear wear traces on the longest side edge. The truncated pieces were found scattered across the settlement surface and do not appear to form any conspicuous concentrations (Fig. 133).

Blades with straight truncation are represented by two examples. They are both on A-blades, of which one is broad, flat and thin. Both have retouch at their distal end. They are respectively 7.7 and 11.4 cm in length and their width is 2.9 cm.

Blades with straight, concave truncation are the most frequent type of blade tool in the assemblage and are represented by 12 examples (Fig. 134b). Two pieces are on broken blades, respectively a proximal and a distal part. Two pieces are on narrow, slender blades, six are on A-blades, one is on a B-blade and one is on a wide, thin A-blade. All have distal retouch. On one piece a corner of the retouched edge has been broken off diagonally. Their length is 4.6-10.7 cm and their width 1.5-4.5 cm. Two of these pieces were made on short, broad blades with a triangular outline. This shape is also known from Vængesø II, but is rare at other coeval Ertebølle settlements in eastern Jutland. This is a local variant.

Blades with edge retouch at the percussion bulb (proximal) end are represented by only two examples at this settlement (Fig. 134e). In one case,

Fig. 133. *Distribution of truncated pieces (mainly on terraces II and III) and blades with fine denticulation (blade saws).*

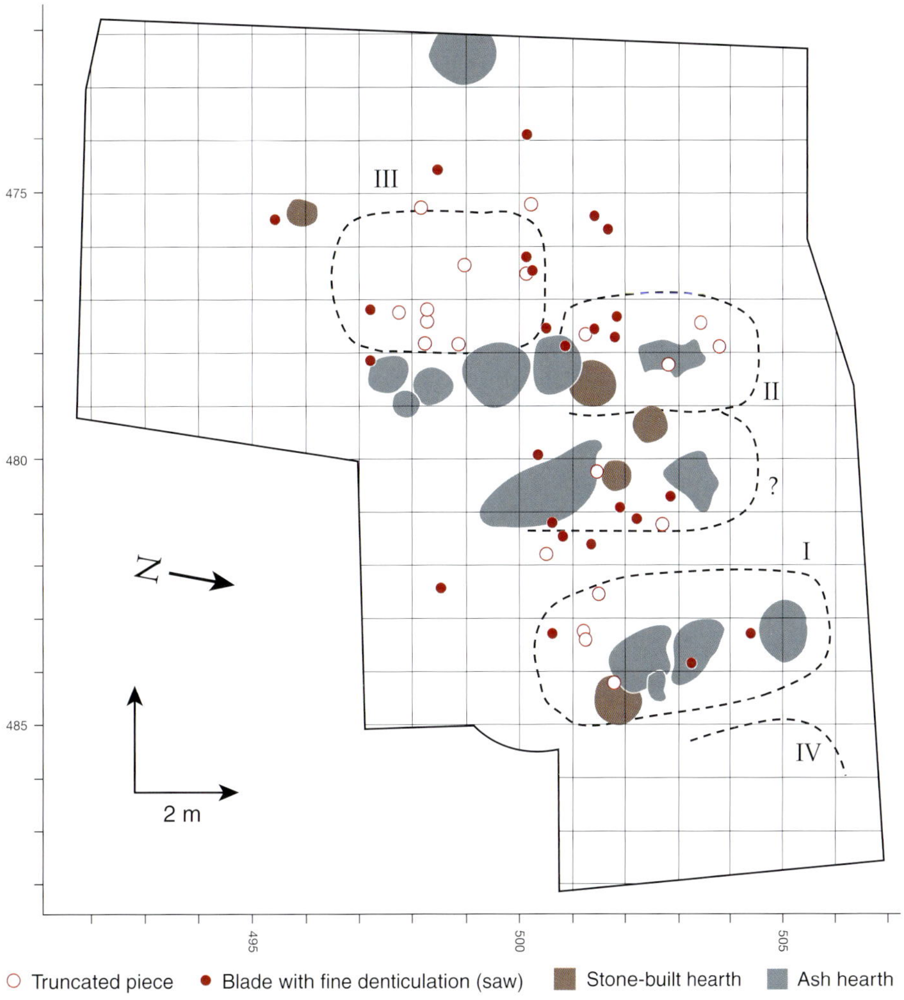

475
480
485
495
500
505
III
II
?
I
IV
N
2 m
Truncated piece
Blade with fine denticulation (saw)
Stone-built hearth
Ash hearth

double-sided edge retouch is seen (handle retouch) at the percussion bulb end; the other only has retouch on one edge. Compared with Vængesø II, where this variant is prominent among the truncated pieces, this type is very rare at this settlement.

Blades with straight, oblique truncation are represented by seven examples (Fig. 134a, f). Of these, one piece is on a short, partially cortex-covered flake. Five pieces are on A-blades, one of which on a wide, flat blade and the others are on irregular B-blades. Remarkably, two are short, almost quadratic pieces. The longest truncated blade has double-sided edge retouch at the percussion bulb end (handle retouch) along a 4 cm section. The smallest example is 3.7 cm long and 3.5 cm wide, the largest is 10.3 cm long and 3.5 cm wide.

Blades with oblique, concave truncation are represented by 12 examples. One is fire-brittled and is finely denticulate along one edge, which is concave (a variant of the blade saws; Fig. 134c). One is on an A-blade, nine are on B-blades and two are broken-off distal ends. The raw material for this group comprises slightly more irregular pieces than the group with straight, concave truncation. One piece has double-sided edge retouch along a 3 cm long section of one edge at the percussion bulb end (propeller retouch), and another also has edge retouch along a 2.6 cm section of an edge, also at the percussion bulb end. Numerous pieces show chips and wear on their longest edge. Their length is 5-10.7 cm and their width 1.8-4 cm.

Pieces with irregular truncation occur as four examples. Three are on blades and in one case the raw material was an irregular flake with concave edges. The width of this piece also increases

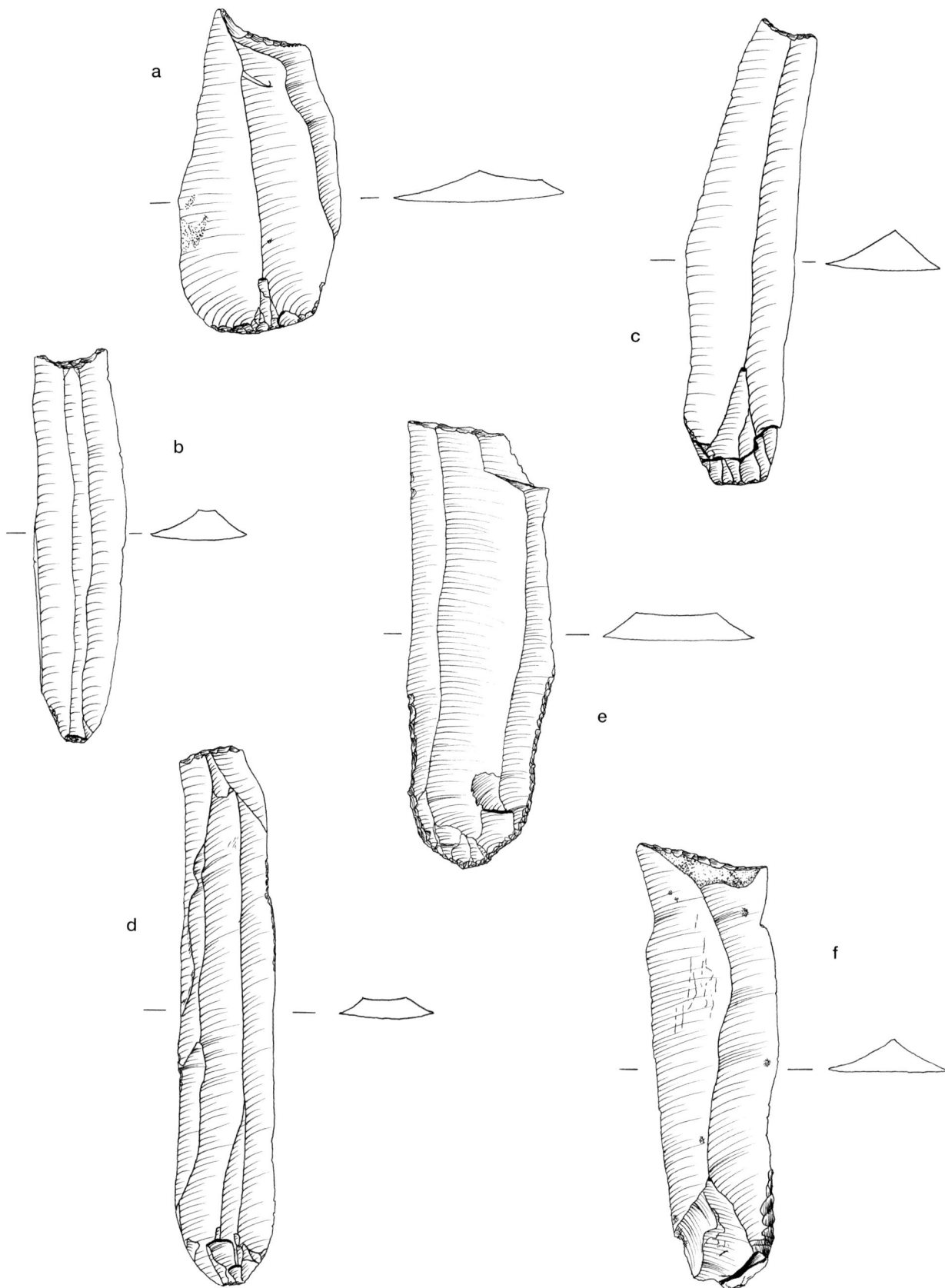

Fig. 134. a-c, f) Blades with concave, distal truncation. d) Blade with weakly convex truncation. e) Blade with oblique truncation and worked handle at its proximal end. Scale 3:4. Drawing: Søren Timm Christensen.

markedly towards its distal end, which has oblique, concave truncation that forms a point at its longest side edge. This edge shows wear damage in the form of both micro- and macroscopic chips. The percussion bulb end is broken off. This piece has a very unusual form and the author has not seen similar tools in other Ertebølle assemblages. Both its form and its wear traces suggest that it represents a knife. Its length is 7.5 cm and its width at the distal end is 5.9 cm. One piece is on a small flake, at the distal end of which is truncation consisting of two concave sections which meet in the middle to form a short point. Finally, there are two pieces on blades (a broken-off distal end and a complete blade) with slightly irregular, slightly curved truncation. Their length is 2-9.6 cm and the width 2.7-2.9 cm. Truncated pieces are one of the commonest tool forms at the Vængesø II and III settlements, but differences can be observed between the morphology of these pieces at the two sites. Firstly, there is a greater number of truncated pieces and also of variants at Vængesø II. Secondly, the raw material employed at Vængesø II was significantly more irregular and consisted to a considerable extent of coarse, irregular flakes, while at Vængesø III there is a dominance of more regular blades. At Vængesø II, this tool group is consequently characterised by numerous large, broad pieces, of which a number have a characteristic, triangular outline (Fig. 50d). This variant is represented by a very few examples at Vængesø III. Furthermore, the type with (handle) retouch at the percussion bulb end is prominent at Vængesø II, but only represented by very few pieces at Vængesø III. It is difficult to explain these differences, but the immediate impression gained is that ad hoc flakes were used for these tools to a much greater extent at Vængesø II than at Vængesø III. If these tools were in particular used for cutting and flensing work (which the wear traces clearly show), this could mean that there was a greater requirement for this type of work at Vængesø II than at Vængesø III. This conclusion is consistent with the interpretation of Vængesø II as a special hunting site located out on the bar between the lagoon and the inlet of Ebeltoft Vig.

Finely denticulate pieces are a common and characteristic type at this settlement and therefore contribute to defining its flint inventory (c. 19% of the flake tools). Twenty-nine examples were recorded, and these form a very uniform and homogeneous group (Fig. 135). The raw material was regular blades. In three cases the choice fell on broad, thin, straight blades. Seven are broken-off percussion bulb ends, one is a middle section and two are distal ends. Three have denticulation on both edges, similar to the piece from Vængesø I (double saw; Fig. 135a; Andersen, S.H. 1975b, 26-27, Fig. 20). In four cases, the denticulation was along a concave edge, which means that these pieces, in terms of their form, are closely related to the curved knives. Their length (intact pieces) is 7.8-11 cm and their width 2.4-3-3 cm.

The finely denticulate pieces were evenly distributed across the settlement surface, but with a particularly frequent occurrence around terraces II and III and on the slope between terraces I and II (Fig. 133). Finely and coarsely denticulate pieces are characteristic types for many settlements from the Ertebølle culture in eastern Jutland and on western Funen, while they appear to be relatively rare in for example the Limfjord area and on Zealand (Jensen, H.J. 1994, 53-55, Fig. 15). Their frequency at Vængesø III is though unusual in relation to other coeval Ertebølle sites. This is a feature that distinguishes the tool inventory of this settlement from that seen at Vængesø I and II, where there were also finely denticulate pieces, but in much smaller numbers.

Blades with coarse denticulation are represented by 18 examples. The raw material was generally irregular blades and blade fragments; in one case it was a broad, thin blade. As a whole, this group consists of used, broken blades. Four pieces are broken-off proximal ends, three are middle pieces of blades and two are distal ends. Nine pieces have denticulation on one edge, the others have denticulation on both edges. In three cases the denticulation is on a slightly concave edge, and in several cases there is a smooth transition between these pieces and the blade saws (true of four pieces). Their length (intact examples) is 6 cm and their width 3.4 cm.

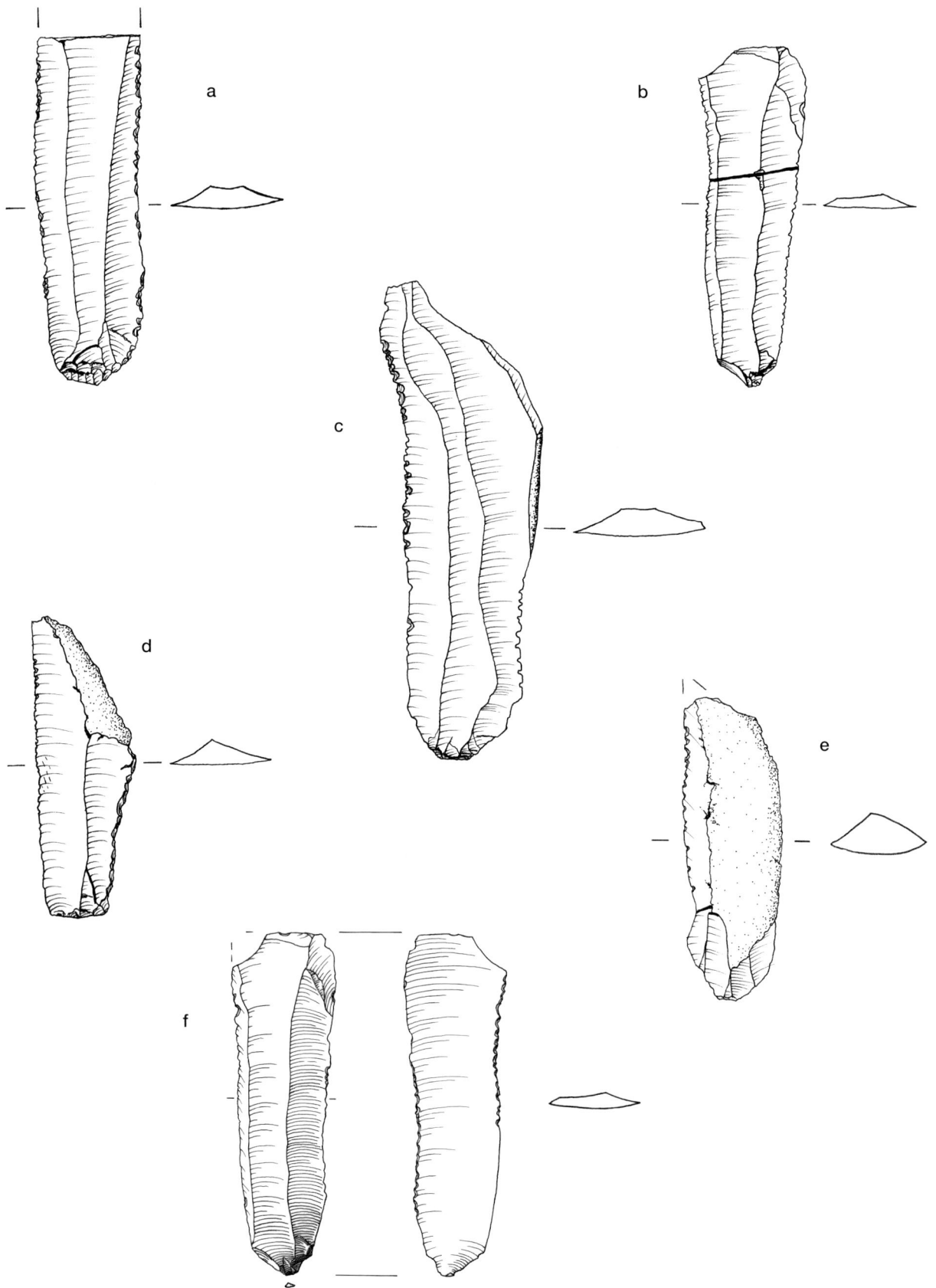

Fig. 135. a-f) Blades with fine denticulation on one or both edges, d) with additional dorsal trimming. Scale 3:4. Drawing: Søren Timm Christensen.

Blades with worked handle at the percussion bulb end are represented by three examples. One of these is made on a thin and regular A-blade, on which the edges have regular edge retouch over a 5 cm long section at the percussion bulb end, thereby forming a handle that is only slightly displaced relative to the side edges (Fig. 134e). The second piece is on a regular A-blade with double, regular edge retouch on a 5 cm long section of both edges at the percussion bulb end, and the third piece is an irregular B-blade. The distal ends of the blades are in two cases broken off, but probably had concave truncation such that the tool originally was a knife with a worked handle. This type is also represented by three examples among the truncated pieces, which suggests that blade tools with this special working of the (proximal) percussion bulb end were originally quite common in the assemblage. Their length (in their present form) is 7.7, 8.3 and 10.3 cm and their width is 3.9, 1.9 and 3.8 cm.

Blades with curved dorsal retouch are represented by nine pieces, which in six cases are on short irregular blades along one curved edge on which there is coarse edge retouch. One piece is on a more irregular flake, on which the edge opposite the curved back has continuous edge retouch. Four pieces are blades/flakes with a white, patinated surface and slight traces of water-wear. One piece is the tip of a blade knife with oblique retouch at the tip (oblique finger rest). Their length is 4-4.6 cm and their width 2.3-3.2 cm.

Fourteen pieces have been identified as *curved knives* (Fig. 136a-b). For a definition of this type, reference is made to H.J. Jensen (1994, 69-70) and S.H. Andersen (2009, 63-64). The raw materials for these were in 13 cases blades or flakes, one edge of which follows either a straight or a concave course and shows macroscopic chips and wear traces. One piece is on a short, wide flake. The pieces from Vængesø III constitute a very uniform group (in terms of form and size), and correspond completely to the previously published definition and description. Their length is 6.6-7 cm and their width 2.3-3.3 cm.

Notched pieces comprise 17 examples, of which four are on A-blades, nine are on B-blades and four are on flakes (Fig. 136c-d). Two pieces are on broken blades (respectively a proximal and a distal end). The

four A-blades are wide and thin. One blade has a retouched notch at one side of its distal end, the others have a notch in one edge. On one flake a notch has been retouched near the percussion bulb (and the opposite, convex edge shows wear traces – it may have been used as a knife). On another flake is a notch in the distal end and in the edge. On ten pieces the notch was formed with retouch and on the others it was made by removing one or two chips from the edge. This group contains one of the assemblage's longest blades. The length of the blades is 5.6-13.5 cm, and their width 1.9-3.6 cm. In the case of the flakes, their length is 4.6-6.5 and their width is 5.4-6 cm.

Pieces with continuous edge retouch are few in number, being represented by 13 examples, of which 11 are on blades. Of these, five are parts of regular blades (proximal, i.e. percussion bulb ends), while the remainder comprises short middle pieces and distal ends. Two pieces are on irregular flakes. A proximal end of a regular blade has double-sided (reverse) edge retouch at the percussion bulb end over a distance of c. 2-3 cm. Their length is 3.5-11.5 cm and their width 2.5-4 cm.

The raw material employed for the *transverse arrowheads* was thin, flat flakes (Fig. 137). In only one case was a biconvex flake used (Andersen, S.H. 1979b, 77-98). Two transverse arrowheads are fire-brittled; one comes from the upper part of the kitchen midden and the other from the pre-midden layer. There is a tendency for the transverse arrowheads from the kitchen midden to have a slightly more patinated surface than those from the deeper layers, where the surface appears more primary. The assemblage from Vængesø III includes a total of 79 transverse arrowheads (40% of the artefact group), which can be classified into a number of form types (Tab. 3).

There are nine fragments of transverse arrowheads, of which four are bases and five are parts of the edge. Two transverse arrowheads are probably of Neolithic date (Fig. 137a-b). On one of these, the edges were formed with reverse retouch; they are also straight and run together to form a pointed base. These pieces both came from the upper part of the kitchen midden – a stratigraphic position that corresponds to their presumed typological age. Three transverse arrowheads differ from the

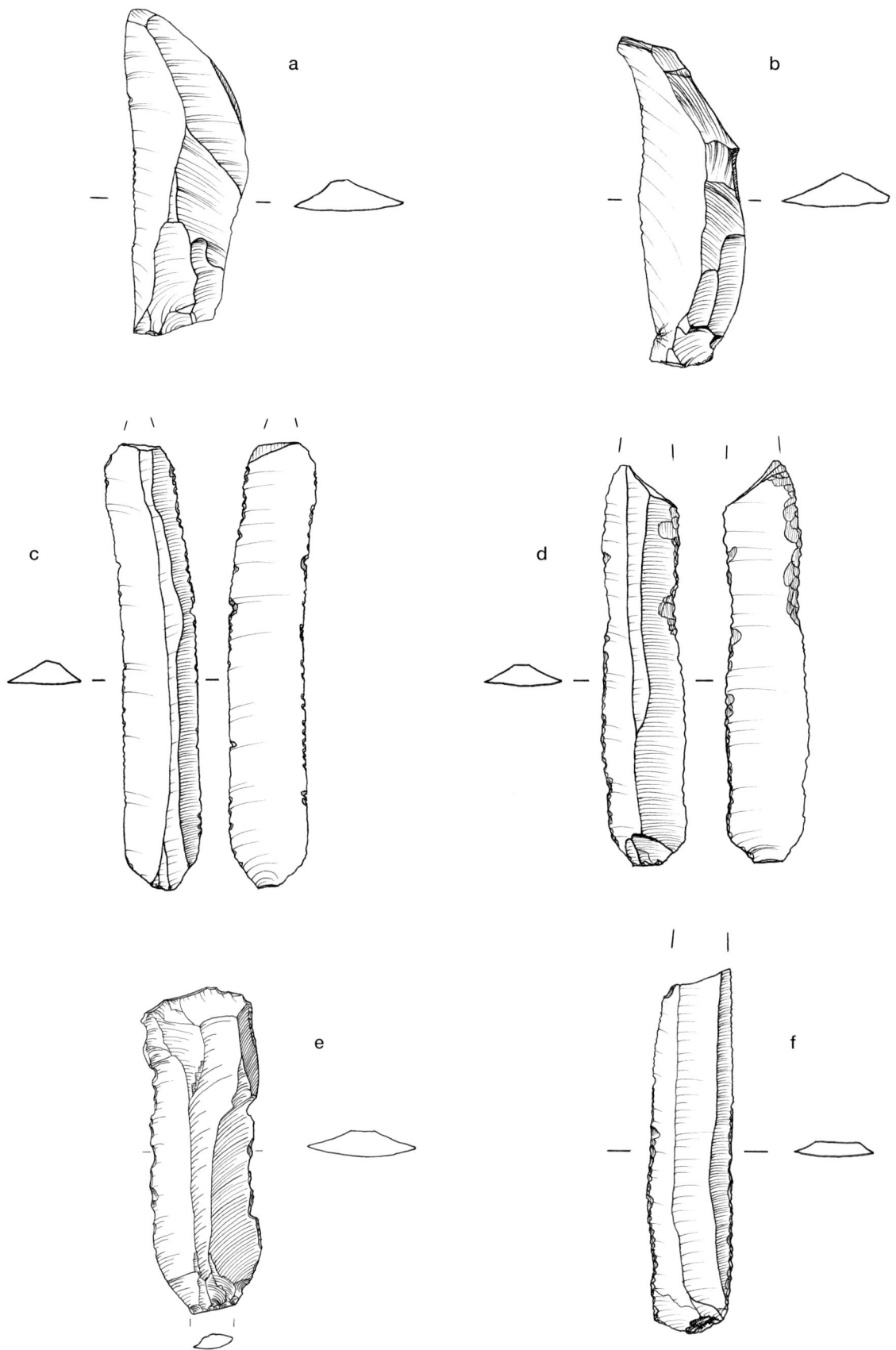

Fig. 136. a-b) Curved knives. c-d) Blades with a notch, denticulation and continuous edge retouch.
e) Blade with coarse denticulation. f) Blade with continuous edge retouch. Scale 3:4. Drawing: Søren
Timm Christensen.

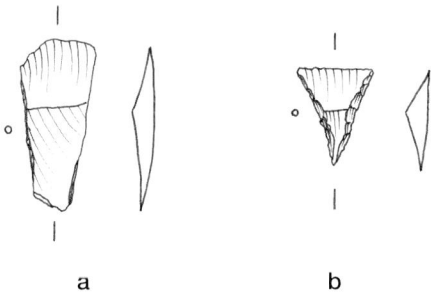

Fig. 137. a-b) Transverse arrowheads from the upper layer in the kitchen midden. c-l) Transverse arrowheads from the middle and lower parts of the kitchen midden; arrows with strongly concave sides dominate in the shell midden. m-v) Transverse arrowheads from the pre-midden layer; arrows with an oblique edge are found in this horizon, cf. Fig. 140. Scale 3:4. Drawing: Søren Timm Christensen.

Upper layer of shell midden

Middle and lower layers of kitchen midden

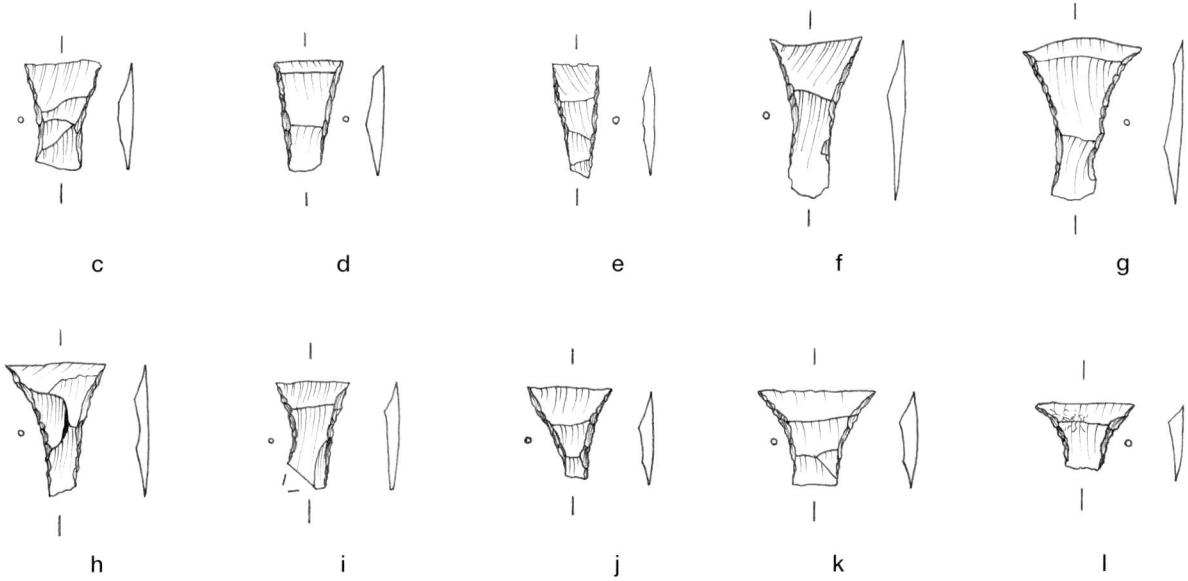

Pre-midden layer

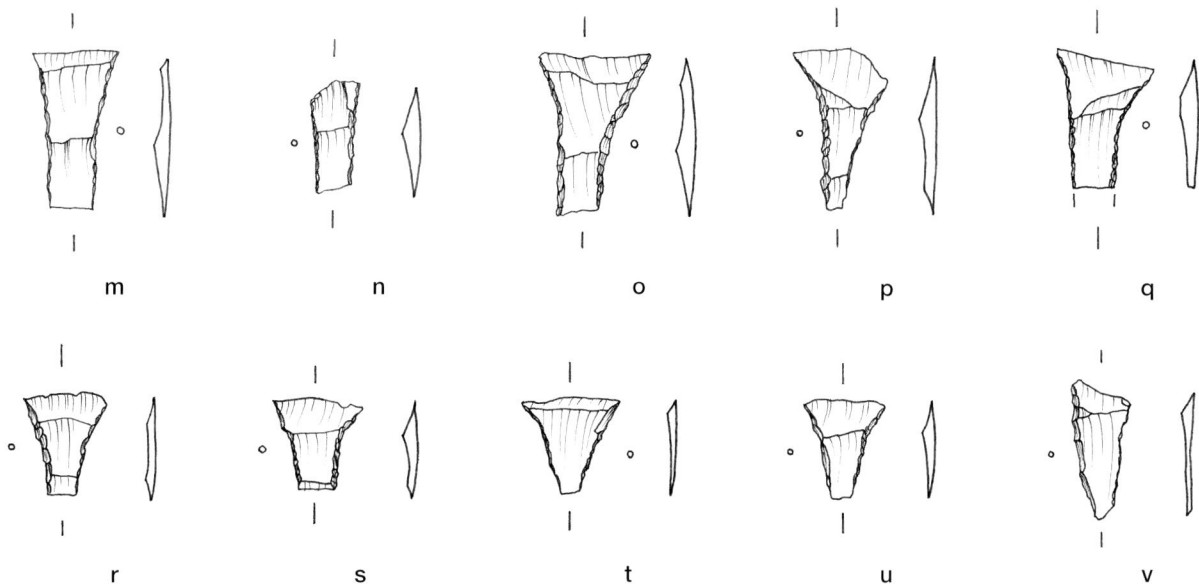

others in that they are both wider and longer than the rest; their length is 2.6-2.9 cm. The dominant types are arrowheads with either slightly or markedly concave edges, which make up respectively 17.7 and 62% of the group (Tab. 3). The other types are of minor significance. If the types are assessed according to where in the deposits they were found, no difference can be established with respect to the pieces with slightly and markedly concave sides. Conversely, the types with slightly or markedly oblique edges are only present in the pre-midden layer, constituting c. 11.4% of the total number. As the latter types (with an oblique edge) are considered to be earlier than arrowheads with concave sides, this difference provides further evidence that the pre-midden layer is older than the kitchen midden, consistent with the stratigraphy and the available radiocarbon dates. The size of the arrowheads varies somewhat, but no difference in size could be established between the types or

between the arrowheads from the two layers. Their length is 1.1-3 cm and their width at the base 0.4-1.3 cm. The majority measure around 1.8 cm in length and have a base width of 1.4 cm. If the transverse arrowheads are divided up according to the layer in which they were found, a distribution pattern emerges that only differs slightly from that presented in Fig. 137. The transverse arrowheads were found all over the settlement surface, but they do show a concentration on terrace II, and especially on the edge of the hearths on this terrace. Conversely, there were very few transverse arrowheads on terrace I and only two on terrace III (Fig. 138). Examination of the horizontal distribution of preforms for these arrowheads (Fig. 139) reveals many at the edge of the ash hearths, especially on terrace II. Furthermore, there are squares in which several examples occur within a very short distance. These concentrations must represent places where the arrowheads were produced.

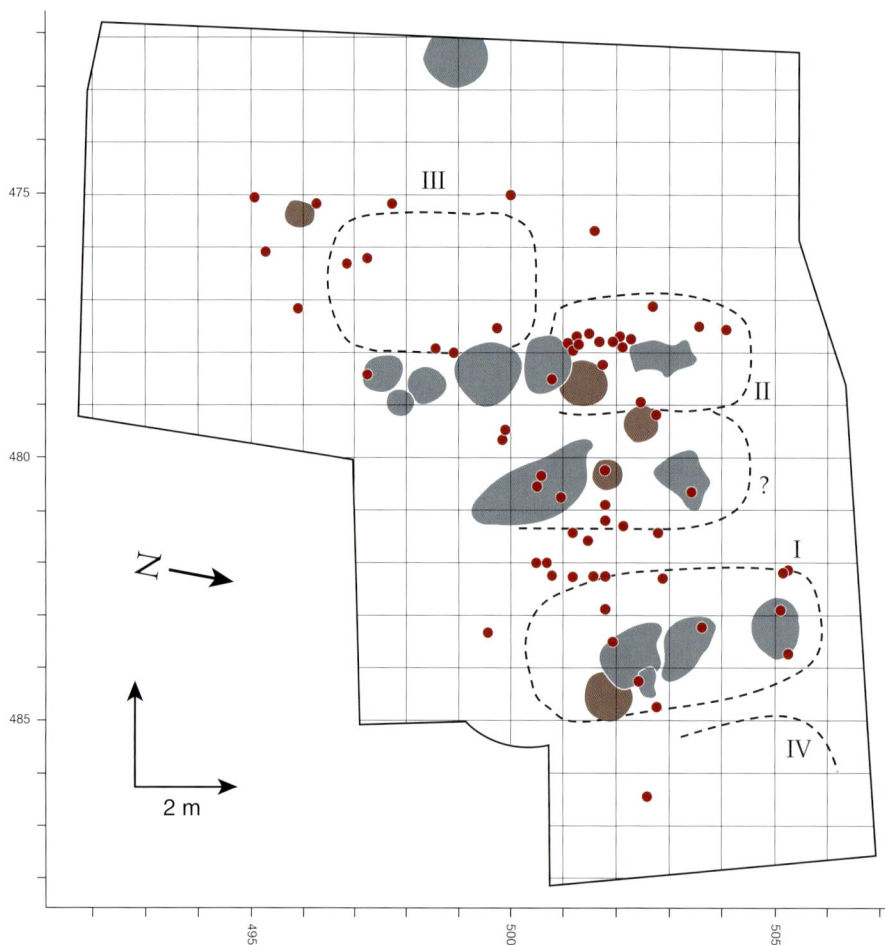

Fig. 138. Distribution of transverse arrowheads across the settlement surface.

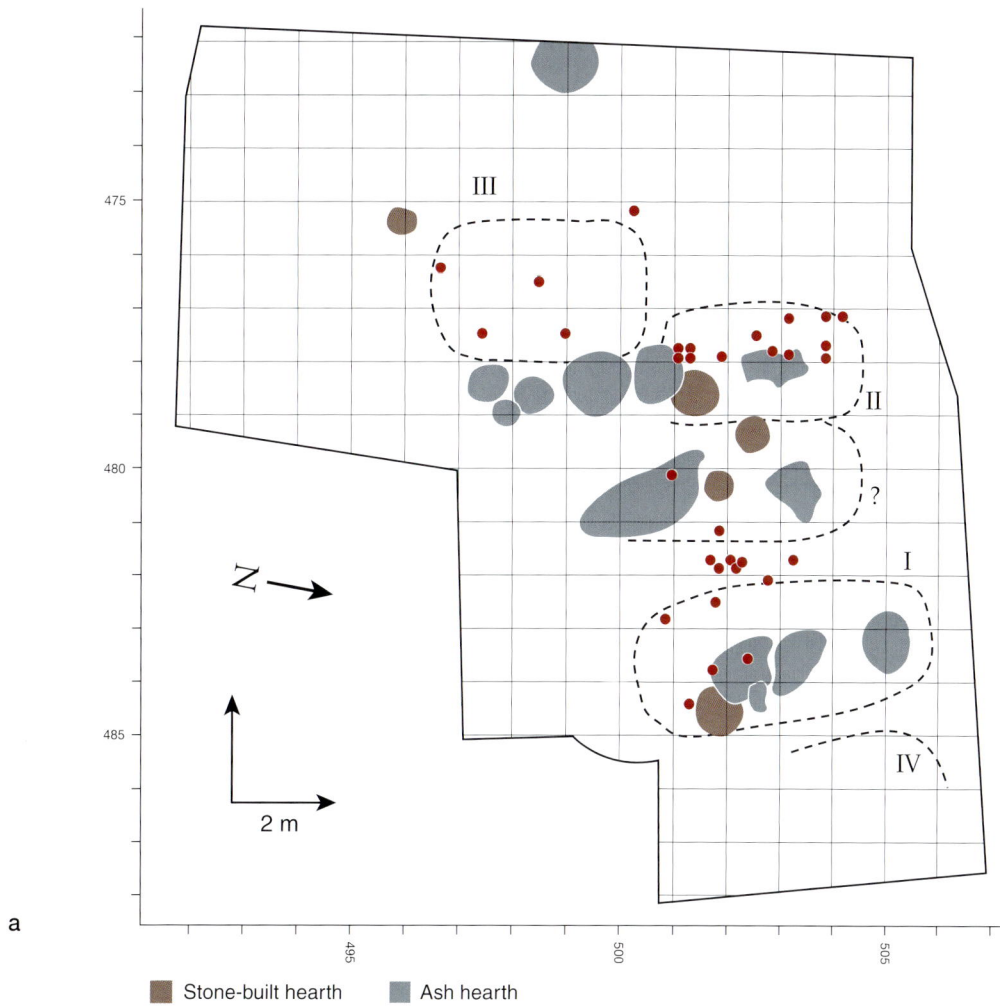

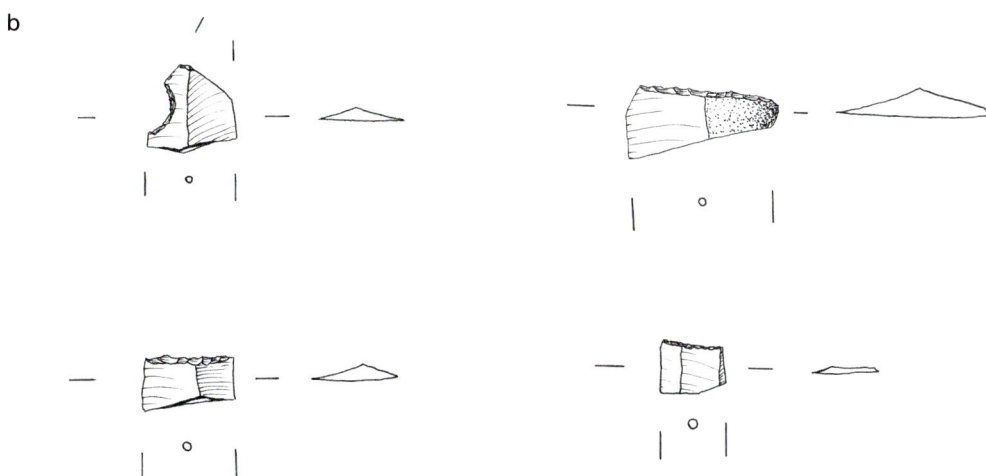

Fig. 139. a) Distribution of preforms and waste from the production of transverse arrowheads.
b) Examples of types of waste from the production of transverse arrowheads. Scale 3:4. Drawing:
Søren Timm Christensen.

Two transverse arrowheads of the type with parallel sides show *use damage from being shot*. This takes the form of a broken-off corner and small irregular chips in the edge. Of the type with slightly concave sides, six show damage in the form of a broken corner and seven have small chips in the edge, and 11 are broken arrowheads from which the base is missing. Of the type with markedly concave sides, one has a broken-off edge, 22 have a broken-off corner, ten lack a base and 26 have chips in the edge (six on the lower surface and 20 on the upper). Among the arrowheads of the type with a slightly oblique edge, two show shooting damage in the form of broken-off parts of the edge. Overall, 38.8% have chips in the edge, 32.5% lack an edge corner, 24.7% have a broken-off base and one example (1.1%) has a broken-off edge.

If all the transverse arrowheads from Vængesø III are matched with a seriation diagram for several Ertebølle settlements in eastern Jutland, it is evident that the locality belongs to the Late Ertebølle culture and is coeval with both Vængesø I and II (Fig. 140). This chronological position corresponds well with the results of the scientific dating and a seriation of the flake axes.

There are 20 *preforms for transverse arrowheads*. In the case of 16, the raw material was short, thin flakes. Six pieces show concave truncation, two have slightly convex truncation (both proximal), eight have straight and oblique (proximal) truncation, three have straight truncation (one with distal, one with proximal) and there is also a chip with a deep, retouched notch in one edge and two transverse, opposing fractured surfaces (micro-

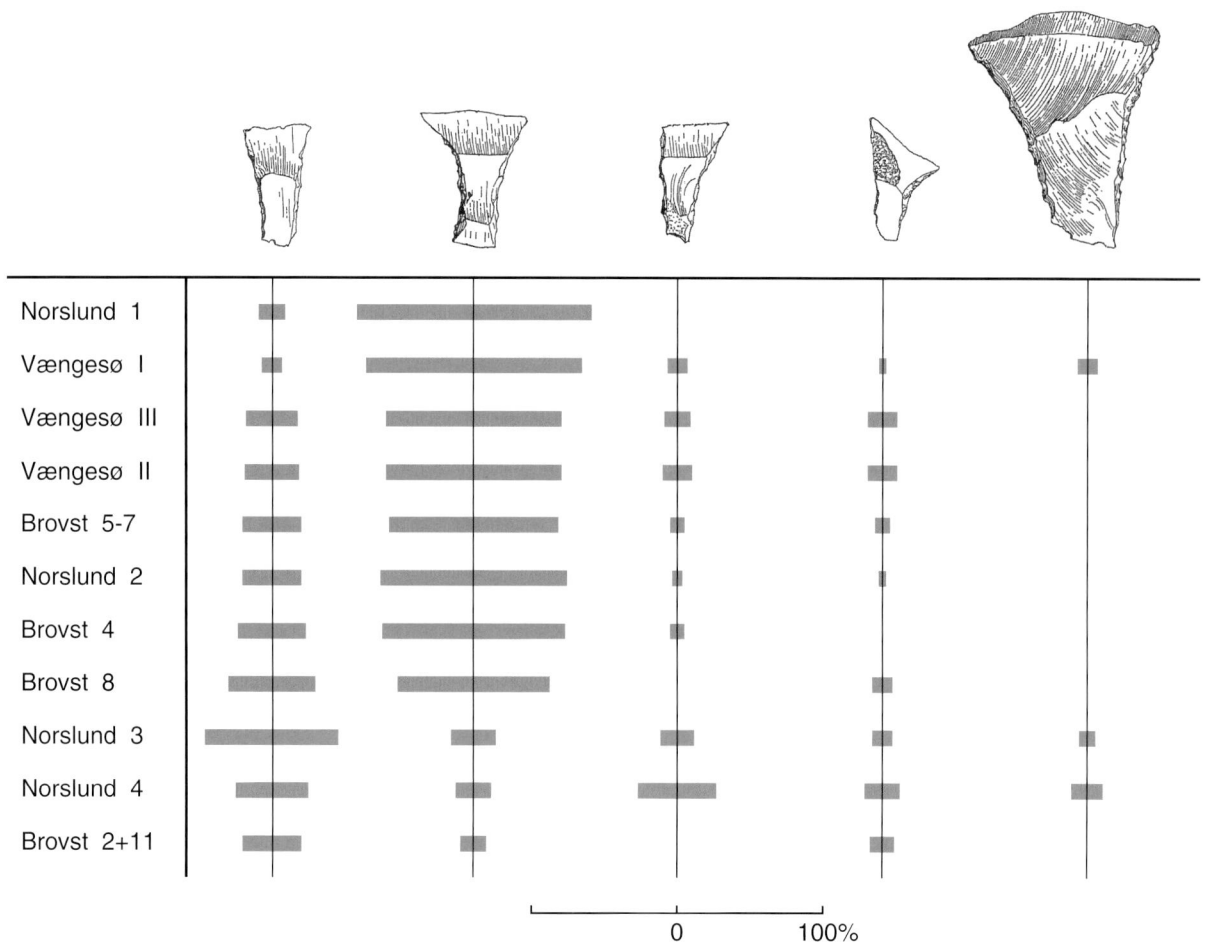

Fig. 140. Seriation diagram for the transverse arrowhead types from the Vængesø I, II and III settlements, compared with the types from the two stratified settlements of Norslund and Brovst. The diagram shows that the three Vængesø settlements should be dated to the Late/Latest Ertebølle culture.

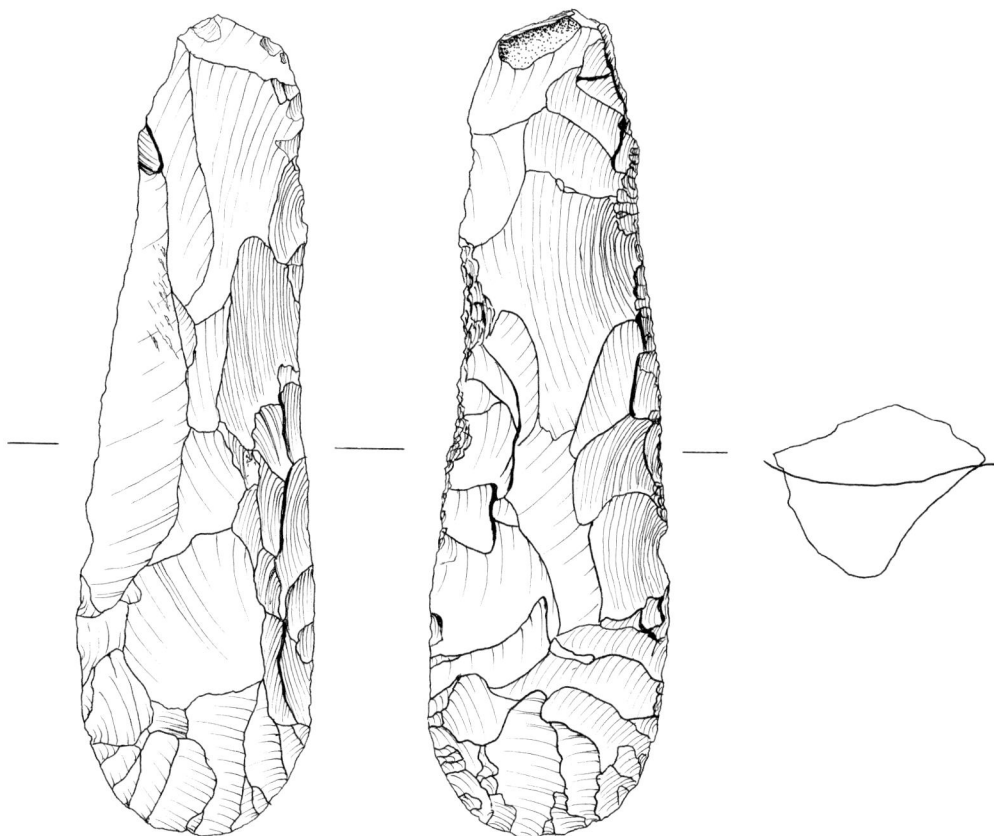

Fig. 141. Symmetrical core adze with bifacial specialised edge working. Scale 3:4. Drawing: Søren Timm Christensen.

burin). Two pieces with straight truncation at the distal end differ from the rest of this group in that they are thicker. These are therefore perhaps not preforms for transverse arrowheads, but maybe the broken-off ends of truncated blades. The length of these pieces is 0.9-4.2 cm and their thickness 1.5-4.5 cm, while two pieces are on slightly thicker flakes (c. 4.5 mm).

Core axes/adzes are rare and only four examples were recovered, constituting 3.3% of the axe group. Two of these are butt sections from symmetrical axes, one is the butt of a symmetrical adze and the fourth is a symmetrical adze with double-sided specialised edge trimming (the only intact example in the assemblage; Fig. 141). It is elongate in outline, guttiform with a regular, rounded edge, which has wear polish on its domed side. The length of this adze is 14.8 cm, its width 4.5 cm and its thickness 3 cm. One of the core axes is fire-brittled.

There are only three *edge flakes from core axes/adzes*, which is consistent with the very small number of core axes/adzes encountered at the settlement. One of these comes from an adze with a double-sided, specialised edge, while the two others are from symmetrical axes. Their length is 5-6.4 cm and their width 4-6.1 cm. A heavily worked (fire-brittled) piece of flint is interpreted as part of the butt of a core axe. This piece appears irregular and thereby differs from the other butt pieces. It measures 8.2 cm in length, 6 cm in width and 2.5 cm in thickness. There is also a short butt fragment of a symmetrical core axe in the assemblage. This measures 3.2 cm in length and 4.1 cm in width. Finally, mention should be made of two butt fragments of symmetrical core axes that are included together with the unipolar cores.

The assemblage includes 100 *flake axes*, representing 83.3% of the axe group. Of these, 79 are symmetrical flat-flaked examples, nine are asymmetrical flat-flaked, one is edge trimmed and 11 are atypical. There are also 19 preforms and fragments. Although the number of flake axes appears large, there are actually fewer flake axes at this site than at the two other, much smaller localities, Vængesø I and II. This difference becomes even more marked when the totals are compared in the light of the area excavated and thickness of the culture layer. A map of the distribution of the flat-flaked flake axes (Fig. 142) shows that they are roughly confined within two areas on the settlement surface, respectively on terrace II and terrace III (especially axes from the kitchen midden). A single square (477/502) was found to contain four flake axes. If the distribution of the flake axe preforms is mapped, there is a clear centre of gravity around terraces II and III, whereas there are only very few down the hillside and on terrace I (Fig. 142). In several places these pieces lay close together, i.e. within c. 0.5-1.5 m. Remains

of damaged flake axes also lay in the same area, showing that they were primarily used (and worn out) on the settlement's highest area. If we turn to the distribution of the edge flakes, these have a clear centre of gravity up on the plateau between terraces II and III. This must mean that the flake axes were in particular used (and resharpened) on this part of the settlement (during accumulation of both the pre-midden and the kitchen midden layers). Examples of the flake axes are shown in Fig. 143. As can be seen from the classification, the flat-flaked form is supremely dominant with 91.2%, while the other types are much less prominent. The raw material was very predominantly a whitish-grey, calcareous type of flint; in two cases a bryozoan-rich type of flint was employed. Six examples are fire-brittled. Measurements of the flat-flaked flake axes show that their length is 4.5-12.5 cm, with an average of 7.5 cm. Their width 3

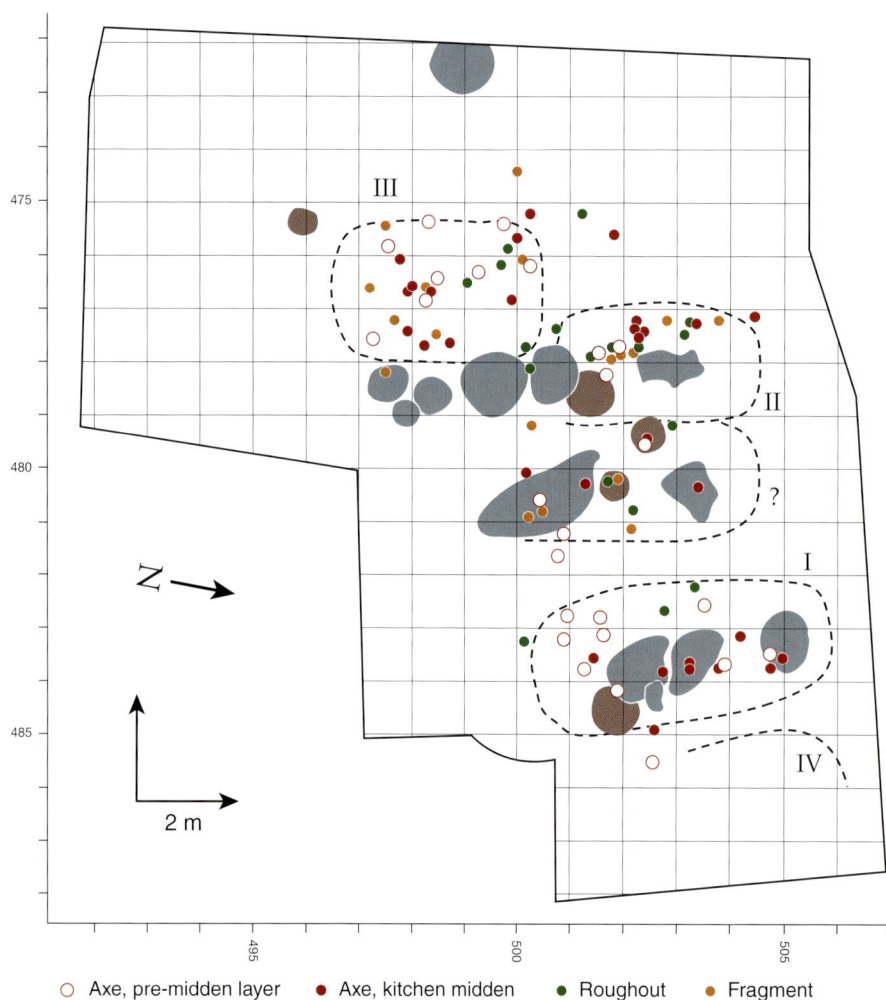

Fig. 142. Distribution of flat-flaked flake axes and roughouts and fragments across the settlement surface. The fragments are associated with the terraces.

○ Axe, pre-midden layer   ● Axe, kitchen midden   ● Roughout   ● Fragment

Fig. 143 (pages 171-173). Flat-flaked flake axes. a, f) Asymmetrical flat-flaked flake axes. b-e, g, h-i)
Flat-flaked symmetrical flake axes. b) Broken into two fragments, which lay 1 m apart. e) and i) reused
as angle burins. Scale 3:4. Drawing: Søren Timm Christensen.

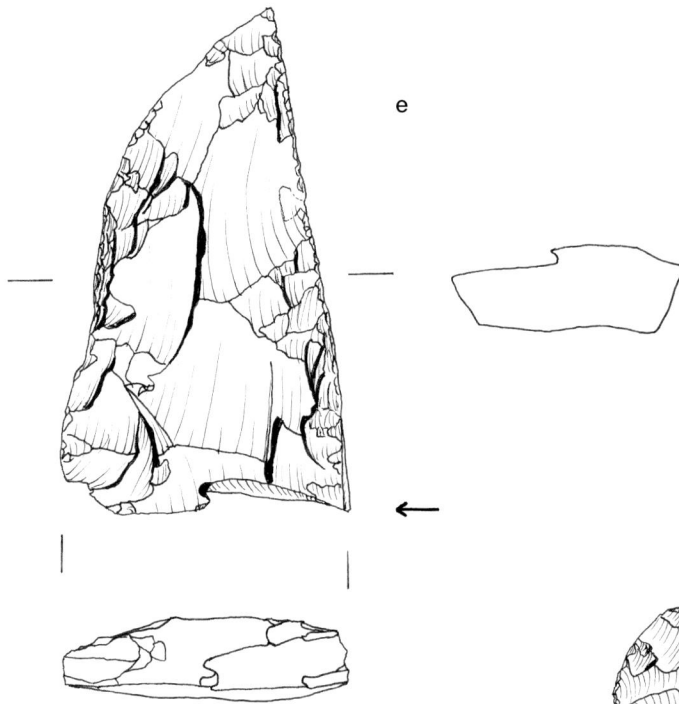

e

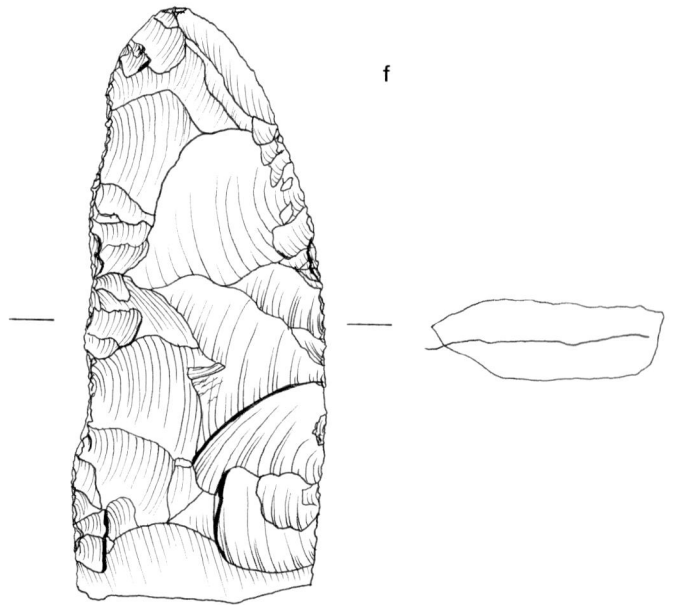

f

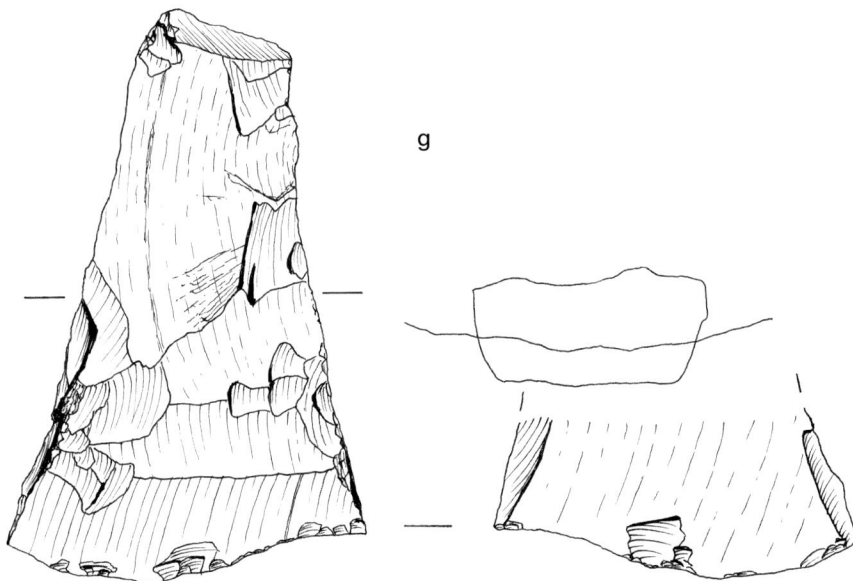

g

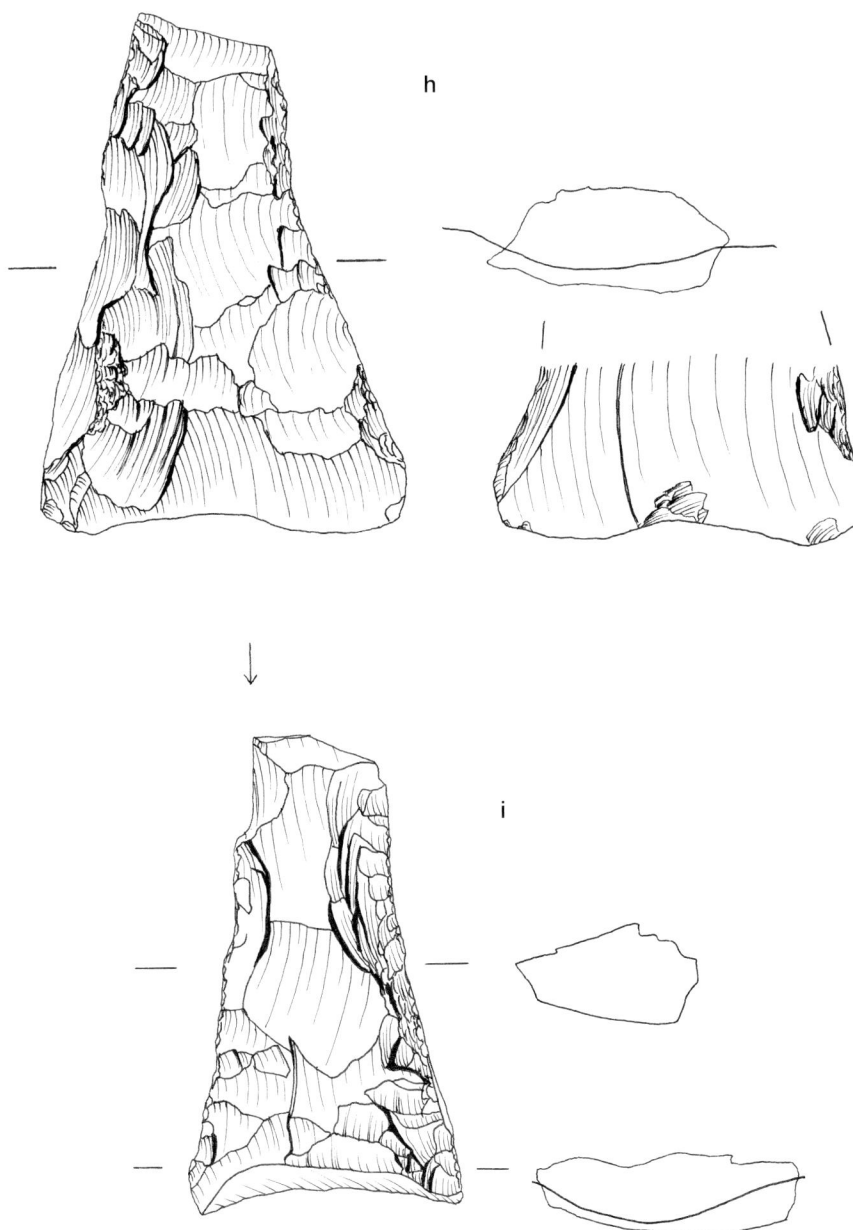

cm from the butt is 2.5-6 cm, with an average of 3.6 cm. Their greatest thickness is confined within very narrow limits, 1-3.5 cm, with an average of 1.7 cm. The edge width is rather more variable, 3-8 cm, with an average of 4.9 cm (Fig. 145b). If these dimensions are compared with those for the flat-flaked flake axes from Vængesø II (length 8.6 cm; see Fig. 59, top and 143, lower), Norslund layers 0+1 and Ronæs Skov (Andersen, S.H. 2009, 75), it is evident that the flake axes from Vængesø III are longer than those from Norslund, but similar in length to those from Ronæs Skov. As for the other dimensions, there is great similarity between the greatest width, width 3 cm from the butt and thickness between Vængesø III and Norslund (layers 0+1), while minor differences are evident between Vængesø III and Ronæs Skov (Andersen, S.H. 2009, 75, Fig. 48). Examination of the sides of the flake axes from Vængesø III shows that 17 (17%) have parallel sides, 57 (56%) have slightly concave sides and 28 (27%) have markedly concave sides (Fig. 145b). This analysis reveals that the

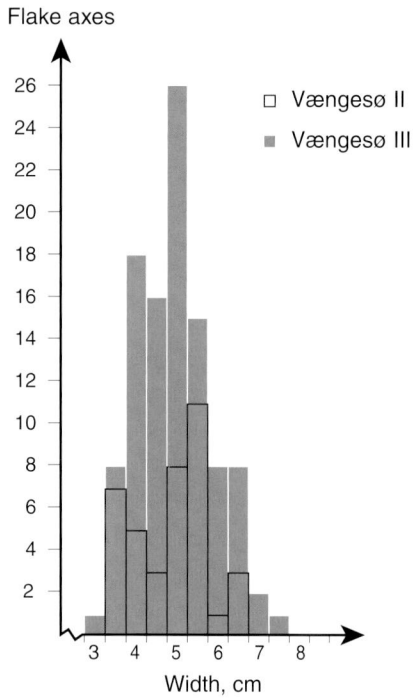

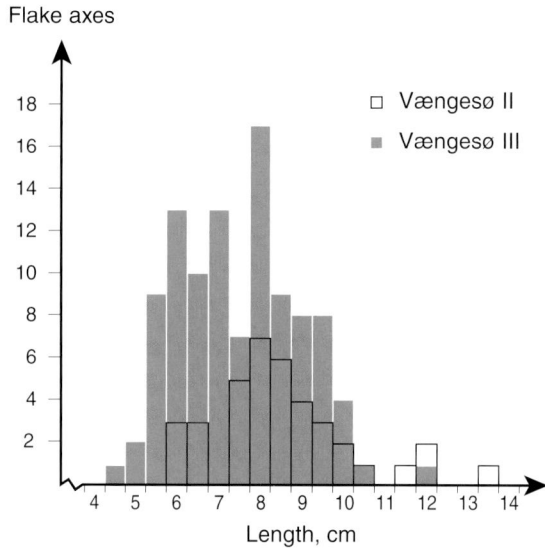

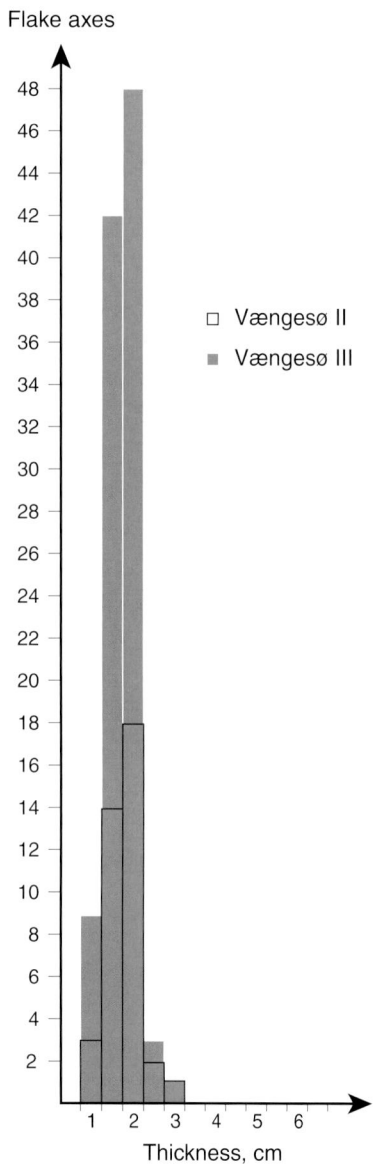

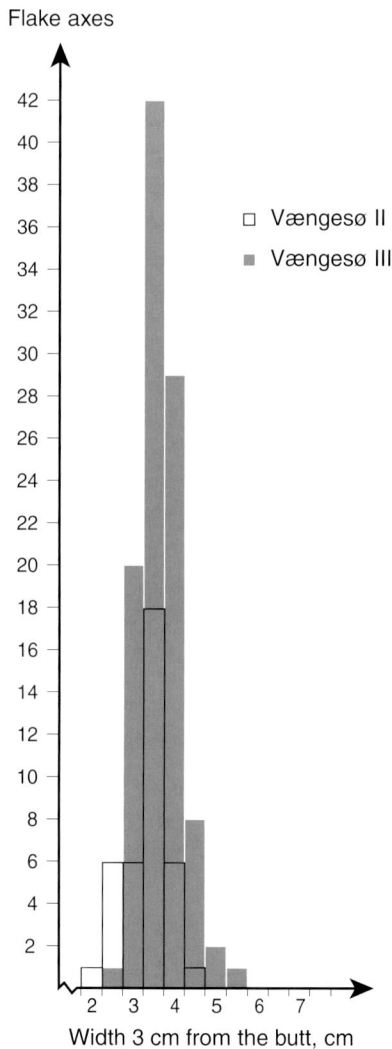

Fig. 144. Dimensions
of the flat-flaked
symmetrical flake
axes from Vængesø
III and Vængesø II.
The flake axes from
Vængesø III are
clearly longer and
wider than those
from Vængesø II,
while other dimen-
sions are the same.

flake axes from Vængesø III belong to a late part of the Ertebølle culture (Andersen, S.H. 2009, Fig. 50), a result that is consistent with the typological dating of the other finds and with the radiocarbon dates. Edge rejuvenation was only observed on six axes (6%) and this differs markedly from for example Norslund layers 0+1, where 37.8% of the flake axes show edge rejuvenation (Andersen/Malmros 1966, 47), Ronæs Skov (33.6%; Andersen, S.H. 2009, 76) and Tybrind Vig (41%; Andersen, S.H.

2013, 104). However, the situation at Vængesø III corresponds to that at Vængesø II, where there was a corresponding low frequency of edge rejuvenation. Apparently, attempts were made to resharpen flake axes on only a few occasions at these latter Ertebølle settlements. As most of the flake axes show damage and/or wear to the edge as a result of frequent and/or hard use, the few limited instances of resharpening must mean that they were swiftly discarded, after which new examples were pro-

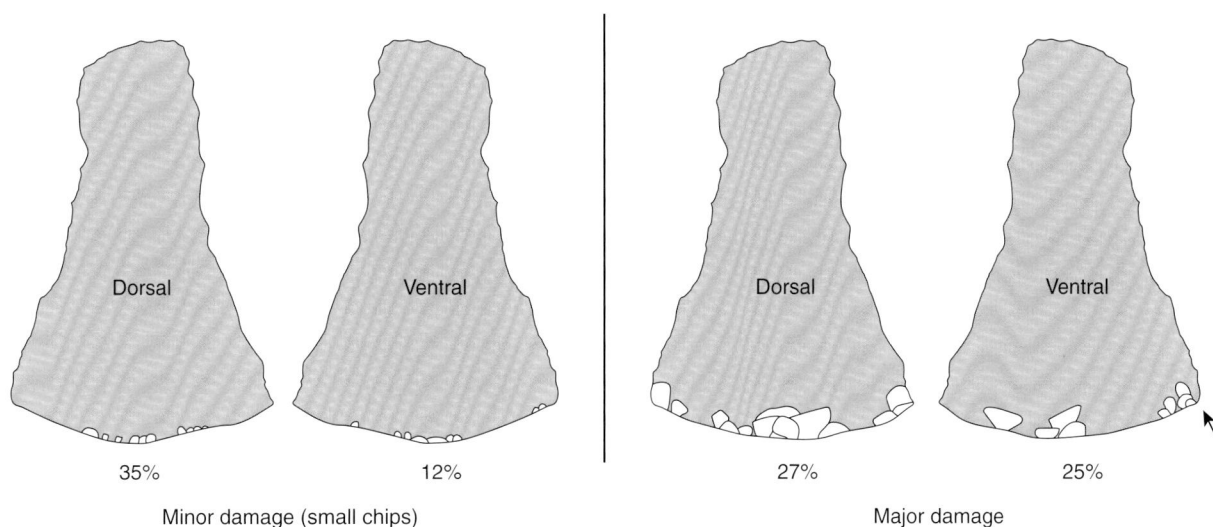

a

Minor damage (small chips) — Dorsal 35% / Ventral 12%

Major damage — Dorsal 27% / Ventral 25%

b

	Total	Flake axe type, outline				Average edge width, cm	Average length, cm
Vængesø III	102	0	17 (16.6%)	57 (55.8%)	28 (27.4%)	4.94	7.51
Vængesø II	47	3 (6.3%)	6 (12.7%)	17 (36.1%)	21 (44.6%)	4.86	8.56

Fig. 145. a) An investigation of the wear traces on the edges of the flake axes shows that the large chips are more or less equally distributed between the dorsal and ventral sides of the axes, whereas minor damage is found predominantly on the dorsal side. The axes also show frequent major damage to one of the corners of their edges (arrowed), cf. Fig. 61; the minor edge damage is more frequent on the axes from Vængesø III than from Vængesø II, while major damage is more frequent on the flake axes from Vængesø II than from Vængesø III. b) The form of the flake axes from Vængesø III. The diagram shows that the dominant types have weakly or strongly concave sides, which is a late characteristic in the Ertebølle culture; the earliest types have convex and parallel sides, cf. Fig. 60.

duced. Examination of the edge section of the flake axes reveals only two examples showing extremely heavy wear. Comparison with the wear on axes used in modern chopping experiments suggests that these two axes were used to work in a hard material, for example antler (Andersen, S.H. 2009, 74, 76, Fig. 47c). The low incidence of such heavy wear damage is consistent with the almost complete absence of worked antler from this locality and helps to underline the special character of this settlement relative to other coeval coastal Ertebølle sites in eastern Jutland (Fig. 145a). Attempts have been made to refit the fragments of flake axes, but in only one instance did it prove possible to reunite two pieces of the same axe which was broken in the middle. The two pieces lay c. 1 m from each other on the plateau (Fig. 143b). Examples of the reuse of flake axes, as regularly encountered at many Ertebølle sites such Ronæs Skov (Andersen, S.H.

2009, 73-77, Fig. 47d-e) are, conversely, very few at Vængesø III; there are only four instances. Three axes have been converted to angle burins (Fig. 143e and i) and one has been reused as a scraper. Most of the flake axes show traces of heavy wear in the form of a chipped edge. Twelve flake axes have a broken butt and in six other cases the right corner of the edge has been struck/broken off. In three cases, this is true of the left corner (when the axe is seen "oriented" in the working position). The fact that it is predominantly the right corner that is damaged can be explained by the user of the axe being right-handed. This would result in a clear tendency for the right edge corner to strike the material being chopped first. In three cases, the axe edge shows traces of the removal of longitudinal flakes without it being possible to determine whether these represent extreme wear or an attempt at some slightly unusual reworking.

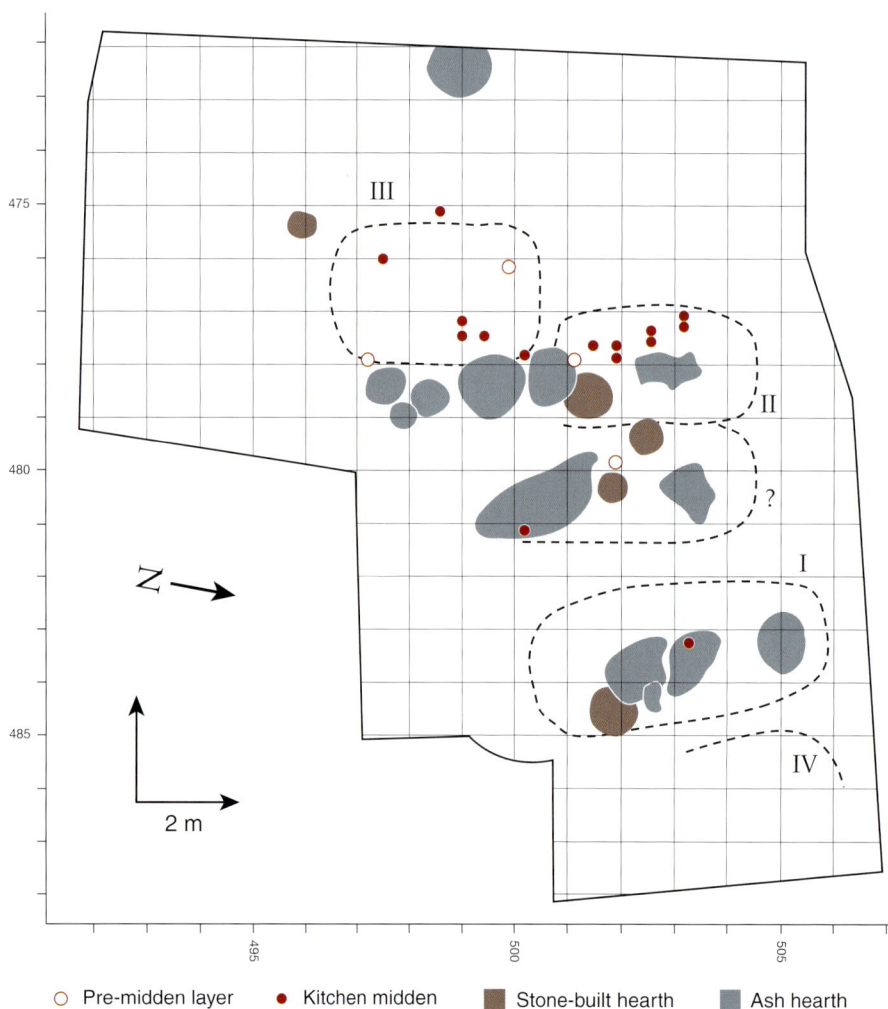

Fig. 146. The distribution of edge fragments from flake axes indicate where the axes have been used and resharpened; these edge flakes are almost only found on terraces II and III, cf. Fig. 121.

○ Pre-midden layer • Kitchen midden ▣ Stone-built hearth ▣ Ash hearth

There are 22 examples of *preforms for flake axes*, where working has stopped at various stages of the manufacturing process. As a consequence, this group is characterised by great irregularity with respect to form, size etc. Four pieces stand out from the rest by representing the final stage of the manufacturing process, where an attempt to remove a transverse (flat-flaked) flake has been unsuccessful such that the flake axe has split along a diagonal fracture. A large number of the characteristic edge and transverse flakes from the working of flat-flaked axes (Andersen, S.H. 2009, 78-79, Figs. 51-52), which are found everywhere across the settlement surface, also shows that production of flake axes was extensive (Fig. 142). Particularly important is demonstration of the fact that the working of flake axes regularly took place in the vicinity of the ash hearths. Flakes recorded from the kitchen midden number 205, and those from the pre-midden layer rather less, 153 examples. If these pieces are mapped (Fig. 121), their dis-

tribution across the settlement surface is seen to correspond with the occurrence of fragments and preforms for flake axes (Fig. 146). It is interesting to note, however, that there are fewer of this kind of flakes on terrace II. In the kitchen midden these flakes are common on the northern part of terrace II and, especially, in the southwestern part of terrace III. As for the pre-midden layer, flake axe flakes are very frequent in the northern part and along the western side of terrace I (Fig. 121b).

Fragments of flake axes are common, being represented by 20 examples, all with one exception from symmetrical flat-flaked flake axes. This further underlines the extensive use of this tool type at the settlement (Fig. 147). It has not proved possible to refit any of the fragments with intact flake axes. There are three butt fragments, all from flat-flaked symmetrical flake axes, broken transversely. Further to these is the butt of an axe that broke leaving a hinge fracture (Fig. 147b). There are three middle pieces and nine edge pieces with

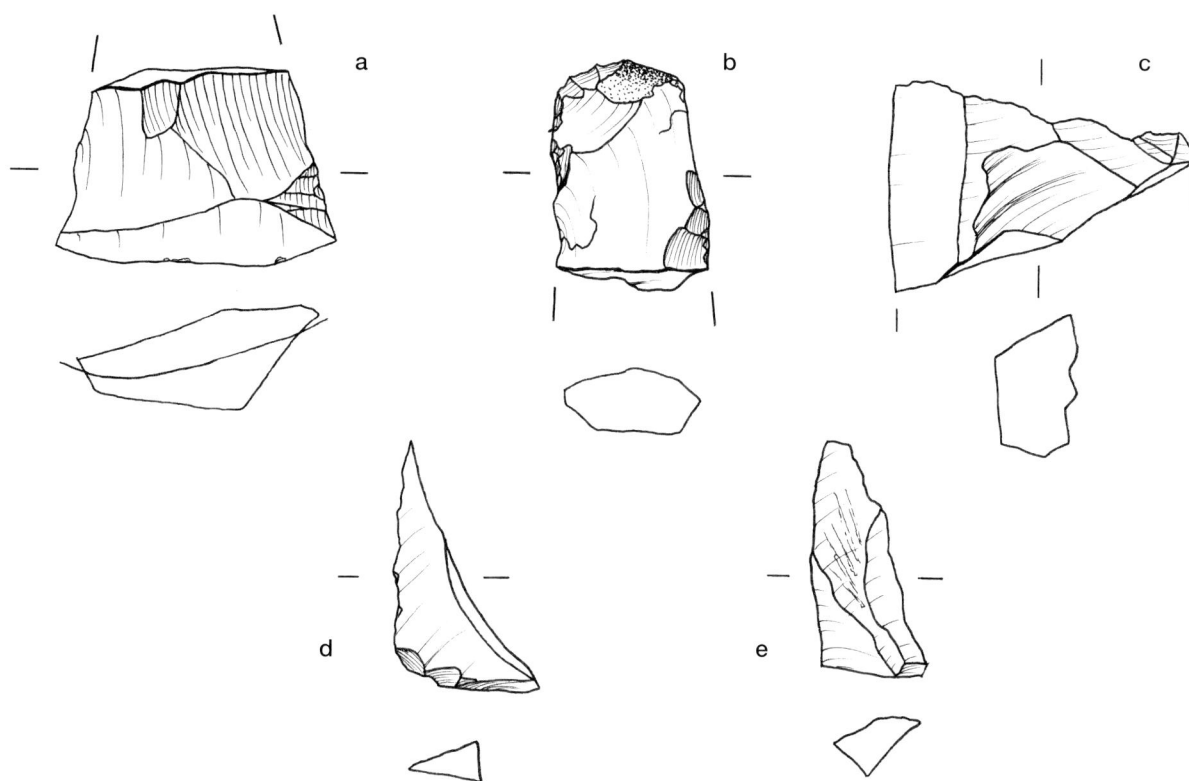

Fig. 147. Fragments of flake axes. a) Broken-off edge. b) Broken-off butt. c) Broken-off edge corner. d-e) Hook-shaped edge rejuvenation flakes. Scale 3:4. Drawing: Søren Timm Christensen.

a break at right angles to the longitudinal axis. One of these (which is also fire-brittled) is from an atypical flake axe. All the edge pieces show a clear, straight break (Fig. 147a). Their size varies from narrow edge sections to several examples of half axes. There are six examples of edge corners, one of which is fire-brittled. Two pieces were broken from the body of the axe – one along the side, the other diagonally. The final two had been struck from the edge section (Fig. 147c). There are six examples of rejuvenation flakes from flake axes, of which four have a hook-shaped outline, while two are straight (Fig. 147d-e). Five are from the pre-midden layer and 15 from the kitchen midden.

Flake chisels are common (13.3% of the axe group), and most of these 12 pieces are flat-flaked (this group also contains the settlement's most

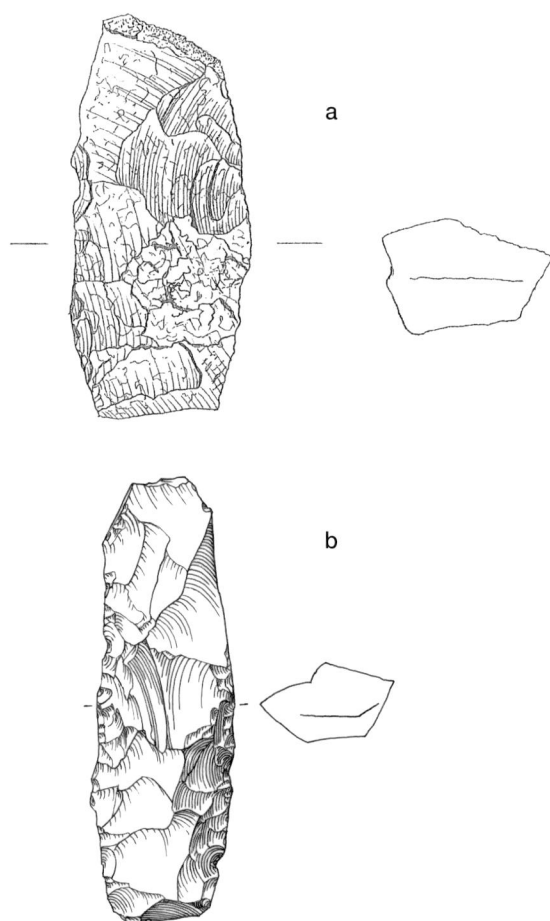

Fig. 148. Flat-flaked flake chisels. a) is fire-brittled. Scale 3:4. Drawing: Søren Timm Christensen.

regular example of a chisel), three are atypical and there is one chisel fragment (Fig. 148). One chisel has been so heavily worked that the original flake surface has been almost completely removed. One example is fire-brittled and another is totally atypical and heavily damaged by use. Four examples have been resharpened and have distinct use damage to their edges. A special variant is represented by four chisels which are made on flat-flaked flake axes, where the edge has been made narrower by striking off one of the edge corners so the resulting chisel is asymmetrical. This subtype has been described and illustrated previously (Müller 1896, 350-351, Fig. 27; Madsen et al. 1900, 39, Pl. V, no. 16). It is characteristic of settlements from the Late Ertebølle culture in Jutland. Another variant comprises chisels on which the edge forms shoulders relative to the sides and lies on the central axis (Fig. 24a). The flake chisels have a length of 6.1-12.7 cm and an edge width of 1.6-3 cm. An asymmetrical flat-flaked chisel (not included in the above average) is unusually small and resembles most of all a piece of "gun flint". It is only 3.4 cm in length and its edge is 2.3 cm wide. One of the two atypical chisels was made on a coarse preform for a flat-flaked flake axe which has been worked such that it is triangular in outline with a 2.6 cm wide chisel-like (and much worn) edge. Its length is 10 cm, width 7.8 cm and thickness 3.5 cm. The other is a rather short example, the butt of which comprises cortex from the original flint core. It has a round/pointed-oval edge and is only 3.8 cm in length. Flake chisels are a characteristic type for the late phase of the Ertebølle culture in eastern Jutland (Andersen, S.H. 1975a), and the relatively numerous examples at Vængesø III also help to underline a relative dating of this site to the Late/Latest Ertebølle culture. Similar pieces were found at both Vængesø I and II.

Spherical flint crushing stones are represented by 11 examples. These are round, almost spherical, and have a surface that is covered with crush marks. Five of them are parts of spherical crushing stones that have broken, and therefore only a smaller (but characteristic) part of their surface shows crush marks. One of these has been used secondarily as a flake core. They measure between 5-6 and 8-8.5 cm in diameter. These spherical flint crushing stones are a very characteristic artefact type at settlements from the Late Ertebølle culture. This type does not occur at settlements from the Early and Middle Ertebølle culture, where there are, conversely, flatter, rounder pieces with crushing marks on their edges (Andersen/Malmros 1966, 58, Fig. 14, x380). The fact that the spherical type is prominent at Vængesø III contributes to underlining the typological dating of this settlement to a late phase of the Ertebølle culture.

Three flint crushing stones differ from the rest by not being spherical. One was made on an elongated blade core with crushing on two opposing sides, resulting in it being slightly hourglass-shaped. It measures 8.5 cm in length, 6.4 cm in width and 6.5 cm in thickness. The second originated as an oval flint nodule, which has crush marks on all its sides, without it having become rounded; it measures 6.8 × 5.5 × 5 cm. The third is an irregular flake core with crushing marks along its sides. The spherical flint crushing stones were found distributed across the entire settlement surface, but there is also the interesting occurrence of four examples on terrace I (Fig. 119). An oviform piece of flint could possibly also have been used and consequently belong to this category, but possible use wear could not be established with certainty.

Hammerstones of rock types other than flint are represented by 15 examples, of which four are of quartzite, ten of fine-grained granite and one of a calcareous flint type. In most cases these are rounded-elongate natural stones on which a pointed end or a projection shows traces of blows and/or impact in the form of crush marks on the surface. Only two examples are of more irregular form, but these also have a projecting point with crush marks on its surface. These stones measure 4.5-9 cm in length. They occur across the entire settlement surface but there is a slight tendency towards a maximum frequency on and around terrace II (Fig. 119). Finally, mention should be made of a 13.5 cm long, 6.5 cm wide and 5 cm thick stone, which is triangular in cross-section

and rectangular in outline. The raw material employed (calcareous flint/quartzite type) and the working distinguishes this from all the other crushing- and hammerstones. This artefact, which is coarsely worked with a longitudinal "trimming seam", has distinct impact marks at one end, which clearly reveal its function as a hammerstone. Its working suggests that the original intention was to produce a core axe, but this was abandoned, after which the stone was used as a crushing- or hammerstone. As it was found uppermost in the subsoil, it must be earlier than or coeval with the first occupation of the site.

Consistent with the small number of burins encountered, there are also few *burin spalls* – a total of ten examples. Six of these are primary with a triangular cross-section, while the remaining four are secondary flakes with a rectangular cross-section. They are narrow and slender (width 0.2-0.5 cm) and none of them comes from the burins that were identified. One burin spall is broken in the middle. All the spalls appear to originate from burins on a break or a transverse blow. They vary in length from 2.1-5 cm. Their distribution is shown in Fig. 132.

There is only one "classic" *micro-burin*. This is the base of a micro-blade that has a deep, retouched notch directly above the percussion bulb. On its ventral side, the piece has an oblique facet. Two other pieces have an oblique facet associated with a concave, retouched edge. This clearly represents micro-burin technique. Similar pieces are always few in number at Ertebølle settlements, but they have for example been found at Ringkloster (Andersen, S.H. 1975a, 45, Fig. 36) and the Egesminde settlement in the former Bjørnsholm Fjord (unpublished; Moesgaard Museum archive no. 3268).

Struck-off percussion bulbs are waste products from the production of transverse arrowheads (Andersen, S.H. 1975a, 55-56, Fig. 46) and five of them were identified at the Vængesø III settlement; three from the kitchen midden and two from the pre-midden layer.

Flint pieces showing evidence of working are common, with 63 examples being recovered. This group is characterised by very irregularly knapped pieces of flint that it is not possible to classify to any of the previous categories. Several of them are coarse flakes with a cortex-covered surface on which one edge shows working. They vary in size from 2 × 2.5 to 7.5 × 10 cm.

A *triangular flint slab* has, through the removal of a few flakes, been given a short tip at one corner. This piece is the only one of its kind in the assemblage and, based on its form and simple working, it mostly resembles the co-called "*Claudi kiler*" from Stavns Fjord on Samsø (Mathiassen 1934, 39-54, especially Pl. III, 7). Its dimensions are 11.5 × 2.8 cm.

Seven *irregular flakes with a partially cortex-covered surface* have a chipped, irregular edge. Two of them are elongate and have a serrated, irregular edge, while the others are on round-oval flakes, on which the edge is chipped. A further four examples also attract attention: These are large, thick and irregular flakes, the edges of which show traces of blows and very heavy wear, resulting from working in a harder material. Two of them are on a calcareous type of flint, while the raw material for the others must be characterised as limestone. Both flakes have been subjected to heavy use and must almost be termed coarse "choppers" (Andersen, S.H. 1975a, 47-48). One of them comes from the kitchen midden and is 14 cm in length, 10.6 cm in width and 4.2 cm in thickness, while the other lacks information on its finds context and measures 8.8 cm in length, 11.2 cm in width and 4 cm in thickness. The wear traces on these pieces show that they have been used for sawing and/or chopping work in a hard material. Several examples of similar pieces were recovered from the small Ertebølle settlement of Dyngby III, where they constitute a characteristic element of the tool inventory (Andersen, S.H. 2004, 17-20, Fig. 7). At the latter site these are (cautiously) interpreted as tools for loosening oysters from their growing places (Andersen, S.H. 2004, 117).

Pieces with coarse edge working/trimming are represented by four examples, where the raw material comprised thick, elongate flakes on which one longitudinal edge has been given a straight or slightly curved form as a result of coarse, contiguous knapping. In one case, the opposing edge (the distal end) shows wear damage indicative of a chopping function, while the other edge has fine wear on the opposite longitudinal side. Their length is 10.1-10.2 cm, their width 4.9-5.4 cm and their thickness 2.5-2.8 cm.

At the base of the secondary pit in the upper part of the kitchen midden was a roughly-shaped *axe blank* of grey, bryozoan-rich flint. The blank was four-sided, elongate and coarsely worked, and in several places it still had intact sections of the original cortex-covered surface. Based on the finds context and the fact that all the flakes were of the same flint type as the blank, a refitting exercise was attempted, resulting in the matching of the blank with six flakes. Due to time constraints, the refitting exercise was not continued to its conclusion, but it appears highly likely that most of the flakes could be refitted. The blank is 26 cm long, 10.5 cm wide and 8.5 cm thick. Its size and form, the type of flint employed and its stratigraphic position all show that it belongs to the Early Neolithic. Together with this flint blank were two thin-walled potsherds (unornamented side sherds) of Neolithic type, which help to underline dating of the flint blank (and the pit) to this period.

A small, thin *flint chip with a polished surface* was also found during the excavation. This is from a Neolithic axe, but its small size does not permit identification of the axe type. The chip measures 1.6 × 2 cm.

Overall, it can be concluded that the flint assemblage from Vængesø III contains all the various flint types characteristic of the Late Ertebølle culture, but their form and, especially, the relative proportions between them, differ from other coeval settlements. The raw material employed was (small) local flint nodules from the coarse sand and gravel deposits around the settlement area. This has influenced the cores which are short and irregular and have cortex-covered surfaces. Unipolar cores dominate. The finds assemblage also shows that there was no significant production of blades, and those that were manufactured are predominantly short, irregular blades of B-type. The group of blade tools is very small and includes only a single scraper, a few drills and a few burins. Conversely, the abundant pieces with concave truncation and the pieces with finely- and coarsely-denticulate edges are particularly characteristic of this settlement. The frequency of truncated pieces corresponds to that seen at Vængesø II. Further to these are numerous transverse arrowheads with markedly concave sides. Flake axes are very common, and debitage from their production shows that large numbers were produced at the settlement. In the case of several of these, production appears to have taken place at the edge of the ash hearths. A small proportion of the flake axes has been resharpened (i.e. rejuvenated) during use. The few core axes with a specialised edge found at this settlement are generally smaller than corresponding examples from other coeval Ertebølle settlements on Djursland, for example Holme Skanse (unpublished; Moesgaard Museum archive no. 1852).

4.3.2 Greenstone/diabase

The outline of a preform for a *greenstone axe* (or coup de poing-/hand axe-formed piece of worked diabase) is guttiform (i.e. drop-shaped) and elongate-triangular. Its cross-section is semicircular as it has a domed-convex and a flat side. Significant areas still have the raw material's original (cortex-covered) surface. Its sides are regular and straight and run together to form a point, which is broken off. The length of the piece is 22.5 cm, width 10.5 cm and thickness 7 cm. It was found in the pre-midden layer. This piece is important as it shows that the production of greenstone axes also took place locally on this settlement (as at Vængesø II), a conclusion that is supported by a further two preforms recovered from the surface of the field. No greenstone axes were found during the excavation, but surface collections at the site have yielded five examples, one of which is unusual in having a central biconical perforation (shaft hole). This is a rare type with a scattered distribution at Ertebølle sites in Jutland (Fig. 149).

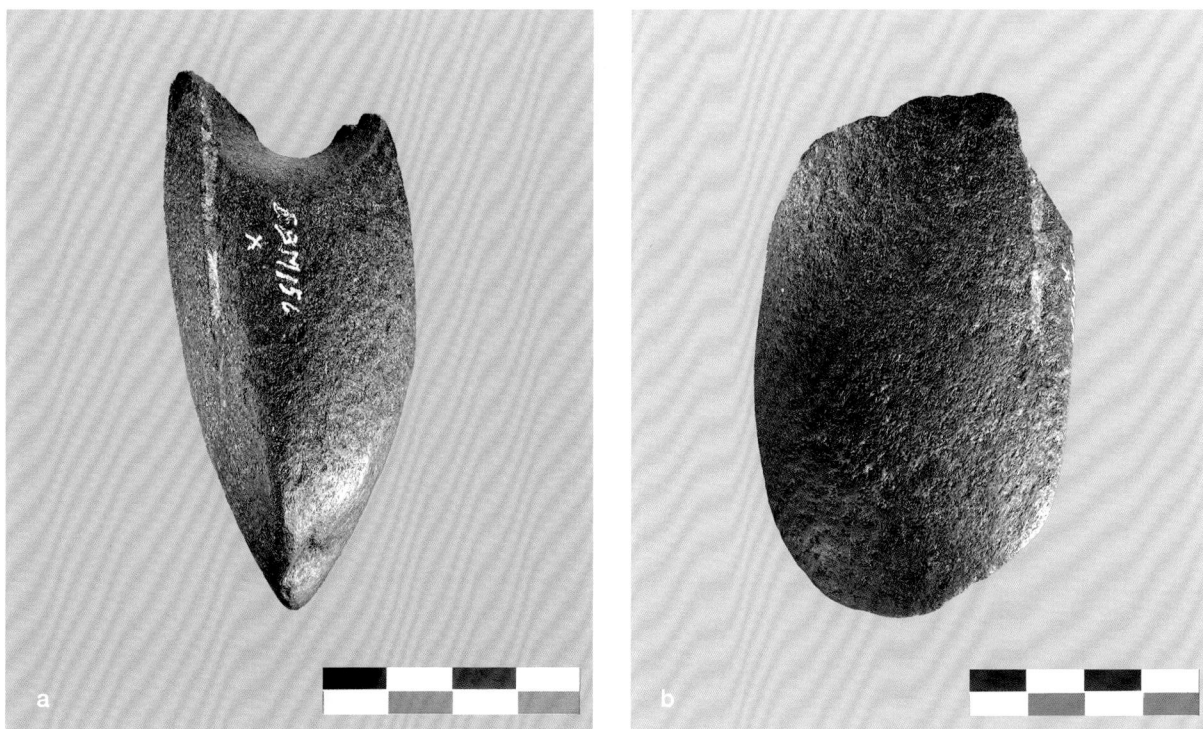

Fig. 149. Edge fragment from a diabase axe with an hourglass-shaped shaft hole. This piece, which was picked up from the surface of Vængesø III, is a rarity, but scattered finds of similar diabase axes are known from a few other Ertebølle settlements across Denmark. Photo: Photo/Media Department, Moesgaard Museum.

Fig. 150. Large pottery fragment in the kitchen midden in square 475/495. Seen looking east. Photo: Lone Ritchie Andersen.

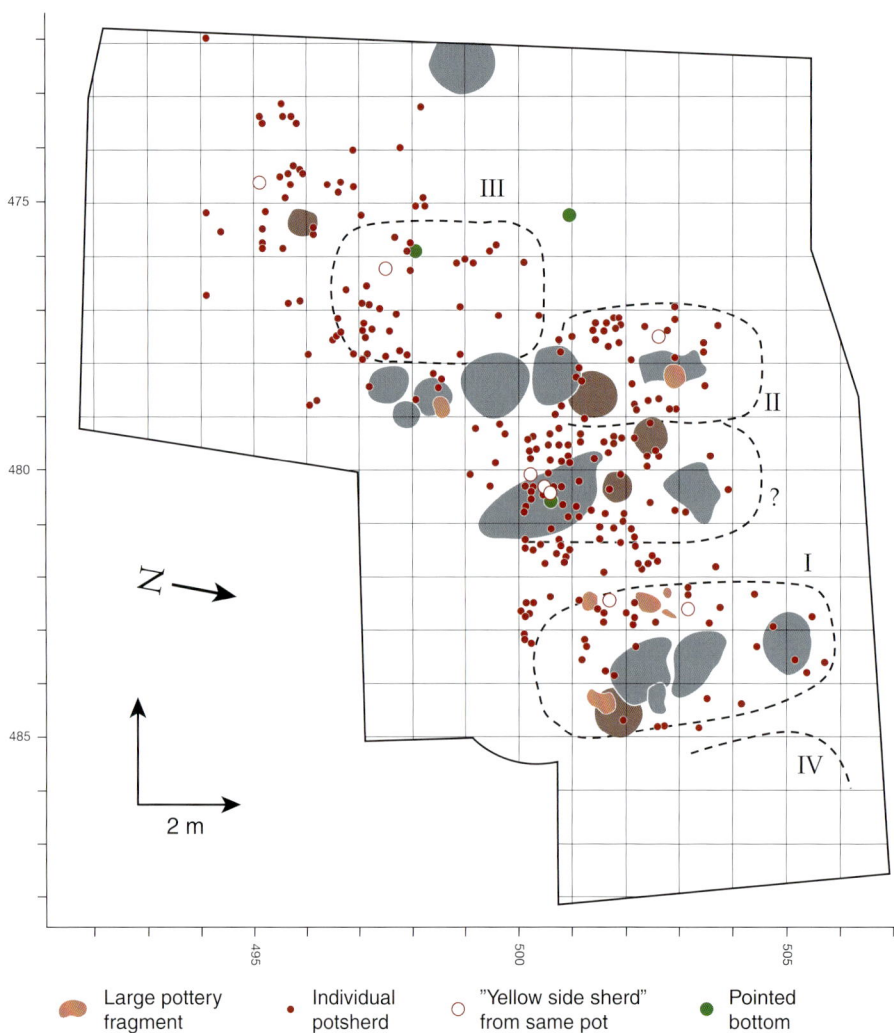

Fig. 151. Distribution of large pottery fragments (they are generally found close to the hearths – cf. Fig. 26), individual potsherds and pointed bottoms of Ertebølle vessels and a number of (yellow) sherds, which presumably originate from the same vessel. The greatest concentration of pottery was found between terraces I and II and to the S-SW of terrace III.

4.3.3 Pottery

Both the kitchen midden and the pre-midden layer contained thick-walled Ertebølle pottery (Fig. 150). The potsherds are generally poorly fired and their size rarely exceeds 3-4 × 3-4 cm. The pottery was found in the form of both single potsherds and larger vessel sections that, in some cases, measured c. 30-40 × 20-30 cm. The latter were particularly frequent on terrace I, but there were also two examples on and close to terrace II (Fig. 151). In most situations, these vessel sections were pressed completely flat and broken into fragments, which made their recovery difficult. In a couple of cases, however, it could be established that they represented vessel sides with a preserved rim. They were brownish-red to reddish-brown on their outer surface and black inside. On one it could be established that the outer surface is blackened from the rim down to the vessel's shoulder, where the colour changes to reddish-brown. This vessel had a height of at least 28 cm. There is charred food crust on the inside of several sherds, but this is thin (less than 1 mm in thickness) and shows no clear structure. Both rim sherds and pointed bases are represented, but these are generally rare. The thickness of the sherds varies from 1.1 cm (U-technique) to 1.8 cm (H-technique). The thickest sherds are 1.7-1.8 cm in thickness and are all constructed in H-technique. A group of eight sherds have a characteristic (and uniform) yellow outer surface. Given their similarity with respect to thickness, construction and colour, they must originate from the same vessel, sherds from which were distributed across part of the settlement surface (Fig. 151). One sherd has a conical hole with a maximum diameter of 0.8 cm (Fig. 152a). The hole was drilled from the outside of the vessel and results from an attempt to repair (clinch) a crack. The sherd comes from a vessel side at the transition between the upper and lower part, and the hole was drilled c. 2 cm above the break in the profile of the vessel side. The latter is 1.1 cm thick, slightly curved, constructed in N-technique and was found in the kitchen midden. There are several similar examples of Ertebølle sherds with "clinching holes" from the Ertebølle midden (Madsen et al. 1900, 75-76, Fig. 6), Flyn-

derhage (Andersen, S.H. 1981b, 118) and Tybrind Vig (Prangsgaard 2013, 286, Fig. 5.10). There is also a number of sherds on which the outer surface has a pattern of deep, horizontal, semicircular (fingernail) impressions. One sherd measures c. 3 × 3 cm, is 0.8 cm thick and is constructed in N-technique. It was found on the surface of the kitchen midden which, in conjunction with its decoration, dates it to the beginning of the Neolithic (Funnel Beaker culture). There are several sherds bearing this ornamentation and it seems likely that they all come from the same vessel.

Pointed bases have been securely identified in three cases (Fig. 151). One is of the type where the point is only slightly demarcated relative to the rest of the vessel, while the point of the two others is much more marked in relation to the actual vessel base. These points are 1-1.3 cm in thickness and

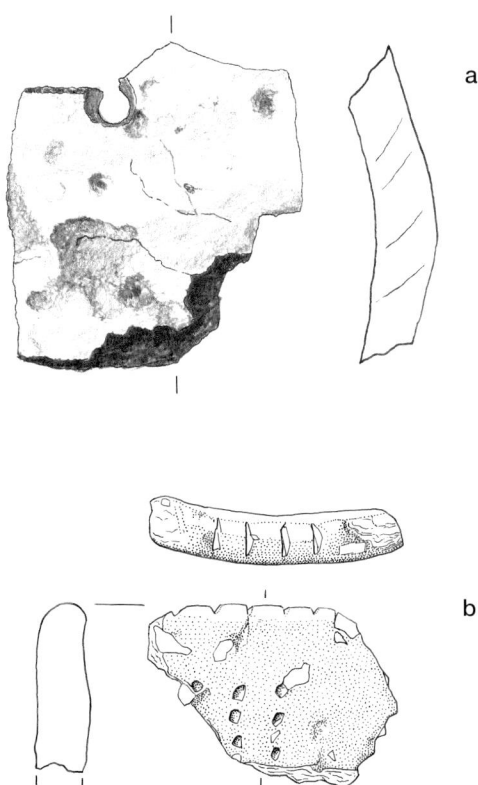

Fig. 152. Ertebølle pottery. a) Thick-walled Ertebølle sherd with "clinching hole". b) Rim sherd from an Ertebølle vessel with dotted outer surface and fingernail marks in the rim edge. Scale 3:4. Drawing: Søren Timm Christensen.

0.8-2 cm in "height". On one base the point is slightly skewed, on the other it is flattened, but at the same time takes the form of a "peg/point" that was "affixed" to the base of the vessel after it had been made. Finally, there is a sherd with a curvature that suggests it comes from very close to a vessel base. It is constructed in H-technique and is 1.3 cm thick. One base came from the kitchen midden, while the remainder derives from the pre-midden layer; one of the latter was found at the edge of ash hearth 6520.

Three *rim sherds* were identified, of which two are constructed in N-technique and one in N-/reverse U-technique. They are 0.8-1.1 cm thick. There are narrow, densely-spaced, right-angled notches on the upper surface of the rim of one sherd. This sherd measures c. 5 × 3 cm and is 0.8 cm thick (Fig. 152b). On its outer surface, c. 1.5 cm below the edge of the rim, are two, perhaps three, parallel rows of small dots/holes. It cannot be determined whether this sherd is from a pointed-based vessel or a lamp, but probably the former. Its closest parallels are seen at the coeval Ertebølle sites of Ringkloster (Andersen, S.H. 1998, 41-42, Fig. 24) and Norsminde (Andersen, S.H. 1998, 42-43, Fig. 25) as well as on the eastern side of the Kattegat at Ordrup Næs (Becker 1939, 263, Fig. 21c). One rim sherd is slightly rounded and slightly thinner than the others (0.7 cm thick). As it was found uppermost in the kitchen midden, it probably dates from the Neolithic, and this would be consistent with its overall form and appearance.

The pottery assemblage includes a c. 2.5 × 2.5 cm rim sherd with a profile that suggests it could come from a *lamp*. Apart from this, no sherds from oil lamps have been encountered in this assemblage.

The abundant pottery (especially in the pre-midden layer) shows that settlement activities must have required a large number of vessels. Considering the settlement's coastal location and its marine-oriented subsistence economy, the absence of lamps is remarkable. This is especially so when compared with the coeval localities of Gudsø Vig and Ronæs Skov, located around the narrowest part of the Little Belt, where seal and whale hunting also formed an important part of the subsist-ence activities, and where the finds assemblage is characterised by harpoons and a relatively large number of lamps (Andersen, S.H. 2009, 2013).

4.3.4 Bone and antler

Artefacts of bone and antler are few in number and represent only a limited selection of types. Consequently, the inventory from Vængesø III has the same character as that of other settlements on this lagoon and is also consistent on this point with other sites of the Late Ertebølle culture, for example Ronæs Skov (Andersen, S.H. 2009). Particularly striking is the lack of antler tools and antler waste, as well as the lack of waste from the production of bone points. Given the areal extent of the excavation, and compared with the material recovered in the excavation of the southern part of the settlement, these absences are not a result of chance, but must mean that the production of tools from these materials only took place to a limited degree here. This observation is also consistent with the very few burins represented in the flint tool inventory.

The assemblage includes a flake of antler with an obliquely cut edge that could be a piece of the edge of an *antler axe*, although other possibilities are conceivable. Due to its size, its function cannot be determined, but this piece is important as it is perhaps the only trace of a possible antler axe at this settlement. It measures 2.1 × 1.7 × 0.5 cm and comes from the kitchen midden.

There are two examples of *split mammal bones*, one of which is a rectangular, 4.9 cm long piece of a tubular bone from a dog (*Canis familiaris*). It is divided longitudinally by two parallel furrows, and at one end the bone has been cut off evenly, while the epiphysis has been retained at the other. Its cross-section is semicircular and it is 1.8 cm in width. It comes from the pre-midden layer. The second example is a rectangular piece of bone with semicircular cross-section, where the bone is split along two parallel furrows. At both ends are traces of transverse sawing. This piece comes from the kitchen midden. Its length is 2.1 cm and its width 1.1 cm. These two pieces could represent waste from the production of pins.

Bone points are represented by ten examples (Fig. 153a-c, f, g), which in the majority of cases have been heavily resharpened (e.g. Fig. 153c). In one instance, the raw material appears to have been whalebone, while the others are made from limb bones of deer species. They are round, triangular or flat in cross-section with distinct side edges. Four examples are intact (but resharpened), while three are broken-off points, one is a middle piece and one is a base. One fragment is the middle piece of a bone point that was split longitudinally. In two cases, the points were reconstructed by fitting together pieces that were found in different places, but only a short distance apart, in the excavation area. The length of the intact bone points is 7.4-9.3 cm and their width/thickness 0.8-1 cm. With one exception (from a layer of fragmented shell uppermost in the kitchen midden), the points are all from the pre-midden layer. Two pieces differ markedly from the rest by being very thin and slender, thereby having a character similar to the group of "pins". Both are completely straight, needle-shaped and with a round cross-section. One has an elongate, guttiform (drop-shaped) outline, but lacks a tip, while the other is completely regular and pencil-shaped (Fig. 153i). Similar slender bone points have not been found at other western Danish Ertebølle settlements, but were encountered at the Sølager (Skaarup 1973, 75, Fig. 24,5) and Bloksbjerg settlements (Westerby 1927, 102, Figs. 30, 31), where they are also referred to as "pins" (Westerby 1927, 102-104, Fig. 31). The length and diameter of these two small points are, respectively, 4 and 0.4 cm and 2.8 and 0.3 cm.

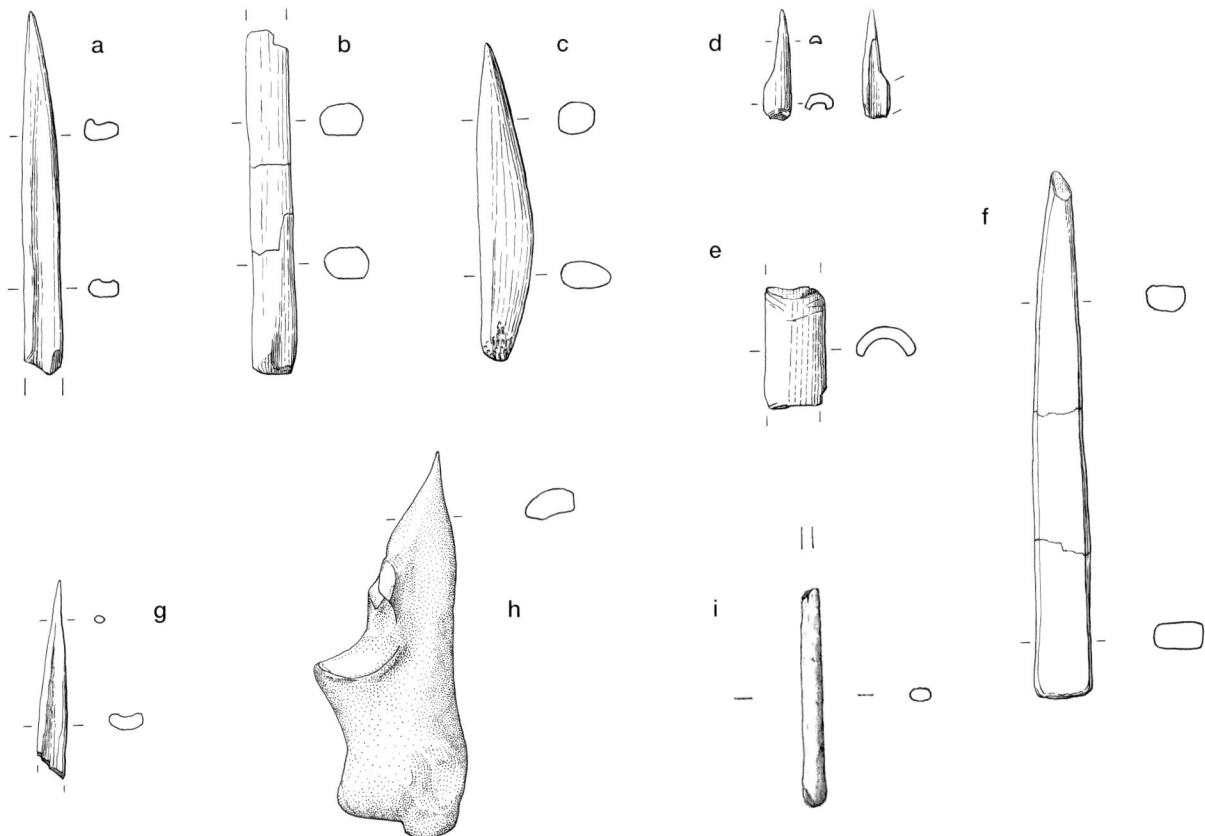

Fig. 153. Bone tools. a-c) Bone points with oval/round cross-section. d) Sharpened piece of bone. e) Rectangular piece of bone with saw marks at both ends. f) Bone point with rectangular cross-section. g) Needle-shaped bone point (broken). h) Small ulnar dagger. i) Short point with oval cross-section. Scale 3:4. Drawing: Søren Timm Christensen.

The finds also contain a small regular point which is cut-off straight at one end while at the other it has a 0.4 cm long, oblique, fractured edge which can be best explained as the trace of a broken-off barb. Its size and shape, and the oblique fracture surface, show that this must be a small *barbed point* of the same type as found at several Ertebølle settlements on Zealand, including Bloksbjerg (Westerby 1927, 105), Sølager (Skaarup 1973, 96, 97-98, Fig. 33,6-7) and Pandebjerg on Nekselø (Brøndsted 1938, 334, 1957, 381). Together with the other artefact types, this point suggests contacts with northwest Zealand. It is 3.8 cm long, 0.3 cm wide and 0.1 cm thick and comes from the pre-midden layer. Another small piece of worked bone possibly also represents part of, or maybe a preform for, a similar point. A short point with a round cross-section has been produced, of which the outermost part is broken off. It can be interpreted as a small, atypical bone point or waste from tool production. Its length is 2.7 cm and its diameter 0.3 cm. It comes from the pre-midden layer. An almost identical piece was found at Sølager (Skaarup 1973, 75, Fig. 24,10).

A 7.8 cm long ulna (elbow bone) of a dog has been worked distally into a point, the outermost part of which is broken off; i.e. a fragment of an *ulna dagger*. A similar (small) ulna dagger was found at Ertebølle (Madsen et al. 1900, 62, Pl. VII, lower row to the left). The length of the latter is 8 cm and its width is 1.8 cm. A similar tool is made from the ulna of a roe deer (*Capreolus capreolus*) and this has clearly been resharpened to a short, *awl-like point* (Fig. 153h). Its length is 9 cm and its width 2.5 cm. Both pieces come from the pre-midden layer.

A *wild boar* (*Sus scrofa*) *incisor* is represented by part of the enamel side, which is split. The wear surface shows clear traces of working caused by scraping and also has an obliquely-cut facet. Its length is 5.5 cm, its width 5.5 cm and its thickness 0.5 cm. This presumably represents waste from the production of a tooth ornament of the same type as that found at Ertebølle (Madsen et al. 1900, 70, Pl. VII, lower right). Carved wild boar teeth are also recorded among the finds from the kitchen midden

at Nederst, located in the middle of Kolindsund (Kannegaard 2013, 208, Fig. 7) and from the kitchen midden at Stubbe Station (Fig. 204a-b). The tooth fragment was found in the pre-midden layer.

There are three examples of the *dorsal spines of spurdog* (*Squalus acanthias*), all from the pre-midden layer. The point of one spine is worked (perhaps for use as a pin), while there is no secure evidence of working on the other two. Similar dorsal spines have been found at several other coastal settlements from the Atlantic and Sub-boreal periods, for example Bloksbjerg (Westerby 1927, 30, 34), Kolind, Dyrholmen and Ølby Lyng (Noe-Nygaard 1971).

A fragment of a *tooth of a killer whale* (*Orcinus orca*) is rather degraded on its surface. However, small working traces (scratches) at the tip show that it has been used in working flint tools (e.g. retouching; Andersen, S.H. 1997, 91-93, Fig. 33). The fact that this is a single find at Vængesø III corresponds to the finds circumstances encountered at several other Ertebølle settlements in eastern Jutland. It provides support for the interpretation that this was a tool with a "special" function, for example a "retoucheur" used in the working of flint. As the tooth is broken, its precise dimensions cannot be given, but its length must have been around 8-10 cm; it comes from the kitchen midden. There is a similar stray find of a killer whale tooth from the Late Ertebølle site Holme Skanse (unpublished; Moesgaard Museum archive no. 1852).

Market gardener P. Poulsen related that he had previously collected three killer whale teeth at Vængesø III and that these lay within c. 10 m of each other.

"*Buttons*" represent a rather unusual artefact type and are represented by three examples (Fig. 154d). The raw material was (rear) vertebrae of porpoise (*Phocaena phocaena*, identified by I.B. Enghoff). An encircling, U-shaped groove has been cut in the edge; this is 0.3 cm deep and extends round half to three-quarters of the circumference. Two examples are well-preserved, while approximately half of the edge has been broken off from the third "button". The uniform material, size and shape of these objects show that this is an established type. Similar or related types have not been found at other Ertebølle sites and their function is uncertain. Their shape, and the wear on one example, do suggest however that they could either be buttons or fasteners for clothing or part of hunting equipment. Their diameter is 2.2-2.4 cm and their thickness 1-1.4 cm. The "buttons" come from the pre-midden layer.

A small tubular bird bone (species not identified) has longitudinal cut marks and ends in an oblique, *irregular, syringe-shaped tip*, while the opposite end is broken. It is 2.2 cm long, 0.3 cm wide at the base and comes from the pre-midden layer.

Pins or points (of bird bone) are the site's commonest artefact type of animal bone and are represented by 12 examples (Figs. 153g and 154c). With a single exception, the raw material was long, narrow strips of very thin, slender bird bones, which have either been produced by the bone being split longitudinally by burin technique, or by being crushed, thereby producing a number of long bone splinters. On one piece, the base of the bone is preserved and the pin has slightly raised edges, i.e. its cross-section is U-shaped. In this respect, these artefacts clearly differ from the bird bone points that have been found at numerous western Danish Ertebølle settlements (Petersen, P.V. 1984, 15, Fig. 12) and which are characterised by having a "syringe tip". The latter artefacts are almost exclusively made from the bones of large bird species, for example swans etc. Only one of the points in this group from Vængesø III is intact (but clearly resharpened). It measures 7.5 cm in length and 0.5 cm in width. Of the others, seven are broken-off tips. The number and shape of these points from Vængesø III are both rather remarkable and, in this respect, put the settlement in a special light. They distinguish it markedly from other Ertebølle settlements in Jutland and also from the other settlements in the Vængesø lagoon.

Two uniform pieces constitute a special group (one of these consists of two parts, found c. 15 cm apart): They are long, narrow, slender bone splinters (probably bird bone) with completely parallel sides. Their cross-section is flat or slightly semicircular. One of these points is almost complete

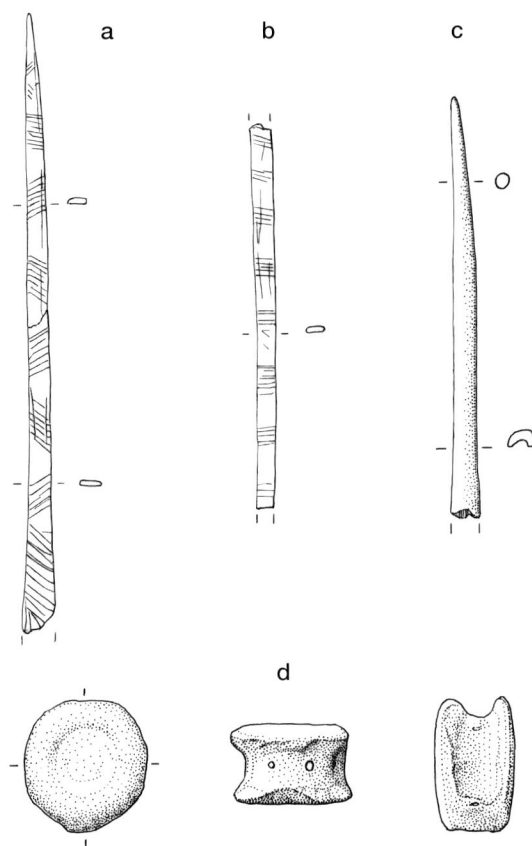

Fig. 154. Bone tools. a-b) Slender bone point ("needle") decorated with transverse and diagonal bundles of lines. c) Simple bone point of bird bone. d) "Button" with circumferential furrow, made from the vertebra of a porpoise. Scale 3:4. Drawing: Søren Timm Christensen.

(only the outermost part of the base is broken off) and it ends in an awl-shaped tip (Fig. 154a). The second has both its base and its tip broken off (Fig. 154b). Both have a surface-covering, incised decoration on the outer surface of the bone in the form of fields with cross-hatching and bundles of incised transverse and diagonal lines. The ornamented fields are separated from each other by blank, i.e. undecorated, areas (Fig. 154a-b). These pieces must be seen as being unique examples, as similar ornamented pins have not been encountered at other Danish Ertebølle settlements. Their function is difficult to elucidate, but their careful shaping and ornamentation suggest that these were probably personal items, for example dress pins or hair pins. The length of the intact pin is

Fig. 155. Decorated needle made of bird bone, cf. Fig. 154. Photo: Lone Ritchie Andersen.

10.7 cm and its width is 0.5 cm. The corresponding dimensions for the other (damaged) example are 6.7 and 0.4 cm (Fig. 155). The pins from Vængesø III are related to those previously published from the Aggersund settlement (Andersen, S.H. 1979a, 39-40, Fig. 28) and (especially) from Tybrind Vig, where this type is common (Andersen, S.H. 2013, 263-264, Fig. 4.47c). The pins/points from Vængesø III are, however, more regular and more carefully worked, with straight, parallel sides. Their uniform size and careful working show that they constitute an established type, and this is further underlined by their decoration. Six pieces in this group are broken-off points, the length of which varies from 2.9-6.3 cm, their width from 0.5-0.9 cm and their thickness from c. 0.1-0.2 cm. The pins come from the pre-midden layer.

The assemblage also includes part of a small implement with a round cross-section, which is broken at both ends. It is possibly a piece of *roe deer antler* or whalebone. Its length is 1.9 cm and its diameter 1.3 cm. It comes from the pre-midden layer.

There is also a splinter of *bone from a large whale* with a blackened outer surface. This shows no definite working traces, but its outer surface is very smooth(-scraped?). It is significant that this piece is part of the assemblage from Vængesø III as it helps demonstrate the site's similarity to both Vængesø I and II, where splinters of (large) whalebones form part of the finds assemblages from both these two

Ertebølle settlements. The length of the splinter is 5.3 cm, its width 2.3 cm and its thickness 1 cm. It is important to underline that, in contrast to the situations at Vængesø I and II, there are no splinters of whalebone of the same species at Vængesø III. Conversely, there are a number of larger (and intact) whale bones at Vængesø III, which is not the case at the two other settlements. There are also whale bones with cut marks and a charred surface at Vængesø III (Figs. 156-157).

In summary, it can be seen that implements of bone and antler are few in number at Vængesø III and also only represent a very few types. Conversely, the assemblage contains two completely new artefacts relative to the inventory of the Ertebølle culture: long, slender ornamented bone pins and circular "buttons" of porpoise bone. Given the fine conditions for preservation of organic material in the cultural deposits, as demonstrated for example by the many millions of fishbones, the absence of bone fishhooks (and especially preforms for these) is surprising. The same applies to the absence of fabricators and antler axes. An explanation could be that fishing was primarily practised using stationary fishing weirs and fish traps, as has been demonstrated by Enghoff (1994, 89). The lack of waste material from the production of bone and antler tools is also striking and must be a consequence of the actual cultural/subsistence economic circumstances associated with this settlement. In particular, it is remarkable that there was not a single piece of antler waste in the pre-midden layer. This material is otherwise very frequent at most coeval Ertebølle settlements of the same size as Vængesø III, for example Dyrholmen (Mathiassen et al. 1942) and Tybrind Vig (Andersen, S.H. 2013).

4.3.5 *Other materials*

The finds also include a dice-shaped, unworked *piece of amber*, measuring 1.9 × 1.6 × 1.4 cm. Its surface is somewhat degraded, but shows no clear traces of working. However, as the piece was encountered in the pre-midden layer, it was presumably brought back to the settlement from the open coast, either in the lagoon or out towards Ebeltoft Vig. A piece of

Fig. 156. Bone of large whale with cut and chop marks on its surface (front and rear). The surface of the bone is charred.

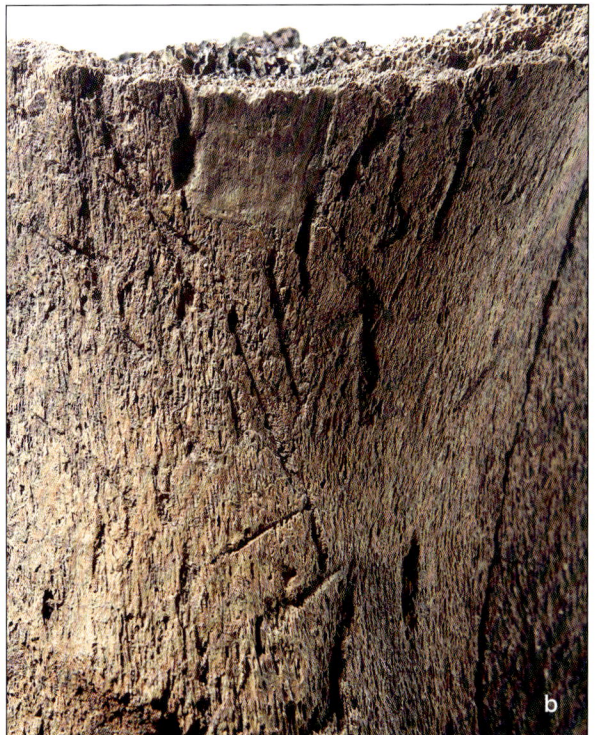

Fig. 157. Close-up of the cut and chop marks on the bone of a large whale, cf. Fig. 156.

unworked amber was also found during the excavation of the male grave in the southern part of the kitchen midden (Asingh 2000, 32-33).

A small lump of *red ochre* was found in the kitchen midden.

Also recovered were pieces of a small *bead made of marine mollusc shell* (mother of pearl). This is round, with a diameter of c. 1 cm. At its centre are traces of a small hole with a diameter of 0.2 cm. Beads of this kind are rare but there are some examples from Ertebølle settlements in Jutland, for example Meilgaard (Andersen, H.H. 1961, 32) and Eskelund (unpublished; Moesgaard Museum archive no. 1564).

4.4 Dating

The above account of the tool/artefact inventory from the pre-midden layer and the kitchen midden clearly demonstrates that this is a settlement from the Ertebølle culture. An analysis of a number of the more chronologically sensitive types, for example flake axes, core axes and flake chisels, transverse arrowheads and pottery, show unequivocally that the cultural deposits should be dated to the Late Ertebølle culture, i.e. corresponding to Dyrholmen II (Mathiassen et al. 1942) and Norslund layers 0+1 (Andersen/Malmros 1966). None of the finds in the assemblage contradict this relative date, which is also consistent with the scientific dates for the pre-midden layer and the kitchen midden. In terms of the tool/artefact types, it is not possible to distinguish between the pre-midden layer and the kitchen midden, and this also concurs with stratigraphic observations and the scientific dates (see below). It is, however, important to underline that this relative date only refers to the northern, excavated part of this kitchen midden. In the light of other kitchen middens in Jutland, the settlement's size, and its elongate form, can perhaps be taken as an indication that it has "grown" along the prehistoric shoreline, i.e. there could be a chronological difference between its various parts. As finds from the excavation of the southern part of the kitchen midden have not yet been published, it is not possible to address this question at present.

There are two radiocarbon dates from the upper shell layer which overlies the kitchen midden. A tooth of a killer whale (*Orcinus orca*) has been dated to 3941-3771 BC cal (1σ; AAR-8117, 5035 ± 55 bp (uncorrected); δ13C 10.83%) and a bone of red deer (*Cervus elaphus*) has been dated to 3969-3803 BC cal (1σ; LuS-7186, 5110 ± 50 bp). These dates show that the upper, thin, cockle-dominated layer above the kitchen midden belongs to the earliest part of the Funnel Beaker culture. This is consistent with the occurrence of a few scattered potsherds of Neolithic type and transverse arrowheads with a pointed base. Furthermore, there is the pit containing flint debitage from the working of a Neolithic axe. The two dates are consistent with the stratigraphic position of the layer, both in the excavation and in relation to the sediment stratigraphy in a wind-throw pit, in addition to the artefacts picked up from the field surface above the *in situ* culture layers.

The lower layer of the kitchen midden is dated to 4442-4269 BC cal (1σ; AAR-8300, 5500 ± 45 bp; bone of large whale (*Cetacea*)). This date is consistent with the stratigraphy and the date for a bone from a male grave in the southern part of the settlement, which gave a result of 4329-4237 BC cal.

A bone of red deer from the pre-midden layer has been dated to 4447-4360 BC cal (LuS-7187, 5570 ± 50 bp).

Collectively, the radiocarbon dates show a chronological sequence extending from the base to the top of the cultural deposits, c. 4450-3700 BC, and they support conclusions drawn from both the stratigraphical observations and the archaeological-typological (relative) dating. The culture layer below the kitchen midden (the pre-midden layer) is stratigraphically earlier than the overlying shell midden, but if the tool/artefact inventories from the kitchen midden and the pre-midden layer are compared, great consistency is clearly evident – both in the individual types and the proportions between the various tool/artefact groups. Only a short period of time apparently elapsed between the depositions of the two layers. If the above dates are calibrated at two standard deviations (2 σ = 95% probability), the results are 4496-4335 BC cal for the pre-midden layer and 4450-4260 BC cal for the lower layer of the kitchen midden, i.e. the date ranges overlap between 4450-4260 BC. This interval must be seen as the most likely time of deposition for the layer, in the given sequence.

A typological analysis of both layer's contents of tools/artefacts shows a clear affinity with the Late Ertebølle culture and also a great deal of concurrence with the finds from Vængesø I and II. Consequently, the terraces (and the other settlement structures) must also be assigned to the Late Ertebølle culture.

4.5 Subsistence economy

A large number of faunal remains in the form of bones and mollusc shells were found which can reveal the inhabitants' subsistence strategy during their occupation of the site. The preservation conditions were good for these types of organic materials and there were bones and shells of marine invertebrates in both the pre-midden layer and the kitchen midden. The quantity of mammal and bird bones was, however, greatest in the kitchen midden, while the pre-midden layer was particularly rich in fish remains. Briefly summarised, the excavation revealed that the inhabitants' subsistence strategy comprised a combination of fishing, hunting on the open sea, gathering of marine/coastal invertebrates and hazelnuts and hunting in the surrounding (primeval) forest. Remains were found of 18 species of fish, 21 kinds of birds and 22 mammal species (Enghoff 2011, 128-141). With regard to fishing and hunting, no significant difference could be demonstrated in species composition between the pre-midden layer and the kitchen midden (Enghoff 2011, 174). The percentage values given in the following sections all derive from the most recent analysis of the faunal material (Enghoff 2011)(Tab. 10).

A small proportion of the faunal remains, a total of 63 examples, shows the influence of fire (Fig. 158), i.e. they are either partially burnt, blackened, grey-/white-burnt or totally white-burnt (calcined). Burnt bones were found of plaice/flounder/dab, cod family, bird (unidentified), seal, pine mar-

ten, dog/fox and of some large animal (e.g. ox). As for the distribution of the burnt bones across the settlement surface, mapping of their finds locations reveals that most came from around the hearths along the western edge of terrace II. There were also some burnt bones by hearth 6911 (between terraces I and II), while there were (surprisingly) none associated with the other hearths (Fig. 158). Overall, there are no indications that the burnt bones (of a wide range of animal species) reflect any kind of pattern, and they must be explained in terms of bones of various prey animals ending up in or near a hearth by chance.

The cultural deposits contained large quantities of fishbones and the overall faunal assemblage indicates that fishing was the most important subsistence activity. In the kitchen midden, the fish remains were most often found in smaller, well-defined areas (patches), as seen at many other kitchen middens, for example Ertebølle (Andersen/Johansen 1987, 46-47, Figs. 12-13), while the quantity and distribution of fish refuse across the settlement surface in the pre-midden layer surpassed anything previously described from the Danish Ertebølle culture. Almost everywhere, this layer comprised a solid, cemented mass of fishbones and other remains. The bones lay both singly and (most frequently) in up to several cm-thick layers ("cakes") on the edge of the grey ash hearths (Fig. 114). In particular, there were abundant fish remains in the previously described "bank" running north-south along the eastern edge of terrace II (Ch. 4.6.2; Fig. 114). Further to this were bodies or patches of clay containing a massive, dense concentration of fishbones that were rather more difficult to explain. In most kitchen middens, for example that at Ertebølle, concentrations of fishbones have been found in delimited heaps or in the form of layers. At Ertebølle, these layers consisted very predominantly of remains of eel (*Anguilla anguilla*) and common roach (*Rutilis rutilus*; Enghoff 1987, 62-76; Andersen/Johansen 1987, 46-47, Fig. 12).

In addition to the large quantities of fishbones, 72 fish otoliths were recovered from the pre-midden layer: 41 of cod (*Gadus morhua*), three of saithe (*Pollachius virens*), 15 from members of the

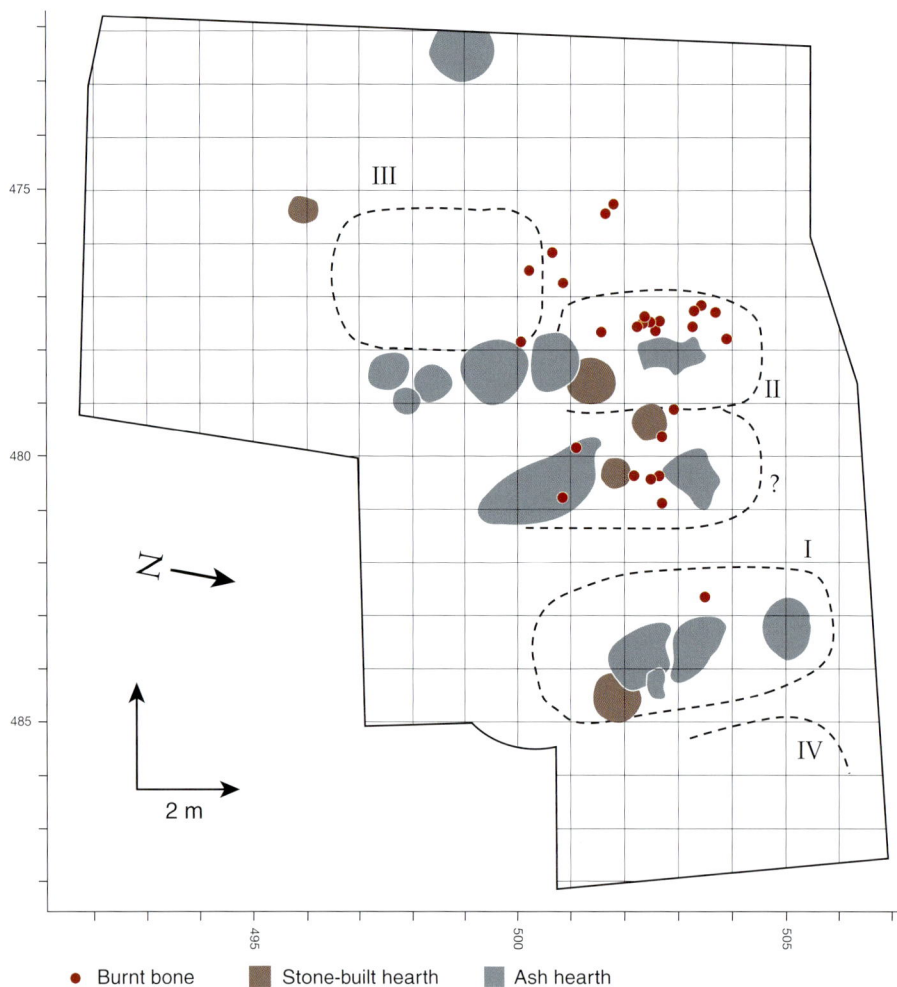

Fig. 158. The distribution of burnt bones across the settlement surface. These were predominantly found associated with terrace II and close to the hearths.

● Burnt bone　　　■ Stone-built hearth　　　■ Ash hearth

cod family (Gadidae) and 13 of plaice/flounder/dab (*Pleuronectes platessa/Platichtys flesus/Limanda limanda*). Three cod otoliths from the pre-midden layer were sufficiently well-preserved for analyses to be undertaken of their growth rings with the aim of determining the season when the fish were caught. These showed that the cod were caught between late summer and early autumn (Enghoff 2011, 158). As mentioned above, fishing activities related to 18 species, all marine. No remains have been found of species that only live in fresh water. There were though remains of eel and three-spined stickleback (*Gasterosteus aculaetus*), which thrive in salt, brackish and fresh water.

At Vængesø III, the dominant species were flat fish, flounder and plaice, together with cod, with c. 34% of the identified remains. These were followed by herring (*Clupea harengus*; 10%) and tub gurnard (*Trigla lucerna*; 5%), the frequency of which surpasses that recorded at other, coeval Ertebølle sites. The tub gurnard is a marine species that is not found in fresh or brackish water and the abundancy of this species shows that the fishing took place in the open sea (Enghoff 2011, 171).

During the excavation, sediment from all the cultural deposits was sieved through a sieve of mesh size 2 mm. Furthermore, as an experiment, a sieve with a 1 mm aperture mesh was employed in some cases, leading to an increase in the proportion of herring bones recovered to c. 23%; probably a better reflection of the actual relative proportions of the various species (Enghoff 2011, 155-158).

Eel was also represented, but its numbers were modest (< 1%) – at least in comparison with the coeval Ertebølle settlements located further north in Jutland, for example Havnø, Ertebølle and Bjørnsholm, where eel completely dominates the species spectrum (Enghoff 1987, 62-76, 1993, 105-118, 1994,

67-68, Tab. 1). The small number of eel remains is striking, because eel fishing on the coasts of Helgenæs has, up until the present day, been very extensive and therefore an important commercial activity (Wendelboe 2012, 374-391; Fig. 168). In general, all the fish species are represented by all parts of their skeleton in the faunal assemblage, and it must therefore be assumed that these fish were brought unprocessed to the settlement (Enghoff 2011, 155).

Bird catching also constituted an important element in local subsistence activities and again it is species of marine and marine-littoral environments that are characteristic. Great or black cormorant (*Phalacrocorax carbo*) is totally dominant (43%), followed by common merganser (*Mergus merganser*; 11%), grebe (*Podiceps* sp.; 9%) and razorbill (*Alca torda*; 7%). Other decidedly marine species include gannet (*Morus bassanus*) and guillemot (*Uria aalge*). The dominance of cormorant corresponds to the situation at Vængesø II (Ch. 3.8). At Vængesø III too, the impression gained is of a likely cormorant colony in the vicinity of the settlement. Perhaps the same colony that was exploited by the fisher-hunters at Vængesø II.

Forest hunting of terrestrial mammals also formed part of the subsistence strategy. Wild boar (*Sus scrofa*) dominates with 16% of the remains (including many young individuals) and roe deer constitutes 9%. Conversely, red deer only constitutes 3%, perhaps due to the settlement's very limited resource area in the immediate surrounding landscape and hinterland. Ox (presumably aurochs) is also represented by a few remains. A piece of roe deer antler is still securely attached to the frontal bone, which suggests that the animal was killed between early spring and late autumn. The bones from the head, body and limbs of wild boar, roe deer, red deer and ox show that these animals were brought intact back to the settlement.

Bones of "fur animals" were, in some cases, found in very discrete heaps, particularly in the deepest parts of the kitchen midden and at the transition from the pre-midden layer. Their horizontal distribution shows that these remains are concentrated predominantly on terrace I and the southern part of terrace III, as well as in the area between terraces I and II (Fig. 115a). In this respect, it is remarkable to note that there are virtually no bones of fur animals on terrace II and around its hearths – an area that is otherwise characterised by great settlement activity (flint-knapping, processing of fish etc.). Slaughtering of prey apparently did not take place in association with this latter structure (Fig. 115a). The "bone heaps" of fur animals correspond to the "shell heaps" that have been mentioned previously (Ch. 4.1) and together they underline the fact that the deposits must have accumulated very rapidly, such that the offal and carrion became swiftly covered and was therefore not accessible to scavengers.

There are numerous remains of dog (8%) and, apart from the remains of two puppies, the majority represents adult individuals (Enghoff 2011, 165). There are also bones of fox (*Vulpes vulpes*), wild cat (*Felis silvestris*), otter (*Lutra lutra*), polecat (*Mustela putoris*) and pine marten (*Martes martes*; 9%). The bones of the latter species (c. 80 examples) were almost all found in a discrete heap located within a c. 1 × 1.5 m area directly east of terrace II (Fig. 115a). Cut marks on the bones show that they represent waste from the slaughtering/skinning and subsequent discard of at least four individuals (Enghoff 2011, 170-172, Fig. 56). The same was also true of badger (*Meles meles*), of which several bones were found on the southern part of terrace III. Similarly, the bones of two juvenile dogs lay within a few adjacent metre squares (Fig. 115), while the bones of the adult animals, and the foxes, were more scattered, though found particularly on the southern part of terrace III and on terrace I (Fig. 115a). Many bones of dog, fox, wild cat, pine marten, wild boar and roe deer show cut marks from slaughtering and butchering/skinning. There are also traces of butchering on some porpoise bones.

There were the same number of species represented in the two culture layers, but with a predominance of bones of seal and dog in the pre-midden layer. Conversely, pine marten was most frequent in the kitchen midden (Enghoff 2011, 169-170). All in all, the faunal assemblage from Vængesø III contains 33% fur animals, suggesting extensive trapping in the surrounding (primeval) forest. This aspect of the economy clearly played a greater role at this settlement than for example at Vængesø II (Fig. 159).

Marine hunting was very extensive and the remains of marine mammals include porpoise (*Phocaena phocaene*), dolphin (*Delphinus delphis*), killer whale (*Orcinus orca*) and sperm whale (*Physeter catodon*). In the same way as at the nearby Vængesø II, this form of hunting puts Vængesø III into a special category with respect to the subsistence economy of the Ertebølle culture at coastal settlements (Enghoff 2011). This is specifically underlined by the numerous bones of grey seal (*Halichoerus grypus*), which dominate the mammalian group with more than 33% of the total remains (Enghoff 2011, 375). In comparison, the proportion of marine mammals on the coeval Ertebølle settlement of Neustadt on the North German Baltic coast is 26% (MN I), i.e. clearly less. Even though seals are represented at almost all coastal settlements of the Ertebølle culture, there are generally only a few bones present (Glykou 2013, 102). On this point, the Vængesø localities differ from the other coastal settlements of the time. With respect to grey seal, many young individuals are represented – perhaps there was a colony in the vicinity? A closer examination of the many seal bones reveals that the animals were brought whole back to the settlement, and distinct cut marks from slaughtering and butchering show that these activities took place on site. The same pattern is seen at the Neustadt settlement in North Germany (Glykou 2014). At Vængesø III, the seal bones were found across the entire settlement surface, but were concentrated particularly in an area on the southern part of terrace III and directly to the east of here. Conversely, no bones of marine mammals were found by the western side of terrace II – an area that is otherwise characterised by numerous settlement activities, for example flint-knapping and the processing of fish. Butchering etc. of seals and whales apparently took place in particular around terrace III (Fig. 115b). The culture layers incorporated several large bones of (large) whales. In this respect, mention should be made of the former Ebeltoft Museum's excavations in the

southern part of the Vængesø III kitchen midden, during which a vertebra of a blue whale or fin whale (*Balaenoptera musculus/Balaenoptera physalus*) – most probably the latter species – was recovered. The piece of large whalebone illustrated in Figs. 156 and 157, exhibiting chop and cut marks, probably comes from a fin whale. Its surface is also clearly fire-blackened.

Comparison of the faunal remains from the pre-midden layer and the kitchen midden reveals an equal number of species that occur with about the same frequency in the two deposits. However, there do appear to be more dog and seal bones in the pre-midden layer and pine marten is most frequent in the kitchen midden. The latter situation is though very probably due to the fact that almost all the bones of this species were found in a single heap in this deposit (Enghoff 2011, 170-172).

Overall, the faunal remains indicate that the subsistence economy at Vængesø III, like that at Vængesø II, was heavily influenced by the marine biotope – as indicated first and foremost by the numerous remains of seals and also those of both small and large whales (Enghoff 2011, 204). The marine aspect of the subsistence economy is more prominent at Vængesø III than at other known Ertebølle coastal settlements. Another feature that characterises Vængesø III is the common occurrence of remains of dog, and a similar situation prevailed at Vængesø II (Ch. 3.8). The fish remains derive from species that only live in saltwater (apart from eel and thee-spined stickleback) and the bird remains too are dominated by marine species, with particular grounds to note the gannet and the guillemot, which only live on the open sea.

Gathering is similarly well documented in the two settlement deposits. This applies in particular to the kitchen midden's vast quantities of shells of marine invertebrates: oysters, cockles, mussels, carpet shells and periwinkles. Mention should also be made of a hazelnut shell (*Corylus avellana*) from hearth 6524 in the pre-midden layer. An evaluation of the abundance of remains of marine invertebrates up through the stratigraphy clearly reveals that gathering during the first phase of the settlement was of a rather random/sporadic character, after which

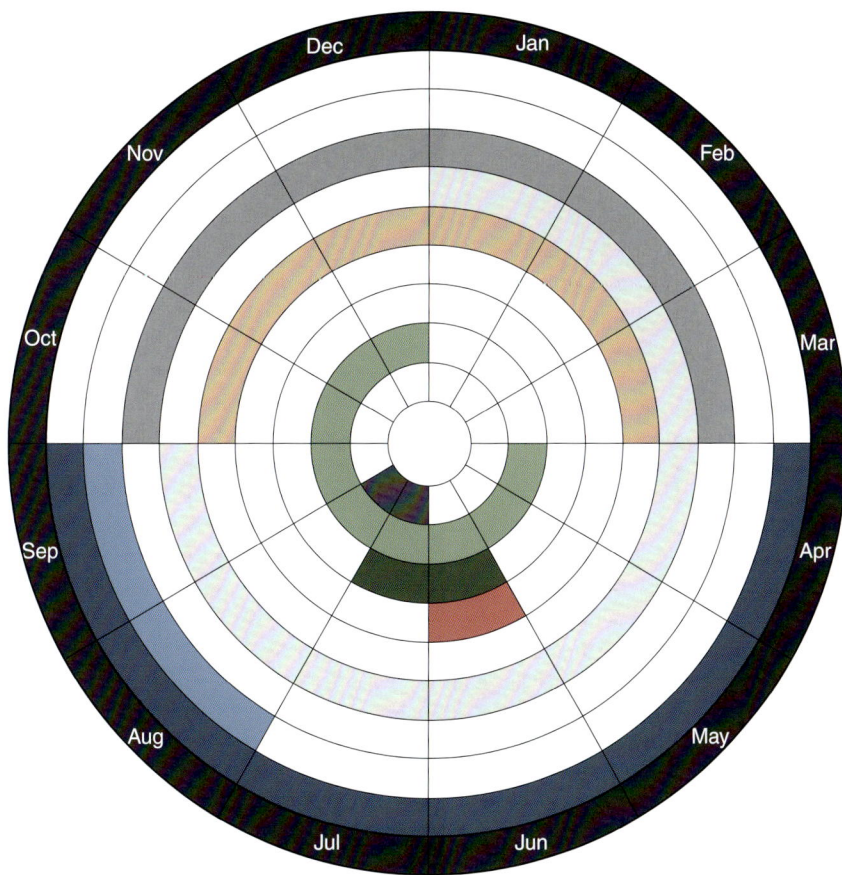

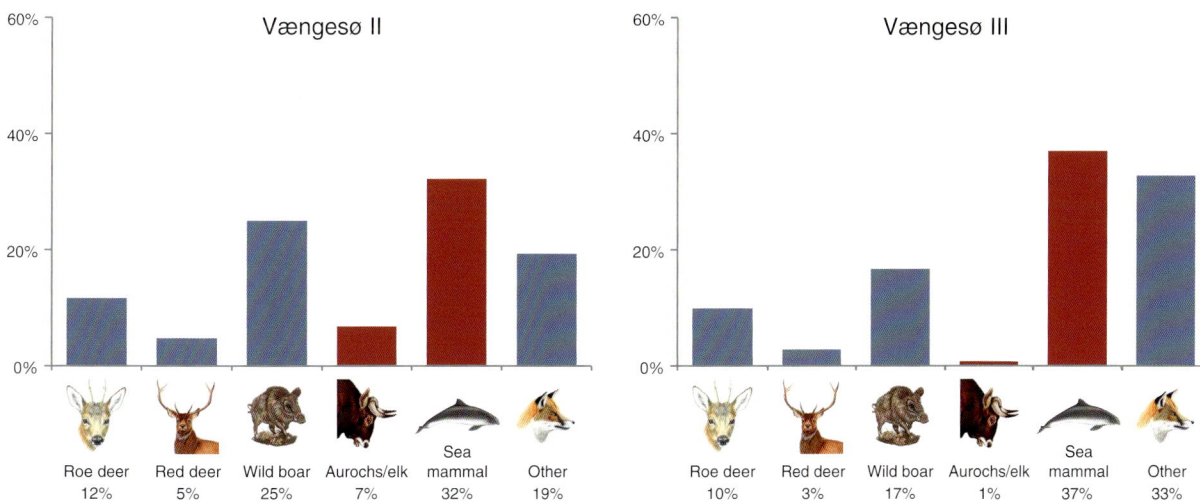

Fig. 159. a) Diagram showing all the observed seasonal indicators at Vængesø III. The analysis indicates that activities took place throughout whole year, but with a predominance in the summer season. Dark blue: Summer fishes. Light blue: Cod otholiths. Grey: Murre. Light grey: Cormorant colony. Light brown: Fur-bearing animals. Violet: Red deer, newborn. Green-black: Roe deer, 1 month old. Green: Roe deer, attached antlers. Black-grey: Grey seal, 6 months old. After Enghoff (2011). b) The relative proportions of the main groups of prey at Vængesø II and III. After Ritchie et al. (in print).

this subsistence activity became heavily intensified during the accumulation of the kitchen midden. In the pre-midden layer, the oysters lay in small "patches" and not in discrete, delimited heaps. They were found spread all across the surface, in contrast to the situation in the kitchen midden deposit. From an overall perspective, oysters are absolutely dominant, followed by periwinkles, cockles, mussels and carpet shells. The latter were found everywhere in the culture layers, both in small, discrete heaps and as such large individuals that they must have been systematically gathered on a par with the other mollusc species. It is remarkable that carpet shells are so abundant at this settlement, as this picture deviates from other kitchen middens in Jutland, where they only occur sporadically. The remains of gathered marine invertebrates at Vængesø III are interesting as there are no other published accounts of kitchen middens reporting so many and so clearly delimited heaps of individual species (Fig. 90c). These heaps are unusual, partly because they are so large, partly because they reveal the systematic gathering of one, and only one, species: for example, the relatively large and delimited heaps of periwinkle shells mentioned earlier.

The dimensions of the periwinkle shells show that these almost exclusively represent individuals of a particular size (and age). It is therefore clear that there was systematic selection/gathering of individuals with a length of c. 2.4 cm. Experts at the University of York could confirm that this size corresponds to an age of about 2-3 years (Milner 2002). Delimited heaps of the shells of oysters, cockles and mussels were found too, showing that these were also prepared as food, eaten and the shells subsequently deposited without being mixed with those of other species. The shell piles must originate from episodes when food waste was not cleared away. That is, they were covered over so rapidly that they did not become spread across the settlement surface and thereby mixed with other food and settlement waste. Tab. 4 details the content of a 5 l sediment sample from an area of the kitchen midden that was dominated by periwinkle shells.

A few mollusc shells show traces of the effects of fire. Moreover, between a third and half of the fish vertebrate are fire-blackened. The oyster shells are generally from small individuals, measuring c. 6-7 cm in length. The largest oysters (from the pre-midden layer) are 9.6 and 11.3 cm long, respectively. As only a small number of shells were measured, these data should be treated with some caution. Measurements of the average length of the oyster shells revealed a gradual decrease in the size (length) up through the stratigraphy (Fig. 93). A similar situation has been observed at numerous other kitchen middens in Jutland, for example Bjørnsholm (Andersen, S.H. 1993), Norsminde (Andersen, S.H. 1991), Krabbesholm (Andersen, S.H. 2005) and Havnø (Andersen, S.H. 2008). This phenomenon could either be a consequence of the gathering activities that took place (Mannino/ Thomas 2001), or possible environmental changes. A random sample of oysters from the pre-midden layer has been analysed by N. Milner and H. Robson with the aim of determining the time of year at which they were gathered. This revealed that the oysters were gathered in the winter and/or spring, i.e. the cooler months of the year (N. Milner/H. Robson, personal communication).

If attention is turned to seasonal indicators as a whole, no crucial differences can be observed between the two cultural deposits (Enghoff 2011, 174). The pre-midden layer shows traces of activity in the summer half of the year, as indicated by both hunting and fishing (roe deer with antler still attached to the frontal bone, juvenile roe deer, fishing for cod and mackerel) and autumn/winter (gathering of nuts, hunting of fur animals, catching of razorbill, guillemot etc., as well as hunting of grey seal). The gathering of oysters took place in winter and spring, i.e. showing a clear tendency for this to have only taken place during cooler months (Robson 2015, in prep.). As for the kitchen midden, there are indications of occupation during both the summer and autumn/winter (Enghoff 2011, 174). As at Vængesø II, the evidence supports an interpretation either in the direction of a series of individual occupations during the course of an annual cycle or permanent year-round habitation. On the basis of the faunal remains, however, the site is interpreted as an all-year-round settlement (Fig. 159a).

4.6 Settlement type

Collectively, the size of the settlement and the thickness of its cultural deposits, the numerous structures/features and the functional compartmentalisation of the settlement surface, the tool inventory and the faunal remains, all suggest a settlement period of some duration. The same indications are given by the various layers in the largest ash hearths (Fig. 105; Schiffer 1987, 233). Further to this is the white-burnt flint found across the entire surface, the occurrence of which is considered to be an indication of more intensive settlement. In general, a threshold value of 2.5% burnt flint is employed to distinguish non-intensive from intensive occupation. With a level of 3.3-3.5% burnt flint, the settlement at Vængesø III must therefore be termed as intensive (Pedersen, K.B. 2009, 122). There were at least 14-15 hearths at the settlement which, based on their delimited form, could have been located indoors (Binford 1983, 157-158). The number of hearths provides no answer to the question of whether there was occupation of the site either by a single group or several groups at the same time. Neither is it possible to give a precise duration for each individual occupation. The fact that the various settlement structures and features could still be identified during the excavation, and had not been erased by repeated subsequent occupations, suggests permanent but relatively short-lived settlement (Binford 1983, 20-21). Further evidence suggesting settlement of a more permanent character is the fact that time and effort was invested in fixed structures in the form of pits, three to four terraces and probably also stationary fish weirs and traps. It is conceivable that the settlement's numerous flake axes could have been used to cut and shape the pointed stakes for these fish weirs. Analyses of the cut marks on the fish weirs' abundant sharpened wooden poles and stakes encountered at (recently published) Ertebølle settlements with good conditions for the preservation of wood, for example Rønæs Skov (Andersen, S.H. 2009, 85), Tybrind Vig (Andersen, S.H. 2013, 120) and the settlements of Halsskov (Pedersen, L. 1997, 138), show that these were produced using flake axes. Similarly, the pits in the settlement surface can be taken as an indication of more permanent occupation of the site. They suggest an investment in facilities for the storage of food, smoking of meat etc. All in all, the evidence therefore suggests that Vængesø III represents a coastal settlement of a more permanent character.

The tool/artefact inventory has, however, a number of special features, and the relative proportions of the various tool/artefact groups also differ from that seen at other coeval Ertebølle settlements of corresponding size in eastern Jutland.

Vængesø III is the largest excavated locality on the lagoon and could very well have been the main settlement for exploitation of the marine resources in the area: I.e. it was a settlement that was surrounded by, and functioned in conjunction with, a periphery of smaller but more specialised hunting stations, i.e. a "collector model" *sensu* Binford (1980; Fig. 169). The faunal remains suggest that it was probably an all-year-round settlement. Seen from a slightly broader perspective, however, the structures and features present and the entire tool/artefact inventory give the impression that this locality is unlikely to have functioned exclusively within its own delimited settlement system. It could have been part of an even larger system that encompassed other settlements – perhaps first and foremost on the "mainland", for example the coast of Helgenæs that extends towards Begtrup Vig (Fig. 3), or the southern part of Mols. This view is supported by indications that some of the tools were brought to the settlement from elsewhere: the few blade tools, the resharpened bone points, the lack of waste from the production of tools of antler and bone, and the potsherd with a clinch hole (suggesting a shortage of serviceable pottery). Similarly, the fact that several large flint artefacts (for example the butts of core axes) were used as raw material for blade production suggests a lack of good flint and, at the same time, that the larger, well-made flint tools were not made on site, but brought from one or other of the nearby settlements. Finally, it should be emphasised that Vængesø III, like Vængesø II, displays continuity of place and subsistence economy on the coast that extends from the Ertebølle culture to the Bronze Age/Iron Age.

4.7 Grave

An inhumation grave was encountered during a small excavation in the southern part of the Vængesø III kitchen midden (Fig. 160; Asingh 2000, 32-33). This contained the remains of an individual buried in an extended supine position with the right arm extended alongside the torso. The skeleton was poorly preserved but it could nevertheless be established that the skull, left upper arm and the upper vertebrae were missing at the time of the investigation. It could not be established whether this lack was due to the unfavourable preservation conditions or whether the bones had been removed. The deceased was buried in the kitchen midden, in a place where it had a thickness of about 0.5 m. No traces were observed of a grave pit or coffin, but this could be due to this part of the kitchen midden having been disturbed by secondary digging activity, primarily in the form of pits etc. from the Bronze Age.

By the pelvis lay a regular (A-) blade with concave truncation (Fig. 161a). This is 10.3 cm long, 2.2 cm wide and 0.6 cm thick. Close to the vertebral column was a further blade with concave truncation (Fig. 161b). This latter piece has a length of 6.9 cm, a width of 1.6 cm and a thickness of 0.4 cm, i.e. slightly less than the first example. Both blades must be perceived as knives, carried in the belt. In terms of form, these pieces differ from the site's other blades/flakes with concave truncation, which are generally shorter, coarser and triangular in outline. Close to the left hand lay a 2.3 cm long and 1.7 cm wide (at the edge) transverse arrowhead (Fig. 161c), and by the left thigh was an irregular non-retouched flake (4.8 cm long, 2.5 cm wide; Fig. 161d). Finally, there was a small piece of amber by the skeleton's hip. Due to its very poor state of preservation, the latter could not be recovered, neither could it be established whether it had been worked. With respect to the flake, the transverse arrowhead and the piece of amber, it is uncertain whether these represent grave goods or randomly incorporated (settlement) waste from the surrounding kitchen midden. As the deceased was buried in the actual kitchen midden, the latter explanation is more likely (even though the position (of the amber) by the hip could suggest the former).

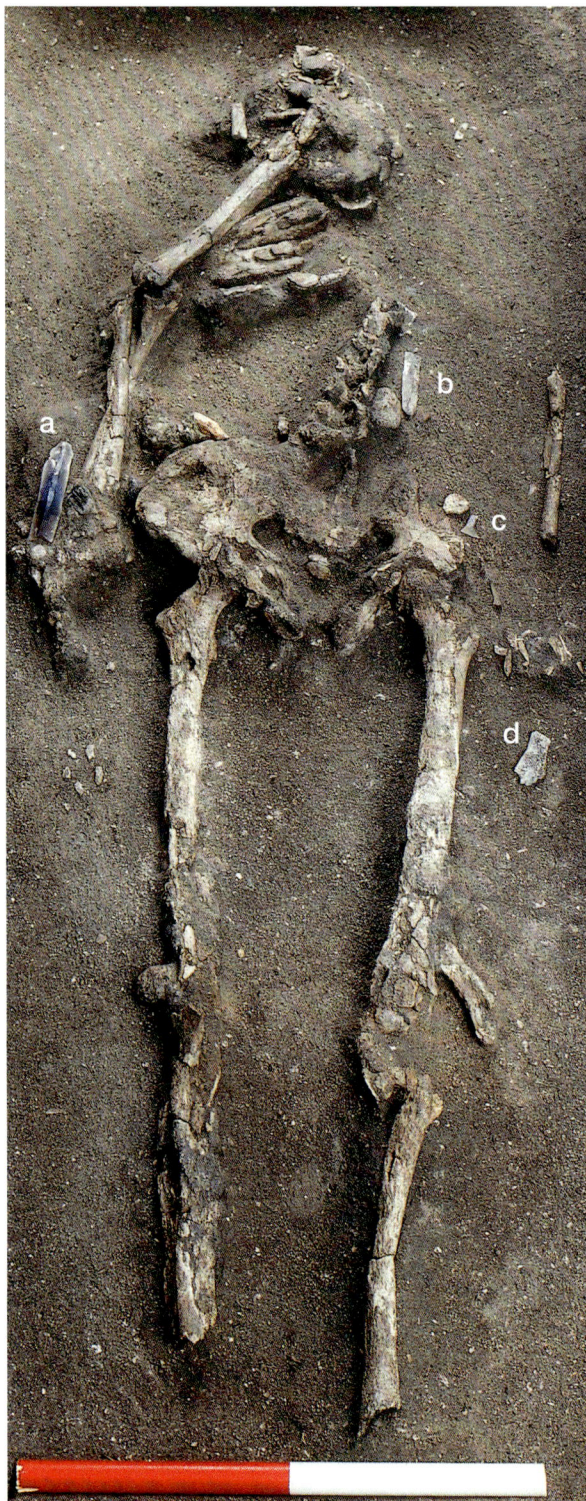

Fig. 160. *The grave containing the skeleton found in the southern part of the Vængesø III site, cf. Fig. 161. After Asingh (2000).*

An appraisal of the grave, together with comparison with other coeval Ertebølle graves, shows that this could be the grave of a man, with the body placed in an outstretched, supine position, accompanied by grave goods in the form of two truncated blades and possibly also a non-retouched flake, a transverse arrowhead and a small piece of amber.

Close to the grave was a large piece from the side of a medium-sized, pointed-based Ertebølle vessel, constructed in reverse U-technique and reddish-brown in colour. The point was only slightly demarcated relative to the lower part of the vessel. Its height was c. 40 cm; there was c. 10 cm from the pointed base to the belly transition, and c. 25 cm from the belly transition to the neck. The rim-neck section was c. 6 cm high and 1.3-1.5 cm thick. There were finger marks on the upper surface of the rim. The vessel fragment lay close to the deceased's left side, but here too is was impossible to determine whether it represented grave goods or settlement refuse. As only part of the vessel was present, the latter seems most likely. Several vessel sides were also encountered in the cultural deposits during the excavation of the northern part of the settlement (Fig. 151), which tends to support the conclusion that the vessel section found by the grave was probably settlement waste.

The grave has been radiocarbon dated to 4329-4237 BC cal (1σ; AAR-4499, 5405 ± 45 bp, corrected for marine reservoir effect to 5460 bp; Fischer et al. 2007, 2133 – Fischer et al. erroneously attribute the date to Vængesø I), i.e. Late Ertebølle culture. This corresponds well with the relative typological dating of the finds from the grave and the surrounding kitchen midden. A chemical analysis of the deceased's bones revealed that the individual had subsisted on marine food – to a very major extent. The ^{13}C value was -11.7‰. A ^{15}N value of 15.3‰ was also obtained for this individual, showing that he predominantly ate food from the highest level in the marine environment's food chain (Fischer et al. 2007, 2132-2133).

The grave is one of several inhumation graves found at Vængesø (Vængesø II), but is several centuries older and stands out by being furnished with

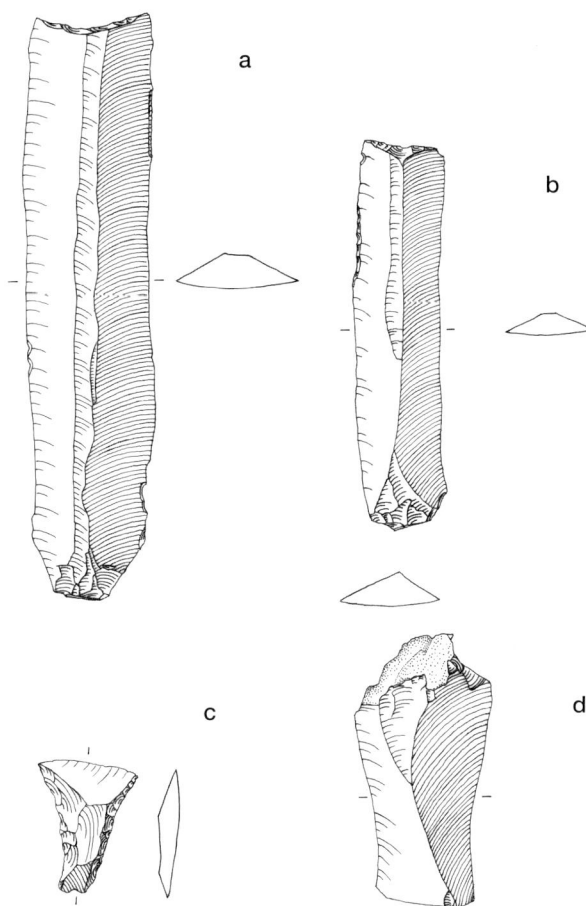

Fig. 161. Grave goods from the grave shown in Fig. 160. a-b) Blades with distal, concave truncation. Other finds from the grave: c) Transverse arrowhead. d) Waste flake. Scale 3:4. Drawing: Pia Brejnholt.

grave goods (flint knives). An interesting aspect of this grave is its lack of a skull, similar to the situation observed at Holmegaard (Ch. 7.3; Fig. 186). Unfortunately, the conditions for observation and preservation at Vængesø III were not so good and it could not be determined whether the man's skull had been removed in antiquity, or whether its absence was due to secondary disturbances, in which case this could suggest some form of trophy or cranium cult.

In the investigation of the extensive faunal material (animal bones) recovered during the excavations, one or possibly two small fragments of human skull were recorded, together with a human tooth, suggesting that secondary disturbance of graves could have taken place. One of the cranial fragments, which measures c. 2 × 2 cm, is burnt and could represent traces of a *cremation grave*. A similar piece of burnt cranium was found at the coeval Ertebølle settlement of Ronæs Skov (Andersen, S.H. 2009, 20-21).

4.8 Conclusion

The Vængesø III investigations relate to a settlement area that comprises part of a large kitchen midden. Judging from the finds distribution, the topography etc., it does however seem that the northern, excavated part of the kitchen midden can be perceived as a discrete entity. Vængesø III is the largest settlement on the Vængesø lagoon and also represents one of the largest kitchen middens in Jutland. The fact that this locality became so large, relative to the lagoon's other settlements, must be a result of several factors. Firstly, it had a larger hinterland than the others, and secondly, it had easy access to drinking water. Moreover, the site had an advantageous position at the mouth of the lagoon, out towards Ebeltoft Vig and Begtrup Vig. This is a hub for several different resources and resource areas: the open sea, the lagoon, the nearby beach-ridge system, the southern part of Mols and the northern part of Helgenæs. Further to this, there was easy access to good fishing places – not just in the Vængesø lagoon, but equally well along the coast of Helgenæs which, right up to the present day, has been renowned for its rich (eel) fishing. In topographic terms, the Vængesø lagoon was a large, natural fish trap, a situation that was probably exploited for this purpose in the Stone Age. Vængesø III differs from the other excavated settlements around the lagoon by virtue of the richness of finds in its cultural deposits, which also contain a huge abundance of fishbones, many different settlement structures and features and an inhumation grave in the southern part. No remains of a "midden" or refuse layer have though been identified at Vængesø III.

The site has a large settlement/occupation surface dating from the Late Ertebølle culture. It is characterised by numerous structures/features of several different types within a relatively small area. The many hearths in particular indicate that the site was visited on numerous occasions. Another characteristic feature of this settlement is the many small and well-delimited heaps of shells of various (marine) mollusc species. They show that there must have been rapid accumulation of the deposits. The numerous areas showing traces of flint-working, which are always closely associated with the ash hearths, point in the same direction. The finds show that it was predominantly the working of flake axes that was undertaken in these places. An important discovery was the demonstration of three (possibly four) elongate and slightly sunken terraces in the hillside. These have the same form, size and furnishing, with hearths arranged along their longitudinal axis (terraces I and II). A common feature is, moreover, that they all lie along (parallel with) the prehistoric coast. They are very uniform and are interpreted as slightly sunken working platforms/terraces. It is, however, also possible that they represent some form of dwelling or that they are not independent structures but represent parts of the floor surface within larger dwellings. Similar terraces were also found at Vængesø I and II.

The flint tools reflect the use of poor-quality raw material that came from the local fluvioglacial deposits. The tool inventory is characterised by small, short cores with a single platform and the production of blades struck with soft technique. The blades are dominated by short, irregular B-blades. Compared with other coeval settlements in eastern Jutland, this site has only a few blade scrapers, borers and burins. Conversely, the blade tools include blades with concave truncation, in addition to pieces with fine denticulation. The settlement also yielded numerous flat-flaked symmetrical flake axes and flat-flaked flake chisels. Characteristic flint debitage reveals the extensive working of flake axes at this site. Core axes are few in number and all have double-sided, specialised edge working. The finds assemblage also includes transverse arrowheads with strongly flared edge corners as well as spherical (flint) crushing stones. The many flake axes probably indicate the extensive production of poles, stakes and rods for fish weirs – an observation that concurs with the many millions of fishbones preserved in the cultural deposits (Enghoff 1994, 89).

Given the good conditions for preservation, there are very few tools of antler and bone – both in terms of type and number. This situation is particularly striking when compared with that at other, coeval Ertebølle sites such as Meilgaard, Dyrholmen and Ertebølle. This finds group is dominated by bone points with a round cross-section, most of which have been resharpened. A slightly unusual find is a point made of whalebone – a raw material that has not previously been identified for this type of tool, but was otherwise commonly employed for the Ertebølle culture's harpoons (Andersen, S.H. 1996, 83-89).

The tool inventory is also characterised by points made from bird bone and splinters of this material, giving these pieces more the character of "pins" rather than actual points. The points from Vængesø III differ therefore markedly from the bird bone points with a "syringe tip" that are otherwise a commonly occurring type at Ertebølle settlements in western Denmark. Artefacts of particular note within this tool/artefact group are the long, ornamented pins that have not previously been found in an Ertebølle context. Similarly, the distinctive "buttons" made from porpoise vertebrae are a new artefact type. The small number of bone and antler tools is consistent with the absence of waste from the production of tools from these materials. For example, there is no antler waste whatsoever, i.e. no discarded tines, antler points with traces of groove-and-splinter technique, "shortening pieces" and pedicels. Similarly, there is an absence of sawn-off bone epiphyses

and pieces of bone showing traces of groove-and-splinter technique. These observations are also consistent with the small number of burins and the observation that only very few of the flake axes show traces of having been used to work in antler. Similarly, the scarcity of fabricators and antler axes is remarkable. The few fabricators that were recovered are of a type also seen at both Vængesø I and II (though in small numbers). The absence of harpoons, and (especially) the waste from their production, is striking, and is particularly remarkable given that the faunal remains demonstrate the extensive hunting of seals and small whales. Finally, the finds assemblage from Vængesø III is characterised by a significant element of pottery in the form of pointed-based vessels, but no finds of "lamps". This is remarkable, given the site's solid economic background in marine hunting of seals and whales.

The subsistence economy was dominated by a mixture of fishing, marine hunting and gathering of marine invertebrates, while hunting and trapping of terrestrial meat animals apparently only played a minor role. Vængesø III does, however, differ from Vængesø I and II by virtue of its much larger element of remains from fur animals and dogs. Marine animals are much more prominent at this settlement (and at Vængesø II) than has been seen to date at other Danish Ertebølle settlements. This applies in particular to the abundance of remains of fish, seals, whales and seabirds. This subsistence economic aspect was supplemented by extensive hunting/trapping of "fur animals".

The settlement has been dated, both archaeologically-typologically and scientifically, to the Late Ertebølle culture and it appears to be (archaeologically) contemporaneous with both Vængesø I and II.

5 Vængesø IV "Tronhøjen"

5.1 Stratigraphy

A minor excavation was undertaken on the edge of a kitchen midden at the locality of Vængesø IV (parish record no. 31, Helgenæs parish, Mols Søndre district, Randers county; Moesgaard Museum archive no. 1963; East Jutland Museum archive no. EBM 158). This lies on the NE/E slope of a steep-sided hillock, with a subsoil of light-brown/yellowish-brown fluvioglacial sand and gravel, which projects to the east and northeast into the now recreated Vængesø (see chapter 1). In prehistory, the hillock was a promontory, which faced eastwards towards the Vængesø lagoon and, to the north, bordered a small marine inlet, which led into a little sound running between Vængesø III and IV (Fig. 3). The kitchen midden also lies directly opposite (west of) the find site for the whale cranium mentioned below. At the foot of the hill are marine deposits (beach ridges) and about 20 m further east, out on the raised marine surface, is a marked c. 1 m high terrace. The limits of the kitchen midden have not been established so it is difficult to give its precise size. However, based on observations of shells on the field surface etc., it can be cautiously estimated to extend c. 20 m (north-south) along the former shoreline and to be c. 10 m wide (east-west), thereby covering an area of c. 200 m²; it must therefore be considered a small site. Three trenches were excavated along a c. 17 m long stretch at the foot of the hillside. In connection with these, three east-west sections,

respectively 3 m, 3 m and 4.2 m in length and running at right angles to the prehistoric coastline, were surveyed and drawn (Fig. 162). A total area of c. 25 m² was excavated, i.e. this was a relatively small investigation. A 0.5-1 m thick sequence of alternating kitchen midden deposits containing the shells of marine invertebrates (predominantly oysters), ash layers and sand/gravel was observed in all three sections; these layers were seen to contain two or three horizontal, more charcoal-rich layers. In the two southernmost sections, the cultural deposits could be followed c. 2 m into the hillside, while in the northernmost trench they extended c. 4.2 m (east-west) and had a thickness of c. 15-50 cm. In the hillside, i.e. to the west, the layers turned obliquely upwards and followed the slope, whereas they were water-lain, i.e. horizontal, towards its foot, i.e. to the east. This applies to both the shell- and the charcoal-rich layers (Fig. 163). In all the trenches, the stratigraphy began with a layer of fine, light sand (subsoil). This was followed by a c. 10-15 cm thick charcoal-rich layer, which sloped slightly towards the east and which could be followed 1.5-3 m into the hillside, where it disappeared (Fig. 164). Above this was a 20-50 cm thick, yellow gravel and sand layer, followed by a series of alternating charcoal and shell layers; the latter varying between one and three in number. The charcoal stripes were c. 5-10 cm and the shell/kitchen midden layers between 10 and 60 cm in thickness. Towards the north, the thin shell layers

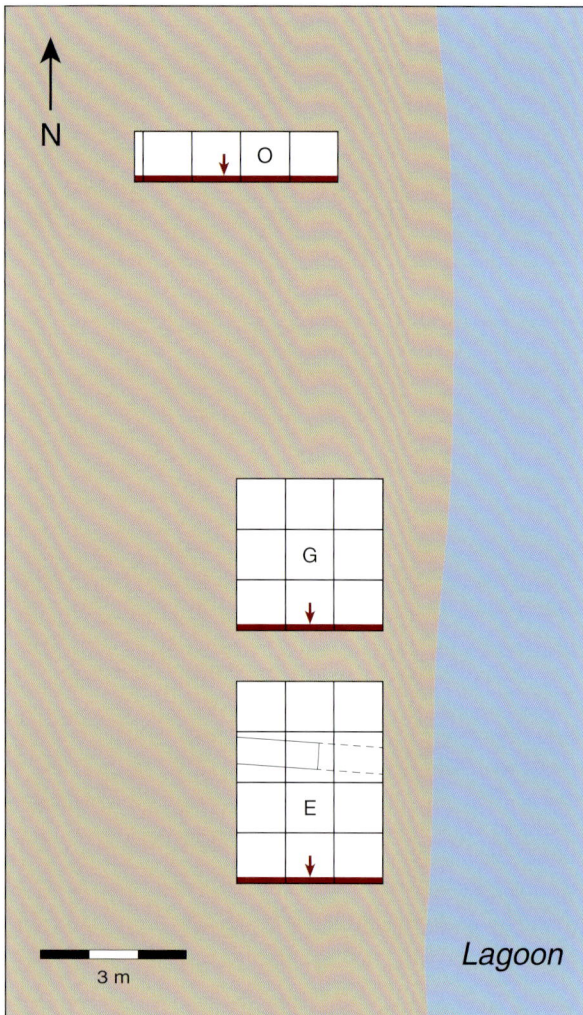

Fig. 162. Plan showing the location and size of the excavated trenches and the recorded sections by the E-NE margin of Vængesø IV. Sections are indicated by thick lines and arrows indicate viewing directions for the sections.

Fig. 163. East-west sections through the stratigraphy at the eastern margin of Vængesø IV. a) Square E. b) Square O. Photo: J.S. Jespersen.

ran together to form a 7-8 cm thick kitchen midden layer. The kitchen midden and the charcoal-rich layers lay obliquely towards the west, but became horizontal towards the east (Figs. 163 and 164). Above this sequence of deposits there was again fine sand. It could not be determined during the excavation whether the sand had slipped down from the hillside or was marine-deposited (or possibly a mixture of the two). The entire stratigraphy lay between 3.4 and 4.6 m a.m.s.l. All the layers contained a little scattered flint debitage, a few flint tools, charcoal and an occasional potsherd. No bone or antler was encountered. The fact that

the stratigraphy was so intact at this locality (in contrast to the situation at the other settlements around Vængesø) was likely due primarily to the site being situated on a steep hillside which, due to its slope, had probably never been cultivated.

The stratigraphy indicates that, at some point, there was a settlement at the foot of the hill around 3.5 m a.m.s.l. This corresponds closely to the findings from Vængesø I and III, where the existence was demonstrated of similar terraces at this level. The sea level subsequently rose and inundated the culture layer, covering it with shingle and sand, i.e. it reached a level of 3.7-3.8 m a.m.s.l. At the same time,

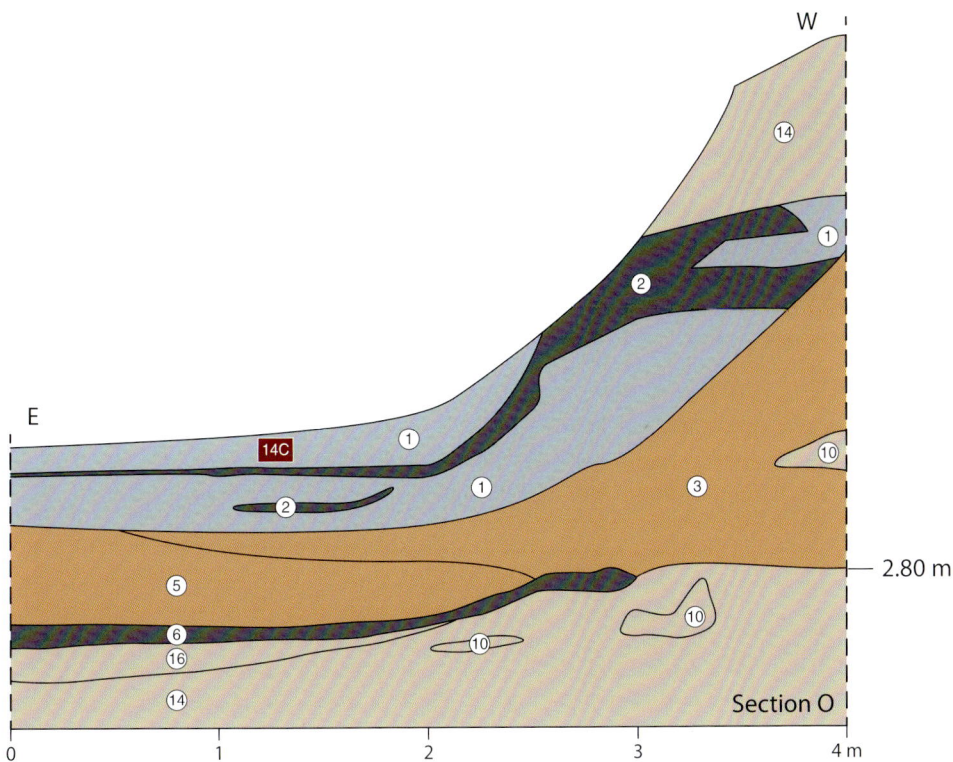

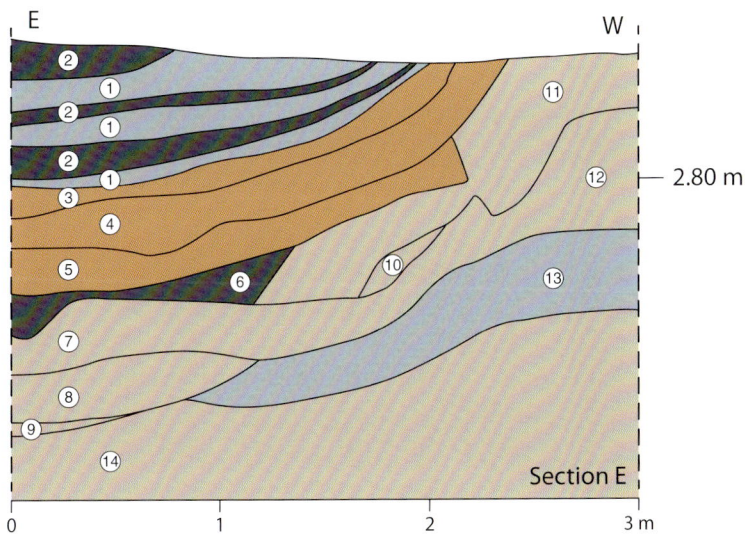

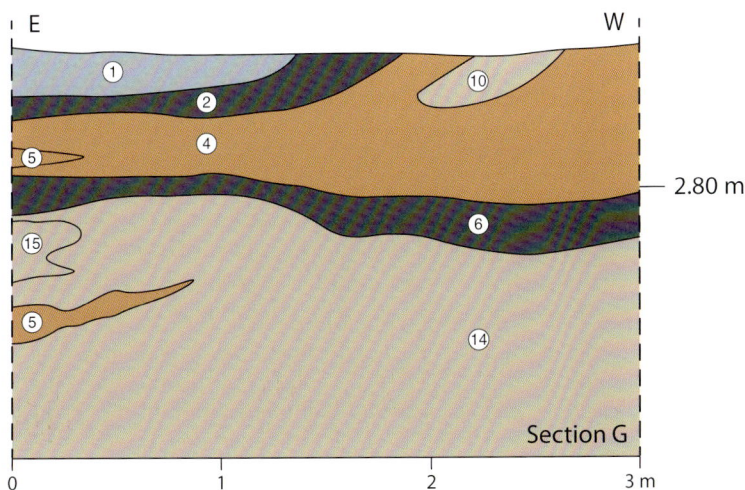

Fig. 164. East-west section evident in the northernmost ditch. 1 Shell layer (kitchen midden dominated by oyster shells). 2 Grey ash layer. 3 Yellow-brown sand layer containing humic material. 4 Grey sand layer containing occasional egg-sized stones. 5 Yellow-brown sand layer with shingle. 6 Grey ash layer. 7 Light-yellow sand layer. 8 Light-yellow sand layer. 9 Grey, stone-less sand layer. 10 Small lumps of yellow clay. 11 Coarse, yellow gravel layer. 12 Yellow sand layer. 13 Grey sand layer. 14 Light-yellow, stone-less sand layer. 15 Grey-yellow shingle layer with comminuted shell. 16 Grey shingle layer. Only layers 1, 2 and 6 are actual culture layers. The position of radiocarbon-dating sample K-3100 is indicated.

some slippage of the hillside probably occurred, sand from which then covered the deepest charcoal/culture layer – especially at the foot of the hill. Subsequently, there was a standstill or a regression in sea level, during which the area at the foot of the hill and up the hillside was occupied (the kitchen midden). Shells and ash gradually slipped down the hillside, forming an increasingly thick culture layer, which at its foot reached a maximum of 4.5 m a.m.s.l. Later, sand again slipped down and out from the hillside, covering the cultural deposits. Even though most of the evidence speaks in favour of this interpretation of the stratigraphy, the very steep course of the kitchen midden from west to east is striking, bringing to mind the previously mentioned terraces at Vængesø I, II and III. Topographically, the hillside at Vængesø IV has the same steep character as the other hillsides, where it was necessary for the inhabitants to dig out terraces in order to create suitable places for occupation. It is therefore possible that the depositional sequence on the slope at Vængesø IV also represents a similar terrace cut into this hillside.

5.2 Finds

The finds are few in number and include three flat-flaked symmetrical flake axes with slightly flared sides (Fig. 165a). One has a rejuvenation flake, which formed the basis for an unsuccessful burin break. Further to these are the basal part of a long, regular A-blade with handle retouch at the proximal percussion-bulb end (Fig. 165b) and the base of a blade with a retouched notch in one side. All these pieces are Late Ertebølle types. In addition, the finds include a short core with a single platform, a curved knife and a coarse, atypical flake with a denticulate edge. These flint artefacts were found in the kitchen midden deposits and uppermost in these was also a small, simple potsherd. This is unfortunately so small and uncharacteristic that is cannot be dated more closely. The sherd has an impression of either a small seed capsule or bud – possibly a flower bud (identified by Eva Koch (1952-2010), National Museum of Denmark).

The Ertebølle flint has a white surface and one of the flake axes is also water-worn, while the other flint artefacts show little or no signs of bleaching or water

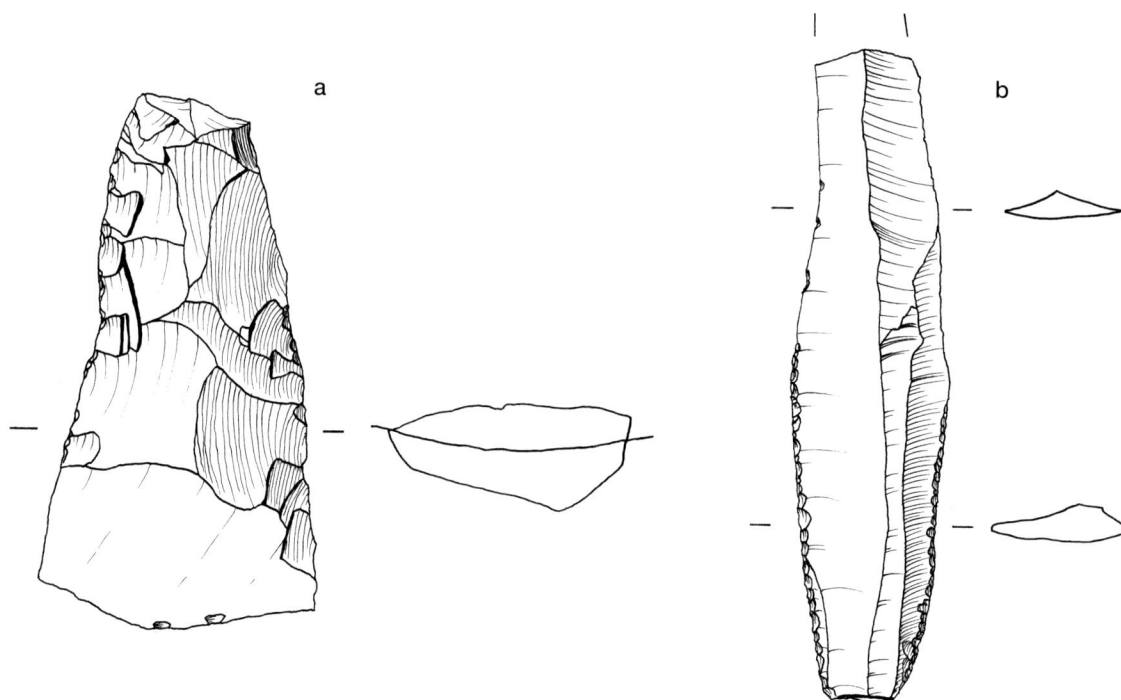

Fig. 165. a) Flat-flaked symmetrical flake axe. b) Regular blade with bifacial edge retouch at the proximal end (handle retouch). Scale 3:4. Drawing: Søren Timm Christensen.

wear. On the whole, there appears to be mixing of water-worn and non-water-worn flint, and surface-transformed or non-surface-transformed flint. This could be due to the finds being a mixture of *in situ* and redeposited artefacts that have either slipped down the hillside or been washed up by the sea.

The kitchen midden is dominated by medium-sized oyster shells, which measure 5-9 cm in length and thereby correspond to the size of the oyster shells from the other settlements around the lagoon. A few shells of cockles, mussels and periwinkles were also observed.

5.3 Dating

The few flint artefacts suggest a date for the kitchen midden in the Late Ertebølle culture, but the characteristic stratigraphy, comprised of shell and charcoal layers, indicates that this could be a so-called "stratified shell midden" with deposits from both the Late Ertebølle culture and the Early Neolithic Funnel Beaker culture. The latter situation has also been confirmed by a radiocarbon date for oyster shells from the uppermost part of the deposits of 3708-3519 BC cal (1 σ; K-3100, 4840 ± 85 bp), corresponding to the Early Neolithic Funnel Beaker culture (TN I). The alternating shell and charcoal layers correspond to well-known Neolithic stratigraphies as seen for example at Norsminde (Andersen, S.H. 1991, 20-24) and Bjørnsholm (Andersen. S.H. 1993, 73). At the same time, this locality has a stratigraphy of the same kind as the ploughed-down (i.e. truncated) parts of Vængesø III.

5.4 Conclusions

The very limited extent of the excavation at Vængesø IV makes it difficult to draw more extensive conclusions about the nature of this site. The few cultural remains and the absence of animal bones raises questions about the site's function in the prehistoric settlement pattern around Vængesø. The locality is very small and the steep hillside would have made occupation difficult – especially for a larger group. Therefore, a terrace was possibly cut into the hillside at this locality. The modest cultural remains found in the cultural deposits and the absence of settlement structures make it very doubtful that the term "settlement" can be applied to this site. It should probably be interpreted as a lookout point or somewhere for short-term occupation when checking/emptying a fishing structure or trap that was possibly built out into the water from the northern tip of the hillock. The north-facing shore, which looked out onto the narrow marine inlet leading from Vængesø into the bay beyond, was an ideal position for a fish weir. The flake axes found here could have been used to sharpen/repair stakes and poles associated with this fishing structure. This interpretation is also consistent with the topography of the site, where the steep hillside was only suitable for short-term occupation involving functions that did not require much space.

5.5 Whale skull

In 1920, the skull of a large whale was found in the marine sand, gravel and shingle deposits at the foot of the Vængesø IV settlement (parish record no. 14, Helgenæs parish, Mols Søndre district, Randers county). It was identified as the skull of a fin whale (*Balaenoptera physalus*, identified by H. Winge; Kinze 2001, 133). In the report on the skull to the Danish National Museum, mention is made of flake axes and greenstone axes being found in the vicinity. These artefacts, together with the depositional circumstances and the numerous Ertebølle sites known in the area, led to the whale skeleton being assigned to the Ertebølle culture and interpreted as representing a hunting site on the shore, where a whale had been butchered (Nordmann 1936, 127-128). A subsequent radiocarbon date for the whale skull, obtained by P.V. Petersen of the National Museum, showed however that it was much later and came from the transition between the Early and Late Bronze Age (K-5661, 2890 ± 80 bp; 1205-945 BC cal (1 σ)). Consequently, there was no chronological link between the whale remains and the Stone Age tools found near it. The author's investigation of the skull in spring 2010 at the Zoological Museum, University of Copenhagen, revealed the presence of distinct cut marks on the external occipital crest. However, due to the poor state of preservation of the surface, it could unfortunately not be determined whether these were made by stone or metal tools. Even though the whale skull had nothing whatsoever to do with the Stone Age tools, this find is interesting for several reasons. Firstly, it shows that, as late as the Bronze Age, whales were either hunted or stranded in Vængesø. Secondly, numerous large whale bones (species unidentified) were found on the nearby southern tip of Vængesø III in archaeological layers which probably date from the Bronze Age.

Skeletal remains of whales have been found in marine deposits of Stone Age date at several locations in Denmark, For example, a humpback whale (*Megaptera novaeangliae*) was discovered in Føns Vang in western Funen (Winge 1904, 150; Andersen, S.H. 2009, 19; Kinze 2001, 141), a fin whale was found at Åsted in northern Salling (Bertelsen 1994, 167; subsequently radiocarbon dated to c. 3800 BC cal, i.e. the Early Subboreal period) and remains of a killer whale (*Orcinus orca*) turned up at Jølby Kær on western Mors (undated find at Morslands Historiske Museum, Nykøbing Mors).

6 Other Ertebølle settlements on and around Vængesø

In addition to the four excavated Stone Age settlements on the shores of Vængesø described above, a number of other sites have been recorded along the lagoon's shores (Fig. 166).

The first of these, named Fuglevad, lies a few hundred metres to the north of Vængesø III, on the southeast slope of a hill. This is an Ertebølle settlement, with no associated kitchen midden, that faced out towards the opening of the Vængesø lagoon into Ebeltoft Vig. The locality is only known from field-surface collections, and over the years P. Poulsen picked up five flat-flaked symmetrical flake axes and several core axes with double-sided edge trimming here. The finds suggest that this is a small Ertebølle locality, which can be dated to the final phase of the culture, i.e. contemporaneous with the other settlements around the Vængesø lagoon presented above.

In the southwestern part of the lagoon is a small north-facing promontory at the foot of a steep hillside. On the northeastern edge of this is a small kitchen midden at about 2.5-5 m a.m.s.l. (parish record no. 32, Borup parish). Its extent has not been determined with certainty, but it apparently only covers a small area of c. 15 × 15 m, within which pieces of oyster shells and a little worked flint have been observed during field-walking.

Parish record no. 33 is a kitchen midden of presumed Neolithic date, measuring c. 15 × 10 m and located by a former coastal slope. Axe blanks and fragments of thin-butted axes have been collected at the site. No trial excavation has been undertaken.

In the southern part of the Vængesø lagoon is a promontory of c. 50 × 50 m that extends out into the former marine area. A kitchen midden measuring c. 20 × 20 m has been recorded here where the artefacts collected over the years include a number of flat-flaked flake axes, fragments of polished thin-butted axes, axe blanks and a point-butted axe (parish record no. 34, Borup parish). In a test pit in the eastern part of the midden, by the base of the promontory, a piece of the rim of a pot (possibly of Ertebølle type) was found c. 10 cm down in the shell layer.

On the south coast of Vængesø, a settlement area has been demonstrated on an elongated islet (c. 100 × 30 m) alongside the former coastline (parish record no. 35, Borup parish). Over an area of c. 25 m in length and c. 10 m in width occurrences of shells and numerous water-worn and surface-transformed flint artefacts have been recorded. These presumably represent a redeposited and ploughed-over kitchen midden.

Parish record no. 36, Borup parish: A kitchen midden in the southeastern part of the Vængesø lagoon. A considerable number of flint artefacts of Ertebølle types have been collected here on a small islet measuring c. 40 × 20 m. A small test pit revealed the existence of a kitchen midden/shell layer of at least 1 m in thickness.

An interesting result of the many years of field-walking over the fields around Vængesø is the collection of a large number of single finds of core

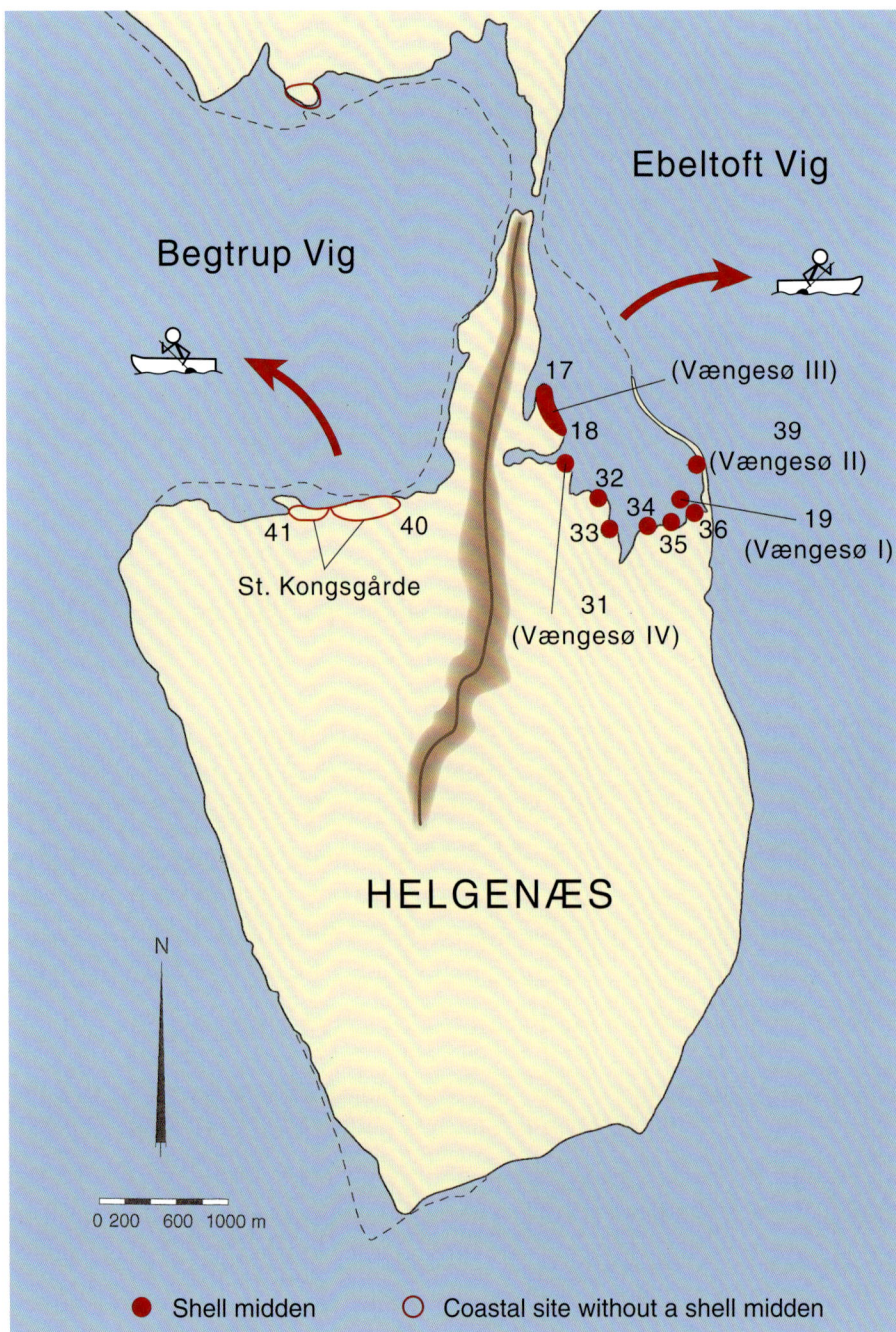

Fig. 166. Map of Helgenæs showing all the known Ertebølle settlements with their parish record number. A bold brown line marks a hilly ridge that forms a topographic boundary dividing the northern part of Helgenæs into an eastern and a western area, containing Stone Age sites oriented towards Ebeltoft Vig and Begtrup Vig, respectively. This division may also have influenced the economic and social organisation and structure of the settlements.

axes and greenstone axes of Late Ertebølle types in the steeply undulating terrain around the former lagoon (especially to the south). The artefacts occur within a belt extending c. 500-750 m from the Stone Age shoreline, after which they cease completely or are extremely rare and scattered. These are single finds, unassociated with other forms of cultural remains, for example settlement traces, at the find sites. Even though there are of course many potential uncertain factors associ-

ated with these finds (see the map presented in Fig. 167), they nevertheless give an impression of the activities of the Ertebølle population in the vicinity/hinterland of the coastal settlements. The axes presumably represent traces of tree-felling activities – probably primarily associated with the production of stakes and poles for the settlements' numerous fish weirs, but also for dug-out canoes and the like. Support for this interpretation of the finds distribution as a reflection of actual prehis-

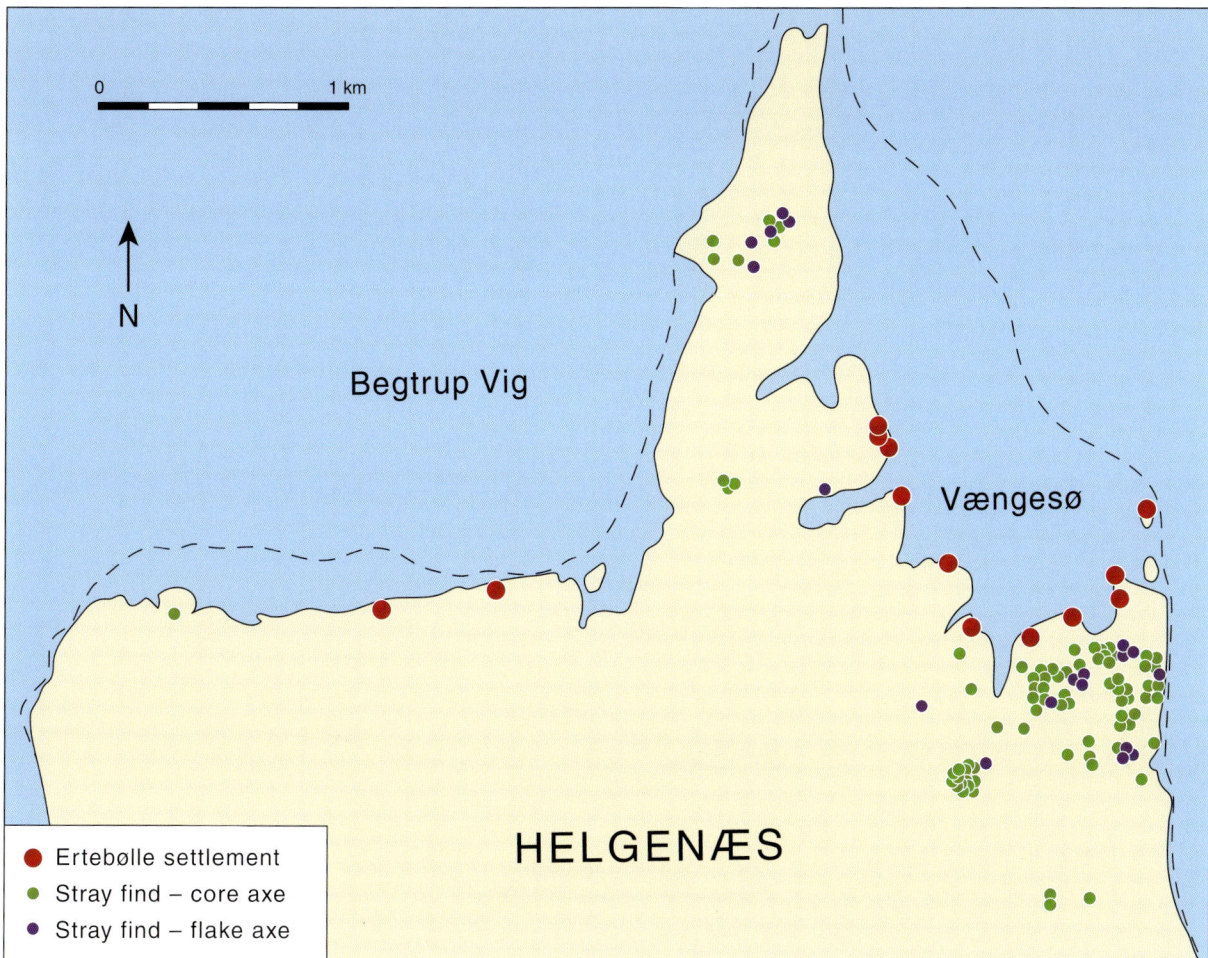

Fig. 167. Map of Helgenæs showing stray finds of core and flake axes outside the settlements in the coastal zone. Although a distribution map of this kind can, of course, be subject to numerous sources of error, the finds probably reflect activities in the area close to the settlements, such as the cutting of hazel rods for fish weirs and the felling of large trees for dugout boats. A similar distribution of stray finds of axes in the landscape was revealed by surveys around the former fjord at Bjørnsholm in north-west Himmerland and around Norsminde Fjord in eastern Jutland.

toric activity is provided by the completely identical picture resulting from intensive field-walking around Norsminde Fjord (Andersen, S.H. 1976, 18-61; unpublished, Moesgaard Museum archive no. 1770) and by the former Bjørnsholm Fjord in northwestern Himmerland (unpublished, Moesgaard Museum archive no. 3232).

Other important Ertebølle sites in the vicinity that should be mentioned include two large coastal settlements located directly west of Store Kongsgårde on the northwest coast of Helgenæs (Fig. 166). These are archaeologically coeval with the Vængesø localities (i.e. date from the Late/Lat-

est Ertebølle culture), and lie only about 1.5-2 km to the southwest. One is located on a beach-ridge system and covers an area of c. 125 × 125 m, while the other is located on a promontory (100 × 50 m) slightly further to the southeast. In the Stone Age, both sites faced out towards the open sea (Begtrup Vig) and solely for this reason they differ markedly from the much more sheltered locations of the Vængesø sites. No traces of kitchen middens have been demonstrated at these two sites, but it should be emphasised that, as archaeological excavations have not been carried out, there is only the evidence provided by years of field-walking/

surface collection. The eastern site has yielded at least 400 flat-flaked flake axes, 20 flake chisels and seven symmetrical core axes with double-sided, specialised edge trimming. In addition to these are many blade tools of Late Ertebølle type, including c. 20 blades with concave truncation and five transverse arrowheads; there are also occasional artefacts from the Neolithic and Bronze Age. Overall, the artefacts recovered from this locality show that it represents a major settlement dating from the Late Ertebølle culture. The other locality (termed Store Kongsgårde Vest) has yielded significantly fewer Ertebølle artefacts; the finds do, however, include c. 35 flat-flaked flake axes, a flake chisel, asymmetrical core axes etc.

There are no faunal remains from these sites, but their location, facing the open sea (and with a limited hinterland), suggests a subsistence economy based on the marine biotope, i.e. fishing, marine hunting and catching sea birds. Both locations reflect major occupations during the Late Ertebølle culture. Given its area and the number of flake

Fig. 168. Map showing the fish weirs that were recorded along the coast of Helgenæs around 1900. After Wendelboe (2012).

axes it has yielded, the Store Kongsgårde locality is considerably larger than any of the Vængesø settlements – it is probably the largest Ertebølle settlement on Helgenæs. If the flat-flaked flake axes are used as a comparative base relative to the Erte-bølle settlements in southwest Zealand, it is evident that the Kongsgårde localities correspond to the largest of these (401-1008 flake axes), which are characterised by being located in the best fishing places (Johansson 1999, 59, Fig. 37). If the flake axes were produced predominantly for the purposes of producing stakes, poles and rods for fish weirs, as suggested by the well-preserved cut marks on the many examples found at submerged Ertebølle settlements such as Ronæs Skov and Tybrind Vig (Andersen, S.H. 2009, 42-44, 84-88, Figs. 20-21, 60-63, 2013, 59-62, 119-122, Figs. 1.30-1.33A, 3.4-3.6), this suggests that the large number of flake axes found at Kongsgårde must reflect extensive fishing activities using stationary fishing structures located offshore from these sites in Begtrup Vig. As these settlements are archaeologically coeval with Vængesø, they make an interesting and important contribution to an evaluation of the settlement density in the Late Ertebølle times in this part of eastern Jutland. As Helgenæs has a very limited topographic depth, it is unlikely that the subsistence economy of these settlements would have been based on terrestrial hunting (as also underlined by the faunal remains recovered from the Vængesø settlements). It is much more likely that their economic base was fishing and marine hunting. In this respect, attention can be drawn to the fact that the (western) coast of Helgenæs was renowned for its extensive eel fishing in both historical and recent times (Fig. 168). Although direct parallels cannot be drawn between the Late Ertebølle period and the present, it is tempting to interpret these large coastal settlements as an indication of similar fishing operations in the Stone Age.

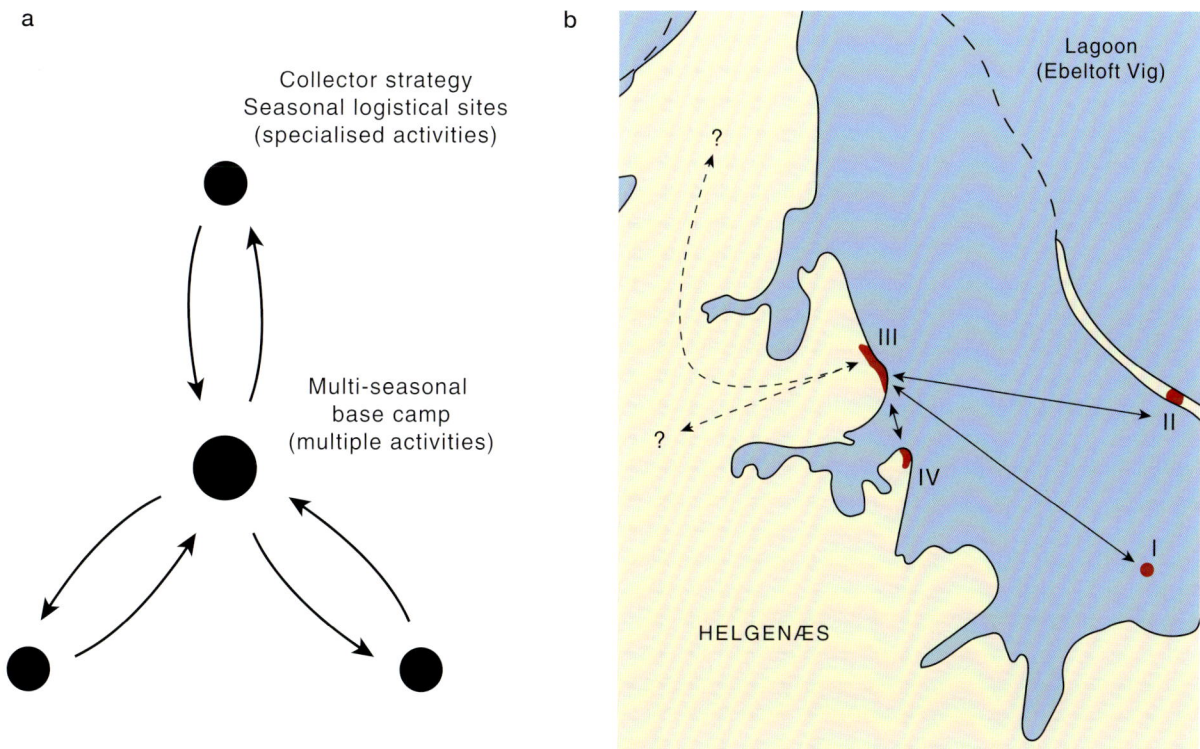

Fig. 169. a) Schematic model of the settlement structure in a "collector system", i.e. with a centrally located base settlement (year-round settlement; e.g. Vængesø III), surrounded by small, more "special-ised" and seasonal localities (Vængesø I and II). After Binford (1982). b) A model of the collector system around the Vængesø lagoon.

7 Holmegaard

· ·

The southeastern part of Djursland is characterised by a very varied landscape, which over short distances alternates between steep-sided gravel and clay hills and low, now peat-covered meadows – remains of a former Stone Age fjord system. According to E. Mertz and A. Jessen, the area has risen c. 5-5.5 m since the Stone Age sea-level maximum (Mertz 1924, 23-24; Jessen 1920, 92). In the Stone Age, the area hosted an extensive east-west-oriented fjord system – "the Stubbe Sø fjord system" (Pedersen/ Petersen 1997, 74). This consisted of a mosaic of islands, peninsulas and promontories separated by inlets and small bays, connected by a sound running east to the Kattegat (Hjelm Dyb; Fig. 1b and Fig. 170). Today, the lake Stubbe Sø represents the western part of this former fjord system. The very varied land-/waterscape here proved very attractive to the groups of Mesolithic hunter-fishers, whose

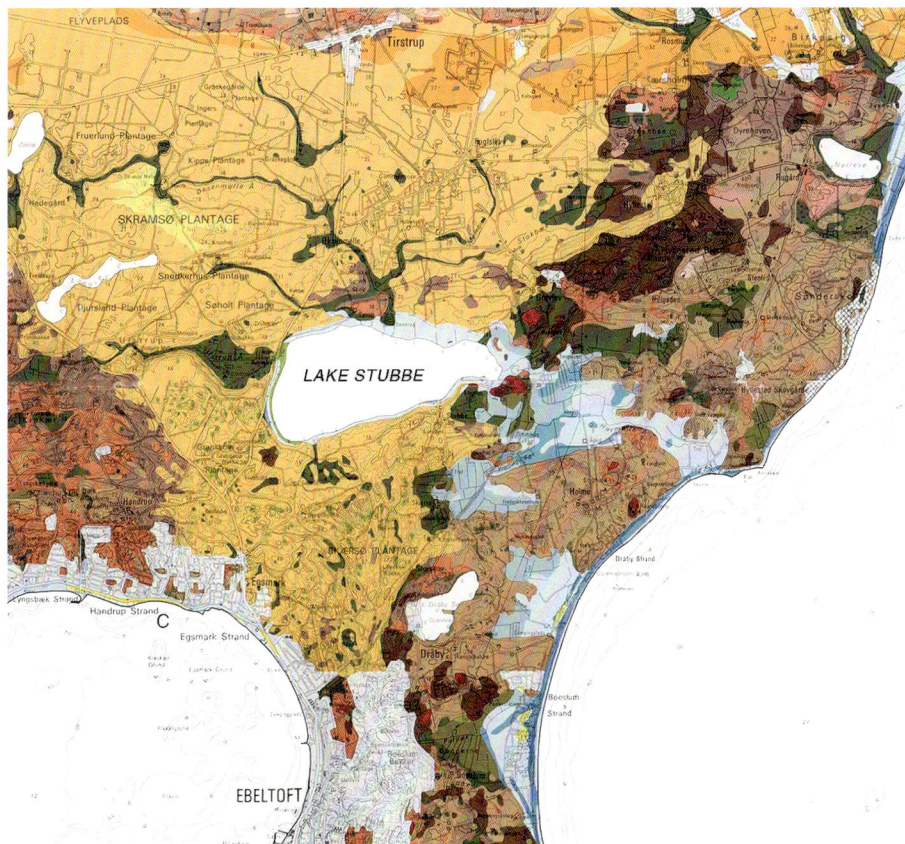

Fig. 170. Geological map of southeastern Djursland. Older marine deposits are shown in light and dark blue, for other soil types see Fig. 2. In the Stone Age, the former Stubbe Fjord linked what is now a lake, Stubbe Sø, with the Kattegat. After Pedersen/ Petersen (1997).

coastal settlements have been discovered in large numbers. In many, but not all, cases, these settlements were associated with kitchen middens. At least 13 coastal settlements of various sizes relating to the Ertebølle culture have been recorded in the area, and the fjord system has one of the densest concentrations of settlements on Djursland from this period of the Stone Age.

The locality of Holmegaard lies on the southwestern "corner" of a c. 400-500 m long, c. 100-150 m wide (E-W/N-S) and c. 18 m high ridge, which slopes down towards the stream Havmølle Å (parish record no. 24, Hyllested parish, Djurs Sønder district, Randers county; Moesgaard Museum archive no. 1532; East Jutland Museum archive no. EBM 27; Fig. 171). In the Stone Age, this hill was an island or a peninsula located approximately in the middle of the former Stubbe fjord – and precisely at the point where it was narrowest (c. 120 m across). Settlement traces have been demonstrated along the entire edge of the hill, but with particular concentrations around its southwestern and southeastern corners. These remains date from both the Mesolithic (most) and the Neolithic.

The Holmegaard kitchen midden's topographic situation is "classic" in relation to the localisation models published in the literature (Fischer/Sørensen 1983, 104-126). During tidal ebb and flow there must have been a very strong current in the narrow channel off the settlement at that time. This is also evident from the adjacent hillsides, which to this day take the form of very steep erosion slopes. The channel, with its strong tidal currents, must have great possibilities for productive fishing.

Fig. 171. Contour plan of the Holmegaard settlement in the Stone Age, showing "Stubbe Fjord" and its immediate environs. The pale areas indicate the maximum extent of the Stone Age sea. 1 Holmegaard. 2 Stubbe Station.

These factors provide an explanation for the concentration of settlements in this very place, and the very favourable location of the Holmegaard kitchen midden within this marine resource area resulted in it becoming the largest in the area.

Directly west of this locality, a lower, sloping area has yielded worked flint from the Early/Middle Ertebølle culture, and to the southeast, numerous flint artefacts have been found dating from both the Mesolithic and Neolithic, but in neither case is there an accompanying kitchen midden. The Holmegaard locality was discovered in 1967, when amateur archaeologist R. Wallin found a well-preserved human skeleton lying *in situ* in the shell deposit during an unsystematic excavation of the midden. Subsequent radiocarbon dating of the skeleton showed it to be of Mesolithic date, more precisely the Middle Ertebølle culture (see below). The discovery was reported to Moesgaard Museum, who carried out a small investigation that same autumn. Back then, the kitchen midden was still very intact and up to c. 50-60 cm in thickness, with a covering soil (plough-soil) layer of c. 20-30 cm. Its estimated extent was c. 20 × 20 m. In subsequent years, the midden became increasingly threatened by ploughing and Moesgaard Museum therefore undertook a further investigation in 1986 – first and foremost to obtain material for radiocarbon dating and to look for further graves from the Ertebølle culture. The kitchen midden still had a thickness of c. 50 cm, but was being rapidly reduced by ploughing. At that time it extended c. 20 m north-south, i.e. at right angles to the former coast, whereas its extent east-west was not established. Outside the coherent shell-rich area, thin shell layers were detected in small hollows in the surface of the subsoil.

The first investigation, carried out in 1967, consisted of a series of seven 1 m² test pits, spaced at 4 m intervals, forming a 30 m long, north-south sequence, running down the hillside and to the fossil marine deposits at its foot. These pits were labelled 1-6 and 12, with pit 1 being furthest up the hillside (Fig. 172). In addition to these, a small trench of 6 m² was investigated around the grave containing the skeleton. This was exposed *in situ*

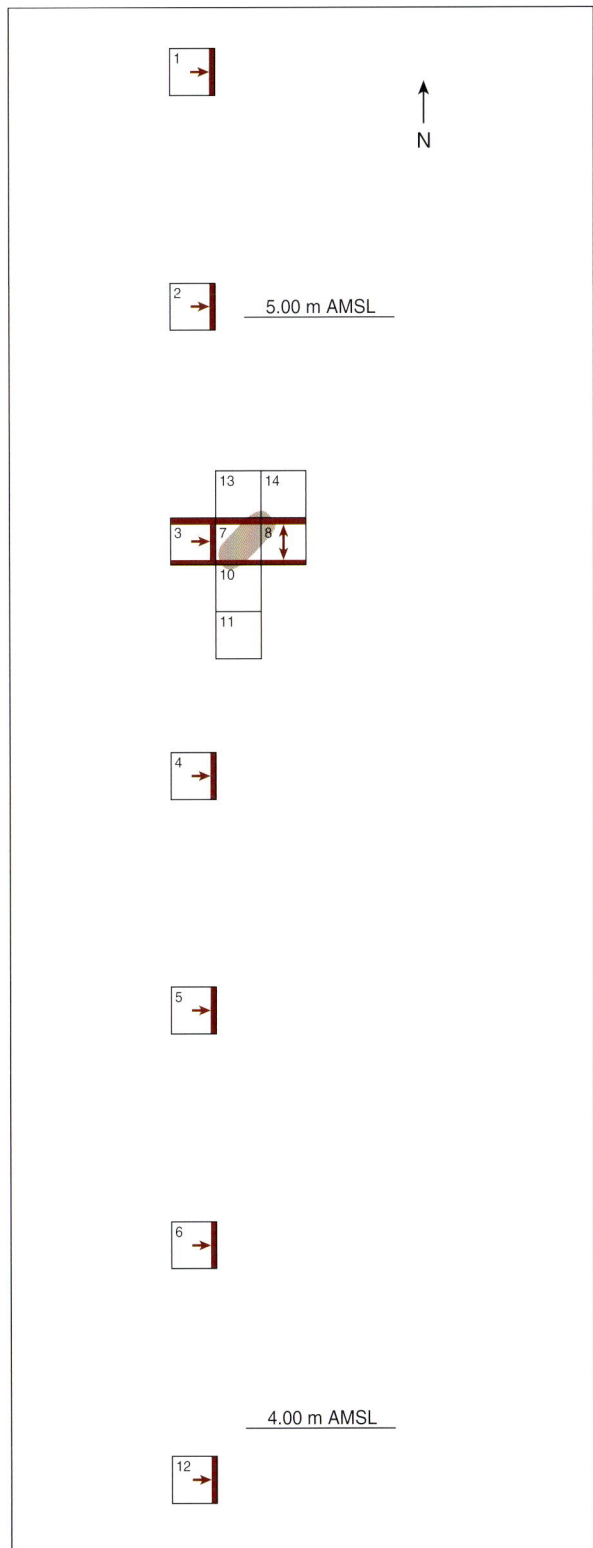

Fig. 172. Plan of the north-south row of test pits running down the hillside at Holmegaard. Pit 1 was located up on the hillside and pit 12 lay down by the prehistoric shore. Sections are marked in red. The viewing directions for the sections are shown with arrows.

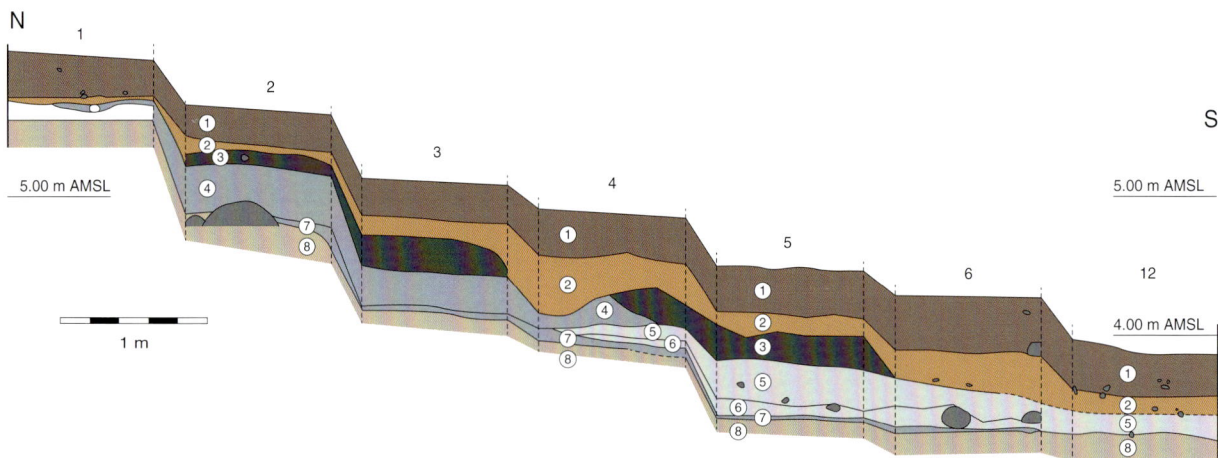

Fig. 173. North-south section drawings for the eastern faces of the test pits, cf. Fig. 172. 1 Plough soil with flint debitage and a little comminuted shell. The flint debitage is slightly water-worn and has a bleached surface. 2 Yellow sand layer with flint debitage and comminuted shell. The flint debitage is slightly water-worn and surface transformed. 3 Black-brown sand layer with flint debitage and comminuted shell. The flint debitage is slightly water-worn and surface transformed. 4 Kitchen midden. Compact shell layer comprised of whole shells (oysters), comminuted shell and flint debitage, which has a transformed surface but is not water-worn. The sand content increases downwards in the layer. In test pit 4, intact oyster shells are evident in the upper moraine deposits. 5 Grey-white sand layer with charcoal fragments in the upper c. 5 cm of the layer. Below this, the layer becomes yellow and without cultural traces. 6 Grey sand layer with a major content of comminuted shell. 7 Dark sand layer with a decreasing content of shells and comminuted shell with depth. 8 Grey-white sandy clay (subsoil).

and then lifted and transported in a block of sediment to Moesgaard Museum, where the excavation was completed. The row of test pits ran directly west of the grave and they were investigated as follows: The upper c. 30 cm (plough soil) was removed by shovel, after which the excavation continued downwards in 10 cm deep spits – referred to as "layers" – until the subsoil was reached (Fig. 174). Tools, animal bones and pottery were recorded by a system of 3D coordinates, while other cultural remains were collected and recorded with reference to the individual excavation "layers". The section at the eastern side of each pit was surveyed and drawn, and additional east-west sections were recorded around the grave (Figs. 173-174).

The second investigation, carried out in 1986, involved a machine-cut, 24 m long, 0.8 m wide north-south trench, which sectioned the site from the ridge, down the slope and into the marine deposits at its foot. As the first investigation comprised individual test pits spaced 3 m apart, and had presented numerous difficulties in establishing and clarifying the stratigraphy of the site, the aim of this trench was to obtain a continuous section through the kitchen midden and also look for possible further Mesolithic burials. The individual metre grids of the trench were labelled A-U, beginning with A in the south. The eastern side of the trench was surveyed and recorded and a continuous column was investigated through the stratigraphy at five selected points: column AE (0.5 × 0.2 m), BH (0.4 × 0.2 m), AL (0.5 × 0.5 m), AN (0.25 × 0.25 m) and AR (0.25 × 0.25 m; Fig. 175). The investigation of the column samples involved recording the positions of tools, cores, blades, faunal remains etc. and the recovery of flint debitage with reference to either 1 or 5 cm thick layers. In addition, a further pit (c. 1 × 1 m) was investigated at the base of grids

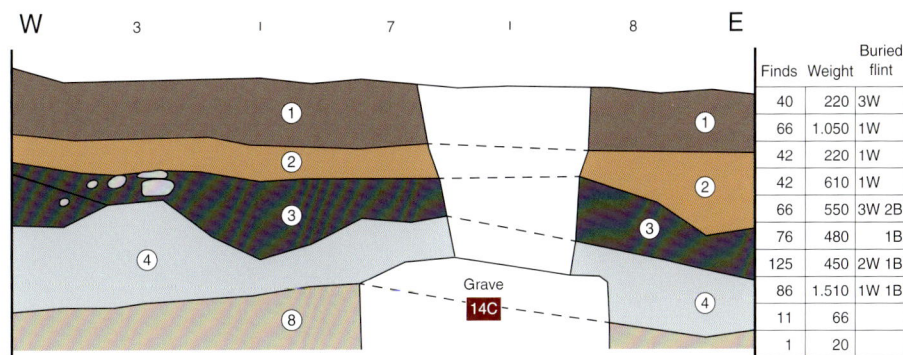

Fig. 174. East-west section over the grave. Stratigraphy as in Fig. 173. Excavation levels, number and weight of flint debris is indicated as well as the number of burnt flint (W = heavy fire affected, B = slightly affected).

Finds	Weight	Buried flint
40	220	3W
66	1.050	1W
42	220	1W
42	610	1W
66	550	3W 2B
76	480	1B
125	450	2W 1B
86	1.510	1W 1B
11	66	
1	20	

E and F (Fig. 175). The layers sampled from the respective columns were dry-sieved in the field, using a sieve with a mesh aperture of 2.5 × 2.5 mm. During the fieldwork, a further 36 soil, charcoal and shell samples were taken for analysis, of which six – from hearths and characteristic layers – were subsequently analysed for charred plant remains – unfortunately with a negative result.

A further trial trench (trench 7) was also cut by machine to the east of the first section. This was 25 m long and 0.45-0.5 m wide and its purpose was to establish the horizontal extent of the kitchen midden to the east. Apart from a multi-burin on a break, no Ertebølle artefacts or shell deposits were found in this direction. At the same time, the section ditch was extended up the hillside and here three parallel, east-west-oriented trenches were opened up 3-4 m apart. Consequently, these ran along the hillside, at right angles to the north-south-oriented trial trench. From south to north, they were labelled trenches II, III and IV. Due to time constraints, however, only the central parts of these trenches were investigated systematically (Fig. 175). Trench II measured 20 × 5 m, of which the central 48 m² was investigated. Trench III measured 18.5 × 3 m, of which the 20 m² in the central part was excavated systematically. In trench IV (14.5 × 2-2.5 m), two small areas of in total 10 m² were investigated. All features, tools, potsherds, animal bones and larger pieces of charcoal encountered in these trenches were recorded in plan and photographed.

The relative locations of the two series of investigations in 1967 and 1986 were not securely determined, but given the topographic conditions and the consistency evident in the stratigraphy, they must lie parallel and very close to each other. The archaeological investigations at Holmegaard therefore comprise a series of test pits and a small trench (1967), as well as a trial trench and three large rectangular trenches on the hillside above the kitchen midden (1986).

The kitchen midden lies on a sloping, southwest-facing hillside (former coastal slope), between 3.4 and 4.6 m a.m.s.l. The hillside continues up to an east-west ridge at 8-10 m a.m.s.l. Observations during the excavations revealed the north-south extent of the kitchen midden to be c. 20-25 m, while it measured c. 15-20 m in an east-west direction. As the original extent and thickness of the deposits could have been reduced by ploughing, especially towards the top of the hill, the above dimensions must be considered as a minimum. It should, however, be pointed out that any ploughing appears to have been of limited extent as all the trenches on the ridge proved to contain areas of *in situ* cultural deposits and an elongated area hosting shell deposits and several stone-built hearths (Fig. 182). Judging from the occurrence of worked flint on the field surface, together with the local topography, this settlement must have had an extent of c. 50 × 50 m. Compared with other examples in Jutland, Holmegaard can therefore be considered a "medium-sized" kitchen midden. As the excavations at Holmegaard were of limited extent and the resulting finds assemblage is consequently rather small, it is only possible to draw some broad, general conclusions.

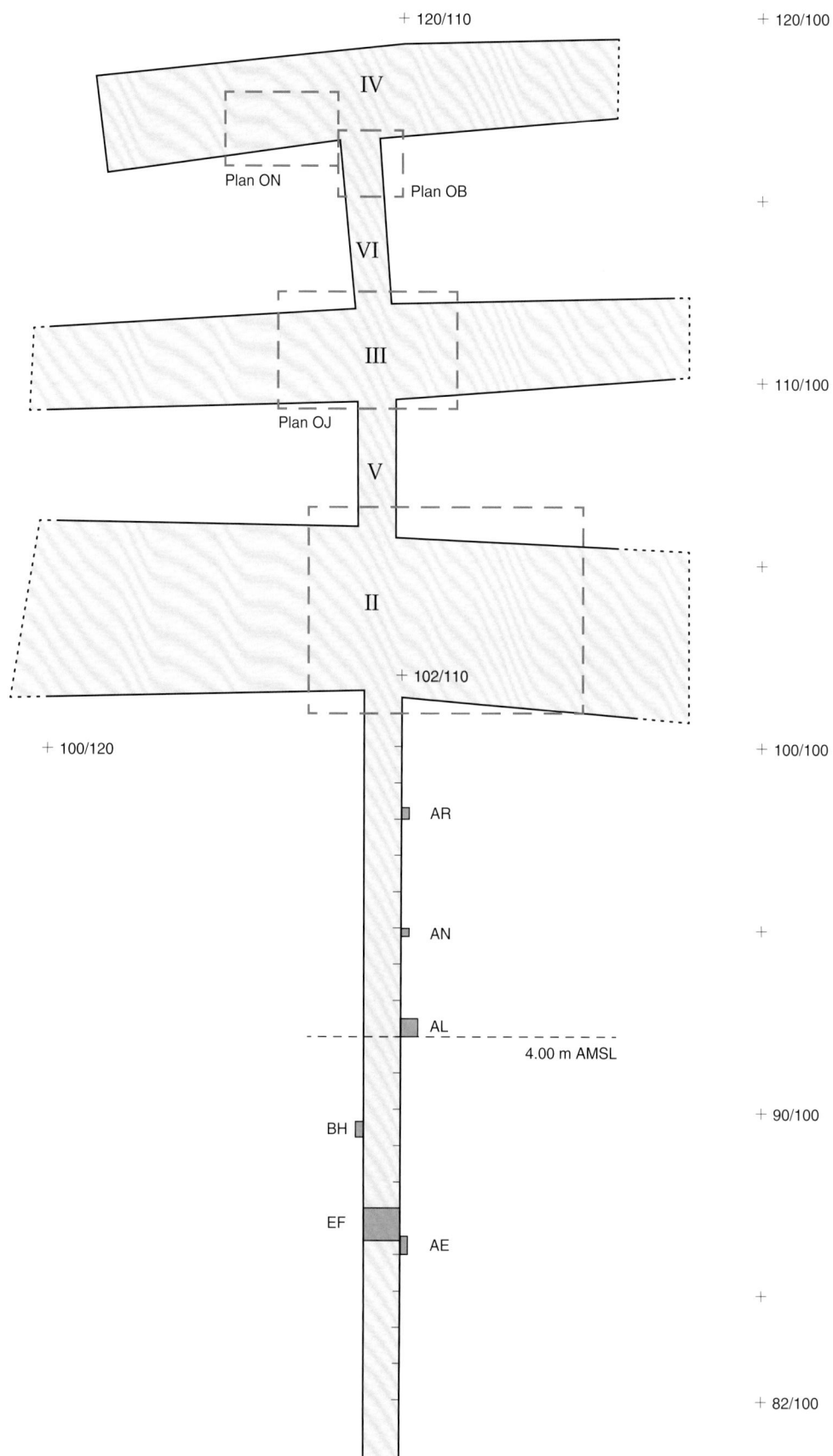

Fig. 175. Plan of the section trench, test squares up on the hillside above the kitchen midden and the systematically investigated test pits in the trench from 1986.

7.1 Stratigraphy

The following description relates to the section shown in Fig. 177. The subsoil consisted of sandy glacial clay (layer 3). From the sloping hillside downwards, the sequence became horizontal and formed a c. 3.5 m wide and c. 0.5 m high bank. At the lowest level, and directly over the subsoil, there was a 0.3-0.4 m thick layer of sand and gravel of marine origin (layer 7), possibly a beach ridge. Above this was a 0.3-0.7 m thick kitchen midden deposit (layer 2), which on the hillside directly overlay the subsoil. The kitchen midden could be followed over a distance of c. 20-25 m (north-south) and became progressively thinner up the hillside, where it disappeared at a level of around 4.5-4.6 m a.m.s.l. To the south, (down the hillside), it could be followed to trench A, where it terminated in a thin stripe at about 3.36 m a.m.s.l. Seen in section, the kitchen midden was ellipsoid in form longitudinally and its surface was evenly undulating. Two component horizons could be distinguished: an earlier, lower part with a loose mass of whole oyster shells (2) and a later, upper part with a more compact mass of predominantly crushed shells, also of oysters (2). In square E and in part of square F, the base of the deposit was irregular where a wedge of periwinkle shells continued into the subsoil, though it was not possible to give an explanation for this phenomenon. The layer of periwinkle shells was covered by *in situ* kitchen midden.

Although heavily dominated by oyster shells, the kitchen midden also contained shells of cockles, mussels and periwinkles (Tab. 6). The shells lay horizontally and the entire kitchen midden was in general horizontally deposited. This fact was further underlined by the hearths and layers of flint debitage and fishbones, which all lay as thin, well-delimited, horizontal layers. In a few cases, it was possible to distinguish discrete shell heaps of individual species – especially periwinkles. At the base of square E there was a discrete heap of periwinkle shells, which measured c. 1.75 m in diameter and 0.3-0.5 m in height. The shells were generally burnt and presumably represent waste arising from a single collecting episode (a meal heap). It is unusual to encounter such a large and clearly delim-

Fig. 176. The machine-cut trench through the kitchen midden. The two systematically excavated squares AN (closest) and AL can be seen in the section, cf. Fig. 177a. Photo: Søren H. Andersen.

ited heap of periwinkle shells in Danish kitchen middens. Four similar, discrete shell heaps were, however, found at Vængesø III (Fig. 90c), but apart from these, the phenomenon has not been mentioned in connection with other kitchen midden sites. The above observations demonstrate that the shell layer accumulated rapidly; because a shell heap such as this would otherwise either have been levelled out or become mixed with the other shell deposits. Everywhere within the shell deposit there were small amounts of sand and gravel, without these forming actual layers. In the deepest layers of the midden, including the deposits around the hearths in squares E and N, a heavy red colouration of the mollusc shells (hematite) was observed in several places.

In squares C and D there were local, up to 15 cm thick, lenses of fine, pale yellow sand lying directly on top of the shell midden (highest level 3.74 m a.m.s.l.) – these presumably represent a marine deposit.

In the 1967 test pits, it could be seen that the thickness of the shell deposits decreased to the east and increased to the west. Furthermore, a c. 2 m wide hollow/pit could be observed in pits 3 and 7. The shell deposit was found to contain charcoal, animal bones, flint debitage and tools of flint, bone

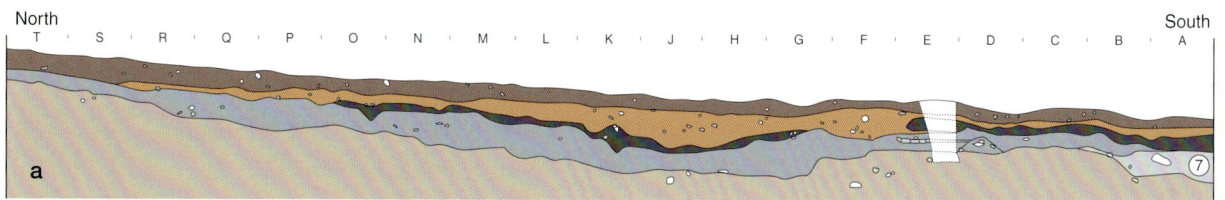

a

Fig. 177 b

North   South

F   E   D

0.5 m

① 4.00 m AMSL   4.00 m AMSL ①

④

Ash lens

4550 BC

5205-5075 BC

5305 BC

②

③

b

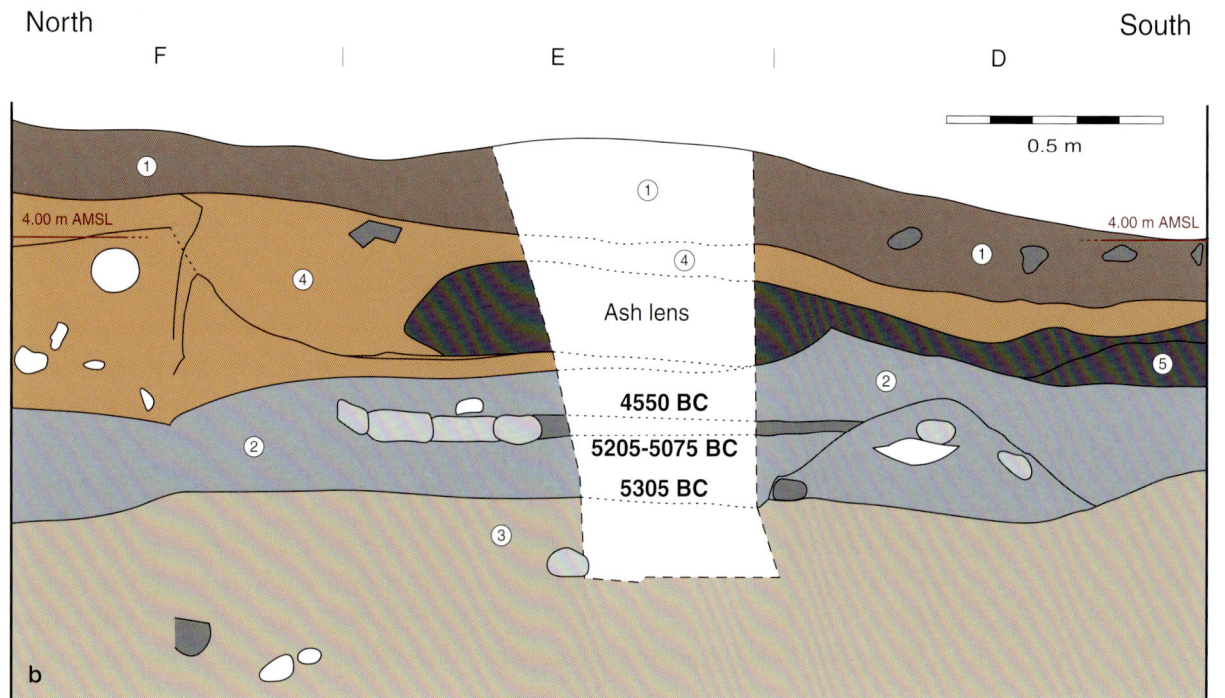

Fig. 177. a) Section drawing of the east face of the trench through the kitchen midden. b) Square E with radiocarbon dates. The latter show that the Holmegaard site is much older than the Vængesø settlements and belongs to the Early Ertebølle culture.

and antler as well as fist-sized cooking stones. The surface of the flint was transformed but not water-worn. Above the kitchen midden (Fig. 177) was a layer of finely-fragmented (comminuted) shells (layer 5), and over this a sand layer containing charcoal and cultural remains (flint, pottery and scattered animal bones – layer 4), the thickness of which varied between 10 and 70 cm. This layer (5) became thicker down the hillside, and furthest to the south (in square A), it lay directly over the marine sand and gravel deposits (layer 7). The flint artefacts had predominantly a white, transformed surface and were in many cases water-worn. The latter was also true of the potsherds, which were small (less than c. 2 cm in diameter) and had rounded, worn edges.

The entire stratigraphic sequence was covered by a 20-50 cm layer of dark-brown, sandy soil containing small stones, of which the upper 20-25 cm was the modern plough soil (layer 1), while the underlying 10-20 cm consisted of older material (colluvium) that had slipped/washed and been ploughed down from the upper part of the hill (layer 1). Layer 1 contained numerous flint artefacts and small pieces of marine mollusc shell (presumably originating from eroded layers at a higher level). In the uppermost 3 m of the section, layer 1 lay directly over the upper surface of the kitchen midden, but further down the slope a layer of yellow sand (presumably marine – layer 4) was wedged in between layer 1 and the kitchen midden. Layer 4 could be followed downwards from c. 4 m a.m.s.l. and it increased in thickness downslope to c. 60 cm, before decreasing again to c. 15-20 cm; it contained scattered flint artefacts. In the middle of the section, layer 4 filled out a large hollow in the surface of the kitchen midden. On the hillside, beneath the dark-brown, humus-rich plough soil, there was a thin culture layer of yellowish-brown, stony, clay-rich sand containing flint artefacts, occasional animal bones, charcoal and scattered potsherds. This graded evenly into the subsoil, which consisted of stony, yellowish, sandy moraine clay. During the excavation, it was extremely difficult to distinguish between the culture layer and the subsoil on the basis of colour and consistency. As the subsoil also contained numerous stones, it was therefore difficult to distinguish between settlement features that included stones and "natural" occurrences of stones of moraine origin. The yellowish-brown, stony, clay-rich sand layers observed here presumably correspond to layers 1 and 4, which covered the kitchen midden (above). For information on the layers' content of artefacts etc.

In the eastern part of trench II, a thin layer of crushed (comminuted) shells (ACO) was encountered which measured c. 2 × 0.8 m and occupied a shallow depression in the surface of the moraine deposits (Fig. 184). This shell layer continued to the south (beyond the excavation trench) and presumably represents the northernmost extent of the kitchen midden. It lay at the same level as the various features in the adjacent trenches, but unfortunately no stratigraphic links could be demonstrated between the shell deposit and the settlement features.

The stratigraphy can be interpreted as follows: The earliest deposits resulted from marine erosion of the hillside, with the sea reaching a level of about 3 m a.m.s.l. Subsequently, the sea level fell and a sand layer was deposited (layer 7). On top of this layer came formation of the earliest part of the kitchen midden (layer 2) and above this a layer of comminuted shells. The latter resulted from erosion of the upper part of the kitchen midden (layer 2), either by the sea (transgression) or due to ordinary surface processes because the layer lay exposed for

some time. The sea then receded once again (regression) and the brownish-black culture layer was deposited (layer 5). Later, the sea level again rose (transgression) and washed over the kitchen midden, depositing the covering sand layer (layer 4) on top of the culture layers (layers 2 and 5). There then followed a period when the sequence of deposits was covered by a thick layer of colluvium (slipped/washed/ploughed-down material), predominantly consisting of soil (layer 1). Uppermost was a cultivation layer from modern times (layer 1). All the layers contained cultural remains, but of varying type, number and date, depending on the preservation conditions and settlement activity. Due to the sloping terrain, and the fluctuations in sea level, it is possible that the cultural remains etc. were transported down the hillside as a result of coastal erosion of the (cultural) deposits located higher up. Consequently, artefacts/shells from other periods could, in theory, be present in the lower-lying deposits. This appears particularly likely in the layers immediately overlying the kitchen midden (layers 5 and 4). Here are typical Ertebølle deposits which must originate from culture layers higher up on the hillside/ridge. Conversely, the kitchen midden itself is very clearly an *in situ* deposit. Furthermore, it must be assumed that ploughing has removed some of the culture layers located highest up (for example possible culture layers on the top of the ridge and the highest part of the kitchen midden). This phenomenon was particularly evident in the northernmost test pit, where the plough soil was in direct contact with the subsoil.

7.2 Settlement features

The investigations on the hillside revealed numerous features that, based on the artefact evidence, must be coeval with the kitchen midden lower down the slope. This interpretation is based on the fact that all the finds from here can be dated to the Early Ertebølle culture. This means that the layout of this site comprised a settlement up on the hillside and a kitchen midden at a lower level down by the shore (see below). Collectively, the finds and features show that the actual settlement was loc-

Fig. 178. The east face (north-south) of test pit 2. Photo: Søren H. Andersen.

Fig. 179. The north face (east-west) of test pits 3 and 7. A small heap of cooking stones from the Neolithic can be seen on the surface of the kitchen midden. Photo: Søren H. Andersen.

Fig. 180. Heap of (Neolithic) cooking stones on the surface of the kitchen midden. Test pit 3. Note how the surface of the kitchen midden consists of crushed shells, cf. Fig. 37. Photo: Søren H. Andersen.

ated at a higher level on the hillside, at the foot of which (near the shore) food waste was deposited, first and foremost in the form of marine mollusc shells, especially oysters, and also animal bones and other cultural remains. The hearths, food waste (remains of meals – especially fish waste) and traces of flint-working do show, however, that people spent time and carried out various activities on the surface of the kitchen midden. The latter must, however, have been inundated at the time of the sea level maximum which, according to the quaternary geological literature, reached a level of 5-5.5 m a.m.s.l. (Jessen 1920, 92; Mertz 1924, 23). No disturbances of the stratigraphy were observed during the first excavation of test pits, but in the trial trench of 1986, traces were evident of three to four windthrows (in squares E, F and G), which had disrupted the upper part of the kitchen midden. Squares BH also revealed a small secondary pit, measuring c. 0.25 × 0.35 m, in the upper part of the kitchen midden. Further to this was plough damage of unknown extent to the highest/northernmost part of the settlement.

7.2.1 Large stones

Isolated large stones were observed in a few places in the kitchen midden (Fig. 178). These included test pit 2 (1967 test pit), where there was a stone measuring c. 50 × 20 cm. Squares D and E (1986 trial trench) also contained two large stones which were rectangular in outline (c. 15 × 13 cm and c. 15 × 20 cm) and at the base of squares E and F there was a large boulder and a number of hand-sized stones, which formed a semicircle (diameter c. 70-80 cm); they were heavily blackened by charcoal. Due to the very limited extent of the excavation, it could not be determined whether these stones repre-sented an independent feature – and in that case, of what kind – or whether there was some link between these stones and the other settlement fea-tures. Further to these examples, heaps of cooking stones were found on top of the kitchen midden in several places in the 1967 test pits (Figs. 179-180). Based on their position in the stratigraphy, these features can be dated to the Neolithic.

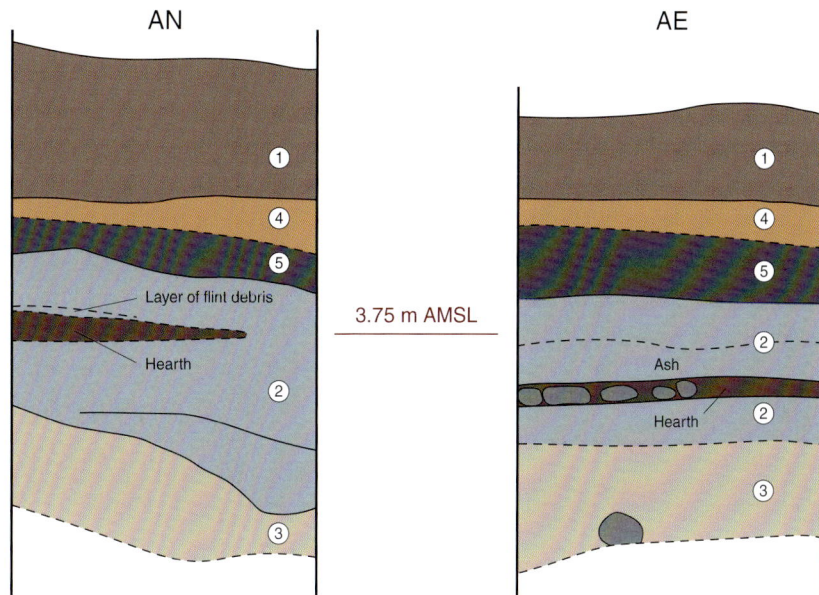

Fig. 181. Detail of section in test square AE and AN. Stratigraphy as in Fig. 173. In square AE, a 10-15 cm thick stone-built hearth (covered by ash) can be seen; in AE the shell layer around the hearth contained numerous fishbones – similar to the situation at Vængesø III, cf. Fig. 114. In square AN is a c. 5-10 cm thick layer of flint debitage close to the hearth (evidence of flint-working).

7.2.2 *Layers of fishbones*

A c. 5 cm thick horizontal layer of fishbones was identified on the edge of the hearth in column sample AE (Fig. 181). Combinations of similar layers of fish waste and hearths are well known from other excavations of Danish kitchen middens, for example Vængesø III (Ch. 4.2.6; Fig. 114) and Ertebølle (Andersen/Johansen 1987, 47, Fig. 12).

7.2.3 *Hearths*

Two types of hearth were demonstrated in the investigations: round features, built of fist-sized stones, and ash layers of varying thickness and diameter. In the 1967 test pits, no *in situ* hearths were found in the kitchen midden, but they were encountered in the trial trench cut in 1986. The difference in the features encountered in these two investigations is striking, but a similar difference in relation to finds and features has been mentioned previously. Four to five round hearths were encountered in the trenches on the hillside above the kitchen midden (trenches II and III – ACJ, ACK, ACL, ACM and ACN, plus perhaps ACG; Figs. 182-184). The features took the form of round accumulations of fist- to head-sized, heat-affected stones (ACJ and ACN) or more diffuse areas con-

taining both heat-affected and non-heat-affected stones and concentrations of charcoal (ACG, ACK, ACL and ACM). Their diameter varied from 60-80 cm, and associated with them were charcoal, fire-brittled flint, flint debitage, lumps of ochre, scattered blade cores, blades and other flint tools. In several cases, the hearth features lay relatively close together (c. 40-60 cm apart), but without it being possible to observe any form of organised system between them. Based on their form, location and associated artefacts, they must belong to the Ertebølle settlement on the hillside.

In the 1986 trial trench, four (possibly five) hearths were evident in the kitchen midden – first and foremost composed of grey, calcareous ash of the same type and composition as regularly described from other kitchen middens, for example Vængesø III (Ch. 4.2.2) and Ertebølle (Madsen et al. 1900, 25-28; Andersen/Johansen 1987, 47-48, Fig. 13). The nature of the investigation (trial trench) meant that it was only possible to give approximate dimensions for these features. In two places (squares E and L), the hearths lay on the surface of the kitchen midden (Fig. 177). They could therefore (theoretically) be later than it, but due to the limited nature of the investigation, this question could not be resolved.

In one case, an ash hearth lay on top of a stone-built hearth in the same square (square E). At its base, the hearth consisted of a 5-10 cm thick layer of heat-affected stones, covered by a c. 15 cm thick ash layer (3.55-3.6 m a.m.s.l.). A corresponding sequence of deposits representing the two types of hearth was also observed at Vængesø III (Ch. 4.2.2) and has been seen at numerous other kitchen middens, for example Havnø (Andersen, S.H. 2008). In square AN, there was an ash hearth at 3.8 m a.m.s.l. (5 cm in thickness and c. 30-40 cm in diameter). In square AL, uppermost in the kitchen midden and occupying the entire length of the square, was a 17 cm thick lens of grey ash with a diameter of c. 1 m (3.5-3.7 m a.m.s.l.). Uppermost in the shell deposit (3.5 m a.m.s.l.) in square K there were the remains of a disturbed hearth, and column sample BH revealed an up to 8 cm thick layer of greyish ash in the upper part of the kitchen midden (3.5 m a.m.s.l.).

7.2.4 A possible dwelling floor?

In the long trial trench cut in 1986, it was clear that the kitchen midden in squares G, H, J and K occupied a c. 3-4 m long (north-south) and c. 25-50 cm deep, flat-bottomed depression in the surface of the subsoil (Fig. 177). It could not be determined whether this depression was artificial (i.e. a man-made hollow) or a geological feature, resulting for example from settlement of the stratigraphy. But as there was an ash-filled pit at the base of the hollow, it seems likely to be the result of human activity here. The same is indicated by the fact that the hollow lay at the very foot of the hillside, where the terrain is flattest. A similar feature was not observed in the test pits of 1967. Due to the very limited extent of the excavation, it was not possible to gain an overall impression of the feature. A cautious interpretation could lie in the direction of a sunken (hut) floor – perhaps associated with a dwelling of the same type as that described from the Ertebølle settlement of Lollikhuse in northern Zealand (Sørensen 1995, 19-29).

7.2.5 Flint-working site

In the middle of the kitchen midden, in square AN (3.9-4 m a.m.s.l.), lay a c. 5 cm thick, dense, horizontal layer of flint debitage, about a quarter of which consisted of small chips. The layer decreased in thickness towards the west, but continued into the adjoining

Fig. 182. The central part of square II (seen from the east). Two (perhaps three) stone-set hearths can be seen in the square. Photo: Søren H. Andersen.

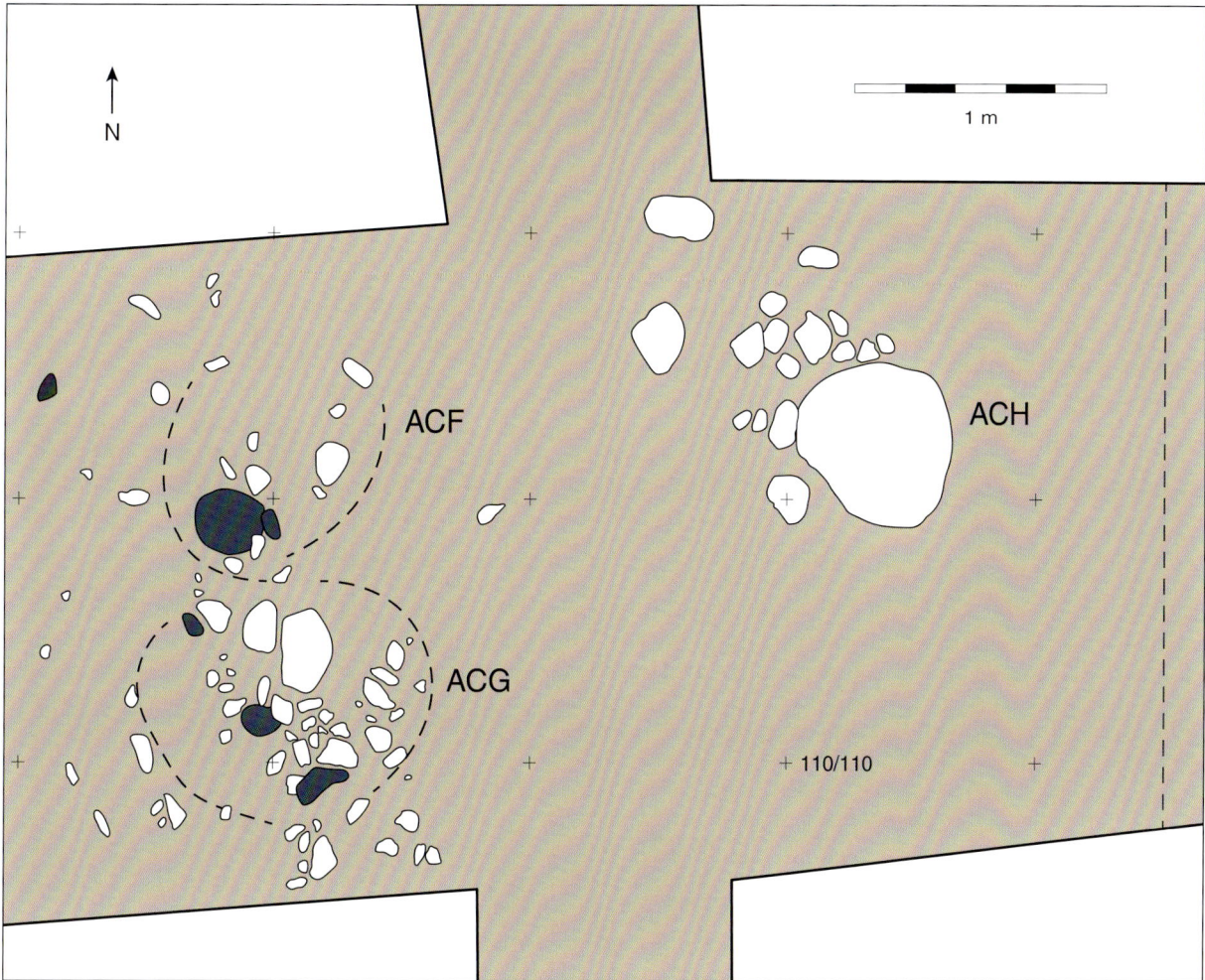

Fig. 183. Plan of the central part of square III with features in the form of stone heaps and areas with charcoal (hatched).

squares in other directions and consequently covered an area of several square metres. Immediately below it was a thin layer of ash and charcoal, which presumably represented the remains of a hearth (Fig. 180). The limited area of the feature, and the abundant waste flakes, showed that flint tools had been worked in the vicinity of the hearth. Similar observations have been made at other Ertebølle kitchen middens, for example Ertebølle (Andersen/Johansen 1987, 46, Fig. 14) and in numerous instances at Vængesø III (Ch. 4.2.10). An analysis of the flint waste reveals that 21 pieces are "winged flakes" arising from working of the edges of one or more flat-flaked flake axes. A similar coincidence between a hearth and an area with working of flake axes was also observed at Vængesø III (Fig. 118).

7.2.6 Red colouration of the shell mass

In several places, but especially at the base of the kitchen midden in the trial trench of 1968, the shells were found to be coloured red by haematite. This reddish-brown compound was found both between the shells and, in many cases, also on their outer or inner surfaces. It should be emphasised that this phenomenon was not due to secondarily precipitated rust deposits. Staining of this kind (i.e. unassociated with a burial feature) is rare and has previously only been recorded during the investigation of a kitchen midden at Nederst in Kolindsund (unpublished; East Jutland Museum, archive no. DJM 2123). Small lumps of haematite were also found in two places in trench II.

7.2.7 Cooking stones

This kind of waste was found all across the kitchen midden and, in general, there were one to two examples per 10 cm excavation layer. There was a slight tendency for the number of cooking stones to increase towards the base of the kitchen midden; most were of granite. During the trial excavation in 1967, three small, discrete heaps of split cooking stones were found (in test pits 1, 3 and 4), which all lay on top of the kitchen midden and must therefore be coeval with or (more probably) later than the Ertebølle culture (i.e. presumably of Neolithic date). They contained 7-17 stones and measured c. 20 × 30-40 × 70 cm. In terms of both their limited size and their content of split stones, they clearly differed from the Ertebølle culture's familiar stone-built hearths: The latter are of greater diameter and only rarely contain split cooking stones.

They most likely represent heaps of discarded cooking stones as seen associated in large numbers with kitchen middens containing Neolithic deposits, for example Norsminde and Bjørnsholm (Andersen, S.H. 1991, 23, Fig. 10; 1993, 68-69, 77-78; Figs. 179-180). Dating of these heaps of cooking stones to the Neolithic is also supported by their stratigraphic position.

7.2.8 Other features

In the squares on the hillside (excavated in 1986), two round features were found with a dark, charcoal-flecked fill. In one of these (ACF), the fill (OC) was surrounded by several head-sized stones, both heat-affected and non-heat-affected. This feature measured c. 1.3 m in diameter. The other feature (ACH) appeared as a c. 1.3 × 1.3 m area, within which lay a large stone (c. 55 × 60 cm), with a heap

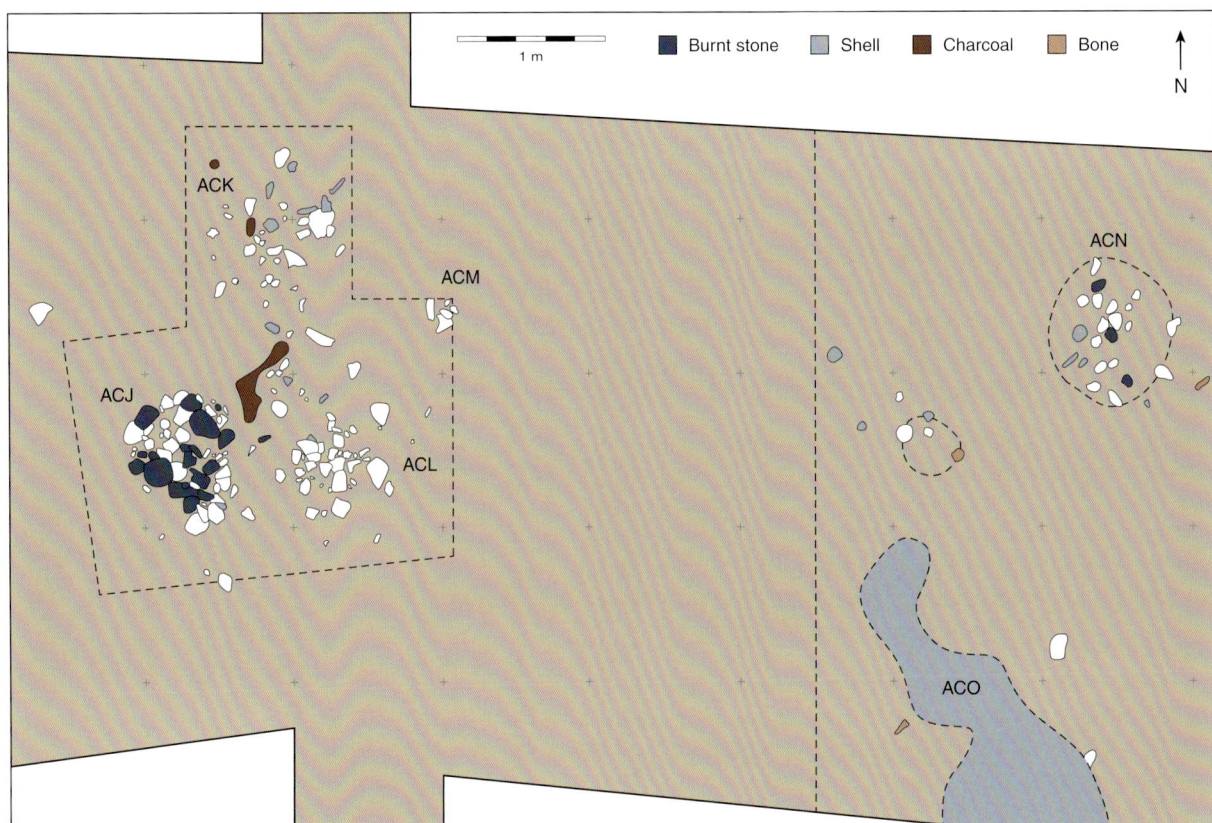

Fig. 184. Plan of the northern part of square II. Note the shell-rich area ACO, which marks the maximum extent of the kitchen midden up the hillside. ACJ is a round collection of stones, ACK and ACL are round collections of stones, ACM is part of a round collection of stones and ACN is a concentration of flint debitage, cf. Fig. 182.

of fist- to head-sized stones at one side (Figs. 182-184). Further to the above, a collection of hand-sized stones was found at the edge of trench IV. Due to its location (at the edge of the trench), this feature was not delimited or investigated further.

7.3 A grave and other human bones/remains

As mentioned previously, the initial reason for investigating this kitchen midden was the discovery of a grave containing a skeleton. This was an inhumation burial which was oriented SW-NE. The skeleton lay *in situ* in an extended supine position with its left arm lying by its side and its head to the southwest (Figs. 185-186). Over the skeleton's legs and feet lay two large stones. No grave goods were found together with the skeleton. With the exception of a small area around the right hand, which was disturbed when the grave was discovered, the bones were very well preserved. The lower jaw lay *in situ*, but apart from two teeth from the upper jaw, the rest of the skull was missing. The presence of the two large stones over the lower legs and feet of the skeleton corresponds closely to the situation in the c. 1500 year later (Ertebølle) graves found at Vængesø II (Ch. 3.4), where there were two large stones over the lower abdomen and pelvic region (Fig. 38). There is also an example from Zealand of an Ertebølle grave with large stones at the foot end, i.e. grave 10 at Bøgebakken (Albrethsen/Petersen 1977, 9, 12f., Figs. 11-12).

The body buried in the grave at Holmegaard was that of a young man of c. 17-20 years of age, whose skeleton showed no indications of illness-related changes. His height is estimated to have been c. 1.65 m. The skeleton was buried in a grave cut about 20 cm into the kitchen midden and its stratigraphic situation demonstrates unequivocally that it was secondary relative to the surrounding

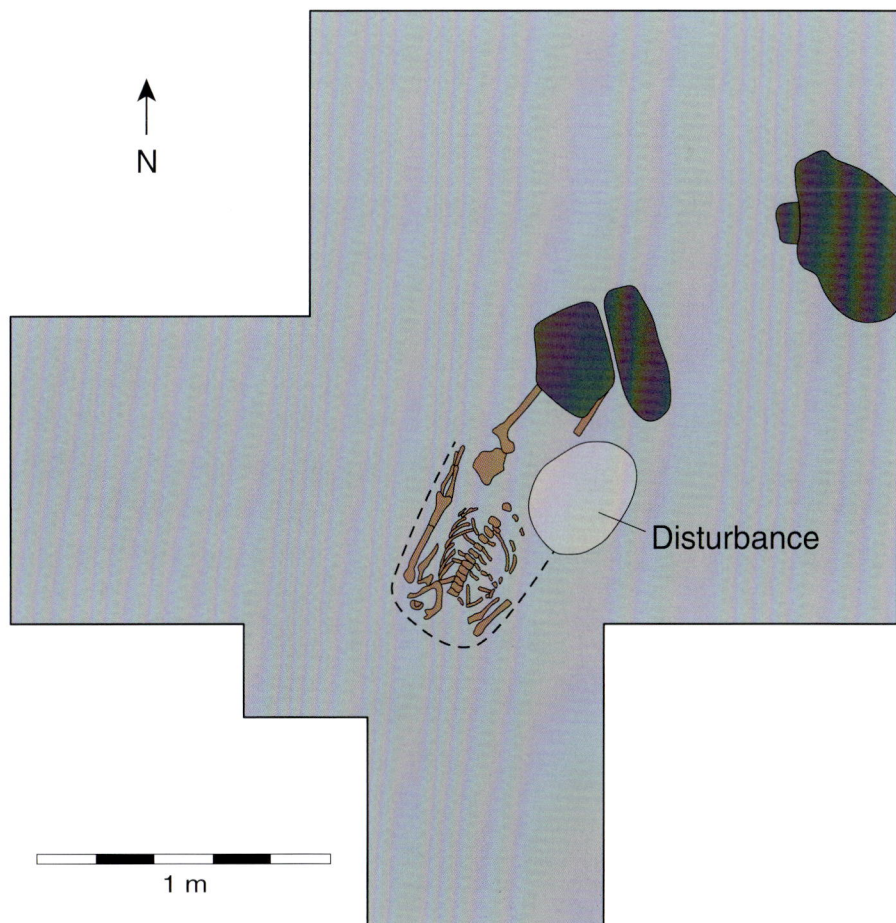

Fig. 185. Plan of the inhumation grave in situ in the kitchen midden. The dotted line marks the edge of the secondary pit in the shell layer, which could be identified in the field. Two large stones cover the lower legs and feet of the skeleton, as seen in the graves at Vængesø II, cf. Fig. 38. Survey: Søren H. Andersen.

N

Disturbance

1 m

Fig. 186. *The skeleton* in situ. *Photo: Søren H. Andersen.*

shell deposits and was therefore of a later date. This observation is confirmed by a radiocarbon date for a bone. The two original dates, produced in respectively Oxford (OxA-118, 6280 ± 130 bp) and Copenhagen (K-3559, 6020 ± 80 bp; Gillespie et al. 1984, 17; Andersen, S.H. et al. 1986, 39-43) were recently corrected to 5719 ± 64 bp (Fischer et al. 2007, 2141), corresponding to 4677-4419 BC cal (1 σ). The skeleton had a $\delta^{13}C$ value of -11.9‰. Originally, ^{15}N values were not measured on the skeleton, but two later analyses at the University of York gave ^{15}N values of 16.1‰ and 15.6‰ (see below). A sample from the kitchen midden (oyster shell), directly beneath the grave, was dated to 4850-4610 BC cal, i.e. consistent with the stratigraphy. The $\delta^{13}C$ value here was +0.6‰ (K-3099; Tab. 7). The grave therefore dates from the Middle Ertebølle culture and is, as a consequence, important because very few other graves are known from this period. A special detail relates to the absence of the skull, and this situation was paid particular attention already during the excavation. Despite very careful investigation and good conditions for observation, no traces of secondary disturbance could be demonstrated around the skeleton's head region. A cautious conclusion must therefore be that the skull was no longer part of the corpse at

Holmegaard

Vængesø III

Vængesø II

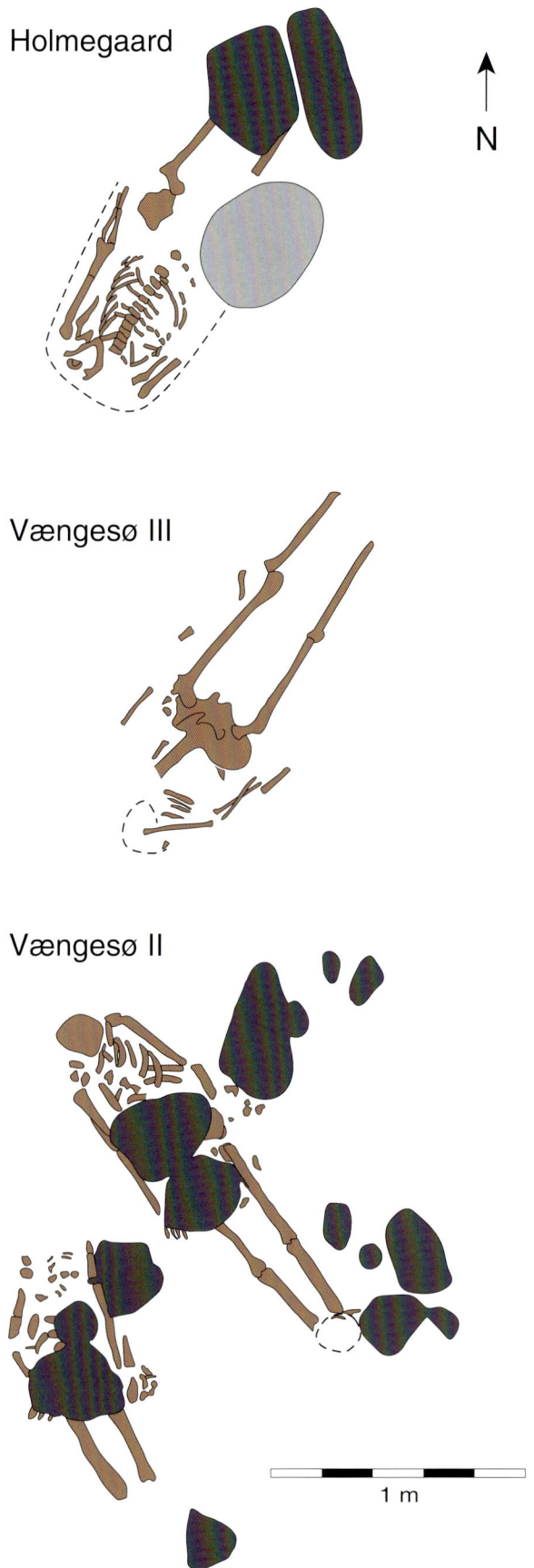

1 m

Fig. 187. *The Ertebølle graves at Holmegaard (above), Vængesø III (middle) and Vængesø II (below).*

burial or that it was removed during or immediately after this event, for example in connection with some form of skull cult or trophy hunt. A sample of DNA material has been extracted from the skeleton, but as yet no results are available from this analysis.

During the excavations in 1967, two further single human bones were found in neighbouring test pits that bordered the grave: a toe joint (phalanx) in test pit 10 (excavation level -60 to -70) and part of an elbow bone (ulna) in test pit 8 (excavation level -60 to -70). Both bones were found in undisturbed layers within a distance of 1-1.5 m from the grave and must also date from the Middle Ertebølle culture. Together with a thighbone (tibia) from the skeleton, the two bones were sent to H.K. Robson at the University of York, England, for ^{13}C and ^{15}N analysis. Rather surprisingly, it turned out that the two bones found singly very probably belonged to the young man buried in the shell midden. As there was no obvious disturbance of the kitchen midden around the grave, there is nothing to suggest secondary movement of elements of the skeleton. However, these are small bones/bone fragments, and it is conceivable that parts of the skeleton could have been (secondarily) disturbed by rodents, for example mice etc. Alternatively, the grave was partially disturbed before it became covered with a layer of shells, resulting in a few bones possibly being moved. Finally, there is the possibility that dislocation and displacement of the layers has taken place over the millennia since the burial.

The ulna had a ^{15}N value of 16.2‰ and a ^{13}C value of -10.7‰. The phalanx had a ^{15}N value of 16.1‰ and a ^{13}C value of -12.3‰. These results show that this individual predominantly obtained his food from the marine environment and from the highest level in the food chain.

These observations relating to the skeleton and the stray finds of bones in the Holmegaard kitchen midden show that dispersed human bones, which are frequently encountered in many kitchen middens, need not necessarily originate from several different individuals or represent manipulation of burials – they can also come from one and the same individual.

7.4 The finds

Artefacts were found everywhere across the excavated area. Due to the difference in size between the two excavations, fewer tools were found in the 1986 excavation than in the 1967 investigation. The following account is therefore predominantly based on the finds from the 1967 excavation. Furthermore, it should be underlined that the site is so small that calculations of the relative proportions of the artefact groups and comparisons with other sites must be viewed with caution.

With respect to the intensity of the cultural remains (especially worked flint) and the feature types, clear differences could be observed between the two excavations. In the test pits of 1967, the kitchen midden was found to contain a significant quantity of flint debitage, with uniform, large quantities present from top to bottom, though with a slight increase towards the base of the deposit (Fig. 174). However, no layers were identified which stood out due to particularly high incidences of flint, for example "old settlement surfaces". In contrast, the trial trench of 1986 yielded significantly less flint, but, in one case, AN, this was evident as a thin, well-defined layer (Fig. 181). This difference is difficult to explain, but it could be due to the fact that the two investigations (involving, respectively, a row of test pits and a trial trench) cut through settlement areas containing different quantities and concentrations of cultural remains. Similar situations have been observed during large excavations of other settlements, for example Ringkloster and Tybrind Vig (Andersen, S.H. 1998, 31, Figs. 12-13, 2013, 69f, Fig. 1.39).

In situ cultural remains were found in all the excavation squares on top of the hillside, but the greatest concentration of artefacts etc. was evident in the kitchen midden on the actual hillside itself and at its foot. As the *in situ* finds are both modest in number and stem primarily from the kitchen midden, all the material recovered from this part of the settlement is dealt with together in the following account.

The flint finds from the layer above the kitchen midden are water-worn and there are also scattered artefacts from the Neolithic and Bronze Age present. All these finds must therefore be considered to be redeposited and there is therefore no certainty with respect to their contemporaneity. As a consequence, they have been omitted from the following account.

Everywhere beneath the plough soil on the hilltop and down the hillside there was a thin, yellowish-brown layer of stony sand containing worked flint, charcoal, occasional bones and potsherds. The great majority of the flint (c. 85-90%) has a bluish-white or white surface, but is not water-worn. Flint of this type only includes Ertebølle types. A small proportion of the flint was completely primary with respect to its colour and surface, being grey or blackish-grey. It presence must be explained in terms of brief visits to the site during the Neolithic. The number of pieces of worked flint varied from 4-192 per m². A total of 1025 pieces of flint debitage were recovered, of which 13 were fire-/heat-affected (1.3%). Further to this were blade cores, blade flakes, scaled flakes, blade fragments and tools as well as a small number of potsherds. The quantity of flint in the individual test pits was very variable. It was though possible to observe a reduction in the amount of worked flint towards the limits of the excavation. The precise extent of the flint-bearing area was not determined, but could be estimated to cover c. 50 × 50 m, i.e. 2500 m².

A general overview of the finds from the test pits shows that they date almost exclusively from the Early/Earliest Ertebølle culture. Very few pieces of flint debitage can, based on their primary surface, be presumed to date from later visits or occupations during the Neolithic, but no secure Neolithic artefact types were recovered from the test pits on the hillside. Conversely, several Neolithic types were encountered in the overlying, secondary deposits at the foot of the hill. A cautious evaluation of the finds assemblage gives the impression of an area where blades, in particular, were produced as well as the raw material for making transverse arrowheads.

On the other hand, the use and discard of everyday tools took place to only a limited extent here, being much more in evidence on the actual surface

of the kitchen midden. The flint debitage, blade cores and tools from these test pits match precisely the material recovered from the kitchen midden.

7.4.1 Flint

7.4.1.1 Debitage, technique and primary working

The kitchen midden deposit encountered in the 1967 test pits was very rich in flint debitage and flint tools throughout its entire depth, but with no particular horizontal concentrations. There was considerably more worked flint in this part of the kitchen midden than seen in most other kitchen middens in Jutland: The number of pieces per 10 cm excavation layer in the 1967 test pits varied from 11-125 and had a weight of as much as 1.5 kg per layer. Due to its white patination, it has not been possible to carry out a detailed investigation of the type of flint used. However, flakes have been found of a very bryozoan-rich material. Moreover, the finds assemblage from the Holmegaard settlement is characterised by numerous flakes of a very calcareous flint type. This gives the flint debitage a very special appearance which helps distinguish it from the other Ertebølle settlements presented here. As Holmegaard lies in a district where Danien deposits of chalk etc. lie close to the surface, and much material has, as a consequence, become mixed up in the moraine material by ice movements (and has been industrially exploited up into modern times), the numerous flakes of this flint type are obviously a result of the exploitation of the local flint resources (Pedersen/Petersen 1997, 22-24, 85-88). For example, a particularly large number of flakes of a very calcareous type of flint were recorded from pit 2, level -30 to -40 cm, and pit 7, level -50 to -60 cm.

The uniform, bleached/whitened and slightly water-worn flint, together with the small and widely-spaced test pits, rendered any attempts at refitting impossible. Nevertheless, two large flakes were found in the kitchen midden in test pit 6, level -70 to -80 cm, which were presumably from the same core (waste from the production of flake axes) and in pit 3, level -50 to -60 cm, a large flake was found that possibly originates from the same core as the pieces found in pit 6. As mentioned above, square N was shown to contain a layer characterised by a considerable content of small flint splinters – a flint-knapping site (Fig. 181). These observations show that working of flint tools took place, at least occasionally, on the surface of the kitchen midden.

The kitchen midden also contained a number of small, rounded pieces of calcareous flint. The weight of the unworked stones in the respective 10 cm excavation layers was determined and found to vary from 0.225-3.775 kg per layer. The flint debitage was found to contain characteristic waste flakes (winged flakes or transverse flakes) from the working of (flat-flaked) flake axes. These flakes were found associated with both the settlement on the hillside and the actual kitchen midden. Flint debitage recovered during the 1967 investigations in the kitchen midden amounted to 3282 pieces, weighing 48.569 kg. Large flakes (greater than 2 × 2 cm) number 3069, whereas there are 213 small flakes (smaller than 2 × 2 cm).

Fire-affected flint was found in all excavation layers in the 1967 test pits. Pieces of white-burnt flint numbered 91 and there were 38 pieces of grey-black, fire-/heat-crazed flint. The amount of heat-affected flint varied from none to four pieces per excavation layer. In all instances, white-burnt flint was most common. There were no clear concentrations of heat-affected flint in particular layers, but the amount did tend to decrease towards the base of the kitchen midden. The fire-brittled flint constitutes c. 2.7% of the flint debitage, i.e. the situation at Holmegaard is on the boundary between high and low settlement intensity, defined as 2.5% burnt flint relative to the total flint artefact assemblage (Pedersen, K.B. 2009, 122).

The *flint technique* was analysed and can be described as follows: The material shows distinct percussion bulbs that are commonly associated with a "lip", whereas percussion bulb scars are rare. Platform remnants are relatively small and narrow on the more regular flakes. Characteristic-

ally though, many pieces have a large platform remnant (0.5-0.7 cm wide), which suggests that hard technique was employed in making a significant proportion of the blades (Petersen, P.V. 1984, 9, 12, Fig. 7). On these latter pieces, the platform remnant is broad and triangular in outline. Platform preparation is only rarely evident and in three cases the platform has cortex present. It is characteristic of the flint technique at this site that a significant proportion of the blades do not show trimming of the platform edge. The dorsal side has, accordingly, a distinct projection ("horn") close to the platform edge. Overall, the flint-working must be considered a mixture of soft and hard technique.

Cores with one platform, and of conical or cuboid form, are the most common form at Holmegaard, where they occur in all variants: from regular, elongate pieces with a trimmed edge opposite the platform face to shorter, completely exhausted pieces (Fig. 188a, b). The length of the conical cores varies from 4.3-9.8 cm, while the more cuboid examples vary from 4.4-6.4 cm. The unipolar core group also contains a small number (eight) that deviate from the above in that the platform face is very short and has, at the same time, a broad, round platform with a denticulate edge. This type, which has been previously described and illustrated in relation to Ertebølle sites (Andersen, S.H. 2013, 81), constitutes a gradual transition, in terms of morphology and size, to the denticulate scrapers. These cores are 2.5-3.8 cm in length.

Bipolar cores are few in number (nine). Of these, five are small, short pieces with platforms that form an acute angle to each other, and where the platform face is formed by negative scars from the two platforms. In one case, these negative scars show that micro-blades were struck from a core of this type. The length of these pieces varies from 4.8-6.5 cm. One core has two parallel platforms and is almost cylindrical in form; its length is 7.2 cm. The three other cores in this group are cuboid, with platforms at an angle to one another. They are 5.3-8.2 cm in length. One core flake provides an illustrative impression of the original size of these blade cores (Fig. 189a).

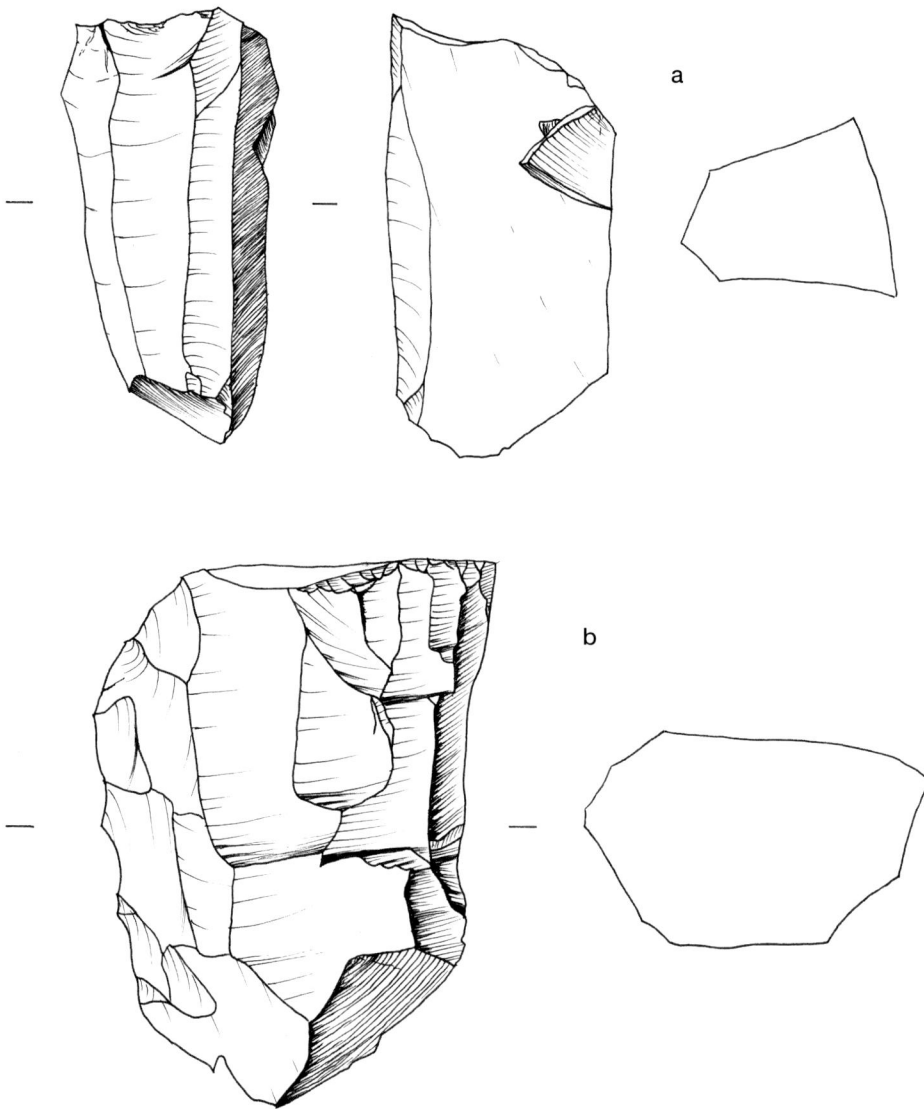

Fig. 188. a-b) Conical blade cores with one platform; b) with a dorsal ridge. Scale 3:4. Drawing: Søren Timm Christensen.

Cores with several platforms (or "nodules") are represented by 13 examples, the majority of which are cuboid in form with traces of cleavage in several directions. One piece is of a very granular and calcareous type of flint. One nodule clearly had a secondary function as a crushing stone, as demonstrated by crush marks on a projecting part of its surface. These pieces measure 4.5-11 cm.

One core stands out from the rest by virtue of its form, which is narrow, elongate and with trimmed side edges such that the core's platform is rectangular in outline and has a weakly curved platform face at one end (Fig. 189b). The flakes produced from it were short and, in several cases, so narrow that they must be termed micro-blades.

Even though the core is shorter and less regular, it is morphologically related to the handled cores known from eastern Denmark and Scania (Petersen, P.V. 1984, 9, 12, Fig. 8). This core is unusual in an Ertebølle context in Jutland, and it is the only one of its type from both Holmegaard and the other Ertebølle sites on Djursland. It was found deep in the kitchen midden and has a transformed, slightly water-worn surface. Both its form and the nature of its surface suggest that it is probably older than the rest of the finds. As a consequence, it represents traces of the Late Kongemose culture at the site, or indicates a very early date for the earliest kitchen midden deposits. Its length is 5.4 cm, width (across the platform) 2 cm and height 3.3 cm.

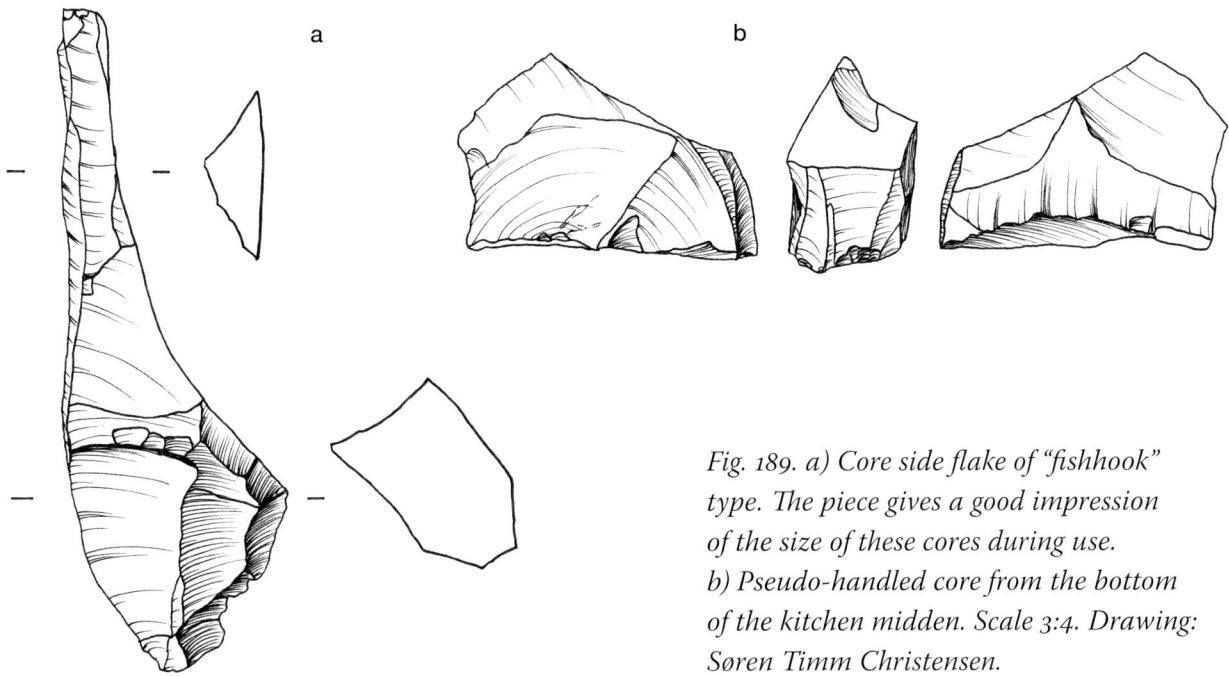

Fig. 189. a) Core side flake of "fishhook" type. The piece gives a good impression of the size of these cores during use. b) Pseudo-handled core from the bottom of the kitchen midden. Scale 3:4. Drawing: Søren Timm Christensen.

Core rejuvenation flakes are recorded in the form of one piece (Fig. 189a)

Scaled flakes, a waste product from the manufacture of transverse arrowheads, are common at Holmegaard, where 23 examples were recorded (Fig. 190). The group can be divided into two forms: a large group (21 examples), the size and working of which is as previously described (Andersen, S.H. 1979b, 77-98) and a (much) smaller group (two examples), where biconvex flakes have been struck from one (or more) right-angled faces, which functioned as a platform. The pieces are on thick, elongate flakes, which measure 10.9-13.6 cm in length, 5.2-6.3 cm in width and 2.6-3.1 cm in thickness. The former group has transverse dimensions of c. 4.5-7.6 × 3.3-7.2 cm and a thickness of 1.4-4.1 cm. The scaled flakes were found both *in situ* on the hillside and in the kitchen midden.

From the *in situ* deposits in the kitchen midden are two flakes from, respectively, the face of a core base and a discoid flake that removed a large part of the platform when it was struck. These measure c. 5 × 5.5 cm. The original size of the cores is evident from a core base flake (stray find) from the kitchen midden, which measures 11 cm in diameter.

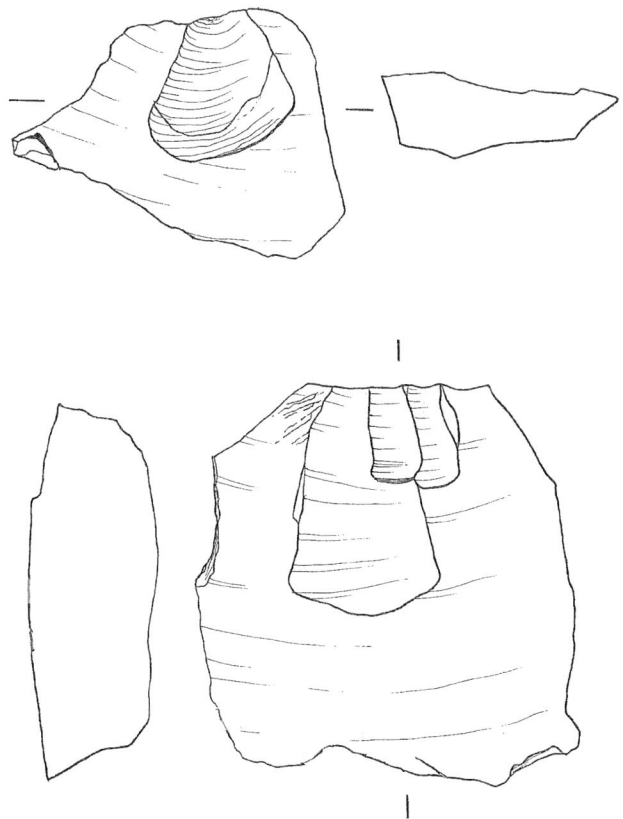

Fig. 190. Scaled flakes from the Early Ertebølle culture. Scale 3:4. Drawing: Søren Timm Christensen.

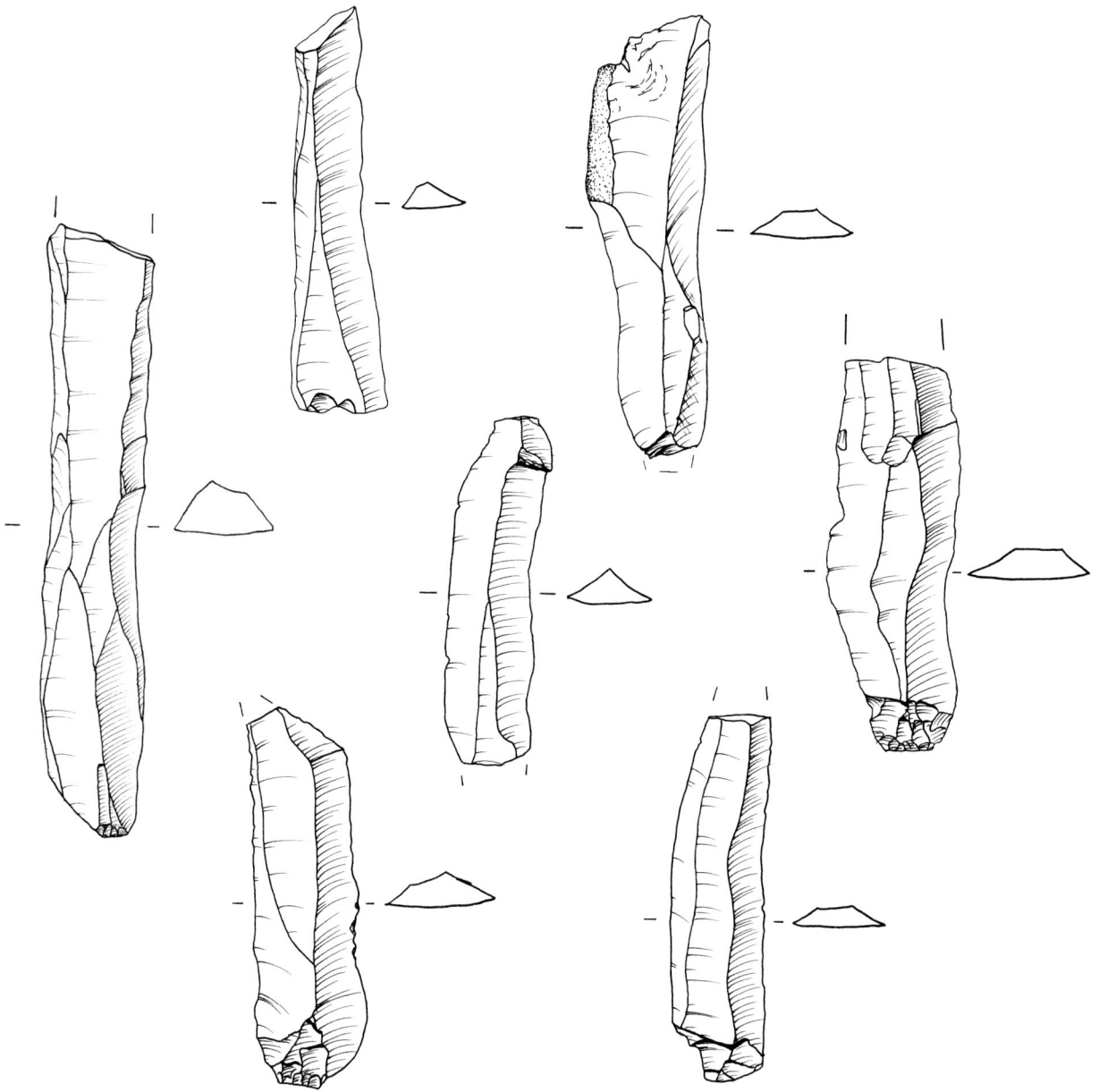

Fig. 191. Selection of blades. Scale 3:4. Drawing: Søren Timm Christensen.

Six flakes originate from the *edge of the core platforms*. In three cases, these pieces were produced by a blow along the edge of the platform, giving them a triangular outline. In two other cases, they had clearly been broken from the core and, finally, there is a more elongate flake with a short piece of a platform edge. The length of these pieces is 2.6-6.3 cm.

(Large) *blades* are common, being represented by 106 examples, of which seven are regular A-blades (6.5%) and 99 are more irregular B-blades (93.5%; Figs. 191-192). Further to these are 20 mi-

cro-blades. The length, width and thickness of the blades are given in the diagrams (Fig. 193). Their average length, width and thickness are 6.95, 2.28 and 0.66 cm. The B-blades from Holmegaard are generally thick and very irregular. A minority of the blades have cortex dorsally. One blade has a completely cortex-covered side and 14 have a small area of cortex dorsally at their distal end. This feature is also characteristic of the blades from Tybrind Vig, where a similar distribution of cortex was also evident on a significant proportion (c. 25%) of the blades (Andersen, S.H. 2013, 86). This

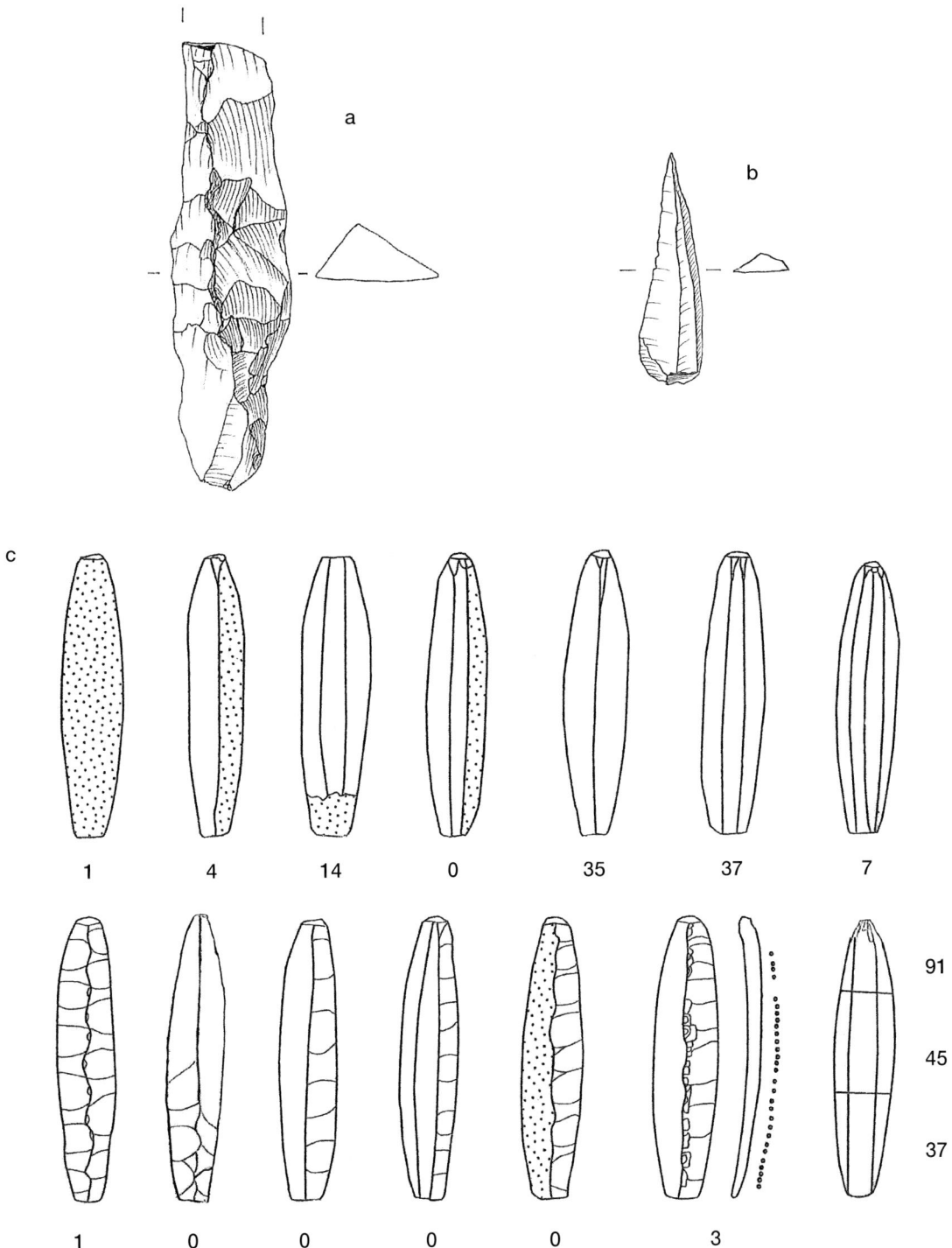

Fig. 192. a) Example of a primary backed blade and b) preparatory flake. c) Diagram showing the site's various blade types and fragments, cf. Figs. 45b and 127. The blade technique at Holmegaard is similar to that employed at the Vængesø sites. Scale 3:4. Drawing: Søren Timm Christensen.

means that many of the blades from Holmegaard must also have been produced from a unipolar, cuboid core, where the end opposite the platform was cortex-covered. About two thirds of the blades have one or two longitudinal midribs (Fig. 192c), which differs from the blades from for example Vængesø III, where there was around half with this feature (Fig. 129). Comparison with the B-blades from for example Vængesø III clearly shows that the blades from Holmegaard are, on average, longer

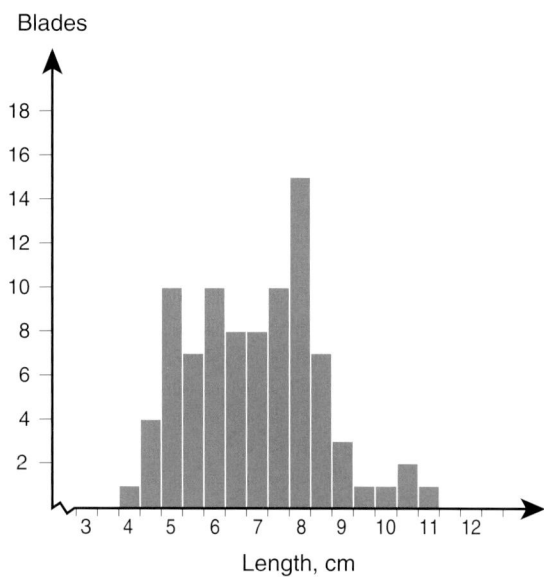

Blades

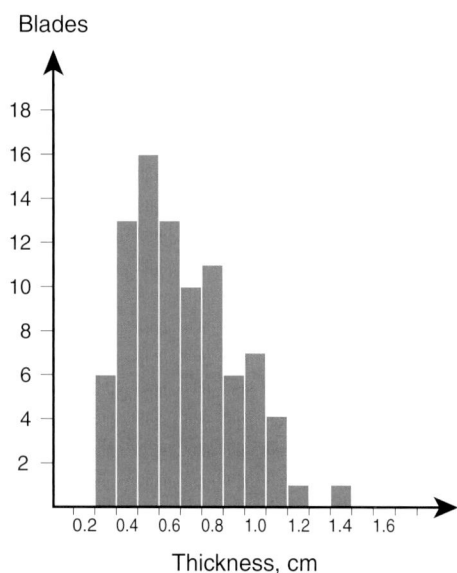

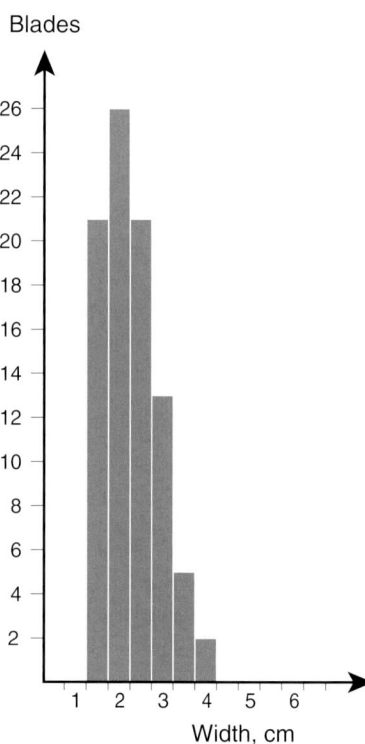

and wider than those from Vængesø. There is also a larger number of micro-blades at Holmegaard. The broad, thin blades that form a characteristic part of the blade group at Vængesø III are, conversely, not represented in the material from Holmegaard.

A total of 238 blade fragments were encountered at Holmegaard (Fig. 192c). Of these, 65 are from the trenches/squares on the hillside and 173 are from the kitchen midden. There are 91 proximal, 45 medial and 37 distal fragments from this deposit.

Preparatory flakes, a form of waste product, are represented by 51 examples. These pieces correspond to those of this type described previously,

i.e. that they are equilateral, triangular in outline and have a longitudinal midrib (Fig. 192b). On the whole, however, the preparatory flakes in this assemblage appear to be slightly shorter and more irregular than those from the Vængesø settlements.

Micro-blades are rare and only 20 examples were identified, of which one is broken. Their length is 3-4.5 cm and their width 0.8-1.2 cm.

Crested blades are few in number, and pieces with a symmetrical back are represented by only one example (Fig. 192a).

Edge flakes with a unilaterally worked midrib are represented by three examples.

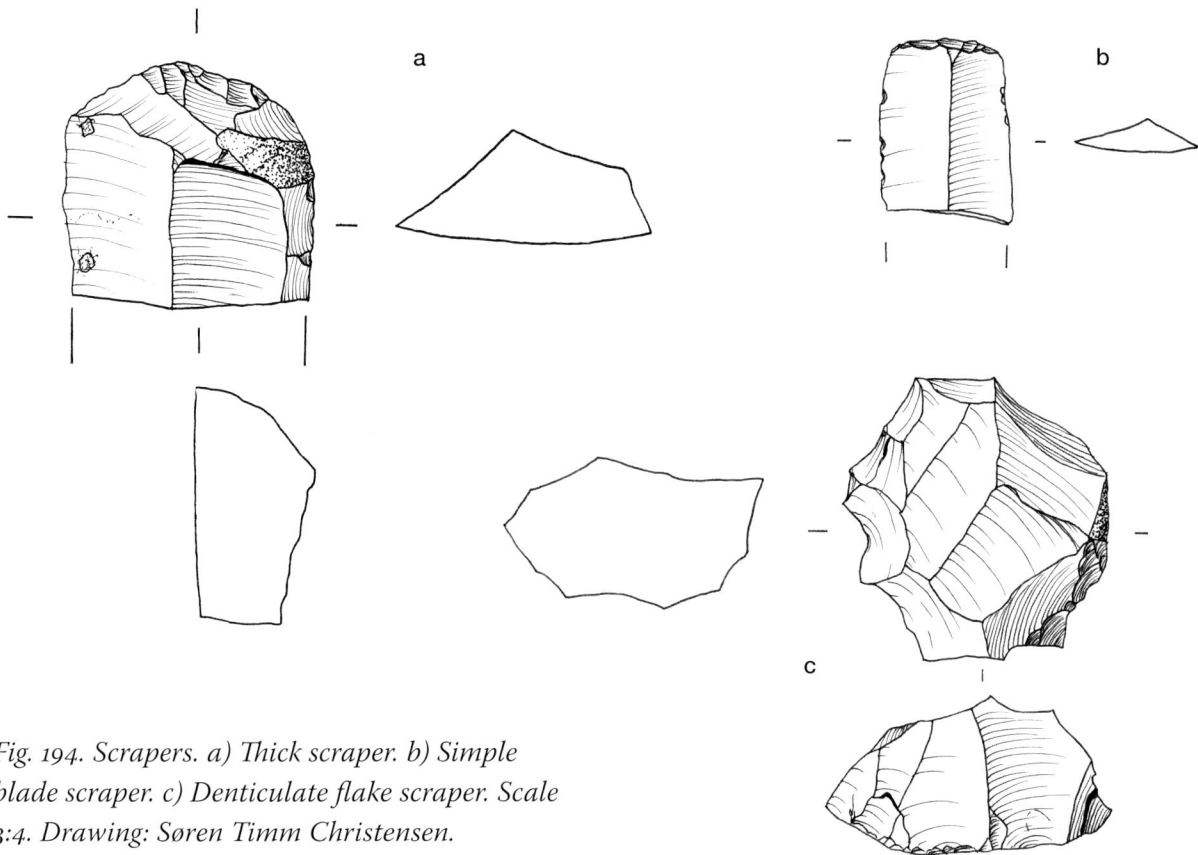

Fig. 194. Scrapers. a) Thick scraper. b) Simple blade scraper. c) Denticulate flake scraper. Scale 3:4. Drawing: Søren Timm Christensen.

7.4.1.2 Artefacts from secondary working

Scrapers are few in number (14.5% of all flake tools) and are represented by only 11 examples, respectively three blade scrapers, the edge of a scraper on a thick flake (Fig. 194a), two denticulate scrapers (Fig. 194c), the edge of a blade scraper (Fig. 194b) and a simple scraper on an oval flake. The flake scrapers measure 4-6.1 cm in length and 3-5.6 cm in width.

Borers are represented by nine examples (12.9% of all flake tools), of which three are oblique borers, one is a flake borer, three are simple borers on irregular flakes, one is a short, regular borer with a symmetrical tip and shoulders and one is a drill borer with a thin tip (Fig. 195). The flake borer has a broken point. An oblique borer was created on the distal end of a wide, regular blade with oblique, straight truncation, one corner of which has been worked into a short borer point. The raw material comprised, in three cases, blades and simple, narrow flakes. The flake borer was made on a piece

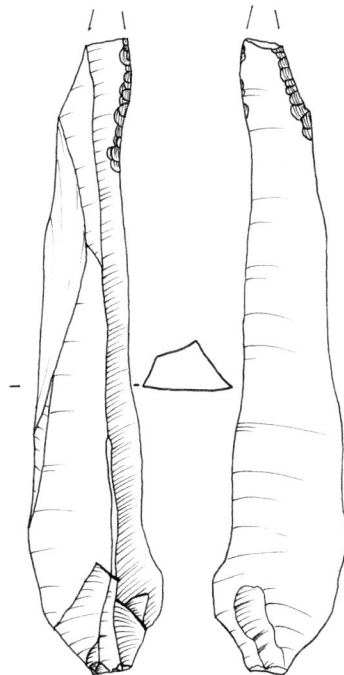

Fig. 195. Oblique borer with broken-off tip. Scale 3:4. Drawing: Søren Timm Christensen.

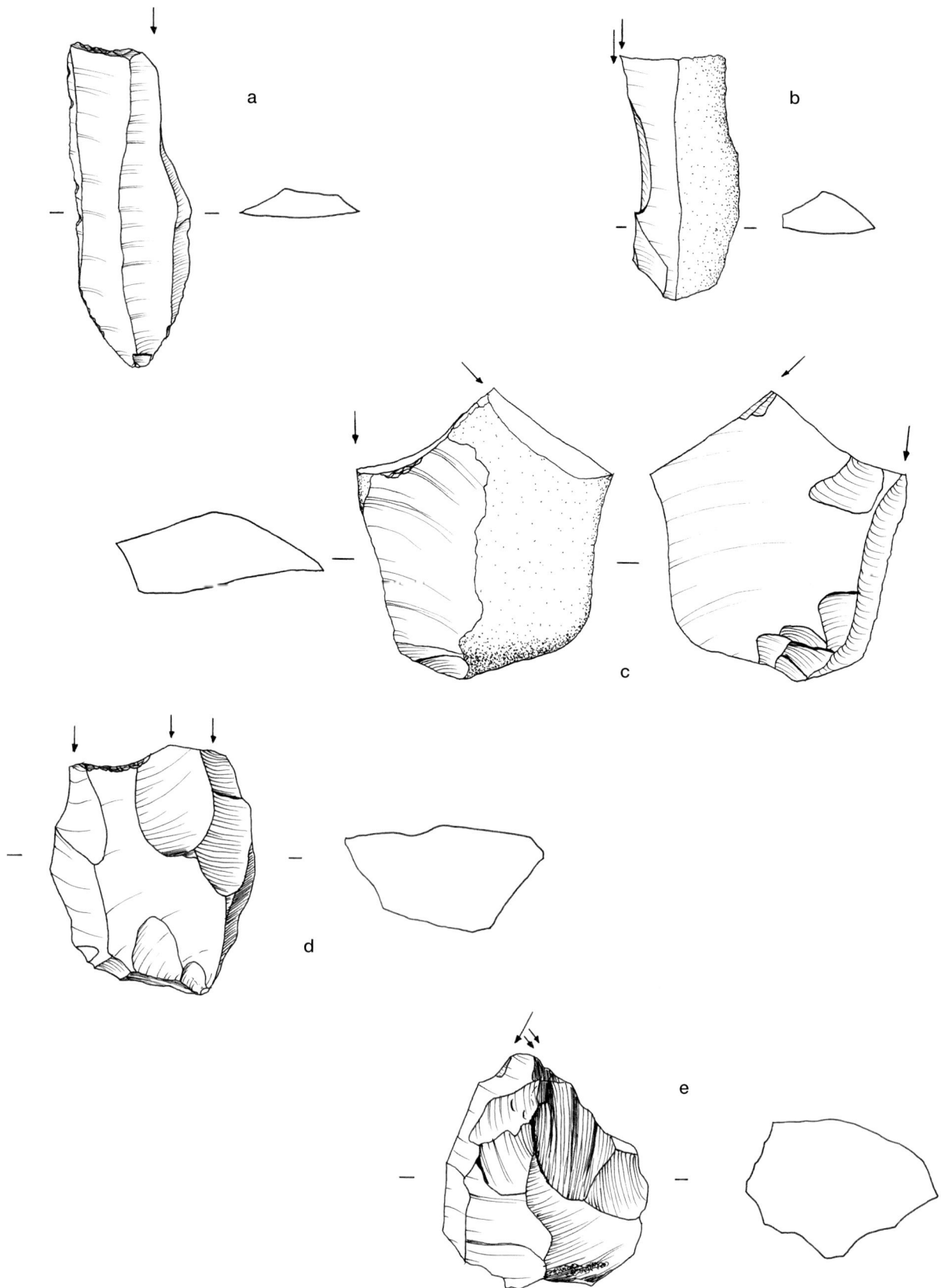

Fig. 196. a) Angle burin on concave truncation. b) Angle burin on a break. c-d) Multi-burins on a break and concave truncation. e) Symmetrical dihedral burin on a thick flake. Scale 3:4. Drawing: Søren Timm Christensen.

of greyish-black, heavily calcareous and bryozoan-rich flint type and measures 7.7 cm in length, 8.5 cm in width and 2.3 cm in thickness.

Symmetrical dihedral burins are represented by four examples, of which one is on a regular A-blade, while the two others are on thick flakes (Fig. 196, c and e). On the former, the burin edge was formed by the removal of two regular flakes, while the edge on the other pieces is the result of several series of flake removals and the sides have chips and retouch resulting from wear. The two last mentioned pieces measure 7.7 cm in length and, respectively, 3.9 and 5.2 cm in width and 0.8 and 1.7 cm in thickness.

Angle burins are common, being represented by 22 examples, in addition to two possible examples. The raw material was both regular A-blades (nine examples; Fig. 196a) and thick flakes (nine examples), of which two have a cortex-covered side. Further to these are four burins on thick B-blades. Simple angle burins on a break are represented by 13 examples (Fig. 196b), four are on transverse blows, five are on truncations (including two multi-burins), one is on a natural surface and three are basal pieces of opposing burins. Finally, there is a single transverse burin. The angle burins on flakes measure 6.1-6.8 cm in length, 3.5-5.8 cm in width and 2 cm in thickness. The angle burins on blades measure 4-10.5 cm in length and 1.6-3.6 cm in width.

Truncated blades and flakes are represented by a total of 12 examples (c. 16.1% of all flake tools). Two flakes have, respectively, concave and straight truncation. The latter piece, which is on a thick, cortex-covered flake, is close morphologically to the denticulate flake scrapers. The length of these pieces is 4.6 cm and their width is 4.3 and 5.4 cm. Three blades and three blade fragments have concave truncation (Fig. 197a-b). The length of the blades is 6.7 cm and their width 2.2-2.8 cm. Finally, there is a group of six short flakes with concave truncation at the proximal (three examples) and distal (three examples – one with reverse retouch) ends. In terms of morphology and size, these are similar to the previously described examples (preforms for transverse arrowheads; Andersen, S.H. 2009, 68-69, Fig. 40i-j). These pieces show that transverse arrowheads were produced at this locality. Their length is 1.9-3.1 cm and their width 1.5-2.5 cm. A blade and two short flakes have straight, oblique truncation (Fig. 197d).

Blades and flakes with continuous edge retouch are represented by a total of six examples: five flakes and two blade fragments (Fig. 197c, f). There are 11 *blades with a retouched notch* and six *blades with denticulate edges* (c. 9.6% of all flake tools), and two examples of blades with dorsal retouch (one is fire-brittled). One of these has heavy, continuous working along a 3.5 cm section of the edge at its proximal percussion bulb end, while the other, in addition to continual dorsal retouch, has oblique retouch at its distal end (finger rest). Their length is 6.2 cm and their width is, respectively, 2.4 and 2.7 cm.

Flakes with a worked handle at the percussion bulb end are represented by only a single example. This is an irregular, pointed-oval flake with an equilateral triangular cross-section and bilateral retouch along a c. 2 cm section of its sides at the percussion bulb end. There is also fine retouch on both sides at the tip of the flake. The working of this piece means that it is related to borers. Its length is 7.2 cm and its width 2.2 cm. Further to this is an irregular B-blade which has, respectively, 2 and 3.5 cm long, regularly retouched edges at the percussion bulb end. These retouched edges are slightly offset relative to the sides of the blade; the distal end is broken off.

There is a base (tang) from a *tanged point*, which has broken (hinge fracture) at the transition to the blade. The tang was worked with reverse retouch, leading to partial removal of the percussion bulb. Its surface is white, fire-brittled and slightly glossy. This piece was found uppermost in the moraine deposits below the kitchen midden. Its length is 1.4 cm and its width 2.4 cm. The morphology of the piece and its context indicate that it is probably the tang of a Lateglacial point/arrowhead. The assemblage also contains the base of a narrow blade with two retouched notches in its edges, close to the percussion bulb. Downwards, it is broken in a hinge fracture. This piece is difficult to classify, but it could also be the base of a Lateglacial point/arrowhead. Its length is 2.1 cm and its width 1.5 cm.

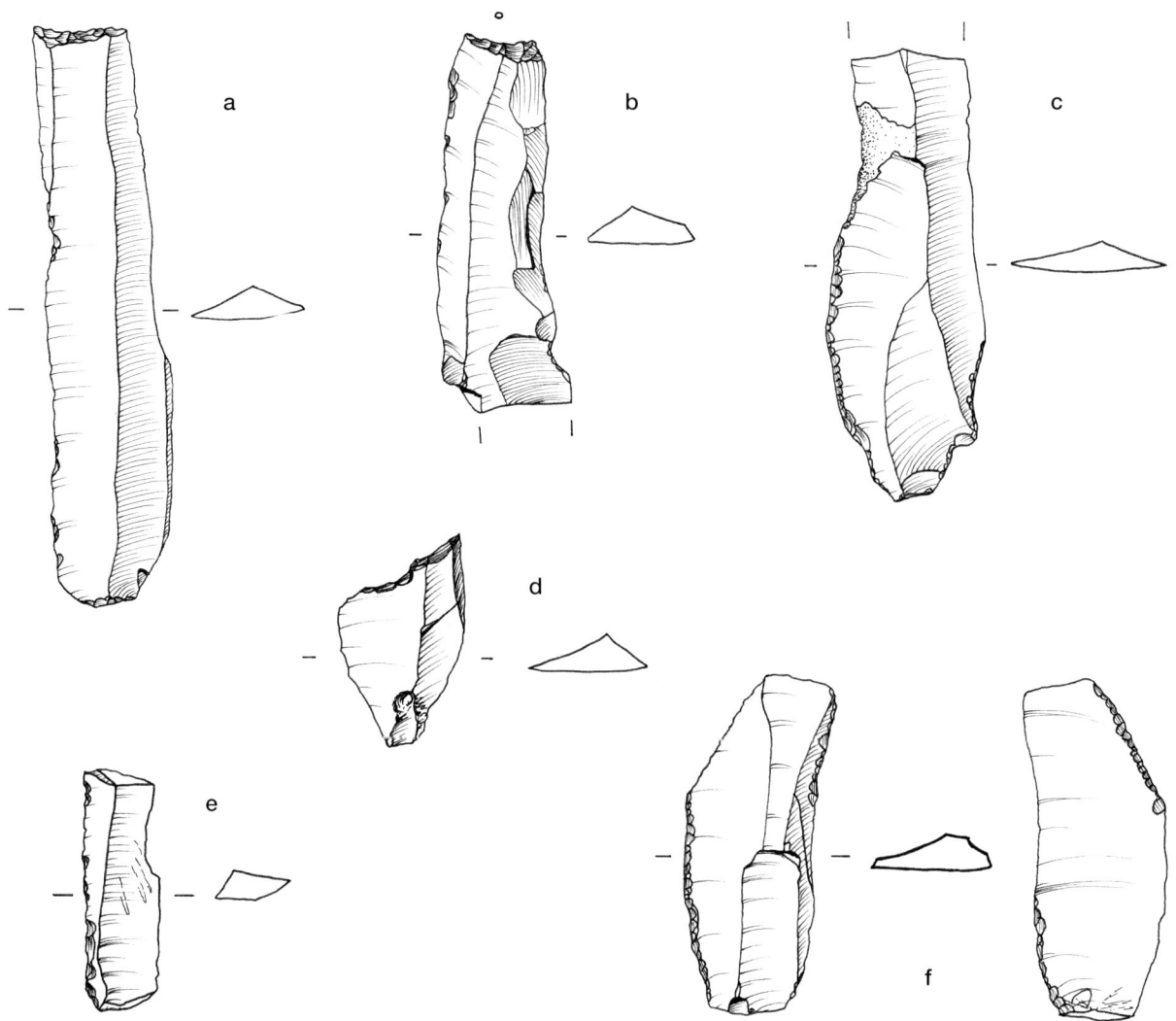

Fig. 197. a) Blade with concave, distal truncation. b) Blade with concave, proximal truncation. c, f) Broken flakes with continuous edge retouch. d) Flake with straight, oblique distal truncation. e) Blade with continuous dorsal retouch at the percussion bulb end. Scale 3:4. Drawing: Søren Timm Christensen.

There are in all 25 *transverse arrowheads* (c. 29% of all flake tools), of which 15 are from the kitchen midden and seven from the hillside, while the remaining pieces are without clear reference. Consistent with the frequent occurrence of scaled flakes, seven of the transverse arrowheads from the kitchen midden (c. 41%) are made on biconvex flakes (Fig. 198, c and i). Of the latter, two have parallel sides, one has slightly flared sides and one has very flared sides, one has a slightly oblique edge and another a very oblique edge. Finally, there is an arrowhead with a pointed base. The classification of the transverse arrowheads is presented in Tab. 5. With two exceptions, all the transverse arrowheads have a white, transformed surface, like the rest of the tool inventory. Among the atypical preforms is a piece made on an irregular, biconvex flake, where the sides of the arrowhead are only coarsely shaped and the base is broken off (Fig. 198c). This preform measures 3 cm in length and 2 cm in width (at the edge). Finally, the piece illustrated as Fig. 198p should be mentioned. This is an oval flake, one side of which has retouch, forming a point. It differs both in terms of working and form from the transverse arrowheads and must almost be termed a lanceolate microlith or an irregular oblique transverse arrowhead. It comes from trench IV on the hillside.

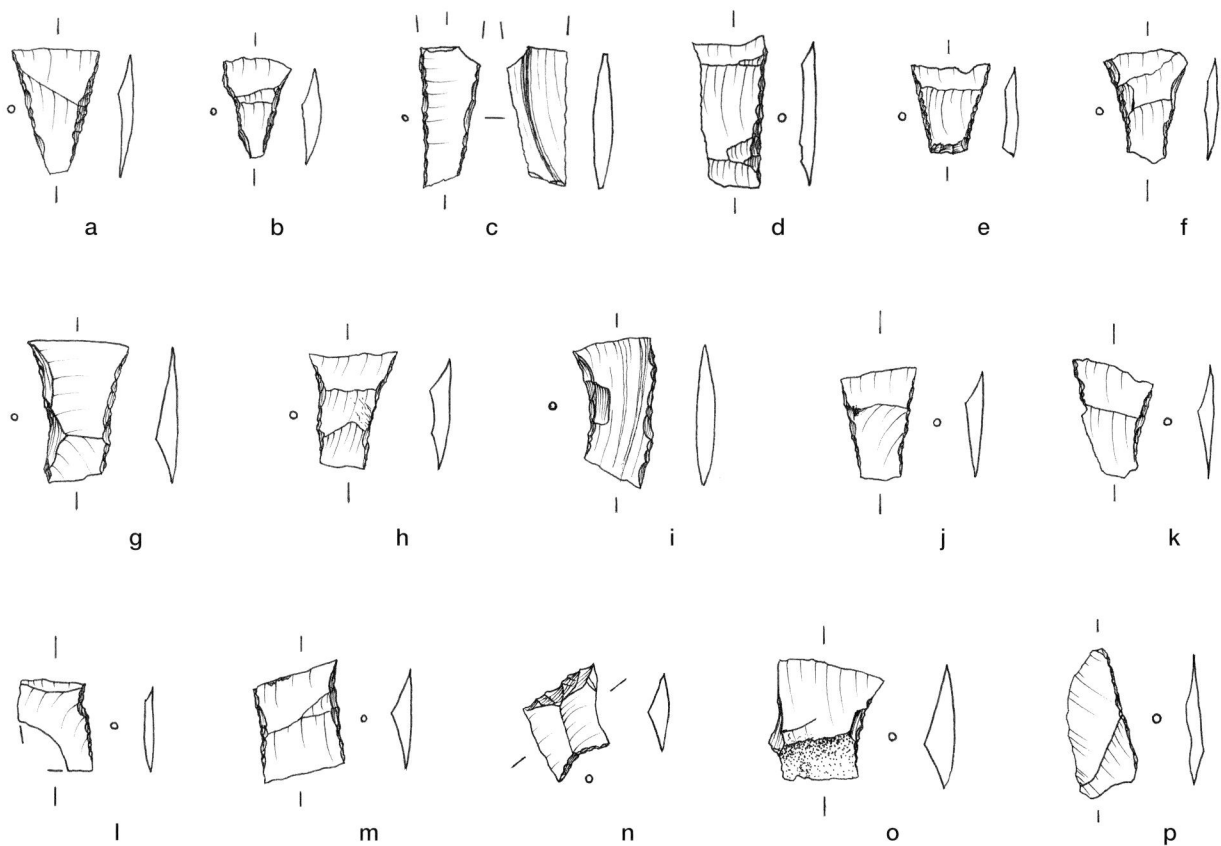

Fig. 198. Transverse arrowheads and rhombic arrowheads from, respectively, the square and the kitchen midden. Note how many arrowheads are irregular and also the four rhombic arrowheads l-o; p) is an oblique transverse arrowhead typical of the transition between the Kongemose and Ertebølle cultures in Jutland. The dominant type is irregular and has parallel sides and an oblique edge. Scale 3:4. Drawing: Søren Timm Christensen.

Core axes are few in number with only three examples, constituting c. 15.0% of the axe group. One of these is of an intermediate form between core and flake axes, i.e. it has been worked like a flat-flaked flake axe, but the working is so extensive that the original flake surface has been almost completely removed. One corner of the edge and the edge itself are also damaged due to heavy use; the edge follows a slightly convex course. Its length is 10.8 cm and its greatest width (in the middle) is 4.5 cm. An elongate, flat, calcareous flint type has a worked edge along one side and is presumably a preform for a core axe. It is 13.3 cm long, 8.2 cm wide and 4.7 cm thick.

The Holmegaard assemblage includes 17 *flake axes* (85.0% of the axe group); it is the commonest axe type at this settlement (Figs. 199a-d and 200a-

c). Many of the flake axes are "thick" and the course of the sides is often parallel or slightly flared, and there are a few examples with convex sides (Fig. 199a-b). *Edge-trimmed flake axes* are only represented by one example, which has concave sides (Fig. 199c). One edge corner is broken off and the edge is chipped. Its length is 6.1 cm and the width of the edge is 4.3 cm. *Asymmetrical flat-flaked flake axes* are also only represented by one example. *Symmetrical flat-flaked flake axes* are the commonest type (13 examples; Figs. 199a-b and 200a). The raw material for these was in one case a very calcareous type of flint. In two cases the sides are convex, in a further two cases the sides are parallel and in six cases they are slightly flared (Fig. 200b). Conversely, there are no axes with very flared sides, which is a late feature with respect to the flake axes

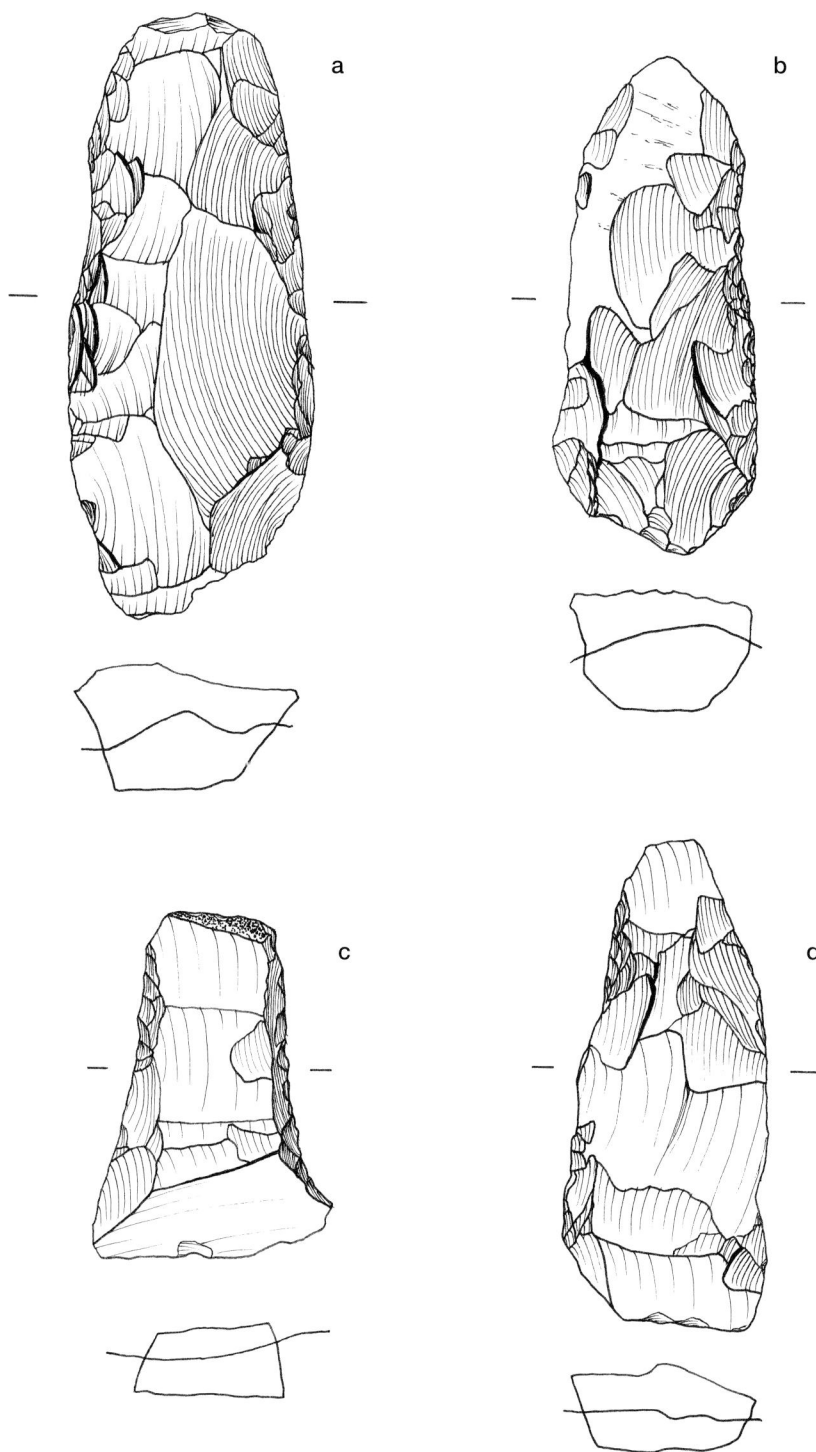

◄► *Fig. 199. a-b)*
Flat-flaked, symmetri-
cal axes with convex
sides. c) Symmetrical
edge-trimmed flake
axe. d) Atypical flake
axe. The dominant
type of flake axe at
Holmegaard has con-
vex or parallel sides
(an "early" typological
feature in the Ertebølle
culture of eastern Jut-
land). e) Diagram of
the sides of the flake
axes from Holmegaard
compared with those
from the Vængesø II
and III sites. Scale 3:1.
Drawing: Søren Timm
Christensen.

at Ertebølle settlements in eastern Jutland. One axe is a typological transitional form between core and flake axes, as is also characteristic of the axes from Norslund layers 3+4 (Andersen/Malmros 1966, 55-58, 72-73, Figs. 12, 23). Similarly, one axe is an intermediary form between an edge-trimmed and a flat-flaked type. One axe is represented by

a broken-off butt. On four axes, the extremity of the butt has been broken off as a result of tension in the shaft – something that has been described previously in relation to the finds from Ronæs Skov (Andersen, S.H. 2009, 71-73, Fig. 46b, e). Two axes show evidence of failed edge rejuvenation, and four flake axes have heavy wear on their edges. Their

e	Total	Flake axe type, outline				Average edge width, cm	Average length, cm
Vængesø III	102	0	17 (16.6%)	57 (55.8%)	28 (27.4%)	4.94	7.51
Vængesø II	47	3 (6.3%)	6 (12.7%)	17 (36.1%)	21 (44.6%)	4.86	8.56
Holmegaard	13	5 (38.4%)	6 (46.1%)	1 (7.6%)	1 (7.6%)	4.20	8.56

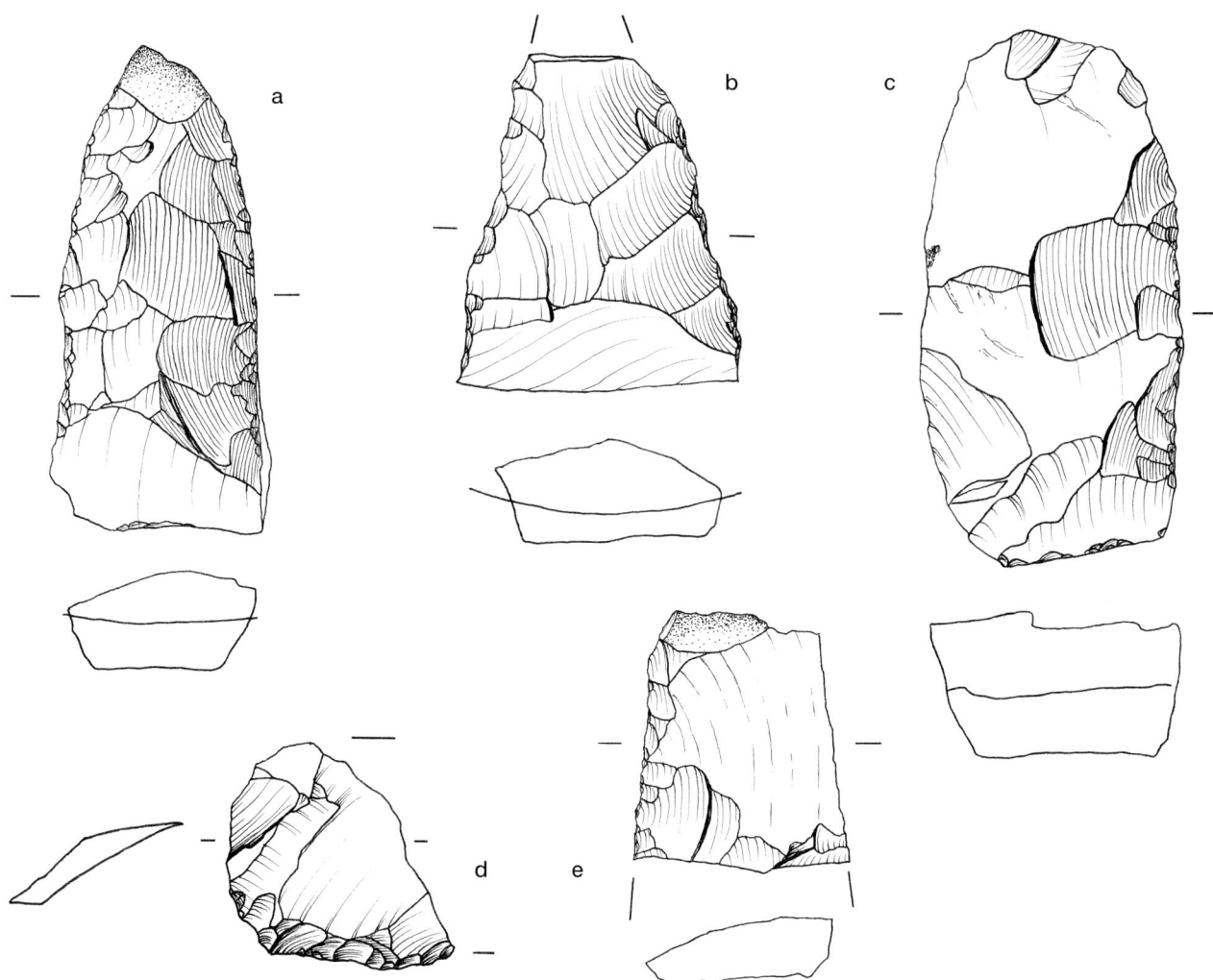

Fig. 200. Flake axes and edge flakes. a) Flat-flaked, symmetrical flake axe with convex sides and pointed-oval butt. b) Flat-flaked, symmetrical flake axe with broken-off butt. c) Flat-flaked, symmetrical flake axe with convex sides. d) Edge flake of core axe. e) Broken-off butt of a flake axe. Scale 3:4. Drawing: Søren Timm Christensen.

length is 6.3-10.2 cm and their edge width 4-5.6 cm. Four examples can be classified as *atypical flake axes* (Fig. 199d). These are very irregular pieces. Nevertheless, chips in the edges of two of them show that they have been used. One axe has the edge broken off. The length of these irregular examples is 5.8-8.4 cm and their edge width is 4-5.3 cm. There are seven *axe fragments*, but due to the gradual transition between core and flake axes in the Holmegaard assemblage, it is difficult to determine the axe type from which they derive. It was though possible to identify the butt of a flake axe (Fig. 200e).

Edge flakes are common and are represented by 27 examples (Fig. 200d). Due to the small morphological difference between the core and flake axes in the assemblage, it has been difficult in some instances to determine whether a particular edge flake comes from one or the other. Furthermore, and for the same reason, it has also been difficult in some cases to determine whether they represent edge flakes or burin spalls. Given these caveats, it is possible to identify ten edge flakes from core axes and 14 edge flakes from flake axes, while three edge flakes are unidentifiable. *Edge flakes from core axes* are characterised by a rhomboid-trapezoid cross-section and they are also thicker than the flakes from flake axes. On seven examples, the edge is chipped and shows clear wear traces. Their length is 3.3-6.1 cm. *Edge flakes from flake axes* are narrower, thinner and have either a triangular or equilateral triangular cross-section. In four cases, the flakes are fishhook-shaped, indicating that the rejuvenation was unsuccessful. Four pieces show traces of attempts at edge removal that have only removed a small part of the damaged edge. Chips are evident in 13 edge flakes. The length of these pieces is 3.7-6.5 cm. Two edge flakes are classified as unidentifiable, but judging from their cross-section, they could be from core axes; one has a chipped and worn edge, the other could also be part of a broken burin spall.

Chisels are few in number, being only represented by four examples, including a *core chisel* (Fig. 201a). Further to this, the assemblage contains one asymmetrical and two symmetrical *flat-flaked flake chisels*, which have slightly convex edges and were produced by a mixture of flat-flaking and edge-trimming (3.1% of the axe group). The length of the chisels is 10.2 cm and the edge width 1 cm. One chisel is fire-brittled and measures 9.4 cm in length, 3.2 cm in width and 1.8 cm in thickness.

Flint hammerstones occur in the form of three small, elongate and rounded flint nodules, showing crush marks over parts of their surfaces. None of these is, however, spherical, or even approximately so, like those known from the Late Ertebølle culture. Further to these are three pieces of flint with crush marks on an edge or a point on their surfaces. The latter are very similar to the flakes with crush marks on the edge that are a characteristic type in the Jutish Early Ertebølle culture (Andersen/Malmros 1966, 65, Fig. 14, x380). Their length is 7-8.2 cm and their width/thickness 5-6.7 cm.

Detached percussion bulbs are a very characteristic type of waste arising from the production of transverse arrowheads (Andersen, S.H. 1975a, 55-56, Fig. 46). Two examples were found

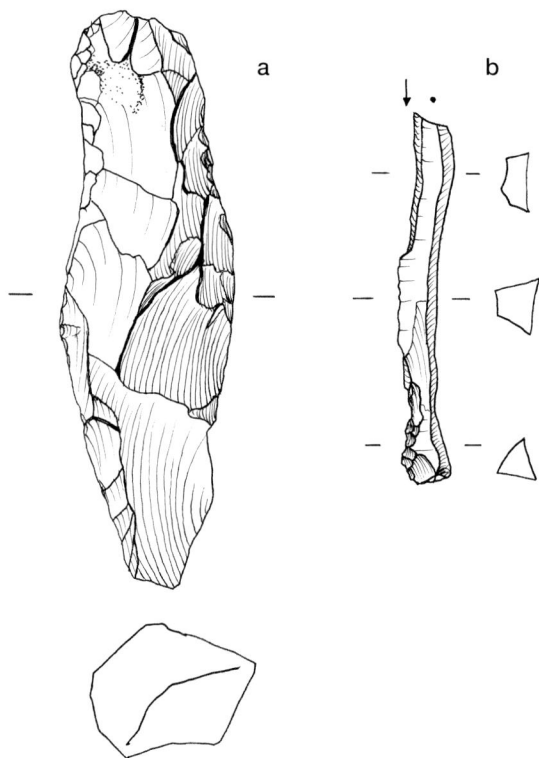

Fig. 201. a) Irregular core chisel. b) Secondary burin spall. Scale 3:4. Drawing: Søren Timm Christensen.

in situ in the middle part of the kitchen midden, i.e. they are from the Early/Earliest Ertebølle culture. They show that transverse arrowheads were made at the site.

Burin spalls are common, being represented by 38 examples, of which 25 are primary and 13 are secondary (Fig. 201b). Morphologically, the burin spalls are closely related to the edge flakes from flake axes, and in several cases it is only a matter of opinion whether the pieces should be categorised as one or the other. The primary examples include three which are so wide that the burin was destroyed in their removal. One example is from a coarse, thick burin, while the others are more slender. Their length is 2.5-7.3 cm.

The secondary burin spalls include three from thick burins, and two are fishhook-shaped. Their length is 1.7-7 cm. None of the burin spalls could be refitted with the burins in the assemblage.

7.4.2 Greenstone/diabase

Included in the stray finds is a *greenstone axe* with a rounded butt. Its edge is broken in a hinge fracture and it has a round cross-section. In terms of its size and morphology, it is similar to previously published descriptions of this artefact type (Westerby 1927, 41-45, Figs. 12-15; Andersen, S.H. 2013, 110, Fig. 2.23a). The axe is 10 cm long, 4.2 cm wide at the edge and 4 cm across at its thickest point. There are also two *preforms for greenstone axes*. One was picked up from the settlement surface and the other was found during the excavations (Fig. 202). The former is an elongate, guttiform piece of diabase, the original surface of which is, to a great degree, intact. Both the size and form of the object show that it was carefully chosen for further working into a greenstone axe. In several places, it has small, localised areas of pecking traces (and in one place perhaps also grinding?). The pointed end has been given a completely round cross-section. Its length is 16 cm, its width 7 cm and its thickness 5 cm. The other example is an elongate piece of diabase with a rectangular cross-section and outline. Two sides of the piece are formed by the original cleavage

planes of the stone block, while the others are lightly rounded as a consequence of the initial pecking work. The ends are blunt and unworked. This preform is 18.5 cm long, 8 cm wide and 5.8 cm thick. Finally, there is a small waste piece of diabase from the kitchen midden. This piece shows that greenstone axes were also manufactured at this locality, with the raw material being locally collected diabase blocks. The diabase artefacts recovered at Holmegaard therefore provide links with the demonstrated production of greenstone axes at Vængesø II (Ch. 3.5.2). Evidence from these three settlements, dating respectively from the Early and Late Ertebølle culture, therefore shows that production of greenstone axes took place on a local basis in eastern Jutland, using raw materials that presumably were obtained from the settlements' near-coastal areas and is therefore not an indication of exchange with more distant regions.

Six oviform or triangular pieces of fine-grained granite have crush marks on a projection or a pointed end, and must have had a hammering or crushing function. Further to these are three pieces of crushed *hammerstones*. These measure 6-9 cm in length, 4-7 cm in width and 2.5-4.8 cm in thickness. An oval hammerstone (quartzite) differs from the rest by being considerably larger and heavier. It measures 13 cm in length, 9 cm in width and c. 6.3 cm in thickness. The marked difference between this and the other stones suggests that this group of artefacts contains hammerstones with different functions.

The assemblage also contains a small *whetstone* of trapezoid outline. It consists of fine-grained sandstone or slate, cloven such that the cleavage plane follows its natural stratification. The cleavage surface has been used for grinding/polishing and is smooth along a c. 3 cm wide band. This object is 8 cm long, 7.1 cm wide and 2.7 cm thick.

7.4.3 Antler and bone

Considering the limited area covered by the investigations, there are relatively large numbers of antler and bone tools from the site. This is true, in particular, of bone points (Fig. 203).

Coarsely-worked

Finely-worked

Unworked

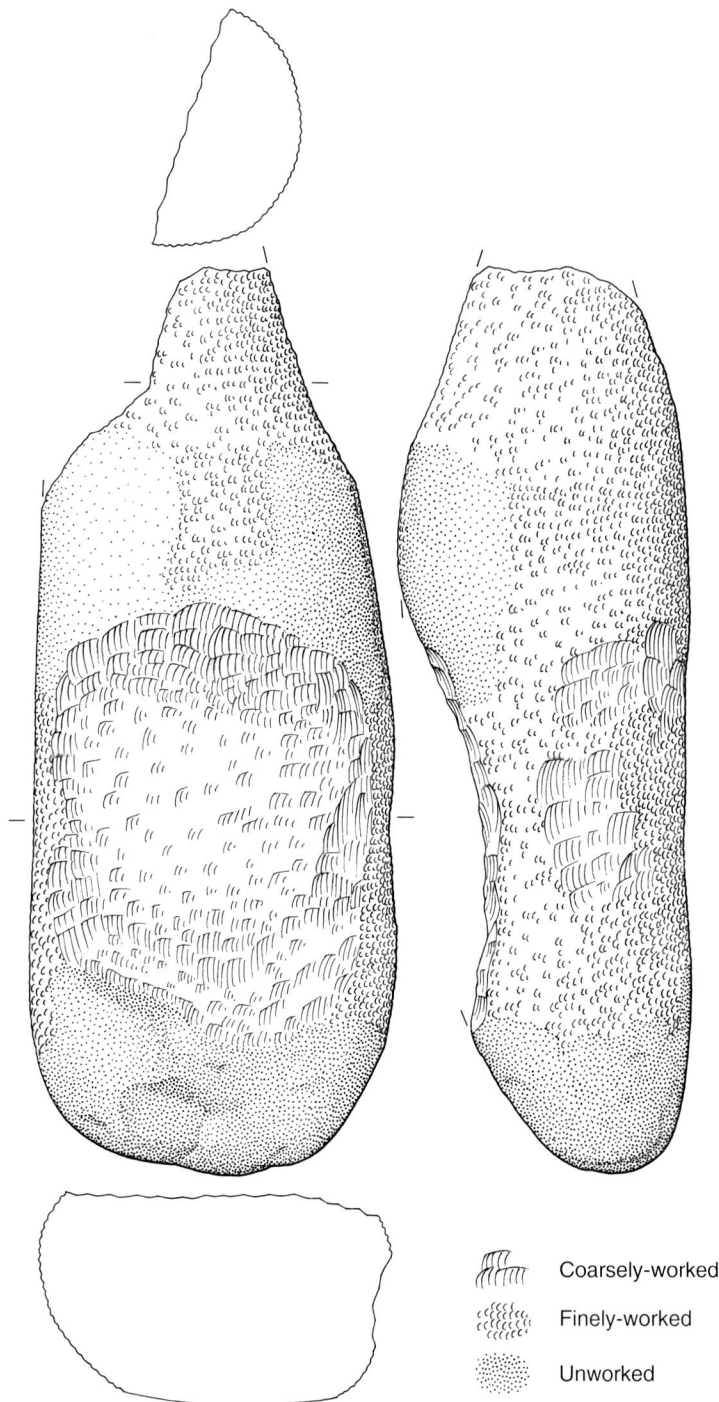

There is a c. 18 cm long piece of *red deer antler with a smooth-polished surface*. The extreme tip is broken off and numerous cut and saw marks are evident at its base which possibly represent the remains of a shaft hole. Its function is unknown.

There are two short *fabricators* with blunt points, from the edge of which chips have split off. Their broad ends shows cut marks resulting from severance from the antler beam. Their length is, respectively, 9.8 and 12.3 cm. There is also a fabricator among the stray finds.

A c. 3 cm long and c. 1 cm wide *chip of red deer antler* has a smooth, oblique termination at one end while the other sides represent fractures. It is presumably a chip from the edge of an antler axe. Due to the small size of the piece and its frag-

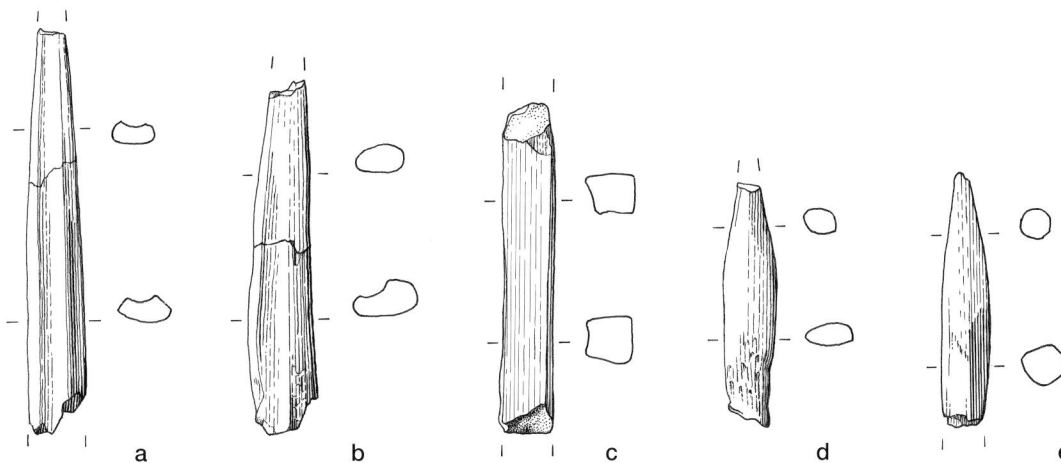

Fig. 203. Bone points. a-b) With side edges. c-e) With a square and round cross-section. d-e) Heavily resharpened. Scale 3:4. Drawing: Søren Timm Christensen.

mentary character, it is impossible to say anything about the type of axe involved.

A curved, flat piece of bone presumably originates from the edge of the tongue-shaped tip of a *skinning knife*. Its length is 2.5 cm.

Bone points with side edges are represented by two examples (Fig. 203a-b). One of these has been heavily resharpened. Its length is 6.2 cm and its width 1.1 cm, while the other piece consists of a broken tip. Its length is 7 cm and its width 0.9 cm.

Bone points with a round or square pencil-like cross-section are represented by two examples (Fig. 203c-e). One of these is a tip with a length of 4.5 cm and a diameter of 0.5 cm (Fig. 203e). The other is a middle section, broken at both ends, with a square cross-section (Fig. 203c). Its length is 5.8 cm and its width 0.8 cm. All the bone points have been heavily resharpened.

A fragment of a red deer metatarsal or metacarpal shows distinct longitudinal traces of splitting; its length is 9 cm.

The assemblage contains two *guttiform pieces of bone*. At one (broad) end there are remnants of the epiphysis of the raw material used and the opposite (pointed) end terminates in a thin, regular, heavily-worked and rounded stump which shows traces of transverse sawing. The length of these objects is, respectively, 3.4 and 4.4 cm and their width 0.9 and 1 cm. Their interpretation is uncertain as they could represent waste from the production of fishhooks.

Even though this is a very small and, in the majority of cases, fragmented antler and bone assemblage, the basic types of the Ertebølle culture are represented. The presence of a skinning knife and two bone points with side edges points towards the Early Ertebølle culture, corresponding to Norslund layers 3+4 (Andersen/Malmros 1966, 66-72, 75-76), and this date is consistent with the flint tool inventory.

7.4.4 Other

Two small lumps of red ochre were found in trench II.

7.4.5 Artefacts from various periods of the Neolithic, Bronze Age and Iron Age

During the excavations, a number of scattered flint artefacts were found of Neolithic date, including several round-oval flake scrapers, the basal piece of a tanged arrowhead (Pitted Ware culture), a chip from a polished flint axe, the butt of an unpolished, thin-bladed axe, a trilateral arrowhead of Late Single Grave culture D-type and a preform for a similar arrowhead. All these objects represent single finds from the deposits above the kitchen midden. However, their presence shows that the site was visited repeatedly during the course of the Neolithic. The locality therefore exhibits a continuous hunting tradition on the coast, as has been demonstrated in recent years at almost all coastal settlements.

No potsherds were found *in situ* in the kitchen midden, which is consistent with the dating of this deposit and its tool inventory. A small number of uncharacteristic, thin-walled side sherds were, however, found in the test pits and trenches on the hillside and in secondary hillwash deposits (colluvium) overlying the kitchen midden. All have very eroded edges and surfaces suggesting that they have been exposed to the erosional effects of frost, redeposition etc., and are therefore not *in situ*. Due to the small size and degraded character of the sherds, they cannot be dated more precisely, but their overall appearance suggests an origin in the Bronze Age or Iron Age.

7.5 Faunal remains and seasonality

The two excavations yielded a well-preserved assemblage of animal bones representing mammals, birds and fish. The material has been examined by U. Møhl and B. Kildeager (mammals and birds) and I.B. Enghoff (random sample of fish-bones), all of the Zoological Museum, University of Copenhagen.

The mammals present comprise aurochs (*Bos primigenius*), red deer (*Cervus elaphus*), roe deer (*Capreolus capreolus*), wild boar (*Sus scrofa*), bottle-nosed dolphin (*Tursiops truncates*), grey seal (*Halichoerus grypus*), otter (*Lutra lutra*), fox (*Vulpes vulpes*), wild cat (*Felis sylvestris*), human (*Homo sapiens*) and, as the only domesticated animal, dog (*Canis familiaris*). Birds comprised white-tailed eagle (*Haliaëtus albicilla*), golden eagle (*Aquila chrysaetos*), swan (*Cygnus* sp.) and various species of duck (unidentified *Anas* sp.). Fish-bones and other remains were exceptionally abundant and occurred both singly and in thin layers as also encountered in for example the Ertebølle kitchen midden (Andersen/Johansen 1987, 46-47, Fig. 12) and at Vængesø III. Remains were identi-

fied of spiny dogfish (*Squalus acanthias*), herring (*Clupea harengus*), eel (*Anguilla Anguilla*), mackerel (*Scomber scombrus*), cod (*Gadus morhua*) and plaice/flounder/dab (*Plaurenectes platessa/ Platichthys flesus/Limanda limanda*). According to I.B. Enghoff, cod appears to be dominant. In one instance, an otolith was found that was probably also of cod (Tab. 10).

Nine shell samples were analysed from the kitchen midden (Tab. 6) and found to include oysters, cockles, mussels and periwinkles. There were also occasional shells of pullet carpet shell (*Venerupis senegalensis/corrugata*), netted dog whelk (*Nassarius reticulatus*) and garden snail (*Cepaea hortensis*). The species composition varies considerably from sample to sample due to the fact that several of the shell samples were taken from local, delimited heaps, dominated by a single species ("meal heaps"). Oyster dominated four of the samples, and cockles were most frequent in two; two samples were dominated by mussels and one by periwinkles. The oyster shells were measured in five different samples, but as the number of shells examined is small, the following dimensions should be treated with caution. The longest oyster shells measured 8 cm and the shortest 3.5-4.5 cm. Their dimensions were very uniform and the average lengths in the five samples were, respectively, 6.5, 6.3, 5.4, 5.6 and 5.7 cm. The shells were generally thin and asymmetrical in outline, which suggests that living conditions were not especially favourable for this species. If these measurements are compared with those from Vængesø II and III (Tabs. 6-8), great similarity is seen in terms of the variation in length. The oyster shells from Holmegaard are, however, significantly smaller (shorter) than those from for example the Ertebølle kitchen midden, where the largest shells had a length of 14-16 cm (Madsen et al. 1900, 90). Seen in relation to the topographical conditions, this is rather a surprising discovery, as it would appear obvious that the narrow channel directly offshore from the settlement would have provided better living conditions and thereby larger individuals (shells) than the more enclosed lagoon at Vængesø. A sample of oyster shells has been analysed by H.K. Robson of the University of York, England, with the aim of determining the season during which these marine invertebrates were gathered. The results show that almost all the oysters were gathered in winter/spring and spring, i.e. in the cool seasons, corresponding closely with the findings from the Vængesø III settlement.

The bone assemblage has not been analysed with a view to determining the season, but does include several summer and autumn indicators (mackerel and eel). Further to these, investigations of the growth lines in the oysters indicate, as already mentioned, that gathering took place during the cold part of the year, i.e. winter/early spring. Over-all the evidence can cautiously be interpreted as indicating either an all-year-round occupation or several visits during different seasons.

7.6 Dating

In addition to the dates for the skeleton in the grave (Ch. 7.3), there are a further nine radio-carbon dates from various places in the kitchen midden (Tab. 7). Five of these are for oyster shells and these form a stratigraphic sequence through the kitchen midden in square E (Fig. 177), while three dates were obtained for red deer bones from layer 5 above the kitchen midden and from the kitchen midden in test pits 3 and 7 (1967 investi-gation). The latter dates were obtained in order to check for a possible reservoir effect and to deter-mine the magnitude of this relative to the dates for the oyster shells. No inconsistencies were revealed between the dates for *in situ* finds of, respectively, oyster shells and red deer bones. Further to these eight dates, there is a date for oyster shells from the kitchen midden from directly below the grave containing the skeleton.

The radiocarbon dates confirm the (relative) archaeological-typological dating of the Holme-gaard kitchen midden, which resulted from a depo-sitional sequence extending over a long period of time, 5300-4700 BC (see below). The deepest part of the kitchen midden is from the period c. 5300-5000 BC, i.e. the Early/Earliest Ertebølle culture or the "aceramic" Ertebølle culture. A single sample of comminuted shells from layer 5 above the kitchen midden (AAR-8122) is from the transition between Middle Neolithic A and B, i.e. from the Funnel Beaker culture to the Single Grave/Pitted Ware culture. All the other dates place the locality in the (Early) Ertebølle culture. The three uppermost dates for the kitchen midden in the 1986 trench show internal inconsistency both with respect to the stratigraphy and in relation to the other dates (as well as the artefact inventory). The explana-tion for this could either be that in this particular area (squares E, F and G), traces were observed of several windthrows, which had disturbed the stratigraphy over and around the hearth in square E (but not the actual hearth and the deposits below it), or that the dates were obtained for shell mat-erial that had been secondarily transported down the hillside and deposited on top of *in situ* kitchen midden deposits at the foot of the hill. Due to these irregularities, the three uppermost and latest dates in this series are not included in the following evaluation. The radiocarbon dates show that the Holmegaard kitchen midden is one of the earliest Ertebølle settlements in Jutland with this charac-teristic type of deposition, and the date for the male skeleton assigns this grave to the Middle Ertebølle culture. Collectively, the dates show that the site was visited over an almost 2600-year period during the Mesolithic and Neolithic, i.e. from the Early Ertebølle culture (c. 5300 BC) to the middle of the Middle Neolithic (c. 2700 BC).

Scaled flakes, and the transverse arrowheads produced from these on biconvex flakes, are a characteristic type for the Early Ertebølle culture in western Denmark and form a prominent part of the assemblage. The working of the flake axes, and the course of their edges, is also typical of the Early Ertebølle culture and further confirmation is provided by the total lack of Ertebølle pottery in the kitchen midden. Finally, attention should be drawn to the "pseudo handled core" and the oblique transverse arrowhead that form part of the assemblage. These characteristic elements, together with the remaining inventory of flint and bone/antler, clearly indicate a relative date in the Early Ertebølle culture. The Holmegaard locality

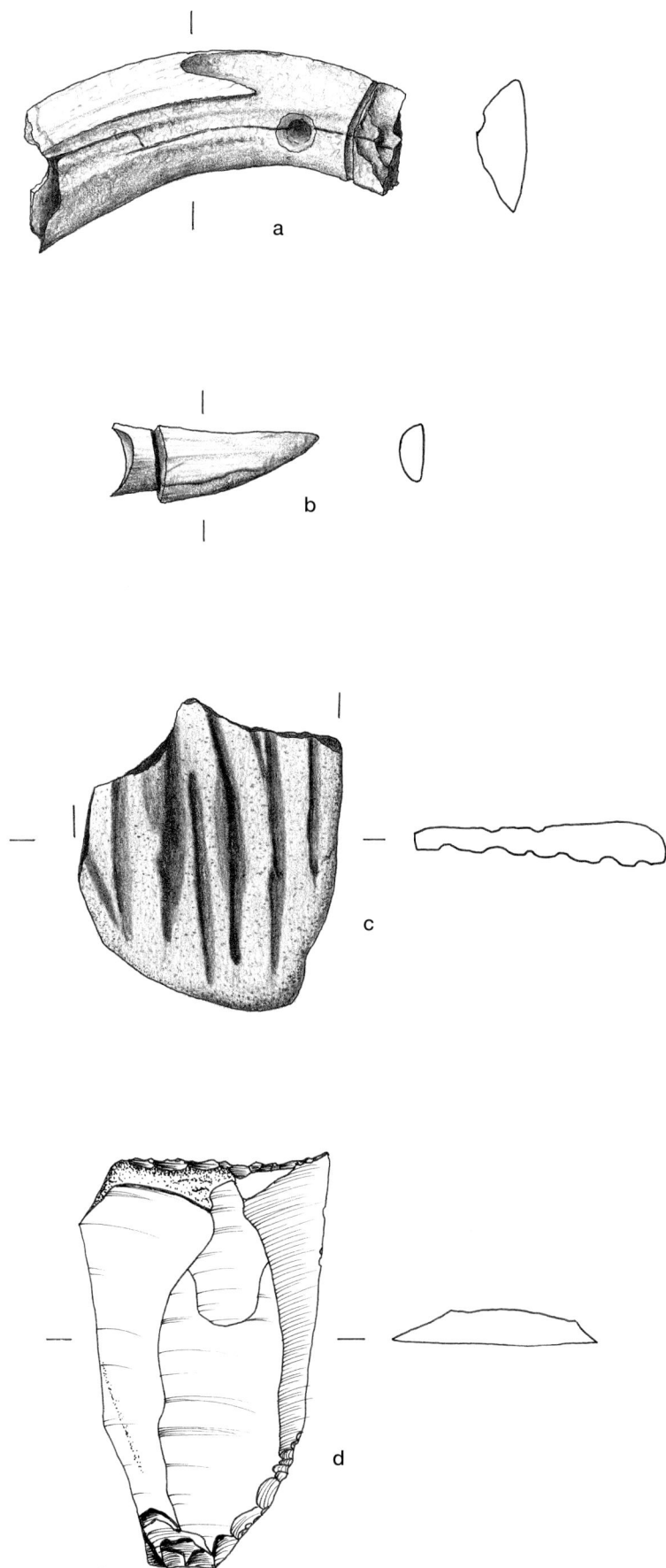

Fig. 204. Finds from the Ertebølle settlement of Stubbe Station, at the eastern end of the present-day lake, Stubbe Sø, cf. Fig. 171. a) Piece of wild boar tusk showing transverse saw marks and an attempt at perforation. Waste from the production of either a rectangular enamel piece or a finger ring. b) Fragment of wild boar tusk from which either a disc or a finger ring has been cut. c) Fragment of a thin stone slab of very fine-grained slate. Longitudinal furrows can be seen on both sides showing that the slab has been used as a whetstone for sharpening artefacts such as bone points. d) Short, broad flake with concave truncation and edge retouch at the base. This type is very characteristic of the Vængesø II settlement, cf. Fig. 50d, and is also represented by a few examples at Vængesø I and III, but is otherwise a rarity. Scale 3:4. Drawing: Søren Timm Christensen.

therefore belongs to the same phase of the Ertebølle culture in eastern Jutland as Norslund layers 3+4 (Andersen/Malmros 1966, 55-78). As the latter has been radiocarbon dated to c. 5400 BC, there is consequently great consistency between the relative dating and the scientific dates.

7.7 Other nearby settlements

A few of the Ertebølle localities in the former Stubbe fjord system have been the subject of minor archaeological excavations (Fig. 170). For example Konens Høj, where an Early Neolithic earthen grave was found, which contained copper ornaments from the Funnel Beaker culture (Stürup 1966, 13-22). The site also yielded an extensive finds assemblage from the Ertebølle culture which has not, however, been analysed.

At the eastern end of the lake Stubbe Sø, c. 1.4 km west of Holmegaard, several small kitchen middens were found on the south side of a small hill (an island in the Stone Age), including one given the name Stubbe Station, which measured c. 30 × 25 m. Kulturhistorisk Museum Randers (now East Jutland Museum) undertook a small excavation (c. 10 m²) here in the 1960s, led by G. Guldager, which cut through a c. 1 m thick kitchen midden layer (East Jutland Museum, archive no. KHM 22/64). A number of artefacts from this investigation are depicted in Fig. 204. Of particular note is the very broad-edged "knife" with distal, concave truncation (Fig. 204d) – an artefact that is morphologically closely related to the truncated pieces from the Vængesø II settlement (Fig. 50d). The other artefacts include two broad A-blades with straight to slightly oblique distal truncation, a narrow A-blade with straight, distal concave truncation, an angle burin on a regular A-blade and three narrow, thin A-blades with straight concave truncation and narrow, regular worked handles.

Attention should also be drawn to a small, flat whetstone with eight narrow, parallel, longitudinal furrows on one side and two furrows on the other (Fig. 204c). This piece, which is broken in the middle, is of very fine-grained mica schist and was presumably a whetstone for bone points and/or

pins. As far as I am aware, this artefact is unique in Danish finds from the Ertebølle culture. The excavation also yielded two pieces of worked wild boar tusk (Fig. 204a-b), which must both be interpreted as waste products from the production of enamel rings. Such rings were not found at the settlement, but were encountered in the large kitchen midden at Nederst in Kolindsund, in the form of a fragment of a broken ring and a waste product from ring production (Fig. 205). They are not known from other Ertebølle settlements/kitchen middens in Jutland and they possibly represent a local type associated with the settlements on Djursland.

7.8 Summary

The investigations at Holmegaard comprised a long trial trench and a series of test pits cutting through the kitchen midden and a contemporaneous settlement area on the hillside above this. The kitchen midden contained one of the inhumation graves from the Ertebølle culture in Jutland and, although a number of burials from the Ertebølle culture have been found in recent years, including several on Djursland (Nederst, Fannerup, Koed and Vængesø), as well as stray, disarticulated human skeletal remains, burials from this Stone Age period remain a rarity. The Holmegaard skeleton's missing skull is of particular interest as this could indicate some form of secondary manipulation of the skeleton.

Also of interest was a flat-bottomed feature observed in the subsoil, which could represent the remains of a dwelling. Hearths were observed in several places in the trial trench of 1986, and layers of fishbones were found associated with these, as well as flint debitage from the flake axe production that took place in close vicinity to them. A new discovery at Holmegaard is that the earliest kitchen middens in Jutland do not consist exclusively of shallow shell deposits, like those seen in Norslund layer 4 and Brovst layer 11, but that this kind of refuse deposit can, at some localities, acquire a considerable thickness (the kitchen midden at Holmegaard is up to 70 cm thick). Another important result is the demonstration of a habitation area up

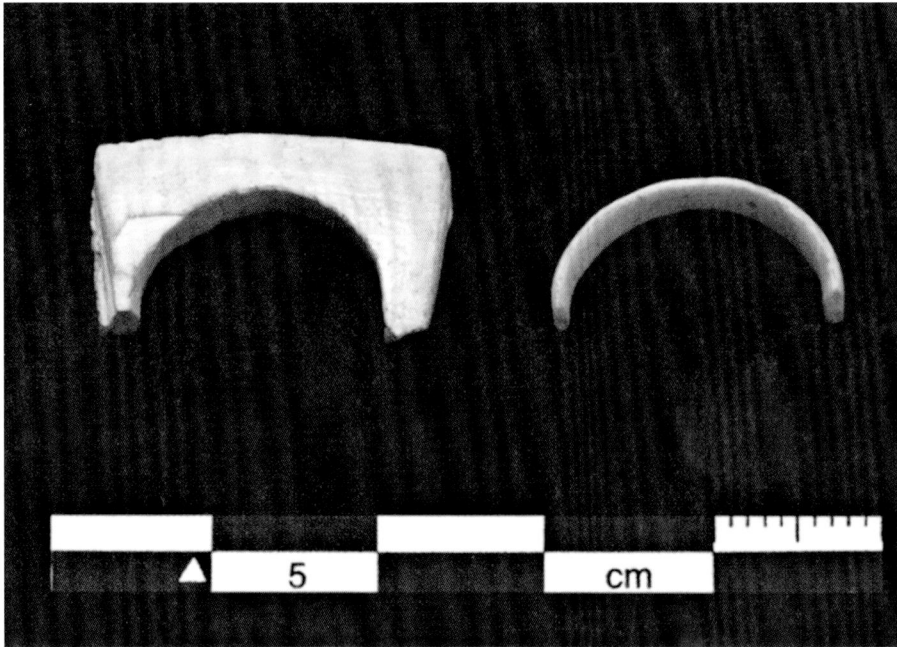

Fig. 205. Waste from the production of bone rings (left) and a broken ring (right) of wild boar tusk from the kitchen midden of Nederst in Kolindsund. After Kannegaard (2013).

on the hillside above the kitchen midden, where several kinds of hearth, small pits and stone-built structures of unknown function were discovered. These features suggest the existence of a shell-free settlement area. The flint tools from the hillside show the deposits here to be coeval with the kitchen midden. The Holmegaard locality therefore reveals the layout of a coastal settlement from the Early Ertebølle culture, with habitation up on the hillside and a kitchen midden lower down by the water. This situation corresponds in full to that discovered in the excavation of the much later Meilgaard kitchen midden (unpublished; Moesgaard Museum archive no. 1700). As for the kitchen midden itself, layers of red ochre were observed in its oldest part. This is an unusual characteristic that has otherwise only been seen at the coeval settlement of Siggård in the former Bjørnsholm Fjord in northwest Himmerland. As layers of red ochre do not occur in kitchen middens dated to the Middle and Late Ertebølle culture, this phenomenon perhaps suggests that red ochre is characteristic of settlements from the Early/Earliest Ertebølle culture.

The tool inventory at the Holmegaard locality is small, but derives from both the habitation area on the hillside and the kitchen midden at its foot by the shore. The blade cores are short and dominated by conical, unipolar examples. The blade production reflects both hard and soft techniques, with hard technique being dominant; B-blades are the commonest type. Scaled flakes are also present, both on the hillside and in the kitchen midden. There are few scrapers and borers, but numerous burins. Of particular note is the small number of knives with a curved, retouched back and blades with oblique, straight truncation, as these are otherwise the commonest types at other coeval sites in eastern Jutland (for example Norslund layers 3+4, Lystrup Enge (Andersen, S.H. 1996) and Dyrholmen I (Mathiassen et al. 1942). An explanation for this could be the small size of the finds assemblage, but the difference could also be due to the settlement activities at Holmegaard being of a different character to those at the other localities. A comparison of the faunal remains from these sites does not, however, reveal any obvious differences. With the exception of the aforementioned blade knives, the remainder of the inventory of stone and antler/bone tools similarly reveals no clear differences between the settlements. There is a dominance of flake axes. The flake axes have convex or straight sides, while the type with strongly flared sides is rare. The transverse arrowheads include examples made on biconvex flakes, and those with parallel sides and a slightly oblique edge dominate. Further to these are a few rhombic examples. A comparison with for example the Norslund settlement shows that this distribution of transverse arrowheads also indicates the Early/Earliest Ertebølle culture. Finally, there is the lack of pottery in the kitchen midden: As the earliest Ertebølle pottery turns up around 4700 BC, its absence indicates that the kitchen midden must predate this date.

The earliest, scant evidence of visits to this locality extend way back to Lateglacial times. A few finds, including a flake core (related to the eastern Danish handled cores) and trapezoid and very oblique-edged transverse arrowheads (and a lanceolate microlith) are, moreover, apparently traces of sporadic visits to the site during the Late Kongemose culture (Fig. 198m-p). The typological analysis of the finds assemblage shows, however, that the Holmegaard kitchen midden belongs to the Early/Earliest Ertebølle culture. The scientific dates reveal that the kitchen midden is from the period 5300-4700 BC. The typological and scientific dating of the kitchen midden therefore concur, and also harmonise with the fact that this locality has no definite traces of Late Ertebølle types such as those which characterise the settlements at Vængesø. With respect to the settlement area on the hillside, all the flint tools – cores, blades etc. – show that this assemblage should also be dated to the Early/Earliest Ertebølle culture. No tools etc. have been found here belonging to later phases of the Ertebølle culture or the Neolithic. A small number of scattered and uncharacteristic potsherds were though recovered, but as none of these were found in association with the demonstrated settlement features, these must be inter-

preted as scattered traces of occupation of the site during a later period – probably the Iron Age.

The subsistence economy in Early Ertebølle times was based on fishing, particularly for cod and flatfish, together with the hunting of meat animals of forest and sea (wild boar, deer and grey seal). There was also bird catching and hunting of fur animals (fox and otter). The diet was augmented by gathering of marine molluscs – especially oysters. Judging from the topographic position of the settlement, together with the faunal remains recovered from it, there is no doubt that animals from the marine environment must have played a dominant role in the overall subsistence strategy. This view is supported by the ^{13}C and ^{15}N isotope analyses of the human bones in the grave, which indicate that a considerable proportion of the individual's food was of marine origin and that, moreover, it came from the highest level in the marine environment food chain.

The Holmegaard locality demonstrates continuity of place on the coast during a long period of the Mesolithic (c. 5300-4700 BC). The settlement had an optimal topographic position in relation to fishing, marine hunting and gathering, which must be the explanation for it being visited and occupied repeatedly during the Late Mesolithic. As Holmegaard is unfortunately the only excavated locality in this part of Denmark that has been published, we are unable to evaluate its relationship to other coeval Ertebølle settlements. But the thickness of the kitchen midden deposits, the duration of the habitation, the nature of the tool inventory and the presence of a grave all suggest that this settlement was both frequently visited and of central significance in the area.

8 Summary and concluding remarks:
Ertebølle sites at Vængesø and Holmegaard

This book presents the results of excavations carried out at coastal settlements of the Ertebølle culture in the southern part of Djursland – at Vængesø, in the northeastern part of Helgenæs, and at Holmegaard, located between Stubbe Sø and the Kattegat. These investigations have contributed much new information and knowledge relating to this culture in eastern Jutland.

Vængesø

At the end of the Mesolithic, Vængesø was a c. 2 km long and c. 0.7 km wide lagoon, linked to the marine bay of Ebeltoft Vig, but sheltered from the open sea by a long, narrow beach ridge formation (Fig. 2). Within a very short distance, there was consequently ready access to several major marine areas (in addition to Vængesø itself). From west to east: the Bay of Aarhus, Begtrup Vig, Ebeltoft Vig and the Kattegat (Figs. 1b-2). As these settlements were located on small islands/peninsulas, a beach ridge and close to the narrowest part of Helgenæs, this resource area was, unlike that of most other coastal settlements of this period, to an extraordinary extent dominated by the food resources of sea and coast. This has heavily influenced the subsistence economy of the settlements and their tool inventories, which differ in several ways from the general situation at the other coastal settlements of the time. Four sites were investigated in the Vængesø lagoon (Vængesø I, II, III and IV), which

constitute a geographically delimited local group within the Ertebølle culture of eastern Jutland (Fig. 3). As significant parts of the settlements' cultural deposits lie in association with coastal slopes, they have to a great extent been protected by land slip and hillwash (colluvium). Consequently, only the uppermost layers have been affected by field cultivation and the like. The kitchen middens at the settlements of Vængesø I, II and III date from the latest part of the Ertebølle culture, c. 4300-4100 BC, but assemblages of water-worn and redeposited artefacts show that there were also settlements in the lagoon during the Early/Earliest Ertebølle culture. Vængesø IV is dated to 3700-3510 BC, i.e. to the Early Neolithic Funnel Beaker Culture.

Even though habitation of the Vængesø settlements occurred particularly during the Late Ertebølle culture, there is evidence at all the sites relating to continued visits during the Neolithic and Bronze Age. Parts of a whale skeleton (found by Vængesø IV) have been radiocarbon dated to the Bronze Age, and numerous pits containing Bronze Age pottery at Vængesø III point in the same direction.

These coastal sites therefore document continuity of both place and subsistence economy through a long period of prehistory, c. 5200-1700 BC. This extended period of use, which is also evident at many other coastal settlements, is a very characteristic aspect of coast-bound settlement – not just at Vængesø, but across the whole of Denmark.

Given the extent of their cultural deposits and the sizes of their artefact assemblages, Vængesø I, II and IV can be considered as "minor" localities, while Vængesø III was one of the largest Ertebølle settlements in Jutland (Tab. 8). Due to the presence of kitchen midden deposits, conditions for preservation are good at all the settlements, which explains the presence of well-preserved faunal remains that are able to shed light on the subsistence economy, seasonal exploitation etc.

As the archaeological investigations were undertaken over a c. 40-year period, excavation/field methods, theoretical questions and finds processing have all changed during this time. Similarly, the extent of the excavations and the parts of the individual settlements that were investigated vary from place to place. These differences have, in some situations, led to difficulties in investigating and analysing the recovered material, and this work has consequently been of varying intensity.

The Vængesø I settlement has been totally excavated, and large areas of the original settlement surface have been investigated at Vængesø II and III. Only short trial trenches and test pits were cut at Vængesø IV. Unlike many other Ertebølle settlements in Denmark, no offshore "dumps/waste deposits" have been found in the marine sediments at Vængesø. This could perhaps be due to the sites being visited so briefly that such deposits did not develop, or perhaps to geological or social circumstances. Consequently, the excavations only relate to settlement surfaces on dry land.

The finds and features associated with the settlements show that these must have been rapidly covered over, otherwise the deposits and features would have become more evened out and disturbed than was found to be the case. The settlement surfaces actually reveal a number of interesting "snapshots" of the situation when they were finally abandoned.

The small sites contain few or no actual features/structures from Ertebølle times. For example, Vængesø I has only one terrace with two stone-set hearths, three small heaps of marine mollusc shells ("meal heaps") and two pits/postholes (Fig. 6). Vængesø II has one terrace and two burials

dating from the Late/Latest Ertebølle culture, but otherwise only few Ertebølle features (Figs. 34-35, 37-38). Conversely, there are extensive stone settings/pavements, hearths and deposits containing cooking stones dating from the Neolithic occupation (Fig. 34).

The opposite is true of the large site of Vængesø III, where many more features and structures are preserved, both in the kitchen midden and in the underlying pre-midden layer. There are several types of hearths (Figs. 101-107), pits (Fig. 116), postholes, three or four terraces (Figs. 88 and 98), areas with numerous cooking stones, abundant fire-brittled flint (Fig. 112), places where flint has been worked and animal prey was slaughtered/skinned (Fig. 115). Further to these are discrete, delimited meal heaps, containing the remains of fish (Fig. 114) and marine invertebrates (Fig. 115), as well as a burial etc. It also proved possible to divide the settlement surface into identified working/activity areas (Figs. 108, 118-121). In particular, the areas around the hearths are characterised by the various activities and functions, for example flint-working, processing of fish and slaughtering of prey animals. Such a well-preserved and detailed picture of a settlement surface from the Late Ertebølle culture has not been presented previously and therefore gives us an important insight into the various settlement activities and where on the settlement surface these took place.

In order to compensate for the sloping terrain on which the Vængesø settlements lie, elongated, horizontal terraces were cut into the hillside. These terraces are oriented such that they all have one long side facing out towards the sea (the lagoon). They are all of the same form and size (c. 6-8 x 2 m, i.e. an area of c. 12-16 m²). Vængesø I (Figs. 5-6) and II (Fig. 36) were each found to have one terrace, while at Vængesø III there were three, possibly four, of these structures (Figs. 88 and 98) and Vængesø IV had possible traces of a similar terrace.

At Vængesø III, these features were not merely cut into the hillside, but also sunk slightly into the subsoil. There are extended rows of hearths running along the longitudinal axis of the terraces, suggesting that the latter were used on several occasions (Fig. 101). One of the features (terrace III) at Vængesø III (Fig. 99) differs slightly from the rest. It has no hearths but, on the other hand, contains numerous cooking stones and heaps of slaughtering waste. This suggests that its function differed from that of the other terraces. No secure traces of postholes or the like were found associated with these structures on Vængesø III.

It remains uncertain whether the terraces represented a particular form of dwelling or a working/activity platform. Their limited size is most indicative of the latter, though the former possibility cannot be completely dismissed. The terraces at Vængesø represent a rare form of feature at Danish Ertebølle settlements. Similar, elongate, slightly sunken terraces have only been found at Vegger (on the Limfjord) and at Kalundborg (Fig. 100). Common to these features is their uniform size, form and the fact that they are cut slightly into a hillside.

Features have been described from several other localities that have been interpreted as possible remains of dwellings. These are, however, characterised by their great diversity and, in this respect, they differ from the Vængesø features in not having the same (uniform) morphology, size or layout; features that are characteristic of the houses and huts of all other prehistoric periods. Examples include that found at Egehøj, near Randers, which was rectangular in form and measured c. 3 x 5 m, and a similar feature at Lollikhuse near Roskilde, which had a floor area of c. 6 x 4 m (Fig. 100).

If a stencil of the same size and form as the presumed dwelling from Lollikhuse is laid over a plan of the settlement surface at Vængesø III, such that the hearths lie along the longitudinal axis of the feature and in the same places as the terraces that have been demonstrated, it is apparent that there is room for two, or perhaps three, dwelling structures of this form and size – i.e. the same as the number of terraces. The possibility that the Vængesø terraces also represent some form of house floor cannot, therefore, be completely dismissed.

An important result of the archaeological investigations at Vængesø is the discovery of a series of burials, in addition to stray finds of individual human bones. Three inhumation graves have definitely been located: two at Vængesø II (Fig. 38) and one at Vængesø III (Fig. 160). A burnt cranial bone from Vængesø III probably represents a trace of a cremation grave, such that two different burial forms have therefore been documented at this site. Stray finds of individual human bones at Vængesø II show that there could originally have been a greater number of graves. This increase in the number of known Ertebølle graves means that Djursland is now the area in western Denmark with the greatest number of graves dating from the Middle and Late Ertebølle culture. Those at Vængesø II are particularly important as they date from the transition between the Mesolithic and Neolithic – a period from which there are, as yet, very few known features of this type.

These are inhumation burials, with the deceased lying in an extended supine position, with their arms by their sides and their head to either the NNW or SSW (Figs. 38, 160, 186-187). In one of the graves at Vængesø II, it could be established that the deceased's feet had been bound together, a phenomenon that has also been seen in graves of the Ertebølle culture in eastern Denmark. In the graves at Vængesø II, the corpse had large stones covering, respectively, its lower abdomen/pelvic region and feet. In the grave at Vængesø III, the upper part of the skull was missing. It is, however, uncertain whether this had been removed as a result of a ritual act or was missing due to secondary disturbance and poor preservation conditions. The missing cranium could perhaps mean that a trophy or skull cult was practised at these settlements in Ertebølle times. The skull in the well-preserved grave at Vængesø II showed evidence of violence to the left side of the frontal bone (Fig. 41) and a thoracic vertebra displayed a circular hole which presumably was caused by a weapon (arrow or spear). The grave at Vængesø III contained two truncated blades, but there were no further grave goods in the other burial features (Fig. 161). From an overall perspective, these new graves are similar in several ways to the Ertebølle graves found at Fannerup and Nederst (both in

Kolindsund), for example the position of the deceased, the bound feet and grave goods in the form of flint knives etc.

Analyses of the stable isotopes of carbon and nitrogen in the bones show that these individuals lived very predominantly on food from the highest level in the marine food chain. The skeletons at Vængesø II were also subjected to DNA analysis, but insufficient DNA was preserved to enable further analysis.

The settlements at Vængesø are generally characterised by a poor flint-working technique. This must be due to access to raw flint being, to a great extent, based on the exploitation of the local occurrences, either in beach ridges or the area's fluvioglacial deposits, which only contain small, irregular flint nodules. There was apparently only limited exchange of raw flint internally between the settlements or with more distant regions. This picture corresponds to the findings from the Aggersund settlement on the Limfjord, where use was similarly only made of local flint, despite the fact that this was of poor quality and that there was also easy access to good and easily available flint within a short distance of the site.

The Vængesø settlements are therefore dominated by short, heavily exploited blade cores with a single platform (Figs. 42, 122-123). The flint was worked using indirect soft technique. The majority of the blades are irregular and micro-blades are rare. The irregular raw material has also resulted in the blade tools being short and irregular relative to those known from other coeval Ertebølle settlements in eastern Jutland and western Funen (Figs. 9-11, 13-16, 47-54, 130-131, 134-136). A small number were, however, made on longer and more regular blades. Some of the equipment could therefore have been brought from other localities, where there was access to better raw material.

The flint tool inventory includes some of the culture's main types, but unlike the other Ertebølle settlements in eastern Jutland of this time, the Vængesø localities have only very few scrapers, borers and burins (Tab. 9). Conversely, pieces with concave truncation are very prominent (Figs. 13a-h, 50, 134). In some instances, the truncated pieces have a worked handle at their proximal end (Figs. 51b-c, 134e). The abundance of these suggests a major local requirement for knives for the slaughtering and butchering of prey animals. Denticulate flake scrapers are also a characteristic element in the tool inventory at Vængesø I (Fig. 9), II and III (Fig. 122), and both finely and coarsely denticulate blades are common (Figs. 14, 52d-e, 135-136e).

An analysis of the transverse arrowheads reveals the type with strongly concave sides to be dominant (Figs. 18, 55, 137). Moreover, a seriation diagram shows that all the settlements belong to the Late/Latest Ertebølle culture (Fig. 140).

Axes are dominated by symmetrical, flat-flaked flake axes (Figs. 21, 58-60, 143-145), relative to core axes, which have specialised, double-sided edge working (Figs. 20, 57, 141). Flake chisels are similarly a characteristic element in the assemblages (Figs. 24, 63, 148). On the settlement surface at Vængesø III, several discrete patches of characteristic flint debitage (always in the vicinity of hearths) showed that flake axes had been manufactured here (Figs. 118, 121).

Greenstone axes are rare finds from the excavations, but occur as stray finds picked up from all the settlements (Fig. 64). A greenstone axe from Vængesø III is perforated by a shaft hole – a very rare type in Jutland (Fig. 149). Vængesø II also yielded the first find from Jutland of a greenstone axe of Limhamn type (Fig. 65), a type otherwise only known from eastern Denmark. Further to this is a unique piece: A fragment of a shoe-last axe, which originates from the regions to the south of the Baltic (Fig. 69).

A completely new aspect with respect to the eastern Jutish Ertebølle settlements was the discovery at Vængesø II of numerous waste flakes of diabase/greenstone. These show that coarse working of this material (for the purpose of manufacturing greenstone axes) took place here (Fig. 66). This discovery shows that the manufacture of greenstone axes occasionally took place at the settlements (on a local level), out on the coast, where there was easy access to boulders of diabase washed out of the moraine deposits.

Tools of bone and antler were remarkably few in number at the Vængesø settlements – both in terms of absolute numbers, relative to the sizes of the excavated settlement areas and, especially, in comparison with other settlements from the same period in Jutland and on Funen. Particularly striking is the small number of fabricators (Figs. 27a, 71) and the almost complete absence of antler axes. Both types are otherwise characteristic of, and common on, other coeval Ertebølle settlements (Figs. 27b, 70). Similarly, the few artefacts of bone and antler that were found are both worn and heavily resharpened. In some cases, there are indications of "recycling"; for example, an antler axe had been made from an antler shaft (Fig. 70). In parallel with the scarcity of bone and antler tools there is also a lack of waste from the production of these artefacts, for example traces from the production of antler axes etc. The fact that this is an actual absence, and not just an expression of poor preservation conditions, is demonstrated by the thousands of well-preserved small, fragile bones of fish, birds and small mammals.

The finds assemblages include simple bone points (Figs. 73, 153), a harpoon (Fig. 74), a few fabricators, a few resharpened ulna daggers (Figs. 72, 153h) and an antler axe, plus small fragments from the edges of antler axes (Fig. 27b).

On the other hand, Vængesø III did yield two completely new bone artefacts that have not previously been recorded in an Ertebølle context: long, narrow, ornamented "pins" of split bird bone (Figs. 154a-c, 155) and circular "buttons" made from the vertebrae of porpoises (Fig. 154d).

The small number of tools and weapons made from these materials concurs with the scarcity of burins encountered at the settlements. Collectively, these observations suggest that tools and weapons of bone and antler were probably not produced at Vængesø but were more probably brought to the lagoon from other areas. A good example of this is provided by the narrow "strips" of antler (blanks) for harpoons found at Vængesø II (Fig. 75). Waste from the production of similar strips is common at most coastal settlements where harpoons have been made. However, as this type of waste is not present at Vængesø II or the other settlements, the blanks must have been brought from somewhere else.

Pointed-based vessels were found at Vængesø I, II and III (Figs. 25, 77, 150-152). At the latter settlement in particular, there were large numbers of potsherds and larger fragments of pots, showing the regular and frequent use of pottery here (Fig. 151). Conversely, remains of "lamps" were not found at any of the settlements. This corresponds to the situation at many other Ertebølle settlements in eastern and northern Jutland, but is nevertheless remarkable given the extensive hunting of seals, whales and sea birds that took place in and around the lagoon. Train oil and blubber extracted from these animals were apparently not used for heating, lighting or cooking at these settlements. The absence of lamps stands in contrast to the situation encountered in excavations of coeval settlements in the narrowest part of the Little Belt (Gudsø Vig, Kolding Fjord and Ronæs Skov) and even further south in Schleswig-Holstein. All these settlements also had evidence of the extensive hunting of porpoises and seals but, in contrast to the situation at Vængesø, they feature a characteristic number of "blubber lamps" in their finds assemblages. The absence of "lamps" at the Vængesø sites further underlines the special character of these settlements. It reinforces both the interpretation of them as "special sites" in relation to all the other known Ertebølle settlements in eastern Jutland from this period and the fact that they were part of a settlement system which included other (more distant) localities, where for example train oil and blubber were used.

Vængesø II also yielded scattered finds of flint tools from various periods of the Neolithic (Figs. 78-79), in addition to potsherds from coarse storage jars of the same data (Fig. 80a-c).

The subsistence economy at the Vængesø settlements was influenced to a great degree by the marine biotope. Activities comprised a combination of fishing, marine hunting of seals, porpoises and large whales and bird catching along the coast and on the open sea. This was supplemented by the gathering of marine invertebrates and hazelnuts. The relative importance of these various subsistence activities cannot be determined with certainty, but the immediate impression is that fishing was one of the most important elements in the subsistence spectrum. But hunting of marine mammals (seals and whales) must also have had great importance, combined with hunting on land in the local forests, which however clearly only played a minor role. The situation at Vængesø IV cannot be assessed, as there are no faunal remains present. Given its location (on a channel between two promontories) and its size, it must be seen as a site that was ideal for fishing and from where, at the same time, marine molluscs were gathered.

The significance of fishing at, in particular, Vængesø III is demonstrated by the identification of remains of 18 fish species (all marine). Furthermore, the amount of fish waste was so great that the cultural deposits included concreted masses of fishbones etc., which often formed dense cakes on the edges of the hearths. The fish remains are dominated by cod and flatfish (Tab. 10).

Almost all coastal settlements of the Ertebølle culture have evidence of the marine hunting of seals and whales, but to date there has been an apparent lack of "specialised" coastal settlements where this subsistence activity constituted one of the primary elements in the food supply. This gap can now be said to have been filled by the findings presented here from Vængesø II and III.

Bones of seals and whales are regularly found at most Ertebølle settlements in Denmark and other countries, but in nowhere near the same quantities as seen at the Vængesø lagoon. Faunal remains recovered from the settlements here show that hunting focussed on grey seal in particular, but harp seal, ringed seal and common seal also feature. Further to these, and featuring to a lesser extent, are remains of porpoise and the slightly larger whale species such as killer whale and bottlenosed dolphin. Evidence from other Danish Ertebølle sites suggests that seal hunting took place primarily from smaller coastal sites. These were located in particular on "outer islands", i.e. small islands with no large adjoining land/hinterland, such as was also the case at Vængesø.

An unusual but common feature of Vængesø I, II and III is the occurrence of splintered bones of large whales (Figs. 28-29, 76). Further to these are the numerous bones of large whales found at Vængesø III (Figs. 156-157), which represent either evidence of active hunting of these animals in nearby waters or (and perhaps more likely) the exploitation of bones of dead whales that stranded, dead or alive, on local beaches.

Similar bone splinters have occasionally been encountered at other Ertebølle settlements in eastern Jutland but are, in general, rare and have never been found to the extent seen at Vængesø. A common feature of these is that they are solid and of more or less the same size (less than c. 30-40 cm in length). They reflect the systematic cleavage and sorting of very large (whale) bones – probably to obtain raw material for the production of for example harpoons, which are commonly made of whalebone.

Ethnographic studies show that whale hunting, in addition to its importance for the food supply and various raw materials, also plays an important social role. This is due, in part, to the fact that this form of hunting demands intense efforts from a large number of hunters and must also be directed and coordinated – often by a leader. There are also important social aspects associated with the very precisely defined rules for the distribution and storage of the prey after the hunt.

Bird catching on the open sea and along the coast constituted an important element in the subsistence strategy at both Vængesø II and III. This activity was directed primarily towards the cormorant, but there are also numerous remains of ducks, geese, razorbill, guillemot, great auk, swan, merganser, grebe and gannet. White-tailed eagle and osprey are also represented in the faunal remains (Tab. 10).

Bones of large terrestrial meat animals – wild boar, red deer and roe deer – have also been found, but remains of the latter two species (especially red deer) are few in number and much less prominent than at other coeval Ertebølle settlements (Fig. 159). The same is also true to some extent of wild boar. This is probably a consequence primarily of the settlements' limited "resource depth", which must have played a decisive role in determining their subsistence base. As these larger animals are unlikely to have lived in the immediate vicinity of the settlements, where the land area is very restricted (islands, isthmuses or promontories), the meat must have been brought to the coastal settlements (for example Vængesø I, II and possibly III) as provisions. In this context, means of transport, in the form of dug-out boats, played an important role. The limited resource depth must also have resulted in lack of fresh water, various raw materials and, as already mentioned above, provisions, having to be taken from the mainland out to the small localities of Vængesø I, II and possibly IV.

In addition to the animal species mentioned above, Vængesø II and, in particular Vængesø III, have faunal elements comprising fur animals (especially pine marten) and dogs. The bones of these animals were found in discrete heaps, representing "slaughtering/skinning waste" by the hearths (Fig. 115).

As for the season of use, the settlements provide only uncertain indications. However, Vængesø III does appear to have been used at all times of the year and therefore either reflects more permanent (all-year-round) habitation or several short visits (Fig. 159).

The gathering of marine invertebrates is evident at all the settlements in the form of shells of oysters, cockles, mussels and periwinkles in the kitchen middens. Oysters are dominant at all the sites and all the individuals appear to have been of the same size (i.e. age). Given the presumed contemporaneity of the settlements, it is not impossible that the oysters were gathered from the same (common) bank located out in the lagoon. There is also clear evidence from Vængesø III of the systematic gathering of pullet carpet shells (*Venerupis corrugata*). Both Vængesø I and III have examples of "meal heaps" located close to and around the hearths (Fig. 90b). Investigations show that the oysters were collected in March-April.

If the settlements are compared with each other, a significant difference can be seen between Vængesø I, II, IV and Vængesø III in terms of size

and the number and diversity of features present. This could be the result of variation in seasonal occupation and/or a different range of functions. The excavation findings suggest that Vængesø III functioned as the area's main settlement and that this locality was linked to a number of minor settlements with fewer subsistence-related functions in the overall settlement pattern.

The limiting nature of the geography must almost unavoidably have led to the Vængesø lagoon functioning as a single discrete hunting ground, exploited by one local group. That is, the settlements functioned as one social and hunting-related entity, which was organised as a "collector system" (*sensu* Binford; Fig. 169).

However, it is also possible that these settlements were *not* component parts of such a system but were, conversely, visited individually, ad hoc, or that they formed part of an even larger settlement hierarchy, which possibly covered all of Helgenæs and southern Mols.

The settlement and subsistence forms described from the sites around Vængesø must have meant that vessels (dug-out boats) were of major importance. The use of boats gave the coastal population a number of obvious advantages: For example, a markedly increased operational radius, a larger transport capacity and also the potential to be a part of a social network extending along the coast. Moreover, locally concentrated or more scattered resources could be more easily exploited and brought back to a centrally located settlement. The use of boats also made it considerably easier to exchange raw materials and information between groups.

The finds assemblages show that the Vængesø area did not function as an isolated entity, but that it had, on several levels, links with the surrounding world. Regionally, there was contact across the Kattegat, for example with northwest Zealand, and across the Bay of Aarhus to other parts of eastern Jutland. The Limhamn axe found at Vængesø II and a dotted potsherd found at Vængesø III both represent unusual types in an eastern Jutish context. Their closest parallels, in geographical terms, lie in northwest Zealand (the distance between Vængesø and the bay of Sejerø (northwestern Sealand) is c. 65-70 km as the crow flies), where they have for example been found at the coeval Ertebølle settlement of Ordrup Næs. The dotted potsherd (Fig. 152b) has, however, also parallels in eastern Jutland (Brabrand, Ringkloster, Norsminde Fjord). Links should therefore also be assumed from Vængesø III across the Bay of Aarhus. The small, short bone points with (and without) a barb (Fig. 153i) are also a rare type in Jutland, but have been found at several settlements in northern Zealand, for example Pandebjerg (Nekselø), Sølager and Nivå.

In international terms, the shoe-last axe found at Vængesø II shows that this settlement also formed part of an even larger network with contacts extending to the south in Europe.

The many years of field-walking and reconnaissance in the area around Vængesø have revealed the existence of a narrow (c. 500 m) coastal belt with an unusual concentration of stray finds of axes of Ertebølle types (Fig. 167). The fact that the finds distribution at Vængesø is neither random nor unique to this area is demonstrated by the existence of identical finds distributions for axes at Norsminde Fjord in eastern Jutland and along the former Bjørnsholm Fjord in northwest Himmerland. These axes could represent remains related to the inhabitants' cutting of hazel stakes and rods for the construction and repair of their fishing structures and traps. The latter probably stood closely spaced along the shores of the lagoon, by all the settlements, as has been shown to be the case at many other Ertebølle settlements, for example Lystrup Enge and Tybrind Vig.

Holmegaard

In contrast to the Vængesø settlements, the Holmegaard kitchen midden runs down and lies at the foot of a steep hillside. It is also located centrally in a narrow former fjord, which in the Stone Age extended from the present-day lake Stubbe Sø out to the Kattegat to the southeast (Figs. 170-171). Both in a local and a slightly broader regional context, the site's position is typical for a Stone Age settle-ment, where fishing constituted a prominent part of the subsistence economy, i.e. located by a narrow channel with strong currents. At the same time, there was only a short distance to the Kattegat coast and with that, the open sea (Fig. 170). The settlement therefore had a much more extensive terrestrial resource area (i.e. greater "resource depth") than those around the Vængesø lagoon.

This kitchen midden is somewhat older than the Vængesø settlements as it dates from the period c. 5300-4500 BC, i.e. the Early/Middle Ertebølle culture (Figs. 1b, 170).

Its ideal location at the narrowest point in the former "Stubbe fjord", with a good potential for productive fishing, resulted in the Holmegaard site being visited and occupied on repeated occasions. It therefore gradually developed into the largest locality on this fjord system, corresponding to the "medium-sized" coastal settlements of the Ertebølle culture.

Excavations encompassed a series of test pits (Figs. 172, 175) and a trial trench giving a longitudinal section through the kitchen midden, as well as three large trenches above and behind the latter. As was the case at Vængesø, no offshore "dumps or waste deposits" were found in the marine sediments by the settlement. As the excavations at Holmegaard were of limited extent, the finds assemblage is very small and, as a consequence, only cautious and general conclusions are possible.

Unlike Vængesø, where the Ertebølle settlements appear to have been of short duration, the dates for various deposits within the Holmegaard kitchen midden show that it accumulated due to visits and occupation over an extended period of c. 1200 years. *The dates also indicate that this is one of the oldest known examples of a kitchen midden in Jutland.* As at Vængesø, the cultural deposits also encompassed traces of later visits/occupation during the Neolithic.

The Holmegaard kitchen midden was found to contain the same kinds of features as those encountered at the Vængesø settlements. Within the actual shell deposits there were both stone-built and ash hearths (Fig. 182-184), as well as areas around these containing evidence of flint-working and the processing and preparation of fish. There was also a rectangular depression in the subsoil, but due to the limited extent of the investigations, it was not possible to arrive at a simple explanation for this phenomenon. It could possibly represent the slightly sunken foundations for a dwelling. The earliest of the kitchen midden's deposits were characterised by concentrations of red ochre. Nothing like this was observed at Vængesø.

In the excavated areas behind and at a higher level than the kitchen midden itself, there was a thin culture layer containing Ertebølle artefacts and numerous types of settlement features, for example stone-built hearths, stone pavements, charcoal-rich patches etc. (Figs. 182-184). This area can be interpreted as the actual habitation area which, judging from the finds recovered, must be coeval with the kitchen midden.

Holmegaard is thereby able to give us an impression of the layout of a coastal settlement from this phase of the Ertebølle period: A habitation area located up on the hillside, at the foot of which, down by the shore, a kitchen midden gradually accumulated. At the same time, everyday activities were carried out here in the form of food preparation/cooking and the working of flint tools. These findings from Holmegaard are important because investigations of the areas behind kitchen middens are still very few and far between.

The skeleton of a young man (Fig. 185), dated to the Middle Ertebølle culture, was found in the kitchen midden. No grave goods were encountered, but the skeleton was covered by several large stones (as seen in similar situations at Vængesø II), and the lower legs appeared to have been bound together. The upper part of the skull was missing, and in this case it could be securely established that this had been removed in the Stone Age. As in the case of the grave at Vængesø III, this could suggest the practising of some form of "skull cult". Chemical analyses of the deceased's bones showed that he had lived very predominantly on food of marine origin, and that this food came from the highest level in the food chain. Despite the low DNA content of the bones, it did prove possible to determine the individual's gender and identify his

mitochondrial variant as belonging to haplogroup U5a2b. This variant has been observed previously in Mesolithic samples from Europe.

If the finds assemblage from Holmegaard is compared with those from the Vængesø lagoon, clear differences are apparent. These arise, first and foremost, from the fact that the Holmegaard settlement is c. 500-1100 years older. A very similar picture of the material culture is, however, familiar from Ertebølle settlements in eastern Jutland of corresponding age, for example the earliest deposits at Norslund and Dyrholmen.

The flint technique is characterised by irregular cores and blades, made using "soft" and "hard" techniques (Figs. 188-189, 191, 193). The dating of the settlement to the Early Ertebølle culture is also reflected in finds of "scaled flakes" – a waste product from the manufacture of transverse arrowheads. These characteristic artefacts only occur during the Early Ertebølle culture in western Denmark (Fig. 190). They were present in both the kitchen midden and the habitation area behind it. The cores include a few examples that are closely related to the so-called "handled cores", which are a characteristic type for the Late Kongemose culture in eastern Denmark (Fig. 189b).

Despite being irregular, the blades are larger than those from Vængesø II and III, probably due to access to better raw material than was the case at the Vængesø settlements.

The blade tools include all the types that are characteristic of this phase of the Ertebølle culture. At Holmegaard, the relative proportions of the various tool groups differ from those seen at Vængesø (Tab. 8). For example, there are more scrapers, borers and burins as well as "knives" with a retouched back (Figs. 194-197).

The transverse arrowhead group is characterised by earlier types with a slightly oblique edge, while the later type, with strongly concave sides that dominates at Vængesø, is less prominent. There are also arrowheads with a rhombic or lanceolate outline. The latter point back in time and probably represent traces of early pre-kitchen midden occupation of the site during the Late Kongemose culture (Fig. 198m-p).

There are more core axes (Fig. 199a-b) and fewer flake axes (Figs. 199c-d, 200a-c) than at Vængesø. The core axes have an oblique edge with no special edge treatment/working. The flake axes include edge-trimmed (Fig. 199c) and asymmetrical examples, which often have slightly convex sides, while axes with strongly concave sides, like those that characterise the Vængesø settlements, are few in number. There is also a preform for a greenstone axe from Holmegaard, which, in this case, has been shaped by pecking (Fig. 202).

As for artefacts of bone and antler, Holmegaard differs from the Vængesø settlements by having a greater number of tools made of these materials. These constitute, first and foremost, simple bone points, which in almost all instances are short and have been heavily resharpened (Fig. 203). These pieces also include a variant with side edges, which represents an early type in the Jutish Ertebølle culture (Fig. 203a). Fabricators and antler chisels also feature in the Holmegaard assemblage.

There is no pottery from Holmegaard, as the site predates the appearance of pottery in western Denmark around 4700/4600 BC.

The subsistence economy at Holmegaard also comprised a mixture of fishing, marine hunting, hunting in the primeval forest and gathering of marine invertebrates. Remains of marine mammals are, however, much less prominent than at Vængesø (Tab. 10). The fish remains are dominated by cod, followed by flatfish, piked dogfish, eel, herring and mackerel. The latter indicates fishing during the summer period. The prominent role of cod corresponds to the situation evident at a number of other coeval coastal settlements from the Early/Earliest Ertebølle culture in eastern Jutland, for example Norslund (layers 3+4) and Lystrup Enge. Judging from the topography of the settlement (by a narrow channel with strong currents), it must be assumed that fishing took place using stationary structures and fish traps/eel pots.

Marine hunting is demonstrated by remains of grey seal and bottle-nosed dolphin, both of which could be hunted in the former fjord and out on the Kattegat coast.

Forest hunting is demonstrated by bones of wild boar, red deer, roe deer and aurochs. The presence of aurochs is consistent with the date of the site as this species was characteristic of Ertebølle settlements of the period, for example Norslund (layers 3+4) and Lystrup Enge. Otter, fox and wildcat round off the picture of forest animals; dog is the only domesticated animal present.

Bird remains are few in number and only comprise bones of ducks and swans, in addition to two birds of prey: golden eagle and white-tailed eagle.

As no excavations have been carried out of other nearby, coeval settlements (unlike at Vængesø), it is not possible to say whether a "collector system" also operated in this fjord. Judging from the areas of the localities and the nature of their artefacts, everything suggests that Holmegaard was the largest settlement on this former fjord. This conclusion is further supported by the various forms of feature that have been demonstrated at this site.

An excavation of a small kitchen midden at Stubbe Station (similarly in the Stubbe fjord system) produced a selection of Ertebølle artefacts (Fig. 204), including a couple of examples of wild boar tusks that had been used as raw material for enamel finger rings (Fig. 204a-b). This artefact type is similarly represented at the large Ertebølle settlement at Nederst in Kolindsund (Fig. 205). Stubbe Station also yielded examples of triangular, truncated flakes (Fig. 204d) of the same type as is characteristic of the Vængesø II settlement (Fig. 50d).

Conclusion

This presentation of the results and findings from the excavations undertaken around Vængesø and at Holmegaard has added numerous new and important elements to our existing knowledge of the material culture, subsistence economy, burial traditions and settlement patterns of the Ertebølle period in eastern Jutland.

In rounding off this account, the question of future plans and priorities arises. The potential at Vængesø for making important archaeological advances and discoveries is far from exhausted. There are several localities in the southern part of the lagoon that have not yet been investigated (Fig. 3) and the same is true of significant parts of the middle and southern parts of the large Vængesø III settlement. Seen from a slightly broader perspective, it would also be obvious to investigate the large settlements at Kongsgårde on Helgenæs (Fig. 166) in order to clarify their position relative to the Vængesø area.

The excavated settlements are all threatened by plough damage, i.e. arable agriculture. It is therefore imperative that protective measures are introduced – first and foremost in the form of a number of local scheduling initiatives, but also continued excavation of either entire areas or smaller parts within the settlements of Vængesø II and III and Holmegaard

9 References

Albrethsen/Petersen 1977
S.E. Albrethsen/E.B. Petersen, Excavation of a Mesolithic Cemetry at Vedbæk, Denmark. Acta Archaeologica 47, 1976, 1-28.

Andersen 1961
H.H. Andersen, Køkkenmøddingen ved Meilgaard. Kuml 1960, 26-35.

Andersen 1981
K. Andersen, Mesolitiske flækker fra Åmosen, Sjælland. Aarbøger for Nordisk Oldkyndighed og Historie 1981, 5-18.

Andersen 1985
K. Andersen, Frihavnen – den første Kongemoseboplads. Fra Nationalmuseets Arbejdsmark 1985, 42-47.

Andersen 1972
S.H. Andersen, Ertebøllekulturens harpuner. Kuml 1971, 73-125.

Andersen 1973a
S.H. Andersen, Bro. En senglacial boplads på Fyn. Kuml 1972, 7-60.

Andersen 1975a
S.H. Andersen, Ringkloster. En jysk indlandsboplads med Ertebøllekultur. Kuml 1973/74, 10-108.

Andersen 1975b
S.H. Andersen, En Ertebølleboplads ved Vængesø/Helgenæs. Hikuin 2, 9-48.

Andersen 1976
S.H. Andersen, Norsminde Fjord undersøgelsen. In: H. Thrane (ed.), Bebyggelsesarkæologi. Beretning fra et symposium d. 7-8. nov. 1975 afholdt af Odense Universitet. Skrifter fra Institut for Historie og Samfundsvidenskab. Nr. 17 (Odense 1976), 18-62.

Andersen 1979a
S.H. Andersen, Aggersund. En Ertebølleboplads ved Limfjorden. Kuml 1978, 1979, 7- 56.

Andersen 1979b
S.H. Andersen, Flade, skælhuggede skiver af Brovst-type. Kuml 1978, 77-98.

Andersen 1981a
S.H. Andersen, Ertebøllekunst. Nye fund af mønstrede Ertebølleoldsager. Kuml 1980, 7-59.

Andersen 1981b
S.H. Andersen, Stenalderen, Jægerstenalderen. (København 1981).

Andersen 1991
S.H. Andersen, Norsminde. A Køkkenmødding with Late Mesolithic and Early Neolithic Occupation. Journal of Danish Archaeology 8, 1989, 13-40.

Andersen 1993
S.H. Andersen, Bjørnsholm. A Stratified Køkkenmødding on the Central Limfjord, North Jutland. With a contribution by Kaare Lund Rasmussen. Journal of Danish Archaeology 10, 1991, 59-96.

Andersen 1995
S.H. Andersen, Coastal adaption and marine exploitation in Late Mesolithic Denmark – with special emphasis on the Limfjord region. In: A. Fischer (red.), Man and Sea in the Mesolithic. Coastal settlement above and below present sea level. Oxbow Monograph 53 (Oxford 1995), 41-66.

Andersen 1996
S.H. Andersen, Ertebøllebåde fra Lystrup. Kuml 1993-94, 7-38.

Andersen 1997
S.H. Andersen, Ertebølleharpuner og spækhuggertænder. Aspekter af marin fangst i Ertebølletid. Kuml 1995-96, 45-99.

Andersen 1998
S.H. Andersen, Ertebølle trappers and wild boar hunters in eastern Jutland. A survey. Journal of Danish Archaeology 12, 1994-1995, 13-59.

Andersen 2000

S.H. Andersen, "Køkkenmøddinger" (Shell Middens) in Denmark: a Survey. Proceedings of the Prehistoric Society 66, 2000, 361-384.

Andersen 2004

S.H. Andersen, Aktivitetspladser fra Ertebølletid. Dyngby III og Sindholt Nord. Kuml 2004, 9-44.

Andersen 2005

S.H. Andersen, Køkkenmøddingerne ved Krabbesholm. Nationalmuseets Arbejdsmark 2005, 151-171.

Andersen 2008

S.H. Andersen, A report on recent excavations at the shell midden of Havnø in Denmark. Mesolithic Miscellany, Volume 19:1, March 2008, 3-6.

Andersen 2009

S.H. Andersen, Ronæs Skov. Marinarkæologiske undersøgelser af en kystboplads fra Ertebølletid. Jysk Arkæologisk Selskabs Skrifter 64 (Højbjerg 2009).

Andersen 2013

S.H. Andersen, Tybrind Vig. Submerged Mesolithic Settlements in Denmark. Jutland Archaeological Society Publications Vol. 77 (Højbjerg 2013).

Andersen et al. 1986

S.H. Andersen/T.S. Constandse-Westermann/R.R. Newell/R. Gillespie/J.A.J. Gowlett/R.E.M. Hedges, New Radiocarbon Dates for two Mesolithic Burials in Denmark. In: J.A.J. Gowlett/ R.E.M. Hedges (eds.), Archaeological Results from Accellerator Dating. Oxford University Committee for Archaeology Monograph 11 (Oxford 1986), 39-43.

Andersen/Malmros 1966

S.H. Andersen/C. Malmros, Norslund. En kystboplads fra ældre stenalder. Kuml 1965, 35-114.

Andersen/Malmros 1985

S.H. Andersen/C. Malmros, "Madskorpe" på Ertebøllekar fra Tybrind Vig. Aarbøger for Nordisk Oldkyndighed og Historie 1984, 78-95.

Andersen/Johansen 1987

S.H. Andersen/E. Johansen, Ertebølle Revisited. Journal of Danish Archaeology 5, 1986, 31-61.

Andersen/Kannegaard 2013

S.H. Andersen/E. Kannegaard, Ka´De li´østers? Skalk 2013-6, 3-7.

Asher 1968

R. Asher, Time´s Arrow and the Archaeology of a Contemporary Community. In: K.C. Chang (ed.), Settlement Archaeology (Palo Alto 1968), 43-52.

Asingh 2000

P. Asingh, Helgenæs – manden i møddingen. In: S. Hvass (ed.), Vor skjulte kulturarv. Arkæologien under overfladen. Til Hendes Majestæt Dronning Margrethe II 16 april 2000 (København 2000), 32-33.

Becker 1939

C.J. Becker, En Stenalderboplads paa Ordrup Næs i Nordvestsjælland. Aarbøger for Nordisk Oldkyndighed og Historie 1939, 119-280.

Becker 1951

C.J. Becker, Den grubekeramiske kultur i Danmark. Aarbøger for Nordisk Oldkyndighed og Historie 1950, 153-274.

Becker 1952

C.J. Becker, Ørnekul paa Nekselø. En sjællands stenalderboplads med hustomter. Aarbøger for Nordisk Oldkyndighed og Historie 1952, 60-107.

Becker 1955

C.J. Becker, Coarse Beakers with "Short-Wave Moulding". Proceedings of The Prehistoric Society 21,No. 7, 65-71.

Bergsvik 2002

K.A. Bergsvik (ed.), Arkæologiske undersøkelser ved Skatestraumen Bind I. Med bidrag av Kristin Senneset, Anne Karin Hufthammer, Kari Loe Hjelle og Einar Alsaker. Arkeologiske Avhandlinger og Rapporter fra Universitetet i Bergen Bd. 7 (Bergen 2002).

Bertelsen, 1994

J.B. Bertelsen, Åsted (hvalskelet). Arkæologiske Udgravninger i Danmark 1993 (København 1994), 167, nr. 287.

Binford 1980

L.R. Binford, Willow Smoke and Dogs Tails; Hunter-Gatherer Settlement Systems and Archaeological Site Formation. American Antiquity 45, 1980, 4-20.

Binford 1982

L.R. Binford, The Archaeology of Place. Journal of Anthropological Archaeology 1, 1982, 5-31.

Binford 1983

L.R. Binford, In Persuit of the Past. Decoding the archaeological record (London 1983).

Boas 1983

N.-A. Boas, Egehøj. A Settlement from the Early Bronze Age in East Jutland. Journal of Danish Archaeology 2, 1983, 90-101.

Boas 2001

N.-A. Boas, Dybdal – en tørvedækket boplads fra Ertebøllekultur på Norddjursland. In: O.L. Jensen/S. A. Sørensen/K. M. Hansen (eds.), Danmarks jægerstenalder – status og perspektiver (Hørsholm 1983), 145-154.

Brøndsted 1938

J. Brøndsted, Danmarks Oldtid I, Stenalderen (København 1938).

Brøndsted 1957

J. Brøndsted, Danmarks Oldtid I, Stenalderen (København 1957).

Canti/Linford 2000
   M.G. Canti/N. Linford, The effects of fire on archaeological soils and sediments; temperature and colour relationships. Proceedings of the Prehistoric Society 66, 2000, 385-395.

Clark 1974
   J.G.D. Clark, Prehistoric Europe. The Economic Basis (Cambridge 1974).

Dudok van Heel 1962
   U.H. Dudok van Heel, Sound and cetacean. Netherlands Journal of Sea Research 1-4, 1962, 407-507.

Enghoff 1987
   I.B. Enghoff, Freshwater fishing from a sea-coast settlement – the Ertebølle locus classicus revisited. Journal of Danish Archaeology 5, 1986, 62-76.

Enghoff 1993
   I.B. Enghoff, Mesolithic eel-fishing at Bjørnsholm, Denmark, spiced with exotic species. Journal of Danish Archaeology 10, 1991, 105-118.

Enghoff 1994
   I.B. Enghoff, Fishing in Denmark During the Ertebølle Period. International Journal of Osteoarchaeology 4, 1994, 65-96.

Enghoff 2011
   I.B. Enghoff, Regionality and biotope exploitation in Danish Ertebølle and adjoining periods. Scientia Danica, Series B, Biologica Vol. I (København 2011).

Fischer 1990
   A. Fischer, A Late Palaeolithic "School" of Flint-knapping at Trollesgave, Denmark. Results from Refitting. Acta Archaeologica 60, 1989, 33-49.

Fischer 2002
   A. Fischer, Food for feasting? In: A. Fischer/K. Kristiansen (eds.), The neolithisation of Denmark. 150 years of debate (Sheffield 2002), 341-394.

Fischer/Sørensen 1983
   A. Fischer/S. Sørensen, Stenalder på den danske havbund. Antikvariske Studier 6, 104-126.

Fischer et al. 1979
   A. Fischer/B. Grønnow/J.H. Jønsson/F.O. Nielsen/C. Petersen (eds.), Stenaldereksperimenter i Lejre. Bopladsernes indretning. Working Papers, The National Museum of Denmark 8 (København 1979).

Fischer et al. 2007
   A. Fischer/J. Olsen/M. Richards/J. Heinemeier/Á.E. Sveinbjörndóttir/P. Bennike, Coast-Inland mobility and diet in the Danish Mesolithic and Neolithic: Evidence from stable isotope values of humans and dogs. Journal of Archaeological Science 34, 2007, 2125-2150.

Gabrielsen 1953
   S. Gabrielsen, Udgravningen på Flynderhage 1945-47.

Aarbøger udgivne af Historisk Samfund for Aarhus Stift XLVI, 5-17.

Gillespie et al. 1984
   R. Gillespie/E.T. Gowlett/E.T. Hall/ R.E.M. Hedges (eds.), Radiocarbon measurement by accellerator mass spectrometry: an early selection of dates. Archeometry 26 (1), 1984, 15-20.

Glob 1952
   P.V. Glob, Danske Oldsager II. Yngre Stenalder (København 1952).

Glykou 2013
   A. Glykou, Seal hunting at the Baltic Sea coast. A case study from the Late Mesolithic and earliest Neolithic Neustadt in Holstein, Germany. In: O. Grimm/ U. Schmölcke (eds.), Hunting in northern Europe until 1500 A.D. Old traditions and regional developments, continental sources and continental influences. Papers presented at a workshop organized by the Centre for Baltic and Scandinavian Archaeology (ZBSA), Schleswig, June 16th and 17th, 2011 (Neumünster 2013), 101-112.

Glykou 2014
   A. Glykou, Late Mesolithic – Early Neolithic Sealers: a case study on the exploitation of marine resources during the Mesolithic-Neolithic transition in the south-western Baltic Sea. In: R. Fernandes/J. Meadows (eds.), Human Exploitation of Aquatic Landscapes. Internet Archaeology 37, Special issue.

Hartz 1999
   S. Hartz, Die Steinartefakte des endmesolithischen Fundplatzes Grube-Rosenhof. Untersuchungen und Materialien zur Steinzeit in Schleswig-Holstein 2 (Neumünster 1999).

Jensen 2002
   C.K. Jensen, En 6000 år gammel hyttetomt ved Randers Fjord. Kulturhistorisk Museum Randers Årbog 2002, 40-46.

Jensen 1994
   H.J. Jensen, Flint tools and plant working. Hidden traces of Stone Age technology. A use wear study of some Danish Mesolithic and TRB implements (Aarhus 1994).

Jensen 1973
   J.Aa. Jensen, Myrhøj. 3 hustomter med klokkebægerkeramik. Kuml 1972, 61-122.

Jensen 2003
   O.L. Jensen, A sunken dwelling from the Ertebølle site of Nivå 10, eastern Denmark. In: L. Larsson/H. Kindgren/K. Knutsson/D. Loeffler/A. Åkerlund (eds.), Mesolithic on the move. Papers presented at the Sixth International Conference on the Mesolithic in Europe, Stockholm 2000 (Stockholm 2003), 230-238.

Jensen 2009
    O.L. Jensen, Dwellings and graves from the Late
    Mesolithic site of Nivå 10, Eastern Denmark. In: S.B.
    McCartan/R. Schulting/G. Warren/P. Woodmann (eds.),
    Mesolithic Horizons. Papers presented at the Seventh
    International Conference on the Mesolithic in Europe,
    Belfast 2005, Vol. I (Oxford 2009), 465-472.

Jensen/Mørck in print
    O.L. Jensen/P.B. Mørck, Rituals reflected in Dwellings
    and Graves from the Late Mesolithic Site of Nivå 10 in
    Eastern Denmark. Papers presented at the Eighth Con-
    ference on the Mesolithic in Europe, Santander, Spain,
    September 2010.

Jensen/Pedersen 2002
    J.F. Jensen/K.B. Pedersen, Jordens nordligste stenalder.
    Nationalmuseets Arbejdsmark 2002, 71-83.

Jensen/Petersen 1985
    H.J. Jensen/E.B. Petersen, A Functional Study of Lithics
    from Vænget Nord, a Mesolithic Site at Vedbæk, N.E.
    Sjælland. Journal of Danish Archaeology 4, 1985, 40-51.

Jessen 1920
    A. Jessen, Stenalderhavets Udbredelse i det nordlige Jyl-
    land. Danmarks geologiske Undersøgelse. II. Række. Nr.
    35 (København 1920).

Johansson 1999
    A.D. Johansson, Ertebøllekulturen i Sydsjælland. Aar-
    bøger for Nordisk Oldkyndighed og Historie 1997, 7-88.

Jønsson/Pedersen 1983
    B. Jønsson/L. Pedersen, Sønderholm. En østsjællandsk
    boplads fra Ertebøllekulturen – kendt, glemt og genfun-
    det. Antikvariske Studier 6, 173-185.

Kannegaard 2013
    E. Kannegaard, Småting fra Nederst. Museum Østjyl-
    land Årbog 2013, 204-209.

Kannegaard 2016
    E. Kannegaard, Late Mesolithic ochre graves at Nederst,
    Denmark: Ochre rituals and customs of personal adorn-
    ment. In: Proceedings from the International Conference
    on "Mesolithic Burials – Rites, symbols and social organi-
    zation of early postglacial communities", Halle (Saale),
    18th-21st September 2013. Tagungen des Landesmuseums
    für Vorgeschichte Halle 13/I (Halle/Saale 2016), 81-93.

Karsten 1986
    P. Karsten, Stenålderen kring Yddingen. Limhamnia
    1986, 65-89.

Karsten 1991
    P. Karsten, Dansarna från Bökeberg. Arkeologiska under-
    sökningar. Skrifter 37. Riksantikvarieämbetet (Lund 1991).

Karsten/Knarrström 2003
    P. Karsten/B. Knarrström, The Tågerup Excavations
    (Lund 2003).

Klassen 2004
    L. Klassen, Jade und Kupfer. Untersuchungen zum Neo-
    lithisierungsprozess im westlichen Ostseeraum unter
    besonderer Berücksichtigung der Kulturentwiklung
    Europas 5500-3500 BC. Jutland Archaeological Society
    Publications Vol. 47 (Højbjerg 2004).

Klassen 2014
    L. Klassen. Along the Road. Aspects of Causewayed En-
    closures in South Scandinavia and Beyond. East Jutland
    Museum Publications vol. 2 (Århus 2014).

Kempfner-Jørgensen/Liversage 1985
    L. Kempfner-Jørgensen/D. Liversage, Mere om Sejerøs
    forhistorie. En stenalderboplads, et kulthus og et flint-
    værksted. Fra Holbæk Amt 1985, 7-27.

Kinze 2001
    C.C. Kinze, Havpattedyr i Nordatlanten (København 2001).

Larsson 1975
    L. Larsson, A Contribution to the Knowledge of Meso-
    lithic Huts in Southern Scandinavia. Meddelanden från
    Lunds Universitets Historiska Museum 1973-1974, 5-28.

Larsson 1985
    L. Larsson, Of House and Hearth. The Excavation, In-
    terpretation and Reconstruction of a Late Mesolithic
    House. In Honorem Evert Baudou. Archaeology and
    Environment 4 (Umeå 1985), 197-209.

Larsson 1988
    L. Larsson, A construction for Ceremonial Activities
    from the Late Mesolithic. Meddelanden från Lunds Uni-
    versitets Historiska Museum 1987-88, 5-18.

Layton 1986
    R. Layton, Political and Territorial Structures among
    Hunter-Gatherers. Man, New Series, Vol. 21, No 1, 18-33.

Liversage 1973
    D. Liversage, Sejerøs forhistorie. Fra Holbæk Amt 1973,
    85-122.

Lomborg 1973
    E. Lomborg, Die Flintdolche Dänemarks. Nordiske For-
    tidsminder, Serie B-in quarto, Bind 1 (København 1973).

Madsen et al. 1900
    A.P. Madsen/S. Müller/C. Neergaard/C. G. Joh.
    Petersen/E. Rostrup/K. J.V. Steenstrup/H. Winge, Af-
    faldsdynger fra Stenalderen i Danmark. Undersøgte for
    Nationalmuseet (København 1900).

Madsen 1992
    B. Madsen, Hamburgkulturens flintteknologi i Jels. In: J.
    Holm/F. Rieck (eds.), Istidsjægere ved Jelssøerne, Ham-
    burgkulturen i Danmark. Skrifter fra Museumsrådet for
    Sønderjyllands Amt 5 (Haderslev 1992), 93-131.

Mahler 1993
    D.L.D. Mahler, Søholm 2. Arkæologiske Udgravninger i
    Danmark 1992, 143-144, Nr. 51 (København 1993).

Malmer 1962

M.P. Malmer, Jungneolithische Studien. Acta Archaeologica Lundensia. series in 8° N° 2 (Lund 1962).

Malmer 1969

M.P. Malmer, Gropkermiksboplatsen Jonstorp RÄ. Kungliga Vitterhets Historie och Antkvitetsakademien. Antikvarisk Arkiv 36 (Stockholm 1969).

Malmros 1995

C. Malmros, Hjortholm-køkkenmøddingen. Sten- og bronzealder omkring Stavns Fjord. In: H.H. Hansen/B. Aaby (eds.), Stavns Fjord – et natur og kulturhistorisk forskningsområde på Samsø (København 1995), 35-67.

Mandrup et al. 2003

P. Mandrup/J.B. Jepsen/C.K. Jensen (eds.), Egehøj. Arkæologiske Udgravninger i Danmark 2002, Nr. 388 (København 2003).

Mannino/Thomas 2001

M.A. Mannino/K.D. Thomas, Intensive Mesolithic exploitation of coastal resources? Evidence from a shell deposit on the Isle of Portland (Southern England) for the impact of human foraging on populations of intertidal rocky shore molluscs. Journal of Archaeological Science 28, 2001, 1101-1114.

Marseen 1953

O. Marseen, Fangstfolk på Selbjerg. Kuml 1953, 102-120.

Mathiassen 1934

Th. Mathiassen, Primitive Flintredskaber fra Samsø. Aarbøger for Nordisk Oldkyndighed og Historie 1934, 39-54.

Mathiassen et al. 1942

Th. Mathiassen/M. Degerbøl/J. Troels-Smith (eds.), Dyrholmen. En Stenalderboplads paa Djursland. Det Kongelige Danske Videnskabernes Selskab. Arkæologisk-Kunsthistoriske Skrifter Bind I, Nr. 1 (København 1942).

Mathiassen 1948

Th. Mathiassen, Danske Oldsager I. Ældre Stenalder (København 1948).

Meiklejohn et al. 1998

C. Meiklejohn/E.B. Petersen/V. Alexandersen, The Later Mesolithic Population of Sjælland, Denmark and the Neolithic Transition. In: M. Zvelebil/L. Domanska (eds.): Harvesting the Sea, farming the forest. The emergence of Neolithic societies in the Baltic region. Sheffield Archaeological Monographs 10 (Sheffield 1998), 203-212.

Mertz 1924

E.L. Mertz, Oversigt over de sen-og postglaciale Niveauforandringer I Danmark. Danmarks Geologiske Undersøgelse II. Række, Nr. 41 (København 1924).

Milner 2002

N. Milner, Incremental Growth of the European Oyster (*Ostrea edulis*). Seasonality information from Danish Kitchen middens. BAR International Series 1057 (Oxford 2002).

Müller 1896

S. Müller, Nye Stenalders Former. Aarbøger for Nordisk Oldkyndighed og Historie 1896, 303-413.

Newell 1981

R.R. Newell, Mesolithic Dwelling Structures: Fact and Fantasy. In: B. Gramsch (ed.), Mesolithikum in Europa 2. Internationales Symposium Potsdam 3. bis 8. April 1978. Veröffentlichungen des Museums für Ur- und Frühgeschichte Potsdam Band 14/15 (Berlin 1981), 235-284.

Nicolaisen 2009

S.R. Nicolaisen, Production and use of Mesolithic groundstone axes and adzes in Zealand, Denmark: Description, production, distribution and status. In: S. McCartan/R. Schulting/G. Warren/P. Woodman (eds.), Mesolithic Horizons. Papers presented at the Seventh International Conference on the Mesolithic in Europe, Belfast 2005, Vol. II (Oxford 2009), 853-859.

Nielsen/Petersen 1993

E.K. Nielsen/E.B. Petersen, Grave, mennesker og hunde. In: S. Hvass/B. Storgaard (eds.), Da klinger i muld... 25 års arkæologi i Danmark (København/Højbjerg 1993), 76-81.

Nielsen 1981

P.O. Nielsen, Stenalderen bondestenalderen (København 1981).

Noe-Nygaard 1971

N. Noe-Nygaard, Spur Dog spines from prehistoric and Early Historic Denmark. Bulletin of the Geological Society of Denmark 21, 1971, 18-33.

Nordmann 1936

V. Nordmann, Menneskets Indvandring til Norden. Danmarks Geologiske Undersøgelser, III. Række Nr. 27, (København 1936), 127-128.

Pedersen 2009

K.B. Pedersen, Stederne og menneskene. Istidsjægere omkring Knudshoved Odde. Forlaget Museerne.dk vol. 3 (Vordingborg 2009).

Pedersen 1997

L. Pedersen, De satte hegn i havet. In: Pedersen/Fischer/Aaby (eds.), Storebælt i 10.000 år. Mennesket, havet og skoven (København 1997), 124-143.

Pedersen/Petersen 1997

S.A.S. Pedersen/K. S. Petersen, Djurslands Geologi (København 1997).

Petersen 1971

E.B. Petersen, Ølby Lyng. En østsjællandsk kystboplads med Ertebøllekultur. Aarbøger for Nordisk Oldkyndighed og Historie 1970, 5-42.

Petersen 1972

E.B. Petersen, A Maglemose Hut from Sværdborg Bog, Zealand, Denmark. Acta Archaeologica Vol. XLII, 1971, 43-77.

Petersen 1978
E.B. Petersen, A Survey of the Late Palaeolithic and Mesolithic of Denmark. In: S. K. Kozłowski (ed.), The Mesolithic in Europe. Papers read at the International Archaeological Symposium on the Mesolithic in Europe, Warszaw 1973 (Warsaw 1978), 77-127.

Petersen et al. 1993
E.B. Petersen/V. Alexandersen/C. Meiklejohn, Vedbæk, graven midt i byen. Nationalmuseets Arbejdsmark 1993, 61-69.

Petersen 1984
P.V. Petersen, Chronological and Regional Variation in the Late Mesolithic of Eastern Denmark. Journal of Danish Archaeology 3, 1984, 7-18.

Petersen/Johansen 1993
P.V. Petersen/L. Johansen, Sølbjerg I – An Ahrensburgian Site on a Reindeer Migration Route through Eastern Denmark. Journal of Danish Archaeology 10, 1991, 20-37.

Prangsgaard 2013
K. Prangsgaard, Pottery. In: Andersen, S.H. 2013, 277-292.

Price/Gebauer 2005
T.D. Price/A.B. Gebauer (eds.), Smakkerup Huse. A Late Mesolithic Coastal Site in Northwest Zealand, Denmark (Aarhus 2005).

Rasmussen 1990
E.H. Rasmussen, Okkergrave fra ældre stenalder på Djursland. Kuml 1988-89, 31-41.

Renouf 1988
M.A.P. Renouf, Sedentary coastal hunter-fishers: an example from the Younger Stone Age of northern Norway. In: G.N. Bailey/J. Parkington (eds.), The archaeology of prehistoric coastlines (Cambridge 1988), 102-115.

Richter/Noe-Nygaard 2003
J. Richter/N. Noe-Nygaard, A Late Mesolithic Hunting Station at Agernæs, Fyn, Denmark. Acta Archaeologica 73, 1-64.

Ritchie et al. in print
K. Ritchie/S.H. Andersen/E. Kannegaard, Skellerup Enge and the distinctive subsistence economy on Jutland at the Kongemose-Ertebølle transition in Denmark. In: Proceedings of the 9th International Conference on the Mesolithic in Europe, Belgrade, Serbia, 14th-18th September, 2015 (in print).

Robson (in prep.)
H.K. Robson, To assess the change of consumption and culinary practices at the transition to agriculture: a multi-disciplinary approach from a Danish kitchen midden. Unpublished PhD Thesis. The University of York.

Rowley-Conwy 1998
P. Rowley-Conwy, Meat, Furs and Skins: Mesolithic Animal Bones from Ringkloster, a Seasonal Hunting Camp in Jutland. Journal of Danish Archaeology 12, 1994-95, 87-98.

Rowley-Conwy 2013
P. Rowley-Conwy, Homes without Houses? Some Comments on an Ertebølle Enigma. In: G.N. Bailey/K. Hardy/Camara (eds.), Shell Energy. Mollusc Shells as Coastal Resources (Oxford 2013), 137-154.

Sergant et al. 2006
J. Sergant/J. Crombé/Y. Perdaen, The "invisible" hearths: a contribution to the discernement of Mesolithic non-structured surface hearths. Journal of Archaeological Science 33, 2006, 999-1007.

Schmölcke et al. 2009
U. Schmölke/A. Glykou/D. Heinrich, 2009, Faunal development in the southwestern Baltic area. Bericht der Römisch-Germanischen Kommission 88, 2007, 205-217.

Sheehan 1985
G.W. Sheehan, Whaling as an Organizing Focus in Northwestern Alaskan Eskimo Societies. In: T.D. Price/J.A. Brown (eds.), Prehistoric Hunter-Gatherers. The Emergence of Cultural Complexity (Orlando 1985), 123-154.

Simonsen 1952
P. Simonsen, Nye Fund fra Himmerlands Ertebøllekultur. Aarbøger for Nordisk Oldkyndighed og Historie 1951, 199-226.

Skaarup 1973
J. Skaarup, Hesselø-Sølager. Jagdstationen der südskandinavischen Trichterbecherkultur. Arkæologiske Studier I (København 1973).

Skaarup/Grøn 2004
J. Skaarup/O. Grøn, Møllegabet II. A submerged Mesolithic settlement in southern Denmark. BAR International Series 1328 (Oxford 2004).

Skousen 1998
H. Skousen, Rønbjerg Strandvolde – en kystboplads ved Limfjorden. Kuml 1997-98, 29-74.

Staal 2009
B. Staal, Statusrapport fra arkæologisk undersøgelse ved STATOIL A/S I Kalundborg forud for byggemodning. KAM 2009-005, sag nr. 09-33 (unpublished report).

Stafford 1999
M. Stafford, From Forager to Farmer in Flint. A Lithic Analysis of the Prehistoric Transition to Agriculture in Southern Scandinavia (Aarhus 1999).

Stürup 1966
B. Stürup, En ny jordgrav fra tidlig-neolitisk tid. Kuml 1965,13-22.

Sørensen 1993
S.A. Sørensen, Lollikhuse – en køkkenmødding ved Selsø. Arkæologi i Frederiksborg Amt 1983-1993. Fra Frederiksborg Amt 1993, 7-37.

Sørensen 1995

S.A. Sørensen, Lollikhuse – a Dwelling Site under a Kitchen Midden. Journal of Danish Archaeology 11, 1992-93, 9-29.

Sørensen 2007

S.A. Sørensen, Limhamnn axes in Denmark. In: B. Hårdh/K. Jennbert/D. Olausson (eds.), On the Road. Studies in honour of Lars Larsson. Acta archaeologica Lundensia. Series in 4° ; no. 26 (Lund 2007), 184-187.

Thomsen/Jessen 1906

Th. Thomsen/A. Jessen, Brabrand-Fundet fra den ældre Stenalder. Arkæologisk og geologisk behandlet. Aarbøger for Nordisk Oldkyndighed og Historie 1906, 1-74.

Tixier 1963

J. Tixier, II. Typologie de l'Épipaléolithique du Margreb. Mémoires du Centre de Recherches Anthropologiques Préhistoriques et Etnographiques (Alger 1963).

Troels-Smith 1939

J. Troels-Smith, Stenalderbopladser og Strandlinjer paa Amager. Meddelelser fra Dansk Geologisk Forening Bd. 9, Hæfte 4, 489-508.

Troels-Smith 1967

J. Troels-Smith, The Ertebølle Culture and its Background. Palaeohistoria 12, 1966, 505-528.

Trolle-Lassen 1986

T. Trolle-Lassen, Human exploitation of the pine marten (*Martes martes* (L.)) at the late Mesolithic settlement of Tybrind Vig in western Funen. In: L.-K. Königsson (ed.), Nordic Late Quaternary Biology and Ecology. Striae 24 (Stockholm 1986), 119-124.

Vedsted 2014

J. Vedsted, Vængesø – et kulturmiljø fra landvinding til naturgenopretning. Museum Østjylland Årbog 2014, 38-51.

Wendelboe 2012

J. Wendelboe, Helgenæs. Historien om et sogn i Danmark (Knebel 2012).

Westerby 1927

E. Westerby, Stenalderbopladser ved Klampenborg. Nogle Bidrag til Studiet af den Mesolitiske Periode (København 1927).

Winge 1904

H. Winge, Om jordfundne Pattedyr i Danmark. Videnskabelige Meddelelser fra Dansk Naturhistorisk Forening, 193-304.

Woodburn 1982

J. Woodburn, Egalitarian Societies. Man, New Series, Vol. 17, No 3, 431-451.

Yesner 1980

E.R. Yesner, Maritime hunter-gatherers: Ecology and prehistory. Current Anthropology 21-6, 1980, 727-750.

10 Tables

<table>
<tr><th colspan="3">Vængesø II – Transverse arrowheads</th></tr>
<tr><td></td><td>Number</td><td>%</td></tr>
<tr><td>With parallel sides</td><td>4</td><td>4.2</td></tr>
<tr><td>With slightly concave sides</td><td>18</td><td>18.9</td></tr>
<tr><td>With very concave sides</td><td>49</td><td>51.6</td></tr>
<tr><td>With slightly oblique edge</td><td>13</td><td>13.7</td></tr>
<tr><td>With very oblique edge</td><td>8</td><td>8.4</td></tr>
<tr><td>With pointed butt</td><td>3</td><td>3.2</td></tr>
<tr><td></td><td>Σ 95</td><td></td></tr>
</table>

Tab. 1. Abundance of the various types of transverse arrowheads at Vængesø II (cf. Tabs. 3 and 5). The dominant types have slightly or strongly concave sides, but there are also a number of arrowheads with a slightly or strongly oblique edge.

Vængesø II – Sediment sample, square 72/49				
	Weight (g)	Number	% weight	% number
Oysters (Ostrea edulis)	325	62	85.8	49.6
Periwinkles (Littorina littorea)	37	27	9,0	21.6
Pullet carpet shells (Venerupis corrugata)	18	7	4.5	5.6
Blue mussels (Mytilus edulis)	11	23	2.8	10,0
Cockles (Cerastoderma edule)	5	3		2.4
Netted dog whelk (Tritia reticulata)	2	2		2.4
Garden snails (Hortensia sp.)	1	1		
Sum of shells	399	125		
Pottery	20			
Gravel 0.3-5 cm/diam.	262			
Fish bones, shell fragments and gravel	183			
Residue (sand)	1732			
Total	2596			

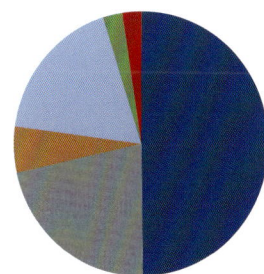

- Oyster (*Ostrea ed.*)
- Periwinkle (*Littorina littorea*)
- Carpet mussel (*Venerupis c.*)
- Blue mussel (*Mytilus ed.*)
- Cockle (*Cerastoderma ed.*)
- Netted dog whelk (*Tritia reticulata*)

Tab. 2. The marine invertebrate content of a c. 2.6 kg sample from the Vængesø II kitchen midden in square 72/49.

Vængesø III – Transverse arrowheads		
	Number	%
With parallel sides	2	2.5
With slightly concave sides	14	17.7
With very concave sides	49	62,0
With slightly oblique edge	4	5.1
With very oblique edge	5	6.3
With straight sides and pointed butt	5	6.3
	Σ 79	

Tab. 3. Abundance of the various types of transverse arrowheads at Vængesø III. The dominant type has slightly or strongly concave sides, while the other types only play an insignificant role (cf. Tabs. 1 and 5).

Vængesø III – Sediment sample from kitchen midden		
Weight (dry):	(g)	% of marine species
Periwinkle	1980	62.2
Oyster (60 individuals)	600	18.9
Cockle (58 individuals)	410	12.9
Pullet carpet shell (27 individuals)	150	5
Mussel (8 individuals)	40	1
Netted dog whelk (1 individual)		
Needle whelk (1 individual)		
Marine shells	3180	
Gravel and small flakes	420	
Dust (fish bones)	1270	
Sand	2140	
Total	7010	

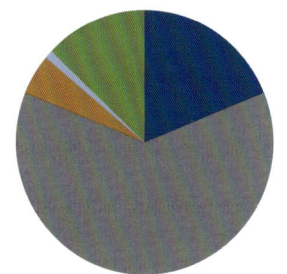

- Oyster (*Ostrea ed.*)
- Periwinkle (*Littorina littorea*)
- Carpet mussel (*Venerupis c.*)
- Blue mussel (*Mytilus ed.*)
- Cockle (*Cerastoderma ed.*)
- Netted dog whelk (*Tritia reticulata*)

Tab. 4. The contents of a 5 l sample from the kitchen midden at Vængesø III. The sample was taken from a discrete meal heap, which almost exclusively consisted of shells of periwinkle.

Holmegaard – Transverse arrowheads		
	Number	%
With parallel sides	4	23.5
With slightly concave sides	1	5.8
With very concave sides	4	23.5
With slightly oblique edge	5	29.4
With pointed butt	3	17.6
Rhombic	2	
Fragments	4	
Atypical preforms	2	
	Σ 25	

Tab. 5. Relative abundance of transverse arrowhead types at Holmegaard (cf. Tabs. 1 and 3).

Σ	No.	Oyster		Cockle		Mussel		Periwinkle		Other	Residue
		Number	Weight %	Number	Weight %	Number	weight %	Number	Weight %	Number	

1532 Holmegård

Σ	No.	Number (Oyster)	Weight % (Oyster)	Number (Cockle)	Weight % (Cockle)	Number (Mussel)	weight % (Mussel)	Number (Periwinkle)	Weight % (Periwinkle)	Number (Other)	Residue
51	OP	12	23.5	33	64.7	1	1.9	5	9.8	1 Venerupis c. 2 Tritia 4 Hortensia sp.	1 fish vertebra
126	RG	69	54.7	8	6.3	26	20.6	15	11.9	5 Venerupis c. 2 Tritia 1 Hortensia sp.	2 flakes 15 fish vertebra
72	SG	53	73.6	2	2.7	16	22.2	1	1.3		1 flake
93	UO	55	59.1	10	10.7	22	23.6	6	6.4		
190	XA	68	35.7	71	37.3	35	18.4	13	6.8	1 Venerupis c. 1 Tritia	2 flakes, 1 helix 4 fish vertebra
67	XB	53	79.1	4	5.9	7	10.4	2	2.9	1 Hortensia sp.	Flint debris + bones
97	VZ	1	1	5	5.1	5	5.1	63	64.9	23 Venerupis c.	
221	SN (bag 1)	69	31.2	19	8.5	85	38.4	42	19	6 Tritia	
211	SN (bag 2)	47	22.2	12	5.6	97	45.9	47	22.2	3 Venerupis c. 5 Tritia	1 fish vertebra

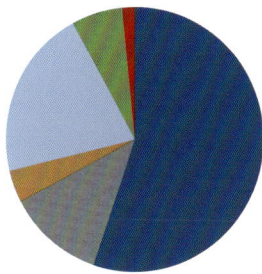

- Oyster (*Ostrea ed.*)
- Periwinkle (*Littorina littorea*)
- Carpet mussel (*Venerupis c.*)
- Blue mussel (*Mytilus ed.*)
- Cockle (*Cerastoderma ed.*)
- Netted dog whelk (*Tritia reticulata*)

Tab. 6. Species of marine invertebrates in nine samples from the kitchen midden at Holmegaard. The samples (OP, RG, SG and UO) form a strati- graphic sequence from top (sample OP) to bottom (sample UO) through the shell layer in square BH. Samples XA and XB represent a similar sequence in square AR; XA is from the uppermost part of the shell layer and XB from the deepest. Sample VZ comes from square E/F and was taken from an ash deposit in the deepest layer of the kitchen midden, while sample SN is from square AE at the base of hearth 2.

Holmegaard – Radiocarbon dates

AAR-7692, 6295±50 bp; 4830-4710 BC cal (1σ)	Oysters, top of shell horizon (layer 2)
AAR-7693, 6130±55 bp; 4680-4470 BC cal (1σ)	Oysters, bottom of shell horizon (layer 2)
AAR-7694, 5895±55 bp; 4360-4260 BC cal (1σ)	Oysters, by hearth in shell layer 2
AAR-7695, 6570±55 bp; 5260-5010 BC cal (1σ)	Oysters, below hearth in shell layer 2
AAR-7696, 6730±60 bp; 5370-5260 BC cal (1σ)	Oysters, bottom of shell layer 2
AAR-8122, 4139±39 bp; 2870-2600 BC cal (1σ)	Red deer bone from layer above shell midden (layer 5)
AAR-8124, 5915±45 bp; 4840-4720 BC cal (1σ)	Red deer bone from top horizon of shell midden (layer 6) pit 3
AAR-8123, 6125±48 bp; 5210-4960 BC cal (1σ)	Red deer bone from bottom layer (layer 6) pit 7
K-3099, 5870±95 bp; 4850-4610 BC cal (1σ)	Oysters, below grave, layer 6

Tab. 7. Radiocarbon dates from Holmegaard. All dates are given at one standard deviation (1 σ) and corrected for marine reservoir effect (= 400 years). M. Kanstrup, AMS-laboratry, University of Aarhus.

Settlement sizes (m) and areas (m²)						
Locality	Well defined	Flint on surface?	Kitchen midden, measurements (m)	Excavated area (m²)	Height (m a.s.l.)	Grave
Vængesø I	X	20 x 20	10 x 10	35	3.6 - 3.75	
Vængesø II	X	60 x 20	18 x 7	130	2.7 - 3.7	X
Vængesø III	X	150 x 10-45	25-45 x 150	165	4.5 - 5.25	X
Vængesø IV			10 x 20	25.5	3.4 - 4.6	
Holmegaard	X	50 x 50	15-20 x 20	89.2	3.5 - 4	X

Area of terraces (m²)	
Locality	
Vængesø I	15 - 24
Vængesø II	14 - 16
Vængesø III	17.9; 12.5; 15
Vængesø IV	

Length of oysters (cm)	
Locality	
Vængesø I	
Vængesø II	5 - 8.5
Vængesø III	3 - 11.3
Vængesø IV	

Tab. 8. Settlement parameters (size, excavated area, height above sea level, presence of graves etc.) or the Vængesø and Holmegaard sites.

Tool groups									
	Vængesø I	Vængesø II	Vængesø III	Holmegaard	Flynderhage	Brabrand	Dyrholmen II	Ronæs Skov	Tybrind Vig
	%	%	%	%	%	%	%	%	%
Scrapers	10,3	2,9	4,1	14,5	21,0	10,9	18,0	13,0	3,6
Borers	5,7	15,4	6,5	12,9	14,5	12,1	8,0	7,0	6,1
Burins	9,4	2,4	3,2	17,7	7,1	13,7	24,0	9,2	9,6
Truncated	16,6	26,2	23,2	16,1	28,3	23,7	21,0	23,8	8,0
Saws	2,0	4,2	19,0	9,6				2,4	4,6
Transverse arrowheads	25,2	47,6	40,0	29,0			27,0	9,2	16,9
Notched pieces	13,0							8,0	6,4
Denticulate pieces	5,0							13,0	8,0
Knives	1,0							6,2	8,9
Core axes	7,8	5,8	3,3	18,7	8,5	11,1	13,9	11,0	21,6
Flake axes	84,9	85,4	83,3	78,1	89,4	88,4	85,7	79,0	71,1
Chisels	7,1	8,7	13,3	3,1	4,0	6,2		5,6	5,1
Greenstone axes	X	1,7		X	1,5	1,2	0,3	4,4	2,0
Pottery	X	X	X				X	X	X

Tab. 9. Percentage distribution of the various tool groups at the settlements of Vængesø I, II and III, compared with the coeval Ertebølle settlements of Flynderhage, Brabrand and Dyrholmen II , Brabrand, Dyrholmen, Ronæs Skov and Tybrind Vig.

Birds – species list				
	Vængesø I	Vængesø II	Vængesø III	Holmegaard
Birds (Aves sp.)	X			
Great cormorant (Phalacrocorax carbo)		X	X	
Goose (Anser/Branta sp.)		X		
Common shelduck (Tadorna tadorna)		X		
Northern pintail (Anas acuta)		X		
Velvet scoter (Melanitta fusca)		X	X	
Eurasian teal (Anas crecca)			X	
Ducks (Anser sp.)			X	X
Razorbill (Alca torda)		X	X	
Common murre (Uria aalge)		X	X	
Great auk (Pinguinus impennis)		X		
Great grebe (Podiceps cristatus)		X	X	
Rednecked grebe (Podiceps grisegena)			X	
Little grebe (Tachybaptus ruficollis)		X	X	
Black-throated loon (Gavia arctica)			X	
Red-throated loon (Gavia stellata)		X	X	
Great northern diver (Gavia immer)		X		
Swan (Cygnus sp.)		X	X	X
Redbreasted merganser (Mergus serrator)		X	X	
Smew (Mergellus albellus)			X	
Common merganser (Mergus merganser)			X	
Merganser (Mergus sp.)			X	
Northern gannet (Morus bassanus)		X	X	
Common eider (Somateria mollissima)			X	
European herring gull (Larus argentatus)			X	
Mew gull (Larus canus)			X	
Glaucous gull (Larus hyperboreus)			X	
Lesser black-backed gull (Larus fuscus)			X	
Gull (Larus sp.)			X	
Golden eagle (Aquila chrysaetos)				X
White tailed eagle (Haliaeetus albicilla)		X	X	X
Western osprey (Pandion haliaetus)		X		
Crow/Rook (Corvus corone/Corvus frugilegus)			X	
Finch (Fringilla sp.)			X	

Tab. 10a Species of birds at Vængesø I, II and III and at Holmegaard.

Fishes – species list				
	Vængesø I	Vængesø II	Vængesø III	Holmegaard
Plaice (Pleuronectes platessa)			X	
Flounder (Platichthys flesus)			X	
Flat fishes (Pleuronectes platessa, Platichthys flesus)				X
Common dab (Limanda limanda)		X		
Cod (Gadus morhua)		X	X	X
Whiting (Merlangius merlangus)			X	
Pollack (Pollachius pollachius)			X	
Gadids (Gadidae)		X		
Spurdog (Squalus acanthias)		X	X	X
Eel (Anguilla anguilla)		X	X	X
Atlantic herring (Clupea harengus)		X	X	X
Turbot (Psetta maxima)			X	
Greater weaver (Trachinus draco)		X	X	
Haddock (Melanogrammus aeglefinus)		X		
Saith (Pollachius virens)		X	X	
Three-spined stickleback (Gasterosteus aculeatus)			X	
Tub gurnard (Chelidonichthys lucerna)			X	
Atlantic mackerel (Scomber scombrus)			X	X
Viviparous eelpout (Zoarces viviparus)			X	
Grey gurnard (Eutrigla gurnardus)			X	
Bull-rout (Myoxocephalus scorpius)			X	
Thornback ray (Raja clavata)			X	

Tab. 10b Species of fishes at Vængesø I, II and III and at Holmegaard.

Mammals – species list	Vængesø I	Vængesø II	Vængesø III	Holmegaard
Swine (Sus sp.)	X	X	X	
Wild boar (Sus scrofa)	X	X		X
Red deer (Cervus elaphus)	X	X	X	X
Roe deer (Capreolus capreolus)	X	X		X
Bovines (Bos sp.)	X	X	X	
Aurochs (Bos primigenius)	X	X		X
Domestic sheep (Ovis aries)		X		
Domestic cattle (Bos taurus)		X		
Human (Homo sapiens)		X	X	X
Seal (Phoca sp.)	X	X	X	
Grey seal (Halichoerus grypus)	X	X		X
Harbour seal (Phoca vitulina)		X		
Harp seal (Phoca groenlandica)		X	X	
Ringed seal (Phoca hispida)		X		
Harbour porpoise (Phocoena phocoena)	X	X	X	
Large whale (Cetacea sp.)	X	X	X	
White-beaked dolphin (Lagenorhynchus albirostris)		X	X	
Bottlenose dolphin (Tursiops truncatus)				X
Killer whale (Orcinus orca)			X	
Common dolphin (Delphinius delphis)			X	
Sperm whale (Physeter macrocephalus)			X	
Atlantic white-sided dolphin (Lagenorhynchus acutus)			X	
Mole (Talpa europaea)			X	
Mouse (Microtus sp.)			X	
Wood mouse (Apodemus sylvaticus)			X	
Water vole (Arvicola terrestris)			X	
Squirrel (Sciurus vulgaris)			X	

Tab. 10c Species of mammals at Vængesø I, II and III and at Holmegaard.

Fur animals – species list	Vængesø I	Vængesø II	Vængesø III	Holmegaard
Badger (Meles meles)		X	X	
Eurasian Lynx (Lynx lynx)				
Grey Wolf (Canis lupus)		(X)		
Otter (Lutra lutra)		X	X	X
Pine marten (Martes martes)		X	X	
Polecat (Mustela putorius)		X	X	
Fox (Vulpes vulpes)		(X)	X	X
Wild cat (Felis silvestris)			X	X
European beaver (Castor fiber)		X		
Dog (Canis familiaris)		X	X	X

Tab. 10d Species of fur animals at Vængesø I, II and III and at Holmegaard.

Vængesø – Radiocarbon dates				
Settlement	Lab ID	14C Age 14C years BP	Calibrated age 68.2% confidence interval(s)	Calibrated age 95.4% confidence interval(s)
Vængesø I	AAR-8298	5479 ±45	4362 BC – 4318 BC [45.3%] 4293 BC – 4263 BC [22.9%]	4445 BC – 4417 BC [6.6%] 4400 BC – 4243 BC [88.8%]
Vængesø II	K-2444	4640 ±100	3629 BC – 3579 BC [9.4%] 3532 BC – 3333 BC [53.1%] 3210 BC – 3190 BC [3.2%] 3151 BC – 3135 BC [2.4%]	3638 BC – 3095 BC [95.4%]
	Aar-8299	5585 ±35	4450 BC – 4436 BC [13.4%] 4426 BC – 4368 BC [54.8%]	4485 BC – 4472 BC [2.7%] 4464 BC – 4349 BC [92.7%]
	K-3920	5156 ±70	4041 BC – 3935 BC [47.6%] 3870 BC – 3809 BC [20.6%]	4226 BC – 4200 BC [2.2%] 4167 BC – 4126 BC [3.8%] 4118 BC – 4094 BC [1.4%] 4078 BC – 3778 BC [88.0%]
	K-3921	5181 ±65	4142 BC – 4136 BC [1.3%] 4052 BC – 3939 BC [57.9%] 3856 BC – 3815 BC [9.1%]	4227 BC – 4197 BC [4.0%] 4170 BC – 4087 BC [10.4%] 4082 BC – 3904 BC [66.3%] 3879 BC – 3799 BC [14.7%]
	OxA-117	5475 ±130	4459 BC – 4225 BC [57.3%] 4202 BC – 4165 BC [6.0%] 4127 BC – 4115 BC [1.7%] 4096 BC – 4075 BC [3.2%]	4582 BC – 4031 BC [93.6%] 4025 BC – 3990 BC [1.8%]
Vængesø III	AAR-8117	5035 ±55	3941 BC – 3853 BC [40.5%] 3845 BC – 3830 BC [5.5%] 3822 BC – 3771 BC [22.2%]	3956 BC – 3707 BC [95.4%]
	LUS-7186	5110 ±50	3969 BC – 3926 BC [25.5%] 3876 BC – 3803 BC [42.7%]	4034 BC – 4021 BC [1.4%] 3993 BC – 3783 BC [94.0%]
	AAR-8300	5500 ±45	4442 BC – 4420 BC [11.5%] 4372 BC – 4324 BC [49.1%] 4284 BC – 4269 BC [7.7%]	4450 BC – 4313 BC [81.3%] 4300 BC – 4260 BC [14.1%]
	LUS-7187	5570 ±50	4447 BC – 4360 BC [68.2%]	4496 BC – 4335 BC [95.4%]
	AAR-4499	5405 ±45	4329 BC – 4237 BC [68.2%]	4346 BC – 4222 BC [77.8%] 4205 BC – 4159 BC [10.0%] 4129 BC – 4070 BC [7.7%]
Vængesø IV	K-3100	4840 ±85	3708 BC – 3616 BC [35.4%] 3611 BC – 3519 BC [32.8%]	3796 BC – 3493 BC [85.3%] 3465 BC – 3373 BC [10.1%]
	K-5661	2890 ±80	1205 BC – 1201 BC [1.1%] 1195 BC – 1138 BC [15.3%] 1133 BC – 974 BC [50.9%] 949 BC – 945 BC [1.0%]	1368 BC – 1359 BC [0.5%] 1295 BC – 891 BC [93.6%] 874 BC – 848 BC [1.4%]

Tab. 11a. Radiocarbon dates from the Vængesø settlements.

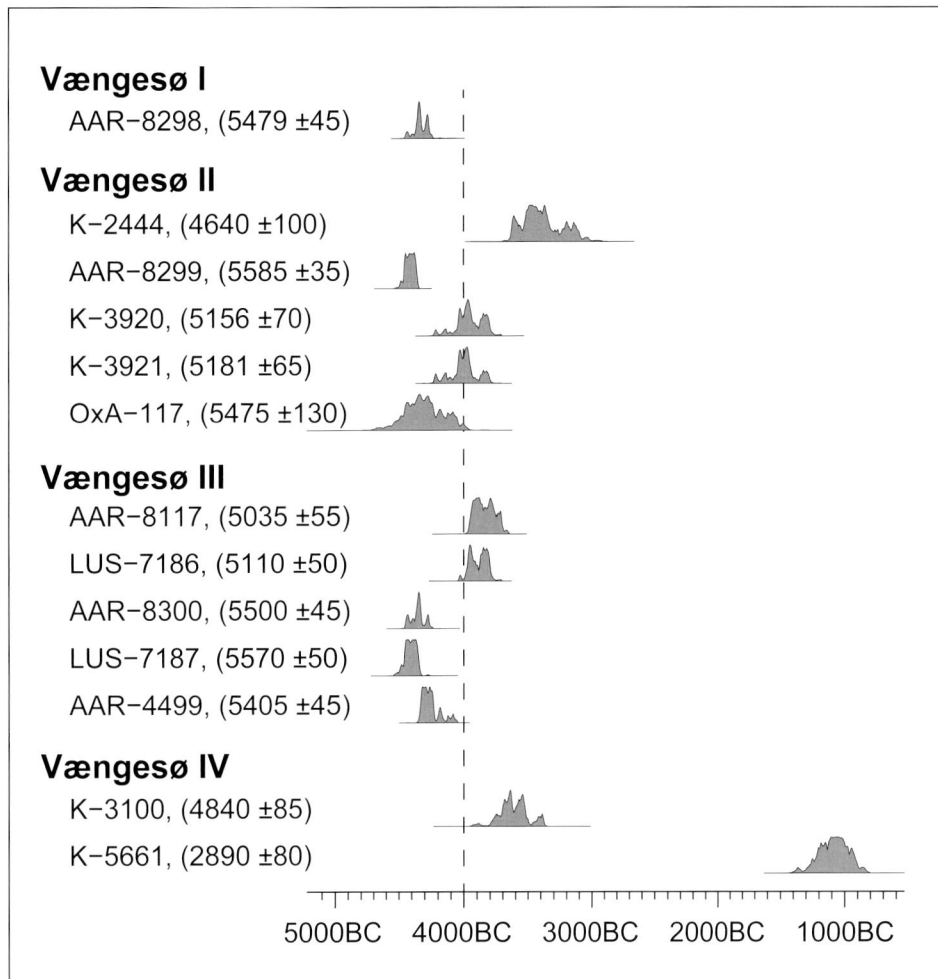

Tab. 11b. Graph of radiocarbon dates from the Vængesø settlements.